Luxemburg International Studies in Political Economy

Series Editors
Jan Toporowski
University of London
School of Oriental and African Studies
London, UK

Frieder Otto Wolf
Institute of Philosophy
Free University of Berlin
Berlin, Berlin, Germany

The Rosa Luxemburg Foundation is one of the largest political education institutions in Germany today. The Foundation's book series Luxemburg International Studies in Political Economy publishes serious academic studies in political economy, broadly conceived to cover critical research in the social sciences on capitalism, as well as feminist and environmental political economy. This series has been supported by the Rosa Luxemburg Foundation, one of the larger political education institutions in Germany today.

Judith Dellheim • Frieder Otto Wolf
Editors

Rudolf Hilferding

What Do We Still Have to Learn from His Legacy?

2nd ed. 2023

Editors
Judith Dellheim
Rosa-Luxemburg-Foundation
Berlin, Germany

Frieder Otto Wolf
Institute of Philosophy
Freie Universität Berlin
Berlin, Germany

ISSN 2662-6373   ISSN 2662-6381 (electronic)
Luxemburg International Studies in Political Economy
ISBN 978-3-031-08095-1   ISBN 978-3-031-08096-8 (eBook)
https://doi.org/10.1007/978-3-031-08096-8

© The Editor(s) (if applicable) and The Author(s), under exclusive licence to Springer Nature Switzerland AG 2023, 2020
This work is subject to copyright. All rights are solely and exclusively licensed by the Publisher, whether the whole or part of the material is concerned, specifically the rights of translation, reprinting, reuse of illustrations, recitation, broadcasting, reproduction on microfilms or in any other physical way, and transmission or information storage and retrieval, electronic adaptation, computer software, or by similar or dissimilar methodology now known or hereafter developed.
The use of general descriptive names, registered names, trademarks, service marks, etc. in this publication does not imply, even in the absence of a specific statement, that such names are exempt from the relevant protective laws and regulations and therefore free for general use. The publisher, the authors, and the editors are safe to assume that the advice and information in this book are believed to be true and accurate at the date of publication. Neither the publisher nor the authors or the editors give a warranty, expressed or implied, with respect to the material contained herein or for any errors or omissions that may have been made. The publisher remains neutral with regard to jurisdictional claims in published maps and institutional affiliations.

Cover illustration: Narodowe Archiwum Cyfrowe

This Palgrave Macmillan imprint is published by the registered company Springer Nature Switzerland AG.
The registered company address is: Gewerbestrasse 11, 6330 Cham, Switzerland

PREFACE TO THE FIRST EDITION

This is the third volume of the series "Luxemburg International Studies in Political Economy".

In 2014, at the International Conference "*The 100th Anniversary of 'The Accumulation of Capital: A Contribution to an Economic Explanation of Imperialism'—A Century-old Work Remains Current, Provocative and Seminal*", Jan Toporowski presented his idea for the series. In an interview about the project he said: "Political Economy has become very fashionable now, for example, among political scientists and heterodox economists. However, much of this literature … is eclectic in its inspiration, ranging from libertarian Austrian ideas, to rather free interpretations of Marxian concepts. This series is distinctive in taking forward the systematic work in political economy from the discussions following Marx's death in 1883, to which Rosa Luxemburg contributed, and showing the relevance of those discussions to problems of capitalism today. For me the key here is the systematic methodology that derives from these discussions, rather than imaginative, but loose, thinking inspired by concepts used in nineteenth century discussions before the emergence of mature capitalism" (Dellheim 2016).

The projected series then started in 2016, with the volume "*Rosa Luxemburg: A Permanent Challenge for Political Economy*" (Dellheim and Wolf 2016). This book helped to at least begin overcoming a still existing fear which has for a long time prevented the European left from any explicit dealing with the entire theoretical legacy of Rosa Luxemburg. One important aspect of this legacy is that Luxemburg—as one of the most fascinating and radical characters in the struggle for liberation and

vi PREFACE TO THE FIRST EDITION

equality—developed a very specific critical relationship with Karl Marx and his theoretical heritage. Accordingly, it was no coincidence that our call for abstracts on the occasion of Marx's 200th birthday began with a quote from Luxemburg: "In accordance with Marx's whole worldview, his magnum opus is no Bible containing ultimate truths that are valid for all time, pronounced by the highest and final authority; instead, it is an inexhaustible stimulus for further intellectual work, further research, and the struggles for truth" (Luxemburg 1918, p. 453). That we returned to this quote on the eve of Marx's 200th birthday was due to the central idea underlying our second volume, dedicated to the unfinished system of Marx's volumes on *Capital*. In following Luxemburg in this respect, we tried to make use of the fragmentary state of the volumes II and III of *Capital* which "provide something infinitely more valuable than any supposed final truth: a spur to reflection, to critique and self-critique, which is the most distinctive element of the theory that was Marx's legacy" (ibid., p. 461). Unfortunately, this spur was not taken up by many of those who followed Luxemburg in her day, as the further development of Marxist theory was dramatically overshadowed and crippled, by reactionary and fascist terror, war and by Stalinism.

> Confronted with further developments of the capitalist mode of production, as well as those pertaining to other forms of societal hierarchies, we urgently have to deal more specifically with the issue of money and finance, still attempting to follow in the very tracks of Marx and Luxemburg. And it is, accordingly, just another consequence of our approach that we now address the work of Rudolf Hilferding and its reception in Marxist debates. The importance of Hilferding's work was already underlined in the call for abstracts to our book on the unfinished volume III of *Capital* (Dellheim, collective, 2016). Consequently, when the second volume of our series, *"The Unfinished System of Karl Marx. Critically Reading Capital as a Challenge for our Times"* (Dellheim and Wolf 2018b), appeared, we already announced that the third one would deal with Hilferding's legacy (ibid., p. 24). The argument for this plan was, on the one hand, that some of our authors referred to Hilferding anyway, given his evident efforts to analyse social and especially economic developments in the world after Marx and Engels. Accordingly, we proceeded from the conviction that a critique of Hilferding's theoretical achievements would be of crucial importance for a deeper understanding of the present societal, economic and political situation—especially of the global financial crisis and its connections to other problems and crises, particularly global warming, the loss of bio-diversity,

PREFACE TO THE FIRST EDITION   vii

militarisation and increasing violence against people, as well as poverty and social exclusion.

Based on his own, specific understanding of Marx—which merits and requires both analysis and criticism—Hilferding showed how the development of banks and joint-stock companies, especially in their expansion towards the control of industry, modified the very structure of societal, economic, political relations, and, last but not least, also of international relations.

Three questions were, or, rather, still are, of crucial interest here. They were already formulated in our call for abstracts written between the 200th anniversary of Marx's birthday and the 100th anniversary of the brutal murder of Rosa Luxemburg on 15 January 1919:

- First, we asked contributors to take a deeper look at the political dimension of Luxemburg's and Hilferding's handling of Marx's theoretical legacy. This is much needed, because any sound critique of their theoretical conceptions should take into account that neither of them were able to refer to all of Marx's manuscripts later published in the (second) MEGA edition. The question we asked pertained to the specific research methodology and the general approach to theoretical work in both Luxemburg and Hilferding, while at the same time looking for an explanation of their very distinct political developments. Hilferding's analyses of banking capital and its relation to other forms of capital, particularly of 'finance capital' as a specific kind of capital collectively accumulated by money capitalists as well as by industrial capitalists, as well his historico-empirical reconstruction of the societal and political consequences this development triggered, opened up a field of important Marxist research and debate. His analysis then significantly influenced the Marxist debates on imperialism, on the prospect of further capitalist development and on the strategic conclusions socialists/communists could or should draw from these findings (Nikolai Bukharin, Vladimir Lenin, Henryk Grossmann, Fritz Sternberg, as well as their supporters and opponents participated in these debates).
- A second question that demands more in-depth scrutiny refers to the consequences of Hilferding's theory of finance capital for the understanding of modern, contemporary processes of the accumulation of capital, for conceiving of its possibilities and perspectives of

development, as well as for working on socialist political strategies of transformation.

- Our third question was about how to deal with Hilferding's legacy as a contribution to the critique of political economy, i.e. as a lasting challenge to the economists of today, in order to find out what could be gained scientifically—in an analysis of reality and in a construction of possible futures—as well as politically—in a diagnosis of possible interventions—by taking up and critically addressing this legacy (Dellheim et al. 2018).

The original interpretation of Hilferding put forward by the influential political economist Joseph Schumpeter (who developed from an early sympathiser of Marx and Engels via conservative to reactionary positions) asserted that Hilferding had shown that capitalism was evolving towards a stable 'general cartel'. This reading of Hilferding was challenged by the Austro-Marxists, who in turn were an important influence on Michal Kalecki and Tadeusz Kowalik, inspiring them to make more critical use of Hilferding's achievements. Their investigations produced a significant legacy of insights, even though they were ignored, falsified, or negated by the Stalinist interpretations which had come to dominate the main thrust of Marxist debates. Proceeding from Kalecki and Kowalik's approach, we shall look at what can be gained today by specifically analysing the accumulation of finance capital—understood as globalised collective capital using credit for mobilising a maximum of resources for its accumulation by primary exploitation (unpaid wage labour) and by secondary exploitation (redistribution, dispossession)—in its relation to the dynamics of societal hierarchies (class, gender, ethnic and cultural origin, individual orientations, etc.) and, at the same time, its effects on the natural environment.

We were very pleased with the resonance our call was met with and the large number of eminently intriguing abstracts, especially from female economists and from scholars from Central and Eastern European countries and from the global South. Unfortunately, the cooperation with many of these authors did not materialise, for very different reasons—some due to very delightful circumstances, like pregnancy and the birth of a child; but also for very sad reasons caused by political repression and economic constraints; or simply due to too busy schedules. We wish the young mother and her new-born baby only the best and express our solidarity with the colleagues living under complicated political conditions. As coordinators of this volume we are grateful to Scott Aquanno (Canada), Patrick Bond (South Africa), John Grahl (Great Britain), Jan Greitens (Germany), Pat Higgins (Poland), Andrew Kilmister (Great Britain), Michael Krätke (Netherlands), Stephen Maher (Canada), Radhika Desai (Canada), Claude Serfati (France), Nikos Stravelakis (Greece), and Jan Toporowski (Great Britain) for their chapters and their constructive cooperation. As some originally planned contributions could not be realised, we were glad that Michael Krätke was able to address several topics in his chapter which otherwise would have been lost to this volume. Not only because of those contributions which ultimately could not be accomplished, we look forward to continuing the debate in this way.

Our book consists of several chapters covering very different aspects of Hilferding's rich, dramatic, and tragic legacy which, moreover, address in different ways the three questions we raised. We very much appreciate that all authors were also interested in the practical perspectives opened up by their contributions. They pursue the aim of helping the reader to understand the recent problems, the reasons for the overall defensive state of progressive alternative forces, and to find ways to overcome these situations of defensive struggles, as well as the underlying structural obstacles for democratic, just, socially and ecologically sustainable solutions for the mounting societal and global problems.

- Michael Krätke offers an overview of the history of Hilferding's seminal work and draws a comprehensive picture of its major theoretical achievements. In so doing, he shows that Hilferding effectively pursued the aim of continuing Marx's analysis of the capitalist mode of production. On the other hand, Krätke presents a full list of major amendments and conceptual changes to Hilferding's theoretical legacy that should allow the reader to begin to understand the phenomena of contemporary financial market capitalism.
- Nikos Stravelakis' chapter is about the key political economy contributions which originated from *Finance Capital*, covering the period from its publication in 1910 to the year 1966. In the author's view, the conclusions of Hilferding, Moszkowska, and Sweezy on economic crisis rely on the neoclassical theory of perfect competition and its 'dark side', i.e. monopoly 'price setting'. In conclusion,

according to the author, the three economists come to reject the Marxian labour theory of value.

- While sharing Krätke's view on Hilferding's aim and efforts, Patrick Bond focuses on Hilferding's contribution to understanding today's conjuncture that combines financial power and vulnerability, or 'financialisation'. But while, in Bond's view, Hilferding contributed in particular to an understanding of how general properties of the capitalist debt system could be advanced beyond the disorganised state of Marx's theory in *Capital* Volume 3, Bond regards a critique of Hilferding as essential for both intellectual and practical purposes.
- Andrew Kilmister provides a detailed comparison between Hilferding's work on finance capital and contemporary accounts of financialisation. He focuses in particular on the work of Costas Lapavitsas. Criticising Hilferding and Lapavitsas, Kilmister shows links between differing conceptions of financialisation and corresponding analyses of the periodisation of capitalism. Finally, he provides a richer picture of the changing periodisation of capitalism.
- By tracing the evolution of state and corporate organisation since the late nineteenth century, Scott Aquanno and Stephen Maher illustrate that a much-needed 'Institutional Marxist theory of corporate governance' should constitute a decisive foundation for the periodisation of capitalist development. They suggest that the 'restructuring of capitalism' since the 2008 crisis has led to the emergence of new consolidated institutional linkages between finance and industry constituting a new kind of 'finance capital' as an organisational form of corporate power.
- Radhika Desai provides an explanation for why Marx's and Hilferding's expectation that the English model of domination of the capitalist mode of production would be superseded by the more productive model of finance capital was not fulfilled. The desire of the United States to emulate British financial dominance ultimately supported the British pattern. Only now, in the twenty-first century, British financial strength and its pattern of dominance are unravelling.
- Claude Serfati analyses finance capital as a main pillar of imperialism. The second pillar, in his view, is militarism—and understanding their respective place in contemporary 'capitalism' requires a clear view of both of these aspects. By critically reading Hilferding, Serfati offers a definition of contemporary finance capital as the intertwining of monopoly industrial, merchant, real estate, land and banking capital

under the control of capital-property and in close relation to militarism.

- Looking at the power of corporations in society, John Grahl shows that Hilferding identified the divorce of ownership and control in the large-scale corporations of his day; and that Hilferding also anticipated the relegation of shareholders to the status of simple 'money capitalists' who traded their economic control for the liquidity of their holdings of securities. Grahl demonstrates how this trend continues into our own day and addresses the resulting lack of social control over large-scale enterprises.
- The history of these large-scale enterprises is connected to the business cycles of capitalist enterprises, as analysed by Michał Kalecki. Proceeding from this link, Jan Toporowski traces the origin of Kalecki's theory of business cycles to Hilferding's account of monopoly capital. Toporowski suggests that Kalecki unconsciously followed Emil Lederer in arguing that cartelisation tended to make business cycles more, not less extreme, but subsequently made the leap from Marx's schemes of reproduction to the modern system of national income accounts.
- While seeing Hilferding's contradictory relation to Marx, Pat Higgins exposes how Hilferding's theories of a moderate, evolutionary socialism produced a syncopated note to the advent of the dominant neoliberal Western ideology in the twentieth century, particularly in Germany. Higgins advocates a revival of Hilferding's moderate, revolutionary democratic socialism.
- According to Jan Greitens, Hilferding was not a Marxist but rather an eclectic. This is illustrated, according to Greitens, by the way Hilferding adopted and used the terms *Gemeinschaft*/community and *Gesellschaft*/society from Tönnies, as well as the literature on American corporate finance, as the basis for his definition of a 'promoter's profit'. Such a profit is primarily capitalised monopoly profit in the process of concentration of production and capital.
- In accordance with the thesis of Hilferding as an eclectic, Judith Dellheim answers the question about his further development of categories of the Marxian critique of political economy—the *Joint-Stock Company* and *Share Capital*—with 'not yet', which leads her to proposing an extended definition of these terms. Such a work process on the history of Marxist economics also shows that left-wing scholars have to deal with the fact that large parts of the left in the West, in

xii PREFACE TO THE FIRST EDITION

their way of thinking and working, are effectively much closer to Hilferding than to Marx and Luxemburg.

- This is another argument for taking a closer look at Hilferding's methodological background, also and especially at his little-known last theoretical text (1940). As a philosopher, Frieder Otto Wolf demonstrates how this text provides an insight into both the creativity and limitations of Hilferding's approach: while Hilferding shows himself, indeed, aware of the major challenges confronting Marxism in its crisis in the 1930s, he displayed a strong tendency to look for solutions in the context of the academic mainstream.[1]
- In his second, new contribution Jan Toporowski presents Ludwik Krzywicki as a significant and instructive forerunner of Hilferding. He outlines Krzywicki's analysis of monopoly finance capital, as published in articles from 1890 and 1905, that anticipates key elements of Hilferding's theory. While lacking the sophistication of Hilferding's theory, Krzywicki's exposition goes beyond Hilferding in two important respects. First of all it argues that the US kind of capital market finance, with investment banks in a coordinating role, is more durable than the bank-based finance capital of Hilferding. Krzywicki also introduced the concept of industrial feudalism, as a static social formation of rigid class boundaries that would emerge in a cartelised economy.
- In a contribution complementing the analysis of the text of Hilferding's last work by Wolf, Michael Krätke informs about Hilferding's long-forgotten still unpublished "notes" to his last work: the 16 pages of "notes" he wrote in addition to his manuscript on the "Problem of History". These notes show many additional reflections and complements to the first draft of the text, together with a long series of footnotes that Hilferding wanted to insert in it. What is more, they show that Hilferding took a fresh start to rewrite several passages of his first draft. These additional texts, although unfinished, as the first draft, serve to clarify some of the ideas Hilferding wanted to develop in this text. A complete reformulation of the main tenets of the materialist conception of history, not more and not less, was what Hilferding intended to achieve.
- Hilferding's important journalistic work is practically disregarded in the literature. Krätke opens the debate on this by presenting an over-

---

[1] The following four entries concern additional texts written for the 2nd edition of this book.

view of this long-forgotten or neglected part of Hilferding's work. Hilferding had worked as an editor, editor-in-chief, and journalist for the most important journals and newspapers in the history of the social democratic movement from 1903 to 1940. He published more than 300 articles in total. Most of his journalistic work was devoted to political and economic analysis. As a journalist, he has described and commented upon the major economic events and crises of his lifetime, the crisis of 1907/08, the German Revolution of 1918/19, the rise and fall of the Weimar Republic, the Great Depression of 1929–1935. During the years of exile, from 1933 until his untimely death in 1941, he has contributed a vast number of newspaper articles, explaining and criticising the economic and political events in Nazi Germany, depicting and analysing the transformation of the German economy into a war economy, and demonstrating the inherent weaknesses and fragilities of the kind of dictatorial capitalism, as well as pointing out how the Nazi state was pushing ever further into the catastrophe of total war. In his journalistic work, he touched many topics that he planned to include in a revised and extended version of his masterpiece 'Finance Capital'.

- In the concluding chapter Dellheim and Wolf explain their interest in a critical re-reading of the works of Eugen Varga. As a former admirer and comrade, and later as a radical critic of Rudolf Hilferding, Varga has been an excellent connoisseur of Hilferding's texts. Re-reading and critically evaluating Varga's critique of Hilferding, as well as Varga's own rich empirical material on the societal and economic development of specific countries, help us to further deal with Hilferding in a productive way. Varga's analyses are also referring to developments after Hilferding's flight from Germany in 1933 and his tragic death in February 1941, up to Varga's own end in October 1964. Their critical re-reading can help to improve current work in political economy concerning economic and political processes. This re-reading will also demonstrate that Varga was not "Stalin's Economist".

  This brief text by the editors is, at the same time, a special kind of call for abstracts or papers for the next volume in the series, inviting contributions to a productive critique of the work of a great internationalist economist and a historical personality.

As it can be concluded from these contributions, Hilferding's reflections still present a substantial challenge to the Marxist mainstream and deserve to be addressed and responded to more elaborately. While unfolding what is still needed for aiming at a society of free and equal individuals living in solidarity among each other and, at the same time, in ecological responsibility, the aim of this volume is to help in radically criticising existing reality and its theoretical and political reflections. We regard Hilferding's legacy not only as an important source of inspiration and a starting point for learning and understanding more about history and contemporary reality, but also for bringing together individuals, socio-political movements, and actors in order to instigate and raise communication, democratic discussion, and common action.

We are grateful to Palgrave Macmillan for the interest in this book on Rudolf Hilferding's legacy, as it already formed part of both of its predecessors and the project of this series as a whole. The general aim continues to be to "analyse capitalist processes, and not its symptoms"—as Jan Toporowski recommended to the current generation of "Marxist" and/or "Marxian" authors (Dellheim, Wolf, 2018a). In this sense, according to Frieder Otto Wolf, we ought to appropriate "Luxemburg's radically critical eyes as tools for reconstructing and prolonging Marx's theoretical arguments on the comprehensive reproduction process of capital as the dominant societal relation" (Dellheim 2016).

We would also like to thank Jan-Peter Herrmann for continuing his excellent translation and editing work, and we appreciate his patience and humour in dealing with complicated authors and editors. Finally, we thank the Rosa Luxemburg Foundation for the support it has given to our project once again.

Berlin, Germany   Judith Dellheim
Berlin, Germany   Frieder Otto Wolf

References

Dellheim, J., and F.O. Wolf. 2018a. The Challenge of the Incompleteness of the Third Volume of Capital for Theoretical and Political Work Today. In *The Unfinished System of Karl Marx. Critically Reading Capital as a Challenge for our Times*, 1–30. Cham: Palgrave Macmillan. https://www.palgrave.com/gp/book/9783319703466.

Dellheim, J., and F.O. Wolf. 2018b. *The Unfinished System of Karl Marx. Judith Dellheim and Frieder Otto Wolf introduce their new book on critical Capital reading.* https://www.rosalux.de/en/news/id/39289/the-unfinished-system-of-karl-marx/.

Dellheim, J., J. Toporowski, and F.O. Wolf. 2018. *Call for Papers On: Rudolf Hilferding's Critical Political Economy.* https://www.academia.edu/37728350/Call_for_papers_on_RUDOLF_HILFERDING_S_CRITICAL_POLITICAL_ECONOMY.

Dellheim, J., and F.O. Wolf. 2016. *Rosa Luxemburg: A Permanent Challenge for Political Economy. On the History and the Present of Luxemburg's 'Accumulation of Capital'.* Cham: Palgrave Macmillan. https://www.palgrave.com/gp/book/9781137601070.

Dellheim, J. 2016. Rosa Luxemburg: A Permanent Challenge for Political Economy. Judith Dellheim in an *interview with Frieder Otto Wolf, Hanna Szymborska, Jan Toporowski and Michael Brie about the new book.* https://www.rosalux.de/en/publication/id/9328/rosa-luxemburg-a-permanent-challenge-for-political-economy/.

Dellheim, J., Collective. 2016. *5 May 2018: The 200th birthday of Karl Marx. Critique of political economy, critique of our society, self critique of the left. Call for Papers on the Unfinished Book III. The Process of Capitalist Production as a Whole. Karl Marx's Capital.* A Critique of Political Economy, Volume III, edited by Friedrich Engels, friend and 'literary executor' (Engels 1891, p. 133). https://www.academia.edu/23053079/5_May_2018_The_200th_birthday_of_Karl_Marx._Critique_of_political_economy_critique_of_our_society_self-critique_of_the_left.

Luxemburg, R. [1918] 2015. The Second and Third Volumes of *Capital*, in *The Collected Works of Rosa Luxemburg*, ed. P. Hudis, Vol. 2, 451–61. London: Verso.

Preface to the Second Edition

Editors and authors are, of course, grateful for the interest of our readers that has made it possible to realise a second edition now. We have made use of this happy occasion to correct mistakes we had overlooked in the first edition, to actualise the texts wherever needed, and to add four texts: one by Michael R. Krätke on the still unpublished notes of Hilferding's last manuscript which had been published post-humously (discussed as such by F. O. Wolf), and another one, also by Krätke, on Hilferding's correspondence; plus a presentation of Krzywicki, the Polish 'equivalent' to Hilferding, by Toporowski, as well as a contribution by the editors opening a perspective on Varga. We hope to fuel the incipient debate on Hilferding by providing access to these materials—which are not merely of biographical relevancy. We also have added a contribution on Eugen Varga, leading on to the next collection of texts planned in this series.

All authors have had the occasion to revise their texts according to the need they could see for this. Accordingly, the new edition will serve as a useful tool for further developing the debate on Hilferding, after it had been unblocked from political fetters resulting from older political antagonisms.

We have become aware that there is an important and specific debate on Hilferding in Japan. Minoru Kurata and Masaaki Kurotaki should at least be mentioned here. Unfortunately, we have not been able to find a Japanese author for presenting this debate authentically, for which we only

xviii PREFACE TO THE SECOND EDITION

have passing references in the volume. This remains an open challenge for further research and debate.[1]

In finishing this volume, while the terrible 'military operations' generated especially by Putin and his narrow power circle are unfolding, we want to underline the deep internationalist character of our work aiming at strengthening critical thinking and emancipatory-solidarity oriented forces.

Berlin, Germany   Judith Dellheim
Berlin, Germany   Frieder Otto Wolf

LITERATURE

Kurata, M. 2009. *Rudolf Hilferding und "Das Finanzkapital"*. Vienna: Koppanyi.

Greitens, J. 2018. *Finanzkapital und Finanzsysteme: "Das Finanzkapital" von Rudolf Hilferding* (Beiträge zur Geschichte der deutschsprachigen Ökonomie, Vol. 40, 2., revised edition. Marburg: metropolis. https://greitens.net/wp-content/uploads/2021/03/Greitens_Finanzkapital-und-Finanzsystem_2018.pdf.

---

[1] A first overview is given in Greitens 2018. And we can refer to Kurata 2009 as a significant example.

Contents

1. Introduction: Critically Returning to Rudolf Hilferding   1
   Judith Dellheim and Frieder Otto Wolf

2. Rethinking Hilferding's *Finance Capital*   11
   Michael R. Krätke

3. From Luxemburg to Sweezy: Notes on the Intellectual
   Influence of Hilferding's *Finance Capital*   53
   Nikos Stravelakis

4. Contradictions in Hilferding's Finance Capital: Money,
   Banking, and Crisis Tendencies   85
   Patrick Bond

5. Finance Capital, Financialisation and the Periodisation of
   Capitalist Development   115
   Andrew Kilmister

6. A New Finance Capital? Theorizing Corporate
   Governance and Financial Power   141
   Stephen Maher and Scott Aquanno

7. Finance Capital and Contemporary Financialization   169
   Radhika Desai

xx CONTENTS

8 Finance Capital and Militarism as Pillars of Contemporary Capitalism 199
Claude Serfati

9 Hilferding and the Large-Scale Enterprise 233
John Grahl

10 Hilferding and Kalecki 251
Jan Toporowski

11 Ludwik Krzywicki's Anticipation of Hilferding 263
Jan Toporowski

12 A Socialist Third Way? Rudolf Hilferding's Evolutionary Socialism as Syncopated Note to Early Neoliberalism 277
J. Patrick Higgins

13 Hilferding as an Eclectic: A History of Economic Thought Perspective on Finance Capital 307
Jan Greitens

14 Rudolf Hilferding on the Economic Categories of 'Joint Stock Company/Share Capital': A Refinement of the Critique of Political Economy? 329
Judith Dellheim

15 Hilferding's Impressive Failure. A Reading of His Last Major Text 367
Frieder Otto Wolf

16 The Forgotten "Notes". Rudolf Hilferding's Still Unpublished Complements to His Manuscript "The Historical Problem" 381
Michael R. Krätke

CONTENTS   xxi

17 **Rudolf Hilferding: A Born Journalist**   393
Michael R. Krätke

18 **Postface: From Rudolf Hilferding to Eugen
Varga—Towards a Further Book Project**   439
Judith Dellheim and Frieder Otto Wolf

Index   451

NOTES ON CONTRIBUTORS

Scott Aquanno is Assistant Professor of Political Science at Ontario Tech University (UOIT). He holds research fellowships from the University of Toronto and previously worked in the bond industry for a major US financial firm.

Patrick Bond, Professor of Sociology at the University of Johannesburg, works on capitalist crisis, global governance, national public policy, political ecology, and urban problems, especially climate change and water. In service to the new South African government from 1994 to 2002, Patrick authored/edited more than a dozen policy papers, including the *Reconstruction and Development Programme* and the *RDP White Paper*. His dozen authored, co-authored, and edited books include *Elite Transition* (2014), *Uneven Zimbabwe* (1998), *Looting Africa* (2006), and *Politics of Climate Justice* (2012). Patrick earned his doctorate in Economic Geography under the supervision of David Harvey at Johns Hopkins University in 1993. He was born in Belfast, Northern Ireland, and has lived in Southern Africa since 1989.

Judith Dellheim is a senior research fellow at the Rosa-Luxemburg-Foundation, Berlin, Germany. She has worked on foreign trade of the GDR. Since 1990, Judith has been working on economies of solidarity, on political parties and movements, and on economic policies. She was a member of the Federal Board of the PDS in 1995–2003, a freelance scientific consultant from 2004 to 2010, and has been a senior researcher at the Rosa-Luxemburg-Foundation since 2011. She is the co-editor of *Rosa*

Luxemburg: A Permanent Challenge for Political Economy and *The Unfinished System of Karl Marx*.

Radhika Desai is Professor at the Department of Political Studies, and Director, Geopolitical Economy Research Group, University of Manitoba, Winnipeg, Canada. She was educated at the Maharaja Sayajirao University of Baroda, India, and Queen's University at Kingston, Canada. She is the author of, for example, *Geopolitical Economy: After US Hegemony, Globalization and Empire* (2013). Her edited or co-edited books include, among others: *Karl Polanyi and Twenty-first Century Capitalism* (2020), *Revolutions*, a special issue of *Third World Quarterly*, Russia, *Ukraine and Contemporary Imperialism*, a special issue of *International Critical Thought* (2016), *Theoretical Engagements in Geopolitical Economy* (2015), *Analytical Gains from Geopolitical Economy* (2015). She also co-edits the *Geopolitical Economy* book series (Manchester University Press) and the *Future of Capitalism* book series (Pluto Press).

John Grahl Professor Emeritus of Economics at the University of Middlesex, is a specialist in the economics and economic policies of the European Union and its member states. He has published widely on developments in industrial relations, social policy, and EU-regional macroeconomics. John's work draws on the broad traditions associated with Marx, Keynes, and other critical and heterodox thinkers. He is a founding member of the Euro-Memorandum Group, which has published an annual critical assessment of EU policies for 25 years. Recently he has concentrated on financial issues, for instance in a forthcoming paper on the dollarisation of the eurozone.

Jan Greitens is Professor of Economics at the Baden-Wuerttemberg Cooperative State University. His research interests lie in the history of economic thought and monetary economics. His recent publications include *Finanzkapital und Finanzsysteme* (2nd ed., metropolis, 2018), his dissertation about Rudolf Hilferding, and *Geld-Theorie-Geschichte* (metropolis, 2019).

J. Patrick Higgins is a PhD candidate at the Faculty of Law and Administration at the University of Łódź, Poland, as well as a member of the research unit, the Alexander de Tocqueville Center for the History of Political and Legal Thought. He has two main research interests: untangling the interconnections between the Austrian School, Walter Lippmann, the ordoliberals, the Chicago school, and the Austro-Marxists, in order to understand the emergence of neoliberalism in the mid-twentieth century; and integrating models from constitutional political economy, the sociology of law, contextualist, and comparative historiography, in order to understand the deep institutional history of Poland from the thirteenth century through its post-communist transformation.

Andrew Kilmister is Senior Lecturer in Economics at Oxford Brookes University Business School. His research interests are in the philosophy of economics, the history of economic thought, and the study of business cycles and financial crises. He is the co-author, with Gary Browning, of *Critical and Post-Critical Political Economy* (Palgrave Macmillan, 2006) and was the editor of the *Journal of Contemporary Central and Eastern Europe* (formerly titled *Debatte*) from 2007 to 2021. Andrew has also published articles and book chapters on European economics and development theory, and his teaching focuses on economic growth and comparisons between orthodox and heterodox approaches to contemporary economic problems.

Michael R. Krätke was Professor of Sociology and Chair of Political Economy at Lancaster University until January 2019 and was previously Professor of Political Economy at the University of Amsterdam. He is a leading scholar on Marxian economics, the history of political economy, and the history of Marxism and socialism. Michael has published 14 books on political economy, as well as more than 250 journal articles and book chapters on various topics, such as public finance, social and economic policy, the history of economic thought, the development of Marxism, the history of modern capitalism and international political economy. He has contributed to major international projects like the Historical-Critical Dictionary of Marxism and the Marx-Engels-Gesamtausgabe (MEGA). His most recent publication is *Friedrich Engels. Wie ein Cotton Lord den Marxismus erfand* (2020, Berlin: Karl Dietz Verlag).

Stephen Maher is Associate Editor of the *Socialist Register*, and a postdoctoral fellow at Ontario Tech University. He is also the author of *Corporate Capitalism and the Integral State: General Electric and a Century of American Power* (Palgrave Macmillan, 2022), and a member of the Toronto-based Socialist Project.

Claude Serfati PhD in Economics, has been Senior Associate Professor of Economics at the University of Versailles-Saint-Quentin-en-Yvelines (UVSQ). He chaired CEMOTEV (UVSQ), a lab collaboration between economists and geographers, and is associate-researcher at CEMOTEV. Besides publishing a number of articles in academic reviews, as well as editing and authoring books, he has contributed as leader and senior manager to a number of international academic projects. Claude's main research fields include the transformations of contemporary capitalism, especially finance capital-dominated globalisation; interrelations between productive and financial activities; transnational corporations as financial groups; modern forms of imperialism; and arms industries, with special reference to science and technology policy.

Nikos Stravelakis returned to academia after a career as a CFO in major Greek firms. He works at the Department of Economics of the University of Athens and is a named partner in a consulting company. His work focuses on Marx's theory of crisis, with an emphasis on the crisis-trigger mechanism. His interest in crisis theory initiated an extensive study on the perceptions of the dynamics of capitalism on the Left and their political repercussions. The chapter included in this volume presents a part of this research. Nikos studied economics as an undergraduate at the University of Athens and as a graduate student first at the New School for Social Research and finally at the University of Athens. He taught and teaches courses and labs in political economy and mathematical economics, and is also a member of the IIPPE, the Greek Association of Political Economy and the Greek Economic Association.

Jan Toporowski is Professor of Economics and Finance at the School of Oriental and African Studies, University of London; and Professor of Economics and Finance at the International University College, Turin. Jan studied Economics at Birkbeck College, University of London, and the University of Birmingham, UK. Before working as an academic he worked in fund management, international banking, and central banking. He has been a consultant for the United Nations Development Programme, the United Nations Conference on Trade and Development, the UN Economic Commission for Africa, and the Economist Intelligence Unit. His research is concentrated on monetary theory and policy, finance, and the work of Michał Kalecki.

Frieder Otto Wolf is Honorary Professor of Philosophy at the Free University (FU) of Berlin. Lecturer in Philosophy at the FU since 1973, he became Honorary Professor in 2007. He has served as a fellow at the Rosa Luxemburg Foundation and sits on the advisory board of several journals. Frieder has published books and articles on political philosophy, the politics of labour, the politics of sustainability, political epistemology, and metaphilosophy, including as co-editor of *Rosa Luxemburg: A Permanent Challenge for Political Economy* and *The Unfinished System of Karl Marx*.

CHAPTER 1

Introduction: Critically Returning to Rudolf Hilferding

Judith Dellheim and Frieder Otto Wolf

In his book, *Rudolf Hilferding. The Tragedy of a German Social Democrat*, William Smaldone sums up: 'The tragedy in Hilferding's life lay in his adherence to a political outlook that was incompatible with German reality in 1933' (Smaldone 1998, 8). Although this may certainly be true, in this, Rudolf Hilferding did not differ from many others, and Smaldone's book itself ultimately says much more about Hilferding's actual tragedy: the talented economist and social democratic politician died in the hell of GESTAPO imprisonment and also played a part in the rise to power of those he had identified as mortal enemies early on, and who were able to maintain that power for many years.

Many of those whom he fiercely opposed and fought against did not survive this period. In fact, many did not even live to see this time, like

J. Dellheim (✉)
Rosa-Luxemburg-Foundation, Berlin, Germany

F. O. Wolf
Institute of Philosophy, Freie Universität Berlin, Berlin, Germany
e-mail: fow@snafu.de

© The Author(s), under exclusive license to Springer Nature Switzerland AG 2023
J. Dellheim, F. O. Wolf (eds.), *Rudolf Hilferding*, Luxemburg International Studies in Political Economy,
https://doi.org/10.1007/978-3-031-08096-8_1

Rosa Luxemburg, because they were murdered by those who paved the way for fascism. Although both of them were members of the same party for a long time, fought for socialism, relentlessly spoke out and stood up against the war, and addressed the same problems, the underlying causes and associated perpetrators both in theory and practice, they were unable to cooperate with one another. The fact that Rosa Luxemburg meticulously and thoroughly studied Hilferding's *Finance Capital* is confirmed by her extensive writings in the form of notes, conspectuses, text and speech drafts (e.g. Luxemburg [1910–1913], p. 152), as well as records and transcripts of her lectures by her students at the SPD's party school (e.g. Walcher [1910/1911], p. 369). Various letters provide further hints in this regard. Unfortunately, she never actually wrote the review of *Finance Capital* she had announced to Kostya Zetkin (Luxemburg [1911a] p. 41) and never referred to the book or its analyses in her own publications. In fact, she even suspected the 'dirt monger Hilferding' (Luxemburg [1911b], p. 142) of having organised the campaign against her *Accumulation of Capital* (Luxemburg 1913c, p. 265): '*Hilf[erding]* is behind this' (Luxemburg 1913a, p. 267), she remarked to Leo Jogiches (see also [Luxemburg 1913b], p. 266). Hilferding, for his part, outwardly ignored Luxemburg's theoretical and political achievements for decades. According to Leon Trotsky, he must have hated her (Trotsky 1929). It was only in 1920, during a very heated argument with Gregory Zinoviev, that Hilferding paid tribute to Rosa Luxemburg, albeit very selectively (Hilferding 1920, pp. 152ff). Zinoviev—on orders of the Executive Committee of the Communist International—had responded to the USPD's request for affiliation by informing them of 21 conditions for membership. In sum, he demanded no less than the USPD's submission, or rather 'Bolshevisation'. Hilferding based his stance on Luxemburg's argument put forward against Lenin, who wanted to develop party members as party soldiers, forging the workers' party as a centralised organisation.

Even though both Luxemburg and Hilferding vehemently rejected Lenin's party concept and its conception of human beings, this does not mean that they shared a common view on the tasks of the workers' party and its members. After all, Hilferding considered the parliament to be the most important field of political struggle, and he developed—despite his explicit demand to be open to argument and despite the aptitude for

1 INTRODUCTION: CRITICALLY RETURNING TO RUDOLF HILFERDING   3

pragmatism[1] he proved to possess during his time as Reich Finance Minister—a peculiar kind of dogmatism. As a result, he turned out, particularly during the crucial years of 1931/1932, to be an opponent of any kind of trade-unionist anti-depression programme because, in his view, government deficit spending contradicted the legitimate boundaries of capitalist economic policy (Stephan 1982, p. 239).

Ever since his experience with Bolshevism and its uncritical followers in Germany, Hilferding had begun to include an undifferentiated anti-communist stance among his political principles. Such positions defended by social democrats facilitated the disastrous Stalinist thesis of 'social fascism', reflecting and reinforcing the historical inability by Social Democrats and Communists to form an anti-fascist alliance. Neither his escape from Germany (Hilferding 1933/1982, pp. 268f, see also Stephan 1982, pp. 279–80[2]) nor the German attack on Poland could convince Hilferding otherwise (Hilferding 1940, p. 290). As early as the 1920s, the independent leftist and brilliant and sharp-tongued journalist Carl von Ossietzky mocked the irrational anti-communist politics as pursued by leading Social Democrats, particularly by such figures as Rudolf Hilferding in his exclusive orientation on parliamentary politics and governmental policies (e.g. Ossietzky 1924/2014, p. 64).

Ossietzky was among the very first victims of the fascists after their all-too-easy assumption of power. Following torture and inhumane incarceration in both prison and in a concentration camp, Ossietzky died in 1938. He had fought passionately for a democratic anti-fascist front, whereas the Bolshevist Zinoviev, even though he had previously warned against the rise of the fascists, had obstructed such efforts. Zinoviev himself also became a prominent victim of Stalin and his followers, whose unscrupulousness and 'successful' elimination (and co-opting) of party members

---

[1] Communist Neugebauer, however, had not simply lied when he remarked: 'the same day that Hilferding declares that the equilibrium of the budget may not be infringed, and that our demands on behalf of the workers must therefore be repelled, his party friends put forward a motion demanding a reduction of the merger tax, a tax break which serves the interests of the trusts. Mr. Hilferding is willing to grant tax relief to the trusts, but he rejects our motion' (BSB/MDZ 1929, p. 184). The motion particularly intended for additional unemployment benefits.

[2] Cora Stephan quotes from a letter by Hilferding to Paul Hertz dated 14 June 1933 in which he provides an explanation for the need to stage anti-fascist resistance: 'Otherwise we will lose our influence in favour of the Communists'.

destroyed millions of lives. These victims included more than a million murdered communist activists.

Among them were high-ranking military staff in the Red Army, some of whom had fought courageously against Franco in Spain. They, of all people, were accused of 'fearmongering' and 'cowardice before the enemy' when they warned of an unpremeditated attack on Russia by Hitler's Germany. They referred in particular to the information provided by German political-economist Richard Sorge (a member of the extended family of Friedrich Adolph Sorge, a friend and comrade-in-arms of Karl Marx and Frederick Engels), who worked for the Soviet enemy reconnaissance in Japan. His analysis, which remains compelling reading to this day, *The Revival of German Imperialism* [*Der neue deutsche Imperialismus*], is based on Hilferding's *Finance Capital* and Lenin's *Imperialism, the Highest Stage of Capitalism*. It contains phrases like 'when Hilferding still was a Marxist' (Sorge [1928/1988], pp. 37, 65). That said, Sorge, at the same time, had some appreciation for the 'renegade' (ibid., p. 37): 'The only one still holding a leading position in the 2nd International who has taken a clear position regarding imperialism is Hilferding' (ibid., p. 152).

Sorge, the anti-fascist spy, was caught, tortured in the most brutal ways, sentenced to death and finally murdered by Hitler's Japanese partners. Stalin apparently did not even attempt to save Sorge's life, given that dead martyrs were far more valuable to him—especially if their early warnings against a German attack on the Soviet Union were about to become more widely known. The anti-fascist Hilferding, for his part, seems to have not made any reference to Sorge the economist in his work. And he certainly did not seek any cooperation with Sorge the communist. And yet one can only agree with Hilferding, when, in 1940, he wrote that 'the Bolshevik economy can hardly be called "socialist"' (Hilferding [1940] 1947). '[F]or to us socialism is indissolubly linked to democracy … the socialist society would inaugurate the highest realization of democracy' (ibid.). Sorge ultimately wanted the same, although he did not grasp Hilferding's fundamental problem: Hilferding wanted to be a Marxist but had never fully grasped Marx's understanding of society and social development. Marx's approach was an empirical and theoretical method closely tied to (even if distinct from) practical intervention and the painstaking organisation of the like-minded it required. Consequently, Hilferding lacked not only any general understanding of Marx's use of dialectics, but both the receptiveness for contradictions and the ability to address them in a strategically productive way—that is, in a way that allowed for increased insight into complex social contexts and for an adequate deliberation on actions and strategies that might have resulted in a more effective kind of left politics.

This was also and in particular analysed very clearly by Hilferding's contemporary Paul Levi (Levi 1927, pp. 1048–50). Following the murder of Luxemburg, Liebknecht and Jogiches, he took over the leadership of the Communist Party of Germany, founded in late 1918/early 1919. He had represented Rosa Luxemburg as a lawyer, advised her as a friend and also been her last lover. However, Levi was expelled from the party for publicly criticising the adventurism of the 'March action' in 1921. His critique of Hilferding, moreover, highlights the great challenge for those involved in this book project who seek to analyse and discuss Hilferding's writings from the perspective of the critique of political economy: to use it as a source of inspiration, to investigate and explain the development of capital relations in connection with other social relations, and to critically reflect and drive forward the scientific, ideological and political engagement with the latter in pursuit of the aim of overcoming them in practice.

This critical approach to Hilferding's work is distinct from that of F. Peter Wagner, who, in continuation of Hilferding's anti-communist attitude, separates him further from the radical left in political terms, thereby levelling precisely his contradictoriness which is so productive. (The important contributions to substantial debate on Hilferding made by Gottschalch, Greitens, Kurata, Pietranera, and Schefold are discussed in the chapters by Greitens, Krätke and Dellheim.) Hilferding, in his contradictions, was capable of extensive political activities and a courageous anti-fascism,[3] in particular with regard to his direct engagement with Goebbels.[4] The fact that the Marx expert, important leftist philosopher and socialist dissident Ernst Bloch refers to scientific social analysis in the critical Marxian tradition as a cold-stream may still be acceptable for Wagner. Wagner, however, considers Bloch's reference to the engaged struggle for

---

[3] The Nazis had a special hatred for Hilferding as finance minister, see http://europeana.eu/portal/record/2022022/11088_2FF551C8_3C99_48E4_9414_652B60694E48.html and http://europeana.eu/portal/record/2022022/11088_35363F83_F7AF_4539_8749_B043EE8C0928.html .

[4] Goebbels stated in the Reichstag on 10 July 1928: 'Go ahead and install Purim as a national holiday, with Hugo Preuss as the father of the constitution and the Jew Hilferding as the executor of the constitution! Then you will have given your republic the holiday it deserves' (Lively applause from the National Socialists—indignant calls from the left ... Delegate Strasser: 'You Jew-servants, you Jew-bandits!') (BSB/MDZ, 1929, p. 151).

socialist values and goals as a 'warm-stream' and his attempts to promote the permanent dialectical process of critical contestation between these two tendencies as a core task of the socialist movement, or of 'Marxism',[5] to be 'confused' (Wagner 1996, p. 186). By contrast, he does praise Hilferding's aspiration for theoretical clarity (ibid.). Socialist Horst Klein makes an effort to organise the engagement with Hilferding the anti-war activist, democrat and theoretician in a way that allows for the emergence or, rather, further development of the communication and cooperation across party boundaries between the social democratic SPD and the socialist DIE LINKE in Germany (Klein 2015, p. 25). He seeks to radically criticise the fateful conflicts between the communist KPD and the SPD and to positively influence today's left, theoretically, politically and culturally, basing himself on both Luxemburg and Hilferding (Klein 2009/2015, pp. 15–9, 23ff).

There seem to be three salient aspects we should like to emphasise concerning the differences of approach that become apparent rather clearly in this volume.

One is simply about what it means 'not to forget class struggle in theory' (Althusser): While it seems to be clear for all to see that this cannot imply in any way to instrumentalise theoretical, empirical or historical analysis and re-construction for political purposes—even if they are more solidly grounded than personal moral stances or party lines—it is to be soberly discussed to what extent this can be achieved within the 'policed areas' of institutionalised academia or the 'tamed struggle' of parliamentary politics. Subservience and conformity do not seem to be a real option for a radically critical scientific approach; radical intentions, however, can never serve as a substitute for ascertaining reality (including its real possibilities). Therefore, explaining and critically dissolving the illusions reproduced by ideological conformism within academic debates remains an indispensable part of real, that is, critical science, while remaining on the lookout for real possibilities of a practical turn for the better in actual class struggles (as well as in other genuine liberation struggles).

---

[5] 'The Kata to dynaton links up [...] with Marxism's *cold-stream*, the cool, sober view [...] on politics as the art of the possible, yet it substantiates in Marx the tense exactness of economic-material determinations of the stations and schedules of historical trajectory and the intervention into that trajectory. While the other, the Dynamei on, which truly constitutes the ontological determination of what is possible, can and must be filled with targeted enthusiasm, thereby corresponding to the *warm-stream* in Marxism' (Bloch 1975, pp. 140–1, italics in the original, translation amended).

The *second* aspect concerns a downside of the same problematique which often seems to be overlooked: concerning oneself only with the consumption of the salaried masses in terms of quantity—as 'underconsumption approaches' tend to do, even among Marxists—amounts to structurally neglecting the overdetermined character of real class struggles which always include an ecological, feminist and internationalist dimension, sometimes positively, but far more often negatively. Being oblivious to the role of these dimensions in the real class struggles as they form the substance of history is therefore tantamount to missing the point of a serious and adequate scientific analysis of the real conjuncture—which is, indeed, the epitome of transition between theory and practice.

The *third* aspect pertains to Marx's understanding of progress, as a quasi-natural process with an in-built teleology towards overcoming the old division of labour within modern society and 'negating' the destruction of natural living conditions accompanying the dominance of the capitalist mode of production. There is a certain contradiction in Marx's theory, namely, between his radical criticism of the 'division of individuals'[6] and his faith in the capacity for progress of human productive powers. We are confronted by a Marxian understanding that this criticism should be somehow connected with an expansion of the means of production in ever-further expanding enterprises, clearly in contradiction to the postulates of a universal development of individual abilities and of a continuous reproduction and further improvement of natural living conditions. While seeing this, Marx also formulated an understanding of the ongoing process of overcoming the old division of labour which does not rely on such a continuous rise in the capacity of the means of production or a corresponding expansion of enterprises. 'Progress', at the end of the day, means nothing less and nothing more, including to Marx, than the real process of criticism and self-criticism of the existing mode of production, that is, of the ways in which the real connection of the labour force with the means of production is historically organised within modern societies— with all kinds of individual, societal, global and, at the same time, ecological consequences, even within the liberated societies which will emerge from the complex historical process of overcoming the domination of the capitalist mode of production over modern 'civil-bourgeois societies'.

---

[6] Critically conceived as the selective development of individual abilities according to the needs of capital accumulation, the reproduction of hierarchies within human modern societies and, again, the destruction of natural living conditions.

While certainly serving as a contribution to a seriously scientific and at the same time radically critical effort, which can provide at least starting points for strategic practical deliberation, this publication aims specifically, and, at the same time, more broadly, to address the international discourse among very different democrats which want to learn from history and come together to fight violence against people and nature. Moreover, the editors of the series and of this volume also and especially address all those engaged in the serious exercise of critical political economy and all those who aim to intervene scientifically, politically and practically into present reality, so as to enable everyone to live in social equality and self-determination, with dignity and in solidarity with one another, as well as in an intact natural environment in the future.

REFERENCES

Bloch, E. 1975. *Experimentum Mundi, Frage, Kategorien des Herausbringens, Praxis*. Frankfurt am Main: Suhrkamp Verlag.

BSB Bayerische Staatsbibliothek, MDZ Münchner Digitalisierungszentrum. 1929. *Verhandlungen des Reichstages*, Bd. 423, 1928 (1929). Berlin; 4. J. publ. g. 1142 y, A-423, urn.nbn:de:bvb-12bsb00000107-7. München.

Hilferding, R. 1920/1982. Revolutionäre Politik oder Machtillusionen? In *Zwischen den Stühlen oder über die Unvereinbarkeit von Theorie und Praxis. Schriften Rudolf Hilferdings 1904 bis 1940*, ed. C. Stephan, 135–165. Bonn: Verlag J.H.W. Dietz Nachf.

———. 1933/1982. Zwischen den Entscheidungen. In *Zwischen den Stühlen oder über die Unvereinbarkeit von Theorie und Praxis. Schriften Rudolf Hilferdings 1904 bis 1940*, ed. C. Stephan, 270–276. Bonn: Verlag J.H.W. Dietz Nachf.

———. 1940. Das historische Problem. In *Zwischen den Stühlen oder über die Unvereinbarkeit von Theorie und Praxis. Schriften Rudolf Hilferdings 1904 bis 1940*, ed. C. Stephan, 298–328. Bonn: Verlag J.H.W. Dietz Nachf.

———. [1940] 1947. State Capitalism or Totalitarian State Economy. *The Modern Review* (June): 266–271. https://www.marxists.org/archive/hilferding/1940/statecapitalism.htm

Klein, H. [2009] 2015. Beiträge zur linkssozialistischen Theoriegeschichte. *Sozialisten im Streit für eine bessere Welt, unter besonderer Berücksichtigung der Ideen von Max Adler, Otto Bauer, Eduard Bernstein, Gustav Eckstein, Rudolf Hilferding, Karl Kautsky und Karl Renner*, Strausberger Studien zur Geschichte (54), 5th Expanded and Improved Edition, Strausberg: Eigenverlag Horst Klein/Hans W. Odenthal.

Levi, P. 1927. Zum Kieler Parteitag, Sozialistische Politik und Wirtschaft, Vol. 5, No. 22, 3 June. In *Paul Levi, Ohne einen Tropfen Lakaienblut, Schriften, Reden*

Briefe, Band II/2: Sozialdemokratie. Sozialistische Politik und Wirtschaft II, ed. Jörn Schütrumpf. Berlin: Karl Dietz Verlag, pp. 1046–1050.

Luxemburg, L. 1910–1913. *Handschriftliche Fragmente zur Entstehung und Entwicklung des Kapitalismus mit Wirtschafts- und weltgeschichtlichen Vergleichen* (Headlines by the Editors). In *Gesammelte Werke*, ed. Rosa Luxemburg, Band 7/1. Edited and Revised by Annelies Laschitza and Eckhard Müller, with a Foreword by Annelies Laschitza. Berlin: Karl Dietz Verlag, pp. 127–236.

———. [1911a] 1987. Brief an Kostja Zetkin Ende März, Friedenau. In *Gesammelte Briefe*, ed. Rosa Luxemburg, Band 4, p. 41. Berlin: Karl Dietz Verlag.

———. [1911b] 1987. Brief an Konrad Haenisch 12. Dezember, Südende, in: Rosa Luxemburg, Band 4, *Gesammelte Briefe*. Berlin: Karl Dietz Verlag, pp. 142–3.

———. [1913a] 1987. Brief an Leo Jogiches, 16. Februar, Berlin-Südende: Rosa Luxemburg, Band 4, *Gesammelte Briefe*. Berlin: Karl Dietz Verlag, pp. 266–267.

———. [1913b] 1987. Brief an Leo Jogiches, 14. Februar, Berlin-Südende, in: Rosa Luxemburg, Band 4, *Gesammelte Briefe*. Berlin: Karl Dietz Verlag, pp. 265–6.

———. [1913c] 1987. Brief an Leo Jogiches 13. Februar, Berlin-Südende. In Gesammelte Briefe, ed. Rosa Luxemburg, Band 4, Berlin: Karl Dietz Verlag p. 265.

Ossietzky, C.V. 1924/2014. Deutsche Linke. In *Carl von Ossietzky. Ein Lesebuch, ausgewählte Texte von Werner Boldt*, ed. W. Boldt, 64–65. Dähre: Ossietzky Verlag GmbH.

Smaldone, W. 1998. *Rudolf Hilferding: The Tragedy of a German Social Democrat.* DeKalb: Northern Illinois University Press.

Sorge, R. [1928] 1988. *Der neue deutsche Imperialismus.* With a Foreword by Jürgen Kuczynski. Berlin: Karl Dietz Verlag.

Stephan, C., ed. 1982. *Zwischen den Stühlen oder über die Unvereinbarkeit von Theorie und Praxis. Schriften Rudolf Hilferdings 1904 bis 1940.* Bonn: Verlag J.H.W. Dietz Nachf.

Trotsky, L. 1929. Mein Leben. https://www.marxists.org/deutsch/archiv/trotzki/1929/leben/16-deutsch.htm

Wagner, E.P. 1996. *Rudolf Hilferding: Theory and Politics of Democratic Socialism.* Atlantic Highlands: Humanities Press.

Walcher, J. [1910/1911] 2017. Aufzeichnungen und häusliche Nachträge des Parteischülers Jacob Walcher zu den Vorlesungen von Rosa Luxemburg (Headlines by the editors) 1910/11. In *Gesammelte Werke*, ed. Rosa Luxemburg, Band 7/1. Edited and Revised by Annelies Laschitza and Eckhard Müller, with a Foreword by Annelies Laschitza, Berlin: Karl Dietz Verlag, pp. 311–408.

CHAPTER 2

Rethinking Hilferding's *Finance Capital*

Michael R. Krätke

FINANCE CAPITAL: A CONTINUATION OF MARX'S *CAPITAL*?

When Hilferding's magnum opus *Finance Capital* was first published in 1910, the author, at the age of 33, was already well known in the community of German-speaking Marxist economists. He had studied medicine at the University of Vienna, opting for a safe, well-paid profession, and graduated as a Doctor of Medicine. From 1901 onwards, he practised as a doctor—specialised in paediatrics—in Vienna.[1] But political economy remained his passion and he continued to study economics, economic history and statistics at the University of Vienna, attending lectures and seminars whenever possible. His teachers, such as Friedrich von Wieser and the

[1] Zweiling, K. 1927. Biographical details about Hilferding can be easily found in Gottschalch (1962), Smaldone (1998) and Wagner (1996). A good overview of the historical context of Hilferding's work on *Finance Capital* can be found in Greitens (2012).

M. R. Krätke (✉)
Amsterdam, The Netherlands

© The Author(s), under exclusive license to Springer Nature
Switzerland AG 2023
J. Dellheim, F. O. Wolf (eds.), *Rudolf Hilferding*, Luxemburg
International Studies in Political Economy,
https://doi.org/10.1007/978-3-031-08096-8_2

old Eugen von Philippovich, certainly were no Marxists. But remarkably enough, the young Doctor Hilferding was allowed into the famous seminar held by Professor Eugen von Böhm-Bawerk, where he sat together with his friend Otto Bauer, with Emil Lederer, Ludwig von Mises and the young Joseph Schumpeter. Böhm-Bawerk was the renowned head of the Austrian school of marginal utility theory and enjoyed a well-earned reputation as an outstanding and sharp critic of Marx's economic theories (see Böhm-Bawerk 1949).

Hilferding belonged to the small but already famous group of 'Austro-Marxists'—together with Max Adler, Otto Bauer and Karl Renner, he formed its inner circle. From 1904 onwards, he acted together with Max Adler as the editor of Marx-Studien, the first truly Austro-Marxist publication, a yearbook, where many of the major works by the Austro-Marxists were published for the first time. Hilferding's *Finance Capital* was published in 1910 as Volume 3 of this yearbook, but also separately as a book in the same year (see Krätke 2019).

Because of this book, Hilferding became the most renowned Marxist economist in Europe almost overnight. He already enjoyed a reputation thanks to his long article on 'Böhm-Bawerk's Criticism of Marx', a response to the critique that Böhm had written after the publication of Volume III of Marx's *Capital*, trying to prove the complete and inescapable failure of Marx's critique of political economy. In his anti-critique, Hilferding had tackled some of the most salient unsettled questions of Marx's economic theory and tried to show that this theory had not been refuted by Böhm once and for all, as many economists believed (see Hilferding 1949).

Hilferding belonged to the first generation of budding Marxists who had had no personal contact with either Marx or Engels. They were confronted with the arduous double task of defending the body of theories they had inherited and of continuing the work their masters had left unfinished. Like Bauer, Hilferding had quite clear ideas about how to meet the challenge of both completing and continuing Marx's analysis of modern capitalism. While working on his manuscript for the book that would become *Finance Capital*, he reported to Karl Kautsky about his plans and the direction of his enterprise.[2] Bernstein and the so-called revisionists had no idea about the direction in which Marx's critique of political economy had further to be developed; they were utterly sterile and did not even

---

[2] Kurata (2009) and Greitens (2012), following Kurata's lead, have provided useful accounts of the making of *Finance Capital*.

imagine what could and should be achieved in this field. Not 'by fiddling with the theory of value but by studying those phenomena that Marx had left out of consideration, in particular in a theory of competition in capitalism, which could, of course, best be studied in New York, we should expect new insights' (Hilferding 1902).[3]

The main source and theoretical inspiration for Hilferding were, of course, the Volumes II and III of Marx's *Capital*, at that time still largely ignored even by the most ardent believers in Marxism. But, as Hilferding clearly saw at the time—much in contrast to the large majority of his fellow Marxists—Volume III was full of gaps, full of unsettled questions, some just alluded to, some hardly touched upon, some bypassed in a rather cavalier manner, acceptable in a first draft but rather inapt for a serious theoretical treatment of the subject matter at hand.[4] As a consequence, nobody could seriously pretend to just 'apply' Marx's theory to a host of new phenomena. That very theory itself had to be completed, elaborated and expanded in order to deal with the many questions that Marx had left unsettled and that even Engels had failed to tackle. Maybe in his original manuscripts Marx had left some hints, or even more than that, which Engels had overlooked and left out in his edition of the Volumes II and III. Hilferding was the first among the young Marxists ever to raise any doubts about Engels's work as editor of Marx's manuscripts. While still working on his analysis and struggling with the many issues that Marx had left unsettled in *Capital*, Volume III, he asked Karl Kautsky whether the original manuscripts by Marx for the second and third volumes were available. He would not have the time to study them right now, but he would really like to do it later. Because he had the 'suspicion that Engels did not always see, what it was all about; some of his polemical remarks against Marx are directly wrong in my view. It would also be interesting to check whether passages that are especially relevant for the investigation of the problem of competition have not been omitted. Transcripts of the manuscripts must exist' (Hilferding 1906).[5] Likewise, he was eager to see the

---

[3] Original in German; the translation is my own.

[4] The original version of Marx's main manuscript of 1864–1865 for *Capital*, Volume III, was published in 1992 for the first time, an English translation is available since 2015 (see Marx 2015).

[5] Original in German; the translation is my own. As the many drafts for the second and third volumes of *Capital* have now been published in section II of the second MEGA, we are today able to answer Hilferding's question. Yes, there are some passages in the manuscripts left by Marx that Engels should have included in his edition. Engels's decision to leave them out, however, can be excused, as Marx himself was not fully aware of the relevance of all the discoveries he actually made.

14 M. R. KRÄTKE

still unpublished manuscript by Engels on the stock market or to learn more about it (see Hilferding 1906).[6]

HILFERDING AND POLITICAL ECONOMY

Kautsky had refused to publish Hilferding's long defence of Marx—his anti-critique to Böhm-Bawerk's highly influential Marx-critique of 1896—in the *Neue Zeit* because it was too long for the journal. But he certainly saw the young man's talent and was eager to win him as a regular contributor for his journal. So, from 1902 onwards, Hilferding was publishing articles on political economy, dealing with the central problems, the specific methodology and the historical context of Marx's critique of political economy (see Hilferding 1902, 1903b, 1904). He was equally welcome to analyse and comment upon actual political problems the socialist movement in Germany and Europe had to face. In these articles, written while he was working on his book, he already gave an outline of his views on the new kind of capitalism that had emerged from the Great Depression and had just experienced its first major crisis in the year 1900. In his article on 'Functional change of the protective tariff', Hilferding anticipated some core elements of his analysis of the most recent changes in capitalism. High finance and industrial capital, acting in close cooperation, had found new ways to use the power of the state in order to exploit the whole of their respective societies and other nations as well (see Hilferding 1903a, pp. 278–279). A second crisis, the world financial crisis of 1907, which had a much larger impact, was soon to follow. Hilferding presented his analysis of the events of the great crisis of 1907 in three longer articles that appeared in the *Neue Zeit* (Hilferding 1907, 1908a, b).[7] Hilferding's reputation as a capable Marxist political economist was soon well established and he was the first to be invited to the German capital to become a lecturer in political economy at the newly founded Party School in

---

[6] Engels's fragmentary text, titled 'Die Börse', was published for the first time much later, in 1933 (see Engels 2003).

[7] It has to be emphasised that apart from *Finance Capital* and his critique of Böhm-Bawerk's criticism of Marx (see Hilferding 1949), Hilferding's work has remained virtually unknown in the English-speaking world. The only exception being Tom Bottomore's anthology of writings from the Austro-Marxist school, published in 1978 (see Bottomore and Goode 1978). For a bibliography of Hilferding's writings, although not complete, see Kurata (1974).

Berlin, a bold enterprise funded and organised by the German Social Democratic Party. Hilferding accepted to move to Berlin, also hoping to arrive at a better place to continue his study of recent developments in world capitalism. Much of the recent economic literature in English was not easily available in Vienna, as Hilferding complained in a letter to Kautsky in March 1905. Only when he had been able to study the most recent literature on money, on banking, on the stock markets and on cartelisation, he would be able to give an adequate presentation of what 'modern capitalism' actually looked like (Hilferding 1905).[8]

At any rate, the move to Berlin and the opportunity to teach Marxist political economy at the Party School must have given a big boost to the young and largely self-taught economist who was eager to learn more about the technicalities of bank and stock jobbery. Unfortunately, Hilferding could not continue his work as a lecturer on Marx's economic theory for very long. As a foreigner—Hilferding was an Austrian citizen at that time—he was not allowed to engage in any kind of political activity on the territory of the German empire—and the German police rightly considered teaching political economy in a Party School to be a highly political activity.[9] Hilferding stayed in Berlin and became one of the editors—and eventually the editor-in-chief of the then leading party journal *Vorwärts* instead.

[8] Still in 1906, his close friend Otto Bauer wrote to Kautsky on Hilferding's behalf, asking him to send some books that Hilferding could not find in Vienna (Bauer 1906).

Although Hilferding wrote in the Preface to his book that the manuscript was already ready by the end of 1905, I doubt that. Once in Berlin, he resumed his work and finished it only at the end of 1909. The books belonging to his personal library, since the early 1950s in the custody of the University of Cologne, show clearly that he continued his study of banking in the Anglo-Saxon countries and in Central Europe for several years. It is remarkable that Hilferding studied German and American textbooks on the techniques and practices of banking—just as Marx had done thirty years earlier (see Hilferding 1957).

[9] His successor became the young Rosa Luxemburg. For some reason, she profoundly disliked Hilferding. Hilferding could only teach his introductory course on Marx's economic theory for a few months, from October 1906 to March 1907. Unfortunately, Hilferding's notes and outlines for his course at the Party School have not been preserved, nor have any notes on his lectures by students survived.

What *Finance Capital* Was All About

In the subtitle to the book, Hilferding made his core intention crystal clear: the book was meant to provide a 'study of the latest phase of capitalist development'. But in order to study and to assess the phenomena of this latest phase properly within the framework set out by Marx, Marx's analysis of capitalism had to be carried further and some of its shortcomings had to be repaired. New tendencies of capitalist development had to be identified and assessed, and new intermediary concepts had to be developed in order to grasp them properly. Accordingly, Hilferding's book was not meant to be a historical study of the last phase in the development of modern capitalism—far from it. The book was meant to continue Marx's theory and critique of modern capitalism. Hilferding wanted to show how to deal with some of the tendencies and phenomena that Marx had already dealt with, although in a rather sketchy form—like, for example, the tendencies towards concentration and centralisation of capital. In order to do this, he had to rethink and, in some respects, redress Marx's analysis. In particular, Hilferding was trying to follow up Marx's fragmentary analysis of competition, of credit, banking and the financial markets in *Capital*, Volume III, taking up the loose ends of this analysis where Marx had dropped them. First, the Marxian theory of money did start with commodity money, and rightly so. But it had to be carried further in order to take into account the recent development of currency systems in the capitalist world. Second, Marx's analysis of competition had remained quite rudimentary and had to be carried further in order to deal with the recent developments of large corporations and of various forms of associations among capitalist firms. Marx's ideas about the importance of joint-stock companies for the development of modern capitalism provided a starting point, but no more than that. Third, Marx's analysis of the basics of credit, banking and financial markets in modern capitalism had remained largely fragmentary; a lot of the tendencies inherent in the modern credit and banking system had just been hinted at by Marx. These sketchy remarks, notwithstanding all the efforts undertaken by Engels to reorganise them into full chapters, had to be supplemented by further argument and rounded out in order to present a somewhat coherent Marxian theory. Marx had left quite a lot of general and rather sweeping statements about the impact of the credit system upon the long-term development of modern capitalism. Following Marx's lead, who had resumed his studies of these matters in the last decade of his life, this broader outlook had to be linked with recent developments in the most advanced capitalist countries of the world. What Hilferding proposed was another kind of revision of Marx's theory, not refuting, but supplementing and elaborating it.

It is a myth, however, that he followed the structure of Eduard Bernstein's book on the *Preconditions of Socialism* and tried to refute it step by step, as Kurata has suggested (see Kurata 2009, pp. 25–29). And the infamous 'Law' or better tendency of the general rate of profit to fall, a law that Marx had never managed to substantiate sufficiently in *Capital*, did not serve as the guiding line of Hilferding's argument in *Finance Capital* either, as Kurz has suggested (see Kurz 2011). As a matter of fact, the tendency of the general rate of profit to fall is mentioned a few times in Hilferding's book, but it by no means served as a guiding line for his argument. Nor has the book been organised along the theory of monopoly or the process of monopolisation, as some commentators believed (cf. Pietranera 1974; Zoninsein 1990). Hilferding had a far more complex task in mind: to develop some concepts, inherited from Marx, in order to make them fit for an analysis of the capitalism of his time. As Bottomore had rightly pointed out, this did entail the development of 'several new concepts', as well (Bottomore 1981, p. 5).[10]

The book was an immediate success and impressed many people. Trotsky, living in Vienna and entertaining quite friendly relations with him at the time, wrote him an enthusiastic letter, addressing Hilferding as *Lieber Finanzkapital-Theoretiker* ('Dear finance-capital theoretician') (Trotsky 1910). Karl Kautsky devoted an extraordinary, long review article to Hilferding's book and praised it highly as a continuation of Marx's *Capital* (see Kautsky 1911). His close friend Otto Bauer, in another lengthy review of the book published in the Austro-Marxist's theoretical journal *Der Kampf*, had even suggested that his *Finance Capital* could be regarded as a direct continuation of *Capital*, Volume III (Bauer 1980, p. 378). He praised Hilferding's vigour in transcending the scope of

---

[10] More than 60 years later, another group of young Marxists in France set themselves the same task. These young economists realised that the analysis of the phenomena of contemporary capitalism could not be carried any further by just repeating the old formula or metaphors that Marxists used to cherish. They were successful in creating a theoretical movement or 'school', the so-called Regulation school, which gained a lot of fame but lost momentum after a few initial efforts. As a theoretical school, setting and working their way through a new agenda of (largely old) problems—from money, the wage labour relationship to the world market—they utterly failed; only a somewhat different phraseology, void of any clear theoretical content, has survived.

18   M. R. KRÄTKE

Marx's theory, even criticising and refuting him where necessary (Bauer 1980, p. 377). Both Kautsky and Bauer had already outlined their own theory of the contemporary phenomenon of high imperialism, pitting all the major capitalist powers of their time against each other in an ongoing race for the appropriation and colonisation of the rest of the world. Bauer did so in his book on the *Question of Nationalities*, first published in 1907, which Hilferding quoted several times in his work (cf. Bauer 1975). In Bauer's view, Hilferding had stayed too close to Marx's manner of presentation and Marx's words.[11]

Heinrich Cunow praised Hilferding's book in another long article, published in the largest and most important journal of the SPD, the *Vorwärts*, a journal addressing a mass audience counting by hundreds of thousands of social democrats. In his view, Hilferding had clearly advanced Marx's analysis in *Capital*, in a systematic wayplaying with Marx's peculiar mode of presentation and phrasing. He had even gone beyond Marx, for instance with respect to the theory of interest and the determinants of the interest rate or with respect to the analysis of crises and cycles, although not without shortcomings (see Cunow 1910).

Bernstein, however, clearly disliked the book. He raised several objections. In particular, he took issue with Hilferding's views on the banking systems in Austria and Britain (see Bernstein 1911). Kautsky's and Bernstein's reviews of the book already set the tone for most of the later criticisms: while Kautsky argued against Hilferding's attempt to extend Marx's theory of money and defended what he regarded as its orthodox version, Bernstein rejected Hilferding's treatment of the relationships between banks and industry. He saw the major flaw of the book in Hilferding's over-generalisation of the kind of relationships that had emerged between German and Austrian banks and industrial capital in recent years. The relations between banks and industry were different in the Anglo-Saxon countries; it was simply wrong to talk about a dominance of banks over industry in Britain. However, he agreed with Hilferding that Marx's views on finance in capitalism needed an overhaul (see Bernstein 1912).[12]

---

[11] Bauer's partly diverging views on the matters addressed in Hilferding's book can be found in the lectures on political economy which he gave for the Austrian Party School (cf. Bauer 1976).

[12] Bernstein was also referring to an earlier attempt to scrutinise the relations between banks and industry (see Kapelucz 1896). Overviews and summaries of the major criticisms of Hilferding's book can be found in Sweezy (1942), Howard and King (1989) and Greitens (2012).

Hilferding had attempted to reformulate and extend Marx's theory of money in order to explain that the changes in the currency regimes which had recently occurred in several capitalist countries had a longer-lasting impact. This effort made a lot of sense and was very much in line with the line of argument presented by Marx in *Capital*—the idea of a change and development of the monetary system within capitalism. Hilferding's explanation had been rejected by most Marxists when it was first published and continued to be rejected in later years. However, his reformulation actually triggered the first international debate on monetary theory between Marxist economists, a debate that started in 1912/1913 with a series of articles in the *Neue Zeit*, and continued until the late 1920s, with no clear result. Again and again, the participants in this long debate tried to explain the coexistence of various types of currencies under the regime of the international Gold Standard, where gold still played a central role, at least on the world market. Again and again, Marxist economists tried to explain the phenomenon of the rising rates of inflation that haunted the capitalist world—and they tried to do so in terms of the changing conditions of gold mining.[13] No comparable debate took place on the issue raised by Bernstein regarding the different types of banking systems and the different forms of investment finance in the capitalist world. However, this critique by Bernstein remained the major objection to Hilferding, leading to the widely shared opinion that he had overstated his case, relying too much upon the German and Austrian type of relations between banks and industry.

Although Rosa Luxemburg ignored him, Hilferding had no reason to complain about the immediate and long-lasting impact of his book on fellow socialists. Obviously, Lenin and Buhkarin's studies of imperialism were strongly influenced by him. Lenin borrowed the term and used it widely in his book on the topic (cf. Lenin 1996). And Buhkarin openly acknowledged that he had been inspired by it and had actually taken it as the starting point of his own analysis (see Buhkarin 2013). While 'imperialism' became the household term to characterise the most recent phase of

---

[13] Hilferding had explained his views further in two articles published a short while before his book (see Hilferding 1909a, b). Today, all this is largely forgotten. Even the best specialists on Marx's theory of money, like the late Suzanne de Brunhoff, have to this day avoided discussing the debates on monetary theory in the era of classical Marxism (cf. de Brunhoff 1976).

20 M. R. KRÄTKE

capitalism and its presence, in the socialist and social-democratic movement all over Europe it was 'finance capitalism'—a term inspired, although not coined, by Hilferding and widely used in the socialist press as well as in the brochures written for educational purposes, especially for the socialist youth organisations (see, for instance, Zweiling 1927). Howard and King have rightly stated that *Finance Capital* 'has proved to be the most influential text in the entire history of Marxian political economy, only excepting *Capital* itself' (Howard and King 1989, p. 100). Joseph Schumpeter, one of the most influential heterodox economists of the twentieth century and a friend from their student days in Vienna, was strongly influenced by it—in particular in his *Theory of Economic Development*, first published in 1911 (cf. Schumpeter 1983).

Hilferding seems to have been aware of the shortcomings of his book. However, he reaffirmed the core thesis of his work on several occasions (see Hilferding 1931a, b). Heavily involved in party politics, as a leading figure of the Weimar SPD, a member of parliament, twice serving as Minister of Finance, and as the editor-in-chief of the SPD's only remaining theoretical organ, *Die Gesellschaft*, his theoretical work came virtually to a standstill.

However, Hilferding continued to investigate the developments in the capitalist world during the following years—until his untimely death in 1941. These later writings, journal and review articles and brochures, have been hardly considered, except for some researchers in Japan (cf. Kamijo 1978, for instance). During the first years of World War I, Hilferding interpreted recent changes in the advanced capitalist countries under the rule of finance capital as shifts towards an 'organized capitalism' that would bring state power and the powers of capital closer together than ever before: a non-democratic form of an organised economy, superseding the anarchy of unregulated markets, that might be able to cater for the material needs of the masses better than ever before (Hilferding 1915). In April 1924, the new theoretical review of the German social democracy *Die Gesellschaft* was launched, replacing Kautsky's *Neue Zeit*, with Rudolf Hilferding as editor-in-chief. He used this occasion to present what he saw as the task of the new journal, meeting a triple challenge to the social sciences (i.e. Marxism) which the development of the last decennium posed: first, to analyse the changes in the capitalist economies, the emergent forms and qualitative changes of 'organized capitalism' which also affected the structure and social psychology of the social classes as well as the relations between state power and the power of associated and (re)organised capital. In particular, he emphasised several secular changes: the hyperinflations of the post-war years and their consequences. That was the 'greatest expropriation process in the history of capitalism, a history abundant with expropriations'. Further, the agrarian revolutions, in particular in East and South-East Europe, and the technological revolutions (Hilferding 1924a, pp. 10, 11f). Second, the changes in the internal political order of capitalist countries due to the advances towards political democracy in the post-war era. And third, the fundamental changes in international politics which had, for the first time, entered an era of true world politics (Hilferding 1924a, pp. 12f, 14f). In the following months, he published a longer text dealing with the new agrarian crisis that had occurred in recent years (Hilferding 1924b), followed by another one on trusts and cartels in England, where he explained why and how the concentration and centralisation of capital was different in England compared to Continental Europe (Hilferding 1924c). In the summer of the same year, he wrote to Kautsky about some issues that were on his mind: first, 'an extension of my theory of money', together with a critique of the most recent English and American literature on crisis, banking and money. And furthermore, the question how central banks could affect business cycles by means of their credit policy (Hilferding 1924e). A few months later, he published another text addressing the salient question of the changing order of the world market and world economy after World War I. A remarkable piece indeed, in which he continued the analysis of world economics and world politics after World War I published a year before (Hilferding 1923). In this much shorter piece, he adumbrated the changes of the world market that had been accelerated by the war. The rise of the Anglo-Saxon world to hegemony, the establishment of the USA as a capitalist world power were among the most important results of World War I. Almost casually, he displayed the framework for his analysis of the rivalries between the great capitalist powers: taken in abstraction, capitalist economies look all the same, but in the territories of different states, capitalist economic structures and dynamics appear in a large variety of shape. The varieties of capitalisms are the result of historical interplays between state power and economic class power. The peculiarities of state powers, even combined with the same economic tendencies, are crucial for international politics. What determines the content of the economic policies in a capitalist state are the relations between industrial, commercial and banking capital, not to forget the relations between industry and agriculture. With that in mind, he gives an explanation of the rivalries between British and American capitalism, focussing upon the struggle between British and American banks for a larger or smaller share in the dominion of the world money and credit markets—the 'most exciting chapter in recent economic history' (Hilferding 1924d). Obviously, Hilferding had advanced in his study of recent developments in the capitalist world economy.

As a leading and widely respected expert in matters of financial and economic politics, he was deeply involved in debates about crisis politics during the first years of the second Great Depression. In public, he criticised the economic policies of governments, not only in Germany, that were unable to pursue at least 'correct capitalist methods' within the framework of a capitalist world economy in crisis, for instance a 'correct banking politics on the international level' (Hilferding 1931b, p. 32). Although he deplored the incredibly low level of the ongoing debates about the crisis on the Left (Hilferding 1931c), he admitted, at least in private correspondence, that he saw correct and purely capitalist ways to handle the crisis, but no socialist solution to it (Hilferding 1931d). The capitalist solution to the great crisis that he adumbrated in 1931, the year of the worst international credit crisis so far, clearly shows that he knew perfectly well and down the last detail how the capitalist world economy worked in terms of trade, currencies, credit relations and banking. Unlike most of his fellow Marxists, he clearly saw both the flexibility and adaptability of capitalism and the possible scope of state action—and remained, more determined than ever, opposed to any kind of collapse theory.

During his years in exile, Hilferding continued to work as an economic journalist and analyst, investigating and commenting upon the events of the world economic crisis and, in particular, on the crisis politics in the capitalist countries. Not surprisingly, his focus was on the economic and financial policies of the Nazi government in Germany. Most of the more than 250 journal articles he wrote during his years in exile dealt with the new economic and financial politics of Nazi Germany.[14] So he became quite familiar with the kind of military Keynesianism that the Nazi government in Germany had practised on a national scale for the first time.

---

[14] Even his last book, a collection of articles published anonymously in Paris 1938, was devoted to an analysis of the successes and failures of the Nazi economy, which he rightly saw as a war economy geared towards total warfare (for details, see Krätke 2019). Hilferding regarded the rise of fascism and the emergence of totalitarian war states in Europe and Asia as a crucial turning point in the history of capitalism. In a letter to Kautsky, dated 2 September 1937, he declared that a "a new analysis of capitalist development, at least since 1914" would be necessary in order to reconsider Marx's and Engels's perspectives for the future of both capitalism and socialism (see Hilferding 1937).

However, Hilferding remained very critical of the hazardous ways in which this Nazi war economy was financed, foretelling inevitable bankruptcy for Nazi Germany in the longer run.

If we can believe the testimony left by Boris Nikolaevsky, who had met and talked to him quite often in Paris, Hilferding planned to get down to a large theoretical work, should he survive. In the first place, as Nikolaevsky reported, Hilferding thought of a new and revised version of *Finance Capital* or about writing a second volume of this work that would offer several corrections and amendments to the first one (Nikolaevsky 1947, p. 6). Being an exiled foreigner trying to evade arrest by the Nazis, he was still able to pen down within just a few weeks—in the library of Arles—a first draft of another major work that he left unfinished. The fragment called *The Problem of History* was published posthumously in 1954 (see Hilferding 1982 [1954]).[15] In this essay, he came back to the problem that had bothered him forty years earlier: during the latest phase of capitalist development, the era of liberal capitalism had come to an end, and the relationship between capital and the state, one of the basic characteristics of modern capitalism, had changed profoundly. In all capitalist countries of the world, capitalists and the capitalist class at large had learned to love and embrace the state. A strong state had become the crucial prerequisite to the economic actions of most, if not all, capitalists in their continuous struggle with other capitalists. To engage and prevail in international competition, capitalists needed the support of a state, and a state strong enough to confront other major powers (Hilferding 1982 [1954], pp. 321–322).

Regarding the rise of fascism, the necessity to revise some of the basic concepts of the research programme called 'materialist conception of history' had become even more urgent. One had to break the spell of Marx's rhetoric and free one's thought from his sweeping metaphors—like the infamous 'base—superstructure' image, an oversimplification that Engels had already tried to rectify and supersede in his last years (cf. Wolf 2008). Hilferding did not shy away from revising some of the traditional formulations of this programme, claiming that politics and state action should be recognised as independent historical forces in their own right (see Hilferding 1982 [1954]). In *Finance Capital*, the orthodox view still prevailed. In Hilferding's analysis of the latest phase of capitalist development, the state stayed out of the picture playing no significant role whatsoever for the ongoing transformations in the capitalist economies.

---

[15] Parts of this manuscript, especially the endnotes, remain unpublished to this very day (cf., my chapter on Hilferding's 'notes' in this volume). For the circumstances of Hilferding's arrest in Arles and his death at the hands of the Gestapo in Paris see Kurotaki (1984).

What Hilferding's Opus Magnum Had to Offer

In a letter to Karl Kautsky, written in March 1906, Hilferding complained that he had to do much work reconstructing and following the lines of argument that Marx had set out in the still widely unread and unknown Volumes II and III of *Capital*, a type of 'reproductive work' that he regarded as rather boring (Hilferding 1906). However, this was necessary and pioneering work, as the second and third volumes of Marx's *Capital* had remained unread and all but forgotten (as they still are today). In particular, Hilferding opened up brand new vistas because he saw the potential of Marx's analysis in *Capital*, Volume II: analysing the different circuits and the turnover of industrial capital, Marx had found the very basis of capital credit (see Marx 1978, Krätke 2022, chapter on 'Money and Credit in Volume II of Marx's Capital'). And his reproduction schemes, providing the foundation for a macroeconomic analysis of a capitalist economy as a whole, also created a valuable starting point for the analysis of the most complex phenomenon of modern capitalism: the phenomenon of cyclical crises.

Marx had only left a very sketchy outline of his ideas about the core category of interest-bearing capital and the modern credit system, largely a collection of materials that he never completed, in spite of many efforts during the 1870s. Engels found this part, which would become Section V of Volume III of *Capital*, by far the most difficult to edit. But any serious attempt to analyse and understand the world of modern capitalism, as it had emerged around 1900, meant returning to these unfinished parts of Marx's theory. Hilferding was the first to try to systematise and to elaborate the theory of credit and finance in Marx (see for Engels's arduous work on Marx's Section V and the conceptual structure of the theory of credit and financial capital that is included in Marx's collection of first drafts and notes Krätke 2020).

He was the first to clearly see the range and scope of Marx's theory of money. A theory that started with commodity money and metallic circulation but did not end there. The real thrust of Marx's theory of money only became visible if one followed Marx's argument up to Section V of *Capital*, Volume III, and his statement that, eventually, all money and all monetary transactions were to be substituted by credit. In the context of the modern credit system, all money had assumed the character of (potential) money capital, and the trade in money and capital brought forth new forms of circulating credit that could fulfil the functions of money.

Hilferding was the first to see the importance of the category of *fictitious capital* which Marx had introduced in a rather casual manner in Section V of Volume III of *Capital*. For Marx, understanding the world of capitalist finance and its phenomena was crucial in order to decipher capitalism as a 'world turned upside down', composed of insane forms of thought and blended together into a veritable everyday life religion. Notwithstanding Marx's failure to elaborate this concept, Hilferding tried to explain how fictitious capital was created, how it circulated and how it could be used to make a profit by a group of capitalists specialising in trading credit (and debts) of all sorts and capital as fictitious commodities.[16] Instead of just enumerating possible forms of securities and negotiable papers circulating in the financial markets, he tried to analyse the emergence of one basic form: shares. The more sophisticated and complicated forms, such as futures and other derivatives, were mentioned but not scrutinised. Hilferding's analysis of the duplication of capital, the transformation of industrial capital into a 'real' capital and a 'fictitious' capital (consisting of shares), his presentation of the double circuit of capital, the circuit of shares alongside the circuit of the 'real' capital was flawed in several respects (see Morioka 1985). But he was the first to try anything like this.[17]

Likewise, he was the first to take seriously Marx's project to develop the concept of competition and to theorise the various processes and relationships belonging to it. He was the first to try to analyse banking capital as a special kind of capital, dealing with specific categories of fictitious commodities (like money, credit, debts and capital) in specific markets. He was the first to engage with the intricacies of the concentration and centralisation of capital—a process that involved the creation of new forms of capital and resulted in new hierarchies between capitals. Individual capitals turning into large corporations and controlling and/or owning other capital in pursuit of long-term strategies to restrict and regulate competition in certain branches of industry and market segments were changing the process of market value formation and price determination.

Last but not least, it should be acknowledged that Hilferding did provide a pioneering analysis of the working and impact of the stock markets

---

[16] What a pity that Hilferding never had the opportunity to study Marx's original manuscripts for Volume II and III. There he would have found a further extension of Marx's rudimentary analysis of modern finance—the concept of *fictitious accumulation*.

[17] See for a recent attempt: Durand (2017).

(or financial markets) in the capitalist world. He even went beyond Marx and Engels's efforts, as he was the first to attempt an analysis of the commodity exchanges that played a crucial role in world trade. The main effect of the financial markets and the specific kinds of capital operating on and ruling them—in Hilferding's view, mainly banks—was to allow and enable, even promote, radical changes in the inner-capitalist relationships. In the longer run, a tendency towards the unification of capitals and capitalists under new oligarchies, the integration and subordination of previously independent forms of capital into a new hierarchy of capital, under the dominance of high finance, had emerged and it would stay and prevail. In Hilferding's view, these structural shifts were the reason for the shifting of political attitudes within the capitalist class which he regarded as the most important cause for the rise of imperialist policies in all the advanced capitalist countries.

HILFERDING AND THE CHANGING WORLD OF MONEY

Of course, Hilferding was right to start his analysis with money. More orthodox Marxists like Cunow would have started with the recent changes in technology and in the organisation of the production process in the factories run by ever-bigger corporations.[18] But the changing monetary order in the capitalist world could be regarded as a symptom, hence as an apt starting point for any analysis of more fundamental changes. When Hilferding wrote his book, the international monetary order known as the Gold Standard had just been established, but not yet completed. In fact, it was an international Pound Sterling standard, based upon the industrial, mercantile and financial predominance of Great Britain and the sheer preponderance of the British Empire. An Empire that was not only by far the largest of all colonial empires run by any advanced capitalist country, but that also controlled all the major sources of gold in the world—in South Africa, in Australia and in North America.

---

[18] This task was actually performed by Otto Bauer twenty years later. He started his great project on the transformations of capitalism since World War I in the 1920s. The first volume of his planned work, the volume dealing with the process of rationalisation in capitalist firms appeared in 1931, the manuscript for the second volume, although far advanced, seems to have been lost, as Bauer himself believed. However, this second volume, Otto Bauer's analysis and explanation of the world economic crisis of the 1930s, the second Great Crisis in the history of modern capitalism, had survived (see Krätke 2008).

For centuries, states had claimed and maintained a monopoly of money, that is the monopoly of money making and money issuing. The seigniorage had always been both a source of income and a symbol of power for the modern state. Since the creation of the first central banks in Europe in the seventeenth century, the guise of the state monopoly of money had changed profoundly. Since the early years of the nineteenth century, states, following the lead of Great Britain, had tried to monopolise the issue of bank notes, gradually suppressing and outlawing the issue of notes by private banks.[19]

Hilferding acknowledged there was a problem to be tackled. Georg Knapp's state theory of money did not come out of the blue (cf. Knapp 1924). The problem, both for monetary theory and for monetary politics, was to find and determine the limits of such state regulation of money circulation. Hilferding insisted upon the original Marxian insight 'that money is a social arrangement in material form' (Hilferding 2006, p. 379). However, he was very well aware that the modern state had always claimed the monopoly of money as one of its core competences and that money and credit had always been strictly supervised and tightly regulated in all advanced capitalist countries.

Accordingly, Hilferding was dealing with currency, not plain money. In particular, he tried to make Marxian head and tail of the currency systems as they existed in the Austro-Hungarian Empire at the time as well as in other countries. Typically, these were mixed currencies, where different sorts of money circulated, in some cases even using gold and silver as metal bases. Paper money, issued and backed by the state, was in use while notes issued by private and central banks circulated as well. Eventually, in some states, central bank notes, backed by public credit and by public credit only, had been privileged by the state, ultimately replacing the notes seen as 'bankers' money' with the central bank notes seen as 'everybody's money' (cf. Krätke 1995b).

Basically, he was dealing with a monetary order or currency, regulated by the state, that was different from all the previous ones and could not easily be classified because it was no longer a currency dominated by state paper or fiat money. The bulk of money in circulation was already credit money, or credit in different guises fulfilling most of the elementary

---

[19] It actually took more than a century to firmly establish the monopoly of central bank notes as legal tender everywhere. In federal states, like the United States of America, the struggle lasted much longer.

functions of money. The state was just stepping in, granting the privileged position of legal tender to one sort of circulating credit paper, the notes of the central bank, above all others.[20]

However, Hilferding did not yet envisage the constellation where in spite of extensive state regulation and central bank control, private banks were able and allowed to create money and increase the amount in circulation just by the very act of granting a loan to one of their customers. As a means of payment, book or deposit money instead of cash (coins and bank notes) had long been established, first in the transactions between businessmen, firms and the state. Later on, the use of money directly created by banks and exclusively based upon bank credit became familiar and even standard practice between businessmen (capitalist producers, merchants, traders, bankers and their counterparts—that is, other industrial producers, merchants, traders and bankers). However, only members of the propertied classes were allowed into this kind of circulation, the so-called moneyed capitalists taking the lead. Members of the working classes were and remained excluded until they became regular bank customers, held bank accounts of their own and employers started paying them by means of regular bank money transfers from account to account. In Hilferding's time, this revolution in the way in which money wages were actually paid was still far away.[21] But the use of book money issued by private banks was already widespread and had dwarfed the role of other forms of money in circulation.

As Hilferding said in a footnote to Chapter Two (the chapter on 'Money in the circulation process'), ignorance of monetary matters was not recommendable to would-be capitalists. To participate in the land's financial and monetary affairs, to claim the lead in financial and monetary politics would require some solid and reliable knowledge of such arcane matters. Otherwise, 'punishment for economic ignoramuses' would be the immediate outcome. That was, of course, evenly true for government officials and for politicians desperate to run the affairs of a modern state.

---

[20] It is a pity that even Suzanne de Brunhoff has avoided a serious discussion of Hilferding's attempt to extend the scope of Marx's theory of money (see Brunhoff 1976).

[21] In Germany and Austria, this profound change did not occur before the end of the 1950s. Still then, the majority of wage labourers—as opposed to salaried employees or white-collar workers—were paid in cash.

HILFERDING AND THE CHANGING WORLDS OF CREDIT AND BANKING

Capitalism had always been a credit economy, based upon debt, from its very beginnings. Moneyed capitalists had thrived on usury practices for centuries, keeping at a distance from the world of commerce and industry while exploiting the efforts of industrial and merchant capitalists and appropriating the spoils generated by capitalist entrepreneurs and managers by means of loans and interests. In *Capital*, Volume III, Marx had praised the recent developments of the credit system, that is seeing it turn into a fully-fledged banking system with a central bank at its heart and many intermediating institutions (like clearing houses) in between. This was the 'most artificial and elaborate product brought into existence by the capitalist mode of production' (Marx 1981, p. 742). For socialists and followers of Marx like Hilferding, it was self-evident that a centralised banking system would play a central role as one of the most powerful levers for any socialist transformation policy.[22] Socialising the banks would secure control of the intermediary system lying at the very core of an advanced capitalist economy.

In the first part of his book, he resumed the rather sketchy analysis of credit relations that Marx had outlined in his manuscripts forty years earlier.[23] Commercial credit—or circulation credit—was the base, as this kind of credit had always been granted by one capitalist to the other, without intermediaries. But the rise of the intermediaries, the banks in various guises, was the one element that changed the world of credit for ever. Following Marx's hints, Hilferding proceeded towards the basic form of industrial credit, that is banks financing industrial investments by industrial capitalists. Marx had already emphasised this function of credit, the mobilisation and the pooling of available, loanable capital in a few large funds, run by the banks. The process of capital accumulation would not only be highly accelerated by bank credits to industrial enterprises, but

---

[22] It was Hilferding's friend Karl Renner, a jurist by training, who emphasised the importance of good knowledge of the intricacies of money, credit and finance for the socialist movement. In order to teach his fellow socialists and the crowd of young budding Marxists more about these matters, he wrote one of the very best textbook introductions to Volumes II and III of Marx's *Capital* (see Renner 1924).

[23] When Hilferding wrote his book, he did not know anything about Marx's later studies of financial markets. Many of Marx's notebooks from the late 1860s and the 1870s had not yet been published. Still today, some of them remain unpublished.

also largely altered because of the long-lasting stakes in industrial capital that banks would acquire.

His analysis of banking capital followed the few sketchy remarks that Marx had noted in his first draft of Volume III in 1865, and had never revised in later years, although he had resumed his study of credit and banking in the 1870s (cf. Krätke 1995a). Hilferding tried to answer the crucial and basic questions: where did the capital of banks come from? How, that is by means of which economic transactions, did banks and bankers valorise their capital? How were they able to make a profit? Whom did banks and bankers exploit and in what ways? How did bankers accumulate capital? How and by what means did banks and bankers compete with each other? The composition of banking capital and its form of circulation was quite different from any other form of capital, given that bank capital was mostly money capital owned by the bank or borrowed from others—private creditors and, quite importantly, from other banks and other financial institutions. With respect to bank profit, Hilferding accepted the rather conventional view that it came from the difference between the interest the banks paid for money they borrowed (capital) and the interest they charged for the loans they made to others. Still, this difference between the interest rates for deposits and those for loans is valid today and one of the bases of the profits banks can make. He forgot, however, about the many financial services the banks were actually providing for and selling to their clients, starting with the keeping and management of private and business bank accounts, and the fees they were charging from their clients. Because of his negligence of bank services and fees, he did not tackle the salient question of whether the employees working for a bank were productive or unproductive workers and how they could and would be exploited by the capitalists and managers running the banks.

Analysing the expansion of joint-stock companies, Hilferding allowed for some oversimplification, focussing solely on the process of founding while disregarding increases of capital stock as well as mergers and acquisitions. In his presentation, the issue of shares lay first and foremost in the hands of banks (or a consortium of banks). Accordingly, the promoter's profit fell to the banks—and this was a new economic category that Hilferding tried to elaborate. This part of his analysis is still valuable today, although he did not explain where promoter's profits—emerging from a difference between two prices, the price of the shares issued and the price of the capital stock owned by the company—came from and where they might fit in with an analysis in value terms.

Hilferding and the Changing World of Corporations

In *Capital* Volume III, Marx had sung the praise of joint-stock capital. As surprising as this may appear to the contemporary reader, Marx saw in the rise of joint-stock companies a remarkable innovation that would have long-lasting consequences for the development of modern capitalism. In his view, joint-stock companies represented a form of 'associated capital', and he considered it a form by which capitalist enterprises were actually transcending the very base of modern capitalism, private property and private ownership of capital by individual capitalists (cf. Krätke 1994). What Hilferding added to this, following some remarks by Engels who had already stressed the emergence of joint-stock companies of a higher order, was the analysis of the special forms that capital accumulation in its 'accelerated' form (as Marx had already emphasised) had assumed. It was not the formation of cartels but the new forms of joint-stock companies, turning into holding and investment companies specialised in the purchase, sale, holding and rearrangement of the shares of other joint-stock companies, that were crucial. This was because these new holding and investment companies were able to create new industrial structures, to conceive of and pursue industrial strategies, to build larger corporations and to forge lasting alliances between them.

Thanks to these new actors, capital could easily be shifted from one branch or sphere of accumulation to another. Industrial capital could be mobilised and restructured, alliances and associations between different groups of capitals could be created without much delay. These holding and investment companies were relying on banks and stock markets and were no longer tied down by the requirements and the very mechanics of the turnover of capital in different branches of industry.

HILFERDING AND THE CHANGING WORLD OF STOCK MARKETS AND HIGH FINANCE

To this very day, capitalism remains the only historical form of an economy based upon a hierarchy of highly differentiated and highly specialised markets. Marx had already indicated that he saw the financial markets—the money market and the capital market—on top, and the labour and commodity markets at the bottom of this hierarchy. Hilferding was the first to try to turn Marx's many scattered remarks on the stock markets into something resembling a coherent theory—and one that would still be in line with the overall pattern of a labour theory of value (cf. Krätke 1995c).

In order to explain the rise of joint-stock companies and the surge of holding and investment companies, and to make some clear sense of the Marxian category of fictitious capital, Hilferding had to deal with the stock markets. First and foremost, he considered them as markets for shares, neglecting sovereign debt, the equity that had still predominated the stock markets until the waves of railway booms in the early nineteenth century had changed them for good. Accordingly, he was envisaging a variety of stock markets that had already prevailed for a while in the advanced capitalist countries and was just about to change in recent times, presenting another historical configuration of financial markets.

Another achievement that should not go unnoticed is that Hilferding was the first to realise the importance of commodity exchanges for any analysis of international trade and the world market. To explain the changes of world market prices and the ways in which world market prices were actually determined in the first place, an analysis of the commodity exchanges was indispensable. Commodity exchanges establish the prices for those commodities that play a central role for the capitalist world market and are traded worldwide. Like the price of cotton during the high times of the English textile industry, when a certain Frederick Engels lived the life of a Cotton Lord in Manchester, the world's leading industrial city. The price of cotton for the English textile industry was determined at the cotton exchanges of Manchester, Bremen and other places. The commodity exchanges were actually the first stock exchanges that introduced the trade in futures, pioneering the markets for derivatives.

Although he did focus on the share markets of his time, Hilferding did not take into account another core market closely linked to them. He did not even try to analyse the markets for enterprises where whole firms and their stocks were sold and bought and where mergers and acquisitions of all kinds were actually forged. This negligence is and seems a little biased because the transactions on this market did involve the banks as well as share markets, with no clear preponderance of one over the other. However, the buoyancy of these markets remained rather modest in Hilferding's time as compared to ours.

HILFERDING'S CONCEPT OF *FINANCE CAPITAL*

Marx had developed a rather complex concept of capital. Capital, he emphasised, should not be conceived of as a thing but as a highly complex economic relationship, or a whole bundle of coherent economic relationships, and as a process, or a complex of processes in space and (historical) time. In order to develop his concept of capital, Marx focussed not on capital in general but on a special kind of capital that he regarded as crucial and epoch-making in the history of modern capitalism: industrial capital. He regarded other forms of capital, like merchant capital or interest-bearing money or the capital acting on financial markets, as secondary forms, subordinated to the dominant form of industrial capital. This was because they did not command productive labour and did not control the process of value and surplus value creation, because they commanded mainly unproductive labour and were only involved in the processes of realisation and (re)distribution of value and of surplus value.

What Hilferding proposed was well in line with Marx's thought. If we can conceive of pure forms of capital separated and pitted against each other by their predominant functions and/or by their respective special fields of economic activity—like industrial production, commerce, banking or trading money and capital as commodities, agricultural production—we can also imagine hybrid and/or compound forms of capital. The rise and fall of such hybrid forms was not new at all; merchant bankers had dominated for long periods in the history of modern capitalism, and they had eventually changed into merchant manufacturers. And Marx himself had expected that industrial capitalists and landowners were to merge in the long run and the class of landed aristocrats was to disappear. The combination of different kinds of capital in new forms was conceivable, even if it was not tantamount to complete mergers of the different forms of capital. A stable association between different kinds of capitalists could do as well.

Hilferding was quite right to regard the analysis of competition between capitals as a clue for any further investigation into the changing patterns of capitalist accumulation. Already Marx had understood that he could not conceive of industrial capital without taking into account the interactions between many capitals and many capitalists. In modern capitalism, the relations of capital to other capital are as decisive as the relationship between capital and wage labour. And the capital–capital relationships, or 'competition', to put it in shorthand, play out on all levels and in all phases of the valorisation process, not only in the marketplace.[24]

Hilferding developed his concept of finance capital step by step. He started with the different and historically changing relationships between the special kinds of capital as they appeared in Marx's presentation— industrial capital, mercantile capital, bank capital.[25] He analysed, first, the different kinds and forms of associations between capitals—combinations, cartels, trusts—as they sprang out of the competition between industrial capitals. These corporations and alliances between corporations, Marx's associated capital in higher potencies, continue to grow and to build new alliances in a more or less distinct form. In order to create and to maintain them, in order to reorganise them, credit was necessary; hence bank capital entered the picture as an intermediary. In the longer run, a new hybrid form of capital arose out of such inevitable cooperations, linkages and finally intertwining of property between industrial corporations and their house banks. Eventually, the different kinds of capital started to conglomerate and amalgamate. Some special kinds of capital lost their autonomy— mercantile capital and the merchant capitalists were downgraded to the status of mere agents, acting on behalf of the higher hybrid form of finance capital. Ultimately, in the new form of finance capital where capitals of different kinds are blended and merged into a new kind of stable inter-capitalist relationship, 'bank capital, that is, capital in money form which is

---

[24] The third pole in the economic field characterising modern capitalism is, of course, occupied by the modern state, a very special economic power in its own right and more than that. Besides the relations between capital and labour and the relations between capital and capital, in every investigation of the basic structures of modern capitalism we have to take the relationships between state and capital into account—as well as the relationship between wage labour and the state. Last but not least, the relations between wage workers and other wage workers should be integrated into this overall picture. As the state only appears as a unified body without any differentiation in philosophical imagination, we are finally obliged to deal with state–state relationships as well.

[25] Obviously, it would have been a good idea to introduce further kinds of capital like agriculture capital and mining capital, or the capital of the extractive industries. Those had remained largely unexplored and undertheorised in the Marxist tradition. Kautsky's early study of capitalist agriculture was one of the rare exceptions (see Kautsky 1988).

actually transformed … into industrial capital', or 'capital at the disposition of the banks which is used by the industrialists' (Hilferding 2006, p. 225). Accordingly, his argument went further via hybrid forms of capital, stable alliances between different kinds of capitalists and, eventually, dependency of one group of capitalists from the other as well as lasting domination of one group of capitalists by another.

As Marx did in *Capital*, Hilferding tried to follow the course of capitalist development at large and to outline general tendencies in capitalism, taking them to their logical end: the process of the concentration and centralisation of capital would lead to ever-larger corporations. The big corporations would try to gain control of each other, either by mergers and acquisitions—a tendency that Hilferding rather downplayed and neglected—or by building ever-larger cartel organisations. And that would lead to the logical end of a 'general cartel'. The process of concentration and centralisation in the sphere of banking would eventually lead to the formation of very large bank corporations and, ultimately, to an all-embracing organisation of the whole world of banking and finance, forming one huge 'general bank'.[26] So it was imaginable that in the end, they might end up organising a unified sort of 'capital in general'. If his main thesis about the domination of industrial capital by banking capital was correct, he was right to assume that the logical end of the tendencies he foresaw would be a unified capital: 'finance capital'. But countertendencies remained in force: cartels broke up, new markets emerged and new ways of competition between capitalist firms were discovered and created. Accordingly, the assumption that the logical, imaginable end of the tendencies in force would also be the historical end of capitalist development was never warranted.

HILFERDING AND THE MARXIST THEORY OR THEORIES OF CRISIS

There was one particular chapter in *Finance Capital* that aroused the ire of Rosa Luxemburg, the chapter dealing with the general conditions of crisis. It was a remarkable chapter in a most remarkable section, the section IV of Hilferding's book, titled 'Finance Capital and Crises'. Six years earlier, Otto Bauer had presented the first systematic exposition of the very diverse bits and pieces pertaining to the Marxian theory (or rather

---

[26] Hilferding wrongly used the term 'central bank' for this, which only caused confusion.

theories) of crisis. Tugan-Baranovsky, the much underrated and today almost forgotten Ukrainian Marxist, had triggered a debate on three closely interconnected core elements of Marx's economic theory, the theory of accumulation, the theory about the falling rate of profit and the theory of crisis. What is more, Tugan-Baranovsky was the first to criticise (in particular the theorem of the falling rate of profit) and to go beyond the texts of Marx in his book (cf. Tugan-Baranovsky 1901). Otto Bauer took a fresh start, announcing that Marx's theory of crisis had to be reconstructed, putting together the diverse building blocks that could be found in *Capital* (Bauer 1979, p. 790). Bauer examined in general terms how and why a purely capitalist economy could fall from a path of growth and prosperity into crisis and depression because of its own inner dynamic, without any external shocks. Taking the credit system into account would in his view largely modify the picture of the business cycle, but not alter the fundamentals, the endemic causes of cyclical crises (Bauer 1979, pp. 803, 804).

Hilferding did not share Bauer's view. He did follow his approach, starting with an investigation of the equilibrium conditions of the process of social reproduction in a purely capitalist economy—an analysis that Marx had left incomplete in volume II of *Capital*. He then tried to explain how and why a sudden turn from prosperity, accelerating accumulation and steeply rising profits to a slump in sales, rapidly dwindling profits and widespread idleness of capital could occur (Chap. 17). Although he made a clear distinction between the long-term trend of the rate of profit and its rise and fall in the course of the business cycle, a distinction that contemporary Marxists use to ignore, he did not succeed. The chapter on the 'causes of crisis' remained more a description of phenomena and symptoms than a theoretical explanation. However, his most important and innovative contribution to the theory of crises came in the following Chaps. 18 and 19: crises in the era of finance capital would inevitably become monetary and crises involving the whole of the financial markets—hence financial crisis. A tendency that Marx had already observed in the 1860s. Hilferding disagreed with Bauer, credit and finance made a big difference. The changing conditions of credit, hence the activities of banks, could alter the course of business cycles—and already had. Credit and finance did add further causes to the onset of crises and changed their character, turning them more and more into financial crises. What is more, bank credit could largely influence the conditions of recovery during and after a crisis (Chap. 19). Whether a crisis would turn into a longer-lasting depression or not was largely dependent upon the ways in which banks and finance capital in particular were handling the overaccumulation of money capital. Hilferding was the first Marxist economist who clearly saw and analysed the role played by credit and banking during the great crises of the twentieth century. Of course, he had been enlightened by the experience of the world financial crisis of 1907 (cf. Hilferding 1907).

How to Continue: How to Rewrite *Finance Capital* for Our Time

Hilferding and his Austro-Marxist friends shared a common belief that can be summed up as follows: Marxism should be regarded as a social science, following a common research programme or paradigm. As the founding fathers Marx and Engels had not been able to pursue their research programme to the end, the primary task for their pupils and followers was not to interpret and reinterpret their work nor to create an ever-larger body of commentaries to allegedly holy texts, but to continue it, filling gaps, solving problems that Marx and Engels had left unsettled. That is what they tried to do in various respects. And that is why, in their reviews of the book, Kautsky and Otto Bauer praised it as looking like a direct addition and complement to Marx's *Capital*. However, this continuation has left a lot of unsettled questions as well.

Hilferding's book has long acquired the status of a classic. Nobody expects that such a book, written and published more than a century ago, could actually offer more than a valuable inspiration and starting point for an analysis of capitalism in the twenty-first century.[27] Obviously, as a study of the phenomena of capitalism as it emerged from the first great depression in the late 1890s, it is largely outdated. Several developments that Hilferding forecasted for the future of capitalism have never come true. Stock markets have never been replaced by banks, the German/Austrian type of universal bank has not prevailed in the long run, nor has the German/Austrian type of relationship between banks and industry. Banks have seldom come to dominate industrial corporations in the long run. Organised capitalism has turned into disorganised capitalism, the relationships between state and capital have changed, although the 'strong state'

---

[27] For a discussion of the salient problem of how to use Marx's theory of capitalism in general for an analysis of recent (or older) changes and developments in the history of capitalism, including its 'contemporary history', see Krätke (2007).

never really disappeared. Merchant capital has never completely disappeared. Colonial expansion and trade protectionism did not prevail in the longer run, free trade returned in a new guise and on an unprecedented scale. Finance capital, as Hilferding saw it, has not prevailed, and the ways in which capitalists form business associations have changed profoundly in the longer run. The unification of all capitalists under the leadership of high finance has never occurred; the capitalist class remains divided into factions. Even the links between capitalists and their respective national states have never been completely severed.

Which elements of Hilferding's analysis are still valid today? Which retain their use value for any effort to continue and further elaborate the critique of capitalism that Marx established, and the Austro-Marxists tried to renew? Some tendencies that Hilferding identified are still valid today, and some phenomena still exist, many of the economic institutions and economic categories that he first scrutinised remain relevant today. To mention just one tendency: the triumphal march of the joint-stock companies has continued unabated since Hilferding's time, and this form of associated capital has risen to dominance at least in the world of big corporations and multinational enterprises. In this respect, both Marx's and Hilferding's forecasts have been largely confirmed. But, on the other hand, some of the shortcomings of Hilferding's work are more evident and more serious today than in his time.

First and foremost, following Hilferding's lead, it is necessary to come to grips with the changing monetary order of the capitalist world as it has emerged since the early 1970s. Although the former money commodity of gold still plays some role as part of the reserves of all central banks, it has been officially demonetised, and convertibility of all sorts of credit and fiat money, regarded as an economic law by Marx himself, has been abolished. All currencies have changed into currencies based upon a mix of public credit, that is bonds issued by the state, and private credit, that is circulating credit created by the banks.

Any analysis dealing with capitalist finance in the post-war era has to take into account the one major change that already occurred during the 1950s and 1960s and was triggered by the rise of the welfare state. Thanks to the establishment of a system of social insurance and allied services guaranteeing a continuous flow of monetary income to all or at least to the large majority of working-class people, the world of credit and finance has changed profoundly. The majority of the population in capitalist countries, far beyond the confines of the propertied classes, have become creditworthy and are no longer restricted to the pawn broker or the practices of chalking up at the grocery shop or the pub. Even in times of unemployment, they became entitled to some regular monetary income and because of the ground-breaking invention of paid holidays and paid retirement, the better paid and fully and stably employed upper echelons of the working class were invited into the world of credit. Step by step, ordinary people living on wages and salaries were allowed, lured and eventually forced into the world of credit, first getting bank accounts and access to moderate forms of circulation credit like overdrafts and credit cards. Second, being granted loans in order to buy consumer goods, consumer durables in particular, eventually even being accepted as debtors for long-term loans like mortgages. And, finally, being admitted into the world of high finance, of financial investments, either individually as depositors, savers, life insurance policy holders and even asset holders, or, even more importantly, collectively, as stakeholders of large pension funds. These funds manage savings and deferred wages in large amounts and have been more or less successful in transforming this kind of money hoarding into accumulated money capital and accumulated fictitious capital. Because of the rise of mortgage finance and pension funds, the working class in contemporary capitalism has clear financial interests of its own and working-class people have become involved in the financial markets, both as actors and at the receiving ends of their vicissitudes. Hilferding could not have imagined anything of this kind in his day.

Accordingly, the whole character of banking and the relationship between bankers and their clients have changed dramatically. Commercial banks are today selling financial services of various kinds to clients who are working-class people in increasing numbers. As a consequence, banks and other financial firms make more and more of their profits from transactions with the non-propertied classes who only own what they can afford thanks to their long-term indebtedness. Or thanks to the credit the banks are willing to grant them, provided they are enjoying a regular flow of money income—either from employment or from welfare state transfers. The thoroughly indebted working class and the continuing involvement of ever-larger strata of the working class in credit and debt relations with the banks have changed the game for the whole financial sector. Banks and other financial firms are no longer restricted to an ongoing struggle over the redistribution of surplus value—already realised or anticipated; they are now able to exploit the mass of the working class directly via credit relations. Just how this secondary exploitation via credit relations (already mentioned by Marx) does work has been left unexplored by Marxist economists.

However, Hilferding's analysis of the basic functions of banks remains sound. But it has to be extended in order to take the various roles of banks as providers of financial services into account. In order to deal with the many specialisations of banks and the differentiation of banking systems, any modern analysis has to deal with the role of investment banks properly. Investment banks, often arising from stockbroker's companies, have led the way towards associate capital in the form of joint-stock companies in the banking sector. While many commercial banks, especially the smaller ones, still retain the form and character of private banks, including a special house bank relationship to a restricted number of carefully selected industrial enterprises, investment banks are predominantly operating on a much wider base and typically acting on international financial markets. Today, they are, more often than not, just at the core of a network of associated or subsidiary financial firms, including specialised intermediaries like investment funds, hedge funds and private equity funds. Accordingly, in the analysis of investment banking, we can forget about deposits and private loans, as well as many financial services, and have to focus on the role of the bank as intermediator in various speculative investments. However, most investment banks (and banks engaging in financial investment activities) are also trading and speculating for their own account. Both commercial and investment banks play a central role in issuing book money—as central banks do—just by granting credits. Hence, today's monetary order in the whole capitalist world is dependent upon bank credit more than ever before.

Hilferding's thesis about the dwindling importance of stock markets as compared to banks was wrong. The relationship between banks and stock markets has developed in a quite different way; in the longer run, it is the banks that have lost ground to the stock markets in nearly all fields of credit. Or so it seemed for quite a long time. Banks appeared to have lost ground in their relationship to industrial capital (and merchant capital and agricultural capital), but they have become core actors on the financial markets. Other kinds of capital specialised in financial transactions, that is, in creating and handling various forms of fictitious capital, have emerged and have become serious competitors to the banks. The relationships between banks, the inter-bank payment and credit system, still the very core of the money market and a crucial part of the capital markets, have retained their importance, while central banks have acquired control over inter-bank money and credit relations altogether.

Merchant capital had dominated the development of capitalism for several centuries. Hilferding considered it a form from the past; he was convinced that merchant capital had already lost its independence and was becoming completely dominated by the banks, and by finance capital in particular. In recent decennia, we have seen a revival of merchant capital and of international, even global merchant corporations in unprecedented forms. Merchant capitalists are selling combinations of consumer goods and personal services, including some kinds of financial services (e.g. credit or debit cards as a means of payment). They manage to do this today in ever-larger networks of retail shops established in all parts of the capitalist world. The new global merchant companies are large enough to turn the directions of mass consumption, to create trends and fashions and to dictate terms to capitalists in the consumer industries. Nowadays, they have become the dominant partners in large parts of the consumer industries, in the worldwide transport industry and, last but not least, in the communication industries. They are no less able and willing to create their own banks and financial agencies of all stripes, at least to acquire shares and stakes in such firms, thus dominating parts of the financial industry as well—at least those parts specialising in consumer credit. As at the peak of merchant capitalism, new hybrids of merchant and industrial (manufacturing) capital have emerged, and in the world of services—product-related personal services—these hybrids reign supreme.

For all transactions in financial markets as for the whole world of contemporary capitalism, the use of various forms of fictitious capital remains crucial. And the 'financial industry' has proven to be quite ingenious in creating new, combined forms of fictitious capital, turning various forms of credit and debt into new, compound securities, easily traded on the international financial markets. They achieve a mobilisation of money capital invested in all kinds of loans, including long-term mortgages, without precedence. As a consequence, relatively stable and long-lasting relationships between banks and other financial firms and their clients are virtually dissolved. Instead, we have ever-changing relationships on a global financial market, although some major parts of it are still regulated on a national or regional basis. Among the various forms of fictitious capital, futures, options and all sorts of derivatives have become predominant in recent times. Derivatives and the trade in derivatives were already in place a long time ago, but the practice of adding specialised derivatives to virtually every kind of equity and security inevitably has multiplied and diversified the volumes and directions of financial transactions on all financial markets. The increasing complexity of these transactions has made further hedging operations highly recommendable and all kinds of insurances, custom-designed for specific risks in specific segments of the financial markets, are offered and traded today. Accordingly, the rudimentary analysis of the share market and the circulation of shares that Hilferding developed in his pioneering study cannot suffice today. We inevitably have to go further, although Hilferding's analysis of the futures trade in commodity markets did provide a good starting point. As Engels had already foreseen in the 1890s, the new quality of the stock and commodity markets introducing futures and options as tradeable commodities on a large scale has triggered new varieties of inter-capitalist competition, outpacing all previous forms.

The real novelty in the world of derivatives has been the emergence of ever-larger varieties of financial contracts, traded as commodities. With rapidly increasing volumes and volatilities, the trade in these new 'financial derivatives' has an impact far beyond the trade in traditional 'commodity derivatives'. They have massively contributed to a veritable reshaping of the trade in financial securities (cf. Bryan and Rafferty 2006). Because of the sheer weight of derivatives in today's financial markets and their common use in virtually all kinds of financial transactions, financial markets have become more thoroughly speculative than ever before.

Recent news about the imminent death of financial intermediaries have been largely exaggerated. The notion of their inevitable decline has gained popularity among many political economists. That is largely due to the emergence and ongoing expansion of so-called shadow banks, or non-banks acting like banks and fulfilling the functions of banks, at least partially and/or temporarily. Today most big corporations are also actors on the financial markets in their own right—and with their own competences—and act not only on their own behalf, but also as intermediaries. In some segments of finance, for instance consumer credit, they have been outpacing banks and other traditional intermediaries. But that does not mean that the intermediaries have disappeared, only that the kind of intermediaries and the types of intermediations in financial transactions have largely changed. Just to mention a few: investment funds of different kinds, more or less specialised, are acting as intermediaries between private wealth owners, pension funds, state funds and other capital funds. Asset managers act as intermediaries between private and collective asset holders and institutional investors of various kinds. As the financial markets and financial market operations grow more and more global, other sorts of intermediaries become increasingly important—intermediaries like the big internationally operating accounting firms and internationally operating law firms, specialising in financial and tax management across borders for an ever-growing clientele.

Stock markets have been radically transformed. In Marx and Engels's time, they were still highly exclusive private clubs of businessmen that were self-organised and self-regulated by their members. Only respectable businessmen, that is gentlemen representing and running a firm of some weight and relevance in the local or international markets, like the young Friedrich Engels, who represented the well-known firm Ermen & Engels in Manchester, could become full members of a stock or commodity market. Today, everybody can buy shares of a stock or commodity market company because they have been transformed into large joint-stock companies run by hired managers and bent on making a profit and paying dividends to their shareholders. Accordingly, today's stock markets are not just well-organised and supervised marketplaces for financial transactions but, by the same token, highly potent financial actors in their own right, operating on these very same marketplaces. The shift towards this form of joint-stock company has triggered a new race on the stock markets, as stock market companies are in permanent competition with each other, vying for ever-larger market shares and trying to gain supremacy in some places by means of mergers and acquisitions. The tendency towards the concentration and centralisation of stock and commodity markets has created an ever-smaller number of very large firms that control the leading financial markets of the world and are even quite successful in controlling the networks between the major financial places in the capitalist world. Dominance in financial markets, not command and control of industrial or merchant capital, is what they are striving for.

What is more, and ultimately most important, in the present world of capitalist finance is that stock markets have been dwarfed by the rise of financial transactions outside of the world of well-organised, specialised and more or less well-regulated exchanges. The majority of financial transactions today take place 'over the counter' (OTC) without any intermediation by capital specialised in financial transactions and/or officially allowed and (as in the case of banks) licensed for such financial transactions. Regarding the surge of over-the-counter finance, all of Hilferding's theses about the shifts between different kinds of capital fall short. On the contrary, the relations between the providers of financial services and the creditors (providers of credit), on the one hand, and their clients have become more short term and volatile than ever before.

Money and credit have been affected by recent changes in the world of financial markets as well. As in earlier epochs in the history of modern capitalism, some kinds of private money, created by capitalists and only in use in transactions between capitalists, have reappeared. Hardly noticed by the larger public, because this time the changes within the monetary order were different. Various forms of fictitious capital, shares and other equities, but also credit and financial market instruments like derivatives, have assumed money functions—but within the confines of financial markets and financial markets only. Shares, for example, are changing hands between capitalists on the financial markets—as a means of payment. Frequently, in the case of mergers and acquisitions, a firm or its shares are bought and paid for by issuing other shares. All kinds of securities, even derivatives, are used as a means of circulation in chains of financial transactions; equities are bought with other equities and/or securities of various kinds. Or they are used to back up credits and to prolong and extend credit chains. But within the realm of the financial markets, only involving and affecting those capitalists that Marx still used to call 'moneyed capitalists'.

Central banks have changed their character considerably since Marx's and Hilferding's days. Marx considered the central banks still to be 'half-breeds', while Hilferding already saw a tendency towards the nationalisation of central banks. Around 1900, more than half of the central banks in capitalist countries were still in private hands; since 1945, more and more of them have been nationalised. Today, only a handful of central banks are not completely owned by the state; the central banks of just a handful of countries—Belgium, Japan, Greece, South Africa, Turkey and Switzerland—still have some private shareholders. The Bank of Japan is the only important central bank in this group. All the others, including the European Central Bank, are state owned and pay dividends or share their profits with the state or the states to whom their equities belong. Accordingly, and notwithstanding any form of official independence, central banks have become core agencies of regulating money circulation and financial markets.

High finance, in Hilferding's view the realm of finance capital, looks quite different today. A large variety of capitalist corporations have entered this sphere, operating on international financial markets, not only owning but actively trading in various forms of fictitious capital, creating new amalgams of different sorts of capital—of banks, of funds, of stock markets, of stockbrokers, of insurances, of trust and various forms of asset managing firms. The tendency towards the concentration and centralisation of capital has brought forth new financial corporations of unprecedented scale and scope. But countertendencies towards specialisation, differentiation and the creation of new breeds of financial institutions and/or new forms of fictitious capital still persist. The realm of currency exchange, by far the largest chunk of worldwide trade (accounting for well over 80 per cent), is concentrated in just eight major currency exchanges.

That Hilferding took the Austrian and German banking system for granted and as a model for the whole of the capitalist world is a myth. *Finance Capital* abounds with comparisons between the German/Austrian type of banking and industrial finance and the Anglo-Saxon. A comparison which became even more accentuated in Hilferding's writings of the 1920s. In our days, we should be warned against sweeping assertions about an ever-increasing alignment between the financial systems of the world. The big financial centres of the world like London, New York and Tokyo are not the same; even between the interconnected financial markets of the Anglo-Saxon world, London and New York, vast differences in kinds and modes of regulation persist. Hilferding did remind us in *Finance Capital* as in various later writings that the impact of politics and state powers remains crucial for the overall structure of the capitalist world, in industry, agriculture, commerce and finance as well.

The Concept of Finance Capital Revisited

Hilferding's basic idea about the emergence of hybrid forms of capital retains its use value for any analysis of contemporary capitalism. But his ideas about the realm of high finance and its relevant actors are lacking the precision necessary to identify and determine the most important financial transactions as well as the most prominent financial market actors of today.

Hence, finance capital could and should be reconceptualised.[28] First, without regarding the relations between capitals operating in the sphere of finance, that is between capital dealing with various forms of fictitious commodities and fictitious capital operating on financial markets and making a profit from such financial transactions exclusively. One could define

---

[28] For a different attempt to do so see Chesnais (2018).

finance capital as capital consisting of money capital (as all kinds of capital do) and of fictitious capital in various forms, engaging in transactions on financial markets and trading with money and capital as fictitious commodities, using and giving credit to other actors on the financial markets. As Karl Renner has shown, although on a completely different empirical basis, it is possible to design the adequate forms of circulation (and turnover) for this kind of capital, introducing specific forms of commodity capital—that is securities and all kinds of negotiable papers that do not have values but mere prices in one or other parts of the financial markets and that do represent fictitious capital.[29]

Second, we should take the relationship between finance capital and other finance capital into account. Finance capital today should be considered as capital active in the financial markets and effectively financing, controlling and eventually even dominating other capital active in the very same sphere of (high) finance: banks controlling other banks and/or other financial corporations, insurance companies controlling banks, hedge funds controlling other hedge funds and/or equity funds, stockbroker companies controlling investment banks and vice versa. As a consequence, financial corporations are rising to prominence that do hold sway over large swathes of international financial markets or maintain a dominant position in at least one or two of the major financial centres of the world. However, many specialisations do continue to exist in the world of finance, both in terms of transactions as well as in terms of the kinds of equities, securities or derivatives traded. In order to scrutinise larger complexes of financial firms, one does not have to suppose a clear tendency towards unification or amalgamation in one direction. Mutual interconnectedness suffices.

Third, one might try to reanimate the spirit of Hilferding and have a closer look at the relationships between finance capital as conceived above and besides all other kinds of capital, finance capital striving for and assuming control of non-financial capital—industrial, merchant or agricultural capital. Still, the revived finance capital concept à la Hilferding suffers inevitably from its built-in bias, the idea of an inevitable preponderance of banking capital over industrial capital. Most multi- and transnational

---

[29] Renner's analysis and his various formulas depicting the special circuits for merchant and banking capital and other forms of interest-bearing capital provide a good starting point. His work, apart from his ground-breaking ideas on the forms and functions of private law (see Renner 2017), remains virtually unknown in the English-speaking world.

corporations today already are hybrids in this sense, comprising industrial, merchant, agricultural and finance capital.

The final step that an analysis in Hilferding's line of thought would require, however, remains difficult to make. When all capitals are dependent upon credit transactions as they are today, and when all credit transactions are passing through financial markets, when, on the other hand, all financial market actors are dependent upon credit, when all speculative actions, whatever their size and scope, are done by credit, the interdependencies between various kinds of capital become quite difficult to pinpoint. The now popular, although ill-defined, term 'financialisation' does refer to a whole bundle of tendencies without any clear hierarchy among them. Again, Hilferding seems a rather modern author in this respect as well, because he insisted upon the predominance of speculation and the speculative nature of most transactions in the financial markets. One can follow his lead and emphasise both the shift towards permanent and systematic over-indebtedness on many sides and the shift towards 'over-speculation' taking hold of and eventually sweeping away even the most cautious of actors in today's financial markets.

Hilferding, although a rather prolific writer, remained famous for just one book. *Finance Capital* was indeed one of the major achievements of the Austro-Marxist school. The book stood for the one big ambition that the members of this school had in common: not to bury Marx under an ever-larger heap of learned commentaries but to praise him—by continuing his work. In his days, Hilferding still hoped to see the unpublished manuscripts of Marx, hoping to gain new important insights from them, at least with respect to the finer tuning of his theory (Hilferding 1928). Today, we have full access to Marx's papers and could praise ourselves lucky to be better equipped for the job.

References

Bauer, O. 1906. Brief an Karl Kautsky, 23. Dezember 1906. In Karl Kautsky Nachlass. Amsterdam: IISG, Signature KDII 471.

———. 1975 [1907]. Die Nationalitätenfrage und die Sozialdemokratie. In *Otto Bauer Werkausgabe*, Band 1. Wien: Europa Verlag.

———. 1976 [1956]. Einführung in die Volkswirtschaftslehre. In *Otto Bauer Werkausgabe*, Band 4. Wien: Europa Verlag.

———. 1979 [1904]. Marx's Theorie der Wirtschaftskrisen. In *Otto Bauer Werkausgabe*, Band 7. Wien: Europa Verlag.

48 M. R. KRÄTKE

———. 1980 [1910]. Das Finanzkapital. In *Otto Bauer Werkausgabe*, Band 8. Wien: Europa Verlag.

Bernstein, E. 1911. Das Finanzkapital und die Handelspolitik. *Sozialistische Monatshefte* 17 (15): 947–955.

———. 1912. Die moderne Finanz im Lichte der Marxschen Theorie. *Archiv für Sozialwissenschaft und Sozialpolitik* XXXV: 217–230.

Böhm-Bawerk, E.v. 1949 [1896]. Karl Marx and the Close of His System. In *Karl Marx and the Close of His System*, ed. P.M. Sweezy. New York: Augustus M. Kelley.

Bottomore, T. 1981. Introduction to the Translation. In *Finance Capital*, ed. Rudolf Hilferding. London: Routledge.

Bottomore, T., and P. Goode, eds. 1978. *Austro-Marxism*. Oxford: Oxford University Press.

de Brunhoff, S. 1976. *Marx on Money*. London: Verso.

Bryan, D., and M. Rafferty. 2006. *Capitalism with Derivatives*. Basingstoke and New York: Palgrave Macmillan.

Buhkarin, N. 2013 [1915]. *Imperialism and World Economy*. London: Martin Lawrence.

Chesnais, F. 2018. *Finance Capital Today*. London: Haymarket.

Cunow, H. 1910. Rezension von Rudolf Hilferding, Das Finanzkapital. *Vorwärts. 2. Beilage des 'Vorwärts' Berliner Volksblatt* 27 (183): 9–10.

Durand, C. 2017. *Fictitious Capital*. London: Verso.

Engels, F. 2003 [1895]. Die Börse. Nachträgliche Anmerkung zum 3. Band des "Kapitals". In *MEGA2*, Vol. II/14, 262–264. Berlin: Akademie Verlag.

Gottschalch, W. 1962. *Strukturveränderungen der Gesellschaft und politisches Handeln in der Lehre von Rudolf Hilferding*. Berlin: Duncker & Humboldt.

Greitens, J. 2012. *Finanzkapital und Finanzsysteme: "Das Finanzkapital" von Rudolf Hilferding*. Marburg: Metropolis.

Hilferding, R. 1902. Brief an Karl Kautsky, 21. Mai 1902. In Karl Kautsky Nachlass. Amsterdam: IISG, Signature KDXII 581.

———. 1903a. Der Funktionswechsel des Schutzzolls. *Die Neue Zeit* 21 (2): 274–281.

———. 1903b. Zur Geschichte der Werttheorie. *Die Neue Zeit* 21 (1): 213–217.

———. 1904. Zur Problemstellung der theoretischen Ökonomie bei Karl Marx. *Die Neue Zeit* 23 (I): 101–112.

———. 1905. Brief an Karl Kautsky, 14. März 1905. In Karl Kautsky Nachlass. Amsterdam: IISG, Signature KDXII 588.

———. 1906. Brief an Karl Kautsky, 10. März 1906. In Karl Kautsky Nachlass, Amsterdam: IISG, Signature KDXII 599.

———. 1907. Die Konjunktur. *Die Neue Zeit* 25 (2): 140–153.

———. 1908a. Die industrielle Depression. *Die Neue Zeit* 26 (1): 591–594.

———. 1908b. Die Krise in den Vereinigten Staaten. *Die Neue Zeit* 26 (1): 526–533.

———. 1909a. Probleme der Bankpolitik. *Der Kampf* 3 (2): 75–84.

———. 1909b. Barzahlung und Banktrennung. *Der Kampf* 3 (3): 126–134.

———. 1915. Arbeitsgemeinschaft der Klassen? *Der Kampf* 8 (10): 321–329.

———. 1923. Die Weltpolitik, das Reparationsproblem und die Konferenz von Genua. *Schmollers Jahrbuch für Gesetzgebung, Verwaltung und Volkswirtschaft im Deutschen Reich* 45 (3/4): 1–28.

———. 1924a. Probleme der Zeit. *Die Gesellschaft* 1: 1–17.

———. 1924b. Handelspolitik und Agrarkrise. *Die Gesellschaft* I (1): 113–129.

———. 1924c. Trusts und Kartelle in England. *Die Gesellschaft* I (1): 296–305.

———. 1924d. Realistischer Pazifismus. *Die Gesellschaft* 1 (II): 97–114.

———. 1924e. Brief an Karl Kautsky, 19. Juli 1924. In Karl Kautsky Nachlass, Amsterdam: IISG, Signature KDXII 636.

———. 1928. Brief an Karl Kautsky, 13. Januar 1928. In Karl Kautsky Nachlass, Amsterdam: IISG, Signature KDXII 649.

———. 1931a. Die Eigengesetzlichkeit der kapitalistischen Entwicklung. In *Kapital und Kapitalismus*, ed. B. Harms. Berlin: Verlag Reimar Hobbing.

———. 1931b. *Gesellschaftsmacht oder Privatmacht über die Wirtschaft*. Berlin: Freier Volksverlag.

———. 1931c. Brief an Karl Kautsky, 15. April 1931. In Karl Kautsky Nachlass, IISG Amsterdam, Signature KDXII 652.

———. 1931d. Brief an Karl Kautsky, 2. Oktober 1931. In Karl Kautsky Nachlass, IISG Amsterdam, Signatur KDXII 653.

———. 1937. Brief an Karl Kautsky, 2. September 1937. In Karl Kautsky Nachlass, IISG Amsterdam, Signature KDXII 668.

———. 1949 [1904]. Böhm-Bawerk's Criticism of Marx. In *Karl Marx and the Close of His System*, ed. P.M. Sweezy. New York: Augustus M. Kelley.

———. 1957. Sammlung Dr. Hilferding. Auflistung der Bücher der Privatbibliothek von Hilferding, geschenkt von Rose Hilferding, Seminar für Politische Wissenschaften, Universität zu Köln.

———. 1982 [1954]. Das historische Problem. In *Zwischen den Stühlen oder Über die Unvereinbarkeit von Theorie und Praxis*, ed. C. Stephan, 298–328. Bonn: J.H.W. Dietz Nachf.

———. 2006 [1910]. *Finance Capital*. London and New York: Routledge.

Howard, M., and J.E. King. 1989. *A History of Marxian Economics*. Vol. I. Basingstoke and London: Macmillan.

Kamijo, I. 1978. Die Ideen Rudolf Hilferdings nach dem Erscheinen seines Werkes "Das Finanzkapital". *Hokudai Economic Papers* 8: 34–38.

Kapelucz, Th. 1896. Industrie und Finanz. *Die Neue Zeit*, 15 (1): 324–331, 374–379, 405–413, 460–468.

Kautsky, K. 1911. Finanzkapital und Krisen. *Die Neue Zeit* 29 (1): 764–772, 797–804, 838–846, 874–883.

———. 1988 [1899]. *The Agrarian Question*. London: Zwan.

Knapp, G.F. 1924 [1905]. *The State Theory of Money*. London: Macmillan & Co.

Krätke, M. 1994. Aktiengesellschaft. In *Historisch-kritisches Wörterbuch des Marxismus*, ed. W.F. Haug, vol. 1, 104–119. Hamburg: Argument Verlag.

———. 1995a. Bank. In *Historisch-Kritisches Wörterbuch des Marxismus*, ed. W.F. Haug, vol. 2, 1–22. Hamburg: Argument Verlag.

———. 1995b. Banknote. In *Historisch-Kritisches Wörterbuch des Marxismus*, ed. W.F. Haug, vol. 2, 22–27. Hamburg: Argument Verlag.

———. 1995c. Börse. In *Historisch-Kritisches Wörterbuch des Marxismus*, ed. W.F. Haug, vol. 2, 290–302. Hamburg: Argument Verlag.

———. 2007. On the History and Logic of Modern Capitalism. *Historical Materialism* 15 (1): 109–143.

———. 2008. Über die Krise der Weltwirtschaft, Demokratie und Sozialismus. In *Otto Bauer und der Austromarxismus*, ed. W. Baier, L.N. Trallori, and D. Weber. Berlin: Karl Dietz Verlag.

———. 2019. Austromarxismus und politische Ökonomie. *Beiträge zur Marx-Engels-Forschung* 2018/2019: 165–220.

———. 2020. Money, Credit and Insane Forms. *Historical Materialism* 29.

———. 2022. *Karl Marx' unvollendetes Projekt*. Hamburg: VSA Verlag.

Kurata, M. 1974. Rudolf Hilferding. Bibliographie seiner Schriften, Artikel und Briefe. *Internationale Wissenschaftliche Korrespondenz zur Geschichte der Arbeiterbewegung* 10: 327–347.

———. 2009. *Rudolf Hilferding und Das Finanzkapital*. Wien: Koppanyi.

Kurotaki, M. 1984. Zur Todesursache Rudolf Hilferdings. *Journal of Miyagi College for Women* 61: 1–21.

Kurz, H.D. 2011. Rudolf Hilferdings Das Finanzkapital. In *Rudolf Hilferding: Finanzkapital und organisierter Kapitalismus*, ed. G. Chaloupek, H.D. Kurz, and W. Smaldone. Graz: Leykam Buchverlagsgesellschaft.

Lenin, W.I. 1996 [1916]. *Imperialism, the Highest Stage of Capitalism*. London: Pluto Press.

Marx, K. 1978 [1885]. *Capital. A Critique of Political Economy*, vol. 2. London: Penguin Books.

———. 1981 [1894]. *Capital. A Critique of Political Economy*, vol. 3. London: Penguin Books.

———. 2015 [1864/1865]. *Marx's Economic Manuscript of 1864–1865*. Leiden: Brill.

Morioka, K. 1985. Hilferding's Finance Capital and Promotor's Profit. *Kansai University Review of Economics and Business* 13 (1–2): 87–110.

Nikolaevskij [Nikolaevsky], B. 1947. Hilferdings Vermächtnis. *Neue Volkszeitung* I: 7, II: 6.

Pietranera, G. 1974. *R. Hilferding und die ökonomische Theorie der Sozialdemokratie*. Berlin: Merve Verlag.

Renner, K. 1924. *Die Wirtschafts als Gesamtprozess und die Sozialisierung*. Berlin: J.H.W. Dietz.

———. 2017 [1904]. *The Institutions of Private Law and their Social Functions*. New York: Routledge.

Schumpeter, J.A. 1983 [1911]. *The Theory of Economic Development*. New Brunswick: Transaction Books.

Smaldone, W. 1998. *Rudolf Hilferding. The Tragedy of a German Social Democrat*. DeKalb, IL: Northern Illinois University Press.

Sweezy, P.M. 1942. *The Theory of Capitalist Development*. New York: Oxford University Press.

Trotsky, L.D. 1910. Letter to Rudolf Hilferding, June 1910, In Estate of Rudolf Hilferding Nachlass, IISG, Amsterdam, Signature TH 16.

Tugan-Baranovsky, M. 1901 [1900]. *Studien zur Theorie und Geschichte der Handelskrisen in England*. Jena: Gustav Fischer

Wagner, F.P. 1996. *Rudolf Hilferding. Theory and Politics of Democratic Socialism*. Humanities Press.

Wolf, F.O. 2008. Engels' Altersbriefe als philosophische Intervention: Worum ging es und mit welchen Mitteln hat Engels eingegriffen? *Beiträge zur Marx-Engels-Forschung NF* 2008: 140–156.

Zoninsein, J. 1990. *Monopoly Capital Theory: Hilferding and Twentieth-Century Capitalism*. New York; Westport, CT; and London: Greenwood Press.

Zweiling, K. 1927. Aufstieg und Niedergang der kapitalistischen Gesellschaft. Berlin: E. Laubsche Verlagsbuchhandlung.

CHAPTER 3

From Luxemburg to Sweezy: Notes on the Intellectual Influence of Hilferding's *Finance Capital*

Nikos Stravelakis

INTRODUCTION AND SUMMARY

This chapter tracks the main ideas and the intellectual impact of Hilferding's *Finance Capital* (Hilferding 1981). It covers the period from 1910 to 1966. The dates were not picked accidentally, 1910 is the year the book was published, and 1966 the year *Monopoly Capital* by Paul Baran and Paul Sweezy (Sweezy and Baran 1968) came out.

In "Finance Capital and the Dynamics of Capitalism", "Luxemburg versus Bauer on Crisis Theory", "The Dominance of Finance Capital 1910–1930", "Moszkowska and Underconsumption Crisis Theories", and "Sweezy-Baran and Monopoly Capital" sections, I will show that Hilferding's book dominated left economic thinking from 1910 to 1930, influencing political decisions and marking confrontations. However, the "great depression" changed things dramatically. The express rejection of

N. Stravelakis (✉)
Department of Economics, University of Athens, Athens, Greece

© The Author(s), under exclusive license to Springer Nature Switzerland AG 2023
J. Dellheim, F. O. Wolf (eds.), *Rudolf Hilferding*, Luxemburg International Studies in Political Economy,
https://doi.org/10.1007/978-3-031-08096-8_3

53

"economic breakdown" by Hilferding damaged his prestige and turned the academic and political interest to the insights of the only prominent figure of the left who challenged his book, Rosa Luxemburg. Her ideas, although presented almost twenty years earlier, influenced the works of Natali Moszkowska and in turn Paul Sweezy as discussed in "Moszkowska and Underconsumption Crisis Theories" and "Sweezy-Baran and Monopoly Capital" sections. The book *Monopoly Capital* (Sweezy and Baran 1968), which closes our reference, brings together Hilferding's monopoly argument and Luxemburg's realization crisis theory. At the same time, the book marked the conclusion of a long period of efforts and queries aiming to build a consistent model of "Monopoly Capitalism". From *Monopoly Capital* onward economists, including mainstream economists, treated this set of theories as a scientific paradigm rather than a variety of insights and ideological perceptions.

Although the chapter belongs to the field of history of economic thought, the arguments discussed herein are highly topical. The unprecedented growth of finance in the era of neoliberalism (1982–2007) and its fusion in all parts of economic and social life triggered fresh interest for this line of thought. As discussed in "Conclusion: Crisis and Finance" section the Baran and Sweezy argument offers analytical explanations both for the supposed "financialization of capital" and the current crisis. In *Monopoly Capital* they argue that finance is one of the most important "unproductive activities" which absorb the ever-rising "economic surplus" in monopoly capitalism. In other words, financial activities induce growth in the otherwise stagnant, owing to monopoly domination, contemporary capitalist economy (Magdoff and Sweezy 1987). In turn, the booming of finance supported an argument, in the category of financialization theories, which claims that the current capitalist crisis resulted from the financial turmoil of 2007/2009 (Magdoff and Foster 2014).

Although Marx also suggests that stagnation and/or weak growth is usually followed by vast amounts of speculative financial investments, his explanation of the economic crisis differs. Profitability and the appropriate rate of profit determine both economic growth and financial asset returns (Stravelakis 2014). In this regard financial turmoil is the trigger rather than the cause of the economic crisis (Shakh 2011).

The last point raises a broader question: Where does this line of thought stand regarding the argument in Marx? I claim that the theories of Hilferding, Moszkowska, and Sweezy develop on a different argument. Moreover, this argument is not based on changes in the social structure and operation of capitalist economies induced by finance. Although the explosion of financial activities following 1980 may have altered the patterns of capital dominance it is the underlying theory of capitalist competition that marks the conclusions in this line of thought. In short, they all adopt the neoclassical theory of "perfect competition", and this determines prices and returns both for commodities (see Appendix 1) and financial assets (see Appendix 2). It is a theory quite different from the "classical theory of competition" which appears in Smith, Ricardo, and of course Marx (Tsoulfidis 2011; Shaikh 1980).

Luxemburg is a different case. Irrespective of any criticism of her arguments, she was the only prominent Marxist theorist of the twentieth century who "adhered the basic lesson of Capital" and this alone was "a great historical contribution" as admitted by one of her critics Henryk Grossman (Grossman 1929, p. 11).

FINANCE CAPITAL AND THE DYNAMICS OF CAPITALISM

When Hilferding's book came out in Vienna in 1910 the reception was triumphant. The most prominent and respected Marxist of the time Karl Kautsky was so thrilled that he named it the "fourth volume of *The Capital*" (Kautsky 1911). His enthusiasm was shared by all the prominent members of the 2nd International, save for Rosa Luxemburg as we will see shortly. The reason was that the book took the discussion away from the question of whether economic breakdown was inherent in capitalism. It argued that capitalism had changed since the times of Marx and its dynamics were now different.

Hilferding suggested that the concentration and centralization of capital will eventually eliminate capitalist competition. The argument develops as follows: Concentrated and highly mechanized industries are expected to grow and embody an increasing part of the economy. These entities depend heavily on investment finance because their establishment and growth require large amounts of capital. For this reason, capital concentration goes hand in hand with the concentration of banks (Hilferding 1981, p. 99). Concentrated banks and financial institutions, in turn, discover in the growth of mechanized large firms new profit opportunities. Through the stock market, especially IPOs and share capital increases, they go after what Hilferding calls the "promoters' profit". The latter is calculated by subtracting corporate cash flows discounted by the dividend rate (or the interest rate plus a risk premium) from the same flows discounted by the profit rate[1] (Hilferding 1981, p. 112). Because the profit rate is assumed greater than the interest rate banks expect considerable profits from these ventures. The profits are realized by funding corporate investments and receiving shares at the "profit rate discounted prices" in return. As these deals increase in number and value, industrial and financial capital eventually amalgamate forming what Hilferding called "finance capital". In other words, through this process, finance capital becomes the main shareholder of both corporations and banks. Therefore, it has no reason to promote price competition and many reasons to control supply by forming new cartels and trusts. On these grounds, Hilferding established his main insight, a world where cartels and trusts would dominate capitalist economies taking the place of free-market competitive capitalism.

Some scholars have suggested that this argument is based on Hilferding's assumption on the rising importance of finance and the consequent broadening of banking activities to include investment banking on top of commercial banking. I disagree, the key assumption Hilferding makes is that, in competitive capitalism, the mechanized companies enjoy a higher rate of profit. The latter implies that companies adopt a technique only if it involves a higher rate of profit at the prevailing price. This conclusion goes together with a specific theory of competition. It is the neoclassical notion of "perfect competition" where capitalist enterprisers are assumed "price takers". In this world, companies have no reason to adopt a technique that lowers their rate of profit because their market share is not threatened. The theory of competition in the classical political economy and Marx is much different. Competition is a war fought by the cheapening of commodities. Therefore, any technique with lower production costs can be adopted. These techniques, however, usually involve higher investment costs because "the productive powers of labor must be paid for" (Marx 1973, p. 776) as Marx states. This is how increased mechanization reflects on a higher organic composition of capital resulting in a falling rate of profit.

The important point for our discussion is that, in Hilferding, the whole argument of the rise of investment banking and the formation of finance capital rests on the idea that both industrialists and bankers get involved exclusively in higher profit rate investments. The only threat they face is that new entries and/or excess productive capacity will push prices down

---

[1] The promoters' profit is very close to what Marx called the "rate of profit of enterprise", the latter is the difference of the rate of profit from the rate of interest. This category is very important in Marx and his crisis theory although Hilferding thinks otherwise (Hilferding 1981, p. 115).

due to oversupply as we will see shortly. This is the reason capitalists are so keen to form cartels and trusts. In the classical theory of competition cartels and trusts cannot stand for long. Corporations will constantly introduce new products and/or new techniques attacking the market share of their competitors.

The theory of competition influences also Hilferding's theory of asset pricing and finance. To find the market capitalization of a company, Hilferding discounts its cash flows with a required rate of return comprising the rate of interest and a risk premium (Hilferding 1981, p. 111). His formula resembles the valuation of assets generating infinite income streams, like perpetual bonds or preferred stock, in mainstream finance theory.[2] The latter indicates that he assumes that the required rate of return is roughly constant since the formula is not mathematically tractable otherwise. Indeed, Hilferding did not pick the formula by chance, his insight is that "promoters' profit" is realized mainly through preferred shares[3] that have a fixed dividend yield per annum (Hilferding 1981, p. 117). Due to the latter, he assumes a fixed rate of return for this category of stocks (Hilferding 1981, p. 118). Things are not very different for common stocks. He states that common stocks have larger price fluctuations due to income uncertainty. This means that variations in corporate profits and/or common stock dividends are the cause of price fluctuations. Corporate profits and dividends, in turn, follow the "general business conditions" (Hilferding 1981, p. 118), in other words, the phase of the business cycle. The idea is that prices adjust to profit/dividend fluctuations to bring common stock returns in line with a roughly constant required rate of return. This is not unreasonable in Hilferding's world. If we keep in mind that corporations undertake investments only if they involve a higher rate of profit, then the general anticipation is that the rate of return will converge to the average rate of profit as investment accelerates toward these industries. This is the reason Hilferding uses the average rate of profit, a slowly changing variable, as the required rate of return for the calculation of corporate value at parity (Hilferding 1981, p. 114).

---

[2] For example, in mainstream theory the formula has the following form for the price (P) of preferred stock:

$$P = \frac{dividend}{rroi} \text{ and rroi = required rate of return.}$$

[3] In other words, he believes that "finance capital" will sell preferred shares to the public to realize their profit and will keep common stocks to maintain control of the companies.

Assuming further that the "interest-bearing capital",[4] holding common and mainly preferred stocks, settles for a rate of return lower than the rate of profit, he concludes that the aggregate value of common and preferred shares stands "somewhat above par" (Hilferding 1981, p. 117). This means that stock prices are not highly volatile and for this reason, financial capital will not have any pressure, due to valuation or actual losses, from holding controlling stakes in industrial companies.

Perfect competition plays a crucial part in this result. In the classical theory of competition, the rate of profit on new investment is the measure that tends to become equalized among sectors (Shaikh 2016). Moreover, it is a highly volatile measure. The relentless introduction of new products and new techniques together with transitory factors, including but not limited to the phase of the business cycle, constantly alters its value. Therefore, valuations cannot rely on constant or slowly varying rates of return. This means also that stock market investments are inherently short-term due to structural uncertainty resulting from capitalist competition. In this world, long-term equity positions held by financial capital are the exception rather than the rule.

These are not simply matters of theory, in a series of papers of the late 1980s, early 1990s, several mainstream economists revealed the empirical failure of constant (or slowly varying) discount factor models like the ones appearing in Hilferding (Shiller 1989; Barsky and De Long 1993). Subsequently, Marxist economists (Shaikh 1997; Stravelakis 2019) have shown that various measures of the rate of profit on new investment are highly volatile and explain the fluctuations of the S&P 500 much better than mainstream models. This is elaborated in Appendix 2 that indicates also why Hilferding's theory cannot explain the volatility and dynamics of stock prices.

Hilferding's argument would be clear by now, if he did not expressly state that in competitive capitalism "the rate of profit declines" (Hilferding 1981, p. 103). As we will see below, on the discussion on Moszkowska ("Moszkowska and Underconsumption Crisis Theories" section), if corporations adopt only a higher rate of profit techniques the rate of profit does not fall unless wages increase (Okishio 1961). Is this an internal

---

[4] The "interest-bearing capital" is a Marxist category and refers to a portion of total capital invested in companies yielding dividends. In the third volume of *Capital* Marx treats the growth of interest-bearing capital as a countervailing influence against the declining rate of profit (Marx 1959, pp. 169, 170).

inconsistency of the argument? I think it is, and it will become evident from discussing Hilferding's crisis theory. His key assertion is that competition is "responsible" for the decline in the rate of profit. The process is described as follows: "[n]ewly invested capital ... obtains extra profit" and the "greater the extra profit ... the more capital flows in these spheres". For this reason, the latter grows disproportionately compared to the rest of the economy. In other words, when the investment expenditure is turned into capacity oversupply "depresses prices". Consequently, the weaker capital is eliminated, and prices move toward new "prices of production". However, these new prices are formed based on a lower average rate of profit. The reason is that, in Hilferding, higher organic composition means that "the same rate of surplus value represents a lower rate of profit" (Hilferding 1981, pp. 261–265). In other words, Hilferding argues, for some miraculous reason, that competition will make companies give away the whole increase in the rate of surplus value, coming from the application of new techniques, to the consumer. Of course, this is wrong; moreover, it has nothing to do with the falling rate of profit argument in Marx mentioned in passing at the beginning of the section. This, together with the determination of monopoly prices in Hilferding, is elaborated in Appendix 1.

Irrespective of these inconsistencies, Hilferding's crisis theory like the whole book was very influential as we will see in the next two sections. For more than two decades Hilferding convinced the majority of the left that economic crisis is a temporary distortion in capital accumulation that had nothing to do with economic breakdown. This was the main reason "Finance Capital" experienced a setback in the years of the "great depression".

But the most influential part of the book was the conclusions on the long-term dynamics of capitalism. At first, Hilferding argued that with the dominance of "finance capital" and the emergence of cartels and trusts, the system would move toward an "organized stage". He claimed that through cartelization, the anarchy of capitalist production and consequently crises will abate (Hilferding 1981, p. 266). In a fully organized and cartelized economy production is planned, therefore there is no reason for disproportional growth of Department I relative to Department II. Consequently, only property relations would stand between the working class and the socialist future. Kautsky and the "center" faction of the 2nd International were thrilled with the idea that most countries will eventually move toward a fully planned capitalist economy (Kautsky 1911). For them, the "organized stage" was the best preparation for socialism, since the only thing the "socially conscious proletariat" had to do was to expropriate the privately owned cartels and trusts (Hilferding 1981, p. 368).

However, there is also a second reading. Hilferding pointed out that a permanent pressing need for capital export characterized the era of "Monopoly Capitalism" (Hilferding 1981, pp. 311–336). Huge monopoly profits in monetary form were expected to accumulate in advanced capitalist countries. This capital would not be able to find employment domestically because of cartelization. Therefore, it would seek investment opportunities in the underdeveloped capitalist and non-capitalist world of colonies and semi-colonies. The Left faction of the 2nd International, dominated by the leading personalities of Rosa Luxemburg and Vladimir Lenin, saw in this reading of the dynamics of capitalism the justification for the impending need for revolution and the overthrow of capitalism. Lenin remained in line with the analysis of Hilferding. Revolution would come from the increasing confrontation between Imperialist countries for markets and investment territory, as well as the insurrection of colonies and semi-colonies against Imperialist rule. Luxemburg accepted the vital need of capitalism for markets and economic territory, but in the context of a different theory as we will see next.

Luxemburg Versus Bauer on Crisis Theory

Motivated by her revolutionary commitment, Rosa Luxemburg attempted to reconcile Imperialism and the breakdown of capitalism. She considered the latter as the "granite foundation of [the] objective historical necessity" of socialism. To understand the meaning of the phrase, we must refer briefly to the debate which followed the publication of the second volume of *The Capital* in 1885. The Russian economist Tugan-Baranowsky, together with other Russian scholars of the time, interpreted Marx's "schemes" of reproduction as a declaration that capitalism is capable of unlimited growth. He suggested that if Departments I and II grew in the right proportion then economic crises will abate (Tugan-Baranowski 1901). Following the end of the "long crisis" in 1896, this line of thought was eventually endorsed by big parts of the 2nd International. In 1910 neo-harmonistic theories advocating balanced growth gained additional prestige through Hilferding's *Finance Capital*. Organized capitalism became the economic solution and the parliamentary path to state control the means for the welfare of the working class. Luxemburg confronted these theoretical and political views with her book *Accumulation of Capital* (Luxemburg 2016a).

In terms of methodology, she stands with Marx, since her effort was to establish an economic crisis theory which is at the same time a revolutionary political agenda. Moreover, certain parts of her work indicate a deep understanding of Marx rarely found in her contemporaries. She is one of the few to consider imperialism and monopoly as phenomena not only of mature capitalism but of early capitalism as well. A perception in the spirit of Marx's works on the East India Company (Marx 1853) and the "modern theory of colonialization" presented in Capital V.I (Marx 1964, pp. 541–549). In this sense, her understanding of the "new phase" of Imperialism at the eve of the twentieth century had to do with the globalization of capitalist relations. In other words, with the process of capital accumulation (Luxemburg 2016) and not the predominance of neoclassical monopoly over labor value theory like in Hilferding. For Luxemburg, twentieth-century monopolies are the "children" of the East India Company rather than neoclassical "price setters". Finally, she seems to have a grasp over the falling rate of profit argument when she states: "a collapse of capitalism due to the falling rate of profit would take a very long time probably as long as the cooling-down of the sun" (Luxemburg 2016b, p. 499). The phrase indicates that Luxemburg understood and accepted the law of the tendency of the rate of profit to fall, but, at the same time, was certain that profits will not decline for this reason in the foreseeable future. She believed that mass production would compensate for the reduction in the rate of profit. The obvious conclusion following this line of thought was that crisis could come only from insufficient demand and Luxemburg turned her attention there. However, she did not elaborate on the idea that profitability boosts effective demand, while the lack of profits reduces demand as well.[5] Luxemburg understood the matter the opposite way. Crisis incurred because the system produced too much surplus value, that could not be realized, rather than too little. This was the reason she attacked the "schemes of expanded reproduction" as if Marx was arguing, like Tugan-Baranowski, in favor of a permanent balance between capacity and demand. She claimed that Marx's "diagram of accumulation does not answer the question who is to benefit in the end by enlarged reproduction" and this issue underlined her whole theory.

---

[5] The discussion of Marx's theory of effective demand is kind of novel in Marxist economics. The paper by Peter Kenway "Marx Keynes and the Possibility of a Crisis" is a good introduction to this subject (Kenway 1980).

The theory argues that the realization of production in capitalism is impossible without demand coming from non-capitalist regions. However, as capital will be exported/invested in non-capitalist regions, as indicated also by Hilferding, capitalist relations will tend to become globally dominant. Non-capitalist regions will become fewer, and their so-much-needed demand will decline. This would cause a rising gap between workers' consumption, capitalist consumption, and the replacement of worn-out machinery on the one hand, and the value of the total product on the other. A "gap" that will become unbridled when capitalism dominates globally. In other words, Imperialism would make capitalism global and at the same time dig its grave. This conclusion rests on Luxemburg's assumption that capitalists have no incentive to close the above-mentioned "gap" by investing in means of production, thereby increasing productive capacity. The reason is that this way they will only realize each other's surplus value. It is a theory that looks at the whole capitalist class as a "single capitalist", in the words of Nikolai Bukharin (Bukharin 1972).

The book gave rise to the first post "Finance Capital" confrontation between the "center" and the "left" of the 2nd International. Otto Bauer contested both the falling rate of profit argument of Marx and the novel theory of Luxemburg as inconsistent crisis theories (Bauer 1912–1913). To support his argument, he presented a reproduction scheme that supposedly incorporated all of Luxemburg's criticism of Marx's expanded reproduction simulations in *Capital* volume II (Bauer 1912–1913). In Chap. 7 of the *Accumulation of Capital*, Luxemburg had pointed out that Marx's "schemes": (1) do not take account of technological advances, (2) do not incorporate a particular rule regarding capitalist consumption and savings/accumulation, and (3) although capitalist consumption increases Marx allocates greater amounts of surplus value for accumulation. In his simulation, Bauer addressed all these issues. He assumed that (1) Constant capital grows twice as much as variable capital, the organic composition of capital increases, and the rate of profit falls; (2) capitalists save/invest a portion of their surplus value in Departments I and II to maintain this rate of accumulation; and (3) consequently both departments grow proportionately. After seven iterations the scheme did not show unrealized production, requiring demand from non-capitalist regions, and at the same time the mass of profit kept growing although the rate of profit was falling. Bauer thought that he had "killed two birds with one stone". He concluded that the economic crisis in capitalism would come only from the disproportional growth of Departments I and II and had nothing to do with something so severe as "economic breakdown". What he had overlooked was that if the iterations were repeated for 35 periods capitalist consumption would fall to zero, in other words, the system would break down because of a lack of profitability resulting from the falling rate of profit. This was the key argument of the book by Henryk Grossman which came out twenty-five years later, in 1929 (Grossman 1929, pp. 29–42).

Luxemburg did not bring out the hidden contradictions underlying Bauer's simulation. However, she showed very strong analytical skills in contesting his crisis theory. The Anti-Critique makes clear that Bauer is suggesting, as J.B. Say, that demand is limited only by production, provided that variable capital grows proportionately to the population and constant capital is in the right proportion to variable capital. Overproduction and thus crisis can appear only in the case that capacity increases in excess of population growth due to the anarchy of capitalist production. But because profits are expected to keep growing this is not a big deal. Production will decline and the system will shortly return to balanced growth. Bauer concluded that "under capitalism there is a tendency for the accumulation of capital to adjust to the growth of population" (Bauer 1912–1913). Luxemburg attacked the conclusion directly. She showed (Luxemburg 2016b) that in the decades prior to WWI the tempo of accumulation was much more rapid than the rate of growth of population in almost all countries. However, the empirical shortcomings of the disproportionality crisis theory did not prevent it from putting all other crisis theories aside for the next two decades of the twentieth century.

The Dominance of *Finance Capital* 1910–1930

The influence of the ideas and insights of Hilferding's book is evident from the fact that they were shared by political groups of the left that were in direct political opposition to each other during the second and third decades of the previous century. The applications of different versions of Hilferding's argument in these confrontations will be briefly outlined in this section.

It is beyond doubt that, the clash which marked not only the period in question but the twentieth century as a whole was that between the Social-democratic and Communist versions of the left. The reason for their separation was the different positions they took regarding WWI. The social democrats through Kautsky (1914) extended Hilferding's idea on the elimination of capitalist competition to the international level. In an article, which appeared in the Die Neue Zeit in September 1914, weeks after the outbreak of WWI, he argued that capitalists could "cartelize foreign policy" as well. The result of the war could be "a federation of the strongest that would renounce arms race". In other words, Kautsky believed that, following the war, Imperialist countries could agree on spheres of influence leading the system to a new stage that of Ultra-Imperialism. These insights took the form of a slogan that advocated in favor of the "United States of Europe".[6] This multinational integration would emerge from the revolutionary overthrow of the German, Russian, and Austrian monarchies and their replacement by republican rule.

Lenin attacked Kautsky's argument by attacking the slogan. His article, titled "On the Slogan for a United States of Europe", appeared in the "Social-Democrat" in August 1915 (Lenin 1974). There he argued that a stable multinational integration is impossible because "Under capitalism, …, no other basis and no other principle of division are possible except force". In other words, conflict cannot abate since Imperialist nations will not stop competing irrespective of monarchical or republican rule. On these grounds, Lenin concluded that "A United States of the World (not of Europe alone) is the state form of the unification and freedom of nations which we associate with socialism". Therefore, for Lenin, imperialism and war took a function of their own and went hand in hand with the socialist revolution.

Shortly afterward similar issues triggered differences between the Russian Communists (Bolsheviks). In his book "Imperialism and the World Economy" (written in 1915) (Bukharin 1929) Nikolai Bukharin argued that internal contradictions had seized to play any part in the economic and political life of advanced capitalist countries. In other words, these countries had reached Hilferding's "organized stage". A crisis could come only from the loss of a market due to war or revolution. Lenin contested this view. He argued that internal contradictions and crises, coming from the disproportional growth between Departments I and II, are present in developed countries at the stage of Imperialism. Lenin's treatment backed policies and slogans condemning Imperialism for the poverty of the masses and justified class coalitions of the working class with the farmers and other urban social groups exploited by monopolies. This was the reason he wrote "Imperialism, the Highest Stage of Capitalism" (Lenin

---

[6] One can make obvious associations with the European Union from the slogan. However, the matter is more complicated and beyond the scope of the present chapter.

1999) one year after endorsing Bukharin's book (where Lenin had written the introduction).

These matters were not put to rest with the triumph of the Russian revolution in 1917, they were broadly and constantly discussed in the communist camp. In his delivery at the first conference of the Comintern (Moscow March 1919) Bukharin (1920) repeated the ideas of his 1915 book. He stated that the anarchy of production has vanished in all capitalist countries through the unification of capitalists in cartels and trusts, as envisaged by Hilferding. Therefore "crisis" is not the result of economic contradictions but of the ruthless antagonism of capitalist countries and their monopolies for markets. This brings war, devastation, and hardship for the working masses of both the winners and the losers of WWI. With the Russian revolution, these masses have awakened seeking organization and action. The latter constituted a qualitative change and introduced the period of "the general crisis of capitalism". Although it was a quite vague notion it was adopted by the conference which resolved in favor of the "export" of the Bolshevik model and the prevalence of the revolution everywhere.

Two years later, in the 3rd conference of the Comintern (Moscow 1921), it was clear that a quick victory of the world revolution was not likely. Acknowledging this fact, Trotsky and Varga tried to sketch a more concrete economic outline of the theory of the "general crisis" (Trotsky and Varga 1921). They argued that WWI had changed the course of the long-term economic dynamics of capitalism. This was not simply the result of the destruction of means of production and infrastructure by war, like in Bukharin (Bukharin 1972, p. 266). The war, argues Trotsky, disrupted the proportionality between Departments I and II because war needs pushed all major war powers to produce means of production instead of means of consumption. This, in turn, disrupted the class equilibrium between "centralized unions" and "centralized industrial capital", as well as the equilibrium between capitalist states. It is an elaboration influenced by the disproportionality crisis theory of Hilferding and Bauer. However, the reason for the (long-term) crisis was not the anarchy of production but war.

In 1923 Trotsky attempted to explain his position in a letter to Nikolai Kondratiev, who was the head of the institute of economic conjuncture of Moscow at the time (Trotsky 1941). The letter includes also a very interesting graph (Day 1976) which follows.[7]

---

[7] I flipped the chart 90 degrees clockwise so that time will appear in the horizontal axis.

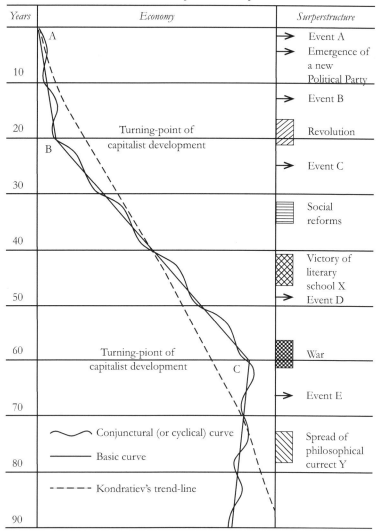

Source: L.D. Trotsky, 'O krivoi kapitalisticheskovo razvitya', in *Vestnik* Sotsialisticheskoi *Akademii*, No.4, April-July 1923.

Trotsky suggested that the war had altered the function of the short cycle. The downside has taken over the upside in the sense that pre-crisis levels of income or production (in other words: proportionality) could not be restored any longer. This would be a consistent argument if the long-term trend became unstable. However, Trotsky suggested that the growth pattern of the world economy will look like the part of the curve to the right of point C. This pictures a stable fluctuation around a negative trend. In this case, the theory is indeterminate. War influences both the short-term economic cycle and the long-term trend. But, what determines the long-term trend (the average rate of accumulation) is never specified. Trotsky acknowledged this problem in the same letter. Nevertheless, he was certain that the long-term trend is determined not by economic factors but by events of the superstructure. On the upper side of the chart, he states as examples: Revolution, Social Reform, War even the dominance of Philosophical Currents and Literary Schools. This is the only certainty underlying his thought.

On these grounds, he criticized Kondratiev for attempting to explain the long-term dynamics of capitalism from economic factors. It was the time Kondratiev presented his work on the "long waves" of capitalist development (Kondratiev 1998); a long-term cyclical pattern of the time series of prices that coincides with major capitalist crises. Marxist economists of the late twentieth and twenty-first century, mainly Ernst Mandel (1980) and Anwar Shaikh (Shaikh 2016), but others as well, have shown that this pattern persists for gold denominated prices throughout the history of capitalism. They have associated this empirical finding with the law of the falling rate of profit.

The chart which follows comes from Shaikh (Shaikh 2016) and shows the recurring and persistent appearance of long waves[8] throughout the history of capitalism irrespective of the political, cultural, ideological, or other circumstances.

---

[8] The bold line is the US golden price index and the lighter line the UK golden price index.

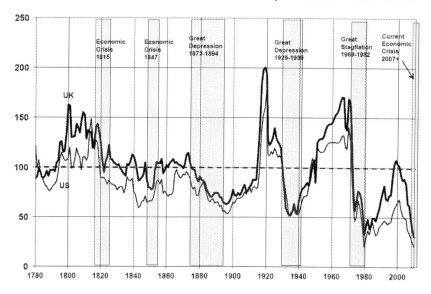

Golden Price Waves and Recurrent Depressions: 1780-2012

The analysis of the economic crisis was not merely a matter of theory, it underlined also policy suggestions. This will become evident below, where I discuss the events which took place in the Soviet Union in 1923. That year production was at 30% of the prewar levels when inflation surged, running at 70% per month. One side effect of the mounting inflationary pressure was the greater increase of industrial commodity prices relative to agricultural prices which made their time-series graph look like an open pair of scissors. This is the reason it went down to history as the "scissors crisis". The figure which follows depicts the time series of the price indexes.

The "Scissors Crisis"
Industrial and agricultural prices in Soviet Union July 1922 to November 1923

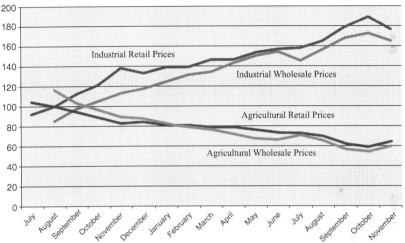

Data based on Biulleten Gosplana 1923 (Gosplan Bulletin 1923), taken from Mark Harrison (2008), "Prices in the Politburo, 1927: market equilibrium versus the use of force." In: Gregory, Paul R. and Naimark, Norman, (eds.) The lost Politburo transcripts: from collective rule to Stalin's dictatorship.Yale-Hoover series on Stalin, Stalinism, and the Cold War. New Haven; London: Yale University Press, pp.224-246.

However, the analogy with open scissors proved misleading. It was understood, mainly by the "left-wing" of the Bolshevik party (Trotsky), as proof that the crisis was due to disproportional growth between sectors. They argued that, in the same way, the US and Europe could not experience growth following the war, the market could not balance the industrial and agricultural sectors in the Soviet Union leading the country to growth. By applying the monopoly model, they suggested that agricultural products were offered at competitive prices while the industrial products in monopoly prices. Therefore, the agricultural sector could not provide sufficient demand for the industrialization of the country. The proposed solution was the immediate implementation of central planning for the industry and the financing of industrialization by suppressing the prices of agricultural products on the basis of their cost of production. It was the policy of "primitive accumulation for socialism" presented by Evgeni Preobrazhensky and summarized in his book *The New Economics*, which came out in 1926, although its main conclusions were discussed since 1920 (Preobrazhensky 1965).

The "right-wing" of Nikolai Bukharin, which stood at the other side of the confrontation, never presented anything even close to a coherent economic model. They simply argued that, if industrial commodity prices were properly controlled, demand from the peasantry would be sufficient to industrialize the country. This was the meaning of Bukharin's moto that industrialization should take place at the "peasants' pace".

Both the "left" and the "right" wings had a superficial understanding of the crisis. The country was undergoing a stagflation episode which was not due to the disproportional growth of Departments I and II. At the same time, political realism dictated that the time was not right for a clash with the peasantry. On these grounds, the party majority consisting of the "center" (Stalin) and the "right-wing" (Bukharin) favored the continuation of the New Economic Policy (NEP) instead of central planning. The implemented policy included innovative ideas like farmer taxation in kind and the circulation of a parallel currency to finance imports between 1924 and 1926. This produced impressive results, by 1926 the economy had recovered to the prewar levels, prices had stabilized and remained stable for the next two years although the country ran budget deficits exceeding 10% of the GDP.

Stalin gained credibility from economic success. His dominance in the party was so overwhelming that he managed to maintain control even when the NEP exhausted its potential in 1928 (Dohan 1969).

Moszkowska and Underconsumption Crisis Theories

The events of the late 1920s were the first setback in the prestige of Finance Capital. However, the real blow came from the outbreak of the "Great Depression". This became obvious in the 1930s when the Comintern turned to Luxemburg's breakdown theory, without referring to her by name. Eugen Varga, who had become the Stalinist authority in economics in the meantime, attempted to cover the absence of a theory explaining economic breakdown. His objective was to associate the Depression with the theory of the "general crisis of capitalism". In the 1935 conference of the Comintern, Varga presented his findings. The theory argued that depression was the result of a decline in "purchase power against expanding productive capacity". However, his argument, like the theory he presented with Trotsky in 1921, was indeterminate. The reason is that both the "general crisis" and short-term economic fluctuations resulted from the same factor, namely the relation of purchase power with productive capacity (Varga 1934).

In the 1930s the depression had turned the economy into a far too serious matter to be left in sketches, insights, and schemes of ambivalent consistency like most of the ideas discussed so far. For the Marxist tradition, the work of Natalie Moszkowska marked a turning point toward scientific analysis. She was a talented economist with important analytical skills, and this became evident from her first book *The System of Marx* written in 1929 (Moszkowska 1929). There, in line with the methodology of Luxemburg, she criticized Marx and attempted to establish a paradigm based on her critique.

For reasons of space, I will not refer to her important discussion of the labor theory of value. I present only her critique of the Marxist theory of the falling rate of Profit (Moszkowska 1935). She suggested that the "countervailing tendencies" have overtaken the law of the falling rate of profit. This was based on the idea that capitalists will not adopt a production technique unless it cheapens the elements of constant capital through the increased productivity of labor. It is an argument we have already met in Hilferding, although Moszkowska deals with it with analytical consistency. She expressly stated, that as a result, the organic composition of capital (c/v)[9] will not rise. What will increase is the rate of workers' exploitation or in other words the rate of surplus value (s/v). Therefore, according to Moszkowska, Marx was wrong and the rate of profit "cannot fall". In the 1960s the Japanese Marxist economist Nobuo Okishio presented this same argument in a formal mathematical manner in what became known as the "Okishio theorem" (Okishio 1961).

As already stated, this result depends on an assumption made by Moszkowska on the nature of technical change. However, in capitalism, one cannot look at technical change in isolation, but in the context of competition. As discussed in "Finance Capital and the Dynamics of Capitalism" section, competition in capitalism is fought by the cheapening of commodities since the main objective is the market share of the competitor. This involves the application of techniques with lower production costs but higher investment costs (Marx 1973). The latter is the reason the organic composition of capital increases and does not remain constant or declines as assumed by Moszkowska.

---

[9] c stands for constant (machinery, energy, and production materials) and v for variable capital (workers).

The analytical question is why Moszkowska, although a deep reader of Marx, did not acknowledge the role of the classical theory of competition in Marx's argument? The answer is that like Hilferding she adopts the neoclassical theory of perfect competition. This is the reason she states that "the law of the falling rate of profit is not a historical law" (Moszkowska 1935). In other words, she claims that the "law" does not hold both in competitive and monopoly conditions. Contrary to Hilferding, Moszkowska was aware that the application of only higher profit rate techniques implies that the rate of profit cannot fall unless wages rise.

For the sake of completeness, I must note that the calculation of the technical and organic composition of capital is part of an ongoing heated discussion. Anwar Shaikh (2016) has shown that the technical and organic composition of capital has increased by more than 20% in the post-war era (Shaikh 2016). Similar findings appear in other recent empirical studies as well (Tsoulfidis and Paitarides 2018). On the opposite side, under a different definition of capital, Paul Zarembka reports relative stability in the ratio of the materialized composition of capital (Zarembka 2015).

Returning to our discussion, the conclusion that the cause of crises is not found in production, like in Marx, leads Moszkowska to search for the origins in the sphere of circulation. Her argument, although influenced by Luxemburg, is different. The cause of the crisis lies in the assertion real wages will either remain constant or rise more slowly than labor productivity, as production becomes more and more rationalized (mechanized). This will reduce workers' consumption as a proportion of the aggregate product. Therefore, a "gap" that cannot be balanced from the increasing demand of capitalists for means of production will appear. This means that the economy will operate below full capacity because the "productive capacity of workers" exceeds their "consumption capacity". Moszkowska presented a clear underconsumption theory. The latter implies also that as the system moves from the phase of "thriving capitalism" to the phase of "late capitalism" the "reserve army of labor", from a transient problem, becomes a permanent phenomenon.

The next question is: How does the combination of these processes produce an economic cycle? With technical development and rising labor productivity, the value of labor-power declines. Consequently, the consumption demand of workers and total consumption demand as a proportion of total produced value drop as well. This leads to overproduction which is equivalent to overaccumulation. The reaction is a decline in production reducing both labor productivity and capacity utilization. The latter results in a decline in the rate of profit below the normal capacity utilization rate. Capitalists react to the negative tendency by laying off workers and reducing investments. This lessens the pace of the decline of the rate of profit and at a certain point, it reverses the trend. The reason is that demand cannot drop below a certain limit. Moszkowska argues that workers' consumption cannot drop indefinitely, at the same time capitalist and middle-class consumption remains constant and state expenditures tend to rise in crisis periods. In short, consumption poses a limit to the decline of production. As a result, at some point, capacity utilization and profits will begin to rise restoring the rate of profit.

Alongside the discussion on this cyclical mechanism, Moszkowska elaborates on a supplemental mechanism for balancing production and demand. This is the non-productive utilization of productive forces. Non-productive utilization, on the one hand, reduces productivity and the total value of output and on the other increases consumption. These processes tend to balance production and demand. The author states as examples of non-productive activities advertisement and sales promotion.

She closes her reference to her crisis theory in the 1935 book with the notice that, as technical progress proceeds, a greater "gap" between "productive power" and "consumer power" will appear following each cycle. This will require an increasing reduction of "productive power", and this involves the danger of a permanent crisis.

Moszkowska elaborated further on these ideas (Moszkowska 1943). She presented the theory of the "social surplus" which represents the difference between full productive capacity output and actual output. The "full productive capacity output" is calculated on the assumption that no part of the means of production and the labor force is employed in non-productive activity (faux frais). On this ground, she explained further her position on the non-productive use of a big part of productive power in the process of development under capitalism. It is the way the system reacts, to the underconsumption of the masses, the underutilization of productive capacity, and the shortage of possibilities for productive employment of idle capital. These ideas are an essential part of the Baran-Sweezy book *Monopoly Capital* (Sweezy and Baran 1968) that closes our reference.

For now, we need to note that Moszkowska managed to put together a consistent underconsumption theory which includes the appearance of cycles and the possibility of systemic breakdown. However, the whole argument rests on the assumption that firms will implement new techniques only when the organic composition of capital remains constant or declining although the "technical composition" increases. This assumption rests on the notion that competition in capitalism operates like the neoclassical notion of "perfect competition".

SWEEZY-BARAN AND *MONOPOLY CAPITAL*

Monopoly Capital is certainly the most popular and appreciated book coming from the Marxist tradition in the west. Howard Sherman in his book review for the "American Economic Review" stated it was "the first serious attempt to extend Marx's model of competitive capitalism to the new conditions of monopoly capitalism" (Sherman 1966). One reason for its broad acceptance, besides analytical consistency, is that it brings together certain insights of Luxemburg with the monopoly theory as presented in Hilferding's "Finance Capital".

In other words, although it elaborates on the ideas of Moszkowska, *Monopoly Capital* begins by accepting that giant corporations set prices while competing to cut costs and promote their products. This means that the assumptions of a stable or rising rate of profit in a competitive economy, which underlies at least the early elaborations of Moszkowska, is not part of the argument in *Monopoly Capital*. However, her insight that the economic surplus will exceed existing consumption and investment plays a central part. Sweezy and Baran argue that, due to weak consumption and investment, growth in modern capitalism is unsustainable. It requires the support of government spending, especially military expenditure, as well as other forms of absorbing the surplus, like finance real estate, and insurance. To put it differently, in *Monopoly Capital*, Sweezy and Baran suggested that, if the economy was left to perform only productive activities, the permanent crisis of capitalism envisaged by Luxemburg and considered as a possibility by Moszkowska would become a reality. They argued that in the absence of external factors "monopoly capitalism will sink deeper and deeper into the blog of chronic depression" (Sweezy and Baran 1968, p. 108).

The reason for the chronic depression is the predominance of monopolies and oligopolies. By oligopoly, they mean the dominance of corporations that are "price makers" contrary to competitive corporations which are "price takers" (Sweezy and Baran 1968, pp. 52–55). When they refer to monopoly and oligopoly, they mean neoclassical monopoly because oligopolies act as a cartel. As stated, in their own words: "the appropriate price theory for an economy dominated by such [big] corporations is the traditional monopoly price theory of...neoclassical economics" (Sweezy and Baran 1968, p. 59).

Mainstream economics is full of theories where sluggish growth and excess capacity appear due to the predominance of "market imperfections". The novelty of the argument in *Monopoly Capital* is that these phenomena reflect an inherent tendency of cartelized oligopoly to expand capacity, and this drives the system to stagnation and crisis. The reason for the crisis is that at the time capitalists have increased their investment expenditure, increasing future capacity, they realize that demand is insufficient for absorbing production coming from the use of the existing capacity. In other words, the central claim of *Monopoly Capital* is that effective demand is persistently sluggish relative to the expansion of productive capacity in modern capitalism. It is a perception influenced by Keynes and Kalecki[10] although the argument is original.

The idea is that cartelized oligopolies tend to implement more productive techniques in order to reduce their costs, increase their profits and maintain their dominant position. At the same time, they decide collectively on prices to maximize the profit of the group. This process makes them sell at, or close to, the price of the profit-maximizing monopolist. The reason is that the most efficient oligopolist (a member of the cartel) imposes his price on the others. In this world, prices do not move downward, because this would mean the dissolution of collective pricing and a price war between the cartelized oligopolists.[11] The latter means also that due to high prices the productive capacity of less efficient oligopolist(s) remains profitable. Therefore, they stay in business and do not turn their plants and machinery obsolete. In other words, they will also plan production given the price at the profit-maximizing capacity utilization. This is the reason excess capacity prevails and the "social surplus", as defined by Moszkowska, will keep increasing both in absolute and relative terms. The

---

[10] The influence of Keynes and Kalecki on "Monopoly Capital" is beyond doubt. There is express reference to the "General Theory", Joan Robinson, Michal Kalecki, and Joseph Steindl in the book (Sweezy and Baran 1968, pp. 55, 56).

[11] This clearly explains why the ideas of Baran and Sweezy diverge from mainstream oligopoly theory. In the latter there is no rule preventing oligopoly prices from declining. For example, in a Cournot duopoly companies have the option to act in collusion by setting prices or independently. In the latter case prices will decline due to competition. In Baran and Sweezy this is not an option and the group of oligopolies behaves like a neoclassical monopoly.

latter means that productive consumption and investment will be a declining portion of the surplus. The reasons are: (1) weak investment in fixed capital restricted to new more profitable techniques, (2) lagged adjustment and declining dividend pay-out relative to (changes in) profit, and (3) any wage increases are passed over to prices. Therefore, in the absence of military expenditures, epoch-making innovations, government spending, advertisement, finance, and non-productive activities in general, either production will remain unrealized or it will shrink further and further. Of course, the whole argument rests on the assumption that the price of the profit-maximizing neoclassical monopolist prevails.

Baran and Sweezy's theory although consistent could not infer economic breakdown unless substantial external factors were lost for world capitalism. The reason is that crisis does not come from declining profitability resulting from production relations but from the ever-increasing "economic surplus". The weak point of the theory is that competition is banned although certain companies enjoy a competitive advantage. In the world of Marx, these companies will use their advantage to attack the market share of their competitors and any collective pricing scheme will be very short-lived.

CONCLUSION: CRISIS AND FINANCE

Following 1990, all these theories, ideas political and policy conclusions, and confrontations were put aside. Most people believed that crises belonged to the past and the market economy was the best way of organizing our lives. Suddenly, the first depression of the new century which started in 2007/2008 made crisis theory respectable once again. Moreover, the current crisis highlighted additional issues. It came at a time capitalism was dominant for a generation, the Soviet Union was history, the labor movement was in retreat, wages and the wage share kept declining, and markets were left to operate uncontested. Therefore, both neoclassical economics and non-economic factors cannot explain its occurrence. This made political economy topical once again.

Because everything started from the financial sector Hilferding's *Finance Capital* was one of the first books people pulled out of the library shelf. However, it was soon understood that it was not relevant (Lapavitsas 2009). The reason is that, as we saw in "Finance Capital and the Dynamics of Capitalism" section, Hilferding does not anticipate financial turmoil to dominate the "latest phase of capitalist development". As far as the economy is concerned, he expected crises to abate since the system was supposed to move toward the "organized stage".

Nevertheless, the theory of Baran and Sweezy is analytically relevant. Based on *Monopoly Capital* they worked on the unprecedented growth of finance witnessed over the past thirty years (Magdoff and Sweezy 1987). As elaborated in the previous section, Baran and Sweezy argued that contemporary capitalism is stagnant by nature. The predominance of monopoly capital prevented potential profits from finding rewarding investment outlets. Therefore, external factors are required if growth is to be injected into the system. However, military expenditures that boomed during the Reagan administration were not considered sufficient to take the system out of stagnation (Sweezy 1980). At the same time, a full-scale war was not an option in the nuclear era. For the same reason, they suggested that fueling peripheral wars, like Korea and Vietnam, was off the table as well. So the task of injecting growth was reduced to what Baran and Sweezy called FIRE (Finance, Insurance, and Real Estate). It is an analytical scheme that justifies the booming of finance following 1980.

But can it explain also the crisis? The *Monopoly Capital* school of thought has argued that the wave of financialization following 1980 gave rise to financial bubbles. In other words, financial accommodation led to the mispricing of financial assets. The resulting "bubble", like all "bubbles", burst in 2007/2008 (Magdoff and Foster 2014). Following the burst of the bubble, the system lost its external growth factor and is currently at its natural condition, that is, stagnation. Again, the explanation is consistent with the theory, but it has two problems. On the one hand, it refers to "bubbles" without a theory of financial asset pricing. To know if an asset is mispriced, you have to know its right price (see also Appendix 2). On the other hand, it cannot explain why the particular financial incidents of 2007/2008 led to ten years of sluggish growth, and this did not happen, for example, in 1987 with the "black Monday" of the New York Stock Exchange.

In "Finance Capital and the Dynamics of Capitalism" section, I referred briefly to a theory of stock pricing based on the rate of profit on new investment. This theory can be generalized to encompass other financial assets as well. Its key feature, that is that financial asset pricing depends on profitability, indicates that although financial turmoil can precede a crisis it is not its cause but its trigger (Shakh 2011; Stravelakis 2014). The cause rests in the underlying conditions of growth and profitability which determine the price of financial assets as well. It is an idea we can find in various parts of

Marx's work, and it constitutes another lesson of Marxist political economy which remains relevant in the twenty-first century (Stravelakis 2019).

Appendix 1: Commodity Prices in Hilferding

When referring to competitive capitalism Hilferding says:

> the tendencies which give rise to a protracted decline in the rate of profit and in its average level, ... can only be overcome by eliminating *their cause— competition* [emphasis added-NS]. (Hilferding [1910] 1981, p. 193)

This is not the case in Marx. In *Capital* Vol.I (Marx [1964], Ch. 12, pp. 220–226) Marx argues that automation becomes the dominant form of increasing the social productivity of labor, and this is done not to get additional profit from other capitalists but to increase the extraction of relative surplus value from workers, the source of profit in capitalism. Mechanization thus results from the labor process itself. This inherent tendency, as we know, leads to an increasing organic composition of capital and a declining rate of profit as presented in *The Capital* V. III (Marx 1959, Part III, pp. 153–171). Competition does not produce this law of capitalist accumulation (i.e., the declining rate of profit) it makes it evident.

This process has an impact on the competition itself. Because capitalist competition emerges out of the fundamental conflicting production relations in capitalism, it is not a game, it is a war fought by the "cheapening of commodities" (Marx [1964], p. 441), it decides who lives or dies. This means that in the Classical/Marxian notion, capitalist competition cannot be abolished for long because it emerges from the production process as a labor process. In the neoclassical world of "perfect competition", competition can be easily eliminated. For this reason, neoclassical economists propose and accept laws and regulations "protecting" competition. In other words, the mainstream theory assumes that the market cannot protect itself from monopolies and cartels.

This explains why Hilferding applies "perfect competition" to justify the tendency toward cartelization. The latter implies also the abolition of the labor theory of value, as admitted by Hilferding himself (Hilferding [1910] 1981, p. 228), and the determination of prices in a similar fashion to that of monopoly prices in neoclassical micro textbooks. The following extract is indicative:

The latter [Monopoly prices-NS] would themselves be determined, however, by the reciprocal relationship between costs of production and volume of output on the one hand, and prices and the volume of sales on the other. The monopoly price would be that price that makes possible a volume of sales such that the scale of production does not increase the costs of production so greatly as to reduce the profit per unit significantly. A higher price would reduce sales, and hence the scale of production, thus raising costs and reducing the profit per unit of output; a lower price would reduce profit so greatly that even the greater volume of sales would not compensate for it. (Hilferding [1910] 1981, p. 227)

The solution to Hilferding's exercise is no other than the familiar figure we have all seen in our neoclassical micro textbooks. Here it is copied from Henderson and Quant *"Microeconomic Theory—A Mathematical Approach"* McGraw-Hill Book Company, Inc. New York 1958, p. 169. Where D is the demand curve, MC is the marginal cost, and MR the marginal revenue.

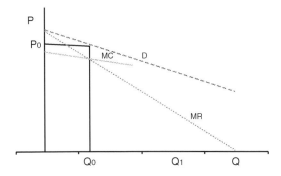

Similarly to Hilferding, the neoclassical economist states: "The monopolist can increase her profit by increasing (or contracting) her output as long as the addition to her marginal revenue exceeds (or is less than) the addition to her cost (MC)" (Henderson & Quant 1958, p. 169).

Appendix 2: Stock Market Prices

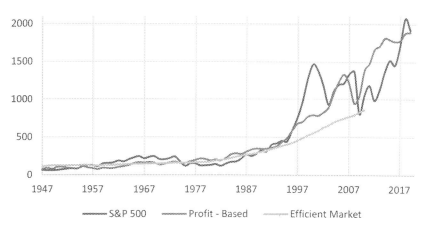

This chart is indicative in many respects. The blue line pictures the real price of the S&P 500 from 1947 to 2019. It is the benchmark for the warranted price data simulation using the Incremental Rate of Profit as the rate of return (brown line) (Stravelakis 2019). The gray line shows the Efficient Market Hypothesis prices calculated by Robert Shiller with a constant discount factor of 7.6%. A constant or slowly varying discount factor appears also in Hilferding for the pricing of common and preferred stock (see "Finance Capital and the Dynamics of Capitalism" section). However, we can see that constant discount factor prices like the efficient market prices are not relevant. This led Shiller to consider the volatility and the diversion in actual prices compared to the "gray" line as an indication of "irrationality" from the side of "economic agents".

The application of the Incremental Rate of Profit as the required rate of return implies that "warranted prices" are the gravity center of actual prices (Shaikh 1997). This leaves room for bubbles or under-pricing. Nevertheless, fundamentals rule in the end. The preceding simulation confirms this insight. In the boom of the 50s and the 60s, actual stock prices exceeded fundamental prices. The opposite happened during the times of the great stagflation (1970–1981) when actual prices underscored warranted prices. This continued in the first years of the neoliberal era. However, following 1985 actual prices overshoot the underlying fundamentals reaching a climax in the dot com bubble (around the year 2000).

The correction that follows was steep but short. Thereafter, actual prices gravitated around fundamental prices. In 2007/2008 stock prices fell shortly after the collapse in the underlying fundamentals. The latter supports the analytical conclusion that the financial crisis was the trigger and not the cause of the depression that followed. This indicates also why the application of the Baran-Sweezy theory (see "Conclusion: Crisis and Finance" section) in understanding the current crisis, although analytically sound, is unsupported. No bubble appears at least in stock market prices following 2000 to justify this reasoning.

REFERENCES

Barsky, R., and J. De Long. 1993. Why Does the Stock Market Fluctuate? *Quarterly Journal of Economics* CVIII (2): 291–311.

Bauer, O. 1912–1913. Die Akkumulation des Kapitals. *Die Neue Zeit*, pp. 831–838, 862–874.

Bukharin, N. 1920. *Programme of the World Revolution*. Glasgow: Socialist Labour Press.

———. 1929. *Imperialism and the World Economy*. New York: International Publishers.

———. 1972. *Imperialism and the Accumulation of Capital*. London: Penguin Press.

Cohen, S.F. 1980. *Nikolai Bukharin and the Bolshevik Revolution*. New York: Oxford University Press.

Day, R.B. 1976. The Theory of Long Waves: Kondratiev, Trotsky, Mandel. *New Left Review*, September, October.

Dohan, M.R. 1969. *Soviet Foreign Trade in the NEP Economy and Soviet Industrialization Strategy*. Ph.D. Dissertation Department of Economics Massachusetts Institute of Technology, Boston.

Eckstein, G. 1913. Rosa Luxemburg: Die Akkumulation des Kapitals: Ein Beitrag zur okonomischen Erklarung des Imperialismus. *Vorwarts*.

Grossman, H. 1929. *The Law of Accumulation and the Breakdown of the Capitalist System*. Leipzig: Hirshfeld (extract translation marxist.org).

Henderson, J., and R. Quant (1958). Microeconomic Theory a Mathematical Approach McGraw Hill Book Company, Inc. New York, Toronto, London 1958.

Hilferding, R. 1981. *Finance Capital—A Study of the Latest Phase of Capitalist Development*. London: Routledge & Kegan Paul.

Kautsky, K. 1911. Finance Capital and Crises. *Social Democrat*, August–December.

———. 1914. Der Imperialismus. *Die Neue Zeit* 2: 908–922.

Kenway, P. 1980. Marx, Keynes and the Possibility of a Crisis. *Cambridge Journal of Economics* 4: 23–36.

Kondratiev, N. 1998. *The Works of Nikolai Kondratiev*. London: Routledge.

Lapavitsas, C. 2009. Financialised Capitalism: Crisis and Financial Expropriation. *Historical Materialism* 17: 114–148.

Lenin, V. 1974. On the slogan for a United States of Europe. In *Collected Works*, ed. V. Lenin, vol. 21, 339–343. Moscow: Progress Publishers.

Lenin, V.I. 1999. *Imperialism the Highest Stage of Capitalism-A Popular Outline*. Sydney: Resistance Books.

Luxemburg, Rosa. 2016a. *Accumulation of Capital. A Contribution to the Economic Theory of Imperialism*. London: Verso.

———. 2016b. *The Accumulation of Capital, Or, What the Epigones Have Made Out of Marx's Capital—An Anti-Critique*. London: Verso.

Magdoff, F., and J.B. Foster. 2014. Stagnation and Financialization. *Monthly Review*, May 1.

Magdoff, H., and P. Sweezy. 1987. *Stagnation and the Financial Explosion*. New York: Monthly Review Press.

Mandel, E. 1980. *Long Waves of Capitalist Development*. Cambridge: Cambridge University Press.

Marx, K. 1853. The East India Company—Its History and Results. *New York Daily Tribune*. https://www.marxists.org/archive/marx/works/1853/07/11.htm

———. 1959. *Capital*. Vol. III. New York: International Publishers.

———. 1964. *Capital*. Vol. I. Moscow: Progress Publishers.

———. 1973. *Grundrisse*. London: Penguin.

Moszkowska, N. 1929. *The System of Marx*. Berlin: Engelmann, H.R.

———. 1935. *Zur Kritik moderner Krisetheorien*. Prague: Michael Kacha.

———. 1943. *The Dynamics of Late Capitalism*. Zurich: Der Aufbruch.

Okishio, N. 1961. Technical Change and the Rate of Profit. *Kobe University Economic Review* 7: 85–99.

Preobrazhensky, E. 1965. *New Economics*. London: Oxford University Press.

Shaikh, A. 1980. Marxist Competition Versus Perfect Competition: Further Comments on the So Called Choice of Technique. *Cambridge Journal of Economics* 4: 75–83.

———. 1997. The Stock Market and the Corporate Sector: A Profit-Based Approach. In *Markets Employment and Economic Policy-Essays in Honour of Geoff Harcourt VII*, ed. M. Sawyer and P.E. Arestis, 389–404. New York: Routledge.

———. 2016. *Capitalism, Competition, Conflict, and Crises*. Oxford: Oxford University Press.

Shakh, A. 2011. The First Great Depression oF the 21st Century. *Socialist Register*, October, 44–63.

Sherman, H. 1966. Monopoly Capital. An Essay on the American Economic and Social Order (Book Review). *American Economic Review* 56 (4): 919–921.

Shiller, R. 1989. Comovements in Stock Prices and Comovements in Dividends. *Journal of Finance* 44 (3): 719–729.

Stravelakis, N. 2014. Financial Crisis and Economic Depression: Post Hoc Ergo Propter Hoc? In *Challenges to Financial Stability–Perspective, Models, and Policies-Volume I*, ed. R. K., 187–210. Warsaw: Assers Publishers.

———. 2019. Marx's Theory of Finance and the 21st Century. In *IIPPE-AFEP Conference*. Lille: IIPE-AFEP.

Sweezy, P. 1980. The Crisis of American Capitalism. *Monthly Review* 32 (5): 1–13.

Sweezy, P., and P. Baran. 1968. *Monopoly Capital*. New York: Monthly Review Press.

Trotsky, L. 1941. The Curve of Capitalist Development. In *Collected Works*, ed. L. Trotsky, vol. 2, 111–114. New York: Fourth International.

Trotsky, L., and E. Varga. 1921. Report on the World Economic Crisis and the New Tasks of the Communist International. In *To the Masses: Proceedings of the Third Congress of the Communist International, 1921*, ed. John Riddell, 102–133. Chicago: Haymarket Books.

Tsoulfidis, L. 2011. Classical vs. Neoclassical Conceptions of Competition. *Discussion Paper No. 11 Department of Economics University of Macedonia*.

Tsoulfidis, L., and D. Paitarides. 2018. Capital Intensity, Unproductive Activities, and the Great Recession in the US. *Cambridge Journal of Economics*, 1–25. https://doi.org/10.1093/cje/bey051.

Tugan-Baranowski, M. 1901. *Theorie und Geschichte der Handelkrisen in England-Studies on the Theory and History of Business Crises in England*. Jena: Gustav Fischer.

Varga, E. 1934. *The Great Crisis and Its Political Consequences on Economics and Politics 1928–1934*. London: Modern Books.

Zarembka, P. 2015. Materialized Composition of Capital and Its Stability in the United States, 1948–2011. Findings stimulated by Paitaridis and Tsoulfidis (2012). *Review of Radical Political* 47 (1): 106–111.

CHAPTER 4

Contradictions in Hilferding's Finance Capital: Money, Banking, and Crisis Tendencies

Patrick Bond

INTRODUCTION

Rudolf Hilferding's (1981) *Finance Capital*, published in 1910, is the most detailed Marxist analysis ever undertaken of the role of finance in the capitalist economy. In spite of errors, the book remains an example of how to develop an applied analysis beginning at the very roots of political-economic theory.

But the errors were profound, and the contrast with classical Marxism is most explicit in comparison to the 'breakdown' theory of Henryk Grossman (1992), who revealed in 1929 several profound flaws in Hilferding's conception of banks and the real economy. Hilferding (1981, p. 368) attributed far too much managerial power to 'six large Berlin banks' whose control "would mean taking possession of the most

P. Bond (✉)
University of Johannesburg, Johannesburg, South Africa
e-mail: pbond@mail.ngo.za

© The Author(s), under exclusive license to Springer Nature Switzerland AG 2023
J. Dellheim, F. O. Wolf (eds.), *Rudolf Hilferding*, Luxemburg International Studies in Political Economy,
https://doi.org/10.1007/978-3-031-08096-8_4

85

important spheres of large scale industry, and would greatly facilitate the initial phases of socialist policy during the transition period, when capitalist accounting might still prove useful." (The difference between German financial-industrial relationships and others in the West meant Hilferding's observations were context-specific.)

Just before he took up his second posting as German social-democratic finance minister in 1928–1929, Hilferding contradicted Grossman: "I have always rejected any theory of economic breakdown. In my opinion, Marx himself proved the falsehood of all such theories" (*Leipziger Volkszeitung*, 27 May 1927). Grossman (1992, pp. 52–53) replied, "No economic proof of the necessary breakdown of capitalism was ever attempted. And yet, as Bernstein realized in 1899, the question is one that is decisive to our whole understanding of Marxism… Marx provides all the elements necessary for this proof." As Grossman (1992, p. 200) concluded in 1929, "The historical tendency of capital is not the creation of a central bank which dominates the whole economy through a general cartel, but industrial concentration and growing accumulation of capital leading to the final breakdown due to overaccumulation."

Hilferding's theory of capitalist self-stabilization was not anticipated by Marx and Engels when *Kapital* Volume 3 was being assembled. Nevertheless, from 1870 to 1920, according to Paul Sweezy [1972, p. 179], it appeared to many observers that a new institutional form—"finance capital"—was achieving hegemony over the entire world economy. Marxists believed that banks and other financial institutions had actually pushed capitalism into a new and perhaps final stage, the era of monopoly, imperialist, "finance capitalism." The leading Marxist theorists of the first decades of the twentieth century—Hilferding, Kautsky, Bauer, Bukharin, Lenin, and others—adopted this broad argument, although there was conflict about whether this final stage was one of strength or one of decay.

However, from 1929 to 1933, the banks that were supposedly at the center of power in this new era of capitalism suffered tremendous bankruptcies, culminating in system-wide crashes that left the financial system in tatters. Yet until then, Hilferding's theory of "finance capital" had much to recommend it, as "the unification of capital. The previously distinct spheres of industrial capital, commercial capital and bank capital are henceforth under the control of high finance." In 1915, Bukharin used the phrase "the coalescence of industrial and bank capital." And in 1917, Lenin termed finance capital "the merging of industrial with bank capital." These definitions each emphasize *institutional power bloc characteristics*, at the expense of failing to draw sufficient attention to the *vulnerability* implicit in financial relations.

In contrast, Grossman's *The Law of Accumulation and Breakdown of the Capitalist System* insisted that overaccumulation was the core contradiction, and the implications for financial crisis were potentially vast, a point demonstrated by stock market meltdowns within seven months of the book's March 1929 publication. The increasingly centralized financial system that Hilferding wrote about—and tried unsuccessfully to regulate when he was German finance minister twice during the 1920s—did not provide capitalism with more stability, but instead with greater vulnerability. Hilferding maintained his thesis as late as 1931 (Sweezy, 1968, p. 298), and it is useful to uncover where his argument came from and went to, in order to assess what mistakes we must avoid today when grappling with financialization's powers and vulnerabilities.

In *Finance Capital*, Hilferding attempts no less than "a scientific understanding of the economic characteristics of the latest phase of capitalist development" (1981, p. 21). The two characteristics most important to this phase are the growth of trusts and cartels and the emergence of banking hegemony. Hilferding's emphasis reflects authentic concerns of the era, for the first few years of the twentieth century, when Hilferding's ideas were forming and the book was written, saw an unprecedented quickening of the centralization of banking capital and important new geopolitical developments. But Hilferding also sought a theoretical framework that might apply across the history of capitalist development. With a work geared to finance and credit, it is not surprising that the defining theoretical idea is exchange, so it is with money that we begin a survey of his thought.

MONEY

The starting point in Hilferding's analysis of the finance capital phase of capitalist development is therefore money. Credit arises from the necessity of 'idle money,' which plays an important role in the relationship of money to capitalist investment. Institutions that develop in response to the functions of money and credit take on new functions of their own. Huge banks, joint-stock companies, trusts, and cartels are logical outcomes of these processes. But inherent contradictions based in the nature of production reassert themselves, leaving the capitalist system in crisis. The institutions of *Finance Capital* develop their own responses to crises, resulting in imperialism and a new role for the state. The arguments are outlined next.

His focus on exchange does not prevent Hilferding from introducing the Marxist categories of commodities, value, and socially necessary labor time within production, since contradictions emanating from this core are the basis for an analysis of the breakdown in capitalist exchange. Within the process of capitalist exchange, money is necessary because 'the law of price' "requires a commodity as a means of exchanging commodities, since only a commodity embodies socially necessary labor time" (1981, p. 35). Money is thus a means of exchange, but it is also a commodity which expresses the value of all other commodities. This dual role—as medium of circulation and measure of value—is important as a contradiction that allows crises to develop, and it will be introduced again later. Some brief explanation is in order as to how money, credit, and financial institutions are related.

As a medium of circulation and as a measure of value, money must be fundamentally tied to commodity production. "The value of money and the price of bullion follow completely divergent courses" (1981, p. 47), so even the power of the state in manipulating coinage or bullion markets is insufficient to prevent the value of money from expressing "the socially necessary value in circulation" (1981, p. 47). Hilferding rejects the quantity theory of money, arguing against the notion that "changes in value are caused by either an excess or deficiency of money in circulation" (1981, p. 56). Instead, money plays an accommodating role. It is brought into circulation according to its supply and the unmet demand for it. Hilferding concludes, "At any given moment, all the commodities intended for exchange function as a single sum of value, as an entity to which the social process of exchange counterposes the entire sum of paper money as an equivalent entity" (1981, p. 56).

However, money must also have its own intrinsic value. Hilferding acknowledges that for two reasons at least, there must be a gold or other metal complement to money. The first reason is the need to settle international balances. Pure paper currency that is not based on metal "would be valid only within the boundaries of a single state" (1981, p. 57). States might be tempted to change the quantity of money in their economies without a corresponding change in the value of commodities. The second reason is that in addition to being a medium of exchange and measure or value, money also logically serves as a store of value, and for that purpose, a metal base is necessary because it is "in a form in which it is always available for use" (1981, p. 58).

Money "as a means of payment" (1981, p. 60) is introduced to describe how as a commodity, money can itself be sold and paid for later in the form of credit money. "This means that the money which is turned over in payment can no longer be regarded as a mere link in the chain of commodity exchanges or as a transitory economic form for which something else may be substituted" (1981, p. 60). In addition to lubricating the exchange process, money—particularly credit money—plays a decisive role in the scope and scale of exchange relationships.

CREDIT

Credit money is treated in a careful, detailed way by Hilferding. Several important characteristics are noted. First, credit money is a function of individual business decisions, not of the state. As such, individual credit money can be created at any time and can be depreciated when loans are not repaid. Second, credit money facilitates a far more rapid velocity of circulation than does money as merely a medium of circulation. Thus, "The greater part of all purchases and sales takes place through this private credit money, through debit notes and promises to pay which cancel each other out" (1981, p. 64). Third, and most importantly in times of crisis, credit money makes "the circulation of commodities independent of the amount of gold available" (1981, p. 64).

Credit money is itself initially and ultimately dependent upon conditions of production and circulation. When an economic crash has occurred, Hilferding notes, a fall in commodity prices "is always accompanied by a contraction in the volume of credit money… [which] is tantamount to a depreciation of credit money" (1981, p. 65). At that point, credit money "becomes suddenly and immediately transformed from its merely ideal shape of money of account into hard cash" (1981, p. 65). It is this contradiction between the financial system and its monetary base that is the hallmark of financial crises.

The relationship of credit to a 'long-wave' economic cycle—as defined by Kondratieff (1926)—which culminates in a crash must be examined closely to understand the full importance of *Finance Capital*. In fact, Hilferding does not use the long-wave description, but his reasoning is quite in keeping with it. He begins by outlining some mechanisms by

90 P. BOND

which credit assumes a greater role in the economy as growth or the capitalist system progresses.

Hilferding looks at the process of growth from the viewpoint of the circulation of industrial capital. Industrial capital is created through the combination of means of production (MP) and labor (L). While in Hilferding's view, it is rare to find loans arranged for the purpose or hiring labor (a mistake discussed below), credit is a common form of financing the purchase of means of production. This is particularly true during the expansionary period, as demand for goods increases, prices rise, the quantity or money demanded increases, and a regular rate of return appears guaranteed. As a result, financiers are more able and ready to extend credit. Indeed, Hilferding argues that "as capitalist production develops there constantly takes place an absolute, and even more a relative, increase in the use of credit" (1981, p. 70). During the expansion, the organic composition of capital increases, as "the growth of M-MP outpaces the growth of M-L, with the resulting more rapid increase in the use of credit compared with the use or cash" (1981, p. 70).

In the process of spurring on production, credit acquires 'a new function' (1981, p. 70), that of taking idle money capital and putting it to use. At the level of the firm, idle money or 'hoarding' plays a role when fixed capital is consumed and needs to be replaced. To preserve continuity in the production process, it is important that the amount of fixed capital consumed be measured in terms of money. This "requires periodic hoarding, and hence also the periodic idleness of money capital" (1981, p. 74), ideally available to a firm through its bank account, where it will earn a rate of return. Idle money is also a factor, Hilferding argues, as surplus value begins to build up in an enterprise but before there is actually enough to use as productive capital for new investment. Idle money increases as fixed capital grows relative to circulating capital, requiring more funds held in a state of readiness.

However, with the development of new technology, the turnover time of capital shortens, leaving idle money less time to be idle. In terms of the long wave, prices start relatively low, technological advances are introduced rapidly, and turnover time is relatively quick. At the cycle's peak, there are greater amounts of idle money available due to longer turnover times, prices are rising, and the demand for credit is higher. Credit is paid for by interest. In his discussion of banks, Hilferding analyzes the nature of the supply of and demand for credit. He notes that interest is utterly unlike profit: "It does not arise from an essential feature of capitalism—the separation of the means of production from labour—but from the fortuitous circumstance that it is not only productive capitalists who dispose over money" (1981, p. 100).

Interest is not autonomous, however: "an increase in production and thus in circulation means an increased demand for money capital which, if it were not matched by an increased supply, would induce a rise in the rate of interest" (1981, p. 103). The amount of cash in the economy, the health of the national currency, and the nature of the gold stock also have a role in mediating the increased demand for money capital, so ultimately, "In a developed capitalist system, the rate of interest is fairly stable, while the rate of profit declines, and in consequence the share of interest in the total profit increases to some extent at the expense of entrepreneurial profit" (1981, p. 104).

Hilferding concludes that "since money is always needed to defray the cost of circulation, and capitalist production has a tendency to expand more rapidly than the supply of money capital, the resort to credit becomes a necessity" (1981, p. 80). A system of managing credit is also a necessity and exists through a complicated maze of financial entities that have a symbiotic relationship to corporate institutions such as joint-stock companies, trusts, and cartels.

Institutions of Finance Capital

First, consider banks. Financial intermediation by banks is necessary, Hilferding argues, because productive capitalists are unable to adequately cancel debts and credits amongst themselves. Productive capitalists may offer each other bills of exchange or other kinds of promissory notes in attempting to realize a balance of payments without the inconvenience of money exchange. But in Hilferding's days, these direct credit instruments were found to be inferior to the credit money offered by banks, both because banks were more creditworthy than individual productive capitalists and because there were efficiencies and economies of scale involved in allowing banks to mediate.

For example, the time period required to verify the quality or a promissory note or the time period required to collect collateral on a note in the event of refusal to pay could be bridged by the use of bank notes. In issuing its own notes—instruments which effectively substituted for the promissory notes offered by productive capitalists—a bank served to guarantee in the public's mind the safety of the investment. The bank also offered a mechanism for sharing the risk of the demise of any given productive capitalist.

In sum, Hilferding argues, credit offered by banks "extends the scale or production far beyond the capacity of the money capital in the hands of the capitalists. Their [productive capitalists'] own capital simply serves as the basis for a credit superstructure…" (1981, p. 84). The spatio-temporal features are vital: "What the banks do is to replace unknown credit with their own better known credit, thus enhancing the capacity of credit money to circulate. In this way they make possible the extension of local balances of payment to a far wider region, and also spread them over a longer time period as a consequence, thus developing the credit super-structure to a much higher degree than was attainable through the circulation of bills limited to the productive capitalist" (1981, p. 86).

Hilferding acknowledges an important role for state intervention in the event of fear that excess bank note issuance might lead to problems in dilution or inconvertibility of the notes. But regulation of credit in this manner "fails as soon as circumstances require an increased issue" (1981, p. 85). Then, when crisis occurs, there is a sharp increase in demand either for high-quality credit issued by the banks thought to be most stable, or for legal tender state paper money.

Hilferding places great emphasis on the distinction between the credit described immediately above (circulation credit) and the credit created through mobilizing idle money (capital credit). The latter is an actual transfer of funds from unproductive sources to productive capitalists, while the former is "merely a substitute for cash" (1981, p. 87). The power of finance capital lies not in lubricating the circulation of credit money, but in supplying capital credit in specified amounts, to specified borrowers, at specified times.

It is here too that the difference between 'financial capital' and finance capital is evident, and that Hilferding's definition of finance capital is understood. The capital of banks is oriented to issuing credit to accommodate circulation. Finance capital, on the other hand, involves the centralization (through the mediation or banks) of productive capital's idle money for the purpose of reinvestment in other productive capital. Productive capital—that is, industrial and commercial capital—is also a lender in this sense, and the bank becomes a borrower. Finance capital, then, can be seen as the 'unification' of banking capital and industrial/commercial capital.

The distinction between providing circulating credit and capital credit is also important to the bank from a technical standpoint. Because it is based on generally short-term notes from productive capitalists, circulating credit is returned to the bank in a manner consistent with the way it was lent; in Hilferding's words, "its value is reproduced during a single turnover period" (1981, p. 91). But capital credit is extended as a kind of long-term investment in the enterprise; its value is returned "in piecemeal fashion, in the course of a long series of turnovers, during which time it remains tied up" (1981, p. 91). Because of this, the provision of circulating credit (more commonly used by merchant or commercial capital than by industrial capital) allows the bank more freedom of action than does the provision of capital credit.

The difference between circulating credit and capital credit can be seen not only in the accounting process for debt repayment, but also in terms of the relative power position of banks vis-a-vis other capitalists. Hilferding develops another distinction in credit categories—that of commercial (or payment) credit as opposed to investment credit—which parallels the circulating credit versus capital credit distinction. In issuing commercial credit, banks do little more than collect bills of exchange, promissory notes, and other forms of payment from industrial and commercial capitalists. The banks are thus heavily "dependent on the state of business and the payment of bills" (1981, p. 92). In issuing investment credit, on the other hand, a bank invests funds in the fixed capital of an enterprise and thereby assumes an entirely different, more important, role.

In terms of relative power, Hilferding notes that "Every merchant and industrialist has commitments which must be honoured on a specified date, but his ability to meet these obligations now depends upon the decisions of his banker, who can make it impossible for him to meet them by restricting credit… the bank is able to dominate and control the function much more effectively" (1981, pp. 92–93). The distinction is also felt across national boundaries, as central banks take on different roles depending on, for example, the pressure to invest in foreign capital or national regulations concerning use of the gold stock. The Bank of England, Hilferding argues, has far less autonomy than the Bank of France, because the former extended largely commercial credit, while the latter, with "its enormous gold reserve and relatively small commercial obligations" (1981, p. 92), served as the principal international investment banker.

One function of the increased power of banks which specialize in investment credit is their ability to affect the profitability of productive capital.

Industrial capitalists can use credit to gain an advantage over their competitors in at least two ways: (1) by borrowing to increase output and thus realize economies of scale I and (2) by borrowing to lower "prices, for that proportion of... output produced with borrowed capital, below production prices (cost price plus average profit) to the point where they equal cost price plus interest" (1981, p. 93). This latter mechanism allows prices to fall but does not affect the capitalists' profits on that proportion of output produced with equity capital. In aggregate, this allows the total sum of profits in the economy to increase (although it does not raise the average social rate of profit) and thus accommodates the system's drive to accumulate.

In the process of achieving greater power over industrial capitalists due to the relationship of dependency on investment credit, the banking industry itself experiences tendencies to greater concentration. This occurs autonomously, because it is efficient to concentrate banking functions to realize economies of scale, particularly as regards international commercial credit. But more importantly, "the concentration of industry is the ultimate cause of concentration in the banking system" (1981, p. 98). In providing a greater volume and more sophisticated kinds of investment credit to ever more dependent capitalists, the banking industry tends to concentration because such credit is the "keystone for all other banking activities in industry, such as promotion and the flotation of shares, direct participation in industrial enterprises, participation in management through membership or the board or directors. In a large number of cases such activities are related to bank [investment] credit as effect to cause" (1981, p. 97). Banks excel at these other functions when they have an inside operating knowledge of the capitalist concern, which is easily acquired through issuing and holding investment credit assets.

The Stock Market

One ancillary function of banks which Hilferding examines more closely is that of share-issuance, a function captured in the investment banking (as distinguished from investment credit) role of banks, in joint-stock companies and the Stock Exchange itself. From a base of power that begins with dependence via capital credit, banks play a vital role in determining the nature and timing of transformation from individually owned enterprise to joint-stock company (or corporation). In Hilferding's time, there were no regulations to prohibit commercial banks from engaging in brokering or issuing shares of stocks. The larger the bank, the more control over the process could be exerted: "The large bank is able to choose the appropriate time for issuing shares, to prepare the stock market, thanks to the large capital at its command, and to control the price of shares after they have been issued, thus protecting the credit position of the enterprise. As industry develops, it makes increasing demands on the flotation services of the banks" (1981, p. 97).

The power of banks relative to others involved in the joint-stock company can be traced to the actual earning mechanism of the new enterprise. The shareholder in a joint-stock company resembles more closely a money capitalist than an industrial capitalist, Hilferding argues, because through the stock market, the capital invested can be regained at any time. "Liquid money capital competes, as interest-bearing capital, for investment in shares, in the same way as it competes in its real function as loan capital for investment in fixed interest loans" (1981, p. 109). Shares are claims to future profits, realized by the sum of dividends and of the increase in value of the shares. Hilferding believes that the yield on such shares will be reduced to the level of the rate of interest in the long-term, as liquid money capital flows around, leveling the rate of return.

The issue unresolved in identifying joint-stock company capital as money capital is the category of entrepreneurial profit. Assuming the joint-stock company return to shareholders is equal to the rate of interest, this entrepreneurial profit can be described as the 'profit rate minus the rate of interest.' Hilferding explains this category in terms of the difference between the total capital stock outstanding and the shares that were issued to represent, in a legal sense only, that capital.

Hilferding remarks that a doubling of capital seems to occur during the transition to joint-stock company status, since the original capital stock has been augmented by the capital raised in sales or shares. The capital receives profit as its return; the share "is a claim to a part of the profit" (1981, p. 110), and not to the actual capital stock invested in the enterprise. But since the interest rate upon which fluctuations in share prices ultimately must rest is independent of the profit rate of any particular enterprise, it is "obvious that it is misleading to regard the price of a share as an aliquot part or industrial capital" (1981, p. 111). Indeed, once the share is issued, "None of the developments or misfortunes which it may encounter in its circulation have any direct effect on the cycle of the productive capital" (1981, p. 113).

96   P. BOND

Hence, in the transformation of profit-bearing capital stock to interest-bearing shares, the capital stock which receives—in Hilferding's example (1981, p. 111)—15% profit becomes shares which receive a 7% rate of return. The difference can be explained by recalling that the shares represent a claim on the profit that accrues to the original capital stock. The original capital, in the meantime, has been augmented by proceeds from the sale of shares. The 'doubling' mechanism has thus made the original capital twice or more valuable than the shares it supposedly is represented by. Because of higher administrative costs associated with the joint-stock company form, the value is typically more than twice as great. This difference is a one-time only profit that Hilferding renames 'promoter's profit' (1981, p. 112) and which accrues to the issuing bank.

By controlling much of the process or joint-stock company promotion, a bank can also affect the rate of return on shares by manipulating the value and amounts of preferred and common shares. This can be done by, for example, allowing or encouraging stock watering or fraudulent activities, if business conditions make such avenues lucrative. By effective watering and manipulation of shares, "the amount of capital necessary to ensure control of a corporation is usually less than [half of the shares], amounting to a third or a quarter, or less" (1981, p. 119). By spreading their resources widely, big capitalists can maintain and distribute control over numerous entities. The joint-stock companies will also have greater ability to utilize bank credit than will individually owned enterprises, mainly because bank familiarity with the joint-stock company as well as internal divisions of labor in the bank and corporation allows for better supervision and for the use of credit in an optimal way (i.e., with the possibility of use for more profitable functions—speculative in nature—than circulation or investment in new fixed capital) (1981, p. 125). As noted above, the use of credit makes the joint-stock company more competitive than the individually owned enterprise that might not have such good access to credit.

If banking capitalists are, through manipulation of shares, through provision of credit and through interlocking board directorships, on a par with leading industrial capitalists—Hilferding calls it a 'personal union' (1981, p. 119)—banks could relatively easily then require that instead of obtaining new credit from them, joint-stock companies acquire needed capital by issuing new shares, again to be accompanied by promoter's profit. In sum, to support the system or joint-stock companies, banks "advance [the initial capital], divide the sum into parts, and then sell these parts [as shares] in order to recover the capital, thus performing a purely monetary transaction (M-M'). It is the transferability and negotiability of these capital certificates, constituting the very essence of the joint-stock company, which makes it possible for the bank to 'promote,' and finally gain control over the corporation" (1981, p. 120). Of course, this is not done without some struggle by the corporations, first for self-determination and second, for a share of the promoter's profit.

One means of avoiding bank dominance might be the stock exchange. As noted above, such a marketplace could support the circulation credit facilities of major industrial capitalists, although with far less efficiency and stability compared to the banks. Similarly, the issuance of securities, detailed above, can be carried out in the stock exchange, but again, with certain important disadvantages which allow investment banks to gain the upper hand in competition. According to Hilferding the main role of the stock exchange comes in the specific form of purchase and sale known as speculation. Unfortunately for those outside the banking industry, even the function of speculation can easily come under bank control.

Speculation is merely taking advantage of fluctuations in prices and has nothing to do with realizing surplus value or profit. Speculators thus do not gain from any outright expansion in the productive capacity represented in the stock exchange, but merely from gambling with one another. Speculators make decisions to buy or sell particular shares of companies based on the two aspects of share price, the level of profit, and the rate of interest. To assess the former, speculators have no inside edge compared to banks, for example. Assessing the latter, in Hilferding's time, was a relatively uncontroversial and steady task.

One aspect of speculation in the stock exchange is that big shareholders manipulate the prices of shares simply in order to siphon off earnings from small shareholders, who are typically too uninformed to keep up with the latest maneuvering. Another aspect is the use of credit to 'buy on the margin,' allowing "the speculator to take advantage even of minor price fluctuations, in so far as he can extend his operations far beyond the limits of his own resources, and thereby make a good profit through the scale of his transactions, despite the small extent or the fluctuations... futures trading, which defers the completion of all transactions to the same date, is the best way to take advantage of credit" (1981, p. 145).

But banks have their own insights into this process, and when the time is right, they can withdraw lines of credit that their small- and mid-sized speculative clients had become dependent upon, thus "putting these clients 'out of commission', making it impossible for them to go on speculating, forcing them to unload their securities at any price, and by this sudden increase in supply depressing prices and enabling creditors to pick up these securities very cheaply" (1981, p. 147). Banks also have some say in the stock exchange when it comes to larger speculators. In obtaining credit on a 'contango basis,' these speculators must temporarily consign to their creditor bank the shares of stock they use for collateral. At the time of shareholder meetings, this is particularly valuable to a bank. In addition, when doing contango business, "the banks can directly influence the rate of interest, because in this case the supply or credit is to an exceptional degree at the discretion of the banks" (1981, p. 148). And through their other relationships to corporations, banks can "carry on all their speculations with considerable security. The declining importance or the stock exchanges is obviously connected with this development or the large banks" (1981, p. 149).

Speculation in a commodity exchange has the important advantage of standardization. The use or futures "makes the commodity, for everyone, a pure embodiment of exchange value, a mere bearer of price… the buyer is spared the trouble of investigating their use value… " (1981, p. 153). As with the stock exchange, bank involvement has a distortive effect: it reduces the return on commercial 'trading' capital per unit, since with greater access to credit, a trader can spread his/her own resources over a larger volume of commodities. The commercial mark-up on these commodities need not be so high, allowing the 'industrial profit' on the commodities to increase. Speculation in commodity markets also assists productive capital, through lowering the circulation time of commodities and providing insurance against price fluctuations. In the process, part of the commercial profit is converted into interest, which goes to the banks.

CARTELS AND TRUSTS

The banks increase their earnings and general control over the economy in the commodity exchange. In order to stabilize the exchange from recessionary forces, banks use their power to encourage cartelization, according to Hilferding. This phenomenon is repeated in the realm of industrial production, as well. In order to understand the tendency to concentration—specifically, the development of monopolistic forms of corporate organization—Hilferding first outlines the competitive forces of capitalism that direct the equalization of the rate of profit. Obstacles to equalization arise, however, as capitalism develops.

To encourage new capital flows into spheres that are experiencing an above-average rate of profit, or to drain resources from spheres that are performing badly, are not easy tasks in highly developed, large-scale areas of business, particularly in two areas: where there is a heavy build-up of fixed capital and where small capital operates individually owned. Both sectors of production tend to become overcrowded and experience below-average rates of profit. Hilferding notes that when certain firms in healthy industries win a competitive struggle and achieve consistently high profits, then banks—which have themselves become concentrated and have spread their interests over a large range of industrial enterprises—stand to lose their investments in the non-competitive firms and industries. "Hence the bank has an overriding interest in eliminating competition among the firms in which it participates" (1981, p. 191). Banks, then, are an obstacle to free competition but support the tendency for the rate of profit to equalize.

The process of bank manipulation of industrial organization is fairly straightforward. The unification of industrial enterprises can take various forms which lead to varying degrees of monopolization: vertical or horizontal integration, mergers, consortia, cartels, or trusts. When bank intervention occurs, the struggle for unification—often a competitive, hard-fought battle—takes on a new, almost preordained nature. When banks facilitate combinations between clients, "unnecessary waste and destruction of productive forces is avoided" (1981, p. 199). For the bank, a number of benefits accrue from facilitating industrial concentration, including greater security and the opportunity to engage in investment banking. While in these arranged marriages, ownership centralizes but does not necessarily concentrate per se (because the resulting enterprise is most likely to be shared by the owners or the premerger firms), production *does* concentrate, leaving Hilferding to remark that this is a "striking expression or the fact that the function of ownership has become increasingly separated from the function of production" (1981, p. 198).

Another outcome of the process of concentration is the attempt of cartels and trusts to try to minimize 'commerce' retail trade, especially—so as to better control prices. In doing so, commercial profit as a share of the total profit on a sale of a commodity declines. The difference can be divided into the other component parts of profit: entrepreneurial profit, interest, and rent. Hilferding asserts that the existence of the monopolistic combine "confirms Marx's theory of concentration, [it] at the same time tends to undermine his theory of value" (1981, p. 228). Price distortions develop that will reduce profits in the non-monopolized industries. Cartels specifically reduce the level of production to elicit greater marginal profits. "Consequently," Hilferding concludes, "while the volume of capital intended for accumulation increases rapidly, investment opportunities contract" (1981, p. 235). One solution to this problem, which Hilferding touches on, is imperialism as understood being necessitated by the export of overaccumulated capital.

At some point, Hilferding notes, the ability to serve advanced cartels requires the amalgamation of banks. Banks must take greater pains to invest in industry rather than in trade or speculation. Hilferding therefore calls "bank capital, that is capital in money form which is actually transformed in this way into industrial capital, finance capital ... An ever-increasing proportion of the capital used in industry is finance capital, capital at the disposition of banks which is used by the industrialists" (1981, p. 225). Thus, banks which as userers were resisted by productive capital, and as money-dealing capital merely accommodated the circulation needs of industrial capital, slowly gained power: the banks "become founders and eventually rulers of industry whose profits they seize for themselves as finance capital" (1981, p. 226). The amalgamation of banks, Hilferding argues, is consistent with the trend toward an "increasingly dense network of relations between the banks and industry... [which] would finally result in a single bank or a group of banks establishing control over the entire money capital. Such a 'central bank' would then exercise control over social production as a whole" (1981, p. 180).

This is one of Hilferding's most controversial predictions, and did not fare well historically. Grossman (1992, p. 198), explained: "Hilferding needed this construction of a 'central bank' to ensure some painless, peaceful road to socialism, to his 'regulated' economy." Also consistent with the trend toward parallel concentration of banks and industry, Hilferding believed, would be a general cartel: "a single body which would determine the volume of production in all branches of industry" (1981, p. 235). Prices and money would no longer matter, and the only conflict would be over distribution. Given these trends, Hilferding concludes that "a fully developed credit system is the antithesis of capitalism, and represents organization and control as opposed to anarchy" (1981, p. 180). This prospect would not theoretically eliminate crises, however. With finance capital in a hegemonic role, economic downturns develop in important new ways.

Capitalist Crisis

Hilferding begins his discussion of crisis consistent with other themes, by emphasizing circulation. According to Hilferding, a likely manifestation of a crisis in capitalist production would be an interruption in the circulation process due to the hoarding of money, the result of which is an inability to purchase the next round of commodities. If this was hoarding of money in its role as a means of circulation, that is, if it only hindered the exchange process and left in its wake a temporary glut of commodities, avenues could be developed to surmount the problem. But the situation is more deeply affected when money has gone beyond a means of circulation to become a means of payment and credit. When a temporary glut becomes a slump under conditions of credit-based production, it may be impossible for producers to meet their debt obligations. The problem expands, as "The chain of debtors resulting from the use of money as a means of payment is broken, and a slump at one point is transmitted to all the others, so becoming general" (1981, p. 239).

Of course, crisis conditions, including the hoarding of money, emanate from contradictions in the production process. Since "Goods are produced in order to obtain a specific profit and to achieve a specific degree of valorizaton or capital" (1981, p. 240), the priorities of production drive consumption. Hilferding thus eschews a narrow perspective emphasizing underconsumption of commodities, in part because the logical solution would not in fact resolve the conditions of crisis: "under capitalist conditions expansion of consumption means a reduction in the rate of profit" (1981, p. 242) because the rise in workers' wages needed to fund consumption would come directly from surplus value extraction. In fact, he later argues, "A crisis could just as well be brought about by a too rapid expansion of consumption, or by a static or declining production of capital goods" (1981, p. 256).

Hilferding considers two versions of why there is a hoard, a glut of commodities, overproduction, overaccumulation, or whatever term is preferred. The two versions are captured in the theories of 'profit-squeeze' versus 'underconsumptionist' tendencies to crisis: as consumption increases, profits are squeezed (because wages rise relative to surplus value extraction); or as profits increase, consumption drops more quickly below levels of production (as workers are unable to afford the goods they produce due to surplus value extraction). Hilferding suggests that with these contradictory tendencies at work, crises in capitalism must be explained not from the standpoint of production and consumption, but instead in the realm or circulation by looking at 'disproportionalities.'

As mentioned above, hoarding of money sets the stage for an interruption in circulation. Hoarding of money is a function of processes that are important in reproduction and balanced accumulation as opposed to production. Hilferding first mentions the need that capitalists have to hoard in order to save to replenish fixed capital that is consumed in the production process. The fixed capital must be replenished in a manner consistent with the amount of circulating capital.

From Marx's reproduction schema, it is necessary to faithfully recreate the ratio of means of production (Department I goods) to means of consumption (Department II goods) if growth is to be steady and positive. But in order to guarantee some consistency within 'the anarchy of capitalism'—for example, to "safeguard against unpredictable consumer wants and constant fluctuations in demand" (1981, p. 246)—some overproduction is necessary. A reserve supply or money and commodities must be hoarded. Hilferding then describes the role of hoarding in achieving an equilibrium in the accumulation process. Once surplus value has been realized in exchange—once the commodity has been sold for money—the capitalist temporarily hoards that surplus value portion of the proceeds while contemplating which sector of production (Department 1 or Department II) will be most profitable for reinvestment.

Hilferding calls these factors in the interruption of circulation 'general conditions of crisis.' An inexorable need to hoard to reproduce capital and to balance accumulation are features of "the dual existence of the commodity, as commodity and as money" (1981, p. 239). To get to the actual causes of crisis, he argues, requires a sense of the basis for disproportional ties between production of Department I and Department II goods. That basis lies in the price structure which signals investment opportunities, which Hilferding describes in terms of the business cycle. At the beginning of the cycle, production expands with "the opening of new markets, the establishment of new branches of production, the introduction of new technology, and the expansion of needs resulting from population growth" (1981, p. 258).

Perhaps the most important facet of the upsurge in business activity is the shortening of the turnover period of capital that accompanies technological progress. Profits rise, as do demand and hence prices, in a self-sustaining upward spiral. However, the system sows the seeds of its own destruction with the introduction of new technology, for the organic composition of capital increases, leaving in its wake an ever-smaller basis for expropriation of surplus value. And, Hilferding argues, even as technological progress allows inefficient fixed capital to be replaced with more efficient fixed capital, the turnover period of capital is lengthened by counteracting tendencies. As the business cycle progresses, one can observe increases in fixed capital relative to circulating capital, shortages in labor and other inputs, overutilization of constant capital leading to physical damage of the means of production, and the development of foreign markets. These factors raise the general turnover period of capital, leading to a declining rate of profit and eventual crisis.

Hilferding notes a problem in the short-term, however, with the rising organic composition or capital scenario. The problem, due again to a faulty price structure, results in new investments occurring in sectors that are particularly prone to the falling rate of profit tendency. Demand for products or heavy industrial sectors typically runs ahead of output, due to the fact that new investment of large amounts of fixed capital in these sectors takes time and is relatively inflexible. With demand outstripping supply in the short-term, prices in heavy industrial sectors can increase at the same time organic composition does. This will signal, incorrectly, that more liquid capital should flow into these sectors. When the new investment in fixed capital in these sectors finally comes on line, supply suddenly increases dramatically, resulting in the disproportionalities which in Hilferding's view are the more proximate 'cause' of overaccumulation and crisis. In other sectors, especially those dependent on raw materials, similar processes of mismatching prices to opportunities for profit exist. 'Convulsions' in raw material supply follow the disequilibrium tendency of demand.

Violent price fluctuations and further inaccurate signals for new investment follow naturally. Reserve money supplies which might have corrected some of the imbalances are often countered by the money supplies that have been hoarded. Accumulation proceeds more rapidly than consumption, and disproportionalities develop throughout the system. Ultimately, Hilferding believes, these factors produce "deviations of market prices from production prices, and hence disruptions in the regulation of production, which depends for its extent and direction upon the structure of prices" (1981, p. 266). Bottlenecks, hoarding, slumps in sales, and crisis follow.

Credit here becomes an especially interesting ingredient. On the one hand, credit could provide the means to rationalize production and *level out* the disproportionalities in pricing. However, upon closer examination, finance *exacerbates* underlying tendencies to crisis. Part of the reason for this can be traced to the dual nature of money as a means of circulation and as a measure of value, which permits the financial system to detach itself from its monetary base. This occurs both because of value changes in money itself—currency becomes unfixed from its gold value—and because credit (centralized idle money) is created in a manner unrelated to the value of circulating commodities.

Certain mechanisms in the business cycle feed off the contradiction in the dual role of money. Hilferding argues that during the expansionary phase of the business cycle, both the system's disproportionalities and the general turnover time of capital increase. To accommodate, more credit is needed. For example, disproportionalities produce gluts in the stocks of commodities in certain sectors, particularly those with rising prices and heavy fixed capital. A ready supply of bank credit to these favored sectors permits producers to avoid equilibrating forces (production or price cuts) so that production levels will continue unhindered by the developing disproportionalities.

Also during the expansionary phase, as fixed capital increases relative to circulating capital, turnover time is extended. In the process, the velocity of the circulation of credit slows, requiring more credit for rollovers, extensions, and renewals. As delays hit one sector and affect payment schedules, they are transferred throughout the economy, requiring ever-increasing credit transactions. Beyond this role in ameliorating certain mechanical problems in managing the growth of the capitalist system during the expansion, credit is also demanded in greater quantities for speculative purposes. As interest rates rise during the expansion, speculation in the stock exchange requires an ever-greater return, and hence more credit. Share prices for joint-stock companies increase, allowing banks more lucrative activity in the promotion of new enterprises. In the commodity exchange, greater demand for credit arises to facilitate the practice of withholding certain commodities from the market in order to artificially inflate their price.

At some point, interest rates are too high to permit profitable speculation, and as banks refuse to extend more credit, the stock exchange can experience a rapid crisis, characterized by an immediate downward spiral in share prices and investor confidence, and ultimately, significant declines in commodity prices. While this has occurred primarily because of a turn-around in the money and credit markets, "it can well precede the onset of a general commercial and industrial crisis" (1981, p. 271). Hilferding hastens to add, "Nonetheless, it is only a symptom, an omen, of the latter crisis, since the changes in the money market are indeed determined by the changes in production which lead to a crisis" (1981, p. 271).

The crisis in the stock exchange is exacerbated by the strain on bank credit in production. As the crisis hits, goods which were financed with bank credit can no longer be paid for at prices high enough to cover interest payments. With falling prices, bank credit cannot be extended at this stage to cover unpaid bills. Defaults increasing, the credibility of the lending institutions comes into question. Runs on banks occur, and "the reversion of the financial system to its monetary base" begins. The limited supply of circulating cash is then subject to hoarding, bid up in value beyond its intrinsic worth, and no longer tied even to its metallic base.

For Hilferding, the relationship of the monetary crisis to the crisis in production varies depending on several factors: the degree to which some banks' credit positions remain unimpaired, the country's gold balances, the role of the state, and the degree of concentration in the banking industry. He concludes ambiguously, by describing certain changes in the character of crises involving the role of banks that can help prevent both the monetary crisis and the crisis in production.

For example, the strength of a country's gold stock can play an important role in managing an economic slide. A deteriorating balance of payments at the peak or expansion weakens the gold stock, since (in Hilferding's day) "gold functions as world money for the settlement of international payments balances" (1981, p. 275). The balance of payments normally swings against economies that are peaking because rising domestic prices encourage imports and leave a weakened balance of trade. A country leading the boom is likely to have the highest interest rates, thus attracting foreign money and further weakening the balance of payments. Speculators finally sense the impending doom and flood the securities market with declining paper money. With gold flight a logical response to these trends, the domestic financial markets are seriously threatened. Conversely, a strong gold policy can ameliorate the conditions of crisis.

The role of the state in mediating the crisis is important in other respects. The most damaging yet widely used tool of the state, Hilferding maintains, is limiting the extension of bank credit. Ideally, the adverse balance of trade experienced by the most advanced capitalist countries during the peak of expansion should be matched by a favorable balance of payments. The best mechanism for this is increased foreign lending. If the banking industry is highly concentrated, Hilferding argues, the risk associated with the conditions of crisis (speculation, default, monetary problems, etc.) can be more widely shared, because banks can spread their resources more widely through different sectors at different stages of capitalist development, and also because depositors are less able to find banks that are unaffected by the crisis.

Power of financiers vis-a-vis commerce and industry shifts in the banks' favor. By the time a banking crisis has arrived, "speculation, in both commodities and securities, has declined considerably in volume and importance" (1981, p. 292). Thus, trends in finance capital might, in Hilferding's view, actually prevent a monetary crisis from occurring. Countervailing forces such as increasing exports, defaults on foreign debt, and an influx of gold during the crisis help limit the damage. But it is clear that a monetary crisis can, quite autonomously, push the productive sector into its own crisis. During the crisis, both industrial and money capital sit idle and liquidity is high. As Hilferding puts it, "Money does not circulate, or function as money capital, because industrial capital is not functioning" (1981, p. 285). It is then in the depth of crisis that the financial system reverts to reflecting the conditions of value production from whence it began.

Hilferding ends his comments on crises by contemplating the Marxist proposition that they deepen and worsen over time. The possibility of crises emanating from the finance capital sector—with "large-scale bankruptcies, and from stock exchange, bank, credit, and money panics" (1981, p. 294)—actually diminishes as finance capital develops, he posits, and the existence or commercial and industrial cartels allows conditions of crisis to be shuffled into non-cartelized industries. As a result, "The difference in the rate of profit between cartelized and non-cartelized industries, which on average is greater the stronger the cartel and the more secure its monopoly, diminishes during times of prosperity and increases during a depression" (1981, p. 298). The ability of monopolies to manipulate prices exacerbates the disproportionalities mentioned previously and prevents the restructuring necessary to end a depression. All of this works over time to further the process of concentration, Hilferding argues. If there is no monetary crash, finance capital, he seems to suggest, may emerge from crises relatively unscathed and able to continue playing a hegemonic role in the economy.

Assessment

Much of the preceding analysis of the relationship of financial phenomena to production, exchange, and distribution stands the test of time. The power of *Finance Capital* is the theoretical base from which the arguments emanate, and it generally appears beyond reproach. Unfortunately, though, the climax to *Finance Capital*—the discussion of crises—is where different conclusions can be drawn, due to contradictions not only within capitalism but within Hilferding's understanding of its dynamics.

Other retrospective objections that should be mentioned pertain to the failure to discuss consumer and government credit (then far less prevalent than today), the emphasis on power blocs, and the political lessons that *Finance Capital* teaches us. The most telling criticism may be derived from the role of financial institutions in major crises during the history of capitalism, both before and after the 1910 book. While Hilferding could draw on major financial meltdowns in the 1840s–1850s and 1870s–1890s, two subsequent crises were more informative about capitalism's dynamics.

The first, from 1929 until World War II, was marked by an explosion of speculation, mismanagement by the strong central bank, and ultimate collapse of both the financial and the productive systems. The second, occurring in fits and starts since the 1970s, can also be characterized by speculative tendencies and the impending prospect of financial collapse at the same time numerous sectors are facing severe productive system decay. These crises have not only persisted over the past four decades—after a period of financial regulation stabilized the system from the 1940s to 1970s—but have become increasingly amplified. The early 1980s' world recession was followed by the late 1980s' financial meltdown in energy and U.S. Savings & Loan housing finance institutions, the mid- to late-1990s' emerging market collapses, the early 2000s' dot.com bubble bursting, the 2007–2009 world financial meltdown catalyzed by a property crash, and the crisis (based likely on corporate debt default) that appears imminent at the time of writing.

For Hilferding, these would be a surprise, for several factors in "militating against a banking crisis" (1981, p. 291) bear repeating: risk can be shared; strong gold and other state policies can shore up the creditworthiness of the system; speculation declines in volume and importance; and joint-stock company production can continue because it need not realize an immediate return. Hence, it is "sheer dogmatism to oppose the banks' penetration of industry… as a danger to the banks" (1981, p. 293). Not only that, "As the power of banks continues to grow, it is the banks which dominate the movements of speculation, rather than being dominated by them" (1981, p. 293).

These arguments, not unreasonable as hypotheses, are in fact untenable given the earlier analysis. There are at least seven reasons to judge Hilferding's approach inadequate.

- First, the disproportionality tendencies Hilferding describes in discussing reproduction schema are demonstrably exacerbated by the growing role of finance capital. With the onset or a production-based crisis, the financial system is bound to suffer.
- Second, while increased concentration or banking allows any given bank's risk to be shared with many more depositors, it seems logical that this would be offset by the growing risk to the general creditworthiness or the entire system as profit rates tend to fall and banks must look further afield to maintain healthy loans and a growing deposit base. (In fact, the stable, steady banking system of the 1950s and 1960s subsequently suffered unprecedented concentration at the same time risk spread out of control.)
- Third, public policy—especially regulation as it has been practiced in the West—makes stability of the banking system a top priority, but some problems are larger than the state alone can handle. The lack, since 1971, of a gold-base to world exchange rates is an important drawback, one that has relieved the U.S. economy of great economic pressure at the expense of a potential gold-hoarding phase.
- Fourth, there is much evidence to suggest that speculation increases immediately prior to a crisis rather than declining in volume and importance. The theory behind it is simple: 'Ponzi financing' forces speculators to borrow both to speculate more and to simply to pay back old loans as their previous investments fail to pan out. Speculation always begets more speculation, for if not, the bubble is burst, and the pyramid scheme topples. The air from a burst bubble tends to be released quickly rather than slowly, as it is not difficult to identify a failed line of investment, and as memories of taking baths, losing shirts, or other graphic descriptions are brought to the fore by the media.
- Fifth, to argue that joint-stock company production will continue unhindered by a banking crisis is to ignore the interplay so well developed earlier in the book. If credit is a key ingredient for the

smooth operation of the stock exchange, and if the stock exchange is crucial in a company's ability to raise funds for increased production (through splits in shares or through the bond market which relies on stock prices), it follows that a banking collapse would affect joint-stock companies quite considerably.

- Sixth, given the tendencies outlined above—especially increasing risk, the breakdown of the state's protective role, and uncontrolled speculation—it is reasonable to attempt to prevent banks from crossing the barriers between banking and commerce, for their own good and for the good of the stability of the system, if such are desirable goals.
- Seventh, given the basic definition of speculation, it is unlikely that banks would be able to harness speculation. Indeed, it is the inability of anyone to harness speculation that causes such severe problems as to make disproportionalities look simple in comparison. As Suzanne de Brunhoff (1976, p. xiv) puts it, Hilferding's dissociation between money and the credit system was "one of the reasons for the overestimation of the role of finance capital."

In sum, the arguments Hilferding makes as to why and how crises can be avoided are all inconsistent with his earlier theory or with proven reality. One reason is that Hilferding neglects government and consumer credit. For Hilferding, credit is based in the needs of firms either to rationalize a plethora of bills of exchange and promissory notes (circulating credit), or to raise funds for new investment (capital credit). By neglecting state debt and consumer finance, Hilferding misses some important phenomena of modern capitalism. One is the ability of the system to raise the social wage of labor through debt, buying labor peace and giving weight to the notion of an advanced capitalist 'labor aristocracy.' Another is the ability of the system to maintain effective demand, buying time and avoiding crises in 'underconsumption' but putting off until later the unavoidable need to repay the debt. In this sense, credit creation begins to simply resemble speculation: gambling that future income will permit the present rate of borrowing.

Earlier in *Finance Capital*, Hilferding had commented, "A bank crash results only from industrial overproduction or excessive speculation, and manifests itself as a scarcity or bank capital in money form, due to the fact that bank capital is tied up in a form which cannot be immediately realized

110 P. BOND

as money" (1981, p. 180). This is the true nature of financial crises, and the later attempt to rationalize a stable banking system was unsuccessful.

In sum, nearly all of Hilferding's previous analysis leads to the logical conclusion that, contrary to finance capital's hegemony during a crisis, banks do indeed lose self-control, as well as control of outside entities and processes. Sweezy (1968, p. 267) may have been correct in this respect when he commented, "Hilferding mistakes a transitional phase of capitalist development for a lasting trend." The transitional phase was one of recovery from the 1870s–1890s' financial crises; these crises would emerge again in the early 1930s and again in recent decades. Part of the reason Hilferding erred in understanding financial crises was his emphasis on bank control of corporations and hence the economy.

During a crisis, banks are the first, not the last, to lose self-control and control of outside entities and processes. Yet Hilferding empowers banks in the finance capital era with tremendous power, offering few caveats. This tends to give a conspiracy theory air to finance capital which is unnecessary given the careful rooting of the issues in the basic capitalist production process. While there are genuine power blocs and institutional symbols in the economy, and while their role may at times be truly autonomous and have strong feedback in the accumulation process, the experience of the 1930s shows that banks are not permanently powerful in, nor permanent symbols of, the last phase or capitalist development.

A final criticism is that in analyzing class fractions, Hilferding is geographically simplistic, leading one to conclude that highly liquid finance capital may be always in harmony with relatively fixed heavy industrial monopoly capital. In reality, when an international bank demands debt repayment from a poor country, it insists that the borrowing country shift to exports, even if these sometimes compete with its hometown capital. The financing of Western deindustrialization by major Western banks as productive capital shifted to Mexico and East Asia is one example.

Financial Power and Vulnerability

What political strategy emerges from the previous analysis? Since finance capital has operated in a somewhat autonomous manner in recent years, and since a banking collapse will further the fractionalization of big capital, it may well be possible to view finance capital as an autonomous target and to consider serious prospects for taking power from a banking system weakened by crisis. In sum, based on Hilferding's analysis rooting credit in money in commodity exchange, and adding the Ponzi nature of credit creation and speculation as the business cycle matures, it is quite natural to conclude that the emergence and power of finance capital does indeed signal a new era of capitalism. It is an era of periodic financial system fragility, a fragility that logically ends in a crash, finally rerooting credit and money back in the process of value production.

But between a new start-up (where credit emanates from idle money and bills of exchange) and the next crash, finance capital can be said to operate autonomously, as if it had a life of its own. Finance capital gains and uses power in ways which Hilferding documents. It allows credit and speculation to career beyond bounds of rationality. And it funnels new investment off into the far corners of the globe, speeding the uneven development of capitalism at the same time it heightens competition and equalizes profits. It is for these reasons that the first major step of any progressive movement upon taking state power, and even in the period ahead of such a revolution, should be to socialize control of finance capital. It is likely that the only opportunity for such a step would be in the shambles following a crash. Moreover, Hilferding concludes,

> The response of the proletariat to the economic policy of finance capital—imperialism—cannot be free trade, but only socialism... The blatant seizure of the state by the capitalist class directly compels every proletarian to strive for the conquest of political power as the only means of putting an end to his own exploitation. (1981, pp. 366–370)

The 2010s–2020s' conjuncture, more than a century after Hilferding's *Finance Capital*, gives us yet more to contemplate, when assessing the ways political power can (and can't) transcend the logic of finance. One moment was the 2009–2014 decision by the main Western governments to print money: 'Quantitative Easing' (QE) in which central banks purchase long-dated state bonds from commercial lenders to swell financial liquidity. The objective was to prop up a world economy whose 2008–2009 financial-asset crash went deeper than ever in modern history, even worse than the first eight months of the global 1929–1930 devalorization that precipitated the Great Depression. Halting and reversing that financial crash did not, however, generate broad-based prosperity—but instead mainly fueled stock market bubbling and extreme inequality. (Japanese experience more than a decade earlier was, similarly, incapable of rebooting productive-circuit capitalism through monetary easing.) And in

2020–2022, a similar burst of financial-asset inflation hit the world economy in the wake of the March 2020 Western central bank QE, deemed necessary because of the COVID-19 pandemic's economic lockdown requirements. But again, the impact was to drive the level of world stock markets (and a few other financial assets) to record levels of market-valuation/GDP ratios (the 'Buffett Indicator')—which in turn generated unprecedented income and wealth inequality.

One additional feature of financial power and vulnerability was the craze in cybercurrencies, which only one country—China in 2021—appeared capable of banning thanks to Beijing's strong exchange control regime and capacity to surveil the citizenry's intimate economic activities. The dislocated, non-grounded feature of Bitcoin was one reason its price rose spectacularly, as national currencies lost favor during the 2010s. Like gold, a scarcity strategy was hard-wired into Bitcoin, although the cybercurrency's 'mining' and blockchain algorithm ('consensus,' ensuring distributed-ledger integrity) required such vast computational power that the energy involved soon created more greenhouse gas emissions than most countries. Most importantly for a working-class strategy of taking state power, the very existence of cybercurrencies prevents a new, progressive government from exercising monetary and fiscal sovereignty, given the likelihood of financial-asset leakage through the ether.

Yet in one other contemporary experience, economic sanctions imposed by the West on Russia following its invasion of Ukraine in February 2022, Hilferding would have nodded with familiarity, rekindling his vision of state power exercised over financial power. After the 2001 attacks by militant Muslims on the World Trade Center and Pentagon, the U.S. Treasury radically improved its capacities to monitor and halt international financial transactions, in a bid to halt 'terrorist' funding. Likewise, within days of Vladimir Putin's assault on Ukraine, there was such an intense sanctions backlash by leaders in Washington, London, Brussels, and Tokyo—even compelling Zurich regulators to comply—that Russians found themselves shut out of Western finance. Well before Putin felt the hits to the Russian real economy—for example, oil and gas flows to Europe and other trade sanctions and corporate divestments—the West's ban on Russian banks (dependent upon the Belgium-based Society for Worldwide Interbank Financial Telecommunications) prevented most international banking transactions. A few countries, including China, had begun to establish escape routes, but not quickly enough (a similar lockout had been used against Iran from 2012–2016, until the nuclear energy agreement Tehran reached with Washington-Brussels restored access). Western financial regulators also seized around half of Moscow's $600 billion in foreign reserves (carelessly still held abroad) and clamped down heavily on several dozen oligarch tycoons (especially those seen as close to Putin) whose Western corporate and property holdings made them vulnerable.

The contemporary frictions between logics of accumulation, centralized capital, concentrations of wealth and uneven capitalist development on the one hand, and the twenty-first century's displays of state power over finance on the other, are thus not necessarily outside the debates in which Hilferding, Grossman, and so many others have engaged for more than a century. Required in all such enquiries is our search for distinctions between the theoretical necessities of capitalism, as opposed to the conjunctural accidents of history. Theorizing finance will never be a finished task, given the geopolitical, territorial, and military noise that, like the Russian example, appear to confound what we see as the logic of capital accumulation. Returning, then, to Hilferding's own deep-rooted convictions about the laws of motion of finance capital power, and correcting these laws to incorporate subsequent lessons regarding structured financial vulnerability, is one entry point to contemporary political economy. Without a history of political-economic thought, it is more difficult to enliven our ever more urgent explorations of class struggles, state power, financial chaos, and deep-rooted capitalist crisis.

REFERENCES

de Brunhoff, Suzanne. 1976. *Marx on Money*. New York: Urizen Books.

Grossman, Henryk. 1992 [1929]. *The Law of Accumulation and Breakdown of the Capitalist System*. London: Pluto Press.

Hilferding, Rudolf. 1981 [1910]. *Finance Capital*. London: Routledge and Kegan Paul.

Kondratieff, N. 1926. Die langen Wellen der Konjunktur. *Archiv fur Sozialwissenschaft undSozialpolitik*, 56: 573–609.

Sweezy, Paul. 1968 [1942]. *The Theory of Capitalist Development*. New York: Monthly Review.

———. 1972. The Resurgence of Finance Capital: Fact or Fancy? *Socialist Revolution* 1 (6): 1–33.

CHAPTER 5

Finance Capital, Financialisation and the Periodisation of Capitalist Development

Andrew Kilmister

INTRODUCTION

Rudolf Hilferding's *Finance Capital* (Hilferding 1910/1981) was acclaimed soon after publication as a significant contribution to Marxist thought and continues to be seen as an important work in the tradition of classical Marxism. Yet in sharp contrast to Marx's *Capital*, there appears to be a general consensus, even among radical writers on finance, that Hilferding's analysis is of historical interest only and cannot be applied to contemporary developments.

A common criticism is that Hilferding generalised the specific cases of Germany and Austro-Hungary in an unwarranted way, presenting these as typical of capitalism in general and neglecting contrasting examples of development such as Britain. Michael Howard and John King write that

---

A. Kilmister (✉)
Oxford Brookes Business School, Oxford Brookes University, Oxford, UK
e-mail: ackilmister@brookes.ac.uk

© The Author(s), under exclusive license to Springer Nature
Switzerland AG 2023
J. Dellheim, F. O. Wolf (eds.), *Rudolf Hilferding*, Luxemburg
International Studies in Political Economy,
https://doi.org/10.1007/978-3-031-08096-8_5

Hilferding generalised far too easily from his own German experience. The economic power of the German banks in the period before 1914 was paralleled (if at all) only in the contemporary USA, and even there not for long. There was never an equivalent phenomenon in Britain or France. (Howard and King 1989, p. 101)

Tony Norfield criticises Hilferding both for failing to relate domestic financial systems to the position that particular countries have in the world market and for exaggerating the role of banks even in countries where finance capital did appear to have played an important role, such as the USA and Japan (Norfield 2016, p. 94). For Norfield, this exaggeration led to crucial political weaknesses; he argues that it led Hilferding to the view that capitalism could be controlled simply by limiting the power of the banks. Both Norfield and Howard and King also highlight what they see as analytical failings in Hilferding's work; in Norfield's view, he misunderstands the forces determining the rate of profit in banking (Norfield, op cit p. 136) while Howard and King criticise his accounts both of economic crises and of capital exports (Howard and King, op cit pp. 100–101). Jan Toporowski is also critical of Hilferding's account of crisis, claiming that it neglects the specific contribution made by the financial system to economic instability and sees finance simply as a passive response to contradictions in the real economy. He writes that

> in line with Hilferding's analysis of finance as coordinating monopoly capitalism, Marxist critics have largely followed the founders of their school of thought to adhere to a "reflective" view that, if financial crisis occurs, it is because it correctly "reflects" critical developments in production: a fall in the rate of profit, increased class struggle, disproportions and so on. (Toporowski 2005, p. 59)

For Toporowski, Rosa Luxemburg's account of international loans, while less orthodox in Marxist terms than Hilferding's work, represented a more creative and ultimately more fruitful approach, owing to its recognition of the autonomous role of finance in generating instability.

Examples such as these could easily be multiplied and, taken together, they converge to a conclusion that, despite Hilferding's localised insights, his work has little to offer in an active way to those trying to understand contemporary financial systems from a radical perspective. At the same time, recent decades have seen a widespread debate on the periodisation of capitalist development in which the concept of financialisation has played a central role (see Albritton et al. 2001 for an important collection of analyses from differing perspectives and Westra 2019 for an overview). This debate was originally stimulated by attempts to understand both the character of the 'long boom' spanning the period from the late 1940s to the early 1970s and the reasons for the ending of that boom and for the consequent slowdown which ensued from the 1970s onwards. An important starting point came from two interpretations of these developments, in which periodisation played a key role, by Ernest Mandel and Michel Aglietta (Mandel 1972/1975; Aglietta 1976/1979), both of which were published at what came to be seen as a central turning point in economic fortunes.

The discussion of periodisation has continued since the initial work of Mandel and Aglietta and has been further encouraged by the emergence of the concept of 'neoliberalism' and by the desire to understand both the character of neoliberalism and the extent to which it represents a distinct departure from previous forms of capitalism (see, e.g., Davidson 2013). Consideration of financialisation has come to be seen as central to this issue but the precise role of financialisation remains controversial. Gérard Duménil and Dominique Levy, for example, structure their account both of the rise of neoliberalism and its crisis around an account of financialisation (Duménil and Levy 2004, 2011), as do the writers associated with the Centre for Research on Socio-Cultural Change (CRESC) (Engelen et al. 2011). On the other hand, the influential work of Robert Brenner (Brenner 2002, 2006) allots a less central place to financial developments while David Kotz explicitly argues against the view that financialisation has been an important cause of the rise of neoliberalism (Kotz 2015, pp. 32–37). For Kotz the line of causation runs the other way, with the rise of the financial sector being seen as a consequence of broader developments within capitalism.

It is notable that despite the wide range of factors considered in this continuing debate, Hilferding's account of finance capital remains to a large extent absent from the discussion. Duménil and Levy point out that the significance of finance within contemporary capitalism is not unprecedented and that Hilferding analysed its role a century ago. However, following this acknowledgement, they develop their own account of recent developments with no further reference to Hilferding's work, and the same is true of the vast majority of recent contributors to debates over financialisation, neoliberalism and the periodisation of capitalism.

Consequently, the question is raised of whether Hilferding's analysis can be used in any way to understand current financial developments or whether it should be seen purely as an account of conditions in early twentieth-century Central Europe. This chapter attempts to investigate the extent to which Hilferding's work retains relevance through comparing his discussion of finance capital with one of the most important recent analyses of financialisation from a Marxist perspective, the work of Costas Lapavitsas and his colleagues in the Research on Money and Finance (RMF) network, based at the School of Oriental and African Studies (SOAS) in the UK.

Hilferding and Lapavitsas: General Considerations

Lapavitsas' account of financialisation has been extremely influential. To a large extent this stems from the fact that it provides the basis for the RMF reports on the origins of the Eurozone crisis from 2010 onwards, an exemplary case of committed Marxist scholarship being integrally linked to political interventions (Lapavitsas et al. 2012). The discussion here, however, will concentrate on his earlier work, in particular his theoretical accounts of the role of money and finance in capitalist societies, one of which was co-authored with the Japanese Marxist economist Makoto Itoh (Itoh and Lapavitsas 1999; Lapavitsas 2003; see also the collection of articles in Lapavitsas 2017) and his discussion of the origins of the 2007–2008 financial crisis (Lapavitsas 2009, 2013).

There are two main reasons for taking Lapavitsas' work as the focus for comparing contemporary accounts of the financial sector with the classical Marxist account provided by Hilferding. Firstly, unlike the majority of writers cited above (with the possible exception of Aglietta), Lapavitsas' main field of interest lies in the theory of money and finance. Consequently, his discussion of financialisation, like that of Hilferding, is rooted in detailed knowledge of monetary thought. Secondly, again unlike other writers in this area, Lapavitsas engages closely with Hilferding's writing and acknowledges Hilferding both as an important contributor to Marxist monetary and financial theory and as a significant influence on his own work. However, Lapavitsas is also strongly critical of Hilferding in a number of ways and takes care to emphasise the extent to which his analysis of financialisation differs from Hilferding's account of finance capital.

In addition to classical Marxism, Lapavitsas' account rests on two further pillars; the Unoist approach to Marxism originating in Japan and a

5 FINANCE CAPITAL, FINANCIALISATION AND THE PERIODISATION... 119

particular interpretation of value theory developed by Ben Fine and his collaborators from the 1970s onwards (Kincaid 2006 provides a useful overview of the background to Lapavitsas' development). As will be seen below, these three influences are closely interlinked in shaping his concept of financialisation. There are also some immediate affinities between them; for example, Lapavitsas refers to the very strong impact of Hilferding's work in developing Japanese Marxism:

> economic thought came to Japan mostly from Europe at the turn of the twentieth century, and perhaps the weightiest part of it was Marxism. Hilferding's book has been used as a standard university textbook for decades during the post-war period; its influence on Japanese Marxism has been enormous. (Lapavitsas 2013, p. 121)

COMMONALITIES BETWEEN LAPAVITSAS AND HILFERDING

There are three aspects to Hilferding's work which Lapavitsas sees as especially important. The first is his insistence that the theory of credit and finance has to be founded on a theory of money rather than the reverse; Marxism requires a monetary theory of finance rather than a financial or credit-based theory of money. Lapavitsas and Hilferding agree on the necessity for such a theory both because the more complex forms of credit and finance cannot be understood without appreciating their grounding in the role of money within capitalist society and also because a central feature of capitalist crises is the flight to money as the structure of credit weakens:

> whenever there is a general disturbance of the mechanism, no matter what its cause, money suddenly and immediately changes over from its merely nominal shape, money of account, into hard cash. Profane commodities can no longer replace it. (Marx 1867/1976, p. 236)

On the basis of this account, Lapavitsas argues strongly against writers like Geoffrey Ingham and David Graeber (Ingham 2004; Graeber 2011) who criticise both Marx and Hilferding for basing their monetary theory on the economics of commodity exchange rather than the politics and sociology of credit and debt; Ingham claims that 'the anachronistic and misleading commodity exchange theory of money is evident in Hilferding's *Finance Capital* which, despite the ostensible critique, was entirely consistent with the orthodox economic theory of the time' (Ingham, op cit

p. 62). While acknowledging the insights of Post-Keynesian monetary theorists such as Basil Moore, Lapavitsas also argues that their emphasis on the endogeneity of the supply of credit money neglects the fundamental relationship between money and real accumulation, an argument which he rests once more on the need to derive credit relationships from basic monetary categories rather than the reverse (Itoh and Lapavitsas 1999, Chap. 10).

In addition to endorsing Hilferding's account of the need to find a theory of finance on a prior analysis of money, Lapavitsas follows quite closely both Hilferding's discussion of the functions of money and the pyramid-like structure of the credit system. Both writers follow Marx in beginning with an analysis of money as a measure of value and then moving on to its functions as a medium of circulation and means of payment. Both see the analysis of the hoarding of money as central and use this analysis as the basis of a criticism of the quantity theory of money. They each then proceed to develop a theory of credit and finance on the basis of money's function as a means of payment, taking trade or circulation credit as a starting point and then showing how this evolves into banking or industrial credit. Their accounts of the development of different kinds of money are also very similar; in particular, they both emphasise the distinction between fiat and credit money and the differing impact of each of these on inflation. In summary, Lapavitsas adopts much of Hilferding's monetary theory, although he develops it further in some key respects; in particular, following Kozo Uno, he highlights the role of the money market in which banks lend to one another, arguing that this was neglected by Hilferding (Lapavitsas 2013, pp. 130–132). He also goes further than Hilferding in discussing the role of central banks, in particular the way in which they sustain a system based on a particular combination of credit and fiat money (ibid., pp. 84–87) and in considering world money (ibid., pp. 101–105).

The second way in which Lapavitsas sees Hilferding making a fundamental contribution to Marxist theory is through his concept of 'founder's' (or 'promoter's') profit and his analysis of joint-stock capital. The central idea here rests on the discounting of future flows of income. Because the rate of interest which is required as a return by shareholders is less than the rate of profit, even when a risk premium is included, the sum of money which can be raised by a company from investors, which is represented by expected future profits discounted at that rate of interest, will exceed the capital required for the company to undertake production and to earn the competitive profit rate. The difference accrues to those starting up the company and is taken by them as founder's profit (Hilferding 1910/1981, Chap. 7). Lapavitsas describes Hilferding's analysis as an important breakthrough in Marxist analysis, both because, taken together with his account of loanable capital, it completes his discussion of the credit and financial pyramid and also because it is central to the explanation of the origins of financial profit. Following Itoh, however, he rejects Hilferding's identification of founder's profit as being equivalent to Marx's 'profit of enterprise' which can be counterposed to interest as a result of the division of overall profit between industrial and financial capital (Itoh 1988, pp. 286–287).

Thirdly, Lapavitsas is in agreement with Hilferding's account of the origins of interest-bearing capital as lying in the idle capital held by industrial enterprises as a result of indivisibilities or breaks in the circuit of capital; for example, enterprises may hold such funds while waiting for machines to depreciate so that new investment is needed or because they need to hold money capital to ensure the continuity of production while waiting for finished goods to be sold (Hilferding 1910/1981, Chap. 4, especially pp. 70–75). Hilferding draws here on Marx's analysis in volume two of *Capital*, and Lapavitsas identifies two strands in Marx's thinking on this question (Lapavitsas 2017, Chap. 6). The first sees the source of interest-bearing capital in the money holdings of a distinct group of financial capitalists who exist separately from industrial capitalists. For Lapavitsas, this conception is analytically and empirically weaker than the view which co-exists with it in Marx and which Hilferding endorses, where interest-bearing capital emerges from the circuit of capital as described above. Such a view both allows the analysis of lending to be grounded in a general account of accumulation and also avoids the tendency to identify finance with the interests of a stratum of rentiers. For Lapavitsas,

> far from being the exclusive property of a layer of rentiers, interest-bearing capital is in large measure the reallocated spare money capital of the capitalist class. By the same token, interest accrues both across the capitalist class and does not constitute the revenue foundation of a separate social group— of the 'monied' capitalists. (Lapavitsas 2013, p. 118)

The involvement of non-financial enterprises in financial activities is an important element in Lapavitsas' account of financialisation, and he goes

122   A. KILMISTER

beyond Hilferding in extending his analysis to the increased mobilisation of workers' savings in financialised capitalism as an element of loanable capital.

DIFFERENCES BETWEEN LAPAVITSAS AND HILFERDING

The presence of a monetary theory of finance, the analysis of joint-stock capital and the discussion of the origins of interest-bearing capital represent important points of congruence between Lapavitsas' account of financialisation and the work of Hilferding. However, there are equally significant differences between their analyses and here the other central influences on Lapavitsas—the Uno School and the value theory developed by Fine—come into play. Again, three issues assume particular importance.

The first relates to the origins of the money commodity. At the start of *Finance Capital*, Hilferding locates the necessity of money in the anarchic and individualised nature of the exchange of commodities and, following Marx, in the contradiction between use value and value, which requires the emergence of a commodity which solely represents exchange value and can be contrasted with other commodities which retain the character of use values. He writes that 'the commodity must therefore become money, because only then can it be expressed socially, as both use value and exchange value; as the unity of both which it really is. However, since all commodities transform themselves into money by divesting themselves of their use values, money becomes the transformed existence of all other commodities' (Hilferding 1910/1981, p. 35). Lapavitsas argues that this account of the development of money is problematic in two ways.

First, while Hilferding shows that money is necessary for the exchange of commodities, this is not the same as showing how money actually developed. Lapavitsas raises a series of questions about the analysis of Hilferding and the elements of Marx's work on which he relies here:

> if a general representative of value existed, the contradictions between use value and value as abstract labour would indeed be resolved. However, how do the contradictions themselves lead to emergence of a general representative of value? What are the economic mechanisms through which value becomes socially represented by money as a result specifically of the contradictions between use value and value as abstract labour? (Lapavitsas 2003, p. 56)

Second, Lapavitsas argues that Hilferding's approach cannot explain the existence of money in pre-capitalist societies. Here he draws particularly on the approach to value theory developed by Fine and others to argue that value as abstract labour exists only in societies based on generalised commodity production, in other words capitalist societies. Hence the emergence of money prior to the development of capitalism cannot be based on the contradiction between value and use value.

Lapavitsas then presents an alternative approach to the development of money which draws heavily on Unoist Marxism and in particular on the work of Itoh (Itoh 1980, Chap. 2). The key idea here is the separation of the form and substance of value. Lapavitsas argues that the money form of value develops prior to the substance of value in pre-capitalist societies, with exchange at the 'edge' of such societies between traders from separate communities playing a central role. The form and substance of value only come together once capitalism has fully developed and abstract labour emerges as the substance of value. Consequently while 'in the capitalist mode of production the forms of value are fully developed and closely related to the substance of value' (Lapavitsas 2003, p. 54), it is also the case that 'money's emergence should be demonstrated exclusively in terms of the form of value. In other words, the roots of money lie in the evolution of the form of value and they are unrelated to the substance of value' (ibid.). The evolution of the money form of value is in large part dependent on social custom and the interaction of such custom within pre-capitalist societies with the exchange that takes place between such societies.

The significance of this derivation of money lies in the more general argument resting on the value theory of Fine and others which Lapavitsas presents in his book *Social Foundations of Markets, Money and Credit*. The central point here is about the connection between economic and non-economic factors. In capitalism, the economic imperatives of generalised commodity exchange and capital accumulation are fundamental to society and shape the character of non-economic relationships. However, those non-economic relationships are not illusory; Lapavitsas argues that within production relations of exploitation depend crucially on relations of power and fiat which are not simply economic in character, while in the sphere of distribution we also see norms of consumption for workers which rely on social custom rather than simply on economic relationships (Lapavitsas 2003, p. 21). This is important because Lapavitsas goes on to argue that not only is there an inherently non-economic element even to commodity production under capitalism but also that capitalism is reliant on a range of kinds of labour which do not produce value, a set both of products and activities which are not commodities and commodities which are not produced by capital rests on the value theory of Fine and others where the non-economic assumes an important role. Examples are state provision of health and education and work in commerce (ibid., p. 26). Centrally for the argument here, the financial sector provides another example.

Lapavitsas writes that 'there are also activities and things that assume the form of commodities, despite being inherently unrelated to commodities' (ibid.). The first example he gives is land, but he then continues by saying that:

> another example is stocks and shares, both of which similarly involve no labour in production. However, they can take the form of commodities because they afford to their owner a claim on profits to be generated in the future. (Ibid., p. 27)

The key consequence of this is that because financial variables are not the result of value-producing abstract labour their prices are strongly affected by non-economic factors. They cannot in the last instance escape from the influence of productive activities, but they have a considerable degree of flexibility:

> the absence of mechanisms anchoring land and stock prices onto the substance of value (in contrast to produced commodities) implies that they also exhibit strong volatility and arbitrariness. Non-economic factors, such as psychological swings of optimism, political change, or even purely institutional manipulation of trading, play a strong determining role for prices of land and financial assets. (Ibid., p. 27)

The impact of non-economic factors on the value of financial assets is thus rooted in the distinction between the form and substance of value, and as shown below, it plays an important role in Lapavitsas' account of financialisation. In addition to discussing the factors listed above, Lapavitsas goes on to discuss the crucial role of the non-economic concept of trust in shaping the credit system (Lapavitsas 2003, Chap. 4; see also Lapavitsas 2017, Chap. 11). As commodity owners, capitalists relate to one another as separate, individual (Lapavitsas' term is 'foreign') entities, linked only by dealings mediated by monetary exchange. But it is essential for credit transactions that relations of trust and power are present among capitalists. Capitalists who engage in credit are already completely related to each other—they are not "foreign" entities engaged in plain buying and selling. (Lapavitsas 2003, p. 68)

Again, the non-economic acquires a high degree of autonomy from the economic but without achieving complete freedom. It is the case that 'capitalists engage in credit operations within explicit relations of trust and power, which directly affect the availability and terms of credit' (ibid., p. 86) but also ultimately that while

> banking credit indeed depends on trust, but the quantities of it that can be made available to capitalist accumulation are not limitless, even when trust between participants is unimpaired.... credit is an economic aspect of the circulation of capital and is therefore ultimately dependent on the processes of production. (Ibid., p. 72)

The second important difference between Lapavitsas and Hilferding relates to the question of the derivation of concrete relationships of financialisation from more abstract categories. Here Lapavitsas argues directly that Hilferding's approach to the periodisation of capitalism (and by implication the approach of classical Marxism in general) is inadequate. He argues that there is a 'leap' from the first three parts of Hilferding's book, dealing with the analysis of finance based on first principles, to the account of crisis and imperialism in the last two parts. For Lapavitsas, 'in line with Marx's dialectical approach in *Capital*, proper analysis of the last two topics would require the introduction of further levels of mediation substantiating the historical evolution of both crises and capitalism in general' (Lapavitsas 2013, p. 50), but 'Hilferding offers little in this respect' (ibid.).

The argument here is connected to ideas drawn from the Uno School. As is well known, Uno's work posits three levels of analysis in the theorisation of capitalism: the theory of a purely capitalist society, the identification of stages of capitalism and the analysis of capitalist history. This clearly provides the basis for an account of periodisation, in which the identification of distinctive stages or periods in capitalist development would form the basis of the second level of analysis, and Unoist work has formed one important strand in the debate over the periodisation of capitalism mentioned above (Albritton 1991). The Unoist justification for separating the account of stages of capitalism from the theory of a pure capitalist society also has close affinities with Lapavitsas' discussion of the relation between the economic and the non-economic, since it is the presence of non-economic factors in the identification of distinct stages of capitalism that necessitates a distinct analysis of such stages. As Albritton writes 'the law of value only works on history in a mediated fashion, since at an historical level, the economic is only relatively autonomous, overlapping with and supported by the ideological, legal and political. It follows that history never approaches asymptotically close to pure capitalism' (ibid., p. 30). Kozo Uno himself provides a criticism of Hilferding along these lines when he writes that

> Hilferding's statement—"Bank capital was the negation of usurer's capital and is itself negated by finance-capital" cannot be supported at all. Usurer capital does not, by its own logic, turn into bank capital, nor does the latter turn into finance-capital. Finance-capital appears only when the capitalist production of use-values physically develops into a new stage. (Uno 1971/2016, p. 174—the passage quoted is from Hilferding 1910/1981, p. 226)

Lapavitsas brings both of these criticisms of Hilferding's approach together when he summarises his approach to periodisation. The relative weight of non-economic factors in the world of finance means that financial systems within capitalism exhibit considerable variety both spatially and temporally, and this variety requires a distinct level of analysis which cannot simply be derived from fundamental principles. Lapavitsas describes Hilferding as seeking an 'endogenous' set of reasons for the emergence of finance capital but he argues against 'endogenous theorisation':

> relations between production and finance tend to be historically specific, and subject to institutional and political factors that shape the financial system. The links between industrial capital and the credit system in the period of financialization have been far more variable than the simple picture of increasing reliance of industry on banks which Hilferding assumed. (Lapavitsas 2013, p. 67)

The third way in which Lapavitsas differentiates his analysis from that of Hilferding is through his criticism of Hilferding for omitting central aspects of capitalism from his analysis, in particular the evolution of production, changes in the labour process and the development of the labour market. He points out that 'if, however, an epochal transformation of capitalism has indeed taken place, its roots are likely to be found in the forces of production and in the labour process. Hilferding does not discuss these issues in any depth' (Lapavitsas 2013, p. 50). Since what is highlighted here is an omission, Lapavitsas does not move on to a more detailed account of the character of Hilferding's analysis here but his own discussion of financialisation does in part differ from Hilferding's through its consideration of issues in the 'real' economy, in particular the impact of changes in productivity, as well as highlighting the impact of financialisation on workers.

To summarise, while Lapavitsas endorses important elements of Hilferding's approach, he differs from him in emphasising the variability of possible relationships between industrial and financial capital as a result of the particular interaction between the economic and non-economic which is typical of the financial sector and of the need to analyse these relationships in the context of distinct stages of capitalism. He also emphasises that movement between these stages is unlikely to result purely from financial developments but will be rooted in changes in production and labour relationships. With these considerations in mind, it is now possible to examine Lapavitsas' own account of financialisation and the ways in which it differs from that of Hilferding.

FINANCIALISATION ACCORDING TO LAPAVITSAS

Lapavitsas starts from the proposition that an adequate account of financialisation has to consider the behaviour of non-financial enterprises, the financial sector and workers and households. Each of these three groups has both shaped and been affected by the growth of financialisation over the last 30 years. Firstly, industrial enterprises (at least large enterprises) have become increasingly 'financialised'. They finance most of their investment from retained profits and have become to a significant extent independent of requirements for funds from the financial system. On the contrary, they themselves have become active players in that system, trading in a range of financial assets. When they do need funds, they obtain them from financial markets, through instruments such as commercial paper for short-term funds and through bonds for longer-term capital. Lapavitsas recognises differences here between national and regional economies; however, he shows that the trend away from reliance on bank funding for investment is exhibited in Germany and Japan as well as in the

USA and UK (Lapavitsas 2013, pp. 217–231). In the majority of industrialised economies which he examines, there has been a tendency for share of trade credit in the assets and liabilities of non-financial companies to decrease and for that of other financial instruments to increase (ibid.). Lapavitsas interprets this as an example of financialisation since, following Hilferding's pyramid of credit, trade credit is the aspect of finance most rooted in productive accumulation, with other elements of finance having a greater detachment.

The loss of business lending to large non-financial enterprises has in turn transformed the behaviour of banks. Financialisation has led them to rely on three other kinds of activity: trading in open markets (especially in Germany and the UK), lending to one another and lending to households. In most of the industrialised countries which Lapavitsas examines (but less so in Japan), there have also been significant changes in bank liabilities with a greater reliance on borrowed funds and less use of deposits. In overall terms, Lapavitsas characterises these developments as involving an increasing detachment of banks from productive accumulation (ibid., pp. 231–238).

The third element of financialisation highlighted by Lapavitsas is what he describes as 'the financialization of the personal revenue of workers and households across social classes' (ibid., p. 38). This involves increasing liabilities for households, partly relating to mortgage debt and loans for consumption and partly to finance expenditure on services such as education and health owing to the increasing withdrawal of the state from these areas. However, it is also the case that household assets, notably pension savings, have become increasingly important for the financial system. Lapavitsas highlights the way in which such assets have been channelled by the banks towards financial markets and the financial profits which have been earned through this. Somewhat controversially, Lapavitsas argues that these relationships have been shaped by imbalances of power and information between banks and households which have allowed for what he describes as 'financial expropriation'. His analysis here is based on a development of Hilferding's discussion of founder's profit and the associated creation of fictitious capital. Lapavitsas argues that if Hilferding's analysis is extended from looking at a 'once for all' transaction when a company is founded to consider ongoing trading in financial assets it can be shown how such trading can generate financial profits through differences in required returns leading to differences in valuation. The advantages in power and information which financial institutions have over households in this process provide the basis for such profits and can be seen as a form of expropriation:

> the path is thus opened for financial institutions to bring to bear predatory practices reflecting the systemic difference in power and outlook between financial institutions and workers. Financial profits could be extracted throughout the lifetime of the security, ultimately deriving from future wage payments. Similar considerations would hold for other consumer borrowing. This is a key aspect of financial expropriation. (Ibid., pp. 167–168)

These three trends provide the basis for Lapavitsas' analysis of the origins of the crisis of 2007–2008. Increased lending to households, fuelled both by a decline in the savings ratio and by low-interest rates, generated a speculative bubble in the US housing market which then burst when interest rates began to rise. The impact of the bursting of the bubble was transmitted through the financial system as a result of the large level of interbank lending, the rise in the proportion of banking activities financed by borrowing rather than deposits and the involvement of banks in trading in open markets. A significant aspect of the causes of the crisis was the change in banking activities resulting from the decline in lending to large non-financial activities, coupled with associated changes in bank behaviour such as the securitisation of loans, reliance on credit-scoring techniques to assess risk and the growth of new financial assets, notably derivatives (Lapavitsas 2009).

It can be seen that Lapavitsas' analysis of financialisation exemplifies in important respects the differences previously highlighted between his approach and that of Hilferding.[1] As outlined earlier, he begins with an account of development in non-financial enterprises and moves from this to consider changes in the financial sector. His account of relations between the financial sector and households draws on his analysis of the importance of non-economic factors, especially relations of power. The speculative bubble he identifies as lying behind the 2007–2008 crisis and other similar phenomena, which have occurred under financialisation, are examples of the relative autonomy of asset prices from underlying value relations. The role of political factors is highlighted strongly, with regard to both the impact of the withdrawal of state involvement in key areas of

---

[1] It should be noted here that Lapavitsas extends his analysis to consider international capital flows and what he terms 'subordinate' financialisation in developing economies. This aspect of his account will not be considered here owing to reasons of space.

social provision on the financialisation of households and the effect of monetary policy on financial relationships. Lapavitsas emphasises continuing national variability within the general framework of financialisation and also stresses the specific institutional factors which have shaped financialisation in particular cases, for example, the role of independent central banks. His emphasis on the importance of institutional structures is reinforced when he moves on from considering the origins of the 2007–2008 crisis to considering its specific impact on the Eurozone (Lapavitsas 2013, pp. 288–305). It is clearly the case that, while highlighting Hilferding's contribution at numerous points, Lapavitsas has provided an account of financialisation which constitutes a distinct alternative to that provided by Hilferding with regard to both specific details and the underlying general approach. Consequently, two questions arise: firstly, that of whether Lapavitsas' account is superior to that of Hilferding or not and, secondly, that of what remains valid in Hilferding's analysis following the criticisms made by Lapavitsas.

Criticisms of Lapavitsas' Approach

Lapavitsas' description of financialisation has been very influential and is compelling in many respects. However, there are a number of issues that are left unresolved in his account and which may indicate a continuing role for the kind of analysis provided by Hilferding, if not necessarily for his specific observations.

A central issue here is that of what has caused the growth of financialisation over the last three decades. Lapavitsas starts by saying that financialisation

> represents a period change of the capitalist mode of production entailing a systemic transformation of mature economies with extensive implications for developing economies, and should properly be examined in these terms. (Lapavitsas 2013 p. 169)

He suggests as a model for such an examination the approach outlined by Trotsky in his critique of Kondratiev. For Trotsky, capitalist accumulation occurs within a 'channel' shaped by various external institutional, political, legal and ideological conditions. Lapavitsas proposes a similar approach to the analysis of periodisation in general and financialisation in particular:

political economy must explicitly specify the "external" conditions, if it is to grasp the direction and changes of accumulation particularly in the context of crisis and historical period change. This insight is crucial to the analysis of financialization. (Ibid., p. 171)

There are three problems, however, with the way in which Lapavitsas implements this approach. Firstly, his account leaves the internal factors affecting capital accumulation unexplained. He outlines developments such as lower GDP growth, changes in the labour force, weak productivity growth and rising inequality but does not connect them to internal causes; they typify the period of financialisation but are not explained in any detail themselves. Lapavitsas makes a rather sweeping statement that 'the material basis of accumulation has been shaped by profound technical change in information processing and telecommunications' (ibid., p. 172) but this is not pursued further.

Secondly, the link between these internal developments and financialisation is not clear. One possible reason for this is that Lapavitsas is sceptical of general accounts of financialisation which see it simply as a 'flight to finance' in the face of weaknesses in the real economy. He criticises the 'Monthly Review' school of Marxist analysis for precisely this failing, arguing that

> if financialization is not explicitly related to the operations of the fundamental agents of the capitalist economy, its content will remain unclear. Unfortunately, the output of the *Monthly Review* current does not offer the requisite analysis, and the same holds for other Marxist work that treats financialization as the flight of capital from a stagnating productive sector. (Ibid., p. 18)

This point is persuasive, but while Lapavitsas describes changes in the behaviour both of industrial enterprises and of banks he does not explain how internal changes in capital accumulation are connected to developments in the financial sector. An example here is the question of the increasing independence of large industrial enterprises from bank finance where he says that

> for the purposes of establishing the underlying relations of financialization, it is not necessary to examine in further detail the forces that determine the balance between 'internal' and 'external' finance for productive capital. (Ibid., p. 220)

132   A. KILMISTER

He suggests, briefly, that new developments in information and communication technologies may have altered investment requirements and speeded up turnover, reducing the need for external funds. He also mentions the possibility that the growth of internal finance may be related to the degree of monopoly. However, neither of these possibilities is pursued in any detail and the causes of this aspect of financialisation remain largely unexplored.

Thirdly, Lapavitsas' account of external, especially political, factors also stands aside from causal analysis in an important way. He argues convincingly that the ascendency of finance depended heavily on state policies, especially the pursuit of low inflation through central bank independence and various forms of national and international deregulation of finance. But he does not fully explain the causes of these policies and in particular whether they acted independently to shape financialisation or were themselves brought about by developments within the sphere of finance. This difficulty is also made apparent by his analysis of neoliberalism. He tends to describe neoliberalism largely in ideological terms; 'neoliberalism has provided the ideology of the period of financialization, the umbrella under which the ascendancy of finance could take place' (ibid., p. 172). As a result, the connection between the broader character of neoliberalism and developments in the financial sector becomes unclear. In particular, the question raised by Kotz of whether neoliberalism in some sense creates financialisation or whether financialisation in contrast requires and brings about neoliberal policies across the economy is not resolved in Lapavitsas' work. Financialisation 'has been accompanied' by neoliberalism (ibid., p. 192) but the nature of their connection is not fully clear.

In summary, Lapavitsas does not fully integrate his account of the various trends within financialisation, which as he says involve changes in the behaviour of both industrial and financial enterprises and households, into a coherent analysis of capitalist development as a whole. He provides a compelling and detailed picture of the changing activities of the various sectors, but he does not fully explain the causal connections between them. This weakness is particularly apparent when his account of the crisis of 2007–2008 is considered. He provides a powerful analysis of the links between firm, bank and household behaviour by showing how trends in industrial financing necessitated new banking strategies focused on households. But it is not clear to what extent this discussion actually differs from the orthodox accounts of the crisis found elsewhere and how much is added to those by the Marxist framework adopted by Lapavitsas. A focus on increased bank lending to financially fragile households, fuelled by reliance on quantitative techniques of credit evaluation and the securitisation of loans and accompanied by bank reliance on interbank lending rather than deposits, which led to a speculative bubble, is surely characteristic of many conventional overviews of the crisis. For Lapavitsas' Marxism to add something really substantial to those overviews, it would need to be more closely related to a broader analysis of the character of contemporary capitalism than it is—and this is surely just where the debate on the periodisation of capitalism becomes most relevant.

Back (or Forward?) to Hilferding

The criticisms set out above of Lapavitsas' approach to financialisation are not in any way meant to diminish its importance. On the contrary, this chapter has concentrated on Lapavitsas' work both because he provides the most convincing Marxist account of financialisation currently available and because of the depth of his engagement with Hilferding's earlier discussion of these issues. However, they do raise the question of whether there are resources in Hilferding's work which might help in resolving some of the difficulties which face current accounts of financial developments.

Clearly, this cannot involve simply applying the concept of finance capital to contemporary capitalism as a general model. The criticisms made by Lapavitsas and many others of the view that banks are currently in some sense fused with and dominant over industrial corporations are valid and important and have been recognised to be so since the work of Paul Sweezy in the 1940s (Sweezy 1942, pp. 265–269; see also the summary of the debate on this issue between David Kotz and Edward Herman in Lapavitsas 2013, p. 56). If Hilferding's work is to retain relevance to the analysis of periodisation today, this will have to result from his general approach rather than his specific conclusions.

Two possible justifications for continuing interest in Hilferding's work can be mentioned initially. Neither of these is fully convincing, but they indicate some of the issues that might be considered in a further more substantial justification. The first approach would be to see Hilferding as identifying a particular stage in capitalist development but one that has now largely been superseded, at least in the major industrialised countries, although it may continue to be relevant for developing economies. According to this view, economies go through a period of 'bank-based development' before moving on to financial systems which allot a more substantial role to markets. The most influential statement of this view is contained in the work of Alexander Gerschenkron (Gerschenkron 1962). Hilferding's work could then be seen as a Marxist variant of Gerschenkron's analysis, allowing the insights involved in the identification of a distinct stage of capitalist development in which banks play a crucial role to be incorporated in the more general periodisation of capitalism.

While the above approach focuses on temporal issues, an alternative viewpoint stresses spatial questions. If it is accepted that capitalism exhibits significant variety across different national and regional units, then Hilferding might be seen as the theorist of bank-based economies co-existing with market-based economies. The question then becomes one, not of markets supplanting banks in a process of temporal development, but of different forms of capitalism typified by different financial systems. The 'varieties of capitalism' literature has become extensive in the wake of the work of Peter Hall and David Soskice (Hall and Soskice 2001). Again, Hilferding could be seen as providing a Marxist basis for the analysis of the variant of capitalism which is centred heavily on bank involvement.

Both of these approaches are attractive in a number of ways as ways of highlighting the continuing relevance of Hilferding and are surveyed briefly by Lapavitsas (Lapavitsas 2013, pp. 38–43). In particular, while the role of banks may have changed significantly from that described by Hilferding in many of the major industrialised countries, there are a number of large middle-income economies where the relationship between banks and industry appears close and significant and where Hilferding's ideas may be useful, notably China, Russia and India. It should also be noted that Hilferding himself was quite aware of the difference between the development of financial capital in the UK and in Germany and Austria and analysed this difference in terms of the historical priority of industrialisation in the UK and its consequences. For example, he refers to the difference between France, Holland and Belgium on the one hand, who provide international investment credit and the UK (Hilferding refers to 'England') which provides commercial credit (Hilferding 1910/1981, p. 92) and to the difference between the UK and Germany with regard to domestic credit, with that provided in the UK being mainly credit for commerce while in Germany industrial credit predominates (ibid., pp. 224–225). On tariff policy, Hilferding writes that 'England's industrial pre-eminence gave her a larger stake in free trade' (ibid., p. 302) while 'the commercial policy interests on the continent were entirely different' (ibid.,

p. 303). In this way Hilferding's own analysis seems connected both to a dynamic view of the role of bank capital in the economic development of 'late industrialisers' and a synchronic view of the differentiation between various capitalist economies, partly caused by the time of their industrialisation.

Neither of these approaches, however, is fully convincing as an argument for returning to Hilferding's work. The problem is twofold. Firstly, the terms of the debates regarding both late industrialisation and varieties of capitalism are primarily set outside Marxism. Consequently, it is not clear just what Hilferding has to offer as a Marxist if his work is primarily assessed within these debates. In other words, the precise contribution which a Marxist account of finance capital can make in this particular context has yet to be identified. Secondly, Hilferding's work is put forward as a general theory of capitalist development. It is also unclear how this purported generality, especially as expressed within the earlier sections of his book which put forward the principles of money and credit, can be made consistent with a view of his work as providing an analysis which is circumscribed either temporally or spatially. The question is whether an analysis supposedly based on general principles of this kind can usefully function as an account of a particular time period within capitalism or variety of capitalist economy.

A third approach to Hilferding's work, which might also be of use in furthering the debate on periodisation, might start from reconsidering the method by which he derives the concept of finance capital from the fundamental nature of money and credit. One of the first things to strike any reader of *Finance Capital* is the strongly unified nature of the argument, the way in which the analysis flows from the basic characteristics of the growth of hoards as a result of discontinuities in the circuits to capital to the development of more and more sophisticated forms of credit and finance through to the relationship between finance capital, crises and imperialism. The analysis flows with an exceptional logical power. However, this is also connected to a crucial weakness in Hilferding's argument: its one-sided nature. Hilferding is able to create an argument with an impressive degree of unity partly because he focuses on one trend within capitalist development to the exclusion of almost all others, the increasing concentration and centralisation of capital and the associated growth of fixed capital and the need for large investment projects. It is this that leads to the growth of ever-larger hoards spurring the development of more complex forms of finance and eventually lays the basis for the fusion between banks and industrial enterprises. It also lengthens the turnover period for capital which both generates increased loanable capital and also increases the dependence of firms on banks.

This trend is a central feature of capitalist development and plays an important role in Marx's own analysis of the growth of machinery and large-scale industry. However, it may well better be seen as a tendency rather than as the kind of deterministic law posited by Hilferding. In other areas of Marx's economic analysis, notably in the discussion of the falling rate of profit, there has been a movement away from highlighting fixed determinations towards analysis of the more complex interplay between tendencies and their countervailing factors. It seems worth considering the possibility that this approach could also form a basis for analysis of the relationship between financial and industrial capital. In such a case, Hilferding's work might be seen not so much as an account of a particular stage in capitalist development or of a particular variety of capitalism but as an analysis of what capitalism might look like in a situation where the tendency towards centralisation outweighs other factors.

It is important here, however, to recognise that this tendency might not be the dominant one if countervailing forces gain strength, and that in such cases a very different relationship between financial and industrial capital from that put forward by Hilferding might obtain. A possible example of this lies in the remarks made by Lapavitsas about the role of information and communication technologies in shortening the turnover of capital and reducing the reliance of industry upon the banks. This might well be one of the relevant forces here, and Lapavitsas is correct in considering the possibility that it may well have shaped recent developments in financialisation. What is needed, however, is to trace back both the tendency towards centralisation and the forces which oppose this to their first principles and to develop on the basis of this an account of the contradictory nature of financial development under capitalism. Hilferding's account would be important here although, as a result of treating one side of this contradictory process as something of an iron law, it provides only one part of a complete account.

An example of how this might work in practice is provided by Hilferding's theory of crisis. This has been widely criticised, in part because the emphasis on disproportionality has been regarded as having reformist implications and as being connected with his views on 'organised capitalism'. It has also been seen as neglecting the role of capital-labour conflict within crises. However, it does have an important strength within the context of the remainder of his analysis. The theory is closely connected with the fundamental factors driving development for Hilferding; it is the rise in fixed capital and turnover time which give rise to the disproportionalities and the credit extended as a result of this rise which masks the underlying problems leading to deeper crises later. Consequently, Hilferding's crisis theory contributes to the unity of his underlying account described earlier. However, it also exemplifies the one-sided nature of that account. Disproportionalities of the kind described represent one aspect of crises, but they are not the only one. In addition to this, the forces leading to crisis may be mitigated by reductions in turnover time or the need for fixed capital. Hilferding's account should be seen as showing a tendency within capitalism rather than an inevitability and needs to be situated within a broader analysis of the many factors shaping capitalist development in general and the role of finance in particular (an important general statement of the need for a multi-causal account of capitalist development is contained in Mandel 1972/1975, Chap. 1).

CONCLUSION

This chapter started from noting that, while Hilferding's account of finance capital commands a considerable amount of respect, his work has played a relatively limited role in the debate over the periodisation of capitalism. This has been the case even though it is widely believed that financialisation is a central concept in understanding contemporary capitalist developments. To explore this further, an important example of current discussions of financialisation, the work of Lapavitsas and his colleagues, was examined. This analysis has important commonalities with that of Hilferding but also makes significant criticisms of his work. Lapavitsas' work also exhibits problems, however, and it is possible to argue that some at least of these problems might be resolved by returning to Hilferding's analysis and recasting it in a less deterministic form. Hilferding can perhaps best be seen as a theorist not of a particular stage in capitalist development or of a specific variety of capitalist regime but as drawing out the consequences of a tendency within capitalism. By embedding his analyses of this tendency within a broader account of the forces which might counter the tendency and the contradictions which might result from this, we can use Hilferding's work as one element in a richer picture of the evolution of capitalism.

REFERENCES

Aglietta, M. 1976/1979. *A Theory of Capitalist Regulation: The US Experience.* London: NLB.

Albritton, R. 1991. *A Japanese Approach to Stages of Capitalist Development.* Basingstoke: Macmillan.

Albritton, R., et al., eds. 2001. *Phases of Capitalist Development: Booms, Crises and Globalizations.* Basingstoke: Palgrave Macmillan.

Brenner, R. 2002. *The Boom and the Bubble: The US in the World Economy.* London: Verso.

———. 2006. *The Economics of Global Turbulence: The Advanced Capitalist Economies from Long Boom to Long Downturn, 1945–2005.* London: Verso.

Davidson, N. 2013. The Neoliberal Era in Britain: Historical Developments and Current Perspectives. *International Socialism* 139: 171–223.

Duménil, G., and D. Levy. 2004. *Capital Resurgent: Roots of the Neoliberal Revolution.* Trans. D. Jeffers. Cambridge, MA: Harvard University Press.

———. 2011. *The Crisis of Neoliberalism.* Cambridge, MA: Harvard University Press.

Engelen, E., et al. 2011. *After the Great Complacence: Financial Crisis and the Politics of Reform.* Oxford: Oxford University Press.

Gerschenkron, A. 1962. *Economic Backwardness in Historical Perspective.* Cambridge, MA: Harvard University Press.

Graeber, D. 2011. *Debt: The First 5000 Years.* New York: Melville House.

Hall, P.A., and D. Soskice, eds. 2001. *Varieties of Capitalism: The Institutional Foundations of Comparative Advantage.* Oxford: Oxford University Press.

Hilferding, R. 1910/1981. *Finance Capital: A Study of the Latest Phase of Capitalist Development.* Ed. T. Bottomore, trans. M. Watnick, and S. Gordon. London: Routledge and Kegan Paul.

Howard, M.C., and J.E. King. 1989. *A History of Marxian Economics: Volume 1, 1883–1929.* Basingstoke: Macmillan.

Ingham, G. 2004. *The Nature of Money.* Cambridge: Polity Press.

Itoh, M. 1980. *Value and Crisis: Essays on Marxian Economics in Japan.* London: Pluto Press.

———. 1988. *The Basic Theory of Capitalism: The Forms and Substance of the Capitalist Economy.* Basingstoke: Macmillan.

Itoh, M., and C. Lapavitsas. 1999. *Political Economy of Money and Finance.* Basingstoke: Macmillan.

Kincaid, J. 2006. Finance, Trust and the Power of Capital: A Symposium on the Contribution of Costas Lapavitsas. Editorial Introduction. *Historical Materialism* 14 (1): 31–48.

Kotz, D.M. 2015. *The Rise and Fall of Neoliberal Capitalism.* Cambridge, MA: Harvard University Press.

Lapavitsas, C. 2003. *Social Foundations of Markets, Money and Credit*. London: Routledge.

———. 2009. Financialised Capitalism: Crisis and Financial Expropriation. *Historical Materialism* 17 (2): 114–148.

———. 2013. *Profiting Without Producing: How Finance Exploits Us All*. London: Verso.

———. 2017. *Marxist Monetary Theory: Collected Papers*. Chicago: Haymarket Books.

Lapavitsas, C., et al. 2012. *Crisis in the Eurozone*. London: Verso.

Mandel, E. 1972/1975. *Late Capitalism*. Trans. J. De Bres. London: NLB.

Marx, K. 1867/1976. *Capital Volume One*. Trans. B. Fowkes. Harmondsworth: Penguin Books in association with New Left Review.

Norfield, T. 2016. *The City: London and the Global Power of Finance*. London: Verso.

Sweezy, P. 1942. *The Theory of Capitalist Development: Principles of Marxian Political Economy*. London: Dennis Dobson Ltd.

Toporowski, J. 2005. *Theories of Financial Disturbance: An Examination of Critical Theories of Finance from Adam Smith to the Present Day*. Cheltenham: Edward Elgar.

Uno, K. 1971/2017. *The Types of Economic Policies Under Capitalism*. Trans. T.T. Sekine, ed. J.R. Bell. Chicago: Haymarket Books.

Westra, R. 2019. *Periodizing Capitalism and Capitalist Extinction*. Basingstoke: Palgrave Macmillan.

CHAPTER 6

A New Finance Capital? Theorizing Corporate Governance and Financial Power

Stephen Maher and Scott Aquanno

One of the most striking gaps in the extensive body of Marxist social science is a substantial theory of corporate governance. To be sure, scholars like Kees van der Pijl and William Carroll have extensively mapped inter-corporate networks of power, thereby gaining valuable insight into contemporary capitalist society.[1] Nevertheless, missing from this literature is an awareness of the institutional formation, restructuring, and internal dynamism of the corporation—and how this is shaped in relation to its insertion within a broader, evolving structure of accumulation. In other

---

[1] And, it should be said, both were greatly influenced by Hilferding.

S. Maher
Toronto, ON, Canada

S. Aquanno (✉)
Ontario Tech University, Oshawa, ON, Canada
e-mail: Scott.Aquanno@uoit.ca

© The Author(s), under exclusive license to Springer Nature Switzerland AG 2023
J. Dellheim, F. O. Wolf (eds.), *Rudolf Hilferding*, Luxemburg International Studies in Political Economy,
https://doi.org/10.1007/978-3-031-08096-8_6

cases, standing in for the corporation as a concrete organization comprised of a specific governance structure is the often highly abstract concept of 'capital.' For instance, while helpful in sharply clarifying the inner logic of capital, Anwar Shaikh's 1000-page magnum opus, *Capitalism*, contains no mention of any actually existing corporation, nor analysis of how specific firms or types of corporate organization emerged and are reproduced. While the structural pressures of capitalism profoundly shape capitalist institutions, focusing on it alone misses what is most dynamic about capitalism: how it is organized and restructured over time. This reflects the tendency for Marxists—including Marx himself—to forsake institutional analysis in the search for general economic laws. Similarly, while insisting on its 'relative autonomy,' Marxist state theorists often depict the state as an agency that *intervenes* in the 'economic sphere,' or *relates to* 'capital,' understood in either case as a functionally integrated, closed system guided by general tendencies or laws described by Shaikh. The deep interconnection between state *political* institutions, and the development of forms of *economic* organization, is rarely explored in any great concrete or historical depth.[2] One of the most striking gaps in the extensive body of Marxist social science is a substantial theory of corporate governance. To be sure, scholars like Kees van der Pijl and William Carroll have extensively mapped inter-corporate networks of power, thereby gaining valuable insight into contemporary capitalist society.[3] Nevertheless, missing from this literature is an awareness of the institutional formation, restructuring, and internal dynamism of the corporation—and how this is shaped in relation to its insertion within a broader, evolving structure of accumulation. In other cases, standing in for the corporation as a concrete organization comprised of a specific governance structure is the often highly abstract concept of 'capital.' For instance, while helpful in sharply clarifying the inner logic of capital, Anwar Shaikh's 1000-page magnum opus, *Capitalism*, contains no mention of any actually existing corporation, nor analysis of how specific firms or types of corporate organization emerged and are reproduced. While the structural pressures of capitalism profoundly shape capitalist institutions, focusing on it alone misses what is most dynamic about capitalism: how it is organized and restructured over

---

[2] For an extensive discussion of this, and an attempt to begin such an analysis, see Stephen Maher, *Corporate Capitalism and the Integral State: General Electric and a Century of American Power*, Palgrave Macmillan, 2022.

[3] And, it should be said, both were greatly influenced by Hilferding.

time. This reflects the tendency for Marxists—including Marx himself—to forsake institutional analysis in the search for general economic laws. Similarly, while insisting on its 'relative autonomy,' Marxist state theorists often depict the state as an agency that *intervenes* in the 'economic sphere,' or *relates to* 'capital,' understood in either case as a functionally-integrated, closed system guided by general tendencies or laws described by Shaikh. The deep interconnection between state *political* institutions, and the development of forms of *economic* organization, is rarely explored in any great concrete or historical depth.

Rudolf Hilferding's *Finance Capital* points to a road not taken toward such a Marxist theory of 'corporate governance': that is, the historically evolved institutional mechanisms and channels for pooling, mobilizing, investing, and accumulating capital, as well as managing production processes. As we will show, Hilferding's work remains foundational for any Marxist analysis of corporate capitalism *methodologically, analytically,* and *politically.* For one thing, it is the core text within classical Marxism addressing the emergence of specific forms of corporate organization, and how these institutions mediate and realize the fundamental structural logic of capitalism. Methodologically, therefore, Hilferding anticipated what we have called Institutional Marxism, discussed below, which seeks to advance a theory of institutions as emergent properties of capitalist society. Analytically, Hilferding's analysis of the tendency for corporate organization to enhance the dominance of money-capital over production, and in particular his theorization of finance capital as consisting not merely of the financial sector, but rather a specific fusion of financial and industrial capital, remains crucial for understanding 'financialization' today. Rather than being characterized by financial parasitism on non-financial firms, as it is often depicted, neoliberal financialization has taken place through a process linking the internal restructuring of the industrial corporation, in connection with the rise of finance across the economy more broadly, such that circuits whereby the dominance of money-capital define the governing institutional logic. This has meant that financiers have become industrialists by gaining control of corporations, as in the nineteenth and early twentieth centuries, as well as the inverse: industrial corporate managers have evolved into money-capitalists. In this chapter, we analyze this dual process, which we argue has resulted in a new fusion of financial and industrial capital—that is, *a new finance capital*—in the period since the 2008 crisis.

Starting from Hilferding's theory of finance capital as a fusion of finance and industry allows us to transcend conceptions of financialization that see this merely as a function of the power of financial institutions, rooting this process in changes to the fundamental structure of the non-financial corporation itself. This, therefore, implies that socialist struggle should be oriented toward a deep and radical reorganization of these institutions. Yet Hilferding's tendency to see financial concentration and corporate organization as leading toward a planned economy and synonymous with the suppression of competitive pressures led him to underestimate this task. Nevertheless, his sophisticated conception of socialist transition still holds important lessons for the 'democratic socialist' left—offering an alternative to Leninist insurrectionism as well as an important corrective to proposals for firm-level democracy and worker ownership advanced by the new socialist movements in the US and the UK. Strongly criticizing the idea that it would simply collapse 'on its own,' Hilferding held that only working-class agency, organized and expressed by a political party, could socialize and democratize the economy. This could best be undertaken, he believed, by waging a class struggle both within the state and beyond it. Socialist revolution was not a matter of 'smashing the state' and declaring 'all power to the workers councils,' as it had been conceived in Russia. Rather, it would entail a prolonged struggle to remove sectors of the economy from capitalist management and market discipline, while building the technical and political capacities to manage it democratically in the service of social need rather than private profit. Accordingly, mechanisms for linking workers' councils with a national planning system had to be devised and built. In his theory and political practice, Hilferding was effectively engaged in a struggle to transform the capitalist state, expanding parliamentary democracy by extending democratic control over production and promoting new forms of workers' democracy.

Toward a Marxist Theory of Corporate Governance

Finance Capital is largely concerned with the impact of the emergence of the corporation on capitalist social relations. Of course, Hilferding understood this not just as a generic bureaucratic organization, but a specifically *capitalist* institutional form, which materialized the dynamics and tendencies Marx outlined. At the same time, the manifold operations and possible permutations of this form were not simply deducible from the operation of the mechanisms analyzed in *Capital*. Marx articulated what remains a singularly compelling model of the logic of capital, but he left scant methodological guideposts for understanding how the realization of this logic across time could lead to the development of new institutional forms. If Marx stressed that only 'real-concrete' history is actual, *Capital* often remained highly abstract—with the real-concrete invoked primarily to illustrate the abstract model. The crucial mediating and determining role of institutions, therefore, remained under-theorized. To a significant extent, this was understandable, as the corporation had barely begun to emerge at the time Marx was writing. It is the subject of only a few short fragments on it in volume three of *Capital*. Although the relationship between abstract model-building and concrete historical analysis was never made clear in *Capital*, Marx does point a way forward in the chapters which identify the *emergence* of capitalist dynamics in nineteenth-century England.

Institutional Marxism (IM) defines 'emergence' as the dialectical process whereby the basic dynamics of capitalist social relations are realized through historically evolved assemblages of functionally interdependent institutional forms. Marx saw this in terms of levels of abstraction, but it bears emphasizing that the causal force and relatively autonomous dynamism of less general (more concrete) levels cannot simply be explained as the mechanistic working out of more basic mechanisms.[4] IM seeks to capture this distinct causal force of institutions as emergent properties of capitalist society, rather than seeing them as epiphenomenal of overarching structural laws. At the most fundamental level, IM starts from the understanding developed within the philosophy of Critical Realism that reality is *stratified*, and composed of hierarchically ordered generative mechanisms. The basic dynamics of capital accumulation theorized by Marx—competition, class struggle, and state power—are situated within this causal structure. Indeed, the complexity of human society means that it must be conceived as an open system, characterized by immense variation in the realization of more basic mechanisms across space and time. Emergence refers to the dialectical process whereby the fundamental dynamics of capitalist social relations are realized through historically

---

[4] See Karl Marx, *Grundrisse*, Introduction, Part III: The Method of Political Economy. The consequence of reifying the most *abstract* level as the essence of *concrete* history is the formulation of an Idealist Marxist, as in the work of Louis Althusser. See Stephen Maher, "Escaping Structuralism's Legacy: Renewing Theory and History in Historical Materialism," *Science & Society* 80:3, July 2016.

evolved assemblages of functionally interdependent institutional forms. In this way, IM seeks to understand the ways in which institutional patterns refract, are transformed by, and establish the conditions for the realization of deeper structural forces—an interaction that results in novel articulations of common mechanisms in distinct contexts.[5]

Hilferding's concern with institutional development across time, and the impact of this on the dynamics of accumulation, led him to adopt a similar methodology in his own analysis—such that 'from *Finance Capital* to his essays and speeches of the 1930s… a new Marxist theory of capitalist development took shape' (Bottomore 1985, p. 64) in his work. Distinct phases of capitalist development, he saw, can be delineated by institutional shifts in the structures and processes through which capital accumulation and the reproduction of class hegemony occurs, including the organized form of surplus extraction and circulation, state structure, modalities of competition, world market and geopolitical relations, and the balance of class forces. Even the most cursory historical analysis reveals that institutional causality exerts substantial force in determining the historical realization of the basic logic of capital in all these areas and more, constraining or expanding the power and range of reproduction strategies available to specific actors embedded within this systemic logic by virtue of their command of institutional resources. Despite the attention paid to corporate and financial institutions, it is revealing of his attentiveness to this causal hierarchy that Hilferding begins *Finance Capital* with an analysis of money, just as Marx began *Capital* by dissecting the commodity. As this suggests, institutions are not the ontological foundation of social reality, but rather emergent phenomena rooted in, but not reducible to, deeper structural dynamics. If the object of *Capital* was to understand how the properties of the commodity embody the logic of capitalist production—which is fundamentally oriented toward producing commodities *as such*, with all the contradictions this entails—the object of *Finance Capital* is to analyze how the coevolution of the corporation, financial system, and capitalist state generated and reproduced the predominance of money-capital.

Finance capital is primarily characterized by the fusion of *bank capital* and *industrial capital*. This occurs through the ascendancy of

---

[5] For a thorough elaboration of the Institutional Marxist framework, see Stephen Maher and Scott M. Aquanno, "Conceptualizing Neoliberalism: Foundations of an Institutional Marxist Theory of Capitalism," *New Political Science* 40:1, March 2018.

money-capital—and thus the increased dominance of the abstract over the concrete. To begin with, the corporation replaces *personal ownership* with *impersonal ownership*. In the prior entrepreneurial era, capitalists directly owned and controlled capital assets (means of production), and raised investment largely through family networks. The corporation's separation of ownership and control, however, means it must engage with financial markets to secure financing. This facilitated the amassing of unprecedented quantities of capital, but it also had the effect of converting industrial capitalists into creditors, or owners of money-capital who have no necessary connection with the uses to which their credit is put. Instead of qualitative capital goods (machinery, buildings, etc.), capitalists owned tradable shares—effectively a draft on future profits generated by assets controlled by professional managers. At the same time, this allowed banks to acquire new importance as shareholders, mobilizers of capital, and organizers of corporations and cartels. As the possessors of the largest pools of money-capital, and capable of generating credit, banks were able to seize control of smaller-scale entrepreneurial firms and merge them into large corporations. As a result, investment banks gained extensive power over industrial enterprises, placing individuals on corporate boards to create interlocking networks of firms they controlled.

Hilferding argues that this formation of finance capital inexorably gives rise to a system of 'organized capitalism,' whereby the banks that dominate networks of monopoly firms steer the economy to overcome the 'anarchy of free-market capitalism on a capitalist basis' (Hilferding 1924/2017, p. 531). Finance capital thus led to the socialization of production through the development of stable linkages across firms and sectors, as large-scale enterprises came to 'agree about their share of the market.' Such cartelization was 'enormously encouraged' by banking interests, as 'reciprocally destructive competition' threatened their existing investments and limited their ability to profitably issue new shares (Hilferding 1931/2017, p. 747). This resulted in what was effectively a planned economic system centered on the investment banks. However, capital's drive for growth meant that competitive pressures were displaced onto the world market in the form of inter-imperial geopolitical rivalry. This took place through the erection of protective tariffs to secure exclusive economic territory for the exploitation by national bourgeoisies, as well as to 'reserve the domestic market for national capital.' Such measures would allow firms to achieve the 'extra-profit' necessary to 'increase their competitiveness on the world market' (Hilferding 1931/2017, p. 748).

Capitalist competition, therefore, fueled the drive for each state to enlarge the economic territory within which its national firms could extract wealth through the export of capital, free from competition by firms located in other states.

For Hilferding, this planned system of production remains distinct from socialism because the productive forces are regulated for the benefit of those classes that own the means of production. However, Hilferding believed it would establish the essential conditions for the democratic administration of the economy. Although organized capitalism changes the character of working conditions by making unemployment less of a threat, it also renders the 'usurpation of economic power' by capitalist owners more apparent and 'unbearable' (Hilferding 1924/2017, p. 532). This has the effect of 'unifiy[ing] the interests of...workers and employees of all types' around the struggle for economic democracy (Hilferding 1924/2017, p. 534). More importantly, it reorganizes the internal logic of firms by eliminating the operation of the law of value (Hilferding 1920/2017, p. 319; Hilferding 1927/2017, p. 572). As organized capitalism centralizes production decisions formally fragmented by market mediation, the different branches of industry become coordinated through scientific planning, suppressing the coercive laws of competition. 'Organized capitalism' thereby effectively consists of a planned economy that is structured to benefit capitalist owners, rather than administered by the state to the benefit of society as a whole. If *Finance Capital* became the key foundation for the understanding of corporate capitalism within the Second International, so too did it pave the way for the widely held but erroneous view—rooted to some extent in the work of Marx himself—that the corporation was a transitional form to socialism. This created the serious misconception that the process of socialization is actually accelerated by the concentration and centralization of corporate power.

As James Clifton argued, large corporations are in fact *more* competitive than smaller firms (Clifton 1977). Capitalist competition is not over sales or market share, but *profits*. Thus 'the key strategic decision of the capitalist is what to invest in and the defining characteristic of capitalist competition is the mobility of investment—mobility over space and between different commercial/financial/industrial activities' (Bryan and Rafferty 2006, p. 167). Competition between capitals takes the form of competition between investment opportunities: low profit rates lead to the withdrawal of investment, while high profits draw increased investment. Such competition takes place not just *between* firms, but also *within* them.

Indeed, an individual *firm* is by no means the same as an individual *capital*. Large corporations undertake a range of separate production processes, each of which can be identified as an 'individual capital.' It is *primarily* individual capitals, not the corporate institutions to which they are articulated, which engage in competition as possible outlets for investment. Since large multi-process firms are also the most mobile, they are also thereby intensely competitive, since such firms have the greatest range of options for investing money-capital across diverse internal operations as well as new external opportunities. While corporations may in some sense be economic planning systems, they are nevertheless about *planning competitiveness*. Importantly, this analysis shows that competition between capitals is internalized not just within the firm, but also *within the money-form itself*. As abstract capital, money-capital confronts the entire range of possible investments as different concrete forms that it could potentially take. In this way, money-capital is the most liquid, and abstract form of capital—and the key locus of capitalist competition.

Capitalism, including finance capital, thrives on competition. Corporations are not merely generic bureaucratic planning machines but are fundamentally organized to reproduce capitalist social relations: raising capital on competitive financial markets, marketing products competitively, allocating investment competitively to maximize profits, and crafting and transacting sophisticated financial instruments that are critical for managing the risks involved in circulating value globally. The functions undertaken by the corporation are distinct to capitalist society, and competitive market discipline plays an essential part in regulating its institutional development. Indeed, as Hilferding shows, an important dimension of competition in corporate capitalism is over *organizational forms*: those organizations that are able to mobilize capital most efficiently will enjoy a range of competitive advantages, thereby swallowing or destroying organizational forms which are less capable, and sparking imitation. The unfolding of corporate organization over time is in this way akin to a process of Darwinian adaptation within a structural environment profoundly shaped by the contradictory logic of capital (Maher and Aquanno 2018). To conceive of the corporation simply as a 'command economy' is to completely misunderstand the dialectical historical process from which different modalities of corporate organization emerge.

The Financialization
of the Non-financial Corporation

Corporate institutions constitute the concrete historical form of the capitalist class at a given moment in time. If the corporation in the *finance capital* era (1880–1929) constitutes one 'type,' that which emerged during the subsequent *managerial* period (1930–1979) is another; the *neo-liberal* firm (1980–2008), another still. It is the function of the state to organize these fragmented systems of *economic* power into a hegemonic *political* order. Indeed, Hilferding's late works are astonishingly prescient in their analysis of the growing capacities of the capitalist state, which played a pivotal role in the demise of finance capital. Though the centrality of investment banks was already on the decline with the broadening of the financial system and breakup of the big family trusts, finance capital was formally brought to an end after the 1929 financial crisis. In the US, a massive state-building effort in the form of the New Deal diminished the role of the banks and established extensive new markets for corporate control to mediate between investors and industrial firms. Particularly noteworthy was Glass-Steagall's separation of commercial and investment banking. Banks opting to pursue commercial banking had to restrict equity holdings and limit seats on the boards of industrial corporations, while investment banks could no longer accept consumer deposits, and thus had reduced leverage. The act thus effectively 'separated financial institutions from corporate boards,' dealing the coup de grâce to finance capital (Simon 1998, p. 1090).

By the 1940s, it was clear to Hilferding that the bank-centric phase of capitalist development he had observed in *Finance Capital* was passing into a new stage, marked by a different institutional configuration of state and corporate power. This was then taking place through the tremendous and rapid expansion of the power of the modern state then taking shape through the rise of Nazism in Germany and Stalinism in Russia, which joined the New Deal in the US in heralding a new era of state-centric capitalist organization. Marxist social science, Hilferding argued, with its focus on economic laws, lacked the tools to grasp the significance of this transformation, focused as it was around state institutions. In a 1941 manuscript he was working on at the time of his suicide in a Nazi prison, Hilferding argued that 'the development of *state power* accompanies the development of the modern economy,' and as a result the state was now 'a power in its own right, with its own agencies, its own tendencies and its own interests.' Consequently, 'the political problem of the postwar period consists in the change in the relation of the state to society, brought about the by the *subordination of the economy* to the coercive power of the state' (Hilferding 1941/1981, pp. 77–78). In this regard, he anticipated the 'state theorists' of a generation later in identifying the impact of the expansion of state institutional capacities on capitalist social relations, and the degree of state autonomy from capital, as the crucial problems facing Marxist social science.

Hilferding's analysis proved incisive. The development of the state economic apparatus and industrial policy dramatically accelerated over the war years and after. In the US, massive state investment during World War II resulted in the *doubling* of production, as well as the formation of a durable military-industrial complex linking the expansive new Department of Defense with large high-tech engineering firms and the vast science and technology apparatus that had emerged around the Manhattan Project, including the university system. This facilitated the consolidation of corporate power in the hands of 'insider' managers, and further reduced the power of external investors. These shifts were underpinned by a tremendous wave of concentration and centralization in the decades following the war, forming the giant corporations that were the foundation for what C. Wright Mills called 'the managerial reorganization of the propertied class' (Mills 1956/2000, p. 147). That the now-'multinational' corporations these managers commanded were substantially autonomous from the banks meant that they had to develop extensive new institutional capacities, including a range of functions necessary to engage with a broader and more competitive financial system (McKenna 1995). At the same time, in marked contrast with the consolidated shareholdings that had existed during the finance capital era, stock ownership was now fragmented and dispersed, preventing the emergence of an oppositional block of ownership power that could challenge this managerial stratum. Shareholder-elected boards of directors, once the centers of corporate control, became backwaters controlled by internal management. This 'Golden Age' of managerial capitalism extended throughout the two-decade-long postwar boom, until the crisis struck once again in the 1970s.

Even as professional insider managers consolidated their position at the top of the institutional pyramid, the diversification and international expansion of the corporations they ruled made it increasingly difficult to manage increasingly complex operations through hierarchical Weberian bureaucracies. This was exacerbated by trends in anti-trust prosecution, whereby price competition was protected by preventing firms from controlling too large a share of the market in any one sector—thereby leading large firms to pursue growth through acquisitions across unrelated sectors (Hyman 2012). Top executives had neither the time nor the industry-specific knowledge to be directly involved in the operations of each business (Chandler Jr. 1962, pp. 299–314; Cordiner 1956, pp. 44–45; Paxton 1955). The answer was centralization-decentralization, whereby operational responsibility for specific businesses would be downloaded to lower-level divisional managers, while investment functions remained centralized in the hands of top executives, now known as 'general managers.' As top executives moved away from *operational* roles in overseeing specific businesses and into general *entrepreneurial* or investment functions, they came increasingly to resemble finance capitalists located at the nexus of finance and industry. These new 'general managers' sought to approximate abstract money-capital, seeking out the most profitable concrete investments both within the firm and outside of it. That 'the top team was now less the captive of its operating organizations also meant that they required 'the financial offices [to] provide more and better data,' which drove the expansion and empowerment of corporate financial operations (Chandler Jr. 1962, p. 310; Cordiner 1956, p. 98; O'Boyle 1998, p. 52). The quantitative metrics these financial units provided constituted *general criteria* on the basis of which *general managers* could assess internal and external operations alike: judging the performance of internal operating units alongside 'new areas for development or expansion in which operating unit executives would have comparatively little interest or knowledge' (Chandler Jr. 1962, p. 310). Increasingly, these metrics were seen in terms of exchange-value: what made qualitatively distinct production processes *comparable* was their quantitative money-value as determined by rates of return.

This was the essence of the *financialization* of the non-financial corporation. Though often conceived in terms of industrial corporations morphing into banks by expanding their financial services investments, this process in fact entails a much deeper institutional reorganization of the corporation from a *system of production* to a *system of investment* (Fligstein 1990). This had three broad dimensions: (1) the conversion of top corporate managers into bearers of abstract money-capital; (2) the reorganization of corporate governance as an internal capital market; and (3) the empowerment of corporate financial functions over the rest of the organization. By the 1970s, corporate planning structures effectively resembled internal capital markets. Top executives saw business divisions not as concrete production processes to be directly managed, but as a portfolio of discrete investments. These divisions competed with one another, and even with outside subcontractors, for a finite sum of investment funds distributed by senior executives. Divisional managers developed business plans autonomously, which they presented to top managers as if they were external investors. In these ways, divisional managers were encouraged to act like owners, making autonomous decisions based on the need to secure investment from corporate planners for their individual business units. Additionally, to the extent possible, managerial remuneration was tied to the contribution of their business unit to the firm's share price (Fligstein 1990; Rothschild 2007; Useem 1993, 1996). Decentralization therefore also meant replacing rigid bureaucratic hierarchies with flexible financial discipline. This was enforced especially by the firm's financial unit, which 'exercised ultimate control over money and personnel' (Cordiner 1956, pp. 66–67; O'Boyle 1998, p. 52).

This was reinforced by the broader rise of the financial sector from the 1970s onward. However, the neoliberal form of financial power was different from that which had existed during the finance capital period. It was characterized not by direct *bank control* of industrial corporations, but rather *polyarchic financial hegemony*, in which constellations of competing financial institutions came together to exert broad influence and discipline (Carroll and Sapinski 2011, pp. 180–195; Glasberg and Schwartz 1983; Mintz and Schwartz 1986, 1987; Scott 1997, p. 139). Bank power was far less centralized, less powerful relative to industrial firms, and its relationship to corporate governance was more substantially mediated by institutions within which 'insiders' retained considerable control. Industrial firms were much larger and more complex, placing a premium on 'insider' knowledge. To be sure, financial hegemony was partly expressed through interlocking directorates possessed by financiers, but boards themselves were less significant institutional spaces for organizing and expressing corporate control than they had been in the finance capital era. In both cases, more significant than these institutional venues were the underlying capital relations that they expressed and facilitated. Such relations are constituted by the functional structure of accumulation—consisting of roles in mobilizing capital such as granting or withholding credit, setting interest rates, and buying or selling large blocks of shares. An important aspect of financial power, therefore, was the extent to which firms had to rely on external financing. With declining profitability and persistent deficiencies in capital formation at the end of the postwar boom, internal financing was constrained, and industrial firms became more dependent on external sources of capital—thereby increasing the relative power of the financial sector. Investors used this leverage to push for further financialized restructuring, including the empowerment of the corporate financial operations with which they were closely linked.

These shifts were further buttressed by a wave of concentration and centralization of equity in the hands of large financial institutions during the 1970s, fueled by the pools of capital that emerged in the form of occupational pension funds. Ironically, the proliferation of such funds 'reflected the strength of unions in collective bargaining in the 1960s,' yet these victories for union power in fact ended up contributing to building financial hegemony, shifting the balance of class forces toward capital and intensifying financial pressure for restructuring non-financial corporations. The state, too, was essential to the tremendous growth of such funds: 'tax advantages for both corporations and workers' played a significant role in the extension of pension plan coverage 'from a fifth of the private sector workforce in 1950 to almost half by 1970' (Panitch and Gindin 2012, p. 121). By the 1970s, pension funds became the largest single holders of corporate stock (Drucker 1976, pp. 1–2; Herman 1982, p. 138; Kotz 1978; Rifkin and Barber 1978, p. 10, 234; Scott 1997, p. 67). The scale of these holdings prevented such big institutional investors from simply following the 'Wall Street Rule' and dumping shares of underperforming firms, as it would be impossible to sell such a large number of shares all at once without seriously depressing their value. This created a further need among investors for new mechanisms for coordination with and oversight of 'insiders.' After the hostile takeovers by the 'corporate raiders' of the 1980s, the power of institutional investors was felt in the wave of proxy fights in the 1990s as the new hierarchy began to crystallize. New institutional linkages were constructed between financiers and the governance structures of industrial corporations, including in the form of 'investor relations' units (Useem 1993, 1996). This, in turn, enhanced the power of corporate finance within the firm, which further pressed financialized reorganization.

In this way, the rise of the financial sector was internally linked with the financialized restructuring of the non-financial corporation. While no major corporation had a Chief Financial Officer in 1963, beginning in the 1970s the trend began to sweep the business world, becoming all but ubiquitous by the 1990s—with diversified conglomerates in the lead. This signaled 'a fundamental redistribution of managerial roles, with greater relevance of financial considerations built into the executive structure and the decision-making process.' Whereas in the past, 'corporate finance had been a back-office function performed by treasurers or controllers, whose duties were confined to tasks like bookkeeping and preparing tax statements.' The CFO was now the company's second-in-command, controlling vast institutional resources. 'Financial' considerations became increasingly paramount, as CFOs 'gained critical say in key strategic and operational decisions, from evaluating business unit performance, inventing new ways to leverage capital, managing acquisitions and divestitures, and fending off hostile takeover attempts, to serving as the company's primary ambassador to investors and financial analysts' (Zorn 2004, pp. 346–347). The CFO's 'investor relations' functions in particular both reflected the rise of finance and contributed to the financialization of the corporation. In addition to supplying data and making forecasts for investors, CFOs also pushed forward the disciplines within the firm necessary to meet these expectations. This included ensuring that financiers 'got their cut' in the form of interest, dividends, and asset valuations—shifting the distribution of profits across the capitalist class as a whole toward the financial sector and culminating in what would be called 'shareholder value.'

New Finance Capital: A New Phase of Capitalist Development?

The irrelevance of boards of directors over the managerial period reflected the empowerment of industrial managers over investors, as boards were basically under the control of insider managers. With the rising power of the financial sector by the 1990s, boards again began to emerge as significant institutional venues for expressing investor power within corporate command and control structures, organizing a constellation of financial interests to finance and govern industrial assets. As the clout of financial institutions and investors grew, financiers successfully pushed for more substantial forms of corporate 'compliance' and 'good governance.' Similarly, major episodes of corruption at Enron and WorldCom paved the way for corporate governance rules that allowed boards to discipline management and initiate key operational and strategic policies. Reforms stressed the importance of having boards composed of a majority of independent members as well as independent board compensation and audit committees, and pushed codes of business conduct to improve transparency.

This restructuring of corporate governance was supported by developments in the state regulatory apparatus, as indicated by the Sarbanes-Oxley Act and especially the SEC's Regulation FD, which greatly strengthened the power and independence of boards. The latter prevented the selective disclosure of corporate information to large investors, ensuring that all shareholders had the same information and that institutional funds were no longer tied to company boards. While these shifts in state policy set the conditions for a different interaction between management and owners, the regulations and restructuring that followed the 2008 subprime financial crisis were even more substantial. Above all, this initiated a process of dual concentration within the financial system: both among a small group of large banks and among asset management firms. Firstly, US regulators looking for a way to stabilize the financial system, amid the seizure of short-term funding markets and the collapse of key asset classes, found a solution in the merger of large banks. Whether this crisis management policy reflected an understanding that larger firms are better suited for global competition, its impact was to create a new class of diversified mega banks, registered in the large increase in the share of system assets of the top five US banks (BIS 2018). It was hoped that these banks, protected by their 'systemically important' status, would be both larger and more stable.

The second aspect of post-crisis financial concentration involved the rise of asset management firms. This took the form of the growing influence of activist hedge funds, such as Elliott Management, Starboard Value, Carl Icahn, ValueAct, Corvex Management, and Bulldog Investors: between 2004 and 2016 these funds increased their assets under management (AUM) by 1400%. Activist funds attempt to extract latent value from underperforming corporations by shaping the composition of boards of directors through proxy contests and better proxy access, which can serve as institutional positions for pushing for a deeper restructuring of assets and labor processes. They also try to influence strategic and operational policies by working directly with managers through investor relations departments (Sawyer et al. 2019). More significant, however, was the historic rise of a small group of asset management firms specializing in passive investment strategies, especially BlackRock, State Street, and Vanguard. Passive funds follow a selected market index (e.g., the NASDAQ or S&P 500) and do not engage in regular trading. As a result, they offer much lower management fees and a long-term investment approach. Indeed, these funds hold shares indefinitely, trading only to reflect the shifting weight of different firms in a given index. Whereas prior to the crisis, 75% of equity funds were actively managed by a portfolio manager, passive funds are now larger in size, with over $4 trillion under management (McDevitt and Schramm 2019). The massive portfolios held by these firms in fact means that they are collectively the largest equity owner in many American corporations (Fichtner et al. 2017).[6] This long-termism has led these funds to undertake more routinized and systematic contact with firms in which they hold stakes.

Paradoxically, then, the aftermath of the crisis saw both a sharp rise in investor *activism* and a simultaneous historic shift in portfolio strategy toward *passive* management. Far from being antagonistic to one another, these two trends are in fact complementary and mutually reinforcing. Moreover, both have encouraged the development and crystallization of institutional linkages between financial institutions and non-financial corporations, which in turn have increased pressure for neoliberal restructuring of corporate governance and the labor process. This all generates great pressure for maximizing shareholder value through cost cutting and enhanced margins, encouraging the implementation of 'lean production' as well as outsourcing and offshoring to precarious and low-paid workforces in both North America and peripheral zones.

State regulation and management was a crucial factor in generating these shifts that followed the 2008 crisis. Perhaps most important of all was the Fed's Quantitative Easing (QE) program. In the process of detoxifying bank balance sheets and backstopping losses, QE pushed up asset prices along the risk spectrum, as private sellers rebalanced their portfolios into riskier assets. This drove a boom in equity prices that made it difficult for investment firms to justify high management costs. In response, institutional investors altered their growth model and began attracting new capital through low-fee passive funds, while hedge funds competed by adopting activist strategies capable of outperforming the market. Moreover, by limiting repo trading and forcing investment banks out of key secondary markets, the tighter liquidity and risk thresholds associated with post-crisis regulation pushed institutional funds away from short-term funding markets and enabled them to expand their concentration of

---

[6] As of 2017 one of Vanguard, Blackrock, or State Street was the largest shareholder in 88% of the S&P 500 companies.

equity ownership. All of this took a significant step forward with the passage of the Dodd-Frank Act, which gave renewed impetus to corporate governance reform that served to further consolidate investor power. The 13 sections of Dodd-Frank dedicated to corporate governance include new 'say on pay' and disclosure rules that have greatly emboldened shareholders.

The importance of these shifts in fund management lies in the new form of organized power that has taken shape as passive institutional funds have integrated their strategies with activist hedge funds. As large long-term holders of corporate equities, passive investment funds have regularly supported activist hedge funds in their attempts to restructure corporate assets to release latent value. They have also reduced market liquidity, encouraging hedge funds to take more long-term strategies themselves. At the same time, these strategies have been supported by and reinforced the empowerment of financial units and competitive logic within non-financial corporations, which push for increased returns from the productive assets they control. This confluence of forces has produced a new constellation of financial power expressed in part through greater contestation over non-financial boards of directors. It has allowed hedge funds to leverage their small ownership percentage to pursue successful activist campaigns, and encouraged large institutional investors to build up sophisticated corporate management teams to further their control over corporate governance (Jahnke 2017, 2019).[7] The result has been a new structure of ownership and control, marked by a *fusion* of finance and industry and the further dominance of money-capital over production: what we call a *new finance capital*. Though financial control is now exercised through shareholder activism, this resembles the system of bank power described by Hilferding, insofar as financiers have come to take a more direct role in the governance of industrial corporations, while industrial managers themselves increasingly resemble money-capitalists.

Concentration in the asset management industry has led to the same type of financial *long-termism* identified by Hilferding, aiming to maximize financial profits through shifts in corporate organization, and striving

---

[7] Jahnke provides a good empirical description of this new form of corporate control. He shows that while 6% of S&P 500 companies reported investor engagement in 2010 this rose to 23% in 2012, 50% in 2014, and 72% in 2017. His research also finds that from June 2016 to June 2017, Vanguard, a major passive investment firm, reported 954 engagements with corporate managers.

to gain 'greater security' for the capital invested by asset managers by increasing the voice of financiers within corporate command and control systems and intensifying the discipline of money-capital (Hilferding 1912/1981, p. 199). The power and autonomy boards amassed during the neoliberal period facilitated greater financial discipline as polyarchic financial hegemony became more centralized, and the linkages between finance and industry more extensive and direct, in the period since 2008. As we saw, in addition to the growing significance of boards of directors, this fusion of finance and industry has been apparent from the emergence of 'investor relations' offices within non-financial corporations; so too was it evident from the reciprocal growth of similar 'corporate relations' units within financial institutions. The latter also serve to coordinate and network with activist investors and influence board policy.

But if all this suggests that a new phase of capitalist development is emerging through the restructuring underway since the 2008 crisis, it is not yet completely clear that this new finance capital represents a permanent shift from the interlocking form of financial, industrial, and state power that constituted the neoliberal form of class hegemony. To be sure, many firms have accepted the demands of activist investors for greater 'shareholder democracy,' stronger boards, or eliminating anti-takeover defenses. At the same time, the intensification of financial discipline has also produced new strategies for insulating corporate governance from financial discipline, such as by limiting shareholder voting rights. The future of these modalities of corporate ownership and control is not yet clear, as the ability for companies to limit financial pressures by instituting classified share voting rights (i.e., in which some shareowners have more voting power than others), executing stock buybacks, and other measures remains to be seen. Similarly, the extent to which the power of large asset management companies is tied to the combination of low interest rates, low inflation, and monetary stimulus through QE is unclear. Higher interest rates may jeopardize the asset inflation that has been central to their ability to concentrate and centralize money-capital, and therefore economic power in relation to industrial corporations. Whether asset managers can sustain their dominant position within contemporary finance in a new macroeconomic environment, including by potentially restructuring their operations as they compete with banks and other financial institutions for savings, is uncertain.

Democratic Control and Socialist Planning

As we have shown, Hilferding's work offers some of crucial foundations for a Marxist theory of corporate governance. It does so in four interrelated ways: (1) developing a theorization of *finance capital* as distinct from *financial* and *industrial* capital, and constituted through the fusion of these two forms; (2) the identification of *money-capital* as the *abstract* form of capital which comes to dominate the *concrete* processes of production through this fusion; (3) an understanding of how institutional forms *emerge* within capitalist society dialectically in relation to the dynamics of capitalist competition, concentration and centralization, the balance of class forces, integration with the world market, and the organization and exercise of state power; and (4) the *periodization* of different 'phases' of capitalist development by reference to the institutional modalities through which accumulation occurs. These constitute some of the key analytical tools for understanding the institutional changes that we have argued amount to a new finance capital, characterized by a fusion of financial and industrial capital. In this process, the increasing mediation of the money-form within corporate governance has meant that the managers of large industrial corporations have become financiers, while financiers have likewise developed increasingly substantial and direct linkages with industrial corporations.

This is not merely of academic interest. Indeed, these tools have never been more essential for political strategy than today, as Bernie Sanders in the US and Jeremy Corbyn in the UK have helped to catalyze a surprising and promising new socialist movement. The policies these leaders have proposed for advancing the socialization and democratization of the economy have consisted primarily of expanding different forms of worker ownership and increasing workers' 'voice' in the management of capitalist firms.[8] Assessing whether these represent meaningful steps toward substantive economic democracy requires understanding how they will impact the actually existing forms of institutional power in which they seek to intervene. This, in turn, must be predicated upon some conception of how these forms take shape and are reproduced. In this regard, as well, Hilferding's work frames some of the crucial questions still facing the socialist movement today and helps to develop a roadmap to socialist transition beyond what has been proposed in the form of worker cooperatives

---

[8] For a thorough discussion of these proposed policies, see Maher et al. 2019.

6 A NEW FINANCE CAPITAL? THEORIZING CORPORATE GOVERNANCE… 161

and other models focused on extending firm-level democracy. Whereas these strategies remain captive to the forces of market competition and profit maximization, Hilferding insists on a struggle to transform the state, especially by developing the capacities to institute a democratic economic planning regime.

Hilferding viewed socialist transition as a process of *extending demo-cratic control* over the economy as a whole by strategically removing specific sectors from capitalist ownership and market discipline and subjecting them to public planning. Therefore, the first task of the socialist movement was to deepen and broaden the democratic capacities of the working class through struggle and popular education. This took place through the organization of a mass party capable of 'transcending the different fractions' within the working class. These divisions develop as gender, race, ethnic, and national identities tend to throw 'workers against each other both concretely and intellectually,' and also as short-term material interests take precedence over long-term political goals (Hilferding 1924/2017, p. 538; Hilferding 1927/2017, p. 575). Hilferding saw this process of politicization and organization as a long process rooted in 'continuous struggle,' through which the building of parliamentary and extra-parliamentary forces would be mutually reinforcing. Running in elections and waging a struggle within the capitalist state would both draw support from, and reciprocally support, the development of durable institutions of working-class power outside of parliament. This included the build-up of public and workplace educational institutions to 'enlighten the popular masses' and foster 'cooperative solidarity' (Hilferding 1918a, p. 292; Hilferding 1920/2017, p. 324; Hilferding 1925/2017, p. 561) The 'psychological transformation' nourished through 'conscious educational work,' he argued, functioned as an essential 'prerequisite for economic democracy' (Hilferding 1924/2017, p. 533).

The transition to socialism would occur through *the transformation of the state*: new forms of workplace, community, and national-level democracy would be organized and linked through the agency of the party, which would restructure the state apparatus to promote and integrate these processes. This struggle would not be consummated in a single revolutionary upsurge. Rather, Hilferding argued that the transition to socialism would take place through a series of ruptures, inflection points, and potential reversals. This process would continue even after the working class had captured political power, since the socialization of the economy could 'occur only in a long-term… evolutionary way' due to the deep organizational and structural basis of capitalist class power (Hilferding 1924/2017, p. 533). Hilferding believed that socialization should proceed from 'capital's strongest economic positions' in a 'step-by-step fashion' until the material and psychological conditions for transition were fully realized (Hilferding 1919a, pp. 301–302). This was because these branches of the economy possessed the technical and organizational capacities that make socialist planning possible. More important, their strategic position in the system of production allowed democratic control to impact profit patterns in other related sectors (Hilferding 1920/2017, pp. 323–325). As a result, taking these 'key positions of economic power' would initiate an 'organized' transformation of the economy, allowing society 'to control all of the positions that form the basis of economic power' (Hilferding 1919a; Hilferding 1924/2017, p. 302).

The path to economic planning regime was developed around a 'combination of socialist and bourgeoisie democracy' (Hilferding 1918b, p. 295). While working through the institutions of liberal democracy in this way opened the door for 'unreliable governments' and 'reactionary impulses,' it established important political conditions for a national planning regime capable of integrating particular community and workplace interests with the society as a whole (Hilferding 1918b, p. 299). In the period of transition, legally protected workers councils would be established within firms still operating capitalistically, which would exercise limited control over 'enterprise operations' (Hilferding 1919b, p. 297). Workers councils would also serve as industrial parliaments for socialized industries, thereby constituting the heart of the socialist planning regime. For Hilferding, the council system possessed the technical and administrative capacities that were indispensable for managing the economy, while preventing the 'bureaucratization of production' by democratizing workplace authority. (Hilferding 1920/2017, p. 316). As the 'permanent representation of the whole working class,' these councils would transfer control over productive assets to workers and consumers, and would also be given certain political functions aimed at advancing and securing the interests of the revolution (Hilferding 1919b, p. 298).

Hilferding's conception of socialist transition thus differed markedly from the Bolshevik call to 'smash the state' in a single blow through insurrection, focusing instead on building the extensive state and working-class capacities necessary to democratically manage a socialist economy while preserving the gains institutionalized within the existing liberal democratic state. Though he saw workers' councils as key organs of workers' power in a socialist society, and sought to develop strategies for supporting their emergence within capitalism to achieve a transition to socialism, Hilferding nevertheless opposed—just months after the Russian Revolution—the slogan of 'all power to the workers' councils' (or Soviets). He did so on the grounds that this would lead to dictatorship, and just as importantly, that individual plants *do not* belong to the workers who work in them, but rather to the entire society. The crucial challenge in this respect was to find ways to *integrate* workplace councils with broader democratic planning structures at the regional and national levels. Society as a whole, not individual workplaces, must democratically determine the division of labor and the relative output of different sectors and branches. For this reason, the 'rights of the councils must be limited' so that production decisions do not 'exclude any part of the population.' To some degree, this could be accomplished by establishing a central workers body, composed of delegates from local councils, responsible for reviewing and submitting legislative proposals. But even this risked corrupting the general will with narrow sectoral interests. Hilferding saw the solution to this in a democratically elected national assembly that worked with the councils to express the interests of the 'whole community' (Hilferding 1919b, p. 297).

Initially, Hilferding focused this strategy on the banking sector, but this changed as he observed shifts in the production process owing to technological advancements. As commodity chains grew more dependent upon the use of synthetic chemistry, he argued that socialization should begin in the energy and raw materials sector (Hilferding 1918b, p. 294; Hilferding 1925/2017). The need for credit during the transition period meant that, in his opinion, big banks could not be immediately socialized but rather would have to be slowly merged 'into a single agency' and gradually 'taken over by society' (Hilferding 1919a, p. 300). This strategy must be placed in the context of Hilferding's argument that socialization is stimulated through 'legislation… placing firms in syndicates,' and the problematic nature of seeing capitalist concentration and cartelization as steps toward socialism in themselves. Nevertheless, it points to the importance of restructuring the financial system and bringing it under public control as a central priority of socialist transition. In any case, it is important to take account of the extent to which Hilferding's strategic reflections begin from a concrete appraisal of class power and corporate organization. This immediately takes him to the central nodes of economic control and patterns of corporate and state governance underpinning accumulation, and to a conjunctural analysis of the social structure, as the basis for socialist strategy.

In the current conjuncture, this draws attention to the forms of financial power consolidated in the post-2008 period. Clearly, it is hard to imagine simply nationalizing the giant asset management firms, or the bank, though this should remain our ultimate goal. In order to get there, socialists can start by devising alternative institutional forms of economic democracy aimed at limiting the impact of the disciplines of competitive pressures. Public banking is one example of such a possibility. These institutions may not directly challenge, or seek to immediately replace, the major institutions of capitalist finance. Rather, they may operate *alongside* these institutions, serving as a proving ground to demonstrate the potential of a more democratic economy to meet social needs, while facilitating the development of the democratic capacities of the working class and socialist activists. At the same time, such projects can serve to build the necessary working-class base for democratic socialists elected at the municipal, state, and even federal level—who can, in turn, nurture these projects with the resources available to them, while raising their profile. In this way, extra-parliamentary forces and those within the state could be reciprocally and mutually strengthened. This is a more productive route than the call to 'break up the banks,' which would not increase democratic control over finance and investment but rather aims to 'restore competitiveness' in the financial sector.

Nor does expanding worker ownership of individual firms through share ownership plans, or granting workers seats on boards of directors, directly contribute to the socialization of the economy. Increasing worker 'voice' through these means merely grants them a larger role shaping competitive strategy to maximize profits—increasing the identification of workers with 'their' firm in competing with others. What is needed to overcome this is a strategy aimed at *socializing* the economy by limiting the mediation of market competition, which ultimately must be replaced by national-level economic planning. Moreover, this must go beyond merely nationalizing corporations or banks, and bringing them under the control of the state. Rather, these institutions must be profoundly reorganized on a new, and radically participatory, basis. First steps in this direction could be taken through the implementation of a Green New Deal, as firms seeking state contracts could be forced to submit to state-imposed planning agreements directing them to produce socially useful goods. It is this conception of socialist transition—as a process of transforming the state to develop the capacities to socialize and democratize all forms of economic and political governance—that should animate strategic debates within the socialist movements taking shape today.

REFERENCES

Bank of International Settlements. 2018. Structural Change in Banking After the Crisis. *Committee on the Global Financial System*, January 24.

Bottomore, T. 1985. *Theories of Modern Capitalism*. Boston: Unwin Hyman.

Bryan, D., and R. Rafferty. 2006. *Capitalism With Derivatives: A Political Economy of Financial Derivatives, Capital and Class*. New York: Palgrave Macmillan.

Carroll, W.K., and J.P. Sapinski. 2011. Corporate Elite and Intercorporate Networks. In *The SAGE Handbook of Social Network Analysis*, ed. P.J. Carrington and J. Scott. London: SAGE Publications.

Chandler, A., Jr. 1962. *Strategy and Structure: Chapters in the History of the American Industrial Enterprise*. Boston: MIT Press.

Clifton, J. 1977. Competition and the Evolution of the Capitalist Mode of Production. *Cambridge Journal of Economics* 1 (2).

Cordiner, R. 1956. *New Frontiers for Professional Managers*. New York: McGraw-Hill.

Drucker, P.F. 1976. *The Unseen Revolution: How Pension Fund Socialism Came to America*. New York, NY: Harper and Row.

Fichtner, J., E. Heemskery, and J. Garcia-Bernardo. 2017. These Three Firms Own Corporate America. *The Conversation*, May 10.

Fligstein, N. 1990. *The Transformation of Corporate Control*. Cambridge: Harvard University Press.

Glasberg, D.S., and M. Schwartz. 1983. Ownership and Control of Corporations. *Annual Review of Sociology* 9 (1).

Herman, E.S. 1982. *Corporate Control, Corporate Power: A Twentieth Century Fund Study*. Cambridge: Cambridge University Press.

Hilferding, R. 1912/1981. *Finance Capital: A Study of the Latest Phase of Capitalist Development*. (London: Routledge).

———. 1918a. Revolutionary Trust. In *Austro-Marxism: The Ideology of Unity: Changing the World the Politics of Austro-Marxism*, ed. M.E. Blum and W. Smaldone, vol. II. Chicago: Haymarket Books.

———. 1918b. Clarity! In *Austro-Marxism: The Ideology of Unity: Changing the World the Politics of Austro-Marxism*, ed. M.E. Blum and W. Smaldone, vol. II, 2017. Chicago: Haymarket Books.

———. 1919a. The Socialisation Question. In *Austro-Marxism: The Ideology of Unity: Changing the World the Politics of Austro-Marxism*, ed. M.E. Blum and W. Smaldone, vol. II. Chicago: Haymarket Books.

———. 1919b. Expand the Council System! In *Austro-Marxism: The Ideology of Unity: Changing the World the Politics of Austro-Marxism*, ed. M.E. Blum and W. Smaldone, vol. II. Chicago: Haymarket Books.

———. 1920/2017. Political and Economic Power Relations and Socialization. In *Austro-Marxism: The Ideology of Unity: Changing the World the Politics of Austro-Marxism*, ed. M.E. Blum and W. Smaldone, vol. II. Chicago: Haymarket Books.

———. 1924/2017. Problems of Our Time. In *Austro-Marxism: The Ideology of Unity: Changing the World the Politics of Austro-Marxism*, ed. M.E. Blum and W. Smaldone, vol. II. Chicago: Haymarket Books.

———. 1925/2017. The Heidelberg Programme. In *Austro-Marxism: The Ideology of Unity: Changing the World the Politics of Austro-Marxism*, ed. M.E. Blum and W. Smaldone, vol. II. Chicago: Haymarket Books.

———. 1927/2017. The Tasks of Social Democracy in the Republic. In *Austro-Marxism: The Ideology of Unity: Changing the World the Politics of Austro-Marxism*, ed. M.E. Blum and W. Smaldone, vol. II. Chicago: Haymarket Books.

———. 1931/2017. Social Control or Private Control over the Economy. In *Austro-Marxism: The Ideology of Unity: Changing the World the Politics of Austro-Marxism*, ed. M.E. Blum and W. Smaldone, vol. II. Chicago: Haymarket Books.

———. 1941/1981. The Materialist Conception of History. In *Modern Interpretations of Marx*, ed. T. Bottomore. Oxford: Basil Blackwell.

Hyman, L. 2012. Rethinking the Postwar Corporation. In *What's Good for Business: Business and American Politics Since World War II*, ed. K. Phillips-Fein and J.E. Zelizer. Oxford: Oxford University Press.

Jahnke, P. 2017. Voice Versus Exit: The Causes and Consequences of Increasing Shareholder Concentration. *SSRN*, September 18.

———. 2019. Ownership Concentration and Institutional Investors' Governance Through Voice and Exit. *Business & Politics* 21 (3).

Kotz, D.M. 1978. *Bank Control of Large Corporations in the United States.* Berkeley: University of California Press.

Maher, S., and S.M. Aquanno. 2018. Conceptualizing Neoliberalism: Foundations of an Institutional Marxist Theory of Capitalism. *New Political Science* 40: 1.

Maher, S., S. Gindin, and L. Panitch. 2019. Class Politics, Socialist Policies, Capitalist Constraints. In *Socialist Register 2020: Beyond Market Dystopia*, ed. L. Panitch and G. Albo. London: Merlin Press.

McDevitt, K., and M. Schramm. 2019. Morningstar Direct Fund Flows Commentary: United States. *Morningstar.*

McKenna, C.D. 1995. The Origins of Modern Management Consulting. *Business and Economic History* 24 (1).

Mills, C.W. 1956/2000. *The Power Elite.* Oxford: Oxford University Press.

Mintz, B.A., and M. Schwartz. 1986. Capital Flows and the Process of Financial Hegemony. *Theory and Society* 15 (1/2).

———. 1987. *The Power Structure of American Business*. Chicago: University of Chicago Press.

O'Boyle, T.F. 1998. *At Any Cost: Jack Welch, General Electric, and the Pursuit of Profit*. New York: Vintage Books.

Panitch, L., and S. Gindin. 2012. *The Making of Global Capitalism: The Political Economy of American Empire*. New York: Verso.

Paxton, R. 1955. *A Case Study of Management Planning and Control at General Electric Company*. New York: Controllership Foundation.

Rifkin, J., and R. Barber. 1978. *The North Will Rise Again*. Boston: Beacon Press.

Rothschild, W.E. 2007. *The Secret to GE's Success*. New York: McGraw-Hill.

Sawyer, M., et al. 2019. Review and Analysis of 2018 US Shareholder Activism. *Harvard Law School Forum on Corporate Governance and Financial Regulation*, April 5.

Scott, J. 1997. *Corporate Business and Capitalist Classes*. Oxford: Oxford University Press.

Simon, M.C. 1998. The Rise and Fall of Bank Control in the United States, 1890–1939. *American Economic Review*.

Useem, M. 1993. *Executive Defense: Shareholder Power and Corporate Reorganization*. Cambridge, MA: Harvard University Press.

———. 1996. *Investor Capitalism: How Money Managers Are Changing the Face of Corporate America*. New York: Basic Books.

Zorn, D. 2004. Here a Chief, There a Chief: The Rise of the CFO in the American Firm. *American Sociological Review* 69 (3).

CHAPTER 7

Finance Capital and Contemporary Financialization

Radhika Desai

It was not free trade England, but the protectionist countries, Germany and the United States, which became the model states of capitalist development, if one takes as a yardstick the degree of centralization and concentration of capital (that is, the degree of development of cartels and trusts) and of the domination of industry by the banks—in short, the transformation of all capital into finance capital.
—Hilferding, Finance Capital, p. 304

Just how much financialization has come to dominate contemporary Western capitalism was underlined when the first and most fulsome response of public authorities to the novel coronavirus pandemic in March 2020—the response that has taken priority not only over saving lives but even over saving economies—was to issue liquidity on a truly epic scale,

---

R. Desai (✉)
Department of Political Studies, University of Manitoba, Winnipeg, MB, Canada
e-mail: Radhika.Desai@umanitoba.ca

© The Author(s), under exclusive license to Springer Nature Switzerland AG 2023
J. Dellheim, F. O. Wolf (eds.), *Rudolf Hilferding*, Luxemburg International Studies in Political Economy,
https://doi.org/10.1007/978-3-031-08096-8_7

169

orders of magnitude greater than in any previous crisis, involving support for a greater diversity of assets (Brenner 2020). The purpose was to reverse the historic plunges in asset markets as they registered the seriousness of the pandemic and the economic damage it could do, plunges that affected even markets for the safest of asset classes, which usually rise during crises.

The intervention was successful, so much so that asset markets recovered within two months and continued soaring even as economies tanked. The pandemic became infamous for minting billionaires at a faster rate than any other period in history. As the pandemic wore on, exposing the productive debility of neoliberal financialized capitalism further, not only did inflation return but, this time around, thanks to practically trillions parked in highly leveraged asset markets in the form of financial wealth of the obscenely wealthy, the conventional remedy—tightening monetary policy—faced an unprecedented obstacle. Reversing over two decades of monetary laxity threatened this wealth. However, so did inflation. Allegedly 'independent' central banks that had done so much to augment the wealth of their political masters were now said to face a tough choice between ensuring monetary stability and ensuring financial stability.

Does Rudolf Hilferding's *Finance Capital* (1910/1981) have anything to contribute to an understanding of financialization, arguably the overwhelming reality of contemporary capitalism? According to the most serious Marxist scholars who have contributed to the vast literature on the financialization of capitalism in recent decades, little. Costas Lapavitsas's verdict is that Hilferding's concept of finance capital, which denoted the relation between banks and industry in the monopoly phase capitalism entered in the late nineteenth century, also considered the most developed and mature form of the relation, needs to be treated 'with considerable caution'. While monopoly has certainly characterized capitalism since the late nineteenth century:

> in practice, a broad range of relations has prevailed among contemporary industrial and financial capitals, often with national characteristics. Moreover, … [contrary to Hilferding] there is no universal long-term tendency for industrial capital to rely on bank loans to finance fixed capital formation.
>
> In short, finance capital does not adequately capture the complexity and range of relations between industrial and banking capital in the course of the twentieth century. (Lapavitsas 2013, 60)

For Lapavitsas, if the concept of finance capital is important, it is only because it focuses attention on the new types of links between bank and industrial capital, 'merely incipient when Marx wrote *Capital*', that had arisen some decades later and were analysed by Hilferding under that rubric.

Meanwhile, François Chesnais employs the term finance capital in Hilferding's original sense 'not for reasons of "orthodoxy" but of analytical clarity'. For him, it designates 'the simultaneous and intertwined concentration and centralisation of money capital, industrial capital and merchant or commercial capital as an outcome of domestic and transnational concentration through mergers and acquisitions (M&As)'. In his analysis of contemporary financialization, including its international aspects, however, he supplements the concept of finance capital in Hilferding's sense with the companion concept of 'financial capital', meaning 'concentrated money capital operating in financial markets' (Chesnais 2018, 5).

The implication here is that *Finance Capital* is outdated, at best a good guide to what happened at a particular stage in the development of capitalism, and perhaps to some limited elements of the structures of contemporary capitalism, but of little general relevance today. If so, this is pretty damning indictment of a work which argued that finance capital was the 'supreme and most abstract' expression of capital (21), 'the highest stage of the concentration of economic and political power in the hands of the capitalist oligarchy ... the climax of the dictatorship of the magnates of capital', and one, it must be pointed out, which was ripe for transformation into 'the dictatorship of the proletariat' (370)[1]. Considering that *Finance Capital* (hereafter *FC*) was considered in its time 'the fourth volume of *Capital*', and given that it was taken up in good part with a further development of Marx's understanding of money and credit, it also puts a question mark over Marx's understanding of these critical matters. Just how much rides on how we judge Hilferding's, and by extension, Marx's understanding of money and finance and their relevance today becomes clearer when we pause to consider that Marx's critique of Say's Law, the pivot of his understanding of capitalism, rested on pointing to the independent role of money in capitalism and Hilferding concurred.

Against these judgements, which, at best, damn Hilferding and, by extension, Marx, with faint praise, this chapter argues firstly that

[1] All references with only page numbers are to *Finance Capital*.

Hilferding's analysis in *FC* has a wider and deeper resonance. He was neither unaware of the varieties of relationships between money and industrial capital to which Lapavitsas refers, nor of 'financial capital' of the sort that Chesnais distinguished from finance capital. In *FC*, Hilferding contrasted the development of the financial sector in 'free trade England' with that of the 'protectionist countries', particularly Germany and the United States. In the former, short-term, market-based, money-dealing capital focused on trading fictitious capital in a parasitical relation with industrial capital have been dominant. In the latter, the 'model states' of finance capital, the relation between the banks and industry in capitalism's monopoly phase—the phase which takes the socialization of labour to its pinnacle as the socialization of labour within giant firms—is one where banks become the effective planners of vast chunks of the economy, engineering their productive and industrial expansion.

We may note two important things about these contrasts. On the one hand, these contrasts resonate with the many overlapping contrasts between two contrasting models of capitalism and the relation of money and industrial capital in them, that have come to pervade the critical literature on capitalism and financialization in recent decades. Linked to Alexander Gerschenkron's (1962) formative idea of 'late development' (itself, as we shall see, part of the Marxist idea of uneven and combined development), they have acquired wide currency in recent contrasts between 'Anglo-Saxon' or 'Stock Market' capitalism and 'welfare' or 'Rhineland' capitalism of the continental variety (made, for instance, by Dore 2000, and Hutton 1995) and in the proliferating literature on models and varieties capitalism (respectively Coates 2000 and Hall and Soskice 2001).

Free trade England model	Protectionist country finance capital
Market capitalism	Relationship capitalism
Short-term capital	Long-term or 'patient' capital
Stock market capitalism	Welfare capitalism
Anglo-Saxon capitalism	Rhineland capitalism
Wall Street	Main Street
Speculative	Productive
Shareholder capitalism	Stakeholder capitalism

On the other hand, Hilferding's contrasts were also rooted in Marx's own historical understanding (on this Hudson 2010 is very useful) of the two very different models of industry-finance relationships. Both saw the

English model as historically closer to pre-capitalist usury which 'just like trade, exploits a given mode of production from outside. Usury seeks directly to maintain this mode of production, so as to constantly exploit it anew; it is conservative, and simply makes the mode of production more wretched' (Marx 1894/1981, 745). In the long history of capital's emancipation from this form, whose culmination would be a developed credit system subordinated to industrial capital, the English model was stuck at the emancipation of commercial capital, while in the protectionist countries, Hilferding's *FC* brings out clearly, finance capital represented the emancipation of industrial capital from the pre-capitalist form.

A second argument this chapter makes is that, in addition to distinguishing these two models and positing a succession from the more primitive English model to the more productive finance capital, Hilferding, following Marx, also gave a historical account of how and why finance capital was triumphing over the English model. His argument here took the form of a version of the logic of uneven and combined development (UCD), a quarter century before Trotsky coined the expression in the first chapter of his famous *History of the Russian Revolution*. This was not surprising because, as I have argued elsewhere (Desai 2013), while Trotsky may have coined the term, the idea can be traced to Marx and Engels and was inherited and developed by Marxists of later generations. Interestingly, as Marcel van der Linden (2012) has demonstrated, Gerschenkron's idea of late development was rooted in this understanding even though, for political reasons, he neglected to reference it.

Many Marxist scholars are simply unaware of the distinction Hilferding made between the free trade English model and that of the protectionist countries even though it was central to Hilferding's argument in *FC* (see, for instance, the discussion in Brangsch et al. 2018, 256-8). More careful scholars, such as Lapavitsas and Chesnais, do note the distinction. Lapavitsas realizes that 'the future of capitalism for Hilferding lay in Germany, a late developer that relied on her banks, not England' (Lapavitsas 2013, 137), rightly references the aforementioned literatures on varieties of capitalism and realizes that contemporary '[f]inancialization … can be considered as the ascendancy of Anglo-Saxon, market based finance' (Lapavitsas 2013, 137). Chesnais, for his part, not only notes the historical differences between the two models, but also discusses contemporary individual national models very intricately.

However, these discussions fail to note roots of these contrasts in Marx's thinking and Marx's and Hilferding's common conviction that the subordination of credit to the needs of industrial capital, the highest form of the relation of finance to industry that Hilferding labelled finance capital, would also form the basis of a transition to socialism. And they do not ask the historical question as to why, if both Marx and Hilferding considered the productive, long-term, finance capital to be the more advanced model of the bank-industry relation, our economies are, over a century later, laden down with the more backward, parasitical speculative, short-term English model. Nor do they ask what this says about Hilferding's and Marx's understanding of money and credit.

The third argument this chapter makes is that the answer to this question lies in a twist of history itself. In the decades spanning the intensification of imperial competition in the last decades of the nineteenth century and in the Thirty Years' Crisis (1914–1945) that opened with World War I, the dominance Britain enjoyed over world capitalism, thanks to her early industrial lead, was successfully challenged by the productively superior 'protectionist' countries, particularly Germany and the United States. The superiority of the protectionist model of finance capital over the English free trade model of short-term credit was becoming apparent, and most observers expected that the world would now witness a number of competing major powers approximating the more advanced model of finance capital. Pressures towards this were noticeable in England itself.

However, as I have argued (Desai 2013), early twentieth century US policy-making elites, who could already see that Britain's hold on the world economy was waning, had begun nursing the desire to replace Britain as the 'managing segment of the world economy', if not by acquiring a comparable territorial empire, then by making the dollar the world's money to replace sterling and New York its financial centre to replace London (Parrini 1969, 13). The outcome of two world wars, both of which boosted the US economy while destroying those of its capitalist rivals, prepared the ground for it to attempt to realize this ambition. It was never realized, not least because sterling and London's centrality to world money was based on Britain's territorial empire, something which the US did not and, in the historical circumstances prevailing, could not have. However, US was sufficiently powerful that its vain pursuit of this ambition put the world on a decades-long detour during which the US financial system was itself transformed into something more closely resembling the English model. Britain's still archaic financial structure played an important ancillary role in this transformation.

Today, as capitalism's most somnolent and difficult decade and a half is followed by the pandemic that has exacerbated as well as exposed capitalism's productive debility and social injustice, that detour may finally be ending. While the core capitalist world will continue its decay as long as working people do not take matters into their own hands, the rise of China's socialist market economy, with a financial sector more closely resembling the finance capital of *FC*, confirms Marx's and Hilferding's analyses about the historically superior finance-industry relation (Desai 2022) and suggests that Marx's and Hilferding's prognostications of the direction of capitalism's development are relevant again, though in an unanticipated manner.

In what follows, we first outline Hilferding's understanding of money and credit, commercial and industrial, and its relation to Marx's. We then examine Hilferding's understanding of the emergence of finance capital in contrast to the English pattern of bank-industry relations. We go on to show how his understanding of finance capital as the most developed form of capitalism, facilitating a transition to socialism, was foreshadowed by Marx in *Capital*, Vol III. We conclude by outlining the explanation, first indicated in my *Geopolitical Economy* (Desai 2013) of why their expectations were not fulfilled, though it cannot be fully fleshed out here.

Hilferding's Understanding of Money

Hilferding's concept of finance capital emerges from his development of Marx's understanding of money and credit to comprehend new developments since Marx's time. Finance capital was only 'the most mature form' of 'the more elementary forms of money and productive capital' (21) discussed by Marx. This aspect of *FC*, which occupies more than a quarter of the book, has been dismissed or neglected. Schumpeter dismissed it as 'old-fashioned monetary theory' (Schumpeter 1954/1986, 881). Later Marxists, whether Sweezy or Lapavitsas or Chesnais, have ignored this aspect entirely, undoubtedly reflecting, at least in part, the considerable confusion caused among Marxists about Marx's views on money by their belief that Marx has a 'commodity theory of money'.

While that matter deserves much fuller treatment than is possible here, we must establish, at least in outline, Hilferding's claim to be taken seriously both as a sufficiently faithful follower of Marx and as having a sufficiently accurate understanding of the capitalism of his time and its monetary and financial aspects.

The belief that Marx had a commodity theory of money is simply wrong. Indeed, a commodity theory of money is an oxymoron because money is precisely that which is *not* a commodity. This is clear, for instance, from the *opposition* of money and commodities that Marx's critique or Say's Law relies on. Marx not only discusses the dynamics of state-issued paper money and various kinds of credit money, but also demonstrates a complex historical understanding of money as predating capitalism. What he does argue is that capitalism needs to impose on money certain commodity dynamics, hence the intrusion of gold and silver, both of which *are* commodities. (I plan to develop this point in a future work. However, its main elements appear in my discussion of the close relationship between Marx's understanding of money and Karl Polanyi's understanding of money as a fictitious commodity, a relationship in which Ferdinand Tönnies is a critical link. See Desai 2020).

The false impression that Marx had a commodity theory of money has certainly been reinforced by the considerable inroads made into Marxism by the antithetical and anti-Marxist neoclassical economics. It has led to the questioning of Marx's analysis of capitalism as contradictory value production on the grounds that it suffered from a 'Transformation Problem' and to the dismissal of the key crisis mechanisms Marx identified, such as its demand deficits and the Tendency of the Rate of Profit to Fall (as discussed in Desai 2010, 2016 and 2020a). Undoubtedly, neoclassical economics's inability to distinguish between money and commodities, and consequent conflation of capitalist exchange with barter, played a role. As both Marx and Keynes pointed out in different ways when they distinguished between a money and a barter economy in their respective critiques of Says' Law, this distinction is critical to understanding capitalism (on this commonality, and connection, between Marx and Keynes, see Sardoni 1997).

In his brief and measured commentary, Tom Bottomore, who introduced the English translation of *FC*, considers Hilferding's discussion of Marx's theory of money 'the least successful part of the book' (Bottomore 1981, 5). On the other hand, however, in a long footnote, he defends it, at least minimally. While he criticizes Hilferding for 'rejecting the possibility of a pure paper currency' and insisting on 'the need for gold in international transactions', he considers Schumpeter's judgement (mentioned earlier) unjust, not least given the less-than-satisfactory prevailing understanding of money in general. Bottomore called for 'a *social* rather than narrowly economic theory of money' of the sort Marxism is capable of (Bottomore in Hilferding 1910/1981, 372, n).

Undoubtedly, Hilferding's is a complex case. On the one hand, he lucidly defended Marx's value analysis (on which any properly Marxist account of money must be based) against Böhm-Bawerk's attack. Hilferding showed that there was no 'Transformation Problem' and acknowledged the centrality of both capitalism's demand deficits and the downward pressure on profit rates (Hilferding 1904/1949, 156, 170, see also Hilferding 1910/1981, 30-31). On the other hand, however, there are distinct signs that the 'policy of theoretical conciliation' (as Bukharin called it, see Bukharin, 1914/1972, 163) that most Marxists adopted towards neoclassical economics did not leave Hilferding unaffected (Desai 2020b).

So, on the one hand, Hilferding appears prey to the neoclassical fairy tale of the origin of money in commodity exchange: 'Money thus originates spontaneously in the exchange process and requires no other precondition' (36). On the other hand, at other places, Hilferding offers precisely the sort of social theory of money Bottomore believes necessary. In the first part of *FC* he says 'money is a knot in the skein of social relationships in a commodity producing society' (34); a commodity-producing society 'only becomes a society through exchange, which is the only social process it recognises from an economic standpoint' (29). He appears to distinguish money from other commodities, at least as a general equivalent: 'Money is … is differentiated from all other commodities by being the equivalent of all of them' (33); and 'Money is … forced into the unique position of acting as a general equivalent for all the others' (33. Emphasis added). He insists that not gold, a commodity, but coins, symbols authorized by the state, are money. Here Gold is only 'money material' (36). Money needs state authorization and that is why it cannot work in international transactions, where barter indeed reigns through gold payments (33): the state establishes the monetary standard in every country, 'outside of which it becomes unacceptable. On the world market gold and silver are accepted as money, but they are measured in terms of their weight' (36) as commodities. Money in the form of coins of currency is not acceptable.

If Hilferding rejects the possibility of a 'pure paper currency', as Bottomore complains, it is only because he emphasizes, correctly, that a capitalist society requires paper money to be governed by the laws of commodity circulation. For Hilferding (and here he references Marx 1867/1977, 224),

The volume of circulation is extremely variable because, given the velocity of circulation of money, it depends, as we know, upon the sum total of prices. This sum changes constantly, and is affected particularly by the periodic fluctuations within the annual cycle (as when farm products enter the market at harvest time, increasing the sum of prices), and by the cyclical fluctuations of prosperity and depression. Hence, the volume of paper money must always be kept down to the minimum amount of money required for circulation. This minimum can, however, be replaced by paper, and since this amount of money is always necessary for circulation there is no need for gold to appear in its place. The state can therefore make paper money legal tender. (38)

Like the chapter on money in *Capital*, Vol. I, the first part of FC also contains extensive discussions of historical instances in which these laws were violated, exploring the effects of such violations, and how bourgeois theory itself, including Ricardo, struggled to impose some commodity discipline on the behaviour of money.

Hilferding's insistence on gold, a commodity not money, as ideally necessary for international transactions also follows Marx and is entirely correct. Only those who look away from the difficulties the use of both the pound sterling in the 'gold standard' era and the US dollar thereafter in international transactions created and continue to create, those who naturalize an international paper money in a capitalist world, can object. (Keynes was keenly aware of the imperial and managed nature of the gold standard as well as the power dynamics of any dollar standard. See also De Cecco 1984, Desai 2013, 2019 and Desai and Hudson 2021).

The Development of Credit: From Circulation to Production

On this account of money in capitalist societies, Hilferding builds his account of credit money emerging from circulation. Here too he follows Marx (Marx 1867/1977, 232-40). Unlike state paper money, credit money 'has no inflexible minimum which cannot be increased'. Rather it 'grows along with the quantity of commodities and their prices' (65). Credit money 'requires special institutions where obligations can be cancelled out and the residual balances settled and as such institutions develop, so is a greater economy achieved in the use of cash. This work becomes one of the important functions of any developed banking system' (66).

Such a system inevitably has a dual character: while it aids 'the expansion of production [and] the conversion of obligations into monetary obligations', it also leads to 'the growth of fictitious capital' (66).

Credit money is, however, a mere promise to pay, second-grade money, fine while the going is good but not 'when the debtor cannot meet his obligation and the promise to pay becomes worthless. Real money must now take its place' (66). So, in a crisis, credit money dries up, prices decline, sales fall and obligations remain unmet. In such circumstances, 'it is perfectly rational policy to expand the circulation of state paper money or the bank notes of the central bank, the credit of which has not been impaired'. In these circumstances, the superiority of central bank credit, paper money and liquid commodities like bullion makes itself felt.

Industrial credit is, however, very different from commercial credit. It is needed not to circulate commodities but to serve industrial investment and rectify certain problems peculiar to it, particularly the need for sizeable hoards of money that it inevitably entails.

While hoards may occur in circulation and commerce, they are essential to industrial investment, occurring at various points in the cycle of industrial capital, whether because of its length, the need to prevent interruptions in production, depreciation or high initial investments. The need for such inactive capital that earns no profit is a problem, 'a mortal sin from the standpoint of capitalists' (74). So, 'every effort is made to reduce this idleness to a minimum' (79). These investment-related hoards become particularly important in the second industrial revolution with its vastly expanded manufacture of producers' goods such as machinery and larger-scale processing of raw materials in the steel and chemicals industries. These forms of investment needed much more capital than previously.

In this scenario, banks help not only to finance the high capital requirements of investment in the monopoly phase of capitalism but also to reduce the idleness of money. Whereas commercial credit is extended by the seller to the buyer, industrial credit, credit for capital investment, requires the transfer of one person's idle money to someone who can 'employ it as capital'. It involves 'a transfer of money which already exists' and, unlike circulation credit, involves little or no economizing of money or reduction in costs of circulation. 'Its primary purpose is to enable production to expand on the basis of a given supply of money' (88).

The provision of industrial credit changes the relationship between banks and their borrowers for good. Where bank credit is confined to commercial credit, the banks' only interest is the condition of an enterprise, its solvency, at a particular time. They accept bills in which they have confidence, advance money on commodities, and accept as collateral shares which can be sold in the market at prevailing prices. Their particular sphere of action is not that of industrial capital, but rather that of commercial capital, and additionally that of meeting the needs of the stock exchange. Their relation to industry too is concerned less with the production process than with the sales made by industrialists to wholesalers.

By contrast, when banks start providing investment credit, the bank

can no longer limit its interest to the condition of the enterprise and the market at a specific time, but must necessarily concern itself with the *long-range prospects of the enterprise* and the future state of the market. What had once been a momentary interest becomes an enduring one; and the larger the amount of credit supplied and, above all, the larger the proportion of the loan capital turned into fixed capital, the stronger and more abiding will that interest be. (94, emphasis added)

This is the crux of his argument about finance capital. Much of *FC* is taken up with discussions of various aspects of money and banking, including the determination of interest rates, the emergence of promoters' profit (a new form of profit Hilferding identified), the functioning of stock and commodity markets and banks, and the new forms crises take in this new stage of capitalism. However, the main trunk of the argument now leads through his discussion of joint-stock companies, the new, more concentrated, form of industrial organization, to the even greater productive centralization involved in the formation of cartels and trusts under the aegis of finance capital and how they lead to imperialism.

The Development of Industrial Organization: From Private Individual to Private Collective Ownership

The transition from commercial credit to industrial credit as the dominant function of banks took place against the backdrop of the second industrial revolution. Under its force, capitalism went from being organized in smaller enterprises producing light industrial consumer goods to much larger units producing heavy industrial producers' goods and from being

7 FINANCE CAPITAL AND CONTEMPORARY FINANCIALIZATION 181

the individually owned enterprise to the joint-stock company, capable of mobilizing larger quantities of capital. There are several elements here.

Ownership of Money Capital, Control of Industrial Capital and Promoter's Profit

First, joint-stock companies separated ownership from control, leading to 'the liberation of the industrial capitalist from his function as industrial entrepreneur' and to the transformation of the owner into a 'money capitalist' (107). Once the money originally invested was transformed into the elements of productive capital, the shares owned by this new type of owner became merely 'capitalized claims[s] to a share in the yield of the enterprise' (110). Their price

> is not determined as an aliquot part of the total capital invested in the enterprise and therefore a relatively fixed sum, but only by the yield capitalized at the current rate of interest. ... It is a claim to a part of the profit, and therefore its price depends, first, on the volume of profit (which makes it far more variable than it would be if it were part of the price of the elements of production of the industrial capital itself), and second, on the prevailing rate of interest. (110)

Hilferding introduces here the category he considers his original formulation, promoters' profit. Since the prices of shares depend on their yield and the rate of interest, the latter forms the floor below which the price-earnings ratio cannot sink in normal circumstances. Therefore, the prices of shares can be pushed up (and their yields, which move in the opposite direction, can be pushed down) to the point where the yield is equal to the going rate of interest, which is determined quite independently by the supply and demand for money.

In these circumstances, promoter's profit is earned by banks who promote or float the shares companies offer to the public when they exploit the 'the difference between capital which earns the average rate of profit and capital which earns the average rate of interest' (the former usually being higher). It becomes possible because banks can raise the price of the shares up to the point where the yield matches the rate of interest, or just below it. Hilferding considered this a new, *sui generis*, economic category belonging to the era of finance capital. It emerges when to loans, the floatation of shares is added as a key line of bank business. Not only can 'bank

182 R. DESAI

capital ... expand industrial credit by the issue of shares', 'encouraged by the prospect for promoter's profit [it] acquires an ever increasing interest in the financing of enterprises. Other things being equal, promoter's profit depends upon the overall level of profit. Hence bank capital becomes directly interested in industrial profit' even more (190). Thus, promoter's profit plays the key role in binding banks to the fate of industry and its profits in Hilferding's conception of finance capital.

The Transformation of Competition: Concentration and Combination

In the age of the second industrial revolution, there was a great 'inflation' (186) in the amount of capital required for initial investment, lengthening the turnover time of capital, making its transfer from less profitable to more profitable sectors more difficult and making entry costs higher (186). All this contributed to a tendency to monopoly, gumming up the processes of competition and equalization of rates of profit. Although the increasing sophistication allows capital to be mobilized with greater ease (187), this does not offset the obstacles the tendency towards monopoly and the 'centralization of capital' places in the path of the equalization of profit rates. On the contrary, it can increase them by removing 'the limitations which arise from the magnitude of the capitals required for new investment' (188). The competitive struggle now transcends the phase when its chief function was to permit the strong to eliminate the weak through price competition. Now, in the branches of industry affected,

> it is well nigh impossible to equalize the rate of profit by withdrawing capital, and extremely difficult to write off the capital. These highly developed industries are precisely the ones in which competition eliminated the small firms most rapidly, or in which there were no small firms to begin with (as in many branches of the electrical industry). Not only does the large firm predominate, but these large, capital-intensive concerns tend to become more equally matched, as the technical and economic differences which would give some of them a competitive advantage are steadily reduced. The competitive struggle is not one between the strong and the weak, in which the latter are destroyed and the excess capital in that sphere is eliminated, but a struggle between equals, which can remain indecisive for a long time, imposing equal sacrifices on all the contending parties. (189)

Thus, to the depression in the rate of profits among small capitalists is added profit depression in precisely the most advanced sectors with the greatest concentration of capital (191). In these circumstances, the banks, which are themselves undergoing a process of concentration of their own (191), often have interests in the losing as well as the winning side.

> Hence the bank has an overriding interest in eliminating competition among the firms in which it participates. ... In this way the tendency of both bank capital and industrial capital to eliminate competition coincides. At the same time, the increasing power of bank capital enables it to attain this goal even if it is opposed by some enterprises which, on the basis of particularly favourable technical conditions, would perhaps still prefer competition. (191–2)

In addition to such concentration, banks also facilitate another sort of amalgamation of industry: combination. Hilferding conceives this as a process through which enterprises expand to include within themselves their backward or forward linkages. In an argument closely matching Marx's (Marx 1894/1981: 213), Hilferding points out that, given the different conditions of production in the extractive industries such that it is difficult to expand production fast enough, boom times result in price and profit rate rises in extractive industries at the expense of processing industries, which also suffer from raw material shortages just when they need more (193–4). In a depression, the tables are turned: 'the drain of money and the curtailment of production are more marked and produce greater losses in the industries which supply raw materials than in the manufacture of finished goods' (194). This discrepancy gives rise to a tendency to the combination of the two sorts of concerns (195) with the initiative being taken by the disadvantaged enterprise. Such combination is also critical to Hilferding's understanding of the new phase of capitalism: it 'involves a contraction of the social division of labour, at the same time as it gives an impetus to the division of labour within the new integrated concern, extending increasing to management functions as well' (196). In Marx's terms, capitalism, having completed the socialization of labour *among* firms in its competitive phase of coordination through 'free' and competitive markets, moves on to socializing labour within firms through ever more intricate technical divisions of labour coordinated through authoritative and planned allocation *within* firms.

Consortia and Cartels

While concertation and combination, whether involving vertical integration or horizontal integration, may take place for technical as well as economic reasons, and involve integration at the ownership level, the formation of cartels and consortia involves 'concentration of production without any concentration of ownership' (199). Banks are also involved in these as they can make their credit more secure and offer greater opportunities for further business, whether in the loan or share floatation departments (199). Cartels, syndicates and trusts, are the organizational forms of concentrated production without concentrated ownership, each representing a greater degree of central control than the previous. The purpose of these forms of productive concentration is the same as the earlier concentration through merger: to restrict competition. They achieve this through agreements on prices and through, where necessary, the elimination of low-productivity plant.

Tendencies Towards National and Imperial Economies

The cartelization of capitalism makes it at once more national and more imperialist. Whereas the likes of List and Carey had supposed that the protectionism necessary for countries to industrialize in the face of British domination of world markets would no longer be necessary once industry in the protectionist country became competitive, Hilferding argues, things turned out quite differently. 'Today it is just the most powerful industries, with a high export potential, whose competitiveness on the world market is beyond doubt and which, according to the old theory, should have no further interest in protective tariffs, which support high tariffs' (307).

This apparently paradoxical outcome is the result of 'a complete realignment of interests with respect to commercial policy' (304). With industrial development, the landowners stop exporting their products and become protectionist, making common cause with protectionist industry and with banks associated with it. Protection itself aids cartelization as does the fact that in countries like Germany, industry did not develop 'so to speak organically and gradually from small beginnings' as in England (305). So the seeds of the transformation of the old 'educational tariffs' of the List variety into the new commercial policy were sowed early on: 'The victory of protectionism in 1879 ... marked the beginning of a change in the function of the tariff from an 'educational' tariff to a protective tariff for cartels' (305).

Not only did protection make it easier to form cartels by keeping foreign competition out, but it also permitted cartelized industry to exploit tariffs in a new way, by keeping domestic prices high and making an extra profit on them by artificially restricting domestic supply (308). For instance, coal and iron producers can appropriate extra profits to industries that use their products by raising prices.

> This extra profit no longer originates in the surplus value produced by the workers employed by the cartels; nor is it a deduction from the profit of the other non-cartelized industries. It is a tribute exacted from the entire body of domestic consumers, and its incidence on the various strata of consumers—whether, and to what extent, it is a deduction from ground rent, from profit, or from wages—depends, as with any other indirect taxes imposed on industrial raw materials or consumer goods, upon the real power relations and upon the nature of the article which is made more expensive by the cartel tariff. (308)

If such domestic price increases reduce the size of the domestic markets, there is always the world market where, thanks again to the new functionality of protection for cartelized industry, cartelized industries can even use the extra profit made domestically to undersell their competitors.

If in the early development of capitalism, the unification of national territory was important, if the development of capitalism had led to the division of the world market into 'distinct economic territories of nation-states' (311), now, with the advance of industry and its cartelization, the expansion of this territory, under the command of a given state, that is to say, imperialism, becomes urgent. '[C]artelization greatly enhances the direct importance of the size of the economic territory for the level of profit (313)' resulting in 'the desire to extend as much as possible the economic territory, surrounded by a wall of protective tariffs'. For now, in addition to the export of goods, the export of capital, 'the export of value ... intended to breed surplus value' (314) whether in 'interest bearing' or 'profit yielding' (315) forms, one of whose purposes is to 'cancel out' 'the falling rate of profit' (314), takes on greater importance. Since all advanced capitalists compete to export capital, to finance capital, free trade appears superfluous and harmful; and it seeks to overcome the restriction of productivity resulting from the contraction of the economic territory [through protection], not by conversion to free trade, but by expanding its own economic territory and promoting the export of capital. (314)

Typically, capital is exported to areas where due to the cheapness of labour and/or raw materials, a higher rate of profit can be expected. Where such price structures restrict the size of the domestic market, loans can be employed to enlarge it.

Hilferding's detailed description of the competitive struggle among the advanced countries to expand their territories, the methods used, the economic effects on the colonies, the inevitable political reaction to them in the form of the rise of independence movements among them, the different situation of England and the new imperialist countries, and the unfolding of the logic of uneven and combined development between them is remarkably accurate. It predicts the coming World War: as England also becomes protectionist:

> The disparity which exists between the development of German capitalism and the relatively small size of its economic territory will ... be greatly increased. ...Germany has no colonial possessions worth mentioning, whereas not only its strongest competitors, England and the United States (for which an entire continent serves as a kind of economic colony), but also the smaller powers such as France, Belgium and Holland have considerable colonial possessions, and its future competitor, Russia, also possesses a vastly larger economic territory. This is a situation which is bound to intensify greatly the conflict between Germany and England and their respective satellites, and to lead towards a solution by force. (331)

The Historical Specificity of Finance Capital

Hilferding's understanding of finance capital, and the specificity of the relation between banks and industry it denotes, is built on the distinction between the antiquated English model and the protectionist countries. In understanding this distinction and its contemporary relevance, we need to understand exactly what Hilferding meant by the domination of finance. Rather than money capital parasitically subordinating industrial capital, the concept of finance capital means, on the one hand, that

7 FINANCE CAPITAL AND CONTEMPORARY FINANCIALIZATION 187

with the increasing concentration of property, the owners of the fictitious capital which gives power over the banks, and the owners of the capital which gives power over industry, become increasingly the same people. As we have seen, this is all the more so as the large banks increasingly acquire the power to dispose over fictitious capital. (225)

On the other hand, 'this does not mean that the magnates of industry also become dependent on banking magnates'. Rather, 'the finance capitalist, increasingly concentrates his control over the whole national capital ... Personal connections also play an important role here'. (225)

Here, Hilferding is developing an important point first made by Marx. Though financial capital is older than industrial capital, though, therefore, early industrial capital encounters an already existing finance capital focused on usury, Marx anticipated that capitalism's maturation would lead to the 'subordination of interest-bearing capital to the conditions and requirements of modern industry', principally through the 'transformed figure of the borrower': no longer a supplicant in financial straits but a capitalist to whom money is lent 'in the expectation that he ... will use [it] to appropriate unpaid labour' (Marx 1894/1981:735). Whereas the initial states of this process of subordination had led to calls for using 'violence (the State) ... against interest-bearing capital [to effect] a compulsory reduction of interest rates', mature industrial capital, Marx opined, would achieve it much more thoroughly and effectively through 'the creation of a procedure specific to itself—the *credit system* [which] is its own creation and is *itself a form of industrial capital* which begins with manufacture and develops further with large scale industry'. When it first emerged, therefore, this more modern credit system, as a creature of industrial capital, took a '*polemical form* directed against old-fashioned usurers' (Marx 1979: 468-9. Emphasis added).

In line with this understanding, Hilferding says

> At the outset of capitalist production money capital, in the form of usurers' and merchants' capital, plays a significant role in the accumulation of capital as well as in the transformation of handicraft production into capitalism. But there then arises a resistance of 'productive' capital, i.e. of the profit-earning capitalists—that is, of commerce and industry—against the interest-earning capitalists. Usurer's capital becomes subordinated to industrial capital. As money-dealing capital it performs the functions of money which industry and commerce would otherwise have had to carry out themselves in the

188 R. DESAI

> process of transformation of their commodities. As bank capital it arranges credit operations among the productive capitalists. (226)

Modern bank capital arose from the 'resistance of "productive" capital, i.e. of the profit-earning capitalists ... against the interest-earning capitalists'. Though '[t]he power of the banks increases and they become founders and eventually rulers of industry, whose profits they seize for themselves as finance capital, just as formerly the old usurer seized, in the form of "interest", the produce of the peasants and the ground rent of the lord of the manor', the relationship never reverts to pre-capitalist forms (95). Instead, there is a further development that results in finance capital which 'appropriates to itself the fruits of social production at an infinitely higher stage of economic development' (226). Such appropriation is not parasitical. On the contrary, it is a higher, more developed, form of capital which seeks constantly to throw itself into production to expand productive accumulation.

The contrast between the early subordination of industry to finance and the later reversal of this relationship overlapped with another, that between England and the 'protectionist countries' that were models of finance capital.

THE GEOGRAPHICAL SPECIFICITY OF FINANCE CAPITAL

Throughout *FC*, Hilferding contrasts English development with that of the protectionist countries: its free trade policy and ideology versus the protectionism of the others; its less elastic monetary system; its very different banking structures; its different, less monopolized and cartelized industrial structure; and, of course, its far larger empire (see particularly, 301–10). The contrast was also a historical one, having to do with the earlier industrialization of England and its consequences for the other countries: English free trade was a result of England's early lead and the decades of industrial supremacy from which the later industrializers had to protect their industry.

In Hilferding's account of the uneven and combined development of capitalism, by the era of finance capital, England was suffering from the disadvantages of her early lead. Contrasting the organizational superiority of German industry over English, Hilferding says,

English industry developed so to speak organically and gradually from small beginnings to its later greatness. The factory was an outgrowth of co-operation (simple division of labour) and manufacture, which first developed principally in the textile industry, an industry which required comparatively little capital. Organizationally it remained, for the most part, at the stage of individual ownership; the individual capitalist rather than the joint-stock company predominated, and capitalist wealth remained in the hands of individual industrial capitalists. (305)

Not only is the English industry less concentrated, but also the relationship of banking to industry is quite different. Whereas in the protectionist countries, bank capital became increasingly important in the financing of industry by the late nineteenth century, laying the basis for the emergence of finance capital, in England

There emerged gradually, but at an increasing pace, a class of wealthy industrial entrepreneurs, owning large capital resources, whose property consisted of their productive plant. Later on, when joint-stock companies acquired greater importance, especially with the development of large transport undertakings, it was mainly these large industrialists who became shareholders. It was industrial capital, in terms of both its origin and its ownership, which was invested in these companies. (305-6)

Not only did industrial and bank capital remain thus separated, like industrial capital, 'bank capital—and notably the capital used in share issuing activities—remained exclusively in the hands of individual capitalists' (306).

In the protectionist countries, as capitalism developed, so too did bank deposits and lending, leading to an increase in 'the dependence of industry upon the banks' (224). Whereas banks had earlier attracted deposits by paying interest from earnings derived from 'speculation and circulation', as capitalism developed, '[w]ith the increase in the available funds on one side, *and the diminishing importance of speculation and trade on the other*, they were bound to be transformed more and more into industrial capital' (224). This situation contrasted with that of England. Whereas in the protectionist countries, bank direction of deposited funds into production kept up a relatively healthy rate of interest, in England, 'the *deposit banks only furnish credit for commerce*, and consequently the rate of interest on deposits is minimal'. In England, 'deposits are continually withdrawn for investment in industry by the purchase of shares', meaning that, 'so far as industry is concerned it involves *less dependence on bank capital in England as compared with Germany'* (224–5. Emphasis added). In the English financial structure,

> the joint-stock banks only provided circulation credit and so acquired little influence upon industry. The bankers who specialized in share issues had equally little influence, since as a result of their activities they had ceased to be bankers and had become, at least to some extent, industrialists themselves. This predominance of capital accumulation in the hands of individual capitalists, one of the earlier and, as it were, organic features of English capitalism, was lacking both on the continent and in the United States. (306)

Moreover, England's vast empire made its own contribution to this structure of English capitalism: 'the large sums flowing in from the colonies, especially India, and from the exploitation of England's trade monopoly, were also accumulated in the hands of individual capitalists' (306), a feature lacking in Germany or the US.

England also had a very different capital export profile. In early capitalism, when England dominated, most international credit was commercial. British banks extended credit to purchasers of British products. In the new phase, however, while British 'credit is not provided exclusively or mainly in the form of commercial credit, but for capital investment', this credit remains in the form of interest-bearing capital; it does not partake in profits. Such investment, for instance when England supplies investment credit by investing in US railway bonds, 'has a negligible influence on the American railway barons' (325). Though Hilferding detects some movement in England towards a more protectionist model, in the main, England remains set in its old ways, supplying chiefly commercial credit or merely interest-bearing investment credit.

By contrast, capital exports from the protectionist countries follow the logic of finance capital already described. Moreover, while the logic may be contrasted, they are also connected.

> [W]e see the strongest drive towards the export of industrial capital in those countries which have the most advanced organization of industry, namely, Germany and the United States. This explains the peculiar circumstance that these countries on the one hand export capital, *and on the other hand also*

import a part of the capital required for their own economies from abroad. They export primarily industrial capital and so expand their own industry, while obtaining their working capital, to some extent, in the *form of loan capital from countries with a slower rate of industrial development but greater accumulated capital wealth.* In this way they not only gain from the difference between the industrial profit which they make in foreign markets and the much lower rate of interest which they have to pay on the capital borrowed in England or France, but also ensure, through this kind of capital export, the more rapid growth of their own industry. Thus the United States exports industrial capital to South America on a very large scale, while at the same time importing loan capital from England, Holland, France, etc., in the form of bonds and debentures, as working capital for its own industry. (326. Emphasis added)

Here, England, Holland and France are the rentier nations while the protectionist countries are the productive ones. While the former earn a lower rate of interest, the latter earn a higher rate of profit.

Finance capital drives the expansion of production instead of squeezing it. Earlier banks supplied only short-term commercial credit, as City of London banks still did in England. The continental bank, however, financed production. As such, it had to 'necessarily concern itself with the long-range prospects of the enterprise and the future state of the market'. The 'momentary interest' in firms to which banks offered commercial credit was displaced by 'an enduring one' in firms to which they offered industrial credit and 'the larger the amount of credit supplied and, above all, the larger the proportion of the loan capital turned into fixed capital, the stronger and more abiding will that interest be' (Hilferding 1910/1981: 95). Such a bank may remain 'the more powerful party' with access to 'capital in its liquid, readily available, form', but it focuses on long-term productive investment (95).

FINANCE CAPITAL AND SOCIALISM

Hilferding has been criticized, even ridiculed, for arguing that finance capital set the stage for socialism through such observations as 'taking possession of six large Berlin banks' would constitute an important step in the

192   R. DESAI

transition to socialism (368. see, for instance, Brangsch, 256). Counter-intuitive as such statements may appear in our age of financialization when financial institutions have wreaked such havoc on our economies, increased inequality, resulted in periodic devastating crises and strangulated production, it should now be clear that this is only because we fail to distinguish between the two models that Hilferding so clearly contrasted. When speaking of finance capital laying the foundations for socialism, Hilferding was referring to finance capital proper, the form it took in the protectionist countries, with its vested interest in the productive well-being of industry, rather than the English model with its more attenuated relationship to industry. Hilferding referred, after all, to six large Berlin banks, not six large London banks. His argument was only a further development of Marx's.

In chapter 27 of *Capital* Vol. III, Marx had seen the emergence of joint-stock companies as a huge advance in the socialization of capital. In joint-stock companies, formerly individual private capital

> receives the form of social capital (capital of directly associated individuals) in contrast to private capital, and its enterprises appear as social enterprises as opposed to private ones. This is the abolition of capital and private property within the confines of the capitalist mode of production itself. (Marx 1894/1981, 567)

Now the capitalist is replaced on the one hand by the manager paid for a particular kind of skilled labour and on the other by a 'mere money capitalist' whose profit 'is still drawn only in the form of interest, i.e. as a mere reward for capital ownership which is now completely separated from its function in the actual production process' (567–8). The result is a historical, rather than merely conceptual, clarification: profit, it is now clear, is

> simply the appropriation of other people's surplus labour, arising from the transformation of means of production into capital; i.e. from their estrangement vis-à-vis the actual producer; from their opposition, as the property of another, vis-à-vis all individuals really active in production from the manager down to the lowest day-labourer. (Marx 1894/1981, 568)

Such 'capitalist production in its highest development' is a

> necessary point of transition towards the transformation of capital back into the property of the producers, though no longer as the private property of

individual producers but rather as their property as associated producers, as directly social property. It is furthermore a point of transition towards the transformation of all functions formerly bound up with capital ownership in the reproduction process into simple functions of the associated producers, into social functions. (Marx 1894/1981, 568)

Engels's observation at this point that tendencies towards cartelization and towards concentrating 'the entire production of the branch of industry in question into *one* big joint-stock company with a unified management' prepared 'in the most pleasing fashion its future expropriation by society as a whole, by the nation' (Marx 1894/1981, 569) is hardly different from Hilferding's proposition about the six large Berlin banks.

Marx continues by observing that '[t]his is the abolition of the capitalist mode of production within the capitalist mode itself ... which presents itself *prima facie* as a mere point of transition to a new form of production' (Marx 1894/1981, 569). Increasing monopoly leads to rising state intervention and 'a new financial aristocracy' with all the speculation and swindling it involves. This, he says, is 'private production unchecked by private ownership' (Marx 1894/1981, 569). The realities of capitalism are exposed: saving can no longer pose as the origin of capitalism when the speculator demands that '*others* should save for him'; abstinence goes by the wayside when luxury 'becomes a means of credit' (Marx 1894/1981, 570). Capitalism, which begins in expropriation comes full circle when the expropriation of small and medium and even some large enterprises by the giant ones, greatly aided by the credit system, lays the foundation of the expropriation of the few remaining owners. The credit system not only accelerates capitalist development, but also accelerates crises and the dissolution of capitalism itself. He concludes:

> The credit system has a dual character immanent in it: on the one hand it develops the motive of capitalist production, enrichment by the exploitation of others' labour, into the purest and most colossal system of gambling and swindling, and restricts ever more the already small number of exploiters of social wealth; on the other hand however, it constitutes the form of transition towards a new mode of production. It is this dual character that gives the principal spokesman for credit, from Law through Issac Péreire, their nicely mixed character of swindler and prophet. (Marx 1894/1981, 572-3. Emphasis added)

Hilferding's views on finance capital representing a stage towards the development of socialism are entirely in line with this vision of Marx.

> The socializing function of finance capital facilitates enormously the task of overcoming capitalism. Once finance capital has brought the most important branches of production under its control, it is enough for society, through its conscious executive organ—the state conquered by the working class—to seize finance capital in order to gain immediate control of these branches of production. Since all other branches of production depend upon these, control of large-scale industry already provides the most effective form of social control even without any further socialization. A society which has control over coal mining, the iron and steel industry, the machine tool, electricity, and chemical industries, and runs the transport system, is able, by virtue of its control of these most important spheres of production, to determine the distribution of raw materials to other industries and the transport of their products. Even today, taking possession of six large Berlin banks would mean taking possession of the most important spheres of large-scale industry, and would greatly facilitate the initial phases of socialist policy during the transition period, when capitalist accounting might still prove useful. (Hilferding, 1910/1981, 367-8)

Indeed, Hilferding adds:

> There is no need at all to extend the process of expropriation to the great bulk of peasant farms and small businesses, because as a result of the seizure of large-scale industry, upon which they have long been dependent, they would be indirectly socialized just as industry is directly socialized. (Hilferding, 1910/1981, 368)

If this view appears to us a strange, perhaps even reactionary, it is because the development of the financial sector took an opposite turn to the one anticipated by Marx and Hilferding. The finance capital of the protectionist countries, with its focus on organizing and expanding production through long-term investment and its development of the contradictions of capitalism to their highest form, did not come to dominate. Instead, it was the more speculative, short-term financial model of England, divorced from production, that dominates the world today, though a variety of other more and less different national financial systems also exist which manage their relationship with this worldwide financial system. We conclude this chapter by reflecting on why this happened.

The Triumph of the English Model and Beyond

The explanation is necessarily a historical, rather than a 'theoretical', one and can only be outlined here.

The age of competing imperialisms, to understanding which *FC* is such a great aid, with its fast-growing contender nations challenging Britain's early industrial supremacy had, as I have argued (Desai 2013), already inaugurated the age of multipolarity in the late nineteenth century. However, whereas most observers anticipated a world of competing powers, the US began nursing a rather more vainglorious ambition—to 'build an international commercial system which would allow American business to topple and replace British business interest as the *managing component of the world economy*' and to 'create new institutional means of performing the politically stabilising task which Great Britain alone had performed before 1914' (Parrini 1969: 1, emphasis added). This ambition could not extend to acquiring a territorial empire to match Britain's; that would involve taking on powerful established empires and rising nationalisms. Therefore, the US confined itself to seeking to make the dollar the world's money to replace the pound sterling and New York its financial centre, to replace London.

This aim was never achieved, nor could it be. Sterling's world role had rested, in any case, on Britain's empire: the key to the operation of the gold standard was Britain's ability to supply the world with sterling liquidity by investing the surpluses it drew from its non-settler colonies, particularly India, to its white-settler colonies and its former colony, the US, both facts pointed to by Hilferding. Without such surpluses, the dollar's world role relied on providing liquidity through current account deficits and this method of providing liquidity was inherently unstable. It was subject to the Triffin Dilemma: the greater the deficits, and thus the liquidity provision, the greater the downward pressure on the dollar's value. This downward pressure originally took the form of the outflow of gold to the point where the US was forced to close the gold window in 1971.

What happened thereafter is deeply connected with contemporary financialization. For, after 1971, the US counteracted the Triffin Dilemma through a series of measures aimed at expanding purely financial dollar-denominated transactions which increased demand for dollars, beginning with the recycling of OPEC oil surpluses in the 1970s and culminating in the blowing of successive financial bubbles, of which the stock market bubble that burst in 2000 and the housing and credit bubble that burst in

2008 were the most recent. Indeed, I have argued that, since 1971, the dollar's world role has been reliant on a series of ever-greater dollar-denominated financializations or asset bubbles.

These financializations required financial structures vastly different from the ones Hilferding described. This transformation was slow and, until quite recently, incomplete. The US lifted capital controls in the 1970s to facilitate them. However, not only had the US financial sector conformed to the finance capital model described by Hilferding in the early twentieth century, Depression-era legislation had turned into one of the most regulated in the world. Its deregulation did not begin until the 1970s and initially remained slow. It accelerated once Alan Greenspan became Chairman of the Federal Reserve in 1987 though the repeal of most important Depression-era regulation, the Glass Steagall Act, had to wait until 1999. In the intervening three decades or so, London, which was and remains one of the most deregulated financial environments in the world, greatly aided processes of dollar-denominated financialization. It was a role which London gratefully accepted, sterling having lost its former position, dollar-denominated transactions became the financial center's new lifeline (see Ingham 1984, Norfield 2016).

London's presence on the periphery of Europe, meanwhile, also played a role in the undermining of the continental model of finance capital. In the early post-war decades, it continued to characterize European capitalism, becoming the core of the famed 'Rhineland Model'. However, a combination of factors including German unification and the advance of European monetary integration set European finance on the road to Western-style deregulation. The City of London enabled the participation of European financial institutions in the US housing and credit bubbles and outside the US and the UK; they were the chief victims when the bubble burst in 2008. The weakening of the European financial sector laid the groundwork for the 2010 Eurozone crisis.

The dollar never stably served the world as its money (Desai 2013) and current trends towards dedollarization amid advancing multipolarity, may well mark the end of the long detour that vain US aspirations to emulating British nineteenth-century dominance had led the capitalist world to. While the end of the detour will not put world history back where it was before the detour began, while, therefore, Hilferding's and Marx's expectations of the relationship between banks and industry will be unlikely to reacquire their former relevance, they can acquire a new one as we seek to make sense of the financialized capitalisms we are left with, particularly when contrasted with China's market socialism, with its greater proximity to both finance capital and socialism.

References

Bottomore, Tom. 1981. 'Introduction to the Translation' in Rudolf Hilferding 1910/1981.

Brangsch, Lutz et al. 2018. 'Marx, Hilferding and Finance Capital' in Walter Baier et al (eds) *Transform! Europe 2018: Integration, Disintegration, Nationalism.* London: Merlin Press, pp. 245-260.

Brenner, Robert. 2020. Escalating Plunder. *New Left Review* II (123): 2–18.

Bukharin, Nicolai. 1914/1972. *The Economic Theory of the Leisure Class.* New York: Monthly Review Press.

Chesnais, François. 2018. *Finance Capital Today: Corporations and Banks in the Lasting Global Slump.* Leiden: Brill.

Coates, David. 2000. *Models of Capitalism.* Oxford: Polity.

De Cecco, Marcello. 1984. *The International Gold Standard: Money and Empire.* 2nd ed. London: Pinter.

Desai, Radhika. 2010. Consumption Demand in Marx and in the Current Crisis. *Research in Political Economy* 26: 101–141.

———. 2013. *Geopolitical Economy: After US Hegemony, Globalization and Empire.* London: Pluto Press.

———. 2016. The Value of History and the History of Value. In *The Great Meltdown of 2008: Systemic, Conjunctural or Policy-created?* ed. Turan Subasat. Cheltenham, UK and Northampton, MA, USA: Edward Elgar Publishing.

———. 2019. C2019. 'The Past and Future of the International Monetary System', ЭКОНОМИЧЕСКОЕ ВОЗРОЖДЕНИЕ РОССИИ 3 (61) 2019 периодическое научное Издание, *EKONOMICHESKOYe VOZROZHDENIYe ROSSII* 3 (61) 2019 periodicheskoye nauchnoye Izdaniye, pp. 35-54

———. 2020a. Commodified Money and Crustacean Nations. In , ed. Radhika Desai and Kari Polanyi Levitt. *The Enduring Legacy of Karl Polanyi,* Manchester University Press.

———. 2020b. 'Marx's Critical Political Economy, 'Marxist Economics' and Actually Occurring Revolutions against Capitalism' in Radhika Desai and Henry Heller (eds) *Revolutions,* a Special Issue of *Third World Quarterly.*

———. 2022. China's Finance and Africa's Economic and Monetary Sovereignty. In *The Quest for Economic and Monetary Sovereignty in 21st Century Africa,* ed. Ndongo Samba Sylla, Kai Koddenbrock, Fadhel Kaboub, Maha Ben Gadha, and Ines Mahmoud. London: Pluto Press.

Desai, Radhika, and Michael Hudson. 2021. Beyond Dollar Creditocracy: A Geopolitical Economy. *Real World Economic Review* 97: 1. https://rwer.wordpress.com/2021/09/23/.

Dore, Ronald. 2000. *Stock Market Capitalism versus Welfare Capitalism*. Oxford: Oxford University Press.

Gerschenkron, Alexander. 1962. *Economic Backwardness in Historical Perspective: A Book of Essays*. Harvard University Press.

Hall, Peter, and David Soskice. 2001. *Varieties of Capitalism: The Institutional Foundation of Comparative Advantage*. Oxford: Oxford University Press.

Hilferding, Rudolf. 1904/1949. *Bohm-Bawerk's Criticism of Marx* in Paul Sweezy, *Karl Marx and the Close of his System* by Eugen von Böhm-Bawerk and *Bohm-Bawerk's Criticism of Marx by Rudolf Hilferding*, London: The Merlin Press.

———. 1910/1981. *Finance Capital: A Study of the Latest Phase of Capitalist Development*. Edited with an Introduction by Tom Bottomore, Tr. Morris Watnick and Sam Gordon London: Routledge.

Hudson, Michael. 2010. From Marx to Goldman Sachs: The Fictions of Fictitious Capital, and the Financialization of Industry. *Critique* 38 (3): 419–444.

Hutton, W. 1995. *The State We're In*. Jonathan Cape.

Ingham, Geoffrey K. 1984. *Capitalism Divided?: The City and Industry in British Social Development*. Basingstoke: Macmillan.

Lapavitsas, Costas. 2013. *Profiting without Producing: How Finance Exploits us All*. London: Verso.

van der Linden, Marcel. 2012. Gerschenkron's Secret: A Research Note. *Critique: Journal of Socialist Theory* 40 (4): 553–562.

Marx, Karl. 1867/1977. *Capital (Vol. I)*. London: Penguin.

———. 1894/1981. *Capital (Vol. III)*. London: Penguin.

———. 1979. *Theories of Surplus Value. Volume III*. London: Lawrence and Wishart.

Norfield, Tony. 2016. *The City: London and the Global Power of Finance*. London: Verso.

Parrini, Carl P. 1969. *Heir to Empire: United States Economic Diplomacy, 1916-1923*.

Sardoni, C. 1997. Keynes and Marx. In *A 'Second Edition' of The General Theory*, ed. G.C. Harcourt and P. Riach. London: Routledge.

Schumpeter, Joseph. 1954/1986. *A History of Economic Analysis*. London: Routledge.

CHAPTER 8

Finance Capital and Militarism as Pillars of Contemporary Capitalism

Claude Serfati

Introduction

This chapter addresses two pillars of theories of imperialism: finance capital and militarism and their place in contemporary capitalism. It looks to two major contributors to the debate on these two issues. Rudolf Hilferding, in his eponymous book, gave the term *finance capital* an incredible popularity. Rosa Luxemburg pioneered ideas on the role of militarism in capitalism. In the Marxist community, a lip service is at best given to her analysis of militarism, while her book *The Accumulation of Capital* has been widely criticised for 'underconsumptionism', a quasi-insult for defenders of a Marxist dogma (an expression she would have considered an oxymoron) (for an overview of the early reception of her book among Marxists, see Gaido and Quiroga 2013).

C. Serfati (✉)
Institut de Recherche Économique et Sociale, Paris, France

CEMOTEV, University of Versailles-Saint-Quentin-en-Yvelines, Versailles, France
e-mail: claude.serfati@uvsq.fr

© The Author(s), under exclusive license to Springer Nature Switzerland AG 2023
J. Dellheim, F. O. Wolf (eds.), *Rudolf Hilferding*, Luxemburg International Studies in Political Economy,
https://doi.org/10.1007/978-3-031-08096-8_8

Both Hilferding and Luxemburg were interested in deciphering the dynamics of capitalism of their time and its transformation into imperialism. The subtitle of Luxemburg's book often omitted is 'A Contribution to the Economic Explanation of Imperialism', while Hilferding's book is subtitled 'A Study of the Latest Phase of Capitalist Development'. But their political evolution and theoretical analysis diverged.

In order to substantiate the fact that finance capital and militarism are core components of contemporary capitalism, this chapter proceeds as follows. The first part explores the double face of capital as social relations, embodied by what I will refer to as capital-in-function (productive capital) and as capital-property. As the importance of this duality of capital is hardly studied in Marxist literature, this chapter takes as a starting point this seminal distinction established by Marx to propose a definition of finance capital. Part 2 analyses the concept of finance capital put forward by Hilferding. Hilferding refers to the duality of capital when he analyses the growth of joint-stock companies and stock markets. He underlines the 'rationalising' role of banks and cartels, in part attributable to finance capital, defined as 'capital in money form which is actually transformed in this way into industrial capital' (Hilferding 1910/1981, p. 225). Then, after a critical reading of Hilferding's definition, based on Marx's analysis of finance, Part 2 presents an alternative definition of finance capital as the intertwining of concentrated (or monopoly) industrial, merchant, real estate, land and bank capital under the control of capital-property (Serfati 2018). It concludes with some hypotheses on the consolidation in present-day capitalism of the power of finance capital and revenue-bearing capital, and why the latter permanently tends to overwhelm 'capital-in-function'. Part 3 bears on the relationships between finance capital and militarism. It highlights the divergences between Hilferding and Luxemburg on this issue, provides some historical evidence of the links between finance capital and militarism and concludes with a discussion of the relevance of Luxemburg's analysis for contemporary capitalism.

THE DOUBLE FACE OF CAPITAL AS SOCIAL RELATIONS

Indeed, Marx never used the term finance capital, and he employed different wordings according to what he wanted to emphasise. In some instances, he speaks of 'moneyed capital in the sense of interest-bearing capital' (Marx 1894/1981, p. 594), and elsewhere he focuses his attention on the 'money-dealing capital' which initially corresponds to 'purely technical movements' which money undergoes in the circulation process of industrial capital (ibid., p. 431). More importantly, Marx observes the two components of the credit system as it develops in capitalism. One observation of his is that when money functions as a means of payment, 'With the development of trade and the capitalist mode of production, which produces only for circulation, this spontaneous basis for the credit system is expanded, generalized and elaborated' (ibid., p. 525). 'Alongside this money-dealing, the other side of the credit system also develops, the management of interest-bearing capital or money capital as the special function of the money-dealers' (ibid., p. 528), referring mainly to banks which centralise money capital and transform it into loanable capital.

The development of capitalism facilitated osmotic relationships between these two components of the 'system of credit'—firstly, 'commercial' credit based on the function of money as a means of payment and, secondly, banks' credit (see Chesnais (2016), Chap. 3, for a discussion of the differences and interactions between the two). Moreover, the development of 'securitisation', which is not new but accelerated during the 1990s and 2000s, increased the degree of interdependence between the 'system of credit' as described by Marx and the stock markets (shares and bonds), which created integrated global financial markets. All the titles circulating in the system of credit and stock markets form fictitious capital (transformation of these property titles into capital through capitalisation or discounting streams of future payments attached to financial assets). As Marx states clearly when he analyses the component parts of banking capital, 'The greater portion of this "money-capital" [with the exception of the reserve fund] is purely fictitious' (Marx 1894/1981, p. 601). Lapavitsas' claim is quite distinct from this, stating that 'loanable capital itself is anything but fictitious [because] it emerges from investment and consumption processes attached to capitalist accumulation' (2010, p. 11). In our view, the fictitious character of any capital is not due to its greater or lesser distance from the real process of production but to the capacity of a property title to generate a revenue, that is, to the function as capital for its holder.

It is widely accepted amongst scholars familiar with Marx's writings that capital is not a 'thing'—a productive equipment or a financial title—but a system of exploitative social relations based on private ownership of the means of production and the 'free' availability of a workforce with the purpose of accumulating wealth in its general equivalent form of money. Capital as a social relation is incarnated in 'real life' in both capital-property and 'capital-in-function' which is located in the process of production. It thus possesses a double face.

The double face of capital and the relationships between capital-property and capital-in-function (or productive capital) are meticulously analysed by Marx in *Capital* but also in *Theories on surplus value*. He sums up his method as follows:

> The starting-point of capital is the commodity owner, the owner of money, in short, the capitalist. Since in the case of capital both starting-point and point of return coincide, it returns to the capitalist. But the capitalist exists here in a dual form, as the owner of capital and as the industrial capitalist who really converts money into capital. (Marx 1861–1863/1989, p. 454)

Here, it is not a question of existence of two capitalists, but one ('the') capitalist. This duality exists because capitalism is not just a mode of production, but a system of exploitative social relations. Furthermore:

> The **social form** of capital—that it is property—devolves on the latter part; on the former part devolves the economic function of capital, its function in the labour process'. (Marx 1861–1863/1989, p. 496, my emphasis)

Hence, Marx's critique of Proudhon, stating

> that capital should not be loaned out and should bear no interest [...] amounts at bottom to no more than the demand [...] that *capital* should *not exist as capital* (italics in the text). (Ibid.)

From a theoretical perspective, we conclude that the revenues gained from the ownership of capital-property's titles cannot be interpreted, as most Marxist scholars claim, as a distributional process that only occurs when capital is loaned by 'moneyed capitalist'—in contemporary capitalism by banks and financial investors—to non-financial institutions. The *quantitative* division of the total profit into profit of enterprise for the capital employed productively and interest for 'capital as such, leaving aside the production process', transforms into a *qualitative* division, a division based on two different agents: industrial enterprises and the banks and other financial institutions (Marx 1894/1981, p. 501). The underlying reason is that capitalism is a social system based on private ownership of the means of production, and the latter which is materialised in financial titles gives their holders the right to appropriate value. Revenues accruing to capital-property reflect this requirement.

The existence of joint-stock companies (JSC) and the corollary development of stock markets reinforce, but do not create, the separation between capital-property and capital-in-function. The process is called 'ossification' by Marx—in modern language, JSCs represent an 'institutionalisation' of the genuine separation of both forms of capital. It is not the stock market which creates this institutionalisation; it works the other way around. The development of stock markets outside of the production process results from the double face of capital. As capital-property's titles could circulate *outside* the production process on specific markets (financial markets), they are an integral component of capitalist social relations. This is evidenced by the fact that

> The employer of capital, even when working with his own capital, splits into two personalities—the owner of capital and the employer of capital; with reference to the categories of profit which it yields, his capital also splits into capital-*property*, capital *outside* the production process, and yielding interest of itself, and capital *in* the production process which yields a profit of enterprise through its function. (Marx 1894/1998, p. 373)

And Marx's conclusion is straightforward: 'Hence the nonsensical pronouncements of those who consider the different forms of surplus-value to be merely forms of distribution; they are just as much forms of production'. Marx makes a similar observation elsewhere, when he writes that profit and interest 'are modes of distribution whose presupposition is capital as agent of production. They are likewise modes of reproduction of capital' (Marx 1857–1858/1986, p. 32).

No doubt that the two last citations, if articulated today, would infuriate those who relegate revenue-bearing capital to a marginal rank compared to the 'real conditions' of capitalist dynamics! Profit and interest are both mode of distribution and mode of reproduction of capital!

It would still be absurd to interpret Marx's remarks as making no distinction between both types of capital. Marx states that '[i]ndustrial capital is the only mode of existence of capital in which not only the appropriation of surplus-value or surplus-product, but also its creation, is a function of capital' (Marx 1885/1978, pp. 135–136). But producing commodities is only a means to generate money as industrial capital (in the sense of machines, buildings, etc.) is an intermediate link in the process of

204   C. SERFATI

value creation and its appropriation by holders of capital-property. It is why the 'accumulation of money capital and of money wealth in general [...] reduces itself to the accumulation of proprietary claims to labour' (Marx 1894/1981, pp. 607).

It is obvious that the development of financial markets and the governmental policies geared towards privatisation have significantly expanded the range of revenues accruing to capital-property. Gains in capital obtained through the circulation of titles on financial markets, fees gained through intellectual property rights and rents drawn from real estate all account for a growing share of surplus value created in the production process. Hence, the denomination of revenue-bearing capital (RBC), not limited to interest as such, is used in this chapter.

In the mid-nineteenth century, capital-property was subordinated to industrial capital, and the reversal of the relation would only occur from the late nineteenth century and imperialist expansion onwards, as evidenced by the consolidation of finance capital. Marx was nevertheless aware of the compulsive pressures exerted by revenue-bearing capital.

> The process of production appears merely as an unavoidable intermediate link, as a necessary evil for the sake of money-making. All nations with a capitalist mode of production are therefore seized periodically by a feverish attempt to make money without the intervention of the process of production. (Marx 1885/1978, p. 137)

The 'fever' manifesting in the early and triumphant decades of industrial capitalism was the announcement of a much larger process, first in the early twentieth century and then in the four last decades.

FINANCE CAPITAL

This part discusses the concept of finance capital. Drawing on a critical reading of Hilferding's seminal work, it proposes to address the concept of finance capital based on the unity of, and separation between, capital-property and capital-in-function. Hilferding, while carefully addressing the relationships between industry and banks and the formation of what he called finance capital, underestimates the radical consequences of this separation.

Hilferding: A Seminal and Biased Work

Upon its publication, Hilferding's *Finance Capital* was considered a major landmark among Marxists and was even read by Otto Bauer as 'a completion of *Capital*', which both 'supplemented and revised volumes II and III' (King 2010). Luxemburg's responses to critics of *The Accumulation of Capital* suggest she was not highly appreciative of Hilferding's book (Luxemburg 1915/1921/2015, in particular in Chap. 2).

Banks 'become to a greater and greater extent industrial capitalists. I call bank capital, that is, capital in money form which is actually transformed in this way into industrial capital, finance capital'. Hilferding (1910/1981, p. 225) is the most famous excerpt of a book far more often cited than read. No doubt that definition was informed by *Capital's* Volume 3, in which Marx addresses the nascent formation of joint-stock companies in relation to the growing role of the credit system. Hilferding's research was also informed by Engels. Engels, in his 1894 foreword to *Capital's* Volume 3, had added to Marx's analysis of the stock exchange dating back to 1865 that stock companies had gradually become the dominant institutions in industry, even for foreign investments, now carried out in the form of shares. In 1890, he wrote that, given the considerable growth of the money market and the market for securities,

> The investment bankers are the owners of railroads, mines, steel mills, etc. These means of production take on a double aspect: business has to be run now with an eye to the interests of direct production, and now with an eye to the needs of the stock-holders in so far as they are money lenders. (Engels 1890)

These insightful remarks were made only a decade and a half before Hilferding started working on his *magnum opus* and obviously inspired the latter.

It is certainly true that *Finance Capital* includes a number of theoretical advances on the formation of monopolies and cartels and the development of fictitious capital which are directly informed by Marx and Engels. According to Guillén (2013), one of the most revolutionary aspects of Hilferding's theory is the category called 'promoter's profit'—the profit (actually a monopoly income) appropriated by finance capital for the mere act of negotiating the fictitious capital, that is, for controlling the issuance and circulation of shares and public and private bonds and securities

(Guillén 2013). According to Lapavitsas and Levina (2011), this insight is of decisive importance for the theory of financial profits on today's financial markets, even though there are problematic aspects to his analysis.

The central aspect of the book, Hilferding's definition of finance capital, was widely accepted. Lenin took it up in his *Imperialism*; Bukharin, despite not citing Hilferding at this point, said that 'finance capital is characterised by being simultaneously banking *and* industrial capital (italics in the text)' (1917/1929); and Trotsky (no longer citing Hilferding) wrote that 'Bank capital merges with industrial capital into financial super-capital' (1939/1970).

Other parts of Hilferding's book have been criticised, including his theory of money, criticised by Kautsky (1912), then noted by Lenin and finally analysed in a more comprehensive manner by de Brunhoff. The latter detects a 'quantitativist' approach to money adopted by Hilferding which is the source of confusion regarding his concept of finance capital (de Brunhoff 1976b, p. 14). Hilferding mixes together two distinct concepts articulated by Marx: *Geldhandlungskapital* (money-dealing capital) and *Geldkapitalist* (money capitalist) (de Brunhoff 1976a). The careful examination of credit and banks by Hilferding, 'but not being organically linked to the theory of money has probably been one of the reasons for the overestimation of the role of "finance capital"' by Hilferding (ibid., p. ix). Disconnecting financing through loans from its monetary base allows Hilferding to conclude that, as banks are at the origin of both loans and money creation, they can fund stock companies on demand. The severity of a crisis triggered by money functioning as a means of payment is ignored by Hilferding and instead substituted with a supposedly non-problematic bank funding of large corporations.

Another critique, put forward by Sweezy, is that Hilferding tried to generalise what was a peculiar German development at the turn of the century, and he overestimated the importance of financial dominance in the latest stage of capitalist development because the large monopolistic corporations actually possess substantial internal funds that make them independent from the stock market and the bankers (Sweezy 1946, pp. 260, 267).

An Alternative Proposal for Finance Capital

Although critiques of Hilferding's definition do make sense, we still think that it is not necessary to 'throw the baby out with the bathwater'. Several dramatic transformations in the capitalist dynamics perceived by Hilferding remain topical. We propose to define finance capital as the intertwining of concentrated (or monopoly) industrial, merchant, real estate, land and bank capital under the control of capital-property (Serfati 2018).

This definition differs from Hilferding's in two aspects. First, he interpreted the separation of capital-property and capital as a progress in the rationalisation of capitalism. In this respect, Chap. 10 is illuminating on Hilferding's perception of capitalist evolution. He contends:

> If this trend were to continue, it would finally result in a single bank or a group of banks establishing control over the entire money capital. Such a "central bank" would then exercise control over social production as a whole. (Hilferding 1910/1981, p. 180)

This is a very one-sided view of the consequences of the centralisation of capital-property that can be contrasted with the observations Marx made when he examined the concentration of capital-property in the hands of the banks:

> Talk about centralization! The credit system, which has its focal point in the allegedly national banks and the big money-lenders and usurers that surround them, is one enormous centralization and gives this class of parasites a fabulous power. (Marx 1894/1981, p. 678)

Hilferding's definition of finance capital as the merger of 'industrial and banking capital', moreover, significantly mitigates Marx's assessment:

> It (the credit, C.S.) reproduces a new financial aristocracy, a new kind of parasite in the guise of company promoters, speculators and merely nominal directors; an entire system of swindling and cheating with respect to the promotion of companies, issues of shares and share dealings. It is private production unchecked by private ownership. (Marx 1894/1981, p. 569)

Marx's remarks on JSC were not ignored by other Marxists. Lenin observes that the capitalist development—having arrived at its imperialist stage—exacerbates the separation between capital-property and capital-in-function, with the consequence that 'the supremacy of finance capital over all other forms of capital means the predominance of the rentier and of the financial oligarchy' (Lenin 1917/2011, Chap. 3). Hence, Lenin criticised the rationalising role of banks envisaged by Hilferding who 'has taken a step backward compared with the non-Marxist Hobson. I refer to parasitism, which is characteristic of imperialism' (Lenin 1917/2011, Chap. 8).

Secondly, as mentioned before, Hilferding identified finance capital with its organisational forms existing at the time in Germany. To his credit, Hilferding did underline the growth in mobility acquired by capital-property in order to correctly reconstruct the process of centralisation of capital in financial institutions (for him, banks) and industry and decipher its role as a counter-tendency to the fall in the rate of profit (see Hilferding 1910/1981, Chap. 14). In the last decade, the mobility of capital-property considerably accelerated owing to the creation of integrated financial markets at the global level. The process of centralisation of capital—that is, according to Marx's definition, the merger of capital-property and 'the transformation of many small into few large capitals'—thus results in the intertwining of monopoly industrial, merchant, real estate, land and bank capital. The mobility of capital-property favoured by financial markets and banks and the tendency of capital accumulation to boost the centralisation of capital accounts for the existence in most developed countries of a dense network of firms based on cross-shareholding and interlocking directorates.

This does not mean that all the institutional units called corporations (or joint-stock companies) conduct business in all the sectors mentioned in our definition. The degree of large non-financial corporations' vertical integration, the extension of activities beyond their 'core business', as well as the scope of banks' control on industrial activities depend on a series of economic, regulatory and cultural factors. To give an example, who would have imagined two decades ago that tech firms Alibaba, Amazon, Facebook, Google and similar would venture into financial services, including payments, money management, insurance and lending, exploiting the large stock of user data collected in their businesses? Benefiting from 'network externalities', 'straddling regulatory perimeters and geographical borders' (BIS 2019, p. 56), those firms pose daunting challenges to regulation authorities and risks to the stability of the system.

TNCs as Core Component of Contemporary Finance Capital

Transnational Corporations (TNCs) exhibit *qualitatively* different features compared to other firms. They represent a category of enterprise *sui generis*, based on a specific organisational structure. The core role, in terms of strategy and profit accumulation, is occupied by the holding company where the centralisation of capital-property is operationalised. The holding company exerts direct and indirect influence on a myriad of affiliates, some of them involved in R&D, production, sales and post-sales activities, while others are created for the unique purpose of generating revenue from money capital valorisation. The predominant logic of valorisation of revenue-bearing capital led us to define them as a core organisational modality of contemporary finance capital, in short: financial groups with industrial specialisation (Serfati 1996).

The 1980s and 1990s saw a considerable strengthening of the weight of TNCs and consolidation of their strategy of financial valorisation of capital. What the literature calls 'global value chains' (GVCs)—in which almost 80 per cent of international production is now realised—are global spaces formed and controlled by large TNCs. They open up a strategic horizon for augmenting the value of capital that reaches far beyond national borders and undermines national regulations. Within GVCs, the asymmetric power relations existing between large TNCs and their suppliers put the former in a position to capture a share of value created in the latter (Serfati and Sauviat 2019). Depressing supplier prices, to say it with Marx, 'has its place in an account of competition, which is not dealt with in this work. It is none the less one of the most important factors in stemming the tendency for the rate of profit to fall' (Marx 1894/1981, p. 342).

Conflation of Profits of Enterprise and Rents in Large TNCs

In sum, one consequence of large TNCs' strategy in the context of the current international macroeconomic setting was the blurring in their total profits from 'profits of enterprise' resulting from a successful valorisation of their productive capital and rents, that is, revenues gained from the valorisation of capital-property. The genesis of the rent concept dates back to the early foundations of political economy. For Smith, wages, profit and rent are the three original sources of all revenue and of all exchangeable value. Ricardo analyses the *differential rent*, which, in contrast to other production sectors, applies only to land and is not determined by the labour and capital incorporated in the production process, but by the technical conditions of production of the least fertile land. Ricardo was criticised by Marx who analysed the *absolute and monopoly rents*, both based on the ownership of property titles conferring exclusive privileges to their holders.[1] *Absolute* rents exist because some people own property titles on portions of land endowed with superior qualities that put them in an exclusive position on the market, while *monopoly* rents are an extension of the same privilege created by or owing to the holding of property titles on any resource and market.

Large TNCs accumulate profits of enterprise (from capital employed productively) and rents through four main channels. Firstly, they accumulate surplus value extracted from the production process organised domestically and by their foreign affiliates, with the opportunity to increase the rate of profit on their capital offshored to emerging countries, given the higher rate of labour exploitation. Then, they also extract rents gained from the asymmetrical power between them and their suppliers along their GVCs. Strategies of squeezing supplier's margins assume various forms, including a reduction in prices and an extension of payment terms. They thus benefit from a redistribution of the surplus value realised in suppliers' firms. The transfer of surplus value created in the labour process realised by suppliers, in favour of large corporations and facilitated by their control on GVCs, is obviously an obstacle to the formation of an average rate of profit, since the latter is conditioned by the 'abolition of all monopolies other than natural ones' (Marx 1894/1981, p. 298). Moreover, they extract monopoly rents gained from an exclusive control over some products which are non-renewable or scarce (hence, monopoly rents), that is, at 'any price determined simply by the desire and ability of the buyer to pay, independently of the price of the product as determined by price of production and value' (ibid., p. 910). At Marx's time, the natural scarcity of a resource was the main cause accounting for this monopoly price, which is why he used a vineyard as an example. It is clear that the creation

---

[1] In his presentation of the concept of rent, Marx establishes a distinction between absolute and monopoly rent as far as their relation to the formation of surplus value and their magnitude compared to production prices are concerned (Marx 1894/1993, p. 910). The underlying privilege to accumulate a rent based on exclusive property rights is still common to both.

of artificial scarcity, for example, through patenting, the support of governmental policies protecting 'their' large TNCs through regulatory and financing measures, and, in the wake of major changes occurring in the 2000s, the consolidation of TNC's GVCs as a way of increasing their power, considerably supports setting monopoly prices on end-markets (for evidence of high margins in smartphone production extracted by Apple, Huawei and Samsung, see WIPO 2017). Finally, large TNCs have increased their financial revenues, that is to say, those gained from their activities on financial markets (in particular in the foreign exchange markets) and from credit activities considered to be lucrative enough to lead them in some cases to create in-house banks.

In the bottom line of TNCs' accounting, 'profit of enterprise' gained from productive activities carried out in their affiliates mix with rents gained from their power over their suppliers, monopoly prices imposed on the market and financial-market revenues. This reflects not only the intertwining of capital-property and capital-in-function, but also the increasing importance of the former in the strategies of TNCs.

Ascendant Domination of Capital-Property and Its Drivers

The increase of revenue-bearing capital (RBC) over the last decades is largely undisputed and generally described by the rather vague concept of financialisation. The growth of dividends accruing to shareholders and interests gained from swelling public debt are often cited, as these two forms of revenue account for the bulk of total RBC. The thriving of RBC in contemporary capitalism still goes beyond these two historical items. To borrow from Luxemburg's apt language, the quest of capital for 'new provinces of accumulation' has become more compelling. This entailed a process of commoditisation based on the creation of private property titles (capital-property). Firstly, from the 1980s onwards, a substantial extension of the domains covered by intellectual property rights (IPRs) was encouraged by governmental policies and the coordination thereof in the World Trade Organization (WTO). A major objective was to dispossess workers of their skills and, firstly, to incorporate the latter as a component of fixed capital and, secondly, to transform tacit knowledge into a commodity priced on financial markets. Then, ruling classes succeeded, buttressed by governmental policies, in enforcing property rights pertaining

212   C. SERFATI

to living organisms. General Electric's patenting of micro-organisms in 1980 was subsequently extended to human genes after the cracking of the human genetic code in DNA sequences. The authorisation was further expanded to encompass patents on plants and seeds, posing a direct threat to the reproduction of communities which were now forced to pay for basic sources of livelihood. It is a reminder of what Marx said with regard to rents: 'One section of society here demands a tribute from the other for the very right to live on the earth' (Marx 1894/1981, p. 908). Finally, the private sphere of human beings opened up a 'new province of accumulation' to capital in its valorisation quest. 'Big data' flows collected from all connected electronic devices (computers, phones, surveillance cameras, etc.) are transformed into lucrative raw material for business, submitting privacy rights to a surveillance regime orchestrated for profit purposes, hence the term 'surveillance capitalism' (Zuboff 2015).

A number of reasons account for the ascendancy of capital-property, some of which are related to the very roots of capitalism, while others are based on asymmetrical class power relations. Firstly, in the process of capitalist production and reproduction, money represents value and wealth in its general form. Money that circulates along the cycle of M-C-M' (M money, C commodity, M'>M) is 'transformed into capital, becomes capital, and, from the point of view of its function, already is capital' (Marx 1867/1976, p. 248). In other words, the ownership of money is potentially the ownership of capital for those who possess social power.[2] And this potential becomes reality when materialised in revenue-generating capital-property titles. This is evident with the 'credit-money [which] springs directly out of the function of money as a means of payment' (Marx 1867/1976, p. 238). In contrast to the money system, the credit system is a creation of capitalism, because it 'presupposes the monopoly possession of the social means of production (in the form of capital and landed property) on the part of private individuals' and is 'a driving force of its development into its highest and last possible form' (Marx 1894/1981, p. 742). Hence, 'Mere money [...] becomes loan capital [...] by its transformation into a deposit, if we consider the general form in the developed credit system' (ibid., p. 642). Throughout the nineteenth century, the credit system, as a form of capital-property bearing revenue, gained considerable momentum with the transformation of the banking

---

[2] With money, 'each individual [...] carries his social power, as also his connection with society, in his pocket' (Marx 1857–1858/1986, p. 94).

system and reinforced the 'compelling motive of capitalist production—money-making' observed by Marx. Over the last three decades, the process of valorisation of 'capital as such', that is, as property rights, advanced considerably.

Secondly, the contemporary thriving of revenue-bearing capital (RBC) has to do with the state of the world economy. The co-occurrence of RBC and the slowdown in productive accumulation in developed countries, also observed by international organisations (IMF 2019), have raised a discussion on the nature of their interrelations. One notable contribution is the analysis by Lapavitsas who, in a Marxist framework, argues that 'there is no direct causation between booming finance and weak production' (Lapavitsas 2010, p. 43). Among most post-Keynesian economists, the thriving of finance directly causes the slowdown of real accumulation, as financial revenues are diverted from an alternative, productive use. For many Marxists, the causality moves in a reverse direction: the crisis of productive accumulation, whatever its causes may be, leads to a surge in financial valorisation. Some argue that the profitability, a proxy of Marx's rate of profit (RoP), triggered the 'great recession' (in 2008) that turned into the 'Long depression' (Roberts 2016). Others challenge the relevance of the fall of the RoP for various reasons, one of them being that no such decline was detected, or because this fall followed the financial crisis. For others, the crisis results from 'A conjunction of a falling RoP and of a roadblock met at C′ of the complete accumulation process (M-C… P… C′-M′, with P being the productive moment), that is in Marxist wordings, a "crisis of realisation" of value' (Chesnais 2016, p. 4).

Thirdly, the social roots of the development of revenue-bearing capital personified in the *rentiers* and their political power have been traced by Marx (see above his remarks on how the development of revenue-bearing capital 'stimulates a new financial aristocracy') and his followers, but also by non-Marxist critics of capitalism (Veblen, Hobson and Keynes).

The social and political bloc which emerged on the basis of finance capital since the 1980s can hardly be underestimated as a driver of the massive surge in revenue-bearing capital accruing to the ruling class (the 'one per cent', whose total revenue is overwhelmingly constituted by the ownership of financial assets). The policies accommodating financial 'vested interests' have created powerful political built-in mechanisms which so far have left the *rentier* class immune to the last four decades of financial crisis. No financial crisis unfolding since the 1982 Mexican default has prevented the growth of revenue-bearing capital. Instead, the 2008 financial crisis boosted the growth of financial assets held by rentiers (or rentier families) and large transnational corporations (on rentier features of the French-ruling class, see Serfati 2015).

'The world-ecological limit of capital is capital itself' (Moore 2015, cited in Chesnais 2016, p. 240). This limit combines with the inability of capital to reach levels of profitability sufficient to raise the level of productive capital accumulation. In our view, despite the rise in the rate of exploitation, the productivity of labour is insufficient to increase the rate of profit, which depends not only on the rate of exploitation but also on the capital-to-labour ratio (capital here means the cost of industrial equipment and raw materials). Hence, the current economic conjuncture considered at its world level could be one in which the crisis results from internal limits to capital accumulation combined with the irrepressible claim by the holders of capital-property—who constitute the upper segments of the ruling class—to receive a growing share of the value created in labour processes. Revenue-bearing capital, today comforted by committed governmental policies, 'appears as a Moloch demanding the whole world as a sacrifice belonging to it of right, whose legitimate demands, [arise] from its very nature' (Marx 1861–1863/1989, p. 453).

Finance Capital and Militarism

This section focuses on the relationship between finance capital and militarism. It highlights the divergences existing between Hilferding and Luxemburg on this issue and concludes with an assessment of the relevance of the latter's analysis for present-day contemporary capitalism.

Hilferding: A Peaceful Imperialism Is Possible

According to some, 'Hilferding's comments could have been taken directly from Rosa Luxemburg (or vice versa); they do not differ on the methods of capitalist expansion' (Brewer 1980, p. 103). This similarity is misleading, given that the differences behind the same terminology could be more substantial than assumed. Hilferding states that the policy of finance capital is bound to lead towards war. He describes the three ways in which capital conquers new territories with the support of force when the process is perceived to move 'too slowly and gradually by purely economic means' (Hilferding 1910/1981, p. 319): the expropriation of the natives, then the introduction of a system of taxation when said natives are no longer sufficiently robust and, finally, capital's attempts to solve the labour problem by introducing foreign labour. By reference to these three ways, he remains within the mainstream framework of Marxist analysis, linking capitalist expansion to the use of violence. Moreover, Hilferding is aware of the ideological justifications for imperialism, stating that 'there emerges in racist ideology, cloaked in the garb of natural science, a justification for finance capital's lust for power' (Hilferding 1910/1981, p. 335).

The risks of armed conflicts and the policy of finance capital leading to war are still mitigated by two factors. Firstly, after envisaging the possibility of an armed conflict between Germany and England (ibid.), Hilferding immediately downplays this risk, based on an interpretation of a balance of power policy 'reminiscent of the balance of power policy of the early stages of capitalism [...] This accounts for the recent international policy of maintaining the status quo'. This claim reflects an underestimation of the severity of economic competition bound to turn into military conflagration, as happened only four years after Hilferding's *Finance Capital*. Secondly, the low-level risk of armed conflict between great powers is reinforced by the existence of international cartels able to put an end to the anarchy of competition and promote a peaceful development of capitalism.[3] This claim is a precursor to Hilferding's proposal made in a 1915 paper on fully 'organized capitalism', according to which a general cartel could be formed (James 1981, p. 856). It is also close to what Kautsky theorised as 'ultra-imperialism' (1914). For Hilferding, the main driver to the cartelisation of foreign policy limiting the risk of war is the role of interest-bearing money capital. Export of capital in the form of credit—rather than the construction of factories—creates a form of solidarity between capitalists from different nations.

This analysis warrants two remarks. The first is that in the conflict between Kautsky and Lenin on imperialism, Hilferding's initial position was somewhere in between (Brewer 1980, p. 107), but as said above, after World War I, he moved closer in the direction of Kautsky's views. The second one is that the pacifying, transnational role of interest-bearing money capital resembles that which Polanyi attributed to

---

[3] This view was already criticised when the book was published in 1910. Julian Marchlewski, in a review of the book published in the SPD's left-wing *Leipziger Volkszeitung*, expressed disagreement regarding the notion that cartels and trusts bring about a peaceful competition, arguing that even among monopoly associations, 'a frantic struggle also rages among the members' (1910/2012, p. 438).

nineteenth-century *Haute Finance*. Briefly stated, the thesis is that *Haute Finance* 'functioned as the main link between the political and the economic organization of the world' (Polanyi 1944/2001, p. 10). Thus,

> by functional determination it fell to *haute finance* to avert general wars. The vast majority of the holders of government securities, as well as other investors and traders, were bound to be the first losers in such wars, especially if their currencies were affected [...] The influence that haute finance exerted on the Powers was consistently favorable to European peace. (Ibid., p. 14)

Polanyi does not dismiss the fact that bankers had no objection to any number of minor, short or localised wars, but their business would be impaired if a general war between the great powers should interfere with the monetary foundations of the system (ibid., p. 11). The reason for this is that cartelisation of *haute finance* transcends national interests, resulting in a state in which 'Trade had become linked with peace' (ibid., p. 15). In hindsight, it is hard to overlook that not only 'localised wars' carried out by the great powers burst out repeatedly under the reign of *Haute finance*, but large-scale wars between them were also common, as evidenced by the Crimean War of 1853–1856 between the Russian Empire on one side and the Ottoman Empire, France, Britain, Austria and Sardinia on the other, or the Franco-Prussian war of 1870–1871.

LUXEMBURG: THE INTERNATIONAL LOANS—PRIMITIVE ACCUMULATION—MILITARISM TRIPOD

A major originality of Luxemburg's analysis is to carefully analyse how finance capital, in the form of international credit, is directly linked to imperialism and armed violence, something too partial for Bukharin who accuses her of treating 'the problem without any regard to the necessity of a specific characterization of capital as finance capital' (Bukharin 1925–1926/1972, p. 253). She writes that foreign loans 'are yet the surest ties by which the old capitalist states maintain their influence, exercise financial control and exert pressure on the customs, foreign and commercial policy of the young capitalist states' (Luxemburg 1913/2003, p. 401). Those remarks have been strikingly confirmed in contemporary capitalism, from the 1982 Mexico default to the numerous financial crisis until the 2008 EU financial crisis.

Luxemburg shows that loan (or credit) money capital often operates through primitive accumulation, that is to say, the direct use of violence in the process of value creation. This analysis is based on Volume 1 of *Capital*. Marx had observed that 'with the national debt there arose **an international credit system**, which often conceals one of the sources of primitive accumulation in this or that people' (Marx 1867/1976, p. 920, emphasis added). Primitive accumulation, Luxemburg comments, is not reserved to early phases of capitalist expansion:

> "Sweating blood and filth with every pore from head to toe" (Marx's *Capital* wordings, C.S.) characterises not only the birth of capital but also its progress in the world at every step. (Luxemburg 1913/2003, p. 433)

Here, Hilferding's and Luxemburg's theoretical approaches can be contrasted. While Hilferding explicitly states that his focus is not on this process of *valorisation* of capital and he is rather concerned 'only with the transformation of the form of value rather than with its origin' (Hilferding 1910/1981, p. 68), Luxemburg draws on Volume 1 of *Capital*, in which the process of value creation is addressed.[4] She thus directs her attention not to the transformation of the form of value, but to one of its major characteristics, namely the different modalities of producing surplus value. This process culminated in a highly uneven integration into the world space of countries and territories differing strongly in their social structures. Thus, finance capital is neither external to capitalist relations of production—as a parasitic activity outside or on top of an otherwise sound productive accumulation—nor can it be identified as an institutional innovation (the 'merging of banking and industrial capital') *à la* Hilferding which succeeds in pacifying capitalist relations and smoothing out economic competition. For Luxemburg, capitalist relations are introduced and consolidated in concentrated form, owing to a flow of accruing revenue from subordinate to metropolitan countries, a process that creates profound imbalances in international economic relations. To sum up, money capital, when materialised as property rights and credit assets, is a

---

[4] There is a certain irony in the fact that Luxemburg, while criticised in Marxist literature *ad nauseam* for focusing on the realisation of value issues, carefully analyses the ongoing process of primitive accumulation, hence value creation, while Hilferding, whose book was hailed by most Marxists of his time, explicitly neglects the value-creation process.

218   C. SERFATI

driver of asymmetric relationships at the global level. And the process is anything but peaceful.

Based on this analysis, it is easy to understand Luxemburg's careful attention to militarism. Indeed, from very early on, she had stressed that for the capitalist class, militarism is 'indeed indispensable—but for whom? For the present-day ruling classes and the contemporary governments' (Luxemburg 1899/1972). And, quite remarkably and unique among Marxists, she was aware of the central role of militarism and its multiple functions almost from the outset of her scholarly engagement. As early as 1898, she laid down the thrust of her understanding of the role of militarism:

> First, as a means of struggle for the defence of "national" interests in competition against other "national" groups. Second, as a method of placement for financial and industrial capital. Third, as an instrument of class domination over the laboring population inside the country. (Luxemburg 1906/1898/2008, p. 63)

All these functions are addressed in *Accumulation of Capital* in an updated way, for example, when she states that military force is used 'for extorting railway concessions in backward countries, and for enforcing the claims of European capital as international lender'.

Still, the ground-breaking analysis is in Chap. 32 on 'Militarism as a Province for Accumulation'. Before turning to her argument, the two following sections provide a historical overview of the connections between militarism and finance capital.

Some Historical Evidence on Connections Between Militarism and Finance Capital

History rather provides evidence for establishing a connection between finance capital and armed violence than a confirmation of Polanyi's assumptions or Hilferding's expectations. Military interventions or threats thereof against indebted countries were not infrequent during the era of classical imperialism. In the last three decades of the nineteenth century, more than 100 interventions backed by military force by the Western great powers in the semi-periphery, mostly in Latin America and the Ottoman Empire, occurred either unilaterally in the case of the United States or 'in concert' by the European powers (von Bernstorff 2018,

p. 248). A significant share of them was motivated by financial defaults. Mitchener and Weidenmier (2005, p. 658) find that defaulting sovereigns between 1870 and 1913 faced threatened or actual military intervention 40 per cent of the time. Finnemore observes that 'Prior to 1907 it was accepted practice for states to use military force to collect debts owed to their nationals by other states' (Finnemore 2003, p. 24). Other scholars add: 'By the turn of the twentieth century, joint military interventions by two or more of the Western powers to protect foreign interests were becoming commonplace' (Johnson Jr. and Gimblett 2012, p. 652).

Arguments for interventions changed over time. At the beginning of the nineteenth century, the desire to collect debt payments was explicitly proclaimed. Over several decades, the tone—but not so much the substance—then changed for a number of reasons, including the cost of military operations, the need to consolidate the use of force on legitimate grounds and, not least, the reluctance of public opinion in some creditor countries (England, France) to see their governments give in to the powerful interests of bondholders. Also, after having previously been limited to defending lenders' interests, 'gunboat diplomacy' increasingly became a component of broader imperialist objectives towards the end of the century.

This is why some historians challenge the notion that the main motive of developed countries' military involvement was debt:

> Debt default and military intervention coincided, not because creditors were taking up arms on behalf of bondholders, but because defaulters happened to be involved in other disputes (civil wars, territorial conflicts, tort claims) that attracted the attention of major powers. (Tomz 2007, p. 153)

While these remarks testify to the fact that military interventions were part of a broader imperialist policy, they do not invalidate that financial interests were a major component in such interventions. In reality, economic and political drivers were often intertwined, as observed by a financial institution in London claiming in 1905 that 'If she [the United States] interferes with matters of finance no doubt that will to a certain extent prevent revolutions in these countries' (Mitchener and Weidenmier 2005, p. 687). And the frequency of wars and revolutions placing many states in temporary default was high (Borchard 1932, p. 141).

At the turn of the century, when military spending rose in all developed countries as a prelude to the world cataclysm, the La Hague Conferences

(1905 and 1907) adopted the Drago Doctrine. Luis Mario Drago formulated a non-intervention doctrine in December 1902: 'The public debt cannot occasion armed intervention nor even the actual occupation of the territory of American nations by a. European power' (Drago and Nettles 1928, p. 214).

Still, despite contrary claims, the La Hague 1907 conference did not prohibit the use of force against defaulting countries, but instead in its *Article 1* stated:

> [The] agreement not to have recourse to armed force for the recovery of contract debts claimed from the Government of one country by the Government of another country [...] is, however, not applicable when the debtor State refuses or neglects to reply to an offer of arbitration, or, after accepting the offer, prevents any *compromis* from being agreed on, or, after the arbitration, fails to submit to the award. (Italics added)[5]

This loose formulation establishing exceptions that allowed for military interventions in fact left the possibility of interventions wide open.

Finance Capital as Sponsor of Wars

This is not the end of the story. Banks, a pillar of finance capital institutions, were involved in arms production and trade. Polanyi himself observes that they were anything but pacifist and had made their fortunes in the financing of wars. Only 'minor, short or localised wars' attracted their interest, however, because their business would be impaired by a general war between the great powers (pp. 9–10). Although it would be reductionist to attribute the causes of wars to 'canon merchants' and their banks, their role is still undeniable. To give an example, the Rothschild banks underwrote the debt of various great powers—France, Britain, Austria and Turkey—during the Crimean War of 1854–1856 even though the family was worried about the impact on its business activities (Ferguson 1999). In all great powers, certain banks, known as the 'armament banks', funded the large companies producing and exporting arms (Engelbrecht and Hanighen 1934).

---

[5] 'Limitation of Employment of Force for Recovery of Contract Debts (Hague, II)', Convention signed at The Hague, 18 October 1907.

Interestingly, far from being exclusively committed to the entrenched national interest, banks contributed to the internationalisation of the industry (Lewinsohn 1935). French banks funded direct foreign competitors to French arms companies, and the same disregard for their home country was also shared by English and German banks (Serfati 2019). To reverse Polanyi's parlance, the growth of trade flows, including with trade deals brokered between rival powers, did not prevent the latter to fuel militarism through very high levels of military spending, albeit paling in comparison to the post-World War II period.

TAKING STOCK OF LUXEMBURG'S ANALYSIS OF MILITARISM WITH A VIEW TO CONTEMPORARY CAPITALISM

As is well known, *The Accumulation of Capital* is concerned with the relations between capital accumulation and its non-capitalist environment. Luxemburg concludes from her comprehensive analysis that

> it is factors such as the burden of taxation, war, and the selling-off and monopolization of the nation's land—factors that belong equally to the spheres of political economy, political power, and criminal law—that are effective in this process of the separation of peasant agriculture from industry. (Luxemburg 1915/1921/2015, p. 286)

The association of militarism (war) and criminal law is no coincidence. Given that they both belong to the so-called superstructure, their role is rather significant. The enforcement of private property rights and the destruction of barter and (commodity) exchange economies as a way of pursuing capital accumulation ('economics') were carried out with the use of force. Luxemburg defines her theoretical approach as follows:

> [P]olitical power is nothing but a vehicle for the economic process. The conditions for the reproduction of capital provide the **organic link** between these two aspects of the accumulation of capital. (Luxemburg 1913/2003, p. 433, my emphasis)

In her argument, Luxemburg refuses to erect an epistemological frontier between infrastructure and superstructure and extends the 'traditional' functions of militarism from a political instrument used for economic purposes to being itself a 'province of accumulation of capital'. She shows that militarism is 'a pre-eminent means for the realisation of surplus value; it is in itself a province of accumulation' (Luxemburg 1913/2003, pp. 434–435). Militarism, buttressed by state legitimation, benefits from the centralised buying power of governments, because in the form of government contracts for army,

> scattered purchasing power of the consumers is concentrated in large quantities [Luxemburg's hypothesis is that arms production is funded out of taxes on wage-earners, C.S.] and, free of the vagaries and subjective fluctuations of personal consumption, it achieves an almost automatic regularity and rhythmic growth. Capital itself ultimately controls this automatic and rhythmic movement of militarist production [...] That is why this particular province of capitalist accumulation at first seems capable of infinite expansion. (Luxemburg 1913/2003, p. 446)

The last sentence is similar to earlier writings stating that 'Militarism thus represents an inexhaustible, and indeed increasingly lucrative, source of capitalist gain' (Luxemburg 1899/1972).

Luxemburg went further on the role of militarism than other Marxists who analysed imperialism as a new historical configuration focused on war in the sense of a political auxiliary of economic competition. The Marxist consensus was summed up by Bukharin as follows: 'War in capitalist society is only one of the methods of capitalist competition, when the latter extends to the sphere of world economy' (Bukharin 1917/1929, p. 54). Luxemburg intended to anchor militarism at the very roots of the capitalist dynamics in an effort to expose any perception of a 'pure capitalism' as illusionary. At first glance, placing militarism at the heart of social relations breaks a fundamental tenet of Marxism, namely the separation between the economic and political-military-juridical sphere in capitalism (Wood 1995; Fine and Picciotto 1992). The use of direct violence within the relations of production (the labour process), at least formally, is not part of the (asymmetrical) relation between capitalists—as owners of the means of production—and workers—as 'free human beings' forced to sell their labour force. The use of 'legitimate violence' is transferred to specific institutions within states. Hence, law and the use of force are two major components of this legitimate violence employed by states to maintain order in social relations.

This separation of economic and political functions should be taken as a conceptual approach to understanding the specificity of the institutional setting of capitalism, and not be transformed into an ahistorical reality. To give an example, while Marx explained that 'The tendency to create the world market is directly given in the concept of capital itself', he never conceived the creation of a world market as a 'levelling playing field' for capitalist competition, no more than the reproduction schemas outlined in *Capital* Volume 2 were addressing a 'pure capitalism'[6] (for the way Marx integrated the world market and the state system in his work, see Pradella 2013). Luxemburg did not attribute this vision to Marx's reproduction schemas either, as she says that Marx 'is anticipating [*vorwegnehmen*] the *real trend* of capitalist development' (Luxemburg 1915/1921, p. 437).

The process of abstraction by which the separation of economy and politics is showed to be specific to capitalism and conceptually established must then be confronted with reality, 'a rich totality of many determinations and relations' (Marx 1857–1858/1986, p. 37). A glance at history illustrates how the economic basis and the political-military-law superstructure are closely intertwined, a feature instrumental and essential for the functioning of capitalism. Indeed, the hypothesis of a central role of political-military coercion in the world reach of capitalism is a common thread running through all early twentieth-century theories of imperialism, despite their differences. The world space (a term that is, incidentally, more adequate than world market) results from the interactive relations between capitalist dynamics and the international system of states (Serfati 2019).[7] As Luxemburg shows, primitive accumulation and 'normal' accumulation were intertwined (Luxemburg 1913/2003, p. 351).[8] The present-day configuration of the world space has not eliminated this combination.

For some Marxist scholars, by contrast, the period of primitive accumulation described by Luxemburg is over and has been replaced by what Ellen Woods defines as the 'empire of capital' (Wood 2003). The 'empire of capital' is the era, setting in over the course of the past decades, in

---

[6] Marx's hypothesis in devising the schemas is to 'treat the whole world as one nation, and assume that capitalist production is everywhere established and has possessed itself of every branch of industry'.

[7] According to Kowalik, Hilferding, Kautsky and Bukharin treated the economics of the new phase of capitalism and the politics of this phase as two separate issues and distinct categories. Lenin understood imperialism as a unity of the economics and politics of this new phase of capitalism (see Kowalik 2014, p. 148).

[8] 'With that we have passed beyond the stage of primitive accumulation; this process is still going on' (Luxemburg 1913/2003, p. 350).

which the subjugation of the whole world to the logic of capital is established. This explains that 'For the first time [since 1945] in the history of the modern nation state, the world's major powers are not engaged in direct geopolitical and military rivalry'. Wood adds that 'Capitalist imperialism has become almost entirely a matter of economic domination' and concludes 'it can be a very bloody business. But once subordinate powers are made vulnerable to those imperatives and the "laws" of the market, direct rule by imperial states is no longer required to impose the will of capital' (Wood 2003, p. 153). Likewise, according to Wood, 'capitalist imperialism extends this purely economic mode of exploitation beyond national frontiers' (Wood 2006, p. 17).

The view adopted in this chapter is different. Neither did wars disappear from the scene since the end of World War II nor did the collapse of the USSR, labelled as the 'empire of evil' by Ronald Reagan, put an end to wars. Militarism and war must be put into a broader context. The era of 'classical imperialism' was marked by the 'globalisation of war' during the early twentieth century. This trend was presciently announced by Engels, writing in 1898:

> [F]inally, the only war left for Prussia-Germany to wage will be a world war, a world war, moreover, of an extent and violence hitherto unimagined. Eight to ten million soldiers will be at each other's throats and in the process, they will strip Europe barer than a swarm of locusts. (Engels 1887/1990, p. 451)

What has emerged from the 1990s onwards are armed conflicts often called 'new wars' or 'resource wars', yet which could better be, defined, in contrast to the preceding era, as 'wars of globalisation' dominated by finance capital. Most wars occurring in less developed countries—particularly in Africa—are a *component* of 'really-existing globalisation'. Local wars where millions of people have perished over the last decades are connected through several channels to world economic flows (trade, finance, arms) and to the geopolitical setting (e.g. the official recognition at the UN of governments involved in those wars which contribute to the reproduction of the ill-named 'world order') (Serfati 2001; Aknin and Serfati 2008).

Wars of globalisation have not ended in the current international context. Instead, they may well go on, fuelled not only by economic distress but also by direct threats to the reproduction of life due to climate change.

The latter, at odds with official discourse along the lines of 'we live on the same planet', produce strong uneven environmental effects on populations, with the poorer share of the world population being directly affected by the consequences of the mode of production and consumption governed by major powers.

In addition to that, we need to connect the role of militarism to the historical world conjuncture that emerged at the end of the 2000s. The '2008 moment' closed the historical period brought about in the early 1990s by the collapse of the USSR (Serfati 2019). It resulted from the conflation of the economic crisis, the changes in the geopolitical setting (weakening of the United States' international position, Russia's assertiveness, emergence of China as a geo-economic power etc.) and social upheavals, with the 'Jasmin Revolution' in Tunisia 2011 as a spearhead of massive popular mobilisation in the Maghreb, Mashriq and Middle East. A new configuration of relations between the economy and the military took place at the world level at the end of the 2000s with a new combination arising between capital accumulation and the international state system. A direct effect of these epochal changes is that in the international relations between dominating countries, economic and military power became closer intertwined at the world level, as evidenced by the centrality of 'national security' in economic policies (Serfati 2020).

To conclude, Luxemburg's analysis of military spending, which is inscribed in her general theoretical framework, has rarely been criticised, as critiques have mainly been centred on her more general 'realisation of surplus-value' approach. Among the few Marxists interested in her analysis of military spending, Grossmann contended that Luxemburg's conception of militarism as a preeminent means for the realisation of surplus value was wrong:

> This is how things may appear from the standpoint of individual capital as military supplies have always been the occasion for rapid enrichment. But from the standpoint of the total capital, militarism is a sphere of unproductive consumption. (Grossmann 1929, pp. 122–123)

Mandel, who, like Luxemburg, converts the reproduction schemas and adds a third department producing military goods, credits Luxemburg for her conception while showing that the permanent armament industry is incapable of solving the problem of realisation inherent in the capitalist mode of production in the course of advancing technical progress (Mandel

1972, p. 281). From what has been developed in this chapter, notwithstanding the flaws in the argument regarding Luxemburg's understanding of Marx's reproduction schemas, placing militarism at the heart of the political economy of imperialism provides a valuable input. And it can be said of Luxemburg's flaws what she herself said of Marx when confronted with a host of 'epigones' criticising her work: 'the difference between an error by Marx and the dim-witted blunders of his epigones—Marx's error by itself [...] is "fructifying" and leads us onward, pointing toward a solution' (Luxemburg 1915/1921, p. 444).

Conclusion

This chapter addressed two pillars of theories of imperialism: finance capital and militarism. It proposes a definition of finance capital based on a definition of capital as a social relation incarnated both in capital-property and capital-in-function (productive capital). The centrality of capital-property is thus rooted in capitalist relations of production, and its ascendancy was reinforced by the political power regained over the last decades by the *rentiers*, a class prospering thanks to the ownership of titles to property rights claiming a growing share of the value created in the production process.

Property rights—which, according to Marx, are 'merely relations of production [...] in legal terms' (Marx 1859/1987, p. 263)—just like militarism, belong to the political sphere. Proceeding in his analysis of the role of law with a somewhat analogous method to Luxemburg on militarism, the Marxist historian E.P. Thompson shows in his major book, *Whigs and Hunters* (1975), that law is 'deeply imbricate within the very basis of productive relations which would have been inoperable without law' (cited in Ireland 2002, p. 128). Likewise, by rejecting a merely 'instrumentalist' role of the law and locating that role instead in the reproduction of capitalist social relations, some Marxist scholars of law have directed attention to a series of observations made by Engels regarding the relation between the economic basis and political superstructure. To give an example, some draw on the distinction he makes between 'essential legal relations', that is to say, those essential legal conceptions that are central to a capitalist economic order, such as property, contract, credit and, on the other end, the law (or judicial practice) (Stone 1985, p. 49).

Capital-property and militarism are two analytical categories useful for our understanding of the contemporary capitalist trajectory. In a context of productive accumulation slowdown, ascending capital-property signifies a considerable increase of value appropriation through rents. Property rights, as the 'legal form' of capitalist relations, have to be enforced, protected and militarily defended. Evidence for this is provided not only by recent history, but also in the present (see the United States' involvement in the Middle East and Latin America and France's military interventions in Africa; for the intertwining of economic, political and military involvement in the sub-Saharan region, see Serfati 2020, 'Frankreichs militärischer Machthebel und die "europäische Verteidigung"', published by the Rosa Luxemburg Stiftung). Ever since Luxemburg wrote *The Accumulation of Capital*, powerful military-industrial systems have been embedded in the economic and political setting of advanced industrial countries. In the context of the '2008 moment', marked by a rise in chaos in some regions (e.g. the sub-Saharan area), the tighter linkage of economic and geopolitical relations in the agenda of major powers is fuelling military spending at an unprecedented level. The interactions between the extension of finance capital under the control of capital-property and militarism merit further attention in research informed by Marx.

REFERENCES

Aknin, A., and C. Serfati. 2008. Guerres pour les ressources, rente et mondialisation. *Mondes en développement* 3 (143): 27–42.

BIS (Bank for International Settlements). 2019. Annual Economic Report, Basel.

Borchard, E. 1932. International Loans and International Law. *Proceedings of the American Society of International Law at Its Annual Meeting* 26: 135–170.

Brewer, A. 1980. *Marxist Theories of Imperialism: A Critical Survey*. London: Routledge.

Bukharin, N.I. 1917/1929. *Imperialism and World Economy*. London: Martin Lawrence. https://www.marxists.org/archive/bukharin/works/1917/imperial/.

———. 1925–1926/1972. *Imperialism and the Accumulation of Capital*. New York: Monthly Press.

Chesnais, F. 2016. *Finance Capital Today. Corporations and Banks in the Lasting Global Slump*. Leiden/Boston: Brill.

de Brunhoff, Suzanne. 1976a. *État et capital*. Paris/Grenoble: Presses universitaires de Grenoble/Maspero.

———. 1976b. *Marx on Money (1976, 1973)*. New York: Urizen.

Drago, L.M., and H.E. Nettles. 1928. The Drago Doctrine in International Law and Politics. *The Hispanic American Historical Review* 8 (2): 204–223.

Engelbrecht, H.C., and F.C. Hanighen. 1934. *The Merchants of Death*. New York: Dodd, Mead & Co.

Engels, F. 1887/1990. Introduction to Sigismund Borkheim's Pamphlet. In Frederick Engels 1882–89, Manuscripts on Early German History. *Marx and Engels Collected Works*, vol. 28. New York: International Publishers. https://www.marxists.org/archive/marx/works/1887/12/15.htm.

———. 1890. To Conrad Schmidt in Berlin, London, October 27. https://www.marxists.org/archive/marx/works/1890/letters/90_10_27a.htm.

Ferguson, N. 1999. *The House of Rothschild: The World's Banker 1849–1999*. New York: Viking Penguin.

Fine, R., and S. Picciotto. 1992. On Marxist Critiques of Law. In *The Critical Lawyers' Handbook Volume 1*, ed. I. Griff-Spall and P. Ireland, 17–20. London: Pluto Press.

Finnemore, Martha. 2003. *The Purpose of Intervention: Changing Beliefs About the Use of Force*. Ithaca/London: Cornell University Press.

Gaido, D., and M. Quiroga. 2013. The Early Reception of Rosa Luxemburg's Theory of Imperialism. *Capital & Class* 37: 437–455.

Grossmann, H. 1929. *Das Akkumulations- und Zusammenbruchsgesetz des kapitalistischen Systems (Zugleich eine Krisentheorie)*. Leipzig: Hirschfeld. Abridged Translation. 1992. *The Law of Accumulation and Breakdown of the Capitalist System*. London: Pluto Press.

Guillén, A. 2013. Contributions of Rudolf Hilferding to an Understanding of the Current Global Economic Crisis. In *Economie Appliquée, LXVI, 2*. Paris: ISMEA.

Hilferding, R. 1910/1981. *Finance Capital. A Study of the Latest Phase of Capitalist Development*. London: Routledge/Kegan Paul.

Ireland, P. 2002. History, Critical Legal Studies and the Mysterious Disappearance of Capitalism. *Modern Law Review* 65: 120–140.

International Monetary Fund (IMF). (2019). World economic outlook: Growth Slowdown, Precarious Recovery, Washington D.C. April.

James, H. 1981. Rudolf Hilferding and the Application of the Political Economy of the Second International. *The Historical Journal* 24 (4): 847–869.

Johnson, T.O., Jr., and J. Gimblett. 2012. From Gunboats to BITs: The Evolution of Modern International Investment Law. In *Yearbook on International Investment law & Policy 2010/2011*, ed. Karl P. Sauvant. Oxford: Oxford University Press.

Kautsky, K. 1912. Gold, Papier und Ware. *Die Neue Zeit* 30 (1), Nr.24 & Nr.25: 837–847 and 886–893. https://www.marxists.org/archive/kautsky/1912/xx/gpcc.htm.

———. 1914. Ultra-Imperialism. *Die Neue Zeit*, September. https://www.marxists.org/archive/kautsky/1914/09/ultra-imp.htm.

King, J.E. 2010. Hilferding's Finance Capitalism the Development of Marxist Thought. *History of Economics Review* 52 (1): 52–62.

Kowalik, T. 2014. *Rosa Luxemburg Theory of Accumulation and Imperialism.* Basingstoke/New York: Palgrave Macmillan.

Lapavitsas, C. 2010. Financialisation and Capitalist Accumulation: Structural Accounts of the Crisis of 2007–2009. https://www.researchgate.net/publication/237138388_Financialisation_and_Capitalist_Accumulation_Structural_Accounts_of_the_Crisis_of_2007-9/citation/download.

Lapavitsas, C., and I. Levina. 2011. Financial Profit: Profit from Production and Profit upon Alienation. *Research on Money and Finance*, 24 May.

Lenin, V. I. 1917/2011. *Imperialism, the Highest Stage of Capitalism. A Popular Outline.* Eastford: Martino Fine Books. https://www.marxists.org/archive/lenin/works/1916/imp-hsc/.

Lewinsohn, R. 1935. *Les profits de guerre à travers les siècles.* Paris: Payot.

Luxemburg, Rosa. 1899/1972. The Militia and Militarism. In *Selected Political Writings by Rosa Luxemburg*, ed. Robert Looker. London: Random House. https://www.marxists.org/archive/luxemburg/1899/02/26.htm.

———. 1906/1898/2008. *Reform or Revolution & The Mass Strike.* Chicago: Haymarket Books.

———. 1913/2003. *The Accumulation of Capital.* London: Routledge.

———. 1915/1921/2015. The Accumulation of Capital, or, What the Epigones Have Made Out of Marx's Theory—An Anti-Critique. In *The Complete Works of Rosa Luxemburg, Volume II, Economic Writings 2*, ed. P. Hudis and P. Le Blanc, 347–450. https://www.marxists.org/archive/luxemburg/1915/anti-critique/index.htm.

Mandel, E. 1972. *Late Capitalism.* London: Verso.

Marchlewski, J.B. 1910/2012. Rudolf Hilferding's Finance Capital: A Study of the Latest Phase of Capitalist Development. In *Discovering Imperialism. Social Democracy to World War I*, ed. Richard B. Day and Daniel Gaido. Chicago: Haymarket Books.

Marx, K. 1857–1858/1986. Economic Manuscripts of 1857–58, Grundrisse. Foundations of the Critique of Political Economy. *Marx and Engels Collected Works*, vol. 28. New York: International Publishers. https://www.marxists.org/archive/marx/works/1857/grundrisse/ch08.htm.

———. 1859/1987. Preface to a Contribution to the Critique of Political Economy. *Marx and Engels Collected Works*, vol. 29. New York: International Publishers. https://www.marxists.org/archive/marx/works/1859/critique-pol-economy/preface.htm.

———. 1861–1863/1989. Economic Manuscripts 1861–63, Theories on Surplus Value. *Marx and Engels Collected Works*, vol. 32. New York: International Publishers. https://www.marxists.org/archive/marx/works/1863/theories-surplus-value/add3.htm.

———. 1867/1976. *Capital: Volume 1: A Critique of Political Economy.* London: Penguin Books.

———. 1885/1978. *Capital: Volume 2: A Critique of Political Economy*. London: Penguin Books.

———. 1894. Capital. A Critique of Political Economy (Vol. III). *Marx and Engels Collected Works*, vol. 37. New York: International Publishers.

Mitchener, K., and M. Weidenmier. 2005. Empire, Public Goods, and the Roosevelt Corollary. *The Journal of Economic History* 65 (3): 658–692.

Moore, J.W. 2015. *Capitalism in the Web of Life*. London/New York: Verso.

Polanyi, K. 1944/2001. *The Great Transformation. The Political and Economic Origins of Our Time*. Boston: Beacon Paperback.

Pradella, Lucia. 2013. Imperialism and Capitalist Development in Marx's Capital. *Historical Materialism* 21: 117–147.

Roberts, M. 2016. *The Long Depression: Marxism and the Global Crisis of Capitalism*. Chicago: Haymarket Books.

Serfati, C. 1996. Le rôle actif des groupes à dominantes industriels dans la financiarisation de l'économie. In *La Mondialisation financière: Genèse, coût et enjeux, François Chesnais*. Paris: Editions Syros.

———. 2001. *La Mondialisation armée. Le déséquilibre de la terreur*. La Discorde. Paris: Editions Textuel.

———. 2015. Imperialism in Context. The Case of France. *Historical Materialism* 23 (2): 52–93.

———. 2018. La domination du capital financier contemporain: une lecture critique d'Hilferding. In *Penser la monnaie et la finance avec Marx. Autour de Zusanne de Brunhoff*, ed. R. Bellofiore, D. Cohen, C. Durand, and A. Orléan. Rennes: Presses Universitaires de Rennes.

———. 2019. France and Political Economy of Contemporary Imperialism. In *The Palgrave Encyclopedia of Imperialism and Anti-Imperialism*, ed. I. Ness and Z. Cope. Cham: Palgrave Macmillan. https://doi.org/10.1007/978-3-319-91206-6_130-1.

———. 2020. La sécurité nationale s'invite dans les échanges économiques internationaux. *Chronique Internationale de l'IRES*, 2020/1 (N° 169): 79–97.

Serfati, C., and Catherine Sauviat. 2019. Global Supply Chains and Intangible Assets in the Automotive and Aeronautical Industries. *International Journal of Automotive Technology and Management* 19 (3–4): 183–205.

Stone, A. 1985. The Place of Law in the Marxian Structure-Superstructure Archetype. *Law and Society Review* 19 (1): 39–68.

Sweezy, P.M. 1946. *The Theory of Capitalist Development*. Londres: Dennis Dobson Ltd.

Tomz, M. 2007. *Reputation and International Cooperation. Sovereign Debt across Three Centuries*. Princeton: Princeton Univ. Press.

Trotsky, L.D. 1939/1970. *Marxism in Our Time*. New York: Merit/Pathfinder. https://www.marxists.org/archive/trotsky/1939/04/marxism.htm.

von Bernstorff, J. 2018. The Use of Force in International Law before World War I: On Imperial Ordering and the Ontology of the Nation-State. *European Journal of International Law* 29 (1): 233–260.

WIPO. 2017. *Intangible Capital in Global Value Chains.* Geneva.

Wood, E.M. 1995. *Democracy Against Capitalism: Renewing Historical Materialism.* Cambridge: Cambridge University Press.

———. 2003. *Empire of Capital.* London: Verso.

———. 2006. Logic of Power. *Historical Materialism* 14 (4): 9–34.

Zuboff, S. 2015. Big Other: Surveillance Capitalism and the Prospects of an Information Civilization. *Journal of Information Technology* 30 (1): 75–89.

CHAPTER 9

Hilferding and the Large-Scale Enterprise

John Grahl

At present a renewed interest in Hilferding's masterwork, *Finance Capital*,[1] is, for obvious reasons, motivated especially by a concern with the increasingly prominent role of finance in economic life. However, the notes which follow depart a little from that extremely topical theme to focus on another, closely related, aspect of Hilferding's analysis, his prescient account of the giant enterprise. It will be suggested that many of his findings remain valid today. However, although the classical Marxist objective of social control over large-scale industry is as relevant as ever, it is necessary to acknowledge that the means of achieving this are unclear since the central Marxist programme of the past—comprehensive state ownership with central economic planning—is no longer plausible.

---

[1] Hilferding [1919] 1981, translation by Tom Bottomore.

J. Grahl (✉)
University of Middlesex, London, UK
e-mail: J.Grahl@mdx.ac.uk

© The Author(s), under exclusive license to Springer Nature Switzerland AG 2023
J. Dellheim, F. O. Wolf (eds.), *Rudolf Hilferding*, Luxemburg International Studies in Political Economy,
https://doi.org/10.1007/978-3-031-08096-8_9

The Dominance of Large-Scale Business

Although other key works in the era of the second international, notably Luxemburg's *Accumulation of Capital* and Lenin's *Imperialism*, provide comparable analyses of the new phase of capitalism, a feature of Hilferding's work is its detailed account of the structural change in the key agents behind the economic transformation which was taking place, that is, towards large-scale business enterprises (including, of course, banks). Hilferding quotes with approval Marx's famous aphorism that the advent of the joint-stock enterprise is 'the abolition of capital as private property within the boundaries of capitalist production itself.'[2] In place of that intuition, however, he develops a full account of the emerging form of enterprise and an assessment of the radical shift in production relations which it brings about. Four aspects will be emphasised here:

- **The separation of ownership and control.** The divorce of the legal proprietors of corporations, reduced—as Hilferding puts it—to the status of simple 'money capitalists,' from the active managers of production and circulation, was subsequently to become a central issue in both heterodox and mainstream economic thought. Marxists tended to see the divorce as preparing the way for full socialisation since the capitalists as owners had rendered themselves functionally redundant and therefore with no strong defence against expropriation. Mainstream economic analysts either sought to revise standard propositions and theorems in the light of the new realities[3] or to save the vision of a 'market economy' by increasingly arcane conceptual devices. The latter tendency in the end led to a programme for the reunification of the divorced parties, either by replacing dispersed shareholders by active venture capitalists with concentrated ownership stakes financed through the bond market or by thorough reforms to corporate governance meant to put the previously passive shareholders back in the saddle. This utopian conception bears no small responsibility for the financial debacles which opened the present century.
- **The extension of conscious co-ordination.** Hilferding, more than other scholars, realised the extent to which conscious social control

---

[2] Ibid., p. 114.
[3] See notably the works of W. Baumol and J. K. Galbraith.

over production was linked to the rise of cartels, monopolies and bank-controlled industrial groups. In particular he considers a deep change in the process by which rates of profit tend to be equalised across different sectors. (He takes such equalisation, not unreasonably, as a criterion for rationality in the allocation of capital resources.) While the growth of individual monopolies, with their capital increasingly immobilised in plant and equipment, tends to impair allocative efficiency by blocking the mobility of competing capitals across sectors, the further growth of concentration and the development of bank-industry linkages restores it in a higher form by aggregating the profits of major groups in a form amenable to their planned reinvestment across wider and wider regions of the economy as a whole. The allocative outcome no longer results from 'the subjective desire for maximum profit which animates all individual capitalists'[4] but from a conscious centralised appreciation of its objective necessity. More generally, there takes place a reversal of relations between markets and business forms. Where earlier market forces dictated the shape of the competitive firm, now the giant firm shapes and reshapes the market itself. In the face of the growing and quite observable autonomy of corporations, the insistence by 'free-market' apologists on the sovereignty of the individual household as suppliers of labour and 'savings' and as consumers of goods and services becomes increasingly formalist.

- **Institutionalisation and political power.** The small-scale firm of Marx's day, often with an individual owner-manager, was institutionalised to a minimal extent. Indeed, hostility to established institutions was a central political stance.

The great problems which agitated the bourgeoisie were essentially constitutional questions, such as the establishment of a modern constitutional state; problems, that is to say, which affected all citizens alike, uniting them in a common struggle against reaction and the vestiges of feudal and absolutist-bureaucratic rule.[5]

The joint-stock company, on the other hand, is necessarily institutionalised, since the limited liability is necessary because the finance of giant

---

[4] Hilferding [1919] 1981, p. 183.
[5] Ibid., p. 337.

236   J. GRAHL

firms by large numbers of shareholders with little or no knowledge of the specific production process required a legal sanction. At first restricted to undertakings for state-promoted purposes, such as trade with a specific region or the launch of a new industry, the corporate form required state approval on a case-by-case basis. In the course of the nineteenth century, corporate form was banalised, with little or no supervision of the projects involved or of the individuals concerned.[6] The economic and social power of the large corporations and the ease with which they could combine to advance their interests gave them immense political power:

> Cartelisation, by unifying political power, increases its political effectiveness. At the same time, it coordinates the political interests of capital and enables the whole weight of economic power to be exerted directly on the state.[7]

In principle, the interests of the cartels are opposed to those of every class in society. In practice all these classes depend on the big corporations as the dominant agents of economic development.

- **The class domination of monopoly capital.** The political power referred to, exercised frequently in the support of imperialist policies, accompanies a class domination more complete than that of the bourgeoisie in the era of competitive capitalism. A key factor in this domination is the co-option and subordination of the landed proprietors who had previously been in conflict with the industrial bourgeoisie. Smaller capitalists, increasingly dependent on their relations with large-scale business, lose their political autonomy in a similar way:

> [T]he old conflict of interest between the bourgeoisie and the petty bourgeoisie is disappearing, and the latter becomes a praetorian guard of big business.[8]

Likewise, a stratum of technically qualified employees benefits from the increased mechanisation which renders many less-skilled workers

---

[6] Sheltering a firm's shareholders from liability for its debts in the event of insolvency logically implies endowing the firm with legal personality. This status was soon abused; in the US, courts were often prepared to accord legal rights to corporations as though they were indeed people. See Bakan 2004.

[7] Hilferding [1919] 1981, p. 338.

[8] Ibid., p. 346.

redundant. They become 'most fervent supporters of large-scale capitalist development.'[9] Hilferding anticipates a key social development then at a very early stage:

> The development of the joint-stock system has a similar effect. It separates management from ownership and makes management a special function of more highly paid wage earners and salaried employees. At the same time the higher posts become very influential and well-paid positions into which all employees apparently have the opportunity to rise. The interest in a career, the drive for advancement which develops in every hierarchy, is thus kindled in every individual employee and triumphs over his feelings of solidarity.[10]

The combined effect of these developments is a much more highly socialised economy, albeit one with sharp, but largely latent, class antagonisms, and still exposed to crises.

MANAGERIAL CAPITALISM

The empirical basis for Hilferding's study was of course the German economy. However, to pursue the developing analysis of the large-scale enterprise, it is useful to switch the focus to the US. (Hilferding himself recognised parallels between the German and American cases, both of which can be contrasted with the British experience, central in the work of Marx himself.)

The remarkable study of Berle and Means[11] is in some respects continuous with that of Hilferding in its exploration of the separation of ownership and control. (Berle and Means both served in Roosevelt's New Deal administration. They drew on the institutionalist approach to economics which was for a time dominant in the US but subsequently eclipsed by the formalism of the neoclassical school. Although neither of them was Marxist, they can be seen as exploring the increasing socialisation of economic relations within US capitalism.)

The work combines detailed empirical surveys of both the economic and the legal status of large corporations. The divorce of managers and owners was by no means complete, but there were strong trends in that direction. Of the 200 largest non-financial corporations in 1929, 88 were

[9] Ibid., p. 347.
[10] Ibid.
[11] Berle and Means [1932] 1991.

identified as under management control, as against 22 either controlled by a sole owner or 1 with a majority equity stake, 41 controlled by a dominant minority shareholder and 47 controlled through some legal device concentrating effective ownership in the hands of an individual or small group. A later edition was able to confirm the postulated trend: in 1963 managerial control extended to no fewer than 169 out of the 200 largest firms.[12]

Berle and Means confirm Hilferding's view of the small shareholder as reduced to the status of a mere money capitalist. With the development of an organised stock market, 'he has, in fact, exchanged control for liquidity. It is thus plain that the concept of a share of stock must now be vigorously changed. Tersely, the shareholder has a piece of paper with an open market value, and as holder of this paper may receive from time to time, at the pleasure of the management, periodic distributions .... This idea does not accord either with the popular or the legal concept of a shareholder. Economically, however, it seems inescapable.'[13]

The legal side of *The Modern Corporation* considers the legal position of management-controlled firms through the examination of many cases (this part of Berle and Means' study is complicated by the fact that corporate law in the US differs from state to state). The courts, in general, found it impractical to enforce shareholder interests in any complete, absolute sense. Although the protection of property and freedom of enterprise are both necessary in the capitalist economy, there is an unavoidable tension between the two principles once ownership and control diverge: rigorous enforcement of shareholder interests may obstruct the efficient management of the enterprise as a whole, and judges tended to define the obligation on managers as being not to shareholders as such, but to the enterprise itself—a consequence of the legal personality necessarily accorded to joint-stock companies.

> The three main rules of conduct which the law has developed are: (1) a decent amount of attention to business; (2) fidelity to the interests of the corporation; (3) at least reasonable business prudence.[14]

[12] Ibid., p. 358.
[13] Ibid., pp. 251–2.
[14] Ibid., p. 197.

After a strictly factual and objective account of the economic and legal status of the corporation, the work closes with some brief but compelling programmatic remarks. The issue is a problem of irresponsible power. If corporations are not required to serve the interests of shareholders, how should they be managed and towards what objectives? The view is

> apparently held by the great corporate lawyers and by certain students in the field, that corporate development has created a new set of relationships, giving to the groups in control powers which are absolute and not limited by any implied obligation with respect to their use. This logic leads to drastic conclusions. For instance, if by reason of these new relationships the men in control of a corporation can operate it in their own interests, and can divert a portion of the asset fund of income stream to their own uses, such is their privilege.[15]

A reassertion of shareholder interests

> would appear to be the lesser of two evils .... A third possibility exists, however .... The control groups have .... cleared the way for the claims of a group far wider than either the owners or the control. They have placed the community in a position to demand that the modern corporation serve not alone the owners or the control but all society.[16]

Berle and Means identify a struggle over the exercise of power comparable to that involved in the reformation of the church.

> The rise of the modern corporation has brought a concentration of economic power which can compete on equal terms with the modern state ... The future may see the economic organism, now typified by the corporation, not only on an equal plane with the state, but possibly even superseding it as the dominant form of social organisation. The law of corporations, accordingly, might well be considered as a potential constitutional law for the new economic state, while business practice is increasingly assuming the aspect of economic statesmanship.[17]

Responding to the challenge of the modern corporation, a vast body of social research in the US has explored the changes in social organisation

---

[15] Ibid., p. 311.
[16] Ibid., pp. 311–2.
[17] Ibid., pp. 211–3.

linked to the development of the large-scale enterprise. In general, the notion of managerial capitalism was accepted by most of the contributors to this literature. Only two of these will be mentioned here. In the view of William Lazonick, 'the most important scholarly work for understanding the evolution of the modern managerial enterprise, particularly in the US context, is that of Alfred D. Chandler, Jr.'[18]

> Chandler argued that when a corporation undertakes an investment strategy to expand into new regional or national markets or to diversify into new product lines, it must also put in place an organisational structure that is capable of administering the more complex set of business activities in which it has invested ... The key features of the multidivisional structure are (1) centralised control by the firm's chief executives over strategic decision-making concerning investment in new markets and products and (2) the delegation of operational decision making to divisions to be monitored as profit centres.[19]

It does not seem exaggerated to see this finding as that adumbrated in Hilferding's account of profit rate equalisation: economic activities can be grouped together not only to increase market power or productive efficiency but also to reinforce control over the allocation of new investments.

A wealth of social research elaborated and corrected the emerging account of managerial capitalism, including influential critiques such as Vance Packard's *Hidden Persuaders* (1957) or William H. Whyte's *Organization Man* (1956). One should mention here also James March and Herbert Simon's *Organizations* (1958), methodologically departing from the strong rationality premise of much formal economic theory in order to build more empirically grounded accounts of the large-scale firm.

Such intellectual developments had a specific political character. Recognising the widespread erosion of market forces and the increasingly socialised nature of the economy, they tended to promote stronger regulation of corporations in order to avoid what might otherwise become the abuse of irresponsible corporate power. One aspect of this, troubling to orthodox proponents of the 'free market,' was the implicit or explicit support that could be derived for notions of a gradual convergence of capitalist and state socialist systems. Alternatively, the growth of giant firms could strengthen the anti-trust tradition in US thinking, leading to demands to

---

[18] Lazonick 1991. The key works of Chandler referred to include Chandler 1971.
[19] Ibid., p. 192.

break up concentrations of economic power or for the introduction of price or profit restraints.[20] The reaction, from the defenders of the supposedly market-based economy, had its centre in the Economics Department of the University of Chicago. The economic difficulties ('stagflation') encountered in the 1970s by the post-war economic model gave them their opportunity.

NEO-LIBERALS AND THE LARGE-SCALE ENTERPRISE

The starting point for neo-liberal analysis of the business enterprise is the seminal paper by Ronald Coase, of Chicago University on 'The Nature of the Firm.'[21] Coase identified a key lacuna in standard microeconomic theory—its lack of any account of the firm as an institution. In the textbooks the firm is reduced to a production function which specifies the technical terms on which factor inputs can be transformed into outputs of goods or services. Questions such as 'why in most firms does the possessor of capital hire labour and not the other way around?,' 'why do we see firms employing workers rather than agreements among self-employed individuals?' or 'what determines the boundaries of the firm?' go unanswered and indeed unasked. Coase addressed this issue by invoking transaction costs, the costs of using the market.[22] Where these costs exceed those arising from the use of administrative procedures within the firm, the activity concerned will be brought in-house. From similar considerations, workers might be hired on general terms permitting their transfer from one function to another in response to unpredictable changes in markets, thus avoiding complex renegotiations in response to every change. If it is the supplier of capital who bears the key risks facing the enterprise, it is logical for the capitalist to employ workers, rather than the reverse. There is no denying the fertility of Coase's analysis. The recognition of transactions costs, together with related concepts of asymmetric information and principal-agent relations, made for more realistic accounts of market exchange. Note, however, that this is a theory of the firm as such, not of the giant firm in particular.

[20] For example, Kefauver 1965.
[21] Coase [1937] 1996.
[22] In categories accepted by Coase himself, transaction costs include search and information costs; negotiation and decision costs; and monitoring and enforcement costs.

Coase's paper stimulated further conceptual work on the nature of the enterprise, but among analysts committed to a free-market interpretation of economic reality, there was a certain reluctance to accept it in full. Coase saw firms as hierarchical structures, as, in the words he borrowed from D. H. Robertson, 'islands of conscious power in this ocean of unconscious cooperation.'[23] Thoroughgoing economic liberals, such as Armen Alchian, rejected the notion of privately exercised power as incompatible with the freedom reigning throughout the market system. Coase had written as though market co-ordination and the co-ordination through authoritarian planning which he found inside and outside the firm, respectively, were in some sense on a par—the choice between them was a practical one. This was unacceptable, Alchian and Harold Demsetz[24] wrote:

> It is common to see the firm characterized by the power to settle issues by fiat, by authority, or by disciplinary action superior to that available in the conventional market. This is delusion. The firm does not own all its inputs. It has no power of fiat, no authority, no disciplinary action any different in the slightest degree from ordinary contracting between any two people.

The alternative was to see the firm not as a hierarchy of power but as 'a nexus of contracts' and it was this notion that prevailed among neo-liberal economists.

Against Alchian, one could ask who, in reality, is deluded. The absence of power relations in the market economy is not an empirical finding but merely an ontological premise. Alternative premises are possible, for instance, that of the feminists, 'the personal is political.' One might take from this the notion that power, the political, pervades all social relations, and especially those between employers and workers, landlords and tenants and so on, as well as those between men and women. Beyond the important legal outlawing of chattel slavery (not, as we are aware, perfectly enforced), there is no substantive reason to claim that power is absent from the capitalist economy.[25] The major contribution of neo-liberal theorists to our understanding of business organisation is impaired by their dogmatic treatment of the price system as necessarily the ideal

---

[23] Coase [1937] 1996.

[24] Alchian and Demsetz 1972.

[25] The parallel and interactive emergence and triumph of liberal ideologies on the one hand and the growth of slave-trading and the slave economy on the other are explored by Losurdo 2014.

form of co-ordination. In his critique of this literature, Lazonick points not only to its meagre empirical basis, but also to its vitiating omission of the key attribute of the modern corporation—economic dynamism.

> Ultimately, the need is for a theory of capitalist development that comprehends the dynamic interaction of social institutions and economic outcomes to enable us to understand their reciprocal and cumulative impacts.[26]

For all its sophistication in the analysis of transactions and contracts, the neo-liberal account continues to see the firm as essentially *adaptive* just as in textbook microeconomics. The innovative character of the corporation is neglected. It is *Hamlet* without the Prince of Denmark.

Indeed the concentration on contracts and transactions seems to result from the extreme individualism of liberal thought as such. It must repeatedly, and never with full success, strive to conjure society and social relations from the interactions of asocial individuals—as far back as the origins of liberalism itself one finds the same dilemma and the serial failure to square this circle.[27] Once the social nature of every agent involved in the enterprise (however sharp their conflicts with each other) is recognised, it becomes possible to refocus on the productive logic which actually drives corporate development even as that development is subordinated to the drive for accumulation.

Neo-liberal enterprise theory tended, as we have seen, to explain and justify actual market outcomes and actual business practices. In the work of Michael Jensen, however, it became highly programmatic, putting forward proposals for business reorganisation which were, for 20 years, extremely influential, and which continue to affect the strategies of business leaders. The context for this initiative was the rising challenge to American industrial dominance from such rivals as Germany and Japan. Jensen identified, very correctly, an unmet need for major restructuring. His own version of neo-liberal enterprise theory[28] emphasised the role of incentives on corporate leaderships; he argued that incentives to improve the efficiency of production had become too weak, because market processes were impaired. In his take on the separation of ownership and

---

[26] Lazonick 1991, p. 277. For an excellent critical survey of theories of the enterprise, see Baudry and Chassagnon 2014.

[27] MacPherson 1962.

[28] See Jensen and Meckling [1976] 1996.

control, he suggested that managements without significant ownership stakes, because their emoluments were related to turnover or other measures of scale, were incentivised to expand the business rather than to make the most profitable use of the resources at their disposal. Product markets were not always competitive enough to correct this situation in firms with some market power. For example, a major oil company might invest in a new oil field even though the return on such an investment was very low. Provided that the returns were not actually negative, the management might expect to benefit from the increased turnover of the firm, while dispersed shareholders, losing by these decisions, were powerless to challenge them.

Jensen's literally reactionary prescription for successful restructuring was to reunite ownership and control. As his doctrines permeated business thinking, the 1980s became the era of the leveraged buyout (LBO). Buccaneering venture capitalists, financed by the issue of junk bonds on a stupendous scale, threatened incumbent, and perhaps somnolent, corporate leaderships, sometimes forcing them to disgorge large sums in the repurchase of their own stock ('greenmail'), to cut back on vanity projects and investments, to outsource and off-shore 'non-core' activities. In sum, however, the impact on powerful corporations was limited. There was a great deal of sharp practice and even corruption in the junk bond market. The social costs in plant closures and abandoned communities were so high as to incline legislatures and judiciaries to reinstall checks and controls on mergers and takeovers which they had happily removed a few years earlier.

A second and more limited version of the Jensen agenda took the form of a drive for shareholder value. Governance reforms might work to align corporate strategies more closely on shareholder interests. Policies might liberalise mergers and acquisitions in the so-called market for corporate control.

It is hardly necessary at this date to describe in detail the debacle to which all this led. Only one point will be made: the shareholder strategy assumes that financial markets are both powerful and efficient, efficient enough to detect and assess sub-optimal corporate performance and then powerful enough to correct it. That both assumptions are invalid was ironically recognised by Jensen himself. An LBO might displace an ineffective management and enhance the value of an enterprise. But what can one do about an enterprise massively overvalued on the stock market? Jensen wryly concedes, 'It is difficult, to say the least, to buy up an overvalued company, eliminate its overvaluation and make a profit.'[29] Of course, contrarian investors might short the company, but as Andrei Shleifer's analysis[30] (and Michael Lewis's book and the subsequent movie) shows, that takes deep pockets, nerves of steel and some residual faith in market valuations: if the company is overvalued today, what is to stop it being even more overvalued tomorrow?

The balance sheet of the neo-liberal challenge to our understanding of the enterprise is surely in heavy deficit. The raiders embarrassed and sometimes disturbed corporate boardrooms; they never came near overthrowing incumbent corporate hierarchies. The basic question remains: how, and in whose interests, is the immense power of the modern corporation to be exercised? What form can effective social control take? The neo-liberal answer was that control can be exercised by the markets, especially the financial markets. Although social control via competitive markets retains some validity for small businesses, when we come to large-scale enterprises, that answer fails both in theory and in practice.

Social Control and the Large-Scale Business

Hilferding saw the future of large-scale enterprise in the same way as Marx. The increasingly social nature of capitalist production would simplify the issue of social control:

> If we now pose the question as to the real limits of cartelisation, the answer must be that there are no absolute limits .... The ultimate outcome .... would be the formation of a general cartel. The whole of capitalist production would then be consciously regulated by a single body .... Price determination would become a purely nominal matter .... The illusion of the objective value of the commodity would disappear along with the anarchy of production and money itself would cease to exist ... This would be a consciously regulated society but in an antagonistic form. Thus the specific nature of capital is obliterated in finance capital. Capital now appears as a unitary power which exercises sovereign sway over the life process of society; a power which arises directly from the ownership of the means of production, of natural resources, and of the whole accumulated labour of the past, and from command over living labour as a direct consequence of property relations .... The problem of property relations thus attains its clearest, most

---

[29] Jensen 2004, p. 12.
[30] The paper cited by Jensen himself is Shleifer and Vishny 1997.

unequivocal and sharpest expression at the same time as the development of finance capital itself is resolving more successfully the problem of the organisation of the social economy.[31]

For those unconvinced by this chiliastic vision—those, that is, for whom Marxist theory is something other than a cult, history can no longer be expected, in Prufrock's words, to squeeze the universe into a ball and roll it towards an overwhelming question. We are confronted not with such a simplification but rather with proliferating complexity. In semi-retreat from the hope of a single decisive expropriation, there is the more practical notion of the 'commanding heights': the view that social ownership of a few, strategically selected, enterprises could be the basis for an assertion of democratic priorities in economic development. If such a programme remains plausible, it must be on a scale wider than a single country such as France where the nationalised giants turned out to be obstacles to the implementation of the common programme rather than levers of control. They were supposed to expand employment and substitute for imports. Their situational logic impelled them to shed labour and internationalise. The outcome was a vast and general waste of red ink.

The same consideration applies to the certainly necessary reinforcement of regulation in the corporate sphere. Issues such as environmental protection and clean-up, enforcement of social and environmental standards across globalised supply chains, an increase by an order of magnitude in the tax contributions of MNCs and, of great material and symbolic importance, the suppression of absurd managerial salaries can be addressed effectively only on a wide transnational basis.

Turning to debates and practices in the mainstream, one can deal quickly with the vogue of 'corporate social responsibility,' the vacuity of which is demonstrated by the simultaneous pursuit of 'shareholder value' by the enterprises concerned. Baran and Sweezy anticipated the whole phenomenon. They quote Carl Kaysen, 'The modern corporation is a soulful corporation.' They comment:

> According to this view, which is certainly very widespread nowadays, the maximisation of profits has ceased to be the guiding principle of business enterprise. Corporate managements, being self-appointed and responsible to no outside group, are free to choose their aims and in the typical case are

---

[31] Hilferding [1919] 1981, pp. 234–5.

assumed to subordinate the old-fashioned hunt for profits to a variety of other, quantitatively less precise but qualitatively more worthy, objectives .... The implications of this doctrine of the 'soulful corporation' are far-reaching. The truth is that if it is accepted, the whole corpus of traditional economic theory must be abandoned and the time-honoured justification of the existing social order in terms of economic efficiency, justice etc., simply falls to the ground.[32]

There are, however, more serious contributions. The 'variety of capitalism' literature emphasises the rather different conduct and governance structures of US corporations on the one hand and those of Japan and Western European countries on the other.[33] A difficulty is the rapidity and facility with which some of the supposedly established European features, for instance, the German financial system, were Americanised.[34] However, the promotion and reinforcement of stakeholder interests (those of employees, suppliers and customers, communities, environmental protection agencies, perhaps others) is certainly a necessary component of any programme for social control.

The role of limited liability perhaps represents an important theme in legal reform. It is a privilege and an extremely valuable one, as shareholders in the banks and other corporations which failed in the global financial crisis—owing billions of dollars—could testify. The privilege could be made the quid pro quo for corresponding duties on those who benefit from it, while limited liability could be denied to investors in socially regressive projects.

Certain mainstream economists have presented critical accounts of the contemporary business enterprise and developed proposals for reform. Colin Mayer relates his proposals for change to the historical use of the corporate form to achieve specific purposes recognised by the state. He proposes a regime where corporations could commit to specific purposes, rather than simply maximising returns to shareholders. He writes, perhaps optimistically,

This simple step of incorporating corporate purpose in company articles of association transforms the whole of the corporate and institutional sector

[32] Baran and Sweezy [1966] 1968, pp. 34–5.
[33] Amable 2003.
[34] Streeck and Höpner 2003.

and, if effectively implemented, provides the answer to how we can escape from the seemingly irresolvable systemic failure we have created.[35]

No comprehensive answer to the challenge of social control can be offered here, largely because the writer is unaware of any such programme. In its absence, reform proposals should draw on all the approaches discussed above.

Instead of a programmatic conclusion, one can return to the separation of ownership and control of which Hilferding offered an early but extremely prescient account and which, as we have seen, the neo-liberal era has failed to reverse. In this context we can mention two conjectures of analytical interest. The first derives from Hilferding's observation that the separation involves the replacement of the industrial capitalist by a paid manager. Clearly the latter, although formally a wage-earner, is not a proletarian; we see today the senior management of large corporations extracting massive sums in what is essentially a form of situational rent. But neither is he a bourgeois—his wealth does not derive from his property but on the contrary—he becomes a proprietor as an expression of his success as a corporate functionary in the same way that successful bourgeois used to turn themselves into landowners. Do we live in a bourgeois society? Does not the concept of a bourgeoisie imply the union of ownership and control which has now disappeared? Michel Aglietta and Anton Brender dared to think so.[36] The social analysis on which they base their programmatic proposals starts from the prevalent status of wage or salary earner. One is confronted not by a simple opposition—owner/non-owner—but by a continuous spectrum from those on the minimum wage to the fat cats at the top of the hierarchy. Certain convergences of ethos and ambition follow, as Hilferding recognised, from that continuity. The corporate elites derive their most certainly exploitative incomes not from ownership but as situational rents based on their control.[37] Meanwhile the trillions of dollars of securities held by middle and higher strata, through their pension funds and other fund managers, offer only meagre returns where these indeed remain positive and the rapidity with which they are traded undermines any notion of control. The Faustian pact of the 'money capitalist'—control abandoned in return for liquidity—is ever more clearly

[35] Mayer 2018, p. 225.
[36] Brender and Aglietta 1984.
[37] Askenazy 2016, reviewed in Grahl 2018.

sealed. Is this still bourgeois society? One can read about that in the pages of Proust or Galsworthy, but does it still exist?

With equal daring, Gérard Duménil and Dominique Lévy draw out the implications of a managerial order that has been somewhat disturbed but in no wise undermined by the neo-liberal assault. Is this still capitalism? They postulate a transition to a mode of production, still riven by class conflicts, but where these are of a different nature from those observed in the era of classical Marxism:

> Managers play a central role in .... two respects, class dominations and sociality: simultaneously as a social class and for being the main agents of socialisation. Managers will be the upper class of managerialism as a new mode of production.[38]

In an era when industrial capitalism as such was still novel and alarming, Hilferding registered, analysed (and frequently anticipated) the profound forces transforming that system. Today the theoretical and practical challenges facing us are just as great.

References

Alchian, Armen A., and Harold Demsetz. 1972. Production, Information Costs and Economic Organization. *American Economic Review* 62: 777–795. Reprinted in Putterman and Kroszner, eds. 1996. *The Economic Nature of the Firm.* Cambridge University Press.

Amable, Bruno. 2003. *The Diversity of Modern Capitalism.* Oxford: Oxford University Press.

Askenazy, Philippe. 2016. *Tous rentiers! Pour une autre répartition des richesses.* Paris: Odile Jacob.

Bakan, J. 2004. *The Corporation: The Pathological Pursuit of Profit and Power.* London: Constable and Robinson.

Baran, Paul A., and Paul M. Sweezy. [1966] 1968. *Monopoly Capital: An Essay on the American Economic and Social Order,* Pelican ed. New York: Monthly Review Press.

Baudry, Bernard, and Virgile Chassagnon. 2014. *Les théories économiques de l'entreprise.* Paris: La Découverte.

---

[38] Duménil and Lévy 2018.

Berle, Adolf A., and Gardiner C. Means. [1932] 1991. *The Modern Corporation and Private Property*, ed. Murray L. Weidenbaum and Mark Jensen, New ed. London: Transaction Publishers.

Brender, Anton, and Michel Aglietta. 1984. *Les Métamorphoses de la société salariale: la France en projet*. Paris: Calmann-Lévy.

Chandler, Alfred D. 1971. *The Visible Hand: The Managerial Revolution in American Business*. Cambridge, MA: Harvard University Press.

Coase, Ronald H. 1937. The Nature of the Firm. *Economica* 4: 386–405. Reprinted in Putterman, Louis and Randall S. Kroszner, eds. 1996. *The Economic Nature of the Firm*. Cambridge University Press.

Duménil, Gérard, and Dominique Lévy. 2018. *Managerial Capitalism: Ownership, Management and the Coming New Mode of Production*. London: Verso.

Grahl, John. 2018. Beyond Redistribution? *New Left Review* 113 (Sept/Oct): 151–158.

Hilferding, Rudolf. [1919] 1981. *Finance Capital: A Study of the Latest Phase of Capitalist Development*. Trans. Tom Bottomore. London: Routledge and Kegan Paul.

Jensen, Michael C. 2004. *Agency Costs of Overvalued Equity*. ECGI Working Paper, May.

Jensen, Michael, and William Meckling. 1976. Theory of the Firm: Managerial Behaviour, Agency Costs and Ownership Structure. *The Journal of Financial Economics* 3: 305–360. Reprinted in Putterman and Kroszner, eds. 1996. *The Economic Nature of the Firm*. Cambridge University Press.

Kefauver, Estes. 1965. *In a Few Hands: Monopoly Power in America*. Baltimore: Pantheon Books.

Lazonick, William. 1991. *Business Organisation and the Myth of the Market Economy*. New York: Cambridge University Press.

Losurdo, Domenico. 2014. *Liberalism: A Counter-History*. London: Verso.

MacPherson, C.B. 1962. *The Political Theory of Possessive Individualism: From Hobbes to Locke*. Oxford: Oxford University Press.

Mayer, Colin. 2018. *Prosperity: Better Business Makes the Greater Good*. Oxford: Oxford University Press.

Shleifer, Andrei, and Robert W. Vishny. 1997. The Limits of Arbitrage. *Journal of Finance* 52: 1.

Streeck, Wolfgang, and Martin Höpner. 2003. *Alle Macht dem Markt: Fallstudien zur Abwicklung der Deutschland AG*. Frankfurt: Campus.

CHAPTER 10

Hilferding and Kalecki

Jan Toporowski

The standard derivation of Kalecki's theory from Marx's work (Feiwel 1977, pp. 56–62; Sawyer 1985, Chapter 8; Sardoni 1989) rests on his well-known reference to Luxemburg in his *Essays in the Theory of Economic Fluctuations* of 1939 where, in stating that capitalists' investment determines their saving, he pointed out that this argument is 'contained in the famous Marxian scheme of "extended reproduction"'. However,

> Marx is interested in finding out, with the help of exchange equations, the pace of investment in investment and consumption goods industries, respectively, which is necessary in order to secure a steady expansion of output … He does not pay attention to the problem of what happens if investment is inadequate to secure the moving equilibrium, and therefore does not approach the idea of the key position of investment in the determination of the level of total output and employment.

J. Toporowski (✉)
Department of Economics, School of Oriental and African Studies, University of London, London, UK
e-mail: jt29@soas.ac.uk

© The Author(s), under exclusive license to Springer Nature Switzerland AG 2023
J. Dellheim, F. O. Wolf (eds.), *Rudolf Hilferding*, Luxemburg International Studies in Political Economy,
https://doi.org/10.1007/978-3-031-08096-8_10

251

Kalecki went on:

> Exactly the reverse attitude is represented by one of his eminent pupils, Rosa Luxemburg. In her *Accumulation of Capital* she stressed the point that, if capitalists are saving, their profits can be "realised" only if a corresponding amount is spent by them on investment. She, however, considered impossible the persistence of net investment (at least in the long run) in a closed capitalist economy; thus, according to her, it is only the existence of exports to the non-capitalist countries which allows for the expansion of the capitalist system. The theory cannot be accepted as a whole, but the necessity of covering the "gap of saving" by home investment or exports was outlined by her perhaps more clearly than anywhere else before the publication of Mr. Keynes's *General Theory.* (Kalecki 1939, pp. 45–46)

Years later, Kalecki admitted to having been influenced in his early intellectual development by another Marxist economist, Mikhail Tugan-Baranovsky (Kowalik 1964, p. 1). Here his interest arose from the consideration of the same question that drew his attention to Rosa Luxemburg, namely the issue of how the surplus or profits of capitalists can be realised in a capitalist economy. In his later years, as he reflected upon the origin of his ideas in the work of Marx and his followers, Kalecki summarised his views on both Marxists in a paper titled 'The Problem of Effective Demand with Tugan-Baranovsky and Rosa Luxemburg', which first appeared in Polish in 1967 (Kalecki 1967).

KALECKI ON HILFERDING

It was not until the end of Kalecki's life that Rudolf Hilferding for the first time was explicitly referenced in the Polish economist's writings. Kalecki's editor observed that 'In the 1920s' Kalecki 'probably read R. Hilferding's *Finance Capital* and Rosa Luxemburg's *The Accumulation of Capital*, among others, but he certainly did not study them at that time' (Osiatyński 1990, p. 425). However, in a final article written with Tadeusz Kowalik, 'Observations on the "Crucial Reform"', published after Kalecki's death, Kalecki examined the legacy of Rudolf Hilferding with regard to the possibility of economic stabilisation of capitalism (Kalecki and Kowalik 1971). Kalecki's comments were rather general, since the detailed remarks on Hilferding in that paper were undoubtedly written by Kowalik, rather than

Kalecki himself: in a subsequent note, Kowalik described their respective parts in writing the article as follows:

> Ultimately, my contribution was limited to presenting the great hypotheses of R. Hilferding, R. Luxemburg, L. Krzywicki and others. In the remaining part of the article my role was distinctly limited. Anyway, even in the first part, Kalecki had a well-formed opinion. He knew well all those hypotheses, except perhaps for Krzywicki's. But he did not want to go back again to the sources in order to check his recollection of them. (Kowalik 1980, p. 634)

Kowalik's summary of Hilferding's views on the question of economic stabilisation, that he compiled for Kalecki, was prefaced by a brief discussion of the difference between what Kalecki and Kowalik meant by 'crucial reform' and the reformism of the German political economist Eduard Bernstein. Kalecki and Kowalik defined 'crucial reform' as occurring when 'the strong pressure of the masses leads to such a radical reform of the system, in spite of the opposition of the ruling class, that, without abolishing existing relations of production, a new valve is opened for the development of the forces of production. There will then be a paradoxical situation: a "crucial reform" imposed on the ruling class may stabilize the system, temporarily at least' (Kalecki and Kowalik 1971, p. 467).[1] Kalecki and Kowalik summarised their interpretation of Hilferding as follows:

> Superficially, it might appear that Hilferding's views did not differ so very much from Bernstein's. Hilferding also attributed crises to the disproportional development of particular branches of industry. He allowed for the possibility of eliminating crises by "organising" capitalism... Anarchy and economic crises could be eliminated only by a "general cartel" in which production would be consciously controlled by a central institution and prices would be only a formal instrument for distributing [total output]. (Kalecki and Kowalik 1971, pp. 468–469)

However, whereas Bernstein thought that capitalism would be transformed in a natural, evolutionary process, the Polish authors quoted

---

[1] Kalecki and Kowalik continued: 'As we argue below, we have to do with just such a situation in contemporary capitalism'. In view of subsequent economic and political developments in the main capitalist countries, this conclusion is perhaps a misjudgement. But since the chapter here is concerned with the place of Hilferding's ideas in Kalecki's analysis, we may leave aside Kalecki and Kowalik's political predictions.

254   J. TOPOROWSKI

Hilferding in arguing that such a transformation was far more revolutionary:

> Planned production and anarchic production are not quantitative opposites such that, by taking on more and more "planning", conscious organization will emerge out of anarchy... to expect the abolition of crises from individual cartels simply shows a lack of insight into the causes of crises and the structure of the capitalist system. (Kalecki and Kowalik 1971, p. 268, quoting Hilferding [1910] 1981, pp. 296–97)

According to the two Polish authors, Hilferding underscored this view by stating that any attempt to enforce a 'general cartel' would fail in the face of opposition from particular industrial cartels and interests, imperialist conflicts between different national cartels, and social class divisions. Yet at the time they were writing (in 1969) the possibility of a general cartel did in fact exist in the United States where, they argued, 'a huge military-industrial complex has emerged which, now with space exploration, plays a predominant part in the ensemble of social and economic relations' (Kalecki and Kowalik 1971, pp. 473–474).

HILFERDING AND THE BUSINESS CYCLE

In their reflections on Hilferding, Kalecki and Kowalik clearly addressed the political controversies that had preoccupied Hilferding during his work on *Finance Capital*, namely the question of imperialism and the reformist political strategy of Bernstein and later Karl Kautsky regarding the possibility of socialism without revolution. Kalecki and Kowalik correctly identified Hilferding as an opponent to this reformist strategy. In particular, they were not concerned with Hilferding's own contribution to economic theory in general, and the theory of business cycles in particular. This aspect of Hilferding's work has been sadly neglected. Schumpeter found his monetary theory 'old-fashioned' and considered the bulk of his work to merely provide 'a hasty generalization from a phase of German developments', however 'interesting and original' (Schumpeter 1954 p. 181).[2] Schumpeter had in mind Hilferding's omission of bank credit as means of payment and the proliferation and circulation of such credit in

---

[2] Schumpeter had greater regard for Hilferding's skills as a finance minister (Schumpeter 1939, p. 715).

capital market-based financial systems. Most monetary theorists have followed Schumpeter in overlooking Hilferding's work, or at least regarding it as a comment on specific circumstances in Central European banking (Ellis 1934, pp. 99–103), whereas Marxists, with the notable exception of the American *Monthly Review* school led by Paul Sweezy, have not been able to come to terms with Hilferding's acceptance, in line with Marx's Volume III of *Capital*, that prices do not reflect the value of labour inputs into production (Hilferding [1910] 1981, p. 228; King 2010; Sweezy 1942, pp. 270–71). As a result, Hilferding's important, albeit unsystematic, initiation of business cycle theory around the question of markets and the modern corporation has been ignored by virtually all commentators.

Hilferding at least managed to identify a key mechanism of industrial fluctuations. His construction thereof derived from the effect of monopolies on the price system and the respective profit margins of cartelised or monopoly businesses, and those of non-cartelised businesses, whose profit margins are subject to competition in their respective markets. The result is that monopolies or cartelised businesses take the lion's share of profits in a boom, while protecting their margins at the expense of competitive businesses in a recession. Hilferding believed that the concentration of banking prevents monetary crises. But the distortions introduced into the price system by monopolies and cartels exacerbate the business cycle. Just a few pages after Kalecki's and Kowalik's reference to Hilferding, cited in the last paragraph of the previous section, Hilferding wrote:

> Cartels ... do not eliminate the effects of crises. They modify them only to the extent that they can divert the main burden of a crisis to the non-cartelized industries. The difference in the rate of profit between cartelized and non-cartelized industries, which on average is greater the stronger the cartel and the more secure its monopoly, diminishes during times of prosperity [with increased demand for all production—JT] and increases during a depression. In the initial period of a crisis and depression the cartel may also be in a position to maintain high profits for longer than the independent industries, thus exacerbating the effects of the crisis for the latter. (Hilferding [1910] 1981, p. 298)

At this point, Hilferding crucially abstained from drawing conclusions about this new business cycle for employment and output, since he was more concerned in that particular chapter about the ownership structure of industry and the factors driving businesses to join cartels. His actual conclusion was:

> [It] is precisely during a crisis and its immediate aftermath that the situation of industrialists is most difficult and their independence most threatened. The fact that just at this time cartel policy denies them any relief in the form of reductions in the price of their raw materials etc., is an important factor in worsening the situation of the non-cartelized industries and accelerating the process of concentration. (Ibid.)

'MANAGED CAPITALISM' AND THE BUSINESS CYCLE

In his later years, Hilferding's scepticism concerning the possibilities of managing capitalism through state coordination of business activities receded as he progressed towards his position of Finance Minister in the Weimar Republic. Proceeding from his notion of a 'general cartel', German and Austrian Marxists discussed the possibilities of stabilising capitalism.

Among those Marxists, Emil Lederer stands out, and not just because Schumpeter deemed him to be 'the leading academic socialist of Germany in the 1920s' (Schumpeter 1954, p. 884) who went into exile, when the Nazis seized power, and ended up teaching at the New School in New York. In 1925 he published a paper on the business cycle, under the title *'Konjunktur und Krisen'* ['Business Cycles and Crises'] (Lederer 1925). In this paper he used the Marxian schemes of reproduction, dividing up the economy into sectors representing wage goods, luxury goods, and investment goods, to examine the factors determining the stability (or instability) of the capitalist economy. He argued that the consumption of government employees and rentiers tends to be more or less constant and, therefore, to stabilise economic activity. However, cartels and monopolies tend to make the system more unstable because cartelised businesses typically overinvest during the boom, while during the recession wages tend to decline faster than the prices of wage goods, thereby squeezing consumption (1925). Lederer's theory, therefore, combines elements of the standard 'Austrian' business cycle theory of Hayek and Mises, who argued that economic booms were driven by excessive investment, with the theory of underconsumption that Marx bequeathed to his followers.

Seven years later, in 1932, Kalecki addressed exactly the same question as Lederer in an article titled 'The Influence of Cartelization on the Business Cycle' for a business weekly (Kalecki 1932). Poland had been hit particularly hard by the economic crisis that followed the Great Crash of

1929, and there was a considerable industrial lobby, as was the case in Germany and the United States, favouring cartels as a means of preventing price deflation.

Kalecki began by dismissing the notion of a general cartel (he called it a 'universal cartel') which he thought was impractical, because

> cartels "succeed" only in industries that show a marked degree of concentration and mass-produced standardised articles. In industries where production is highly fragmented or the output of particular factories covers a wide range of different products, the fixing of prices and quotas is virtually impossible. Cartels in such industries either cannot be organised or cannot achieve the required coherence. (Kalecki 1932)

One of the key arguments in favour of cartels is that they stabilise prices either through government regulation or through agreement among producers in cartels. But Kalecki argued that this does not stabilise output, because cartelised producers either supply non-cartelised industries or produce goods that are consumed by workers and capitalists in those industries. If one assumes that profit margins remain the same for all producers, then the effect of partial cartelisation is to reduce fluctuations in investment. But this occurs at the cost of increased fluctuations in workers' incomes and, hence, reductions in consumption during the recession and increased consumption in the boom, both of which represent consequences of price-fixing agreements in cartels. Assuming that more stable profits in the cartelised sector result in more stable investment, it is possible to infer that partial cartelisation neither increases nor decreases fluctuations in output but instead causes shifts in the capacity utilisation of particular industries and in the incomes of workers. However, this suggests that more stable profits in cartels result in a more stable flow of investments. Kalecki pointed out two other considerations that would apply. First of all, because of price-fixing, cartelised businesses will have lower profit margins during boom periods. If those businesses nevertheless invest on the same scale that they would in a competitive system, then this will cause prices and profit margins in the non-cartelised sector to rise, inducing increased output in that sector. In a recession, the reverse happens: cartelised businesses have higher profit margins than they would have in a competitive system, but still invest at the same lower level that they would have done in a competitive system. Prices as well as profit margins in the non-cartelised sector decline, causing a drop in output by independent businesses.

Kalecki's argument is somewhat tortuous in this part of his article, but essentially it states that even under the assumption that cartelised firms maintain the same levels of investment as they would in a system of free competition, 'the more extreme fluctuations of profits in the non-cartelised industries result in more extreme fluctuations in their production, and hence in total output' (Kalecki 1932).

He reinforced this argument by suggesting one additional reason why cartelisation would lead to more extreme business cycles: cartels control prices by means of production quotas, which are usually determined by productive capacity. In the struggle for markets (or market shares), firms in a cartel would therefore tend to overinvest in a boom phase to obtain higher production quotas. In a recession, cartels would protect their firms' profit margins from being squeezed by lower demand at the cost of a lower capacity utilisation: rather than eliminate their excess capacity, firms will prefer to sell capacities (and the attached quota) to another firm in the cartel (Kalecki 1932). This failure to eliminate excess capacity and the related disincentive for further investment then became the foundation of Josef Steindl's later theory of industrial maturity and stagnation (Steindl 1952).

Kalecki concluded that 'in a partially-cartelised system, business cycles will be more extreme than in a system of free competition. In particular, *cartels aggravate the course of a crisis*, not primarily because of rigid prices, but because their *higher profits* than in other industries at this time *are not accompanied by correspondingly greater investment*' (Kalecki 1932, emphases in the original).

In one other respect, Kalecki followed a parallel path to that of Hilferding. Both of them based their analysis on Marx's 'schemes of reproduction', demonstrating how profits are realised as money (Kalecki 1968/1984; Hilferding 1910/1981, pp. 248–256; see also Kowalik 2014, Appendix 1 and chapter 9). As a result, both Kalecki and Hilferding took the total mass of profits or surplus as given, rather than determined by profit margins or some 'productivity' of capital, and assigned the price system the function of distributing those profits around capitalist enterprises. But it was Kalecki who was able to work out what determines that mass of profits, and, more precisely, how that mass is then distributed between monopolists, cartels, and independent businesses to exacerbate the business cycle.

A year after publishing his article on cartelisation, Kalecki published his famous essay on the theory of business cycles that was to establish him as one of the co-founders of the Keynesian Revolution in economic theory. At the end of the original version of this essay, he devoted a section to the question of cartels, using arguments that resembled those contained in his earlier article. However, he now considered the situation in a wholly cartelised economy in the sense of Hilferding's 'general cartel'. In this system, profits are equally determined by investment and remain unchanged. Hence, capitalists cannot increase their profits by increasing prices or depressing wages. All that they can do, by increasing prices or lowering wages, is to reduce workers' incomes and their consumption in a similar way as occurs in a partially cartelised economy (Kalecki 1933). However, he dropped this section from subsequent editions of his essay, and the section, together with the earlier article on cartelisation, was only included in the publication of the English edition of Kalecki's *Collected Works* in the 1990s (Osiatyński 1990).

Conclusion

It is tempting to see Lederer as the 'missing link' between Kalecki and Hilferding, as suggested by Dickler (1981, p. 296). However, Lederer's business cycle theory did not make the leap from Marx's schemes of reproduction to modern national income accounts, as Kalecki was able to do on the basis of his work with Ludwik Landau on Poland's national income data. Furthermore, there is no evidence that Kalecki was familiar with Lederer's work. The Austrian/German/American is not mentioned in any of Kalecki's writings, nor did he refer to him in discussions with his closer circle, although Lederer's business cycle theory was known in Poland prior to World War II. The case for Kalecki's understanding of Hilferding's *Finance Capital* is much stronger. Kalecki adopted and reinforced Hilferding's early critique of monopoly capitalism by showing how it destabilises capitalism. In his business cycle theory, Kalecki assumed that he was addressing the unfinished ideas of Marx and Rosa Luxemburg. In truth he was addressing the political economy of Rudolf Hilferding.

REFERENCES

Dickler, R.A. 1981. *Emil Lederer und die moderne Theorie des wirtschaftlichen Wachstums' Nachwort zu Emil Lederer, Technischer Fortschritt und Arbeitslosigkeit. Eine Untersuchung der Hindernisse des ökonomischen Wachstums,* 263–327. Frankfurt am Main: Europäische Verlagsanstalt.

Ellis, H.S. 1934. *German Monetary Theory 1905–1933.* Cambridge, MA: Harvard University Press.

Feiwel, G.R. 1977. *The Intellectual Capital of Michał Kalecki.* Knoxville: University of Tennessee Press.

Hilferding, R. [1910] 1981. *Finance Capital a Study of the Latest Phase of Capitalist Development.* London: Routledge and Kegan Paul.

Kalecki, M. 1932. Wpływ kartelizacji na koniunkturę. *Polska Gospodarcza* 13 (32): 932–933.

———. 1933. *Próba teorii koniunktury.* Warszawa: Instytut Badań Koniunktur Gospodarczych i Cen.

———. 1939. *Essays in the Theory of Economic Fluctuations.* London: George Allen and Unwin.

———. 1967. Zagadnienie realizacji u Tugana-Baranowskiego i Róży Luksemburg. *Ekonomista* 2: 241–249.

———. [1968] 1984. The Marxian Equations of Reproduction and Modern Economics. In *The Faltering Economy the Problem of Accumulation Under Monopoly Capital,* ed. J.B. Foster and H. Szlajfer. New York: Monthly Review Press.

Kalecki, M., and T. Kowalik. 1971. Observations on the 'Crucial Reform'. In *Collected Works of Michał Kalecki Volume 11 Capitalism: Economic Dynamics.* Oxford: The Clarendon Press.

King, J.E. 2010. Hilferding's Finance Capital in the Development of Marxist Thought. *History of Economics Review* 52 (Summer): 52–62.

Kowalik, T. 1964. Biography of Michał Kalecki. In *Problems of Economic Dynamics and Planning Essays in Honour of Michał Kalecki.* Warszawa: Panstwowe Wydawnictwo Naukowe—Polish Scientific Publishers.

———. 1980. *Komentarz Tadeusza Kowalika' in Michał Kalecki Dzieła tom 2: Kapitalizm Dynamika gospodarcza.* Warszawa: Państwowe Wydawnictwo Ekonomiczne.

———. 2014. *Rosa Luxemburg Theory of Accumulation and Imperialism.* Basingstoke: Palgrave Macmillan.

Lederer, E. 1925. *Konjunktur und Krisen. Grundriss der Sozialökonomik,* 354–413. Tübingen: J.C.B. Mohr.

Osiatyński, J. 1990. Editorial Notes and Annexes. In *Collected Works of Michał Kalecki Volume I Capitalism: Business Cycles and Full Employment*. Oxford: The Clarendon Press.

Sardoni, C. 1989. Some Aspects of Kalecki's Theory of Profits: Its Relationship to Marx's Schemes of Reproduction. In *Kalecki's Relevance Today*, ed. M. Sebastiani. New York: St. Martin's Press.

Sawyer, M. 1985. *The Economics of Michał Kalecki*. Basingstoke: Macmillan.

Schumpeter, J.A. 1939. *Business Cycles a Theoretical, Historical and Statistical Analysis of the Capitalist Process. Vol. II*. New York: McGraw-Hill Book Company.

———. 1954. *History of Economic Analysis*. London: Allen and Unwin.

Steindl, J. 1952. *Maturity and Stagnation in American Capitalism*. Oxford: Basil Blackwell.

Sweezy, P.M. 1942. *The Theory of Capitalist Development Principles of Marxian Political Economy*. New York: Oxford University Press.

CHAPTER 11

Ludwik Krzywicki's Anticipation of Hilferding

Jan Toporowski

Some ten years before the end of the nineteenth century, and twenty years before the publication of Hilferding's *Das Finanzkapital*, the Polish Marxist, journalist and sociologist, Ludwik Krzywicki (1859–1941) published an important article that laid out recent trends in industrial capitalism. The article, and three later ones published in 1905, strikingly anticipated many of the ideas that were later to appear in Hilferding's book. The brevity of Krzywicki's analysis lacked the scholarly sophistication of Hilferding. But it had the advantage over Hilferding's account in that Krzywicki, and later Lange, rooted their understanding of finance capital in the capital market operations of modern corporations, rather than in the commercial banking practices of the Berlin clearing banks. Moreover, in at least two aspects the articles went beyond the analysis given by Hilferding. In the first place, Krzywicki pointed out that the American trust form of monopoly finance capital was more durable than the bank-based finance capital that featured in Hilferding's book. Secondly,

J. Toporowski (✉)
Department of Economics, School of Oriental and African Studies, University of London, London, UK
e-mail: jt29@soas.ac.uk

© The Author(s), under exclusive license to Springer Nature Switzerland AG 2023
J. Dellheim, F. O. Wolf (eds.), *Rudolf Hilferding*, Luxemburg International Studies in Political Economy,
https://doi.org/10.1007/978-3-031-08096-8_11

Krzywicki advanced beyond the hints at social contradictions in Hilferding by arguing that monopoly finance capital would give rise to a specific socio-economic formation in which a capitalist industrial society becomes stratified into relatively closed social classes defined in relation to their property or their professions. He called this formation industrial feudalism and argued that it would suppress the economic and social dynamism by which capitalism overthrew feudalism. In this respect Krzywicki's analysis looks forward to Lenin's analysis of monopoly finance capital in his essay on imperialism and to the more recent account of modern capitalism provided by Paul Baran and Paul M. Sweezy.

The paper is in three sections. The first section introduces the Polish sociologist and political economist Ludwik Krzywicki, who first put forward the concept of industrial feudalism as a consequence of monopoly finance capital. In a second section, Krzywicki's subsequent views on industrial feudalism are summarised. A third section summarises the discussion about Krzywicki in the period after his death. Finally, a brief conclusion summarises and suggests what may still be relevant in Krzywicki's analysis to twenty-first century capitalism.

FINANCE CAPITAL INTRODUCED

Towards the end of his life, the Polish economist Michał Kalecki (1899–1970) sat down with his friend, the distinguished political economist Tadeusz Kowalik (1926–2012) to reconsider the reasons for the durability of capitalism and the possibility of a 'crucial reform' that they defined as 'such a radical reform of the system … that, without abolishing existing relations of production, a new valve is opened for the development of the forces of production.' (Kalecki and Kowalik 1971/1991, p. 466). Inevitably, perhaps, much of their discussion centred around similar discussions that were taking place in that remarkably fertile period of the development of Marxist ideas, in between the death of Engels in 1895 and the First World War. A key text from that period was Rudolf Hilferding's *Finance Capital*, in which Hilferding suggested in *Finance Capital* that the formation of cartels may give rise to the emergence of a 'general cartel' that would 'resolve the basic economic contradictions of capitalism'. Kowalik wrote:

> We find a certain anticipation of Hilferding's vision of a general cartel much earlier in the works of the Polish sociologist Ludwik Krzywicki, who noticed

11 LUDWIK KRZYWICKI'S ANTICIPATION OF HILFERDING   265

strong tendencies toward "industrial feudalism". This was a vision of a 'nation-estate'—a kind of feudal estate embracing the whole country—with a hierarchical social structure governed by a financial oligarchy. Krzywicki linked this vision with the simultaneous... [spread of mass conformity within society including also] the working class, which would derive certain material benefits from this "estate". This is why he attributed considerable stability to the system of industrial feudalism, apparently even seeing it as a threat to the eventual socialist alternative. (Kalecki and Kowalik 1971/1991, p. 469)

Krzywicki put forward his idea in a handful of articles that he wrote from the start of the 1890s, some two decades before the publication of Hilferding's *Finance Capital*. However, a striking difference lies in that, whereas Hilferding based his analysis of monopoly or finance capital on the coordination of capital by banks, Krzywicki recognised the emergence of an American form of monopoly based on the functioning of the capital market, that is, the market for stocks issued by corporations. This meant that Krzywicki's analysis was strikingly more comprehensive of mature capitalism, and it is arguably more applicable in the twenty-first century, than the bank-based finance capital of Hilferding. Kowalik had come across Krzywicki's articles on monopoly finance capital in the course of writing his doctoral thesis on Krzywicki in the first half of the 1950s. In that thesis, Kowalik devoted a whole chapter to presenting Krzywicki as a pioneer of the monopoly capital approach to late capitalism.

As the paper by Kalecki and Kowalik indicates, by the 1960s Krzywicki was known in Poland as an industrial sociologist and the patron of the Institute of Social Economy (*Instytut Gospodarstwa Społecznego*) where he pioneered a radical form of social research based on extensive interviews with workers, peasants and the unemployed. He wrote the Introduction to Kalecki's study of wages in a market economy, 'Money and Real Wages' (*Płace nominalne i realne*) (Krzywicki 1939/1991; see also Toporowski 2018, pp. 16–17). However, at the time of his articles on America, Krzywicki was a leading figure among Polish followers of Karl Marx, respected in those circles for his work translating Marx's *Capital* and for his correspondence with Friedrich Engels. The sectarian divisions among Polish Marxists, in Krzywicki's time and when Kowalik was writing his thesis, were apparent in the chapter in his book that Kowalik devoted to 'The Krzywicki Controversy' (*'Spór o Krzywickim'*) over the question of

266   J. TOPOROWSKI

whether Krzywicki was a real Marxist or not (Kowalik concluded that he was! Kowalik 1959, Chap. 5).[1]

Krzywicki's analysis of monopoly finance capital and its associated concept of industrial feudalism appeared first in an article that he wrote at the end of 1889 for the Warsaw weekly *Prawda* (or 'Truth', not to be confused with the Russian organ of the Russian Social Democratic Party, with the same name in Russian, established much later in 1912). The Polish weekly was the journal of Polish 'positivists' who advocated social and industrial reform, in contrast to the 'romantic' nationalism of activists agitating for Polish independence. At the time when Krzywicki was writing for it, *Prawda* had become an unofficial forum for discussions in socialist circles (Holland 2007, pp. 96–97). The article therefore preceded the publication of volumes 2 and 3 of Marx's *Capital*. Krzywicki reported efforts to construct a coal cartel and quoted the English economist Herbert Foxwell arguing that after a century of competition, economies now faced the problem of how to understand monopoly. According to Krzywicki, some economists like the German Lujo Brentano, or the Austrian politician Karl Vogelsang, favour cartels out of nostalgia for a mythical feudal past of social stability. Such cartels were driving out competition from their markets, Krzywicki argued. But, the purpose of monopoly was not to introduce new techniques and improved products, or lower prices, as happened under competition, but to obtain and keep a higher profit margin.

Krzywicki gave examples of cartels emerging in France and Germany. However, he argued that in these countries they could only be temporary. Legal challenges reduced many cartels to informal 'understandings' among the firms that combined together in them. Cartels would hold in poor trading conditions when factory owners sought protection from those conditions in such agreements. But in a boom, firms had greater incentives to break ranks.

According to Krzywicki, the situation in America was different. Here, more permanent arrangements were secured by handing over shares in particular factories to 'trusts'. The trusts did not issue their own shares, but $100 certificates of deposit, which could be bought and sold on stock markets at prices depending on the demand for the certificates. The certificates gave no title to ownership, or even to the profits of the companies organised in the trust. But the right to an income was guaranteed by the

---

[1] A summary biography of Krzywicki is provided in Kołakowski 1978, pp. 194–197.

'trustees' of the trust. In this way arose the separation of ownership from control of the industry: the trusts held controlling shares of the stocks in the companies, but the holders of the deposits in the trust had no influence on the management of those companies. Krzywicki noted that some 80% of sugar refining capacity on the East coast was controlled by the Sugar Trust (Krzywicki referred to it as the Sugar 'Company'). Even more extensive were the activities of what he called the 'Oil Raffineries (sic) Trust', which undertook common infrastructure investments, such as oil pipelines. The activities of these trusts were now widely known as a result of investigations by commissions of enquiry into their activities set up by state assemblies in New York and Massachusetts.

In his 1889 article, published at the beginning of 1890, Krzywicki revealed the link between these monopolies and the social structures of 'industrial feudalism'. Why, he asked, were Brentano and Vogelsang so favourable towards cartels? The two advocates of cartelisation were not concerned with the technical significance of monopolies, but with counteracting the 'anarchy of the market and the associated rise of social democracy.'

> They dream of a specific society. Private property exists, but the entrepreneurs of each profession constitute a single cartel whose executive collects statistics on demand in the industry, sets down production quotas divided up among the individual producers, and delivers the final product to the consumers. Workers have complete certainty about their prospects, and secure earnings and pension rights. In this way the anarchy of the market is removed together with the main source of workers' grievances, but rents from property are retained. In the final analysis, this is "capitalist socialism" or rather, on closer inspection, industrial feudalism. Political representation is organised on the basis of profession, with its principal heading the factory like a baron his subjects... This is the social order for which yearn Vogelsang and, less obviously, Brentano and the followers of Rodbertus.

Krzywicki concluded that this could not be the end of the story. The centralisation of ownership and production created by the monopolies prepared them organisationally for their takeover by the 'organised social will' that constitutes real socialism (Krzywicki 1890/1957).

Krzywicki's article is striking not only for its anticipation of Hilferding's idea of *finance capital* linked to monopolies, which Krzywicki was able to show in its American capital markets setting, that was to become predominant at the end of the twentieth century.

268   J. TOPOROWSKI

Krzywicki also raised two aspects of this finance capital that would be taken up a quarter of a century later by Lenin in his famous study of imperialism. One of these was the elimination of the 'anarchy of the market' by the planning associated with the calculations of finance capital. The other aspect was the emergence of an 'aristocracy of labour' given improved wages and pensions to move the labour movement away from socialism. This differs from the later view of Lenin, who followed Hilferding in regarding the better working conditions of workers as being paid for from the profits accruing out of imperialist exploitation (Lenin 1917/1968). Krzywicki did not advance any theory of imperialism: at the time when he was writing, Poland was not an independent state, still less an imperial one. The 'Congress Kingdom of Poland' where he was active was a part of the Russian Empire, but an empire whose social and economic backwardness evoked considerations of economic development, rather than imperialism.

KRZYWICKI AND MONOPOLY CAPITAL AFTER CHICAGO

In 1893, Krzywicki visited America, and stayed there for six months. He attended the Chicago World Fair, where he was impressed by the technological achievements of the monopolies that he was criticising. This experience was to affect his early, pessimistic, view on the economic consequences of monopoly. However, he did not change his views on the social and political consequences of the monopolies, and he retained his interest in the economic, social, and political significance of the new corporate behemoths at least into the early years of the new century. His last work on the subject appeared, as the 1905 Revolution was getting under way. That work took the form of three articles, in effect a long essay in three parts, in a political and literary weekly called 'Ogniwo' (chainlink) that was published in Warsaw and was associated with the Polish Socialist Party. Krzywicki edited the weekly along with Stanisław Posner of the Polish Socialist Party and a leading freemason, Stanisław Stempowski.

Krzywicki's essay appeared under the overall, and suggestive, title 'Morganizacja przemysłu' (The Morganization of Industry). The title referred to the process of creating the holding company structures that allowed a trust to control its member companies: 'Morganization' was the term then used in the US in honour of the leading exponent of this art of corporate restructuring. J.P. Morgan was by then locked in a political struggle with the US President Theodore Roosevelt over the President's campaign to break up the trusts dominating the American economy. According to Krzywicki 'In Morgan, the greatest magnate of economic life, are concentrated all the tendencies of capitalism....' This power came from his control of railways and his position as director of shipping, electricity and other trusts.

'But Morgan only holds the highest position among the commanding heights. Next to the Morgan clique are four other groups [of investment banks combining trusts—JT]: Gould Rockefeller, Harriman-Kuhn Loeb, Vanderbilt, and the Pennsylvania group, have divided among themselves the whole railway network.' Rockefeller controlled the oil industry through his Standard Oil Company. 'Like a spider spins his web and, placing himself at its centre detects every movement of any thread, the Morgans and the Rockefellers have captured the arteries of social life and, having taken over these positions, they dictate the rules to industrialists, and turn manufacturers into their vassals' (Krzywicki 1905c).

Krzywicki did not use the term 'industrial feudalism' in this essay. But he argued that 'these plutocrats, having taken into their hands control over American industry, have turned into "sociocrats", in other words they are starting to shape the world in accordance with their will and their outlook. There is a fantasy novel of the well-known English writer Wells [in which] the whole world is concentrated into the hands of one syndicate; the masses are deprived of all cultural advantages and kept compliant through their own ignorance and the most advanced instruments of control, while those who could oppose the rules with their energy and intelligence, are kept enchanted in a "garden of delights", where they lose their powers, health, life… It is in this direction that Morgan and Company are pressing their republic' (ibid.).

Krzywicki was alluding here to Wells' novel *The Time Machine* which presents a dystopian future in which the cultured have become the ineffectual 'Eloi' people, while the working class have been reduced to an animal-like existence underground as the light-fearing 'Morlocks', whose labour makes it possible for the Eloi to continue their agreeable existence. (In the novel, however, the Morlocks sustain themselves by eating the Eloi.)

In the first part of his essay, Krzywicki revealed the sources of his information on the trusts, in the work of John Moody, better known today for the credit-rating agency that was to emerge from that work, and a Representative of Maine in the US House of Representatives, Charles E. Littlefield. Moody had published an annual listing of the largest trusts, and Littlefield was involved in presenting evidence on antitrust legislation to the House Judiciary Committee. Krzywicki highlighted the paradox of the standard economic theory of the firm, according to which the firm is supposed to produce up to the point where its (rising) marginal cost curve meets the price or average revenue curve. Beyond that point of production, firms are supposed to start making losses on their marginal production. The paradox arises because the capital and output of the new companies was much larger than the possible profitable production envisaged by this theory. Although he did not write this explicitly, the paradox is resolved once it is understood that what neo-classical economists refer to as the 'theory' of the firm, using this marginal cost analysis, does not represent how any actual firm operates. It is merely a theory of how production in one plant should be regulated in order to maximise profits. Trusts are firms that allow their directors to control the operation in a number of plants. Obtaining control of a whole industry, a trust may obtain the two benefits that economic centralisation brings: the technical progress and cost-saving that Krzywicki had observed in Chicago. In this respect, Krzywicki modified his earlier view that monopolies stood in the way of technical innovation (Krzywicki 1905a. See also Kowalik 1959, pp. 242–244).

Krzywicki's second article was devoted to explaining the working of the trusts dominating the American steel industry. He explained that Morgan had come to an understanding with the two industrialists dominating that business, Andrew Carnegie and Charles M. Schwab, and with the financier John D. Rockefeller to establish the United States Steel Corporation, with interests covering not only the United States, but also France and Germany. The corporation issued capital far in excess of the value of its actual productive capital. But this 'watering down' of the capital, through the over-issue of stock, or over-capitalisation, merely showed that the 5% return on the shares reflected a true rate of profit of some four times that amount (Krzywicki 1905b). In the final part of his essay, Krzywicki argued that, apart from maintaining the lavish lifestyle of the financiers and industrialists who toiled over the direction of their empires, the profits of the trusts were used to sustain corporate restructuring and the creation of new trusts under their control (Krzywicki 1905c).

The 1905 Revolution must have taken Krzywicki away from his interests in monopoly finance capital in general, and American capitalism in particular. In December *Ogniwo* was closed down by the Tsarist authorities as part of their efforts to suppress the unrest gripping the main industrial centres of the Russian Empire. The dress rehearsal for the October Revolution was followed, in October 1907 by the dress rehearsal for the 1929 Crash. A dramatic fall in stock prices on the New York Stock Exchange led to the failure of an investment fund, the Knickerbocker Trust. The failure caused a run on banks in New York and other financial centres in the US and then abroad, spreading even as far as Britain and Italy. Morgan was the informal lender of last resort to the New York banks and contributed to the crisis when he ran out of gold to assist them with their payments. The American antitrust investigations were now reinforced by a Congressional review of banking and monetary arrangements that eventually gave rise to the establishment of the Federal Reserve System in 1913 and ushered in a new era of corporate domination.

Krzywicki's Finance Capital Forgotten

Krzywicki never came back to his analysis of finance capital. He spent his later years working on anthropology and industrial sociology, rather than political economy. By the 1930s, he was known in Polish Marxist circles mainly for his contribution to translating the first volume of Marx's Capital into Polish, and his interpretation of Marx's philosophy. Oskar Lange represented a younger generation of political economists in an article about Krzywicki published in 1938, that put him forward as a proponent of an anthropological interpretation of historical materialism (Lange 1938/1970). But, writing in America in the 1940s, and unaware at the time of Krzywicki's earlier writings on the subject, Lange himself came up with a very similar analysis of its monopoly finance capital, including the centralised control by investment banks over industrial capital, and the resulting social atrophy (Lange 1941–1944/1973; Lange and Lerner n.d.).[2]

After Krzywicki's death, unusually of natural causes, in Warsaw in 1941, his name came to the fore in the lively discussions that accompanied the fall of the Stalinist leadership in Poland in 1956. Addressing a stormy Congress of Polish Economists in June 1956, the leading Polish Marxist Oskar Lange denounced the 'atrophy of Marxist thinking in Poland' that he said had given rise to the crisis in Communism. 'In this atrophy of Marxist thought, the failure to take advantage of our own great

---

[2] A different view was presented by the son of the Vice-President of the First National Bank of New York, Paul Sweezy in Sweezy 1941/1953.

272 J. TOPOROWSKI

intellectual resources, we also failed to take full advantage of the treasury of ideas of the outstanding representative of progressive intellectual thought, Ludwik Krzywicki.' (Kowalik 2007, p. 7). Nine volumes of his collected works were published in Poland. But only the first of his articles on monopoly was included. As mentioned above, Krzywicki was the subject of Tadeusz Kowalik's doctoral thesis (Kowalik 1959), and a book by the distinguished Marxist journalist Henryk Holland that was being prepared for publication when its author apparently committed suicide in suspicious circumstances. Holland's book was not to come out until 2007, and discusses Krzywicki's philosophical and sociological works, rather than his political economy.

In his extensive survey of Marxism, the Polish philosopher Leszek Kołakowski devoted a short chapter to Ludwik Krzywicki that is perhaps the only summary in the English language of Krzywicki's work. However, the chapter significantly omits mention of Krzywicki's writings on monopoly finance capital, and the concept of industrial feudalism to which it gave rise. But in passing he mentioned the main features of the new social formation to which capitalism may give rise:

> In his preface to the Polish translation of Kautsky's book on the *Economic Doctrines of Karl Marx*... [Krzywicki] stated that the new order that would result from the evolution of capitalism and the polarization of classes might be the work of either the proletariat or the bourgeoisie. In the former case there would be collective ownership of the means of production; in the latter, private ownership and wage-labour would remain, but be subordinated to the state organization. In later articles he repeated this view more than once... capitalism would succeed in curing the anarchy of production and competition by transforming the whole of production into a state monopoly. This would mean a kind of state capitalism more or less similar to that envisaged by Rodbertus or Brentano: the workers would enjoy social security and economic planning would be introduced, but the basic features of socialism would be missing, namely the abolition of wage-labour and the control of production by the entire working class. (Kołakowski 1978, p. 200)

Writing in political disgrace after his dismissal in 1968 by the Communist authorities from his position at Warsaw University, Kołakowski concluded rather differently from Kowalik ten years earlier (see reference to 'The Krzywicki Controversy' in the previous section):

Krzywicki... did much to introduce Marxist ideas and methods into Polish intellectual life, but the flexibility and eclecticism of his approach was one of the reasons why Polish Marxism failed to take on orthodox forms and tended to dissolve into a general rationalist or historicist trend. In this sense Krzywicki—like Labriola in Italy, though for slightly different reasons—was perhaps, from the Marxist point of view, not so much a battering-ram as a Trojan horse. (Kołakowski 1978, p. 207)

CONCLUSION

Writing his analysis of monopoly finance capital in the form of commentaries and newspaper articles, Ludwik Krzywicki could not match the sophistication and creativity that Hilferding was able to bring to *Finance Capital*. But without the benefit of reading the Second and Third volumes of Marx's *Capital* Krzywicki's articles nevertheless are no mean achievement that repays study today. In particular, they make up for their analytical artlessness by their deeper understanding of finance capital organised around capital markets and investment banking, rather than the clearing bank system that appears today, in the twenty-first century, to be a transitional form of finance capital. Krzywicki added to this a suggestive analysis of industrial feudalism as the social formation created by monopoly finance capital: a situation in which the economy is stabilised, but social mobility is denied. In the twenty-first century, when Keynesianism is widely accepted as the expression of government policies stabilising monopoly finance capital, it is worth remembering that the elimination of economic instability is no guarantee of the satisfaction of the legitimate social and personal ambitions of working people and their families. In our recent study of wealth distribution, Hanna Szymborska and I show how Krzywicki's industrial feudalism—the confinement of individuals and their families into the social or wealth classes into which they were born—takes place today through the increasing need for private asset ownership to move between classes (Szymborska and Toporowski 2022). Behind this lies Krzywicki's prophetic analysis of monopoly finance capital and his anticipation of Hilferding.

Acknowledgement The author acknowledges financial support from the Leverhulme Trust and the Institute for New Economic Thinking. I am grateful to Thomas Ferguson, Riccardo Bellofiore and Grzegorz Konat for helpful comments on an earlier draft.

REFERENCES

Baran, Paul A., and Paul M. Sweezy. 1966. *Monopoly Capital: An Essay on the American Economic and Social Order.* New York: Monthly Review Press.

Hilferding, Rudolf. 1910/1981. *Finance Capital: A Study of the Latest Phase of Capitalist Development.* London: Routledge and Kegan Paul.

Holland, Henryk. 2007. *Ludwik Krzywicki—nieznany (Ludwik Krzywicki—unknown).* Warsawa: Książka i Prasa.

Kalecki, Michał. 1971/1991. Class Struggle and the Distribution of National Income. *Kyklos* vol. 24 No. 1, pp. 1–9. In *Collected Works of Michał Kalecki Volume II Capitalism: Economic Dynamics*, ed. J. Osiatyński. Oxford: The Clarendon Press.

Kalecki, Michał, and Tadeusz Kowalik. 1971/1991. Observations on the "Crucial reform". In *Collected Works of Michał Kalecki Volume II Capitalism: Economic Dynamics*, ed. J. Osiatyński. Oxford: The Clarendon Press.

Kołakowski, Leszek. 1978. *Main Currents of Marxism Its Rise, Growth and Dissolution Volume II: The Golden Age.* Oxford: The Clarendon Press.

Kowalik, Tadeusz. 1959. *O Ludwiku Krzywickim Studium Społeczno-Ekonomiczne.* Warszawa: Państwowe Wydawnictwo Naukowe.

———. 2007. '*Słowo wstępne' (Introduction) in Henryk Holland Ludwik Krzywicki—nieznany (Ludwik Krzywicki—Unknown).* Warsawa: Książka i Prasa.

Krzywicki, Ludwik. 1890/1957. Nowoczesny prad monopolowy (The new monopoly current). In *Idea a życie z wczesnej publicystyki (1883–1892) (Ideas and Life from Early Journalism 1883–1892)*, ed. Ludwik Krzywicki, and intro. Henryk Holland. Państwowe Wydawnictwo Naukowe: Warszawa.

———. 1905a. Morganizacja przemysłu I (The Morganisation of Industry Part I). *Ogniwo* 17: 377–378.

———. 1905b. Morganizacja przemysłu II (The Morganisation of Industry Part II). *Ogniwo* 17: 402–404.

———. 1905c. Morganizacja przemysłu III (The Morganisation of Industry Part III). *Ogniwo* 17: 427–428.

———. 1939/1991. Preface to "Money and Real Wages". In *Collected Works of Michał Kalecki Volume II Capitalism: Economic Dynamics*, ed. J. Osiatyński, 519–521. Oxford: The Clarendon Press.

Lange, Oskar. 1938/1970. Ludwik Krzywicki—Theorist of Historical Materialism. In *Papers in Economics and Sociology 1930–1960*, ed. O. Lange, and trans. P.F. Knightsfield. Oxford: Pergamon Press.

———. 1941–1944/1973. A Democratic Program for Full Employment, trans. 'Demokratyczny program pełnego zatrudnienia'. In *Dzieła tom 1 Kapitalizm* (Collected Works Volume 1, Capitalism), ed. Oskar Lange. Warszawa: Państwowe Wydawnictwo Naukowe.

Lange, Oskar, and Abba P. Lerner. n.d. *The American Way of Business The Role of Government in a System of Free Enterprise*. Delhi: Pranava Books India.

Lenin, Vladimir I. 1917/1968. Imperialism the Highest Stage of Capitalism. In *Selected Works*. Moscow: Progress Publishers.

Sweezy, Paul M. 1941/1953. The Decline of the Investment Banker. In *The Present as History Essays and Reviews on Capitalism and Socialism*. New York: Monthly Review Press.

———. 1942. *The Theory of Capitalist Development Principles of Marxian Political Economy*. New York: Oxford University Press.

Szymborska, Hanna, and Jan Toporowski. 2022, January 18. *Industrial Feudalism and Wealth Inequalities*. Working Paper No. 174, Institute for New Economic Thinking, pp. 1–24.

Toporowski, Jan. 2018. *Michał Kalecki: An Intellectual Biography Volume 2: By Intellect Alone*. Basingstoke: Palgrave.

CHAPTER 12

A Socialist Third Way? Rudolf Hilferding's Evolutionary Socialism as Syncopated Note to Early Neoliberalism

J. Patrick Higgins

INTRODUCTION

Rudolf Hilferding's 1941 death in Gestapo captivity barely captured any international notice, a strange fate for a man who at one point was hailed as both a top intellectual and politician within Marxist and socialist circles for nearly two decades (Smaldone 1998, p. 3). Indeed, Hilferding's reputation, like the Austro-Marxists and Social Democratic parties in the 1920s and 1930s to which he contributed, has suffered historically, variously condemned as straying too far from Marxism (Zoninsein 1990), too orthodox (Gates 1974), advocating ambiguous and incoherent political practices (Blum 1985; Leser 1976), and responsible for the collapse of the Weimer Republic and the rise of National Socialism (James 1981; Bottomore et al. 1978). Hilferding, as finance minister and adviser to several different coalition cabinets, prominent politician, and prominent

J. P. Higgins (✉)
University of Łódź, Lodz, Poland

© The Author(s), under exclusive license to Springer Nature
Switzerland AG 2023
J. Dellheim, F. O. Wolf (eds.), *Rudolf Hilferding*, Luxemburg
International Studies in Political Economy,
https://doi.org/10.1007/978-3-031-08096-8_12

277

278   J. P. HIGGINS

party intellectual, has received much blame, especially for the latter (Winkler 1990; Gourevitch 1984; Breitman 1976; Gates 1974).

Hilferding's main accomplishment, *Finance Capital*, was hailed by Otto Bauer and Karl Kautsky as a 'Fourth Volume' of Marx's *Capital* itself (Coakley 2000; Zoninsein 1990) and cemented his place as a leading socialist politician in the Second International (Smaldone 1998, p. 40). Even Lenin was influenced by his ideas,[1] though with the success of the radical Soviet revolution in Russia, Lenin denounced Hilferding as an 'ideologically bankrupt leader of the Second International' and as part of the 'miserable petty-bourgeois, who were dependent on the philistine prejudices of the most backward part of the proletariat' (quoted in Smaldone 1998, p. 81), and as an 'ex-Marxist' (Coakley 2000). Stalin denounced the Austro-Marxists in 1913 as 'fellow travelers of the bourgeoisie', expelling them from the Second International (Johnston [1972] Johnston 1976, p. 99). Trotsky himself wrote the stinging criticism that Hilferding 'remained a literary official in the service of the German party—and nothing more' and that his character was 'furthest from that of a revolutionary' (quoted in Smaldone 1998, p. 57). Thus, critics of Hilferding attacked both his theory and his practice, and he has the unique distinction of being simultaneously exhorted as a champion and master of Marxist theory and accused as a vanguard of the bourgeois classes within one decade of his life!

Recently, there has been something of a rehabilitation of Hilferding, the Austro-Marxists, as well as the various failed attempts to re-establish social democracy in the German-speaking world during the 1930s. Hilferding and others are now understood to have done the best they could in a chaotic situation (Smaldone 1988; Wagner 1996). Even Wilhelm Röpke, one of the pioneers of neoliberalism, tentatively defended the German Marxists, conceding that some of the earliest critics of National Socialism were the Marxists, even if they mistakenly viewed it as another form of capitalism (Röpke 1935, p. 88). This was due to the unique Austro-Marxist conception of the state, which was not simply reducible to class and therefore to economic power, but was independent

---

[1] The influence of Hilferding on Lenin's thought is well-documented in academic literature. Lenin himself makes the admission, on the first page of *Imperialism*, where he references Hilferding's magnum opus, *Finance Capital* as '[a] very valuable theoretical analysis of "the latest phase of capitalist development" as the subtitle of Hilferding's book reads' (Lenin 1916, p. 1). For other sources of Hilferding and Lenin's relationship, see Zarembka (2003), Coakley (2000), Smaldone (1998), Zoninsein (1990), James (1981), and Sweezy (1949).

of the economy as a separate, theoretically neutral sphere of contention (Bottomore et al. 1978; Hilferding [1940] 2010, [1910] 1981; Bauer [1927] 1978; Adler [1933] 1978). The renewed interest in Austro-Marxism is not just due to historical revisionism, however, as Hilferding's analyses of the separation of ownership and management, the interlocking of bank capital and financial capital, and the internationalisation of capital and capitalism's ability to stabilise itself by spreading crises deserve deeper consideration in a world of austerity and 'too big to fail'.

While these concerns still linger today, these themes were particularly important for the first half of the twentieth century and were very much 'in the air' on both sides of the Atlantic. Hilferding was a direct contributor to the intellectual milieu of his time particularly from 1910 to 1935. One of the most surprising of his contributions was the emergence of early German neoliberalism as one of the many 'third ways' that tried to navigate between Marxism (i.e. strong socialism) and *laissez-faire* (i.e. strong capitalism). He contributed in two aspects: historically and ideationally. In terms of the former, albeit occasionally discarded in the literature as a minor point, Hilferding expressed some interest in attending the August 1938 Colloque Walter Lippmann in Paris, but he was rejected due to his status as a 'politician' (Denord 2009, p. 47). The second aspect is that many of his ideas of gentle, parliamentary evolutionary socialism, rather than hard, militarist revolutionary or dictatorial socialism, were also quite close to emerging conceptions of the 'Third Way', albeit from the left.

Both aspects will be examined via the theoretical metaphor of the syncopated note, which deviates rhythmically from a musical piece's main theme and serves to accent it by way of contrast.

SYNCOPATION AS HISTORICAL AND CONCEPTUAL METAPHOR

Syncopation is one of the most 'familiar and widely used concepts in discourse about rhythm, but is difficult to define precisely' (Temperley 2010, p. 371), and it is still a vague and contested term. However, its one important feature is that 'syncopation and emphasis' depend on 'unambiguous differentiation' from the natural flow of the music. Historically, it has been treated as beginning with a weak beat and ending with a stronger one (Gatty 1912, p. 369), though modern music theory approaches have examined the phenomenon more deeply. Generally, the trend is to move away from the more precise definition of types of beats or emphasis and explore how syncopation helps define the overall feeling or structure of a piece.

One of these approaches seeks to group the temporal sequence of notes, that is, rhythm, by 'family', or to group types of rhythm according to broad characteristics, such as whether they reinforce the overall flow of the piece, disturb the beat, or cause breaks in the flow of the piece, for example, rests or ties. This second category, *syncopation*, 'anticipates the beat and lasts throughout its onset and therefore disturbs the meter' (Cao et al. 2014, pp. 444, 450, 465). Similarly, it is also 'defined as the contradiction, though not overturning, of a dominant metric structure by rhythmic stresses' (Leong 2011, p. 111), in the sense that a '*syncopated* note has an onset on a metrical unit of lesser importance than one that occurs prior to the onset of the next note, and so it tends to disturb the meter for the moment' (Cao et al. 2014, p. 447). Finally, it is also considered as a form of displacement, rather than disagreeing or suppressing. In this manner, 'syncopation features stresses, events, or pulses in unexpected locations, often coupled with their absence from expected locations' (Leong 2011, p. 123).

Synthesising these varying definitions, albeit closer to the modern understanding, syncopation is understood here as that which anticipates the beat and lasts throughout the metre but highlights it more strongly through general contrast than interference or outright contradiction would. Translating this into historiographical terms, a syncopated idea, person, or event is that which helps to shape a subsequent event by way of anticipation and contradistinction, but is also historically simultaneous to it. In this sense, it is similar to a critique in that it opposes an idea and, through its opposition, clarifies it; yet it is different in that it also helps contribute to its emergence, if only indirectly. Syncopation is thus a judgement of contribution to the milieu. In other words, a person, idea, or event that is *syncopated* to a second person, idea, or event may be an element from a totally separate intellectual tradition that briefly intersects with the second phenomena at a stage in its development, someone whose work contributes to a minor or secondary point of a theme but not its overall movement, someone whose earlier analysis or description of a phenomenon was intended for one use but co-opted for another, or someone who may have been a founding father of a movement, but who quickly diverged from it.

Hilferding's Evolutionary Socialism as Syncopated Note to Neoliberalism

The metaphor of Hilferding's evolutionary socialism as syncopated note to the emergence of early German neoliberalism is relevant on two levels: the purely historical and the ideational level. As mentioned earlier, Hilferding sought to participate in the Colloque Walter Lippmann, which was a gathering of German, French, and Austrian, but also some American and British economists, businessmen, and philosophers in August 1938 with the stated purpose of reinvigorating liberalism in light of the Great Depression as well as the dark cloud of totalitarianism that was descending upon Europe. In terms of syncopation, Hilferding's explicit rejection by the organisers of the conference, because he was a 'politician', sheds light on the emerging neoliberal movement. Their use of supposedly neutral policy or economic terminology aside, there are clear political principles, especially anti-socialist in character. This seems curious, given the diversity of intellectual and methodological participants who attended the Colloque, many of whom were politically active before, during, or after the War, and many of whom had socialist leanings or positions that were at least sympathetic towards it, and many of the attendants did not join the core of the growing neoliberal movement and the Mont Pèlerin Society (Reinhoudt and Audier 2018, pp. 53–78). Hilferding's historical involvement with the neoliberals vis-à-vis the Colloque meets the criteria of syncopation in that he was excluded yet did not turn against the movement as such, at least not explicitly. There seems to be no concrete evidence that Hilferding was particularly aware of the attempts to reinvent liberalism by threading the needle between *laissez-faire* and collectivism, and if there was any opposition to such attempts, it would have rather originated from a general rejection of liberalism as bourgeois ideology than specific opposition to any particular ideas, persons, or movements. Hilferding was more concerned with his own personal safety than with any deeper theoretical reflection on the history of the European political economy in the last few years of his life.

However, Hilferding as syncopated note to the emergence of German neoliberalism also occurred ideationally, as a leftist version of the 'Third Way'. This will be elaborated below, after a few clarifying comments on the nature of neoliberalism as a third way.

The Third Way: The Walter Lippmann Colloquium to German Neoliberalism

In his lectures on biopolitics and governmentality, Foucault (1994) was one of the first to extensively discuss the August 1938 Colloque Walter Lippmann in Paris, and it has remained an item of interest in the neoliberal scholarship as its possible birthplace ever since (Mirowski and Plehwe 2009). The occasion was to celebrate and discuss American journalist Walter Lippmann's recent book, *The Good Society*, which presented critiques of both *laissez-faire* and a totalitarian collectivist economy and was concerned with issues such as the separation of ownership versus management, large-scale industrial planning (economic calculation), the importance of a legal framework to manage the economy, and appropriate versus inappropriate forms of government intervention in the market economy (Lippmann [1937] 2005). Over the five days of the conference, the participants discussed a variety of topics, from the causes of the decline of liberalism (limitations imposed by imperialism, demographic growth), the nature and causes of crises under liberalism (to what extent they were politically tolerable, whether they were inevitable or could be managed, whether their causes were structural or exogenous), the nature of liberalism, its history, and whether it could be revived. Throughout the conference, there was a vague consensus that the project of liberalism had utterly failed and needed to be completely re-examined, although there was disagreement as to *why* it had failed: Lippmann, Rüstow, and Röpke believed that the problem was rooted in *laissez-faire* itself and that there were necessary interventions for the state to pursue in order to protect the market, whereas Ludwig von Mises contended that political interventions had prevented any genuine *laissez-faire* from truly evolving, and these interventions had crippled liberalism, causing it to fail (Reinhoudt and Audier 2018).

These tensions remained throughout the neoliberal group, with the Germans developing the model of a social, political, and legal order that reinforced, restrained, and complemented the market, whereas the Mont Pèlerin Society and American libertarian movements followed Mises' critiques (Burgin 2012). The German movement, sometimes referred to as ordoliberalism, was centred around the works of Röpke, Rüstow, Walter Eucken, and others, and many of them had been ardent anti-Nazis, returning to Germany after World War II, where they became strong contributors to the political and economic scenes over the next two decades. Röpke shared and developed Rüstow's and Lippmann's criticism of *laissez-faire* into what he referred to as the 'Third Way', which explicitly rejected both socialism and capitalism (ibid., pp. 81, 143; Röpke [1942] 1992). This approach was suspicious of the concentration of economic power as well as political power, and explicitly sought to offset them against each other, simultaneously constituting the first reference to 'neoliberalism' (or neo-liberalism) in the literature (Gerber 1994; Megay 1970; Oliver 1960; Friedrich 1955). Characteristically, Röpke distinguishes 'capitalism' from the 'market', the latter of which must be embedded in an 'extra-economic', that is to say, social, political, legal, and moral order in its own right, in order to thrive (Röpke 1960, pp. 87–129).

Röpke represents two important shifts: a suspicion of capitalism and a desire to embed and constrain it as part of a greater social order, and an acceptance of active, democratic politics to maintain such an order. These two points—a rejection of the antagonism between the social and the economic, as well as the active role of the political in reconciling these two, will be points where Hilferding's evolutionary socialism converges as a leftist third way, and which the rest of the paper will be dedicated to elaborating more explicitly.

Trouble Brewing in Vienna: Hilferding's Intellectual Environment

Hilferding was born to a Polish Jewish bourgeois family that had immigrated to Vienna and considered themselves to be liberals, secular, and German. Vienna, a diverse and culturally rich, tumultuous capital city of an equally diverse and tumultuous Austro-Hungarian Empire, was increasingly divided due to class divisions, nationalism, and rising anti-Semitism. In his youth, Hilferding chose to become a social democrat, rejecting aesthetic escapism and Zionism to focus on practical matters. He entered the University of Vienna, where he was drawn to economics, studying under many influential thinkers of his time, including Eugen von Philippovich as well as the founders of the Austrian School Friedrich von Wieser and Eugen Böhm-Bawerk. He also studied under Carl Grünberg, one of the most prominent Marxists at the university, as well as Ernest Mach, a leading positivist philosopher (Smaldone 1998; Wagner 1996). Many of his fellow students would also become prominent Austrian scholars in politics and economics: Ludwig von Mises, Otto Bauer, and Josef Schumpeter (Michaelides et al. 2007; Mises 1978). A particularly formative event for many of these students was the famous 1905 seminar held by Böhm-Bawerk, in which he strongly criticised Marxism. Otto Bauer was Marx's principle defender and drew admiration from both sides of the debate for his intellect (Shulak and Unterköfler 2011; Michaelides et al. 2007; Caldwell 2004; Mises 1978).

At the time, university reforms were being implemented, with the Austro-Hungarian Empire adopting the German university system, giving professors greater freedom (Mises 1969). During this time, neo-Kantianism and critiques of the German Historical School (Köhnke 1991; Wiley 1978; Mises 1969) were undermining traditional, orthodox 'Hegelian' Marxism, such as that preached by Karl Kautsky, the so-called pope of Marxism (Steele 1992), and other German orthodox Marxists (Bottomore et al. 1978). In short, this volatile mix of cultural, political, and intellectual diversities created the ideal conditions for a rethinking of Marxism, the breeding ground of Austro-Marxism.

The Gauntlet Is Thrown: The 1905 Böhm-Bawerk Seminar, Hilferding's Anticritique, and the 'Austrianisation' of Marxist Capital Theory

The closing decades of the nineteenth century saw Marxist theorists battling with many difficult theoretical and practical problems, the most significant of which was the theory of capital and economic crises, as well as the labour theory of value. The success of the marginalist revolution and its subjective theory of value as well as the inconsistencies in Marx's own thought revealed by the publication of the third volume of *Capital* (1894) (Howard and King 1989, p. 108) forced many Marxists to re-evaluate the social labour theory of value as well as the theory of capitalist crises; money also became a topic of heated debate (Michaelides et al. 2007; Evans 1997, Milios 1994). Marx had argued that crises resulted from the contradictions inherent in the anarchic nature of capitalist production, particularly the social production of commodities versus their private consumption (Smaldone 1988). However, how crises arose was not entirely clear, and three models were present in the Marxist literature: crises due to over-accumulation of capital, underconsumption of capital, or the decline of profits (Milios 1994). Ukrainian socialist economist Mikhail Tugan-Baranovsky remained committed to Marxism for ethical reasons, but recognised that Marxist economics had to be reworked, admitting that the marginal-utility and labour-production economic theories were opposites, and sought a way to make them compatible with each other (Howard and King 1989, pp. 109–10; Nove 1970).

Tugan-Baranovsky attempted to resolve both issues by injecting subjectivism as well as an organic theory of capital into Marxism. In order to understand how multiple sectors in a capitalist economy were connected, he advanced theories of cyclical growth based on the proportionality of investment/malinvestment of capital depending on which industries proved the most profitable. He contended that crises occurred when the equilibrating process among sectors was disrupted (Howard and King 1989, pp. 102–3) and that both the under- and over-production theories were thus incorrect, as the real issue was that the market in capitalism continuously expanded and restructured itself (Milios 1994; Nove 1970). This theory is quite similar to the Austrian School's understanding of capital, value, and economic crises as malinvestment of capital, which, as it were, represented the strongest influence on his thinking (Howard and King 1989, p. 109).

Tugan-Baranovsky's work was known to revisionist German socialists in the 1890s, and after his work was translated from Russian in 1900, it was taken very seriously in the German-speaking world indeed (ibid., p. 96). Tugan-Baranovsky was to become perhaps the largest influence on Hilferding's own theory of finance capital, and in 1902 he wrote a review of Böhm-Bawerk's *Karl Marx and the Close of His System* (1896) (Smaldone 1998, p. 27), but Hilferding was also able to drink from the river at its source, so to speak, and participated in Böhm-Bawerk's seminar in 1905. The experience of writing his 'anticritique' of Böhm-Bawerk and attending the seminar surely provided much of the material for his *Finance Capital* (1910).

Böhm-Bawerk's critique of the Marxist labour theory of value is still regarded as one of the strongest challenges to Marxism,[2] and much of

---

[2] The power of his critique is still considered by contemporary Marxist thought. In his introduction to Hilferding's response, titled *Böhm-Bawerk's Criticism of Marx*, Sweezy acknowledges that it was a major impetus for the energy of reformist socialism at the turn of the twentieth century. One student of the history of the debates recounted in 1939 that:

> Böhm-Bawerk anticipated nearly all the attacks on Marxism from the viewpoint of those who hold the political economy to centre on a subjective theory of value. On the whole, little has been added to his case by other critics; their important contributions are outside the theories he chose to contest. (Sweezy 1949, p. x)

Mises' (Steele 1992) and Hayek's (1931a, b) own critiques are simply elaborations or qualifications of it. The gist of his argument was that there is a fundamental contradiction at the heart of Marxism: that labour as the source of all value directly contradicted the idea that the unique composition of capital per industry created different profit rates.

Böhm-Bawerk argued that either goods sell at prices in direct proportion to their labour values and that in this case rates of profit will permanently differ based on the capital or labour intensity of the productive process, or that rates of profits are equalised by competition and thus prices never converge with labour values (Steele 1992, p. 138; Böhm-Bawerk [1949] 1896, p. 28). In short, the equalisation of profit rates from capital within the capitalist economy indicated that it had to be more than just the quantity of labour, that contributed to the production of value, for example competition and scarcity. The process of the adjustment of profits within a capitalist system can only occur through competition, and only in non-capitalist societies where the workers control their own means of production is price solely determined by value. He concluded that Marx could no longer maintain that labour was the sole determinant of value after he began his third volume and that he was left with the option to either sacrifice the consistency of his system or its logic, and that Marx chose the former, seeking to mitigate its contradictions by exploring competition. However, Marx did his best to belittle or avoid competition and instead employed a static model in which competition was merely the reference to the movements of supply and demand in the long run and that prices reach their 'true value' only in competition (ibid.).

Hilferding's response to Böhm-Bawerk followed Tugan-Baranovsky in absorbing some elements of the Austrian school, both in thought and in practice (Darity and Horn 1985; James 1981). Sweezy contends that it was not so much a *defence* of *Capital* as it was an 'anticritique', that is, a retaliation against Böhm-Bawerk's attack (Sweezy 1949, p. xxiii). This demonstrates that although Hilferding rejected the Austrian School, which he referred to as a 'psychological' school of economics (Hilferding [1920] 1949), he was clearly prepared to go beyond orthodox Marxism.

Hilferding first engages Böhm-Bawerk on a philosophical level: his criticism of Marx is invalid, Hilferding argues, because the subjectivist school proceeds from the individual and the individual's subjective understanding of value, whereas Marxism departs from the point of society (Hilferding

[1920] 1949). As society exists as a whole, it does not simply exchange commodities, and thus the true basis of value in society is labour which reflects the social structure and relationships (ibid.). Economics must be a historical and a social science that concerns itself with the transition of goods to commodities, that is, when the economic system becomes a system based on exchange. Consequently, the purpose of Marxist economics is to uncover the 'laws' which govern the motion of capitalist society, that is, how the exchange of labour value and commodities in society is produced by and reproduces the social relationships in that society (ibid.).

Fundamentally, Marxist economics approaches the economy from a totally different angle than the Austrian subjectivist school, which from its very founding philosophy seeks out precisely ahistorical laws of economics, whether under Menger's Aristotelianism or Mises' apriorism (White 2003). As such, Austrian economics and Marxist economics ultimately hailed from paradigms so divergent that, if one attempted to transpose one into the other, a contradiction ultimately emerges (Lavoie 1985).[3] Therefore, Böhm-Bawerk asks the wrong question when he makes the argument that skilled labour cannot be understood as a single multiplication of unskilled labour, for it is the society which determines value, rather than purely economic processes. It was Böhm-Bawerk's confusion of price with value, due to his Austrian economic theory, that drove him to mistakenly view Marxism as contradictory (Hilferding [1920] 1949).

In his criticism of Böhm-Bawerk, Hilferding repeatedly emphasises the importance of social relationships, and while Hilferding thought he remained within the Marxist tradition (James 1981) and that he was merely expanding Marx's work on monopolies (Arestis and Sawyer 1994; Hilferding [1910] 1981), he diverged from Marx in the theory of money and competition (Zoninsein 1990). Hilferding, as Tugan-Baranovsky, had converged with Austrian models of money, particularly Menger's view of money as a socio-historical creation (1892), as well as Böhm-Bawerk and Mises' understanding of capital as heterogeneous (Boettke 2008; Böhm-Bawerk [1884] 1890; Mises [1912] 1981).

---

[3] Lavoie (1985) argues that this was one of the strongest elements in the complex and confusing 'socialist calculation debates' that occurred in the 1920s. Neither party was able to fully understand each other, and as such, the debate essentially was never completed, but merely faded into the background as more important political and economic concerns, for example, fascism, emerged and this impasse to a very real extent has defined the course of modern economics.

While much of Hilferding's treatment of financial economics was shaped by the Austrian understanding of money, he was also profoundly influenced by neoclassical economics' conception of perfect competition. This also significantly broke with the orthodox Marxist belief that competition would eventually result in monopolisation and concentration (Steele 1992, pp. 272–74). Zoninsein (1990) claims that Hilferding's theoretical work on 'monopoly capitalism' was due to replacing Marxist understanding of competition with the neoclassical one, which, in agreement with the Austrian School, contended that monopolies were aberrations of the market system that occurred due to state interference (Reinhoudt and Audier 2018; Lippmann [1937] 2005; Gerber 1994; Darity and Horn 1985; Mises [1920] 1979; Megay 1970).

Hilferding's position in his anticritique of Böhm-Bawerk represents a synthesis of these approaches. He wrote:

> For society is the only accountant competent to calculate the height of prices, and the method which society employs to this end is the method of competition [...] it is society which first shows to what degree this concrete labor has actually collaborated in the formation of value, and fixes the price accordingly [...] This is the conception in accordance with which the theory of value is regarded, not as a means "for detecting the law of motion of contemporary society" but as a means of securing a price list that shall be as stable and as just as possible. (Hilferding [1904] 1949, p. 147)

In other words, a simple labour theory of value is not enough, and Hilferding essentially transforms Marxism from a labour theory of value, to a social theory of value, where society itself is the mechanism by which prices are determined, rather than the market. The Marxist economist was to determine what proper balance of social arrangements, that is, 'competition', created 'stable and just' conditions, that is, a 'price list'. He had reached the conclusion that understanding the economy as a self-enclosed historical product was insufficient, and that more emphasis was needed on the interrelation between contemporary political and economic practices (Daly 2004, p. 6). This challenged orthodox Marxism in that the state was not purely a phenomenon that passively acted according to laws as if following a schedule of historical development, but that it could play an active role. If the political was aligned with society as the 'accountant' that was competent enough to create a just order, then the economic sphere would naturally follow suit.

Hilferding's interpretation of Tugan-Baranovsky and his response to Böhm-Bawerk thus anticipated the rise of neoliberalism as well as the market socialist position, as both challenged the idea that the state and society were simply reflections of the system of production. Neoliberalism was explicitly opposed to *laissez-faire*, and market socialists and revisionists were opposed to orthodoxy for the same reason: the state was assumed to play a passive role vis-à-vis natural, historical, or economic forces, and thus neither classical liberalism nor orthodox Marxism created a positive political theory of the state.[4] Walter Lippmann called for a new, positive theory of the state because he felt that in an era of economic depression and uncertain, rapid industrialisation and urbanisation and tensions within the Western political system (both the instability of colonialism and the post-Versailles peace) liberalism needed to supply it or else it would be swept away by more radical ideologies, that is, totalitarianism. Although Hilferding could not have anticipated the rise of totalitarianism, he certainly addressed many of the same issues that Lippmann reflected upon some 25 years later, such as the increasing problems of industrial capitalism, the rise of nationalism, and the decline of the Austro-Hungarian Empire.

As a syncopated note, Hilferding not only helped prepare the milieu for later thinkers' critiques of capitalism and imperialism[5] but also sustained his own vision through his personal pragmatic politics as a member of the Social Democratic Party. In his life as a politician, his evolutionary and parliamentary socialism converged with the general feeling of searching for a third way. However, his parliamentary politics emerged from his mature economic thinking, presented in *Finance Capital* (1910) as well as

---

[4] This is, essentially, Foucault's entire thesis in his lectures on neoliberalism as the political technology that enables the rise of biopolitics: that the government was not merely a reflex of the economic system, and, while its possibilities were shaped by the material constraints of the time, they were also shaped by the ideological space as well, that is, that it was the rise of political economy as a science which enabled the formation of governmental reason with regard to the economic space (Foucault 1994).

[5] It was Hilferding's conjunction of neoclassical and marginalist economics that would make *Finance Capital* so penetrating and important. Caldwell (2004) and Foucault (1994) posit that the debates of the neoliberals with socialists, Marxists, and fascists—which the neoliberals broadly referred to as collectivists, statists, or interventionists—proved to be the 'road to Damascus' necessary for their full maturation, and Kirzner (1988) and Lavoie (1985) describe the dialogue as one reason for an increased self-understanding on the part of both the Austrians and the socialists. Furthermore, Hilferding's analysis reveals two tensions within the neoliberal cadre: that of competition and of markets (Izzo and Olga 1997).

290   J. P. HIGGINS

from the political theories of Max Adler in the 1920s and 1930s. Both will be briefly addressed in the following.

FINANCE CAPITAL

Finance Capital was hailed by Otto Bauer and Karl Kautsky as something of a fourth volume of *Capital*, which confirmed Marx's prediction of the concentration of capital, but asserted that it leads to a qualitative change in the nature of capitalism itself, as a new phase. However, it also demonstrates Hilferding's mature thinking about money (Trevor 1997) where his anticritique of Böhm-Bawerk inspired him to reinvent Marx's theory of value as a 'critical social theory'. This reframed the labour theory of value and the 'laws of motion' of capitalism as social, rather than natural laws (Wagner 1996, pp. 28, 32). This allowed for a Marxist theory that was more subtle and flexible than doctrinaire orthodoxy, but also made it vulnerable to being diluted by broader theories and approaches. Another consequence was that the political and economic systems were more autonomous and their relationship more complex. He asserted that the defence of the labour theory of value was no longer essential to the labour movement, and that much of the technical-economic theory was a distraction from working, political solutions (ibid., pp. 37–39). He was also concerned that capitalism was no longer simply capitalist versus worker, but that competition also existed among capitalists (Smaldone 1998, p. 24). In this sense, Hilferding moved away from the traditional Marxist understanding of competition as anarchic, closer to what the Austrian School would consider as *rivalrous*, that is, that competition is not a detriment to markets, but rather that it *constitutes* markets and is something natural rather than an aberration.[6]

[6] Much of Böhm-Bawerk's criticism of Marx is clarified by Lavoie's (1985) explanation that a major difference between socialist and Marxist economics, as variants of classical economics, and the Austrian School is that the Austrians view competition as rivalrous, that is, that market interactions are fundamentally a clash of human practices in continuous disequilibrium. The market system thus does not always stabilise in a manner beneficial to society—if at all—and it actually may be quite disruptive in the long run. The Marxists establish a long-term equilibrium, and from this point, they view rivalry and competition as anarchistic and detrimental to society, rather than as inherent to complex production (ibid., pp. 22–7). As such, competition and its role are only grudgingly acknowledged by Marx where 'anarchism' rather means dis-coordination than total chaos; thus, while Marx acknowledges competition, he views it as an outgrowth of the capitalist system that is necessarily alienating and detrimental (ibid., pp. 36–9).

The introduction of competition among capitalists required the development of new economic phenomena in order to reconstruct capitalism, both analytically and in practice. This latest phase of capitalism produces a new form of capital, *finance capital*, which unites banking capital with industrial capital, though banks are superior in the relationship (Arestis and Sawyer 1994; Lachmann 1944). This is due to the control that banks exercise over the flow and quantity of money. As the means of production become increasingly complex and specialised, more and more exchange is needed, but the medium of exchange needs to become more and more general, until a universal form is reached: money. *Finance Capital* thus comports with the theory of the origin of money hypothesised by Menger (1892), but Hilferding goes further and agrees with Ernest Mach that money has effectively become the ego of society, to which all other things can be reduced and fetishised. Money is now the symbol of society itself, and the state's primary function is henceforth that of the guarantor of money (Hilferding [1910] 1981, p. 31).

As Tugan-Baranovsky, Hilferding was convinced by 'bourgeois' economics' description of modern capitalism, though he continued to disagree with it normatively. Though the Austrians had a more neutral outlook on money, Hilferding contends that it has several negative consequences: it separates use value from exchange value and facilitates the equalisation of profit rates through the shifting of the base of society from labour to monetary and industrial capital. This further conceals the inequality of labour. Hilferding believed that the theory of labour was no longer a fixed concept, but more of a general approach to economic history and that the process of equalisation of profit rates was the true driver of capitalism. The anarchic and competitive nature of capitalism, along with necessary human error, led to uncertainty, which was compensated for by holding large portions of money or capital in reserve in order to compensate for delays in commodity circulation, that is, the necessity of liquid reserves while waiting for payment (Hilferding [1910] 1981).

Taking his cue from Böhm-Bawerk's work on the heterogeneity of capital ([1884]1890), Hilferding recognises that not only is there an uneven distribution of the spread of capital throughout various sectors in the economy, but also there are both qualitative and quantitative changes in the capital structure (Blumen 2008). Furthermore, the Austrians point out that the process of production itself also requires the use of capital as an intermediate good (Hayek 1931a, b). The speculative nature of capitalism, which locks capital out of circulation as an emergency reserve, the usage of capital as an intermediate good, and the heterogeneous nature of capital combine to create economic crises that are due to disproportionality in the capital structure, and hence in prices (Michaelides et al. 2007; James 1981). However, Hilferding's understanding of credit money transforms this whole argument, wherein banks, which do not suffer from the same problems regarding the circulation and production of their capital, are in a unique position to effectively smooth out capitalist crises by providing a more efficient reserve of money capital, freeing up capital and increasing circulation (Hilferding [1910] 1981).

Banks, therefore, stabilise and expand the amount of capital in circulation, activate idle capital, and, due to the unique nature of banking capital, are able to absorb money and interest capital from all segments of society, further increasing the power of capitalists (ibid.), and to reach across international borders. Along with the increasing power of banks and banking capital, Hilferding believes that the rise of modern corporations goes beyond the original scope of Marx's analysis (ibid., pp. 114–16) and that stock capital is 'fictitious capital' which does nothing else but increase the profits and power of its shareholders. Hilferding notes that corporations allow for a disproportionate expansion of the power of capitalists, for under a normal firm one would have to have complete ownership to exercise sovereignty over the capital, but under a corporate format one must only be a majority shareholder.

As such, stock capital allows for a maximisation of external capital for the minimum of one's own capital, which allows for interlocking corporate director boards. Banks, therefore, have greater security in corporate investments as they translate into stock, which grants ownership. Furthermore, given that corporations are legal entities and independent of the size of individual shares of capital that compose them, it is much easier for a corporation to expand than an individual enterprise. In its capacity to assemble capital, the corporation is thus similar to banks, except that it employs fictitious capital instead of shares, rather than money capital (ibid., pp. 118–22).

In the modern era of capitalism, banks are thus the driving force of the economy, and Hilferding argued that they would continue to accelerate the concentration of capital in an ever-decreasing number of individuals through a process of cartelisation (Smaldone 1998, p. 44). Cartelisation also does not stop the anarchy of production or crises, but rather shifts the burden of the crises onto smaller firms, which furthers cartelisation as larger firms continuously absorb smaller firms until a giant grand cartel forms, where a central bank controls the entire economy (Hilferding [1910] 1981). Against this backdrop, Hilferding believed that the very nature of capitalism had changed: finance capital and shareholder anonymity had displaced the capitalist entrepreneur, and the merging of banks with industrial capital had eliminated free competition through market organisation (Botz 1976). Hilferding also thought that technology would facilitate a new restructuring of capitalism, allowing cartels to produce more profit, and that capitalism would not fail due to the reduction of socially necessary labour time given the rise of machines (Michaelides et al. 2007), thus breaking with the Marxian assertion that labour is the sole source of value (Darity and Horn 1985).

Hilferding's conclusion broke with the Marxist view of crises, believing that perhaps a breakdown of capitalism was not inevitable, but that a general cartel would be able to remove the anarchy inherent in the capitalist system and that this would allow for a transition directly into socialism (Smaldone 1998; Wagner 1996; Hilferding [1910] 1981). Hilferding believed that cartelisation of the banking industry effectively colonised the state and produced imperialism,[7] a scenario in which the state would work to continuously increase the economic sphere of influence to facilitate further capital concentration and production (Smaldone 1988). However, Hilferding believed at the same time that the worker movement would not benefit from warfare and thus sought how to organise 'for the revolution' rather than organise 'the revolution' (ibid.). There was thus a significant tension within Hilferding's thought: while he believed that there was an increasing tendency towards warfare due to finance capital, he deemed this unnecessary and instead supported parliamentarian practices.

This new understanding of money, capital, and competition broke down the notion of monolithic, antagonistic social groups and cleared the way for conceptualising a political sphere distinct from both the social and the economic. Furthermore, the understanding of money as a social product guaranteed by the political, rather than as a reflex of the economic system, also cleared the path for an active state and an active monetary policy. Finally, Hilferding's concern with cartelisation and the damaging effects of unrestrained 'economic' phenomena, for example, the

---

[7] This line of thought was a significant influence on Lenin's own *Imperialism* ([1919] 2010), but Lenin took it further, reasoning that banks used financial capital to control industries through direct manipulation of credit and interest rates in addition to ownership of stock ventures (Lachmann 1944).

fetishisation of money, created the impetus for the distinction and demarcation of the economic from the political and from the social. Other contemporary groups, such as the Fabians and the Georgists, were also concerned with such issues. Lippmann, Röpke, Hayek, and Mises were all sympathetic to socialism in their youth, and even though they all ultimately abandoned it, they recognised that unbridled capitalism could be destructive.[8] Finally, all of them—albeit to varying degrees—argued against a pure *laissez-faire* system as had developed in the nineteenth century, paving the way for an active state. One major difference remained: none of the neoliberals themselves were active politicians. To complete this comparison, it is therefore necessary to return to the reason why Hilferding was supposedly banned from attending the Colloque Walter Lippmann: his political practice.

MARX WITHOUT HEGEL: AUSTRO-MARXISM AS NEW POLITICS AND NEW PRAXIS

From its very inception, Austro-Marxism was a political programme that was multidisciplinary and pragmatic; the trinity of Karl Renner, Max Adler, and Hilferding met at the Fabian circle *Zukunft* and shared a commitment to democratic socialism but also their opposition to both Kautsky's orthodoxy and Bernstein's revisionism (Bottomore et al. 1978; Leser 1976). Max Adler, the chief philosopher of the group, attempted to revise Marxism with neo-Kantian ideas and transform it into an ethic of socialised humanity (Adler [1925] 1978; Bauer [1937] 1978) as well as a 'sociology of revolution'. These positions nicely dovetailed Hilferding's separation of the political, the social, and the economic (Wagner 1996; Hilferding [1910] 1981, [1904] 1949; Sweezy 1949; Adler [1933] 1978), clearing

---

[8] A key point of ordoliberalism/German neoliberalism is the tension emerging from the view that the foundation of the market system was competition, whereas society thrives on unity and the elimination of competition (Hartwich 2009; Boarman 2000; O'Leary 1979; Röpke [1942] 1992). As such, several of the neoliberals were concerned with the construction of liberalism and the construction of a *good society*, which extended far beyond the simple economic relations that Mises concerns himself with, and in their humanist critiques (Boarman 2000; Friedrich 1955), they share many points with socialists and Marxists. However, unlike Marxists, they believe that this tension is a question of balancing the social and economic spheres or putting them in their proper order, for example, the *Ordnungsökonomik*, rather than something that is fundamentally fatal to the political and economic systems.

the way for parliamentary Marxism instead of the revolt of the proletariat. It was quite close to the Marburg German Social Democrats who advocated creating a 'foundation for evolutionary socialism and parliamentary democracy', with a corresponding political strategy of gradualism (Wiley 1978, p. 174). He concluded that 'The Marxist as theorist does not stand in contradiction with the Marxist as politician [*sic*]' (Adler [1928] 1978, p. 138). Adler wanted to avoid both a violent revolution and bourgeois parliamentarianism by distinguishing political from social revolution: the job of the Marxist was to educate the population and help it develop a desire for revolution, which would lead to the social reorganisation of the means of production, through a strong Social Democratic Party.

The other major philosophical influences on Hilferding were his professors Ernst Mach and Carl Grünberg, who took positivism in different directions. Mach divorced the ethical strands in neo-Kantianism from positivism to establish a foundation for critical science (Bottomore et al. 1978, pp. 15–16). Grünberg disentangled historical materialism from philosophical materialism and was also active in the workers' movement and championed attempts to create a truly scientific Marxism to defeat bourgeois economics (Wagner 1996). On the other hand, Grünberg did not believe in meta-historical laws of motion, but that every historical period was moved by unique historical laws that had to be discovered (Held 1980), thus sharing the socio-historical relativism of Mach except for his 'evolutionary' emphasis.

Thus, to Hilferding, Marxism was more of *an orientation to the world*—a critical historical-materialist model for social science—and not a dogma to be followed, while he personally cited Marx's own opposition to 'the planting of a dogmatic flag'. Hilferding believed that 'the effective power of Marx's thought stemmed not from any particular claim that he had made, but from the spirit in which he had worked' (Smaldone 1998, p. 17). This flexible perspective is the key to understanding Hilferding's pragmatic, parliamentary politics in which he would have to accept 'non-socialist fiscal policies' for which he is so often blamed (Smaldone 1998; Winkler 1990; Gourevitch 1984; Breitman 1976; Gates 1974).

Hilferding's Evolutionary Socialism as Pragmatic Political Praxis

The final point of reflection on Hilferding's syncopation to early neoliberalism is that he did not want to overthrow the political system of his time but rather sought its reformation, namely by reinventing both the political doctrine and the institutions to support it. While neoliberalism would go on to reshape the world via a series of international think tanks and policy research centres, in its beginnings it was supported by Walter Lippmann, who was no stranger to the political elite, as well as many economists and politicians who helped rebuild West Germany's political and economic systems after the war. The Austro-Marxists and Social Democrats whom Hilferding supported pursued an approach that was not too dissimilar, maintaining a network of newspapers, party schools, labour unions, and political parties. That neoliberalism succeeded while moderate socialism failed is not a reflection on the socialists' lack of effort. With the rise of National Socialism in Germany and Austria, the Great Depression, and the continued economic strain due to punishing war reparations, the moderate socialists in central Europe simply found themselves in an impossible situation. It is nonetheless worthwhile to examine how Hilferding attempted to pragmatically navigate the increasingly difficult situation he found himself in, as a kind of 'stress test' for the feasibility of democratic and parliamentary socialism, with lessons still relevant today.

The Austro-Marxists argued that the break-up of the old monarchies after World War I had brought about a balance of class power and that hence the state was now neutral (Leser 1976). Accordingly, much of their efforts became focused on trying to educate the masses in order to establish a working-class consciousness *for* the revolution rather than organise *the* revolution (Smaldone 1998). By 1906 Hilferding was known for being a sound theorist of Marxism and took a position as a teacher at the German Social Democratic (SPD) Party School, giving up his life as a physician and fully committing himself to politics. At the time, the SPD was undergoing a difficult period of internal debates, with Bernstein adopting a revisionist position, Kautsky taking the more orthodox stance, and Rosa Luxembourg advocating for a more revolutionary approach, and Hilferding's talents as a public speaker, public intellectual, and commitments to pragmatic politics and parliamentarianism allowed him to become something of a moderating force among the factions (Smaldone 1998; Wagner 1996). Hilferding's first major political contribution was his work on the general strike which he sought to incorporate as part of the socialist political parliamentary repertoire derived from the position of the working class in society, rather than as an extra-parliamentary tactic. In his view, the strike should be used to uphold and protect the suffrage of the workers and the legality of the workers' movement itself. However, using it carelessly or too frequently would only unite the other parliamentary factions against labour (Smaldone 1998, pp. 25–6; Wagner 1996, p. 53).

Hilferding's advocacy of the general strike was complementary to his view of parliamentary democracy, for, while the capitalist classes rule but do not necessarily govern, the parliament is still an overall reflection of the capitalist structure itself (Wagner 1996, p. 52). Hilferding recognised that parliamentary democracy had the *potential* to achieve parity of all class and social democracy, but did not *guarantee* this and that there was a growing paradox in Austria and Germany in the sense that there was a concentration of both state and economic power as well as parliamentarianism, which meant that whichever class or political party governed had increased power (Hilferding 1905). Thus, it was possible for social democracy to grow in numbers but actually lose power because of governing coalitions of liberal or reactionary anti-proletarian parties, and Hilferding consequently declared that the general strike had to be used based on the specific political context and that, while it should always be used to retain the gains made by the workers' movement, its use depended on the concrete social context of the country. Due to the differing composition of political and class interests in Austria and Germany, there could be no single universal blueprint for the general strike (ibid.).

Hilferding's position on the general strike was in effect a political compromise with forces within and outside of the social democratic movement and demonstrated his commitment to socialist democracy as the voice of parliamentary politics on behalf of the international workers' movement *in addition to* his view for pragmatic politics. Hilferding did not believe that the labour unions were acting as a cartel for labour as a commodity and that the labour movement could enter into parliament and transform bourgeois parliamentarianism into social-democratic parliamentarianism (James 1981). Within the social democratic movement, there was unease concerning the question of the strike, with revisionists fearing that overuse of the strike would impede any attempts at coalition building, while the orthodox feared that the usage of the general strike at the wrong time or too often would endanger the gradual transition from liberal capitalism to social democracy and thus should only be a defensive tactic. The Bolshevists and radicals, for their part, were willing to use the strike as a means of breaking down the capitalist social order and igniting the revolution (Smaldone 1998; Wagner 1996).

The themes of commitment to working-class unity, social-democratic parliamentarianism, the balance of class forces, gradualist economic and social revolution, and willingness to compromise would comprise Hilferding's view of politics, his role as a Social Democratic politician, and in his multiple terms as finance minister. His adoption—or at least toleration—of marginalist, non-Marxist economic analysis would actually converge with several of the 'orthodox' economic policies of his time and would lead the Social Democratic Party into several failed coalitions that tried to shore up failing democracy in Germany and Austria (Smaldone 1998; Wagner 1996; Breitman 1976), while he favoured deflationary or at least anti-inflationary economic policies as well as supporting the gold standard (Darity and Horn 1985; Gourevitch 1984; Gates 1974).

The difficulty that Social Democrats faced was trying to balance what was politically feasible versus what was economically sustainable for their gradualist vision of social, economic, and political change. They believed that if they were unable to retain their position in parliament, then they could not ensure that there was progress towards socialism. However, in order to maintain their position in parliament, they had to make compromises or were vulnerable to crises and the capricious whims of public opinion, which made them—more often than not—reinforcers of the status quo.

Breitman contends that Hilferding

> had a tendency to oppose limited correctives for the problems of the business cycle. In theory, they preferred more far-reaching plans for changes in the relationship between the state and the private sector, which were supposed to reduce the competitive friction and waste they saw as inherent in capitalism. Since their own approach was usually politically unfeasible, they contented themselves with the observation that greater economic concentration at least seemed to be preparing the way for a socialist economy. Anything that resembled a gift to business, or any policy that threatened to unleash another inflation was suspect. Therefore, the socialist economists offered few positivist proposals. (1976, p. 375)

The opposition towards the adoption of demand-stimulus or deficit-financing models, such as Keynesianism, in a world of increasing economic desperation and shifting public debate and electoral fortune, would be a parallel Hilferding shared with the neoliberals, as before Lippmann converted to a strong advocate of Keynesianism, he was also suspicious of debt-financing and retaining the gold standard (Goodwin 2014). Röpke (1933, 1937) and Hayek (1931a, 1932a, b) also advocated for the importance of sound monetary policy, particularly the gold standard, and were especially suspicious of doctrines of 'forced savings' or any other effort by the government to impact the value of money and credit, and hence the business cycle. With the onset of the Great Depression, those who argued for more conservative, traditional monetary policy lost the public debate, and Hilferding's position as finance minister in coalition governments was never stable or long lasting. Similarly, with the exception of German reconstruction, the neoliberals were often left out in the cold and on the margins of academia for the next quarter of a century until the Keynesian consensus in mainstream economic thought began to break down in the 1970s.

While the neoliberals found themselves in the political wilderness, the situation in Germany and Austria would soon become a question of life or death for the moderate socialists. The SPD found itself in a period when there were a variety of 'socialist' parties and ideologies, especially within Germany. One of the most devastating legacies of World War I was the division of the international labour movement into Christian centrist socialism, National Socialism, democratic socialism, communism, Bolshevism, anarcho-socialism, and others. The split between Hilferding and Lenin simply exemplifies how Hayek's view in *The Road to Serfdom* ([1944] 2007)—that socialism is better at breaking down the old liberal order than defending against fascism—seems to be on the whole true, at least in the case of Germany and Austria. His argument was that socialism had effectively become a victim of its own success, that there were so many different varieties of socialism that none of its representatives could hold power or stabilise for long (ibid., p. 146). The SPD and Austro-Marxists found themselves in the impossible position of being too embedded in the state and locked in a tight competition for labour and working-class votes to effectively react to the rising National Socialist threat. Ironically, Hilferding's political strategy of gradual electoral coalition building, educating and building political consciousness among the working classes, and pursuing stable monetary policy had left them perfectly vulnerable to an external, extra-parliamentary threat.

300 J. P. HIGGINS

The rise of totalitarianism concerned both the neoliberals and the moderate socialists, though the neoliberals, by and large, escaped unscathed, with Röpke and Rüstow fleeing into exile in Turkey or Geneva, Hayek and Mises fleeing to Great Britain and the United States, and Eucken remaining in hiding in Freiburg for the entire duration of the war. Hilferding never had a chance to see the rise of moderate, parliamentary social democracy flourish in Europe, briefly fleeing to Paris only to be caught, dying in Gestapo captivity in 1941.

Conclusion

Rudolf Hilferding's ideas anticipated many of those harboured by the early neoliberals, especially those in Germany. His concerns about cartelisation and the dangers of the unbound competition were resolved by a rethinking of Marxist theories of money, competition, economic crises, and pragmatic, parliamentary politics. His belief in the neutrality of the state and the separation of the economic, political, and the social spheres created an active and pragmatic, albeit somewhat conservative and vague, theory of Marxist politics that tried to balance theoretical updating with the issues and needs of its time and an effective political practice. This anticipates and parallels the early neoliberals' search for a way to update liberalism to overcome its contemporary crises and to develop political theories and corresponding practices for an active state, rather than *laissez-faire*. Indeed, if not in substance nor in form, but in general orientation towards the social world, there are many parallels between Hilferding and the early neoliberals as co-seekers of an elusive Third Way that are worth exploring.

References

Adler, M. [1925] 1978. The Relation of Marxism to Classical German Philosophy. In *Austro-Marxism*, ed. T. Bottomore and P. Goode, 62–68. London: Cox & Wyman.

———. [1928] 1978. The Sociology of Revolution. In *Austro-Marxism*, ed. T. Bottomore and P. Goode, 136–146. London: Cox & Wyman.

———. [1933] 1978. Metamorphosis of the Working Class. In *Austro-Marxism*, ed. T. Bottomore and P. Goode, 217–248. London: Cox & Wyman.

Arestis, P., and M. Sawyer, eds. 1994. *The Elgar Companion to Radical Political Economy*. Brookefield: Edward Elgar Publishing.

Bauer, O. 1927. 1978. In *What Is Austro-Marxism? In Austro-Marxism*, ed. T. Bottomore and P. Goode, 45–48. London: Cox & Wyman.

———. [1937] 1978. "Max Adler: A Contribution to the History of Austro-Marxism." In *Austro-Marxism* edited by Tom Bottomore and Patrick Goode, 48–52. London: Cox & Wyman Ltd.

Blum, M.E. 1985. *The Austro-Marxists 1890–1918: A Psychobiographical Study.* Lexington: The University of Kentucky Press.

Blumen, R. 2008. *Hayek on the Paradox of Saving.* Ludwig von Mises Institute. http://mises.org/daily/2804. Accessed 7 April 2012.

Boarman, P.M. 2000. Apostle of a Humane Economy: Remembering Wilhelm Röpke. *Humanitas* 13 (1): 31–67.

Boettke, P.J. 2008. Austrian School of Economics. In *Concise Encyclopedia of Economics.* Library of Economics and Liberty. http://www.econlib.org/library/Enc/AustrianSchoolofEconomics.html. Accessed 17 October 2012.

Böhm-Bawerk, E. [1884] 1890. *Capital and Interest: A Critical History of Economical Theory.* Trans. William A. Smart. Library of Economics and Liberty. http://www.econlib.org/library/BohmBawerk/bbCICover.html. Accessed 17 October 2012.

———. [1896] 1949. *Karl Marx and the Close of His System*, ed. Paul M. Sweezy. New York: August M. Kelley.

Bottomore, T., P. Goode, and eds. and trans. 1978. *Austro-Marxism.* London: Cox & Wyman.

Botz, G. 1976. Austro-Marxist Interpretation of Fascism. *Journal of Contemporary History* 11 (4): 129–156.

Breitman, R. 1976. On German Social Democracy and General Schleicher 1932–33. *Central European History* 9 (4): 352–378.

Burgin, A. 2012. *The Great Persuasion: Reinventing Free Markets since the Depression.* Cambridge/London: Harvard University Press.

Caldwell, B. 2004. *Hayek's Challenge: An Intellectual Biography of F.A. Hayek.* Chicago: The University of Chicago Press.

Cao, E., M. Lotstein, and P.N. Johnson-Laird. 2014. Similarity and Families of Musical Rhythms. *Music Perception: An Interdisciplinary Journal* 31 (5): 444–469.

Coakley, J. 2000. Rudolf Hilferding (1877–1941). In *A Biographical Dictionary of Dissenting Economists*, 2nd ed., 290–298. Northampton: Edward Elgar Publishing.

Daly, Glyn. 2004. Radical(ly) Political Economy: Luhmann, Postmarxism and Globalism. *Review of International Political Economy* 11 (1): 1–32.

Darity, W.A., Jr., and B.L. Horn. 1985. Rudolf Hilferding: The Dominion of Capitalism and the Dominion of Gold. *The American Economic Review* 75 (2): 363–368.

Denord, F. 2009. French Neoliberalism and Its Divisions: From the Colloque Walter Lippmann to the Fifth Republic. In *The Road from Mont Pèlerin: The Making of the Neoliberal Thought Collective*, ed. Philip Mirowski and Dieter Plehwe, 45–67. Cambridge; London: Harvard University Press.

Evans, T. 1997. Marxian Theories of Money and Capital. *International Journal of Political Economy* 27 (1): 7–42.

Foucault, M. 1994. *The Birth of Biopolitics: Lectures at the Collège de France 1978–1979.* New York: Picador and Palgrave Macmillan.

Friedrich, C.J. 1955. The Political Thought of Neo-Liberalism. *The American Political Science Review* 49 (2): 509–525. Markets vs Capitalism Distinction of Ordos vs Paleoliberals.

Gates, R.A. 1974. German Socialism and the Crisis of 1929–1933. *Central European History* 7 (4): 332–359.

Gatty, R. 1912. Syncopation and Emphasis. I. *The Musical Times* 53 (832): 369–372.

Gerber, D.J. 1994. Constitutionalizing the Economy: German Neo-Liberalism, Competition Law, and the 'New' Europe. *The American Journal of Comparative Law* 42 (1): 25–84.

Goodwin, C.D. 2014. *Walter Lippmann: Public Economist.* Cambridge: Harvard University Press.

Gourevitch, P.A. 1984. Breaking with Orthodoxy: The Politics of Economic Policy Responses to the Depression of the 1930s. *International Organization* 38 (1): 95–129.

Hartwich, O.M. 2009. Neoliberalism: The Genesis of a Political Swearword. *The Center for Independent Studies.* Occasional Paper 114.

Hayek, F.A. 1931a. The 'Paradox' of Saving. *Economica* 32: 125–169.

———. 1931b. Reflections on the Pure Theory of Money of Mr. J.M. Keynes. *Economica* 33: 270–295.

———. 1932a. Money and Capital: A Reply. *The Economic Journal* 42 (166): 237–249.

———. 1932b. A Note on the Development of the Doctrine of 'Forced Savings'. *The Quarterly Journal of Economics* 47 (1): 123–133.

Held, D. 1980. *Introduction to Critical Theory: Horkheimer to Habermas.* Berkley: University of California Press.

Hilferding, R. [1904] 1949. *Böhm-Bawerk's Criticism of Marx*, ed. P.M. Sweezy. New York: Augustus M. Kelley.

———. 1905. Parliamentarianism and the General Strike, Trans. by Jacques Bohomme. *Social Democrat* 9 (11): 675–687. http://www.marxists.org/archive/hilferding/1905/11/parliamentarianism-strike.htm.

———. [1910] 1981. *Finance Capital. A Study of the Latest Phase of Capitalist Development*, ed. T. Bottomore, Trans. M. Watnick and S. Gordon. London: Routledge and Kegan Paul. http://www.marxists.org/archive/hilferding/1910/finkap/index.htm.

12 A SOCIALIST THIRD WAY? RUDOLF HILFERDING'S EVOLUTIONARY...   303

———. [1920] 1949. Paul M. Sweezy, (Ed.) Böhm-Bawerk's Criticism of Marx. New York: Augustus M. Kelley.

———. [1940] 2010. State Capitalism Or Totalitarian State Economy? Transcribed by S. Palmer. *The Modern Review*, June 1947, 266: 71. http://www.marxists.org/archive/hilferding/1940/statecapitalism.htm.

Howard, M.C., and J.E. King. 1989. Russian Revisionism and the Development of Marxian Political Economy in the Early Twentieth Century. *Studies in Soviet Thought* 37 (2): 95–117.

Izzo, Herbert J., and Olga F., trans. 1997. Report of the Sessions of the Walter Lippmann Colloquium. *Studies of the International Research Center for the Renewal of Liberalism* I: 1–94.

James, H. 1981. Rudolf Hilferding and the Application of the Political Economy of the Second International. *The Historical Journal* 24 (4): 847–869.

Johnston, W.M. [1972] 1976. *The Austrian Mind: An Intellectual and Social History 1848–1938*. Berkeley: University of California Press.

Kirzner, Israel M. 1988. The Economic Calculation Debate: Lessons for Austrians. *Review of Austrian Economics* 2 (1): 1–18.

Köhnke, K.C. 1991. *The Rise of Neo-Kantianism: German Academic Philosophy Between Idealism and Positivism*. Trans. R.J. Hollingdale. Cambridge: Cambridge University Press.

Lachmann, L.M. 1944. Finance Capitalism? *Economica* 11 (42): 64–73.

Lavoie, D. 1985. *Rivalry and Central Planning: The Socialist Calculation Debate Reconsidered*. Cambridge: Cambridge University Press.

Lenin, V.I. [1916] 2010. *Imperialism: The Highest Stage of Capitalism*. New York: Penguin Group.

Leong, D. 2011. Generalizing Syncopation: Contour, Duration, and Weight. *Theory and Practice* 36: 111–150.

Leser, N. 1976. Austro-Marxism: A Reappraisal. *Journal of Contemporary History* 11 (2/3): 133–148.

Lippmann, W. [1937] 2005. *The Good Society*. New Brunswick: Transaction Publishers.

Megay, E.N. 1970. Anti-Pluralist Liberalism: The German Neoliberals. *The Academy of Political Science* 85 (3): 422–442.

Menger, C. 1892. On the Origin of Money. *The Economic Journal* 2 (6): 239–255.

Michaelides, P., J. Milios, and A. Vouldis. 2007. *Schumpeter, Lederer, and Hilferding on Economic Development, Credit, and Business Cycles*. Presented at the 9th Conference of Greek Historians of Economic Thought, Thessalonica, 11–12 May 2007. Retrieved August 8, 2012, from http://users.ntua.gr/jmilios/MichaelideMiliosVouldisGHET2007.pdf.

Milios, J. 1994. Marx's Theory and the Historical Marxist Controversy on Economic Crisis (1900–1937). *Science & Society* 58 (2): 175–194.

Mirowski, Philip, and Dieter Plehwe, eds. 2009. *The Road from Mount Pélerin: The Making of the Neoliberal Thought Collective*. Cambridge: Harvard University Press.

Mises, L. [1912] 1981. *The Theory of Money and Credit*. Indianapolis: Liberty Fund. Library of Economics and Liberty. http://www.econlib.org/library/Mises/msT.html. Accessed 17 October 2012.

———. [1920] 1979. Economic Calculation in the Socialist Commonwealth. Auburn, AL: Praxeology Press of the Ludwig von Mises Institute.

———. 1969. *The Historical Setting of the Austrian School of Economics*. New Rochelle: Arlington House.

———. 1978. *Notes and Recollections*. Spring Mills: Libertarian Press.

Nove, Alec. 1970. M. I. Tugan-Baranovsky (1865–1919). *History of Political Economy* 2 (2): 246–262.

O'Leary, J.P. 1979. Wilhelm Röpke and the Problems of Contemporary International Political Economy. *World Affairs* 4: 307–312.

Oliver, H.M., Jr. 1960. German Neoliberalism. *The Quarterly Journal of Economics* 74 (1): 117–149.

Reinhoudt, J., and Serge Audier. 2018. *The Walter Lippmann Colloquium: The Birth of Neo-Liberalism*. Cham: Palgrave Macmillan.

Röpke, W. 1933. Trends in German Business Cycle Policy. *The Economic Journal* 43 (171): 427–441.

———. 1935. Fascist Economics. *Economica* 2 (5): 85–100.

———. 1937. Explanatory Note on the Review of Röpke's 'Crises and Cycles'. *The American Economic Review* 27 (1): 108–109.

———. [1942] 1992. *The Social Crisis of our Time*. New Brunsweck, NJ: Transaction Publishers.

———. 1960. *A Humane Economy: The Social Framework of the Free Market*. Chicago: Henry Regnery Company.

Shulak, E.-M., and H. Unterköfler. 2011. *Eugen von Böhm-Bawerk: Economist, Minister, Aristocrat*. Ludwig von Mises Institute. https://mises.org/library/8-eugen-von-b%C3%B6hm-bawerk-economist-minister-aristocrat. Access 11 December 2020.

Smaldone, W. 1988. Rudolf Hilferding and the Theoretical Foundations of German Social Democracy, 1902–33. *Central European History* 21 (3): 267–299. https://doi.org/10.1017/S0008938900012218.

———. 1998. *Rudolf Hilferding: Tragedy of a German Social Democrat*. DeKalb: Illinois University Press.

Steele, D.R. 1992. *From Marx to Mises: Post-Capitalist Society and the Challenge of Economic Calculation*. La Salle: Open Court Publishing Company.

Sweezy, P.M., ed. 1949. *Karl Marx and the Close of His System by Eugen Böhm-Bawerk and Böhm-Bawerk's Criticism of Marx by Rudolf Hilferding*. New York: Augustus M. Kelley.

Temperley, D. 2010. Modeling Common-Practice Rhythm. *Music Perception: An Interdisciplinary Journal* 27 (5): 355–376.

Trevor, E. 1997. Marxian Theories of Money and Capital. *International Journal of Political Economy* 27 (1): 7–42.

Wagner, F.P. 1996. *Theory and Politics of Democratic Socialism.* Atlantic Highlands: Humanities Press International.

White, L. 2003. *The Methodology of the Austrian School Economists.* The Ludwig von Mises Institute. http://mises.org/pdf/methfinb.pdf. Accessed 1 August 2012.

Wiley, T.E. 1978. *Back to Kant: The Revival of Kantianism in German Social and Historical Thought 1860–1914.* Detroit: Wayne State University Press.

Winkler, H.A. 1990. Choosing the Lesser Evil: The German Social Democrats and the Fall of the Weimar Republic. *Journal of Contemporary History* 25 (2/3): 205–227.

Zarembka, P. 2003. Lenin as Economist of Production: A Ricardian Step Backwards. *Science and Society* 67 (3): 276–302.

Zoninsein, J. 1990. *Monopoly Capital Theory: Hilferding and Twentieth-Century Capitalism.* New York: Greenwood Press.

CHAPTER 13

Hilferding as an Eclectic: A History of Economic Thought Perspective on Finance Capital

Jan Greitens

SOCIETY AND COMMUNITY: THE TRANSFORMATION OF CAPITALISM

While working on his book *Finance Capital* (1910), Rudolf Hilferding published an article titled 'Zur Problemstellung der theoretischen Ökonomie bei Karl Marx' (on the problem of theoretical economics in Karl Marx's work, 1904) in the journal *Die Neue Zeit*. In this article, Hilferding deals with Marx using the concepts of *Gemeinschaft/community* and *Gesellschaft/society* developed by Ferdinand Tönnies, which he quotes from the first edition of the book *Gemeinschaft und Gesellschaft* (1887). Not only during this period but during his entire life, Tönnies was an important influence in Hilferding's intellectual development (Greitens 2018, pp. 377ff). The essay reads like the extended version of the first

J. Greitens (✉)
Duale Hochschule Baden-Württemberg, Mosbach, Germany
e-mail: Jan.Greitens@mosbach.dhbw.de

© The Author(s), under exclusive license to Springer Nature Switzerland AG 2023
J. Dellheim, F. O. Wolf (eds.), *Rudolf Hilferding*, Luxemburg International Studies in Political Economy,
https://doi.org/10.1007/978-3-031-08096-8_13

307

paragraphs of *Finance Capital*. The terms *Gemeinschaft/community* and *Gesellschaft/society*, which Tönnies used to address economic questions in a narrower sense (Lichtblau 2000, p. 426), run through Hilferding's articles. For Hilferding, these questions regarding the 'social order' (*soziale Ordnung*) are at the heart of theoretical economics (Hilferding 1904, p. 108).

Tönnies (1887, pp. 17, 233) separated the natural and organic connection between humans in a *Gemeinschaft/community* and the mechanical connection in a *Gesellschaft/society*. 'The theory of *Gemeinschaft* is based on the idea that in the original or natural state there is a complete unity of human wills' (Tönnies 1887, p. 22).

> The theory of *Gesellschaft* takes as its starting point a group of people who, as in *Gemeinschaft*, live peacefully alongside one another, but in this case without being essentially united—indeed, on the contrary, they are here essentially detached. [...] Nothing happens in *Gesellschaft* that is more important for the individual's wider group than it is for himself. On the contrary, everyone is out for himself alone and living in a state of tension against everyone. [...] Nobody wants to do anything for anyone else, nobody wants to yield or give anything unless he gets something in return that he regards as at least an equal trade off. (Tönnies 1887, p. 52; these sentences are quoted in Hilferding 1904, p. 106 and explained p. 105f)

The law that regulates the exchanges of goods is also the law of motion in a society (Hilferding 1904, p. 107). As exchange becomes the paradigm of society, Tönnies follows Marx and connects this idea to a value theory based on work (Tönnies 1887, p. 54ff). Hilferding describes a society by the production of exchange value, while in a community the use value is the focal point (Hilferding 1904, p. 111). Behind Tönnies' construction lies a dialectical argument, in which the era of community was followed by an era of society. Tönnies' projected end of society is not followed by barbarism, but instead by a 'new community' with the labour movement as its driving force (Rudolph 1991, p. 309). In 1919, Tönnies states that the goal of the labour movement is to restore the community (ibid.). For Tönnies, communism means common property, whereas socialism means that the state owns the property. Communism is community-based, while socialism is a kind of society (Kozyr-Kowalski 1991, p. 329). Hilferding's idea of a consciously organised society (first defined by Hilferding in this essay, 1904, p. 109) is shaped by Tönnies' definition:

In a more perfect version of *Gesellschaft*, every commodity would be produced in the correct amounts and sold at its proper value by one single unified capitalistic concern which had complete foreknowledge of normal demand. (Tönnies 1887, p. 79)

Finance Capital was translated into English only once. This honourable task was done by Morris Watnick and Sam Gordon in 1981 and determined how the book was viewed by all non-German-speaking readers. The first paragraph is the following:

> *Die menschliche Produktionsgemeinschaft kann prinzipiell auf zweierlei Art konstituiert sein. Sie kann einmal bewußt geregelt sein. Die Gesellschaft—mag nun ihr Kreis die selbstwirtschaftende patriarchalische Familie, den kommunistischen Stamm oder die sozialistische Gesellschaft umschließen—schafft sich die Organe, welche als Vertreter des gesellschaftlichen Bewußtseins das Ausmaß und die Art der Produktion festsetzen und das gewonnene Gesellschaftsprodukt unter die Mitglieder verteilen.* (Hilferding 1910, p. 2)

The translation by Watnick and Gordon states:

> In principle the human productive community may be constituted in either of two ways. First, it may be consciously regulated. Whether its scale is that of a self-sufficient patriarchal family, a communistic tribe, or a socialist society, it creates the organs which, acting as the agents of social consciousness, fix the extent and methods of production and distribute the social product thus obtained among the members. (Hilferding 1981, p. 27)

Already in the first two sentences, Tönnies' terms *Gemeinschaft/community* (here presented as 'production community,' which the translators call 'productive community') and *Gesellschaft/society* appear. These terms give the entire book its framework; the 'latest phase of capitalism,' as the subtitle of *Finance Capital* is, moves between these two poles. Unfortunately, the term *Gesellschaft/society* is left out in the translation, and thus the central dialectic approach, the driving force in Hilferding's book, is missing.

The translators were unaware of the significance of Tönnies and his terms for Hilferding's work, so that in their translation, the terms community and society were not retained strictly. Probably, these terms were understood by the translators as a matter of group size, as the word 'scale' shows in the preceding translation where Hilferding lists several types of community. Based on this translation, the intended meaning is hard to detect.

The idea of a conscious regulation, which Hilferding would later call a (conscious) organisation in the concept of *Organized Capitalism* (1927), is also introduced in the first sentences.

The paragraph proceeds:

> *Wie, wo, wieviel, mit welchen Mitteln aus den vorhandenen natürlichen und künstlichen Produktionsbedingungen neue Produkte hergestellt werden, entscheidet der Pater familias oder die kommunalen, Landes- oder Nationalkommissäre der sozialistischen Gesellschaft, die, sei es, aus persönlicher Erfahrung die Bedürfnisse und Hilfsquellen der Familie kennend, sei es mit allen Mitteln einer organisierten Produktions- und Konsumtionsstatistik die gesellschaftlichen Erfordernisse erfassend, in bewußter Voraussicht das ganze Wirtschaftsleben nach den Bedürfnissen ihrer in ihnen bewußt vertretenen und durch sie bewußt geleiteten Gemeinschaften gestalten.* (Hilferding 1910, p. 2)

The translation by Watnick and Gordon is as follows:

> Given the material and man-made conditions of production, all decisions as to method, place, quantity and available tools involved in the production of new goods are made by the *pater familias* [accentuation missing in Hilferding 1910], or by the local regional or national commissars of the socialist society. The personal experience of the former gives him a knowledge of the needs and productive resources of his family; the latter can acquire a like knowledge of the requirements of their society by means of comprehensively organized statistics of production and consumption. They can thus shape, with conscious foresight, the whole economic life of the communities of which they are the appointed representatives and leaders in accordance with the needs of the members. (Hilferding 1981, p. 27)

This is a description of the *Gemeinschaft/community* in Tönnies' sense, where the term *sozialistischen Gesellschaft* (socialist society) stands out. Only communism is again a (production) community, while there is a transitional phase—a socialist society—which is a conscious organisation of a societal economy (see also Hilferding 1904, pp. 106f). Here together with the subtitle, one finds clearly at the beginning of the text that Hilferding wants to describe a process, a development.

The paragraph proceeds:

> *Die Menschen einer so organisierten Gemeinschaft beziehen sich in ihrer Produktion bewußt aufeinander als Teile einer Produktionsgemeinschaft*

13 HILFERDING AS AN ECLECTIC: A HISTORY OF ECONOMIC THOUGHT... 311

[accentuation by Hilferding is missing in translation]. *Ihre Arbeitsordnung und die Verteilung ihrer Produkte unterstehen der zentralen Kontrolle. Die Produktionsverhältnisse erscheinen als unmittelbar gesellschaftliche Verhältnisse, die Beziehungen der einzelnen, soweit sie das Wirtschaftsleben betreffen, als von der gesellschaftlichen Ordnung bestimmte, ihrem Privatwollen entrückte gesellschaftliche Beziehungen. Das Produktionsverhältnis selbst wird unmittelbar verstanden als von der Gesamtheit bewußt gesetztes und gewolltes.* (Hilferding 1910, pp. 2f)

The translation by Watnick and Gordon is as follows:

The individual members of such a community consciously regulate their productive activity as members of a productive community. Their labour process and the distribution of their products are subject to central control. Their relations of production are directly manifest as social relations, and the economic relations between individuals can be seen as being determined by the social order, by social arrangements rather than by private inclination. Relations of production are accepted as those which are established and desired by the whole community. (Hilferding 1981, p. 27)

The description of this transitional phase is continued. A *zentrale Kontrolle* (central control) is introduced. It is this role which, in the further course of the book, will be played by the forces of finance capital, the amalgamation of bank and industrial power. Hilferding speaks of *gesellschaftliche Ordnung*, which is translated as 'social order.' A more precise term in the sense of Tönnies and Hilferding would be 'societal order,' as Hilferding defines the socialist society as a society that has the conscious production of use values as its goal (Hilferding 1904, p. 111 footnote).

The second paragraph of *Finance Capital* starts with a precise definition of *Gesellschaft/society* as coined by Tönnies:

Anders die Gesellschaft, die dieser bewußten Organization entbehrt. Sie ist aufgelöst in voneinander unabhängige Personen, deren Produktion nicht mehr als Gesellschafts-, sondern als ihre Privatsache erscheint. Sie sind so Privateigentümer, die durch die Entwicklung der Arbeitsteilung gezwungen sind, miteinander in Beziehung zu treten; der Akt, in dem sie dies tun, ist der Austausch ihrer Produkte. Erst durch diesen Akt wird hier, in der durch Privateigentum und Arbeitsteilung in ihre Atome zerschlagenen Gesellschaft Zusammenhang hergestellt. (Hilferding 1910, p. 3)

This paragraph is translated by Watnick and Gordon as follows:

> Matters are different in a society which lacks this conscious organization. Such a society is dissolved into a large number of mutually independent individuals for whom production is a private matter rather than a social concern. In other words, its members are individual proprietors who are compelled by the development of the division of labour to do business with one another. The act by which this is accomplished is the exchange of commodities. It is only this act which establishes connections in a society otherwise dismembered into disparate units by private property and the division of labour. (Hilferding 1981, p. 27)

Apart from Tönnies, Hilferding, with his focus on financial economics, can also rely on a tradition of German-speaking economists such as Adam Müller, Karl Knies, or his Viennese contemporary Johann von Komorzynski, who all describe money as the way to reunite the divided *Gesellschaft/society* for production (Greitens 2022, pp. 279, 290ff, 303f). Valentin Wagner called this tradition the *sozialrechtliche Kredittheorie* (Wagner 1937, pp. 51ff), which means credit as a social and judicial instrument. In this sense, Hilferding concludes the second paragraph:

> *Denn erst durch ihn geschieht die Verbindung der durch die Arbeitsteilung und das Privateigentum zerlegten Gesellschaft zu einem Ganzen.* (Hilferding 1910, p. 3)

which is translated by Watnick and Gordon as follows:

> A productive community must express itself in such acts of exchange because only in this way can the unity of society, dissolved by private property and the division of labour, be restored. (Hilferding 1981, p. 28)

The reunification of the individuals is only necessary in a *Gesellschaft/society*. Unfortunately, the translators use both terms, 'community' and 'society,' in their cumbersome translation of this sentence. This makes it impossible to figure out the intended meaning.

In the same paragraph, Hilferding defines the phase of the *sozialistischen Gesellschaft* (socialist society) whose emergence he wants to describe in his book:

> *Nur als Vermittler des gesellschaftlichen Zusammenhanges bildet aber der Austausch den Gegenstand theoretisch-ökonomischer Analyse. Denn auch in*

einer sozialistischen Gesellschaft mag Austausch statthaben. Aber es ist ein Austausch nach stattgefundener, von der Gesellschaft irgendwie mit Willen und Bewußtsein normierter Zuteilung. (Hilferding 1910, p. 3)

This paragraph is translated by Watnick and Gordon as follows:

> Exchange is the subject matter of theoretical economics only because, and to the extent that, it performs this mediating function in the social structure. It is of course true that exchange may also take place in a socialist society, but that would be a type of exchange occurring only after the product had already been distributed according to a socially desired norm. (Hilferding 1981, p. 27f)

The translators left out the words *mit Willen und Bewußtsein* (with will and consciousness), which is the central role of finance capital in the transformation of capitalism.

The Development of Capitalism in Finance Capital

In the first two paragraphs of *Finance Capital*, Hilferding clarifies what he wants to do in his book: to describe and explain the development from a society of capitalist anarchy to a society of a consciously organised capitalist economy by the forces of finance capital. Then, in a political overthrow, the society becomes a consciously organised socialist economy, that is, a socialist society. The further transformation to a communist community is not described in *Finance Capital*. For Hilferding, communism is not 'subject of theoretical economics' (Hilferding 1904, p. 107).

In this framework, Hilferding implicitly uses a step model. In the beginning, capitalism prevails against the previous, feudal economic order (Greitens 2017, p. 153ff; Greitens 2018, p. 181ff). This early competitive capitalism was already analysed and explained by Karl Marx. Before the socialist society can begin, capitalism enters a second phase in which the system modifies itself. This idea is at the centre of *Finance Capital* and can be divided into five steps.

Step 1: Capitalism of free competition

- Competitive capitalism exists, as described by Marx.
- Marx's theory of value applies in this anarchic, capitalist economy.

- The economy is not highly concentrated, and the financial system consists of *Geldhandlungskapital* (money-handling capital), which refers to bills of exchange.

Step 2: Financial system development

- The formation of limited-liability companies, such as joint-stock companies, enables larger investments and mobilises capital through the fungibility of the fictitious capital at the stock exchanges.
- A financial system gradually develops to meet the growing demand for capital.
- The concentration and centralisation of capital in the industry begins.

Step 3: Concentration in the economy

- Due to economies of scale and scope, concentration and centralisation in the industry continues.
- With the increasing liquidity needs of the companies, banks play a central role as the provider of this liquidity.
- The banks promote monopolisation in the industry to hedge their investments.
- The capital needs of the industry and those within the promoter's business cause banks to concentrate on fulfilling these demands.
- The importance of the stock exchanges decreases, and a bank-based financial system emerges because this type of financial system allows a stricter control of the bank clients.
- The concentration and centralisation in the industry rise up to a general cartel.
- The applicability of Marxian value theory weakens: 'It seems that the monopolistic combine, while it confirms Marx's theory of concentration, at the same time tends to undermine his theory of value' (Hilferding 1981, p. 228).

Step 4: Emergence of finance capital

- Banks merge into one monopolistic bank. Thereafter, finance capital emerges as a centralised power over the entire economy.
- The rule of the capital magnates takes central control over the economy.

- Value theory is no longer relevant.
- The economy is consciously organised but in antagonistic form by the capitalists.
- 'The tendency of finance capital is to establish social control of production, but it is an antagonistic form of socialization, since the control of social production remains vested in an oligarchy' (Hilferding 1981, p. 367).

Step 5: Overthrow of capitalism towards a socialist society

- A political revolution changes ownership and puts the conscious organisation in the hands of the proletariat.
- 'Finance capital, in its maturity, is the highest stage of the concentration of economic and political power in the hands of the capitalist oligarchy. It is the climax of the dictatorship of the magnates of capital. [...] it makes [...] the internal domination of capital increasingly irreconcilable with the interests of the mass of the people, exploited by finance capital but also summoned into battle against it. In the violent clash of these hostile interests the dictatorship of the magnates of capital will finally be transformed into the dictatorship of the proletariat' (Hilferding 1981, p. 370).

The driving forces in this process are the following transformations:

(1) monetary and financial system development, and
(2) concentration and centralisation in the industry.

Regarding the monetary and financial system, Hilferding describes the evolution of a bank-based financial system, which not only includes the institutions of the financial sector itself but is based on a broad understanding of financial systems. Hilferding begins with a monetary theory that money is of fundamental importance in the organisation of an economy. Additionally, he stresses the importance of new types of enterprises, joint-stock companies, and their corporate governance structures (Hilferding 1910, p. 120ff). Market liquidity at the stock exchanges is the prerequisite for the liquidity of fictitious capital and thus for the mobilisation of capital. Nevertheless, these market-based institutions are not as dominant in Germany as they are in England. In particular, the stock exchanges initially developed in a complementary manner to banks, but they lose their relevance when the banks become dominant. With the development of the bank-based financial system, the settlement of all financial transactions and the provision of liquidity are monopolised by banks until they ultimately control the entire economy.

Regarding concentration and centralisation in the economy, in competitive capitalism, the capitalists are subjected to the pressure of competition. The concentration and centralisation of capital, especially with the new joint-stock companies, lead to greater freedom of action for the capitalist. The businessman is reduced to the role of owner and the managers lead the large companies (Hilferding 1910, p. 154).

In the term 'finance capital,' the two transformations come together. The tendency to establish a general cartel and the tendency to form a monopolised bank coincide and their amalgamation leads to the power of finance capital (Hilferding 1910, p. 319). Hilferding provides the following definition:

> 'I call bank capital, that is, capital in money form which is actually transformed in this way into industrial capital, finance capital. So far as its owners are concerned, it always retains the money form; it is invested by them in the form of money capital, interest-bearing capital, and can always be withdrawn by them as money capital. But in reality the greater part of the capital thus invested with the banks is transformed into industrial, productive capital (means of production and labour power) and is invested in the productive process. An ever-increasing proportion of the capital used in industry is finance capital, capital at the disposition of the banks which is used by the industrialists.' (Hilferding 1981, p. 225)

Hilferding describes many reasons why the banks wield so much power over the industry. Two groups of arguments are central. First, the banks control the liquidity of the companies, supply of credit money, and higher liquidity of bank assets (equities, loans, and others) compared with the less liquid industrial assets such as machinery. Second, the construction of corporations is considered as a tool to obtain power over companies with a relatively small amount of their own capital (Hilferding 1910, p. 138ff).

Hilferding does not want to destroy the complex institutional network of the organised economy under the rule of finance capital but wants to change the ownership to transform the economy into an organised economy in the form of a socialist society. According to *Finance Capital* (1910), this change of ownership is to occur by means of a political overthrow. Later, during the democratic Weimar Republic, Hilferding wanted to reach this goal with 'economic democracy' (e.g. Hilferding 1927).

Hilferding is acknowledged for having scientifically investigated the widespread term 'finance capital' to describe the power of banks and formation of huge industrial conglomerates. He was the first to identify the fundamental aspects of a bank-based financial system in contrast to market-based forms. Particularly striking is his broad analysis, which begins with a monetary theory and extends the argumentation stringently to the financial system. His analysis also includes factors outside a narrow economic perspective, similar to the 'varieties of capitalism' approach applied today (e.g., with reference to Hilferding by Mettenheim 2011). In this respect, finance capital for Hilferding means the description of an economic style (*Wirtschaftsstil*) with the banks as central actors, which had a long historical continuity and existed until 20 years ago, for example, under the term 'Deutschland AG' (Greitens 2017, p. 153ff).

PROMOTER'S PROFIT IN LIGHT OF HILFERDING'S CONTEMPORARY SOURCES

Hilferding's Private Library

In 1956, Hilferding's second wife Rose bequeathed his private library to the Seminar für Politische Wissenschaften of the University of Cologne, whose director at the time was Heinrich Brüning, with whom Hilferding had worked closely during his chancellorship. In a letter of thanks dated October 15, 1956, to Rose Hilferding, Hermann Josef Unland from the Seminar states that seven boxes weighing 637 kg had arrived in Cologne on October 12, 1956 (Archiv der sozialen Demokratie, 1/ RHAB 1/2).

In 1957, an inventory was published in a brochure by Unland. The list includes 609 titles (Hilferding 1957). For a long time, the collection was accessible in its entirety at the Seminar für Politische Wissenschaften. It was later incorporated into the central library of the university, where the collection lost its coherence. Since 2018, Hilferding's private library has been made available again at the University and City Library of Cologne (https://www.ub.uni-koeln.de/sammlungen/hilferding/index_ger.html).

The database of the University of Cologne today contains 698 titles from the collection. The difference results from various ways of counting (e.g., in 1957, the 19 volumes of the book series *Internationale Bibliothek* were summed up in one position). Furthermore, 68 publications from the 1957 list are missing. These are mostly books (by authors such as Marx, Sombart, Oppenheimer, Luxemburg, and Kautsky) that were presumably available in several editions at the library and were therefore sorted out. Among them was Hilferding's edition of Bruno Buchwald's textbook *Die Technik des Bankbetriebs* (1904), which is elementary for Hilferding's understanding of the banking business (Greitens 2018, p. 386f). However, nine works that were not on the list in 1957 have now been added.

Before 1910, 167 works were published. This does not mean that Hilferding possessed them before that year, let alone read them. However, 22 works quoted in *Finanzkapital* can be found in the library in exactly the edition cited. In 1904, Hilferding wrote a review of Luigi Cossa's 'Die ersten Elemente der Wirtschaftslehre' in *Die Neue Zeit* (XXII, Vol. 2, pp. 703–704). In the book in the private library (signature HILF388), exactly those passages are highlighted, which Hilferding quoted literally in the review (esp. p. 9). In the writings of Hobson (signature HILF248), Greene (signature HILF156), Meade (signature HILF200), and Liefmann (signature HILF389) are the same blue and grey underscores that can be found in the relevant passages in *Finance Capital*. This fact once again proves the high relevance of these authors for Hilferding's *Finance Capital* and the continuity of the library can be concluded up to Hilferding's early Viennese period.

Further on, the example of the promoter's profit, which can be regarded as his most famous discovery (Schefold 2000, p. 15), will be used to show the extent to which Hilferding's personal library can contribute to clarifying his ideas.

The Concept of Promoter's Profit

One central driving force behind the rapid expansion of joint-stock companies is the opportunity to quickly earn high profits, that is, *Gründergewinn* (promoter's profits). The shareholder is only a money capitalist and can get his capital back at any time.

> The shareholder, on the other hand, if we consider him only as a money capitalist, will make his capital available to anyone so long as he gets interest on it. (Hilferding 1981, p. 108f)

Therefore, competition for money capital exists between the two forms of investment in equity (shares) and debt (bonds), thereby leading to price convergence.

> Liquid money capital competes, as interest-bearing capital, for investment in shares, in the same way as it competes in its real function as loan capital for investment in fixed interest loans. The competition for these various investment opportunities brings the price of shares closer to the price of investments with a fixed interest, and reduces the shareholders' yield from the level of industrial profit to that of interest. (Hilferding 1981, p. 109)

Hilferding does not elaborate on this development, but speaks of a 'historical process' that goes hand in hand with the development of joint-stock companies and stock exchanges. As long as this process is not complete, the dividend still includes interest and profits.

> The competition for these various investment opportunities brings the price of shares closer to the price of investments with a fixed interest, and reduces the shareholders' yield from the level of industrial profit to that of interest. This reduction of the share yield to the level of the rate of interest is a historical process which accompanies the development of stocks and the stock exchange. When the joint-stock company is not the dominant form, and the negotiability of shares is not fully developed, dividends will include an element of entrepreneurial profit [*Unternehmergewinn*] as well as interest. (Hilferding 1981, p. 109)

For joint-stock companies, this condition means that they only have to earn the average rate of interest for their shareholders and not the average profit because shareholders only expect dividends as high as interests.

> To the extent that the corporation is prevalent, industry is now operated with money capital which, when converted into industrial capital, need not yield the average rate of profit, but only the average rate of interest. (Hilferding 1981, p. 109)

As under normal circumstances the average profit is earned, an additional profit remains in the company. This profit is capitalised and distributed through the promoter's profit to the company founders. It is the difference between capital which earns the average rate of profit and capital which earns the average rate of interest. This is the difference which appears as 'promoter's profit,' a source of gain which arises only from the conversion of profit-bearing into interest-bearing capital. (Hilferding 1981, p. 112)

The issued equity is chosen as large as possible when going public to achieve the largest possible promoter's profit. The foreseeable profit must be sufficient to pay dividends on the rate as interest for the entire issued capital in shares.

The shares are issued; that is, sold for money. One part of this money constitutes the promoter's profit, accrues to the promoter (say, the issuing bank) and drops out of circulation in this cycle. The other part is converted into productive capital and enters the cycle of industrial capital. (Hilferding 1981, p. 113)

Hilferding (1981, p. 112) describes the promoter's profit as a separate category, an economic category *sui generis*; this is a formulation that Marx had previously applied to money as interest-bearing capital. 'Promoter's profit, or the profit from issuing shares, is neither a profit, in the strict sense [phrase in the translation cannot be found in Hilferding 1910], nor interest, but capitalized entrepreneurial revenue [*Unternehmergewinn*, earlier translated as "entrepreneurial profit," which is clearer]' (Hilferding 1981, p. 174). The promoter's profit can be realised in all capital transactions in which the income on the capital is higher than the interest, that is, in conversions into joint-stock companies and capital increases.

[The bank] merely supplies the market with a certain amount of money capital in the form of fictitious capital, which can then be transformed into industrial capital. The fictitious capital is sold on the market and the bank realizes the promoter's profit which arises from the conversion of the industrial capital into fictitious capital. (Hilferding 1981, p. 128)

Discussions on Promoter's Profit

The weakness in Hilferding's argument is obvious:

he simply takes the difference between the rate of interest and the rate of profit for granted, and offers no explanation of its origin or persistence. (Howard and King 1989, p. 96)

Hilferding has merely taken from Marx the fundamental separation between profit and interest. However, the question remains how Hilferding imagined the historical process of reducing the dividend to the interest rate, which he does not explain any further.

Many ideas about this process have been expressed, and the following approaches can be distinguished:

- *Speculation*: The promoter's profit is often described as simple financial speculation. The background for Hilferding should have been the bubble of 1873 (e.g., Kim 1999, p. 108). However, Hilferding (1981, p. 112) explicitly rejects this interpretation and considers the speculative phase of capitalism to be over after the panic of 1873:

  > The mass psychoses which speculation generated at the beginning of the capitalist era, in those blessed times when every speculator felt like a god who creates a world out of nothing, seem to be gone for ever. (Hilferding 1981, p. 294)

  Since then, the market has become unemotional: 'prose has vanquished the poetry of gain' (Hilferding 1981, p. 294).
- *Risk premium*: Another interpretation concerns the question of risk. In the neoclassical tradition of Miller and Modigliani (1958), the promoter's profit is described as a premium for the higher risks involved in equity investments (e.g., Boyer des Roches 2015 or Streissler 2000, p. 60). Hilferding (1981, p. 127) mentions a risk premium in his definition of promoter's profit but rejects a greater significance.
- *Goodwill*: Another line of argumentation refers to the existence of goodwill. Under the act of 1896, companies listed on the stock exchange must exist for at least one year. In the period between the formation of the company and its public offering, goodwill can therefore be created, which can be distributed to the founders during the issuance of the shares (e.g., Fritsch 1968, p. 158 or Morioka 1985, p. 99f). Dieudonné (2016, p. 14) sees the idea of goodwill as the basis for the promoter's profit based on the work of Thorstein Veblen (there is no evidence for this; e.g., Veblen is not in Hilferding's library). To explain the promoter's profit in an above-average market success before a company's public offering would ignore Hilferding's claim to describe a normal and average phenomenon.

- *Monopoly position of the banks*: Pietranera sees the concentration of the banks as the cause of the promoter's profit because this concentration allows charging monopoly prices for the shares (Pietranera 1974, p. 46). The reduction of dividends to the level of the interest rates is due to the influence of the monopoly capital (ibid., pp. 57f). The connection of the promoter's profit with the monopolistic position of the banks can be found in *Finance Capital* (Hilferding 1981, p. 128): 'The more powerful the banks become, the more successful they are in reducing dividends to the level of interest and in appropriating the promoter's profit.' This condition explains who gets the promoter's profit but not their existence.
- *Liquidity*: The different liquidity of fixed capital compared to shares must result in different valuations, that is, the capital market is not homogeneous. The shareholder must be satisfied with the interest rate as the price for higher liquidity of his investment. Hilferding is not looking for mechanisms that could lead to an equilibrium. Instead, he describes an institutional development resulting from this imbalance in the form of the promoter's profit and the intertwining of industrial and bank capital (Schefold 2000, pp. 15, 20).

Hilferding's Sources Behind the Promoter's Profit

Hilferding's library astonishingly contains several American textbooks about corporate finance. In his book *Modern Business Corporations* (1906, signature HILF58), William Wood writes in the chapter 'Promoter's Profits':

> The promoter has to create value to entitle him to profit. He provides a new or original means of making money, and makes the means productive through the development of a "going" concern for the utilisation of that means. His profit, though large, is legitimate profit. It is arrived at usually as follows. From the figures of the technical expert on the proposition, the promoter arrives at a conclusion as to the total net profits of the business when it has been developed. If he is a conservative man, he capitalises his business on the basis of its average earning capacity with only enough "water" to provide for increased earnings. If the proposition was one worth his efforts, it was a proposition which could be capitalised at a figure greatly in excess of what he paid for it in its undeveloped condition, and also in excess of this cost price and the development cost combined. The difference between these costs and the sum which he receives for the stock represents

13 HILFERDING AS AN ECLECTIC: A HISTORY OF ECONOMIC THOUGHT... 323

his profit. [...] The association of individuals in the promoter's corporation is not fortuitous, but is the result of the work of a trained business agent, the promoter, who is working for his own profit, and is earning his profit by assembling the business proposition and by securing the incorporators and other investors. (Wood 1906, p. 16)

This passage is marked by Hilferding in the copy in his library and describes the mechanism of receiving capitalised profits by issuing a larger number of shares.

Thomas L. Greene, who is cited by Hilferding in *Finance Capital*, wrote in the same year in his book *Corporate Finance* (signature HILF200):

The unwillingness of the average investor, individual or institutional, to put his money at any business hazard, is one of the main causes for the continued fall in the average rate of interest. Capital competes with capital for safe investments. The demand for security in loans gives the business firm or corporation its opportunity. If perfectly sound in condition and management, it can borrow its outside capital at a low rate, and so increase its own profits. (Greene 1906, p. 3)

Here, Hilferding's argument of decreasing earnings on shares to the level of interest is described (Greitens 2013, p. 31f).

Also, a copy of Edward S. Meade's *Trust Finance* (1907) is in Hilferding's library and, as we can see from his marks, he read the book in detail. It combines the question of concentration in the economy with financial questions, as later done in Hilferding's *Finance Capital*. Furthermore, the book covers some basic rules of calculation, for example, 'The value of a security is the capitalization of the income which the security produces' (Meade 1907, p. 116).

In considering Hilferding's reference to Meade's work, we can infer that the former must have seen in the latter's book a fundamental empirical confirmation of his theory. This American example illustrates the processes of concentration and the financial sides of this development, such as the low dividends and the promoter's profits (e.g., p. 122).

Meade's approach is also theoretical, and in these sections many pages are marked by Hilferding as well. In Meade's discussion of the promoter's profits, the essential principles of the promoting business, which generates the promoter's profit, are the sale of the certificates of this capitalization to the investor either directly or through the agency of middlemen for a sum of money exceeding the amount necessary to purchase and develop the resource which it is intended to exploit. The difference represents the promoter's profit, a characteristic feature of corporation financiering. What has the promoter done to entitle him to this large profit? He has produced no coal; that is done by the company to which he turns over his options. Nor has he risked an amount of money in any way comparable to the profit which he has made. [...] Judged by the canons of what is generally considered to be legitimate money-making, the promoter has done nothing [...]. And yet the profits of the promoter are as legitimate as are the profits of any of the more familiar professions. The promoter is a creator of value. He brings into existence a means of producing wealth which did not before exist. (Meade 1907, p. 56)

Meade (ibid., p. 57) adds:

What is the justification for the promoter's profit? The answer to these questions lies in the nature of the transaction. Neither the owner nor the investor can do the work of the promoter, and they have, therefore, no claim to his profits.

In addition to the general approach to the promoter's profit (the issuance of more shares than necessary), the legitimacy of the promoter's profit, as a means of enabling future profits, is emphasised.

The value of each of the plants which it was proposed to include in the new trust was based upon its earning power. That earning power [...] was greatly reduced by competition. The promoter expected to option each plant at a figure which should represent its past earnings, organize a company with a capitalization which should represent the increased earning power of these plants when competition had been eliminated, and sell the stock of this corporation to the public. [...] By combining a large number of small holdings under one ownership, and properly equipping the property for large operations, the value of coal-land can be increased from $20 to $100 per acre. Out of the securities, representing this valuation, even at a discount of 50 per cent, the promoter can equip the property and have a large profit remaining. [...] This, then, was the advantage which the trust promoter sought to obtain—to capitalize the economies of combination, sell the certificates of the capital, and obtain a share of the proceeds as his own profit'. (Meade 1907, pp. 63–64)

Meade describes the promoter's profit very clearly as monopoly profits, as whose organisers the promoters are paid.

Hilferding had intensively studied the contemporary literature on American corporate finance. This literature describes in detail the developments that Hilferding discusses in *Finance Capital*: corporate mergers, intensive promoting business with high profits, and low returns as an investor on the stock exchange. In these works, the promoter's profit turns out to be monopoly profit resulting from high concentration, which is capitalised and handed out to the promoters. Hilferding's achievement consists in his ability to integrate this corporate finance literature into his Marxian theory of profits and interest.

The idea of a new, innovative, and small company, which is today associated with the term *Gründer/promoter*, is not the understanding Hilferding had. In his description of a mature and consciously organised economy, promoting means above all the merging of existing companies. The promoter's profit is the yield received for forming a trust.

CONCLUSION

Hilferding was not an orthodox Marxist but an eclectic. He wanted to take up new ideas and interpret them within a Marxist framework, as he had explained in the foreword of the first volume of the *Marx-Studien* (Adler and Hilferding 1904, p. VI ff). This was proven by two examples: first, the terms *Gemeinschaft/community* and *Gesellschaft/society* from Tönnies, which Hilferding used as the basis for his description of the development of capitalism; and, second, the literature on American corporate finance, which Hilferding used as the basis for his definition of promoter's profit. Evidently, for Hilferding, this profit is primarily capitalised monopoly profit in the concentration process.

The analysis of Hilferding's personal library is helpful in exploring these backgrounds. Unfortunately, the library has only received limited attention in the research done on Hilferding. In addition, as honourable as the translation of Hilferding into English is in principle, the translation is not always as precise as necessary to make these connections visible.

REFERENCES

Adler, M. / Hilferding, R. 1904. Vorwort. *Marx-Studien*, Vol. 1, V-VII. Wiener Volksbuchhandlung.

Archiv der sozialen Demokratie, Friedrich Ebert Stiftung, Bestand Rose Hilferding.

Boyer Des Roches, J. 2015. Bank Rate, Profit of Enterprise, Risk Premium and Promoter's Profit in Marx and Hilferding, International Conference: MEGA and Marxian Discourses on Economic Crises, 2015, Tokyo, Japan, hal-01497162.

Dieudonné, M. 2016. Credit, Shares and Goodwill: A Veblenian Trinity, hal-01264730.

Fritsch, B. 1968. *Die Geld- und Kredittheorie von Karl Marx*. 2nd ed. Frankfurt: Europäische Verlagsanstalt.

Greene, T.L. 1906. *Corporate Finance*. 3rd ed. New York: G.P. Putnam's Sons.

Greitens, J. 2013. Marxian and Non-Marxian Foundations of Rudolf Hilferding's Finance Capital. *The History of Economic Thought* 55 (1): 18–35.

———. 2017. Der Begriff Finanzkapital in der Prägung durch Rudolf Hilferding. In *Handbuch Reichtum*, ed. Nikolaus Dimmel et al., 152–163. Innsbruck: Studienverlag.

———. 2018. *Finanzkapital und Finanzsysteme, 'Das Finanzkapital', von Rudolf Hilferding* (2nd ed.). Marburg: Metropolis Verlag.

———. 2022. *Geld-Theorie-Geschichte* (2nd ed.). Marburg: Metropolis Verlag.

Hilferding, R. 1904. Zur Problemstellung der theoretischen Ökonomie bei Karl Marx. *Die Neue Zeit* 1 (XXIII): 101–112.

———. 1910/1947. *Das Finanzkapital, Eine Studie über die jüngste Entwicklung des Kapitalismus*. Berlin: Dietz Verlag.

———. 1927/1982. Die Aufgaben der Sozialdemokratie in der Republik. In Stephan, Cora, ed., 1982. *Zwischen den Stühlen oder über die Unvereinbarkeit von Theorie und Praxis. Schriften Rudolf Hilferdings 1904–1940*, 212–236. Berlin: Dietz Verlag J.H.W. Nachf.

———. 1957. *Sammlung Dr. Hilferding*. Seminar für Politische Wissenschaften, University of Cologne.

———. 1981. *Finance Capital, A Study of the Latest Phase of Capitalist Development*. London: Routledge & Kegan Paul.

Howard, M.C., and J.E. King. 1989. *A History of Marxian Economics, Volume 1, 1883–1929*. Princeton: Princeton University Press.

Kim, K.-M. 1999. *Hilferding und Marx: Geld- und Kredittheorie in Rudolf Hilferdings 'Das Finanzkapital' und im Marxschen 'Kapital'*. Köln: PapyRossa-Verlag.

Kozyr-Kowalski, S. 1991. Ferdinand Tönnies über den historischen Materialismus. In *Hundert Jahre 'Gemeinschaft und Gesellschaft'*, ed. Lars Clausen and Carsten Schlüter, 321–335. Opladen: Leske & Budrich.

Lichtblau, K. 2000. 'Vergemeinschaftung' und, Vergesellschaftung' bei Max Weber. *Zeitschrift für Soziologie* 29 (6): 423–443.

Meade, E.S. 1907. *Trust Finance, A Study of the Genesis, Organization, and Management of Industrial Combinations.* New York: D. Appleton and Company.

Mettenheim, K. 2011. *Varieties of Finance Capitalism, Corporate Governance and Competitive Advantage.* http://paperroom.ipsa.org/app/webroot/papers/paper_26142.pdf.

Miller, M.H., and F. Modigliani. 1958. The Cost of Capital, Corporation Finance and the Theory of Investment. *American Economic Review* 48 (3): 261–297.

Morioka, K. 1985. Hilferding's Finance Capital and Promoter's Profit. *Review of Economics and Business* 13 (1): 87–110.

Pietranera, G. 1974. *R. Hilferding und die ökonomische Theorie der Sozialdemokratie,* Trans. Sophie G. Alf. Internationale Marxistische Diskussion, No. 48. Berlin: Merve Verlag.

Rudolph, G. 1991. Ferdinand Tönnies und die Lehren von Karl Marx, Annäherung und Vorbehalt. In *Hundert Jahre 'Gemeinschaft und Gesellschaft',* ed. Lars Clausen and Carsten Schlüter, 301–230. Opladen: Leske & Budrich.

Schefold, B. 2000. Rudolf Hilferding und die Idee des organisierten Kapitalismus. In *Vademecum, Kommentarband mit Beiträgen zur Faksimile-Ausgabe von 'Das Finanzkapital',* 5–32. Düsseldorf: Verlag Wirtschaft und Finanzen.

Streissler, E. 2000. Rudolf Hilferding und die österreichische Schule der Nationalökonomie. In *Vademecum, Kommentarband mit Beiträgen zur Faksimile-Ausgabe von 'Das Finanzkapital',* 53–65. Düsseldorf: Verlag Wirtschaft und Finanzen.

Tönnies, F. [1887] 2001. *Community and Civil Society.* Trans. José Harris and Margaret Hollis. Cambridge: Cambridge University Press.

Wagner, V.F. 1937. *Geschichte der Kredittheorien, Eine dogmen-kritische Darstellung.* Wien: Springer.

Wood, W. 1906. *Modern Business Corporations, Including the Organization and Management of Private Corporations with Financial Principles and Practices.* Indianopolis: Bobbs-Merril.

CHAPTER 14

Rudolf Hilferding on the Economic Categories of 'Joint Stock Company/Share Capital': A Refinement of the Critique of Political Economy?

Judith Dellheim

This chapter takes up the argument of the chapter '"Joint-Stock Company" and "Share Capital" as Economic Categories of Critical Political Economy' (Dellheim 2018, pp. 265–98) in our previous volume in this series, *The Unfinished System of Karl Marx. Critically Reading Capital as a Challenge for our Times*. The reason is a simple one: Marx's analyses from the mid-1840s to the end of his productive period and his final letters place a major focus on the joint-stock company and share capital. These works helped him—as well as his followers—to understand the movement of the capitalist mode of production and the problems of a radical critique thereof, and to further develop the critique of political economy. Rudolf

---

J. Dellheim (✉)
Rosa-Luxemburg-Foundation, Berlin, Germany
e-mail: judith.dellheim.fellow@rosalux.org

© The Author(s), under exclusive license to Springer Nature Switzerland AG 2023
J. Dellheim, F. O. Wolf (eds.), *Rudolf Hilferding*, Luxemburg International Studies in Political Economy,
https://doi.org/10.1007/978-3-031-08096-8_14

329

Hilferding's *Finance Capital* was an attempt to pick up on Marx's works in order to

> arrive at a scientific understanding of the economic characteristics of the latest phase of capitalist development. In other words, the object is to bring these characteristics within the theoretical system of classical political economy which begins with William Petty and finds its supreme expression in Marx. (Hilferding [1910] 1981, p. 21)

By 'these characteristics', Hilferding was referring to 'those processes of concentration which, on the one hand, "eliminate free competition" through the formation of cartels and trusts, and on the other, bring bank and industrial capital into an ever more intimate relationship' (ibid.). He wanted to investigate to what extent 'the legal forms in which industrial enterprises are established have a specific economic significance; and this is a problem which the economic theory of the joint stock company may perhaps contribute in finding a solution' (ibid.). But a further characteristic of the 'latest phase of capitalist development', especially discussed by Rosa Luxemburg, should be added: the increased and growing aggressiveness of the capitalist elites and their political and state partners towards Europe and the world, especially with regard to the conquest and defence of colonies. Hilferding is widely regarded as the pioneer of a new theory of the jointstock company (e.g. Kurata 2009, p. 26), based in particular on chapter 7 of his *Finance Capital*. The aim of my chapter in the previous volume was to illustrate how exactly Marx had developed the categories of joint-stock company and share capital and analytically distilled 'the economic characteristics of the latest phase of capitalist development'—and now I shall analyse how Hilferding proceeded from these Marxian categories. On the one hand, this served to find out more about the way Hilferding formed his thoughts and proceeded in his work, and about what lessons can be learned from this. This accounts for various passages in the following pages, which do not concern the joint-stock company/ share capital directly, but rather focus on Hilferding's methodical approach. A second objective is to critically examine, through scrutiny of the supposedly 'Marxist' social analysis in Hilferding's texts, the emancipatory substance of these texts. This endeavour is essentially linked to the search for the causes of the structural weakness of emancipatory-solidary agencies today and ways to overcome it. The initial finding was already quite striking: Hilferding only very vaguely referred to the contexts in which Marx developed the categories of 'joint-stock capital' and 'share capital' and scarcely looked at the question of how and why he had done so, nor did he ascertain the consequences this had for Marx's subsequent work. A number of problems with Hilferding's texts arise from his approach to analysing and reflecting societal (and particularly economic) developments. This raises the question why Hilferding failed to develop an adequate sensitivity for environmental problems and their consequences for socialist politics, despite an ongoing critical public discussion on these matters already during his day.

The first central thesis of this chapter can be formulated as follows: Hilferding's greatest strength is his exquisite knowledge of the actions of banks and other enterprises, as well as his ability to grasp and logically develop specific economic processes. His main shortcomings, on the other hand, are a number of erroneous conclusions resulting mainly from his failure to fully and critically appropriate Marx's scientific legacy—despite his in-depth study of select writings of Marx and his numerous references to these works. The attribute 'critical' aside, this criticism may appear somewhat shallow and dogmatic, but it nevertheless points to a problem which large sections of the left have in common with Hilferding: their approaches to thought and theoretical work are based on a certain conception of Marx (regarding Hilferding: see Gottschalch 1962, p. 249) which has not been radically and (self-) critically challenged. Frequently, as the argument goes, there is not enough time to trace Marx's development of categories during his work on the Critique of Political Economy, because, after all, 'one must proceed to the real problems of today', as fast as they develop. Yet even though the problem of an adequate reading of the development of categories in *Capital* may appear *de facto* irresolvable, it must at least be considered and reflected in one's own work. My second central thesis is therefore that the categories of 'jointstock company' and 'share capital' in Hilferding's work must be discussed and criticised in the context of a radical critique of previous and current modes of socialisation.

This chapter proceeds from a brief focused reflection of the book chapter mentioned at the beginning (Dellheim 2018, pp. 265–98). This is followed by a discussion of Hilferding's passages which are relevant for substantiating the central theses in the temporal order of their composition. At the heart of this study lies Hilferding's *Finance Capital*. The argument then culminates in a few answers to the question formulated in the title: towards a critique of Hilferding's categories of 'joint-stock company/share capital' as well as other questions raised below.

A Brief Reflection of 'Joint-Stock Company' and 'Share Capital' as Economic Categories of a Critical Political Economy

My chapter in our book on Marx led to, or, rather, reinforced, the following insights:

1. Marx's interest in the joint-stock company dates back as early as to the 1840s, beginning with his efforts to prove that the possibility for the emancipation of the exploited, disenfranchised, downtrodden and aggrieved arises within the contradictory processes of socialisation. He considers the organisation of solidarity in the struggle against the existing social conditions the elementary starting point for such emancipation. This includes, in particular, the competition among the 'bourgeois' who drive that socialisation forward while obstructing the organisation of solidarity among the oppressed, especially the workers. Socialisation always implies the development of inter-human relations, in their metabolism with nature as well, in the course of which the spaces expand in which people relate to and depend on one another. Socialisation occurs mainly via the continuous social division of labour and the resulting processes of exchange of the products of labour. This includes processes of the concentration of the means of production, as well as the formation and disintegration of monopolies, setting social relations of power in motion.

2. The joint-stock company served the ruling elites' collective resource mobilisation for the conquest of new territories, the robbery of property and natural resources, slavery and private enrichment in the beginnings of capitalist modernity. It represented the economic precondition for the thriving of manufacture and was accompanied by the development of the debt and credit system as well as of speculation—that is to say, the so-called primitive accumulation of capital, or, in other words, the prevailing of the capital relation in the emerging modern societies. Joint-stock companies were initiated by state agencies, and have served, ever since their inception, as 'powerful levers for the concentration of capital' (Marx [1867] 1976, p. 918), or capital accumulation. The latter unavoidably leads to violence against people and nature—and it is based on two functions: the mobilisation of resources for surplus value production and the realisation of surplus value through dispossession and redistribution, the

14 RUDOLF HILFERDING ON THE ECONOMIC CATEGORIES OF 'JOINT...

use of money as money capital, and the production of this very surplus value by workers (and the appropriation thereof by the capitalist). With capital accumulation, or the socialisation of labour in a capitalist form, or, in still other words, with the development of the capitalist mode of production, above all the agencies and sites of surplus value production and capital accumulation as well as the relation of capital vis-à-vis 'the state' change. New markets emerge, and expand, and they destroy the previous systems of exchange. Over the course of the development of joint-stock or capital companies, their very sources of accumulation, or financing, undergo a change (Toporowski 2018, pp. 420–1).

The joint-stock or share capital company evolves into a form of enterprise held by owners of capital, or as a form of enterprise which realises both functions of capital accumulation (i.e. the mobilisation of resources for capitalist production, as well as production of surplus value) and for that purpose moves share capital—as associated fictitious interest-bearing capital. Its progress is accompanied by expanded commodity production and circulation as well as by the socialisation of labour, during the course of which the capital relation continues to evolve. Mutually interlinked with this is the contrary development of the qualification of the labour force, as embodied in the labourers, the development of the means of labour and production, as well as of technologies and new forms of labour organisation, of the division and centralisation of management and of administrative tasks. The socialisation of labour occurs in an interaction between the concentration and centralisation of production, or capital, and their counter-tendencies, with a simultaneously ongoing change and expansion of relations of competition and monopoly, as well as the combined effect of primary exploitation (production and appropriation of surplus value) and secondary exploitation (different forms of redistribution benefiting the exploiters and their partners, and a simultaneous interaction between distinct societal hierarchies). This complex process of socialisation as socialisation of labour also has a military dimension from its beginning (Suvanto 1985).

3. The development of the joint-stock company marks the transformation of the industrial capitalist's function as entrepreneur into that of money capitalist. In the joint-stock company, and particularly in the cooperative enterprise (taken over and managed by workers),

workers have acquired capabilities—over the course of the progress in and interplay of the factory and the credit system—which makes capitalists redundant for the organisation of societal production. With the generalisation of joint-stock companies (respectively share capital companies), the economic preconditions for starting to build a new society—of the free and equal living together in solidarity in an intact natural environment—are now given. The emancipated agencies, or classes, could organise a plan-based, solidary and ecological mode of socialisation and profoundly transform the societal mode of production and life.

4. Along with capital accumulation, certain tendencies evolve simultaneously which block the realisation of the depicted ideal society: wage earners are unable to develop a spontaneous solidarity of interests, let alone to live in solidarity with the colonised. Capital accumulation ties wage earners to capital in increasingly more complex ways, so that they are unwilling (or unable) to escape their adjustment to functions related to the production and realisation of surplus value. The members of bourgeois society are incapable of conceiving of a realistic societal alternative in their complex everyday life, or they are unable to imagine that they themselves might be capable of realising such an alternative. The emancipatory possibilities, for workers and for society as a whole, as well as for the preservation and improvement of natural conditions of life, are progressively destroyed.

This motivates—at least—the following: in which way and to what extent does the study of Hilferding's literary legacy help us to answer the following questions?

- Why does the society of the free and equal, living together in solidarity and in an intact natural environment, which Marx envisioned, continue to be impossible, or is increasingly made impossible?

- How is this fact linked to a generalisation and refinement of the joint-stock company/share capital company[1] as a form of collective enterprise of capital owners?

Finally, proceeding from these questions, the conclusions arising from these findings will be discussed.

Share Capital/Joint-Stock Company in Hilferding: A Refinement of the Critique of Political Economy?

In order to answer these questions, and against the backdrop of the preceding considerations, it is particularly Hilferding's treatment of three problems raised by Marx that appears relevant in this context. This treatment articulates the following problems:

(a) The thesis of the separation of capital ownership and capital function in the joint-stock company as the crucial

result of capitalist production in its highest development is a necessary point of transition towards the transformation of capital back into the property of the producers, but no longer as the private property of individual producers, but rather as their property as associated producers, as directly social property. It is furthermore a point of transition towards the transformation of all functions formerly bound up with capital ownership in the reproduction process into *simple* functions of the associated producers, into social functions. (Marx [1864/1865] 2016, p. 537)

(b) The orientation regarding the necessary future emergence and reproduction of 'associated producers', and indeed their socialisation of societal production and reproduction, thereby introducing a new mode of the reproduction of modern societies.
(c) The organisation of solidarity among and on the part of wage earners in the struggle for emancipation and for the equality of all. Another question demanding an answer would thus be whether

---

[1] In this chapter, the term 'joint stock company' stands generally rather for share capital companies than for the specific legal form of the German 'Aktiengesellschaft'. The joint stock company which has been discussed by Marx and Hilferding is a kind of a share capital company, as it has historically first emerged.

and how Hilferding discusses the fact that the capitalist mode of production continues to progress, despite the separation of capital ownership and function; that the mode of socialisation of the 'associated producers' would no longer function according to the elementary principle of the concentration of the means of production and expanding production sites; that the building of solidarity among wage earners, the oppressed and the exploited is the precondition for societal progress.

Of equal interest is the following question: if and to what extent Hilferding engages with Marx's understanding of society (see above, Greitens) and, especially, with his method of research and presentation?

On the Path to 'Finance Capital'

Towards the end of the nineteenth century, German Social Democracy debated a potential collapse of the capitalist mode of production. Eduard Bernstein rejected this possibility (Bernstein [1899/1921] 1984, p. 5). He sought to examine whether Marx's theory accounted for historical development and the present at the turn of the nineteenth/twentieth century in a way that was sufficient to justify any engagement with it, and thereby increase political efficacy (ibid., pp. 28–30). This debate is important for an understanding of Hilferding's scientific and political work. He was rather oblivious to the fact that Bernstein had not understood Marx's critique of Hegelian philosophy: social contradictions can only be resolved, if the agents and their interests—moving in and with those contradictions—change qualitatively, so that new relations emerge among them. These interests are crucially related to the aim and mode of organisation of societal labour—and to the appropriation and distribution of its products. Bernstein accuses Marx of having 'abandoned' the counter-tendencies to the concentration and centralisation of capital he himself discerned, 'so that the social effect of the antagonisms appears much stronger and direct than it is in reality' (Bernstein [1899] 1993, p. 57). According to Bernstein, 'By virtue of its form the joint-stock company tends to be a very significant counterweight to the centralisation of wealth through the centralisation of business enterprises. It permits an extensive division of already concentrated capital and makes it unnecessary for individual magnates to appropriate capital for the purpose of concentrating business enterprises' (ibid., p. 58). Bernstein concluded that it was therefore not the task of social

14 RUDOLF HILFERDING ON THE ECONOMIC CATEGORIES OF 'JOINT...   337

democrats to fight the magnates, seeing as they were bound to perish in the objective economic processes. Initiating a socialist socialisation of production through a revolutionary rupture of the capital relation, he argued, did not constitute a subject of meaningful political debate at the time (Bernstein [1899/1921] 1984, pp. 216–17). This motivated Hilferding, too, to prove that despite, or more precisely because of the development of the joint-stock company, the concentration and centralisation of production and capital ultimately had become a dominant feature. Hence, the discussion concerning the joint-stock company assumed a programmatic and strategic dimension in the tremendously active Social Democrat Hilferding from the very outset, which accounts for his arguments that go beyond the joint-stock company/share capital company as such. 'The bourgeoisie only holds political power insofar as it is able to gain control over the state organisation by virtue of its economic influence' (Hilferding [1903], p. 17, translation amended). From this perspective, state organisation is neutral, and the opponents of the bourgeoisie thus have to direct their thought and action primarily towards the state. However, the state, as the administrative entity organising complex, contradictory societal contexts, has an interest of its own: it has to harmonise the conflicting interests of its components according to areas of responsibility, territories and administrative levels, which in turn engage more or less directly with highly diverse agencies. Furthermore, it must persuade the ruling elites, which engage in in fighting among and between themselves, to reach an understanding with regard to their costs and the coercive apparatus required for the preservation or modification of societal normality. There are conflicts of interests in which the specific economic interests, political views and favoured social theories, ideologies and values of the agents involved do, indeed, clash with one another. In Great Britain and in France, the bourgeoisie managed to take over political control after they previously succeeded in developing economic and political power outside the state structure. Hilferding does not see this, arguing instead:

> The parliament … firstly, renders the economic power of the individual bourgeois commensurable, directly comparable to one another … Secondly, it brings to bear this power in a uniform manner as organised class power and becomes the tool through which the bourgeoisie transforms its economic power directly into political power. And yet, it does not suspend … the peculiar separation of political and economic power, which results exclusively from modern development. And it is precisely this separation that

338 J. DELLHEIM

makes it possible to change the nature of parliamentarism itself, to transform bourgeois parliamentarism, the bourgeoisie's device for dominating the state, into a device for the dictatorship of the proletariat. (Ibid., pp. 18–19, translation amended)

This contradicts historical experience. In April 1869, the cavalry and gendarmerie attacked legally striking workers at the Cockerill Ironworks company in Seraing, Belgium, killing many people.

When these days of horror had passed away, it became bruited about that Mr. *Kamp,* the mayor of Seraing, was an agent of the Cockerill Joint Stock Company, that the Belgian Home Minister, a certain Mr. *Pirmez,* was the largest shareholder in a neighbouring colliery also on strike, and that His Royal Highness the Prince of Flanders had invested 1,500,000 francs in the Cockerill concern [i.e. group—J.D.]. Hence people jump to the truly strange conclusion that the Seraing massacre was a sort of joint stock company *coup d'état,* quietly plotted between the firm Cockerill and the Belgian Home Minister, for the simple purpose of striking terror unto their disaffected subjects. This calumny, however, was soon after victoriously refuted by the later events occurring in Le Borinage, a colliery district where the Belgian Home Minister, the said Mr. *Pirmez,* seems not to be a leading capitalist. (Marx [1869] 1985, p. 47)

The example illustrates that there is no total separation of powers between the state, parliament and the power of capital owners. Why should the owners of capital heed a parliamentary decision and do something which they are not inclined to do because of their personal interests and are not effectively forced to do so, because of their powerful societal position? Hilferding remarks on the approximation of the interests between the *Junkers* (country squires) and major industrialists:

They have joined forces for the common robbery of the public ever since the stock system allowed for the increasing participation of agrarian capitalists in industrial interests and the cartel organisations began to render the protectionist tariff desirable even for the most advanced export industries … This union has been strengthened by the common interest in the state's politics of power, which includes militarism, marine militarism and colonial expansion… (Hilferding 1904a, 1905, pp. 809–10, translation amended—and, as I should like to add here, by the hatred towards the socialist workers' movement)

This, however, should effectively constitute an argument to convince Hilferding to revise his stance on the general strike—'...the general strike is to be applied only as a defensive means to protect against violence which would make a peaceful development impossible' (Hilferding 1903, p. 23, translation amended)—so as to also, and particularly, apply it in the struggle to force those in power to abandon their imperialist colonial politics. The dominant forces driving forward the latter, according to Hilferding, are 'Bank capital and heavy industry—especially the electricity, arms and iron industry—which in Germany are so closely intertwined' (Hilferding 1907, p. 36, translation amended). The German workers' movement retorted to this with 'the free self-determination of the people in domestic politics, democracy in legislature and administration. This struggle for democracy, however, is condensed ... in the question of equal suffrage in Prussia' (ibid., p. 42, translation amended). Hilferding wants to oppose the coalition of *Junkers*, industrialists and bankers primarily by use of bourgeois democracy's toolkit. His main aim is not the struggle of the labour movement for these tools in order to use them in more profound conflicts to overcome existing relations of domination, precisely because, in his view, political struggles ought to be confined to parliamentary contestation and legislation.

On 'Finance Capital'

Hilferding considers finance capital, which is linked to the joint-stock company, to be the 'most mature form of the same relationship that can be discerned in the more elementary forms of money and productive capital. Accordingly, there emerges the problem of the nature and function of credit, which in turn can be dealt with only after the role of money has been clarified. This task was all the more important because, since the formulation of the Marxian theory of money, many important problems have emerged ... which monetary theory up to now has apparently been incapable of resolving' (Hilferding [1910] 1981, pp. 21–2). The first aspect about this passage that is striking is that changes in production as a result of scientific discoveries and technological innovations in the context of the military build-up, the accelerated exploitation of labour and the destruction of their natural conditions of life, are not mentioned. Secondly, the two questions and problems formulated at the end of our first section are not reflected on by Hilferding. To Marx, the activities of socially heterogeneous labour forces, who are related to one another via the societal division of labour and the corresponding processes of exchange on the market, represent a crucial starting point for his analysis of value. The constitution of the labour force, the constellation (*Gestalt*) of the means of production, the combination and organisation of specific labour processes all determine the quantum of societal labour which a collective, or an 'organ' in the system of the social division of labour, expends on average for the production of a commodity. This organ may well be also a monopolistic firm in the form of a joint-stock company. It produces a specific commodity within a certain amount of time, which is then offered on the market. Here, the tendency of the exchange of equivalent quanta of soci etal labour expended on average and thus its societal recognition takes effect. That said, in the capitalist mode of production these are not quanta of labour which the labour collectives expend that receive social recognition on the market. It is the labour quanta which are required on average for the valorisation of the specific capitals invested. The way that the capitalists or their managers reflect 'the market' and the (average) societal demand for specific commodities and organise the production accordingly certainly has to do with market processes and the weight of monopolies in the societal reproduction process. The fewer monopolists exist (respectively, the weaker they are in relation to non-monopolists) the more will the competition among the largely equally powerful producers and buyers determine the exact configuration of the mass and structure of the capital required on average for profit realisation and for the realisation of expended capital. Money serves here both as the measure for capital consumption and capital valorisation, and as means of commodity exchange, that is, the organisation and realisation of capital accumulation. It is able to fulfill this function because it 'moves' along with the socialisation of labour, because it represents a specific autonomous expression of processes of value transfer, value formation and value realisation, as it is ongoing within the production and circulation of commodities. Money, with its functions and its value substance, constitutes a specific commodity itself. The concentration on the abstraction present in the value relations, however, does not eliminate the other societal relations and processes which take effect in the formation and circulation of such quanta of objectified societal labour. Money is therefore the expression of the totality of societal power relations which take effect in the targeted expenditure of societal labour, in its recognition as socially necessary labour and in the circulation of its products. Historically, gold and silver emerged as money commodities, and gold ultimately triumphed—and (still) remained the actual money commodity at the time that *Finance Capital* was written.[2] To Hilferding, however, the existing mass of commodities appears as the measure of value and the determinant of the value of paper money, the latter of which, when issued in a particular value, he then declares to be the measure of the value of commodities:

> And as before, money [as paper money, J.D.] continues to serve as a "measure of value". But the magnitude of its value is no longer determined by the value of the constituent commodity, gold, or silver, or paper. Instead, its "value" is really determined by the total value of commodities in circulation, assuming the velocity of circulation to be constant. The real measure of value is not money. On the contrary, the "value" of money is determined by what I would call the *socially necessary value in circulation*. (Ibid., p. 47)

Kautsky, in his critique of Hilferding's passage on money (Kautsky 1911, 2000), referred to it as an 'academic whim' (Kautsky ibid.). He would later notice his mistake.[3] He was also mistaken in his assessment that 'the whim' 'has no effect upon him, either theoretically or practically' (Kautsky ibid.). For Hilferding (see also Hilferding [1912] 1982, p. 46), money is above all a means of circulation (Behrens 1976, p. 219). Hence, his explanation of the emergence of credit from within 'commodity circulation itself, from the change in the function of money, and its transformation into a means of payment after being a medium of circulation' (Hilferding [1910] 1981, p. 69)] is hardly convincing. After all, the commodities need to be produced and the producers require means of circulation. Hilferding develops his argument as follows: the banks collect money from all members of society in order to provide it to certain suitable individuals for a given period of time. When these individuals are productive capitalists, the money becomes money capital serving the movement of productive capital. Depending on whether it is constant or variable, fixed or circulating capital, refluxes of money occur. The deposits are moved as interest-bearing capital and function as assets or items in the books. The bank acts as intermediary of monetary transactions, which it expands while

---

[2] The author in no way negates that a demonetisation of the money commodity has taken place in recent history. But the process of reproduction cannot take place without the compensation of the expenditures of capital through the sphere of circulation, in which these expenditures are put in proportion to the commodities required for such a compensation.

[3] Kautsky in his criticism of Hilferding (Kautsky 1912a, 1912b).

simultaneously depressing the minimum level of money capital needed for the circulation of corporate capital, or joint stock.

> When it invests its capital in a capitalist enterprise the bank becomes a participant in the fortunes of the enterprise; and this participation is all the more intimate the more the bank capital is used as fixed capital. (Ibid., p. 91)

At the same time, the bank will spread its investment risks. Overall,

> the bank's influence over the enterprise increases ... It is the bank's control of money capital which gives it a dominant position in its dealings with enterprises whose capital is tied up in production or in commodities. (Ibid., p. 95)

The actual practice, however, could have demonstrated to Hilferding that industrial enterprises pursue risk diversification, too. Take, for example, the Siemens & Halske corporation, which had 1900 different businesses including eleven different banks (Baudis and H. Nussbaum 1978, p. 90). Furthermore, the situation of credit banks in Germany worsened significantly during the 1920s because business enterprises kept their reserves to a large extent inside their own enterprises. They had a major demand for operating resources and sought to strengthen their position vis-à-vis the banks. Correspondingly, the banks were largely excluded from the administration of the businesses' primary and operating reserves. The latter consolidated their self-financing, set up financial departments and often created their own corporate banks, such as the Krupp corporation's *AG für Unternehmungen der Eisen- und Stahlindustrie* and the IG Farben conglomerate's *Deutsche Länderbank* (M. Nussbaum 1978, p. 312). It is not exclusively the banks which are relevant in the mobilisation of resources of surplus value production and its realisation, but rather the agencies of money capital involved, which include more than just banks, as, for example, insurance companies. In 1906, there was a total of 5060 joint-stock companies in Germany and limited joint-stock partnerships (Rahlf 2015, p. 254). Hilferding speaks exclusively of the joint-stock company, the starting point of which is the bank. This is neither historically nor logically convincing. Joint-stock companies, or share capital companies, even were created to counteract a dependency on banks. The industrial capitalists, who became creditors or money capitalists with the rise of the joint-stock company, receive interests for their invested capital. They are shareholders who decide over the amount of capital they invest and who are liable only for this capital. The realisation of profit, at least at the prevailing rate of average profit, represents the original motivation for the foundation of the joint-stock company (Hilferding [1910] 1981, pp. 107–8). The premium for the shareholder is generated because the supply of available money capital for the investment in shares, according to Hilferding, is lower than that for the fixed-interest investment. This greater (in-)security, in his view, constitutes the reason for a greater or lesser availability of money capital. From the diversity of this relation between supply and demand then results a variation in interest revenue (ibid., p. 108). It should be added, however, that interest earnings in the capitalist mode of production are ultimately linked to the creation, regulation and realisation of surplus value. And people employed by finance institutes are exploited, too. Back to Hilferding, however, the expected share revenue, he continues, is determined, under otherwise stable conditions, by the average rate of profit. The shareholders are entitled to an aliquot part of the revenue and must be granted the right to retrieve their capital in the form of money capital at any point in time. This is possible through the sale of shares (or their entitlement to the joint-stock company's profit) via the stock exchange. The price of these shares is the capitalised part of profit due, and it depends on the volume of expected entrepreneurial earnings and the applicable (or expectable) rate of interest.

When profit is capitalised and determines the price of the share, fictitious capital enters the equation: in contrast to industrial capital and its profit, 'fictitious capital' exists only in an accounting sense and is treated as 'share capital'. It is the lump sum price of an expected revenue. Share trade is thus a trade with titles to income. The sum of the 'share capital' as the aggregate price of capitalised revenue or titles to income need not coincide with the sum of the money capital previously converted into industrial capital (ibid., pp. 110–11).

> [T]he difference which appears as 'promoter's profit', a source of gain which arises only from the conversion of profit-bearing into interest-bearing capital ... is neither a swindle, nor some kind of indemnity or wage. It is an economic category *sui generis*. (Ibid., p. 112)

This may require a more precise explanation: a significant part of the money represented in differing form—as the totality of societal power relations that take effect in the expenditure of average societal labour for capital accumulation, or the use of capital which is invested for the purchase of shares—is already the result of the appropriation of surplus value. Accordingly, it is supposed to mobilise surplus labour and in fact realises surplus value through the purchase of means of production. When workers purchase shares, they finance renewed primary and secondary exploitation, frequently in other regions of the world, together with their exploiters—the capitalists and the *Junkers*. Share profit and the promoter's profit are related to real primary exploitation in the past and present, to be expanded in the future, which is complemented by secondary exploitation and subsequently expanded once again. As this movement of surplus value takes place on the basis of real production and circulation, production increases, circulation expands, a new concentration of the means of production occurs, the turn-over of energy, materials and transport, including the corresponding impact on people and their natural conditions of life, is further increased. More and more people are involved in the societal division of labour, drawn into specific social contexts, in order to be exploited, and to become accustomed to it, as well as to participate in the exploitation of others. The kind of large enterprises in production and circulation relevant for these expansion processes historically emerged and evolved as joint-stock companies. Hilferding's focus of interest remains on the circulation of fictitious capital, and he establishes that shares (S) are issued and sold for money (M). The amount of money is then divided into the promoter's profit (m_1), which is withdrawn from circulation, while the other part of the money (M_1) is converted into productive capital and enters the cycle of industrial capital. A renewed circulation of the shares sold requires additional money as medium of circulation (M_3). The movement S-M_3-S takes place on the stock exchange. Correspondingly, Hilferding presents the following 'scheme of circulation':

$$
\begin{array}{c}
\mathbf{M_p} \\
\mathbf{M_1-C<} \quad .... \mathbf{P} .... \mathbf{C_1 - M_2} \\
\mathbf{S<} \qquad \mathbf{L} \\
\mathbf{m_1} \\
\\
| \\
\\
\mathbf{M_3} \\
\\
| \\
\\
\mathbf{S}
\end{array}
$$

(ibid., p. 113)

Here, C stands for commodity, Mp for means of production, L for labour force.

The trade with shares, as with fictitious capital, requires new cash and credit money, that is, new bills of exchange. These are now covered by the capital value of the shares. This 'capital value' in turn depends on the yield, that is, on the sale of the commodity which the joint-stock company produces and sells at production prices (cost price plus average profit). Credit money is indirectly covered by the commodity value. While the volume of payments in trade are determined by the value of commodities, the latter is in turn covered by the amount of profit realised. The required money as real means of circulation is limited by the movement of shares (ibid., pp. 113–4).

Hence, the formula for the promoter's profit (P) is as follows (ibid., p. 114):

$$P = \frac{100Y}{d} - \frac{100Y}{p}$$

In this, p stands for average profit, d for dividend—the capital enterprise's profit distributed to the shareholders—and Y for the yield of the enterprise. Administrative costs of the enterprise (e) then need to be deducted from the initial Y, resulting in (Y-e). Or, to put it more precisely:

$$P = \left[(Y-e):d \times 100\right] - \left[Y:p \times 100\right]$$

The promoter's profit can be obtained during each capital increase in already existing joint-stock companies, given that the yield exceeds the average interest (ibid., p. 128). In his summary, and, moreover, his answer to and explanation of the question of discretionary power over the joint-stock company, Hilferding provides the following definition:

> The corporation is an association of capitalists. It is formed by each capitalist contributing his share of capital, and the extent of his participation, his voting rights, and the degree of his influence, are determined by the amount of capital he contributes. (Ibid., p. 118)

Exercising control over the joint-stock company requires a maximum of half its capital, which doubles the power of major capitalists. The discretionary power over outside capital is thus crucial for exercising control over the corporation. Each capital in its own right is therefore—as a result of the development of the credit system—simultaneously *per se* an exponent of borrowed capital belonging to others. The capital of the major shareholder is thus such an exponent in two senses: their capital controls that of the other shareholders and the overall capital draws the capital of others, as loan capital for the enterprise. If an even further-reaching system of interdependent joint-stock companies is then created, the financial power is exponentially increased:

> With the development of the joint-stock system there emerges a distinctive financial technique, the aim of which is to ensure control over the largest possible amount of outside capital with the smallest possible amount of one's own capital. (Ibid., p. 119)

Hence, the number of major capitalists who have invested their capital in joint-stock companies grows. As a member of the supervisory board, the major shareholder receives a share of the profits via bonuses and is able to influence the company's management and use the knowledge about what goes on inside the company for future transactions. A select circle emerges the members of which are represented in a large number of supervisory boards of joint-stock companies—either through their own capital power or as representatives of the concentrated power of the capital of others (bank directors).

> There develops a kind of personal union, on one side among the various corporations themselves, and on the other, between the corporations and the bank; and the common ownership interest which is thus formed among the various companies must necessarily exert a powerful influence upon their policies. (Ibid., pp. 119–20)

In a footnote on the 'personal union' Hilferding remarks:

> A personal union is the starting point or culmination of combinations among companies which, for external reasons, must remain organizationally and institutionally separate, but can attain their full effectiveness only by combining their forces in a single top management ... The combination of the political and economic organizations of the working class through a unified leadership at the top reinforces the strength of both types of organization. (Ibid., Footnote #16 on p. 119, see p. 398)

Hilferding's conclusion regarding the desirable personal union between the leadership of the workers' party, its parliamentary group and the trade union leadership is essentially linked to his understanding of politics—and it raises the question whether a reactive approach to opponents based on their respective power structures and logic can lead to sustainable success for emancipatory-solidary agency. Which are the implications for any strategy that is effectively addressing the given reality? Furthermore, it should be added that the agents of capital accumulation seek to eliminate competition, whenever they see fit, while they tend to promote it, when they can benefit from it. This occurs, on the one hand, through the pursuit of major projects such as shipbuilding to engage in conquests and, secondly, via the development of new business fields, for example, in the context of financing and making use of such major projects, or via the privatisation of public services and the alteration of economic framework conditions (economic laws, free trade agreements, etc.). The functionaries of capital seek to realise maximum planning and ensure the necessary proportions in production and operational procedures in the enterprises they control, but they also want to disrupt or prevent the planning and stability of their competitors, as far as possible without any harm to themselves. They concentrate and centralise capital, when it is beneficial to them—and they break up capital, destroy and decentralise it, whenever this seems even more beneficial, and they are, in fact, able to do so. They call for 'the state' when they want resources to be redistributed, developed and secured in their favour, but they call for 'freedom from the state's patronising' when advantageous to them. This pragmatism can intensify conflicts of interest between capitalist elites, but may also facilitate coalitions of common interest. Yet Hilferding—in utter negation of real history and its antagonisms—develops the joint-stock company without any reference to the state (although a central factor in his version of the theory of 'organised capitalism'), but instead always via describing the activities of the bank which constantly appeals to the money market and engages in stock trading. But the exploitation of bank tellers is not an object of Hilferding's high interest.

> It is the transferability and negotiability of these capital certificates, constituting the very essence of the joint-stock company, which makes it possible for the banks to "promote", and finally gain control of, the corporation. (Ibid., p. 120)

348   J. DELLHEIM

The best way to guarantee this, according to Hilferding, is through the direct presence of bank directors in the supervisory boards of joint-stock companies:

> In fact the corporations—especially the most important, profitable and pioneering ones—are governed by an oligarchy, or by a single big capitalist (or bank) who are, in reality, vitally interested in their operations and quite independent of the mass of small shareholders. Furthermore, the managers who are at the top of the industrial bureaucracy have a stake in the enterprise, not only because of the bonuses they earn, but, still more important, because of their generally substantial shareholdings. (Ibid., pp. 121–2)

Yet the joint-stock company can take advantage of the fact that it can organise money capital itself and exhibits clear advantages compared to the individual enterprise: it can raise and accumulate capital more easily, it is more likely to be granted credit, it is more robust economically and in a more favourable position with regard to technological developments, price competition and efficient business management (ibid., pp. 122–5). However, these advantages are only mobilised for the benefit of a small minority: the owners of the respective dominant share package (ibid., p. 127). And, according to Hilferding, these are above all the bank capitalists:

> As intermediaries in the circulation of bills and notes, the banks substitute their own bank credit for commercial credit, and as intermediaries in the conversion of idle funds into money capital, they furnish new capital to producers. They also perform a third function in supplying productive capital … by converting money capital into industrial capital and fictitious capital … the bank … supplies the market with a certain amount of money capital in the form of fictitious capital which can then be transformed into industrial capital. The fictitious capital is sold on the market and the bank realizes the promoter's profit which arises from the conversion of the industrial capital into fictitious capital … This function of the bank, to carry out the mobilization of capital, arises from its disposal over the whole money stock of society, although at the same time it requires that the bank should have a substantial capital of its own. Fictitious capital, a certificate of indebtedness, is a commodity sui generis which can only be reconverted into money by being sold. But a certain period of circulation is required before this can happen, during which the bank's capital is tied up in this commodity. Furthermore, the commodity cannot always be sold at a particular time, whereas the bank must always be prepared to meet its obligations in money.

14 RUDOLF HILFERDING ON THE ECONOMIC CATEGORIES OF 'JOINT... 349

Hence it must always have capital of its own, not committed elsewhere, available for such transactions. Moreover, the bank is compelled to increase its own capital ... The more powerful the banks become, the more successful they are in reducing dividends to the level of interest and in appropriating the promoter's profit. (Ibid., pp. 127–8)

Although Hilferding is entirely fixated on banks, there are other major financial market agencies as well. And he is not very interested in analysing the accumulation of capital as creation, realisation, distribution and redistribution of surplus value with the consequences for societal and ecological living conditions in total—that is, the development of capital relations and societal power relations more generally.

It is proven that, in the long term, the banking sector, or money capital, grew faster than the real economy[4] between 1850 and 1937—except for the war-related slump (Rahlf 2015, p. 216). The proportion of credit banks and savings banks in bank lending to non-banking enterprises rose substantially—from around 34 to 74%. Over the same period, bank lending to non-banking enterprises increased almost ten-fold overall (calculation by Rahlf 2015, p. 218). Furthermore, concentration and centralisation processes as well as the personal union of agencies in both industry and banking can also be statistically confirmed (Windolf 2006, p. 213). That said, statistical evidence for the following statement of Hilferding's is rather more difficult to provide:

An every-increasing part of the capital of industry does not belong to the industrialists who use it. They are able to dispose over capital only through the banks, which represent the owners. (Hilferding [1910] 1981, p. 225)

Comprehensive studies of the financing of major corporations in the German chemical and electrotechnical industry prior to World War I (Feldenkirchen 1985) provide a quite diverse picture: overall, the relation between banks and industry differed significantly depending on the industrial branch and economic position of the respective enterprises. While the banks' influence in the electrotechnical industry was greater, at least by tendency, it was only weak in the chemical industry.

---

[4] The term 'real economy' is controversial. The role of the financial sector in the economy belongs to the economy and is connected to the production and reproduction of goods, as it is certainly expressed by Rahlf.

350   J. DELLHEIM

Generally, a comprehensive dependency of industrial enterprises on banks cannot be confirmed, but rather a mutual dependency, in which, however, cause and effect cannot be isolated. What Hilferding asserted as a supposed fact in 1910, namely the dependency of industrial enterprises on banks, at any rate was no longer tenable at the moment of publication. (Ibid., p. 118, translation amended)[5]

By contrast, it can be corroborated that the number, share capital and average capital stock of joint-stock companies and limited joint-stock partnerships grew between 1896 and 1929 and that crises, processes of concentration and World War I have caused discontinuities. Likewise, we may note that the number of limited liability companies increased dramatically between 1913 and 1925, only to decrease just as dramatically after 1933 (Table 14.1). Both processes could be related to the low requirements regarding the disclosure of the books, which certainly appeared appealing to many at first, but was hardly in the interest of the Nazis.

Table 14.1   Joint-stock companies (including limited joint-stock partnerships) and limited liability companies (LLC) in Germany between 1886 and 1939 (in euros)

	Joint-stock companies (including limited joint-stock partnerships)			LLC		
	Number	Capital stock		Number	Share capital	
		Million euros	Average in thousand euros		Million euros	Average in thousand euros
1886	2143	2493	1163	–	–	–
1896	3712	3500	943	–	–	–
1906	5060	7081	1399	–	–	–
1913	5486	8874	1618	26,790	2422	90
1919	5345	10,371	1940	32,670	2931	90
1925	15,171	9913	653	64,398	–	–
1929	11,545	12,307	1066	43,600	–	–
1933	9292	10,811	1163	41,076	–	–
1939	5357	10,399	1941	23,505	2381	101

Source: Rahlf (2015, p. 254), author's own rendering

[5] Bernstein had accused Hilferding of an inaccurate use of statistics in *Finance Capital* (Bernstein 1911, pp. 947–55).

14 RUDOLF HILFERDING ON THE ECONOMIC CATEGORIES OF 'JOINT... 351

In 1926, German firms' share capital dominated the banking sector, the energy and raw materials sector, transport and industry more generally (percentage of total capital of each industry sector):

Mining 93%
Iron mining and extractive metallurgy 80%
Iron, steel and metalware production 26%
Electrotechnical industry 87%
Chemical industry 83%
Textile industry 37%
Wood/Woodworking industry 6%
Food and beverage industry 41%
Garment industry 11%
Banking 74%
Total 65%
Or, in other categories:

- Raw materials industry 89%
- Manufacturing industry 57%
- Trade and transport 58%. (See H. Nussbaum 1978, p. 258)

It can be said that the cooperation between owners of money and industrial capital for the valorisation of capital had a decisive impact on the economic and particularly on the industrial development in Germany. Moreover, it can be shown that these owners of capital had highly concentrated and centralised capital at their disposal: the German capital market was dominated by six major banks—the 'Berlin High Street Banks' [*Berliner Großbanken*] (M. Nussbaum 1978, p. 268). Numerically, the Deutsche Bank's share of these major Berlin-based banks was around one quarter. Following its merger with the Disconto-Gesellschaft in 1929, this share rose to about 40% (Lehmann 1996, p. 11). The highly concentrated and centralised capital which is formed and used in the cooperation between owners of money and of productive industrial capital or, rather, for the valorisation or the accumulation of capital, can by all means be referred to as 'finance capital'. It is a monopoly capital which extends the monopoly of the means of production causing the production of surplus value by wage labourers to the subordination of weaker capital owners doing the same and of other economic agencies both of which are in such a relation of dependency on the owners of finance capital that they have to accept economic conditions dictated by the collective owners of finance capital, intending to valorise their capital to the maximum and realising a project which, firstly, is relevant to the reproduction and development of the existing social life. So 'the market' is not a market of equals and 'the competition' is not a competition of equals (Dellheim 2021, pp. 384–386). The cooperation of capital owners (and their leading managers) as a whole accomplishes the two functions of capital mentioned above and may also be brought to bear in a corporation organised as joint-stock company with its own financial department or its own bank. The main agencies in this cooperation—the capital owners and their managers—can, furthermore, be regarded as the nucleus of a capital oligarchy, for they determine economic and social developments, following their respective own interests. However, there are also always contradictory relations between this nucleus and certain agencies within the state (which itself may be a shareholder), namely 'in politics', being used as the decisive dimension for the major undertakings which motivated the formation of the joint-stock companies in the first place. And this is relevant for the societal everyday life at all the distinct administrative levels. All actors involved can be shareholders. Major projects in many ways affect the interests of ruling elites, concerning tax and budgetary policies, economic law, the regulation of labour relations, as well as international politics. How else would Germany have been able to prepare and wage two criminal world wars, restore its 'economy' after World War I and 'cope' with the consequences of the world financial crisis in the 1930s? This had not by any means necessarily involved a disappearance or only a weakening of competitive relations. The totality of competition in such a constellation is far richer than, say, the competition between the producers of identical or similar commodities. It also always entails the rivalry over spaces and resources, relying upon state cooperation—for what is at stake is simply profit, wherever it may be made. These facts (as well as other aspects related to a broader social analysis taking these facts seriously) constitute a strong argument against such merely formal 'logical' conclusions as the following, drawn by Hilferding:

> Once finance capital has brought the most important branches of production under its control, it is enough for society, through its conscious executive organ—the state conquered by the working class—to seize finance capital in order to gain immediate control of these branches of production. (Hilferding [1910] 1981, p. 367)

After 'Finance Capital'

This hope expressed in 1910 had not materialised ten years later, and Hilferding presumed that a development had set in, because

> the capital masses can increasingly no longer be commanded by large anonymous corporations, joint-stock companies or banks. Instead, in capitalism, an ever more sharply pronounced personal dominance of individual capital magnates becomes manifest. (Hilferding [1920], p. 115, translation amended)

The real novelty about this was the presence of such magnates inside the government (M. Nussbaum 1978, p. 6). Yet the personification of economic relations by specific individuals and the reality of impersonal capital power do in fact constitute a real contradiction—which manifests itself in the fetishism of the commodity and in the money fetish, that is to say in the 'power of financial markets'. Furthermore, capital competition certainly persists, and it can even increase, especially with the magnates being part of the government. Hilferding identified the second half of the 1890s as the beginning of a new phase of industrialisation, in which an 'extraordinary structural transformation of European capitalism' (Hilferding [1931], p. 240, translation amended) took place. This included 'the emergence of the joint-stock company' in reaction to international competition (ibid.): the statistics alone show that talking about such an *emergence* is inaccurate. In the literature on economic history the *expansion* of the joint-stock company as a form of enterprise in Germany after 1871 is explained as, firstly, originating from those needs of specific capital elites who may have been faced with international competition. Secondly, changes in economic law in the course of German unification are relevant here: the cancellation of the obligation to hold a licence for joint-stock companies, guarantees for free enterprise and the freedom of movement, and favourable conditions for the development of the credit system (see also Baudis and H. Nussbaum 1978, p. 95). All these tendencies have increased and intensified the constraints of competition. 'Capitalist competition in the early days of capitalism was characterised by the circumstance that one major capitalist wiped out many small capitalists' (Hilferding 1931, p. 241, translation amended)—a tendency which, however, was now no longer valid.

354   J. DELLHEIM

> Given that competition becomes so costly, ... the question arises whether capitalist competition cannot be replaced by the *organisation of the entire branch of production* by an understanding between the former competitors. And this understanding occurs when the individual large enterprises are able to agree on their respective market share, and this agreement then manifests itself through the formation of large capitalist monopolies ... This tendency ... is now greatly promoted by the interest of the banks ... They are ... opposed to that mutually competitive underbidding, which may endanger their customers, poses a threat to their credits and inhibits their business opportunities. (Ibid., pp. 241–2, translation amended)

Here, again Hilferding conceives competition far too narrowly—because he associates it only with specific industries—and has no relevant interest in thoroughly exploring the contradictory movement of competition and monopoly building, as it is characteristic of capital. He shows how capital or investment credits tie up bank capital and, at the same time, are the cause for technical and economic concentration, as well as productivity increases in production.

> The struggle over the investment of capital *compels capital to pursue an ever-increasing influence on state power*, and to strengthen this state power in order to harness the invigorated state power for its own economic interest. (Ibid., p. 243, translation amended)

To Hilferding, the state continues to be neutral—regardless of its dramatic history. That is the reason why he does not consider state agencies to be members of the capital oligarchy. The conflict between the government and the Rhenish-Westphalian Coal Syndicate in 1902–1904 alone could have shown Hilferding that 'the state' can by all means pursue its own interests (Baudis and H. Nussbaum 1978, pp. 142–59). In Germany, prior to World War I and in the context of its immediate preparation, the competition between two main groups of capitalist economic elites, or capitalist oligarchies, and conflicting interest groups in the government and state became tangible (ibid., p. 256). After World War I, the Prussian state and the Reich government intensely intervened in 'the economy'. The Reichsbank also intervened—increasingly against the interests of the local municipalities, the German states and the credit banks. The latter were first shaken up by inflation, subsequently suffered from the corporations' strategy of self-financing, and, once they were in a weakened position, were struck by the global financial and economic crisis. In his reaction, Hilferding asserted

> that the capitalists are unable to protect their own credit organism even in the slightest from senseless and privately dictated claims, even though they thereby paralyse it entirely. They have not done it even though they hold in their hands the means to do so. Because ... the money economy and, consequently, and retroactively, the credit economy ... is regulated by the state almost from the outset, in a deliberate dependency on the central bank. (ibid., p. 258, translation amended)

According to Hilferding, the state had been hijacked by the capitalists, but he goes on to conclude that the crisis had now definitely weakened:

> to a certain extent the fighting capacity of the working class, and weakens its influence in several countries, while the obvious failure of capitalism, the crisis of capitalist production, on the other hand, intensifies those tendencies that lead to a greater degree of planning, supervision and the strengthening of state influence. (Ibid., p. 264, translation amended)

Hilferding does not enquire into the mistakes and shortcomings on the part of labour, which, of course, had to react to the 'failure of capitalism', yet could have taken advantage of the situation of crisis in order to change the societal balance of forces. In September 1931, a Reich Commissioner for the Banking Sector was appointed who was granted the power to issue directives to banks and to inspect their books. In Hilferding's view, this was a positive measure that reflected progress in the law on stock companies and antitrust legislation (Hilferding [1931], p. 265). He was in fact involved in imposing it, and he suggested control and regulation laws for share commerce (Pünder [1931]). The law on stock companies banned joint-stock companies from owning more than 10% of their own share capital. Subsidiaries were not allowed to acquire shares of their own parent corporation. In order to regulate the competition among banks, a regulation of the interest rates for bonds and partial debentures was decreed. The government now also started intervening in the banks' staffing decisions. The corresponding government meetings over the summer of 1931 saw the participation of IG Farben's finance manager Schmitz, who was simultaneously a member of the Deutsche Bank supervisory board and the Reich Credit Society [*Reichskreditgesellschaft*]. This redeployment of staff strengthened the role of the Deutsche Bank (M. Nussbaum 1978, pp. 319–20). In 1931, the Reich granted guarantees for large credits and frequently became a major shareholder of ailing enterprises. Finance Minister Dietrich and Reich Chancellor Brüning had close ties to IG Farben and were advised by Schmitz at all times. The latter served as chairman of the IG Farben—the company which has later been involved in the production of the poison gas Zyklon B for killing humans by gas showers and supplied it to the death camps—from 1935–45.

The members of the capital oligarchies initially had no trouble cooperating with the Nazis, and many became Nazis themselves. Monopoly companies that had been nationalised under Brüning, such as the mining corporation Gelsenkirchener Bergwerks Aktiengesellschaft (GBAG), were re-privatised. Hilferding's hopes were shattered. At first, he had been unable to imagine a fascist regime in Germany, then he thought it would not last and finally he despaired.

Some Conclusions

The joint-stock/share capital company as such accelerates the concentration and particularly the centralisation of capital, as well as capital accumulation, the socialisation of labour and of production as exploitation; it intensifies speculation, supports the use of violence against people and, not least, advances the destruction of the biosphere. Those active in the immediate production process are increasingly deprived of any tangible connection with others who are involved in the creation and realisation of the final product. The competition between wage/salary earners within the system of the social division of labour is often complemented by the competition for the transformation of their monetary income and assets into an exclusively interest-bearing kind of money capital. The exploited, in fact, thereby compete for the biggest possible share of the primary and secondary exploitation of those who are even weaker than themselves. The ownership of shares, especially of one's own employer company, further ties workers to capital. At the same time, the fetishisation of social relations and processes constantly reproduces itself and even enlarges its hold on the reproduction process of the societies involved. Those forces of living labour which suffer from an increasing difficulty of expressing solidarity—as competition is further aggravated, in both its breadth and its depth—are hit the hardest: those who are unable to partake in the game of competition, the poorest in all societies, those who depend most on solidarity. While reading *Finance Capital*, Rosa Luxemburg expressed her impression that Hilferding was 'only writing around the problem in a supposedly Marxist manner, but has failed to find the solution' (Luxemburg [1911] 2011, p. 297). The question here is, of course, who identified which problems, when and why. The debate on *Finance Capital* probably has brought out what Luxemburg had missed: Hilferding's contrary treatment of monopoly (which later allowed him and the reformists to systematically overlook the capitalist monopoly as a result and as promoter of the accumulation of capital, closely linked with the centralisation of capital, as well as with competition, crises and an aggressive external expansion). On the one hand, Hilferding has reflected this and has explained the development of trusts, cartels, corporations and the export of capital as driven forward, especially, by the major shareholders of joint-stock or share capital companies. On the other hand, what he has derived from these developments and their results has been the possibility of a planned capitalism, the exclusion of destructive competition, as well as of deeper crises, and, accordingly, a tendentially peaceful development, a steady weakening and overcoming of all antagonistic societal contradictions. The reason for this problem lies in Hilferding's limited ability to understand the economic development in the framework of the complex and contrary development of modern bourgeois societies: his simplified and harmonising perspective brings him to overestimate the counter-tendencies to competition and anarchy, as well as the possibility of common interests between different types of capitalists and capitalist elites. Some authors like Behrens link this weakness to Hilferding's break with the Marxian labour theory (Behrens 1976, pp. 219–220, see also Stravelakis 2021). The first element of this break was mentioned in connection with the false understanding of money reflected in the 'socially necessary value in circulation'. The second element is the explanation of the

> 'monopoly price' which 'can indeed be fixed empirically, but its proper level cannot be apprehended in an objective theoretical manner, only grasped psychologically and subjectively....If monopolistic combinations abolish competition, they eliminate at the same time the only means through which an objective law of price can actually prevail. ... It seems that the monopolistic combine, while it confirms Marx's theory of concentration, at the same time tends to undermine his theory of value'. (Hilferding [1910] 1947, p. 228)

But in markets shaped by alliances or in the monopolistic business relations, with their corresponding purchase and sales prices, it becomes apparent to what extent this societal labour receives social recognition or devaluation. The monopolistic cost price is depressed below this level in the non-monopolistic enterprises by the position of monopoly in the field of the supply of particularly productive and cheap raw materials, in the field of scientific and technical invention and development, or in the field of the supply of particularly highly specialised and productive labour—and also in that of relatively cheap labour (for mass production). The mass of surplus value, that is, the quantity of monopoly profit produced, that is, squeezed out of the individual workers and employees working in the monopoly enterprise, on the other hand, is greater, as a rule, than the mass of surplus value or profit obtained per worker by smaller capitals (Autorenkollektiv 1986, pp. 516–517). This is true wherever monopoly companies compete with non-monopolistic companies in technically and technologically distinguishable branches of production. Using the term and conception of 'monopolistic reproduction price' (ibid., p. 519) can help here to explain that the market price must realise the monopolistic cost price and surplus value at a necessary level (in the presence of industries with different organic compositions of capital and different turnover times) in order to make a proportional economic development possible. Accordingly, the monopolistic reproduction price as 'a mediating category between value and price' (ibid.), through which the necessary proportions of the development of productive power are implemented in a way deformed and distorted by monopolistic exploitation. At the same time, the monopoly companies try to assert their 'changing needs of capital accumulation' (ibid., 517–519) in this very process. Under the conditions of conglomerates, transnational production chains, integrated technologies and blurring sectoral boundaries, there is a growing tendency for the monopoly enterprises to operate increasingly with internal transfer prices, that is, in such a way that the individual production price of the specific kind of commodity calculated is more strongly influenced by considerations internal to the enterprise. A difference becomes apparent here between the price that is calculated for the output from the reproduction expenditures of the specific commodity produced in capitalist way and the price the calculation of which is based upon the necessary reproduction expenditures of the capitalist enterprise. The conditions of competition for the specific types of commodities determine this difference. The capitalist elites orient themselves towards an obligatory patenting of research and development services, even of biological organisms; this development pushes them towards the monopolisation of the fields of their concrete reproduction needs. These phenomena are linked to the exclusion of agencies from participation in common goods, to monopoly pricing and to the expansion of trans- and international rent relations: monopolised conditions of production and reproduction and progressive transnational division of labour, linked to an increasing intra-industrial division of labour, which explains the growing weight of absolute rent compared to differential rent (see also Ricci 2019, pp. 234–235). The emergence of the respective proportions for the continuation of the international division of labour cannot take place solely through monopolistic reproduction prices, or, in other words, these prices are shaped by extra-economic moments to a relevant degree. The production of the proportions required for social reproduction is becoming more and more complicated and increasingly turns into a matter which the capital elites have to negotiate with their state and supra-state partners (Dellheim 2021, pp. 380–384, see also Serfati in this book).

But for Hilferding's later political role another fact seems to be significantly more important than the labour theory: the words solidarity and solidary appear 14 times in *Finance Capital*, but they are not once relating to workers or to the colonised. Such problems as he describes by referring to Marx seem to be of little interest to Hilferding. Luxemburg's confidant Paul Levi has already aptly summed up the general character of Hilferding's theory of 'organised capitalism' in the formula of 'Bernstein-Hilferding' (Levi [1927], p. 1049). We may expand this to include their common weakness of failing to proceed in a more dialectical fashion and of being self-critical. And yet we can certainly agree with Gottschalch (1962), Greitens (2012), King (2010), Kurata (2009), Schefold (2001), Smaldone (1998) and many other critics of Hilferding in that his economic writings are indispensable for modern critical political economy. Hilferding's notion was certainly accurate when he concluded: 'My analysis of the economics of the corporation goes considerably beyond that provided by Marx' (Hilferding [1910] 1981, p. 114). This also applies to the explanation of the functional mode of banks, the shareholder and stock system and joint-stock company, as well as a number of links between the credit system, joint-stock companies, share capital, the formation of monopolies and finance capital. Hilferding's knowledge of the business processes and economic context is impressive. The demonstrated differences between the individual enterprise and the far more independent joint-stock company, generalisations of economic laws according to Marx with the inclusion of the joint-stock company, the perspectives and role of the shareholder, the explanation of stocks/shares, dividend, founder's profit and their movements, the orientation on the role of the personal union (ibid., pp. 119–20)—all these elements underscore the extent of Hilferding's effective contribution to the critique of political economy. In other words, we may just as well list the tasks that remain to be resolved:

- A critique of Hilferding's literary legacy regarding the explanation and overcoming of socialisation processes in the evolution of capital relations—which are intertwined with other relations of domination—in their metabolism with the natural world.
- The critique of the movement of value and money separated from societal labour, of the joint-stock company/share capital company as specific unity of two functions of capital accumulation—of the organisation of accumulation sources for surplus value production and the realisation of the surplus value on the one hand, and of surplus value production on the other—and, of course, of the role of share capital in that process.
- The critique of a mode of socialisation that concentrates the means of production, while reproducing structures of domination in production and consumption which block the development of the conditions for a self-determined life within an intact natural environment.

This list brings together those things which Hilferding himself never has addressed in an explicit and coherent way. What prevented him from doing so were his technocratic understanding of society and his reductionist reference to the Marxian legacy, his consistently selective use of statistics and of historical literature, only for the purpose of supporting his own assumptions, as well as his insufficient reflection of societal developments in his own lifeworld and his insufficient critique of his own views on these, as well as his generally 'mechanicism' which tended to ignore (or just to circumscribe) real contradictions in modern bourgeois societies—and (last, not least) his attitude of almost total ignorance vis-à-vis Luxemburg and other political opponents.

The question whether Hilferding accomplished a refinement of categories in the critique of political economy raised in the title of this chapter therefore needs to be answered with a paradoxical 'not yet', which simultaneously poses the challenge of presenting a more comprehensive definition: to begin with, under the new economic law, the joint-stock company represents a legal form of enterprise, behind which we find a collectively organised unit pursuing the realisation of the two functions of capital accumulation (mobilisation of accumulation sources and the production and appropriation of surplus value). It is, thus, an organisation for the pursuit of primary and secondary exploitation. It is both the result and an aggravating moment of capital centralisation, and it is marked by the fact that (a) the ownership of capital is separated from the function of capital, that (b) the members of the collective as shareholders are money capitalists and that (c) an enterprise is 'founded' for the increase of stock capital and that way the 'promoter's profit' is realised. This is essentially the expected capitalised entrepreneurial profit. The joint-stock company in this sense circulates fictitious capital while real capital is valorised (including within the enterprise itself). Decision-making powers and the distribution of the dividend are determined in accordance with the money capital contributed to the company and the corresponding proportion of share capital. In the course of the competition among the shareholders, those who command the most capital assert themselves, although they do not necessarily have to be majority shareholders. They are always linked to a financial institution, which in turn can also be independent. From this position, they control the corporation. Moreover, they act as initiators of a new 'foundation' of these companies, via an increase in share capital, and they appropriate the largest part of the promoter's profit. The corporate activity as a whole is decisively mediated via the expanding money functions, above all in the form of credit, and it has an altering effect on the money substance as the totality of societal relations, especially power relations. Over the course of a few decades, a de-monetisation of the commodity of money has also taken place. Left-wing scholars in particular have to address the fact that large parts of the left in Germany and Western Europe—even in the case of a clearly articulated rejection of 'organised capitalism' and of anti-communism, of the Stalinist defamation of Luxemburg, and despite an explicit adherence to Marx—are generally much closer to Hilferding in their intellectual approaches than to Marx or to Luxemburg. Many on the left have not internalised an understanding of progress guided by real socialisation, proceeding from people who act independently, in solidarity and in an ecologically sustainable way. The course correction needed in this respect would simultaneously entail a heightened awareness for the interplay of concentration, centralisation and decentralisation of resources and decision-making, which, when adhering to the primacy of decentralisation, would allow for a maximum of freedom and equality of individuals, a maximum resource efficiency and a minimisation of the consumption of above all non-renewable resources and of the impact on the natural conditions of life.

The critique of political economy, in this perspective, faces the challenge of determining which agencies and tendencies have a constructive and which have a destructive impact on the possibilities of a realisation of this ideal. Hence, the task at hand is the development of a category system which explains the movement of socialisation within the capitalist mode of production itself and the tendencies towards a kind of alternative socialisation which must be enabled, reinforced and realised. The critique of political economy would thus provide scientific insights for policies which would place the question of the substance of work on the same level as the remuneration and conditions of work; the agencies of these initiatives would embrace ongoing struggles in solidarity and stand by the side of those whose brutal exclusion often prevents them from taking up the fight in the first place. The critique of political economy, with an additional focus on the natural conditions of life and on the issue of the commons, may thus help to activate and mobilise against all efforts aimed at advancing the two functions of capital accumulation just referred to. These functions and share capital—and especially capital relations more generally—would ultimately have to be driven back in structural terms, and eventually be overcome.

REFERENCES

Autorenkollektiv. 1986. *Politische Ökonomie des Kapitalismus. Lehrbuch.* Berlin: Karl Dietz-Verlag.

Baudis, D., and H. Nussbaum. 1978. *Wirtschaft und Staat in Deutschland. Eine Wirtschaftsgeschichte des staatsmonopolistischen Kapitalismus in Deutschland vom Ende des 19. Jahrhunderts bis 1945 in drei Bänden, Band 1.* Berlin: Akademie-Verlag.

Behrens, F. 1976. Rudolf Hilferding. In *Grundrisse der Geschichte der politischen Ökonomie*, Band II, 216–220, Berlin: Akademie-Verlag.

Bernstein, E. [1899] 1993. *The Preconditions of Socialism.* Edited by Henry Tudor. Cambridge/New York: Cambridge University Press.

———. 1911. Das Finanzkapital und die Handelspolitik. In *Sozialistische Monatshefte.* 15 = 17 (27. Juli 1911), H. 15, 947–55. https://www.marxists. org/deutsch/referenz/bernstein/1911/07/finanzkapital.htm.

————. [1899] [1921] 1984. *Die Voraussetzungen des Sozialismus und die Aufgaben der Sozialdemokratie, eingeleitet von Horst Heimann.* Berlin, Bonn: J.H.W. Dietz Nachf.

Dellheim, Judith. 2018. 'Joint-Stock Company' and 'Share Capital' as Economic Categories of Critical Political Economy. In *The Unfinished System of Karl Marx, Critically Reading Capital as a Challenge for Our Times*, ed. J. Dellheim and F.O. Wolf, 265–298. Cham/Basingstoke: Luxemburg International Studies in Political Economy. Palgrave Macmillan.

————. 2021. 'Kein Kampf für Classenprivilegien und Monopole'. Zur Kategorie 'Monopol' in der Kritik der politischen Ökonomie und zu ihrer Anwendung in moderner 'Globalisierungskritik'. In *Auf den Schultern von Karl Marx*, ed. T. Sablowski, J. Dellheim, A. Demirović, K. Pühl, and I. Solty, 377–394. Münster: Westfälisches Dampfboot.

Feldenkirchen, W. 1985. Zur Finanzierung von Großunternehmen in der chemischen und elektrotechnischen Industrie Deutschlands vor dem Ersten Weltkrieg. In *Beiträge zur quantitativen vergleichenden Unternehmensgeschichte*, ed. R. Tilly, 94–125. Stuttgart: Klett-Cotta. https://nbn-resolving.org/urn:nbn:de:0168-ssoar-338309.

Gottschalch, W. 1962. *Strukturveränderungen in der Gesellschaft und politisches Handeln in der Lehre von Rudolf Hilferding.* Berlin: Duncker&Humblot.

Greitens, J. 2012. *Finanzkapital und Finanzsysteme: 'Das Finanzkapital' von Rudolf Hilferding.* Marburg: Metropolis.

Hilferding, R. [1903] 1982. Zur Frage des Generalstreiks. In: *Stephan, Zwischen den Stühlen oder über die Unvereinbarkeit von Theorie und Praxis. Schriften Rudolf Hilferdings 1904 bis 1940*, ed. C. Stephan, 13–24. Berlin/Bonn: Verlag J.H.W. Dietz Nachf.

————. [1904a] 2005. Parlamentarismus und Massenstreik. In *Neue Zeit*, 804–16. nz_mktiff.pdf.

————. 1905. Parliamentarianism and the General Strike. *Social Democrat* 9 (11): 675–687. Trans. Jacques Bohomme. https://www.marxists.org/archive/hilferding/1905/11/parliamentarianism-strike.htm.

————. [1907] 1982. Der deutsche Imperialismus und die innere Politik. In *Zwischen den Stühlen oder über die Unvereinbarkeit von Theorie und Praxis. Schriften Rudolf Hilferdings 1904 bis 1940*, ed. C. Stephan, 25–42. Berlin/Bonn: Verlag J.H.W. Dietz Nachf.

————. [1912] 1982. Geld und Ware. In *Zwischen den Stühlen oder über die Unvereinbarkeit von Theorie und Praxis. Schriften Rudolf Hilferdings 1904 bis 1940*, ed. C. Stephan, 43–54. Berlin/Bonn: Verlag J.H.W. Dietz Nachf.

————. [1920] 1982. Die politischen und ökonomischen Machtverhältnisse und die Sozialisierung. In *Zwischen den Stühlen oder über die Unvereinbarkeit von Theorie und Praxis. Schriften Rudolf Hilferdings 1904 bis 1940*, ed. C. Stephan, 110–32. Berlin/Bonn: Verlag J.H.W. Dietz Nachf.

364   J. DELLHEIM

———. [1931] 1982. Gesellschaftsmacht oder Privatmacht über die Wirtschaft. In *Zwischen den Stühlen oder über die Unvereinbarkeit von Theorie und Praxis. Schriften Rudolf Hilferdings 1904 bis 1940*, ed. C. Stephan, 239–67. Berlin/Bonn: Verlag J.H.W. Dietz Nachf.

———. [1910] 1947. *Das Finanzkapital. Eine Studie über die jüngste Entwicklung des Kapitalismus*, Berlin: Verlag JHW Dietz Nachf.

———. [1910] 1981. *Finance Capital. A Study of the Latest Phase of Capitalist Development*, London: Routledge and Kegan Paul.

Kautsky, K. 1911. Finanzkapital und Krisen, *Die Neue Zeit* 29-I, 1911, 22, 23, 24 & 25, 764-772, 797-804, 838-846 & 874-883, https://marxists.architexturez.net/deutsch/archiv/kautsky/1911/xx/finanzkapital.pdf.

———. 1912a. Gold, Papier und Ware. *Die Neue Zeit* 30-I., 1912, 24 & 25, pp. 837–47 & 886–93. https://www.marxists.org/deutsch/archiv/kautsky/1912/xx/gold.pdf.

———. 1912b. Gold, Paper Currency and Commodity, translated by Daniel Gaido. https://www.marxists.org/archive/kautsky/1912/xx/gpcc.htm.

———. [1911] 2000. Finance-Capital and Crises. In *Social Democrat*. London, Vol. XV, No. 8, 15 August 1911, transcribed by Sally Ryan. https://www.marxists.org/archive/kautsky/1911/xx/finance.htm.

King, J.E. 2010. Hilferding's Finance Capital in the Development of Marxist Thought. *History of Economics Review* 52 (1): 52–62.

Kurata, M. 2009. *Hilferding und das 'Finanzkapital'.* Wien: Koppanyi.

Lehmann, K. 1996. *Wandlungen der Industriefinanzierung mit Anleihen in Deutschland 1923/24–1938/39*. Stuttgart: Franz Steiner Verlag.

Levi, P. [1927] 2016. Zum Kieler Parteitag, Sozialistische Politik und Wirtschaft, Issue 5, No. 22, 3 June. In Paul Levi, Ohne einen Tropfen Lakaienblut, *Schriften, Reden Briefe*, Band II/2: *Sozialdemokratie. Sozialistische Politik und Wirtschaft* II, es J. Schütrumpf, 1046-50. Berlin: Karl Dietz Verlag.

Luxemburg, Rosa [1911] 2011. Letter to Kostya Zetkin, 22 March 1911. In *The Letters of Rosa Luxemburg*, ed. G. Adler, P. Hudis, and A. Laschitza, 296–7. London/New York: Verso.

Marx, K. [1864/1865] 2016. Marx's Economic Manuscripts of 1864–1865. In *The Role of Credit in Capitalist Production*, ed. Fred Moseley, 535–40. Leiden/Boston: Brill.

———. [1867] 1976. *Capital, Volume 1*. London: Penguin Books.

———. [1869] 1985. The Belgian Massacres. To the Workmen of Europe and the United States, https://www.marxists.org/archive/marx/iwma/documents/1869/belgian-massacre.htm.

Nussbaum, Martha 1978. *Wirtschaft und Staat in Deutschland. Eine Wirtschaftsgeschichte des staatsmonopolistischen Kapitalismus in Deutschland vom Ende des 19. Jahrhunderts bis 1945 in drei Bänden*, Band 2. Berlin: Akademie-Verlag.

Pünder, H. 1931. Notiz über Ministerbesprechung am 5. August 1931. In *Bundesarchiv*, R 43 I/1451, 61–74. http://www.bundesarchiv.de/aktenreichskanzlei/1919-1933/0000/bru/bru2p/kap1_1/para2_178.html?highlight=true&search=Hilferding&stemming=true&pnd=&start=&end=&field=all#highlightedTerm.

Rahlf, T. (ed.) 2015. *Deutschland in Daten. Zeitreihen zur Historischen Statistik*. Bonn: Bundeszentrale für politische Bildung. http://www.bpb.de/shop/buecher/zeitbilder/211002/deutschland-in-daten.

Ricci, A. 2019. Unequal Exchange in the Age of Globalization. *Review of Radical Political Economics* 51 (2): 225–245.

Schefold, B. 2001. Rudolf Hilferding und die Idee des organisierten Kapitalismus. In: *Private Versicherung und soziale Sicherung*, ed. Herausgegeben von Hans-Christian Mager, Henri Schäfer, und Klaus Prüfer, 478–501. Marburg: Metropolis-Verlag.

Smaldone, W. 1998. *Rudolf Hilferding: The Tragedy of a German Social Democrat*. Northern Illinois: University Press.

Stravelakis, N. 2021. Hilferding's Monopoly Theory and the Labor Theory of Value. *Academia Letters*, Article 2759. https://doi.org/10.20935/AL2759.

Suvanto, P. 1985. *Marx und Engels zum Problem des gewaltsamen Konflikts*. Helsinki: SHS.

Toporowski, J. 2018. Marx, Finance and Political Economy. *Review of Political Economy* 30 (3): 416–427. https://doi.org/10.1080/0953825 9.2018.1496549.

Windolf, P. 2006. Unternehmensverflechtung im organisierten Kapitalismus. Deutschland und USA im Vergleich 1896–1938. *Zeitschrift für Unternehmensgeschichte* 51: 191–222.

CHAPTER 15

Hilferding's Impressive Failure. A Reading of His Last Major Text

Frieder Otto Wolf

There is a postulate in the tradition of hermeneutics—as a specifically theologico-philosophical approach going back to Philon of Alexandria and the 'church father' Origines[1]—that the influential German Heideggerian philosopher Hans-Georg Gadamer[2] aptly summarised as the 'anticipation of perfection'. This is, without any doubt, unacceptable within a sober, materialist theory of interpretation. And yet, the effort to look out not only for what a text—especially a philosophical one—effectively achieves, but also for what it begins to make visible, but then masks again by a sudden turn in its course of argument, is a task a materialist reading should not avoid.

[1] Most impressively represented and summarised by the late Paul Ricoeur (2016).
[2] In his ideological career, as a pupil of Martin Heidegger actively involved with German fascism, as well as flirting with Stalinism after the war, see Orozco (1995).

F. O. Wolf (✉)
Institute of Philosophy, Freie Universität Berlin, Berlin, Germany
e-mail: fow@snafu.de

© The Author(s), under exclusive license to Springer Nature Switzerland AG 2023
J. Dellheim, F. O. Wolf (eds.), *Rudolf Hilferding*, Luxemburg International Studies in Political Economy,
https://doi.org/10.1007/978-3-031-08096-8_15

367

Hilferding's last theoretical text, *The historical problem* (*Das historische Problem*) written in 1940,[3] does indeed merit such a critically constructive treatment: it outlines a critique of the notion of 'historical materialism' dominant within the Marxist tradition to which he himself had belonged (p. 303); it provides a first formulation of the problematic of 'implementation' (*Umsetzung*)[4] (p. 299), which became a central category in later social democracy; it sketches a radical notion of 'the total state' (pp. 300ff.) that goes beyond current constructions of historical 'phases of capitalism'; it raises, addresses and ultimately fails in solving the problem of theoretically conceiving historical singularities in the Marxist tradition (pp. 300f.), and it quite pertinently raises the real problem of theoretically analysing acting subjectivity (p. 302)—that is, in Althusserian terms, of ideology in the singular[5]—, again, only to relapse into some kind of common-sensical 'psychology': 'The result seems to be that in place of a connection [*Zusammenhang*], [which is], at least to some degree, objectively given, a purely psychological problem [should be addressed]' (p. 302).

THE 'MATERIALIST CONCEPTION OF HISTORY'

Hilferding's most general point about the 'materialist conception of history' ought not to be simply brushed aside and interpreted as a sure sign of his 'revisionism': at least since Mehring's introduction of the term 'historical materialism', which was taken up and, as it were, officialised, by the old Engels[6], a strong leaning towards the kinds of reductionist materialism criticised by Marx, for example in his *Theses[7] on Feuerbach*,[8] has exerted a

---

[3] The following refers to Hilferding (1940), in the form published by Cora Stephan in 1982. Translations are my own.—In the second edition of this book I can now refer the reader to Michael Krätke's report on the still unpublished notes Hilferding had prepared for this text. These notes do not seem to invalidate my reading of the main text.

[4] In the 1970s, this notion of '*Umsetzung*' became central to an important phase of social democratic reformism in the Federal Republic of Germany (see Pöhler and Peter 1982; Peter 2003).

[5] Which traditional Marxism had attempted to address the somewhat obsolete category of 'consciousness', with a first high point in György Lukács's theory of 'imputed consciousness' (see the overview in Milner 2019).

[6] who then had a hard time combating the reductionism of the 'Young Ones' in his letters of the 1890s (see Wolf 2009).

[7] The promotion of these notes to 'theses' by Engels is part of a problematic history of reception (see Wolf 2006).

[8] See Labica (1984, 1998).

15 HILFERDING'S IMPRESSIVE FAILURE. A READING OF HIS LAST MAJOR... 369

patently problematic influence within the Marxist tradition,[9] indeed giving rise to 'recurrent misunderstandings and infertile polemics' (p. 303[10]). Hilferding's proposal to replace even the much more cautious formulation of a 'materialist conception of history', which was a real part of Marx's own self-reflection, does not do justice to the problems involved.

As he himself is eager to make explicit, this amounts to systematically neglecting the breakthrough Marx achieved in conceiving elements of a 'science of history' and concretising it for modern societies,[11] against which the 'sociology' of Max Weber's (and others) militated as a 'bourgeois alternative'—alongside the new economics of the 'neo-classics' and the new politics of the 'general theory of the state' (emerging in Germany[12]): although Hilferding is able to see that 'materialistic' could take on a new meaning, going beyond Marx's earlier programmatic notions of 'naturalism' and 'humanism' (p. 306) and describing 'in a newly circumscribed sense a kind of synthesis of both notions' (ibid.), he sides with Max Weber against some seemingly 'deterministic' formulations of Marx—which do indeed deserve some clarification[13]—in claiming that 'knowledge [*Erkenntnis*] of the conformity to laws [*Gesetzmäßigkeit*] within history comes to its boundaries [*auf Schranken stößt*] [due to the occurrence of 'violence' [*Gewalt*]], so that we cannot talk about necessity in the sense of Marx, but only about chance in the sense of Max Weber'.

---

[9] This was exemplified by Plekhanov—and not overcome by Lenin's mainly political criticism of his kind of Marxism. On the contrary, this tendency strongly helped to shape the Stalinist tendency Hilferding was confronted with.

[10] In the following text, all quotations from Hilferding's essay 'Das historische Problem'—in my own translation—will be referred to by simple page numbers in brackets. The edition by Cora Stephan—see https://www.cora-stephan.de/home/—seems to be trustworthy, even though the entire book seems to deserve the distancing note formulated by Hilferding's heir on the last page (p. 336)—with an almost non-sensical title, affirming the incompatibility of theory and practice, and mentioning Hilferding's name only in the sub-title, and with some dubious commentary by Stephan who has no understanding at all for Hilferding's claims to scientific analysis, nor for his notion of *Marxist* social-democratic politics.

[11] This 'science of history', in its concrete elaboration, has 'morphed' into the *critique of political economy*, as well as the into the *critique of politics* (cf. Balibar et al. 1979)—which raises a good number of interesting epistemological questions we cannot pursue here.

[12] In the United States, the beginnings of 'political science' in the 'progressive era' can be analysed as an alternative and parallel development which was to become hegemonic in the course of the twentieth century, whereas in France the current of 'institutionalism', as elaborated by Maurice Hauriou, should be seen as another parallel development.

[13] For a deeper discussion see, for example, Jossa (2018).

I am convinced that it will be helpful to think that Hilferding here—in exile and with little access to books—was using the name of Marx to denote the dominant kind of Marxism—that is, a strongly economistic reading of Marx (in which he himself had been an active participant[14]). Marx's own, and publicised, position on historical determinism was clearly different[15]—without, however, arriving at the kind of indifferentism and subjectivism defended by Max Weber.[16]

Hilferding is clearly referring back to a reading of Marx's theory in a perspective of economic reductionism, devoid of any reference to the role of violence in history,[17] let alone of class struggle within theory.[18] And he seems to anticipate later attempts to throw out the baby of Marx's theory of the domination of the capitalist mode of production in modern bourgeois societies with the bathwater of economic determinism, as for example in Giddens 1983.

However, this reading is not just a figment of his imagination. It is an important historical reality, and his essay deserves closer scrutiny. In doing so, we have to keep in mind that it was written at the very midnight of the twentieth century, when it was not yet possible to foresee the eventual defeat of the German Nazi bid for world power with any degree of realistic certainty, and when the historical crisis of Marxism was at its peak—and unable to find an adequate response.[19]

[14] In this sense, Stephan's proposal to read this last text by Hilferding as an exercise in self-critique (p. 297) is justified.

[15] A helpful analytical summary of the relevant contributions to this debate can be found, for example, in Sherman (1981).

[16] The degree to which Weber's radically subjective approach has left readers puzzled can be gauged by comparing the readings of his epistemology by Kolko (1959) and Wolin (1981). Still helpful for getting a clearer perspective is a systematic comparison of the theories of 'modern society', as elaborated by Marx and Weber, which has been realised within West-Berlin Marxism. See Bader et al. 1976. A rather dazzling complexity of the much-needed debate has been constructed by Greisman and Ritzer (1981).

[17] As it was classically discussed by Engels as early as in 1887 (https://marxists.catbull.com/archive/marx/works/1887/role-force/ch01.htm)—with a misleading translation of 'Gewalt' by 'force' instead of violence in the very title.

[18] As discussed by Althusser (1971, pp. 11 ff).

[19] Horkheimer and Adorno's sketch of the *dialectic of enlightenment* originates in the same 'night of the century'—and likewise fails to directly address, let alone overcome, the historical crisis of Marxism.

A New Phase of History Under the Impact of War

Hilferding starts impressively by referring to the 'historico-political experience' (p. 298) of his own generation, stressing the 'uniquely singular nature' of the events it witnessed (ibid.). By comparing these events to the 'downfall of the Roman world' (ibid.) and to 'the discovery of America and the maritime way to India' (p. 299), he hints at least at the need for a discussion of deep historical transitions[20]—which he immediately cuts short, however, by switching to the 'decisive' role of violence [*Gewalt*] (ibid.). He adds a radical critique of economism:

> And the relation [supposedly between violence and economic exchange] is by no means of such a kind that the economy determines the content, the aim and the result of violence; the result of the violent decision, from its side, determines the economy. (Ibid.)

He goes on to sketch a theoretical conception of violence as a force of radical historical contingency: 'Violence, however, is blind, its results cannot be foreseen' (ibid.). And this is why, then, as already quoted, he considers it justified to side with Weber against Marx.

Let us return to his central thesis about the new 'phase which changes the very foundations historical life has had so far' (p. 299): 'with the war of 1914 humanity entered into such a phase' (ibid.), while the outbreak of the war still 'followed the old conformity with the law [*alte Gesetzmäßigkeit*] [of historical development]—and can, accordingly, be analysed with regard to its causes (ibid.). Such an analysis can expose the relevant 'capitalist developments' which define the 'sociological conditions …, within which military conflict [*kriegerische Auseinandersetzung*] becomes possible and is determined in its content and in its extent' (ibid.).

The Issue of 'Implementation'

According to Hilferding's new analysis, however, an important change has to take place at this very point of the historical process: 'For the economic relations [*Verhältnisse*] need a transposition [*Umsetzung*] into the political' (ibid.). And Hilferding goes on to stress the irreducible specificity of this process of 'transposition into the political'—which in subsequent

---

[20] As was realised, to my mind, by Balibar and Wallerstein (1991).

Marxist debates has been discussed under the heading of the 'relative autonomy of the political':[21] 'This transposition is a process by which the immediately economic interests and motives undergo a transformation [*Umwandlung*]' (p. 299). Against reductionist notions, Hilferding stresses that the 'political superstructure of society is a power in itself' (ibid.) and he refers back to the history of European modernity in which 'the development of state power has taken place at the same time' as 'the development of modern economy'—and, as he adds, more importantly, that the 'steady increase of state-power' in this historical process is easily overlooked because of 'the restriction of an arbitrary exercise of power' that took place in this process (ibid.). In other words, as Hilferding summarises, 'state power even in the heydays of liberalism has been objectively stronger than in times of absolutism' (ibid.).

For his own day, the interwar years, Hilferding ventures a diagnosis of its central 'political problem' (p. 299) applying his argument to the new historical conjuncture, which consists, in his view, in 'the change of the relation of state power to society' (ibid.): by means of what he conceives as 'a subjection of the economy to the discretionary power [*Verfügungsgewalt*] of the state' the very state 'becomes a totalitarian state' (ibid.).

Hilferding goes on to discuss a widely used analogy between the pre-1914 era of 'neo-mercantilism' and the classical mercantilism (p. 300) of early modernity:[22] whereas these models of economic politics by state action have created conditions for the 'unfolding' of the 'autonomy of economic development' (ibid.), the 'total state subjects the economy to its own needs' (ibid.)—and thereby 'replaces the economic aims of the individual agents of production with its own purpose as a state [*Staatszweck*]'. In discussing his own analysis of 'why this has come about and where it leads' (ibid.), he applies it directly to the problem of social consciousness: 'Societal consciousness only exists in its political form, as a consciousness of the leading instance of the state [*Staatsleitung*]'. And as 'a unitary and purposive consciousness' it 'has the organic means at its disposal, [i.e.] the ever-growing state apparatus, required for making its will effective' (ibid.).

---

[21] See Balibar et al. (1979), as well as Albo and Jenson (1989).

[22] I have not been able to identify the specific debate Hilferding was referring to here. The term is still actively in use today. For a historical background overview, see O'Brien and Clesse (2002).

According to Hilferding's analysis, 'the development since 1914 is characterised by the rapid degeneration [*Entartung*] of this state power' (p. 300). Here the text seems to be slightly elliptic: in the supposed process of an 'autonomisation of its intrinsic self-interests [*Eigeninteressen*] and tendencies vis-à-vis society' (ibid.), also characterised as an 'extension of its [i.e. state power's] competencies to areas hitherto wholly or partly free from the state [*staatsfrei*]' (ibid.), 'to the point of a submission [*Unterwerfung*] of the domain of the economy and of economic agents which had so far been regulated autonomously' (ibid.), a 'subordination [*Unterordnung*] of the hitherto [existing] socially unconscious [*gesellschaftlich Unbewussten*] to the state's consciousness [*Staatsbewußtsein*]' (ibid.), an 'elevation [*Erhebung*] of state consciousness to dominating society' (ibid.). In conclusion, Hilferding sums up these findings in a thesis marking his distance from a kind of Marxism for which almost everything is explicable in terms of 'laws of development': 'It is a singular phenomenon in a singular situation [as it has] emerged from the impact of the violence of war [*kriegerische Gewalteinwirkung*]'.

This notion of implementation is taken up and discussed again—with steady reference to Marx—in the main part of Hilferding's text: against the danger of 'substituting' the (objectively defined) 'interests' 'far too directly and far too exclusively as the historically efficient causes' (p. 316), Hilferding takes up an undeveloped distinction to be found in Marx's preface to his *Contribution to the Critique of Political Economy* of 1859—'between the material transformation [*Umwälzung*, which also translates as revolution] of the economic conditions of production, which can be determined with the precision of natural science', on the one hand, and 'the legal, political, religious, artistic or philosophic—in short, ideological forms in which men become conscious of this conflict and fight it out', on the other,[23] to further develop his conception of implementation as a specific task of translating the 'objective revolutions in the relations of production into motives for action' (p. 316).

---

[23] https://www.marxists.org/archive/marx/works/1859/critique-pol-economy/preface.htm.

The Underlying Problem of Theory

In the ensuing part of his essay, 'The Theoretical Problem' (pp. 301–4), Hilferding articulates his central theoretical thesis around the notion of a 'sublation [*Aufhebung*] of the societal domain, as it had hitherto been an area free from state intervention [*staatliche Einwirkung*], regulated by autonomous laws' (p. 301). He defends the thesis that in the new phase of history, ushered in by the historical break of 1914, the 'self-regulation of the economy is abolished' (ibid.), and thereby its 'sphere of autonomy' (ibid.)—with the effect of 'sublating the autonomy of the economic sphere of society'—and with it also the 'rights of persons [*persönliche Rechte*]'. Here, Hilferding seems to be unaware of the class domination permeating modern bourgeois societies in spite of their superficial realm of 'Freedom, Equality, Property, and Bentham' (Marx [1867] (1976), p. 280)—and yet he has a real point here: the relation between the legal order and state power has changed profoundly in the development of the 'capitalist state', as indeed occurred during the twentieth century,[24] 'completely changing the foundation upon which societal relations have so far been shaped [*gestaltet*]' (ibid.): 'Their functional dependencies turn into totally different ones, and thereby the entire complex of historico-societal laws is changing, as it has determined the course of historical events' (ibid.).

In other words, Hilferding goes very clearly beyond the theses of a transition to a modified form of the domination of modern bourgeois society by the capitalist mode of production, as they had been developed, more or less simultaneously, in the form of a theory of 'state monopoly capitalism' (Eugen Varga[25]) or of 'organized capitalism' (James Burnham): he sees a transition towards a radically new historical situation in which 'the absolutisation [*Verabsolutierung*] and autonomisation [*Verselbständigung*] of state power modifies or abolishes in any case the causal connexions in the form in which they have existed so far' (p. 301). And he draws the radical conclusion that 'the object of inquiry ceases to be the relation of the economy—in its widest possible meaning—to politics, their mutual conditionality and their acting upon each other', stating positively that 'state power has subdued the economy, determines its movement, has become its master'. Hilferding explicitly rejects any idea of

---

[24] This even became the *ratio essendi* of a specialised journal: 'Capitalistate', published in the 1980s—and now apparently vanished from all libraries and catalogues.

[25] Judith Dellheim has alerted me to the historical fact that Varga has been a critic of the Stalinist notion of 'state monopoly capitalism' (cf., for a thorough analysis, Gannage 1980).

interaction here: 'It [state-power] alone determines its behaviour in relation to the economy it has subjugated, and the economy does not determine the will of the state' (ibid.). He goes on to reject the objection that state power, at any rate, remains bound by the 'extent of the available [*vorhandenen*] means of production' (ibid.): such 'technical limitations' will, without any doubt, always exist. They may, however, become the 'object [*Inhalt*] of state politics' (ibid.), supposedly with the aim of changing them. Most importantly, Hilferding stresses once again, 'the autonomy, the socio-economic independence of this important, hitherto fundamental sphere of society has ceased to exist' (p. 301 f.)—with the important effect that this is also true of 'the regular [*gesetzmäßig*] influence it has exercised on the conscious sphere of society thus far, i.e. the [sphere of the] state' (p. 302).

This, according to Hilferding, brings about a profound epistemological change:

> The place of the problematic [*Fragestellung*] of the science of history [pursued] so far is taken by a new one, resulting from the change of the causal nexus of society [*gesellschaftlichen Kausalzusammenhangs*]. (p. 302)

This new problematic is formulated by the question, bluntly formulated, of 'what actually determines the substance of state politics' (ibid.).[26]

OBLIQUELY ADDRESSING THE PROBLEMATICS OF SINGULARITY AND OF SUBJECTIVITY

The question raised by Hilferding with regard to the new historical conjuncture he sees rising since 1914 is evidently of more general relevance: if, as Marx had indeed underlined, the critique of political economy means dealing with the structures, processes and trends of the domination of the capitalist mode of production 'in its ideal average', the question of how to grasp what Lenin called the 'concrete analysis of the concrete situation' requires a type of inquiry that goes well beyond this kind of general theory. The issue of singularity, which Hilferding regarded as central to the new period of history, as diagnosed by his theoretical intervention in 1940, would therefore have already been required in the analytical work

---

[26] At this very point, Hilferding has come to the brink of discovering the problematics of Marx's *critique of politics* (cf. above, note 11).

that went into making Marx's critique of political economy effectively relevant for critical, let alone revolutionary politics.

Hilferding, however, seems to avoid drawing such conclusions—simply by falsely historicising the matter: in the past, an economistic version of Marxism is declared to have been pertinent, while in the new age, ushered in by the first Great War of the twentieth century, Marxist analyses of class struggle are put aside in favour of an analysis of violent domination and wars.

A similar category mistake hindered his second major intuition from bearing fruit: Hilferding rightfully stresses that there is a problem in the Marxist tradition concerning the analysis or the dealing with the subjective conditions of critical or revolutionary practice—but he does not take long to shift from addressing these problematics of subjectivity to embracing 'psychology'—40 years after the publication of Freud's seminal work on the 'interpretation of dreams', and although he refers to him (p. 317 n. 7), Hilferding—resorting to the subterfuge of simply using 'psychology' as a 'historian' (ibid.), comparable to 'great artists' like Zola (p. 318, n. 7)—still adheres to the common-sense idea of a science of the human soul as it emerged with European modernity.[27] Nor does he refer to the still recent attempts within the Marxist tradition to develop a notion of 'class consciousness' and the ways it is constituted[28]—starting with Lukács's reflections on the idea of an 'imputed consciousness'.[29]

This lends his problematisation an impressively radical character: in principle, he seeks nothing less than an adequate understanding of the ways in which acting (individual or collective) subjectivities react to the singular conjunctures in which they find themselves—and refuses, rather convincingly, to find an answer in general theories about 'class consciousness'. Instead, he proposes to focus on the problematics of the relation of what he calls 'class interest'—that is objectively pre-defined interests of social categories, especially of classes[30]—and 'class consciousness', based

---

[27] It seems that he even refused to take notice of the 'Grundlagenstreit' between radically different approaches to psychology as a science that has been ravaging the emerging discipline since the end of the nineteenth century (see the more recent examples of Holzkamp 1973; Gröben and Westmeyer 1981).

[28] See the recent overview in Milner (2019).

[29] See the comprehensive study by Bewes and Hall (2011).

[30] He quite convincingly proposes to distinguish between Marx's reconstruction of the fundamental classes of modern bourgeois society (incomplete in *Capital*) and Marx's exercises in class analysis in his later political writings (p. 322).

on the transformation of this particular interest in a universal claim on and for society (p. 323). In so doing, he underlines the important role of the state (p. 323f.) and the function of intellectuals (p. 325) in what he conceptualises as a 'process of transformation' with 'two components' (p. 324):

> The immediate (material) interest of the social group ... assumes a fundamental role, the assertion [*Durchsetzung*] of which constitutes the aim of the social and political action of the group, which the construction of a new ideational edifice is supposed to serve.

—with a tendency towards completeness and systematicity:

> this will then constitute, according to this aim, a comprehensive and complete system of a societal new order, in which the consciousness of interest then dissolves. (p. 325)

Unfortunately, Hilferding did not have time to critically pursue the alleys of thinking considered and developed thus far in the concluding parts of his essay. And the dominant forms of scientific common sense—a somewhat mechanistic dichotomy between causal determination and indeterminacy and a relegation of the task of understanding acting political subjectivities to the well-trodden, but ineffective paths of 'psychology'— were not critically addressed by him as such, let alone overcome. A certain fragmentation of Hilferding's specialised efforts in political economy which, at the end of the day, remain within mechanistic horizons; his personal training as a medical doctor and his broad experience as a social democratic politician (both of which should contribute towards adopting a broader and more complex approach) seem to present a considerable challenge to further research.[31] Still, his last text remains an important testimony to the historical crisis which has held Marxism in its grip since the new age of global history, which Hilferding at least tried to understand.

---

[31] Michael Krätke's report on Hilferding's unpublished notes to this essay (in this 2nd edition of this volume) constitutes an important first step in fully understanding what Hilferding has been trying to do.

References

Albo, G., and Jane Jenson. 1989. A Contested Concept: The Relative Autonomy of the State. In *The New Canadian Political Economy*, ed. Wallace Clement and Glen Williams, 180–211. Montreal: McGill-Queen's University Press.

Althusser, L. 1971. Ideology and Ideological State Apparatuses. Notes Towards an Investigation. In Id., *Lenin and Philosophy, and Other Essays*, Trans. Ben Brewster, 85–126. New York: Monthly Review Press.

Bader, V.-M., J. Berger, and H. Ganßmann. 1976. *Einführung in die Gesellschaftstheorie. Gesellschaft, Wirtschaft und Staat bei Marx und Weber*. Frankfurt a.M.: Campus.

Balibar, É., and I. Wallerstein. 1991. *Race, Nation, Class. Ambiguous Identities*. London; New York: Verso.

Balibar, Étienne, C. Luporini, and A. Tosel. 1979. *Marx et sa critique de la politique*. Paris: Maspéro.

Bewes, T., and T. Hall. 2011. *Georg Lukacs: The Fundamental Dissonance of Existence: Aesthetics, Politics, Literature*. London; New York: Bloomsbury.

Gannage, C. 1980. E.S. Varga and the Theory of State Monopoly Capitalism. *Review of Radical Political Economics* 12 (3): 36–49.

Giddens, A. 1983. *A Contemporary Critique of Historical Materialism*. London: Polity Press.

Greisman, H.C., and G. Ritzer. 1981. Max Weber, Critical Theory, and the Administered World. *Qualitative Sociology* 4 (1): 34–55.

Gröben, N., and H. Westmeyer. 1981. *Kriterien psychologischer Forschung*. München: Juventa.

Hilferding, R. 1940. Das historische Problem. In (1982) *Zwischen den Stühlen oder über die Unvereinbarkeit von Theorie und Praxis. Schriften Rudolf Hilferdings 1904 bis 1940*, ed. Cora Stephan, 298–328. Berlin; Bonn: Dietz Verlag J.H.W. Nachf.

Holzkamp, K. 1973. *Sinnliche Erkentnis*. Frankfurt a.M.: Athenaeum.

Jossa, B. 2018. Is Historical Materialism a Deterministic Approach? The Democratic Firm and the Transition to Socialism. *Review of Radical Political Economics* 50 (1): 82–98.

Kolko, G. 1959. A Critique of Max Weber's Philosophy of History. *Ethics* 70 (1): 21–36.

Labica, G. 1984. *Le marxisme-léninisme. Éléments pour une critique*. Paris: Bruno Huisman.

———. 1998. Engels and Marxist Philosophy. *Science & Society* 62(1). Friedrich Engels A Critical Centenary Appreciation: 13–34.

Marx, K. [1867] (1976). *Capital: Volume 1: A Critique of Political Economy*. London: Penguin Books.

Milner, A. 2019. Class and Class Consciousness in Marxist Theory. *International Critical Thought* 9 (2): 161–176.

O'Brien, P.K., and A. Clesse, eds. 2002. *Two Hegemonies: Britain 1846–1914 and the United States 1941–2001*. Aldershot: Routledge.

Orozco, Teresa. 1995. *Platonische Gewalt. Gadamers politische Hermeneutik der NS-Zeit*. Hamburg: Argument Verlag/Ariadne.

Peter, G. 2003. *Wissenspolitik und Wissensarbeit als Gesellschaftsreform: ausgewählte Beiträge zur Arbeitsforschung 1972–2002*. Münster: LIT.

Pöhler, W., and G. Peter. 1982. *Erfahrungen mit dem Humanisierungsprogramm. Von den Möglichkeiten und Grenzen einer sozial orientierten Technologiepolitik*. Köln: Bund Verlag.

Ricoeur, P. 2016. In *Hermeneutics and the Human Sciences: Essays on Language, Action and Interpretation*, ed. J. Thompson. Cambridge: Cambridge University Press.

Sherman, H. 1981. Marx and Determinism. *Journal of Economic Issues* 15 (1): 61–71.

Wolf, F.O. 2006. Marx' Konzept der 'Grenzen der dialektischen Darstellung'. In *Das Kapital neu lesen*, ed. J. Hoff et al., 159–188. Münster: Westfälisches Dampfboot.

———. 2009. Engels' Altersbriefe als philosophische Intervention: Worum ging es und mit welchen Mitteln hat Engels eingegriffen? *Beiträge zur Marx-Engels-Forschung NF* 2008: 140–156.

Wolin, Sheldon S. 1981. Max Weber: Legitimation, Method, and the Politics of Theory. *Political Theory* 9 (3): 401–424.

CHAPTER 16

The Forgotten "Notes". Rudolf Hilferding's Still Unpublished Complements to His Manuscript "The Historical Problem"

Michael R. Krätke

THE MANUSCRIPTS OF 1940/1941

Rudolf Hilferding wrote his last unfinished manuscript, starting in September 1940, in quite precarious circumstances. The manuscript in his handwriting is dated 29 September 1940; he probably worked on this until January 1941. As far as we know, Hilferding wrote this text in a library in Arles, a rather small provincial town in the Provence, at that time under the authority of the Vichy-regime in France. As a refugee, Hilferding did not carry any books with him, so he must have been using the public library that he found in town. Boris Nikolaewsky reported that he had eagerly browsed the library of the Archeological Institute in Arles. From the end of September 1940 to early January 1941, he could enjoy the

M. R. Krätke (✉)
Amsterdam, The Netherlands

© The Author(s), under exclusive license to Springer Nature Switzerland AG 2023
J. Dellheim, F. O. Wolf (eds.), *Rudolf Hilferding*, Luxemburg International Studies in Political Economy,
https://doi.org/10.1007/978-3-031-08096-8_16

381

peace of this place—before he was arrested by the French police, and, shortly afterwards, handed over to the Gestapo.[1]

According to Benedict Kautsky, Hilferding's second wife, Rose Hilferding, had been able to save and preserve the manuscript of her late husband. Obviously with the help of some friends in France. In 1948, she wrote in a letter to Benedikt Kautsky that she had received the original manuscripts of "Finance Capital" but did not mention the manuscript of "The Historical Problem".[2] When still in the USA, she sent the latter manuscript to Benedikt Kautsky, who published it after his return to Austria. Probably, Rose Hilferding has transcribed and typed both her husband's first manuscript and the manuscript of the "notes", before she sent them to Benedikt Kautsky.[3] In the 1950s, Hilferding's unfinished manuscript was published posthumously twice, first in 1954 in an academic journal in Germany, the "Zeitschrift für Politik", then again in 1956 in the theoretical journal of the Austrian socialist party, "Die Zukunft".[4]

What the Hilferding papers in the custody of the International Institute for Social History (IISH) in Amsterdam show are three different documents: first, a handwritten manuscript, in two notebooks, A5 format, the first version of the text. The handwriting is Hilferding's. Second, a typoscript of the same text which has probably been written by his wife Rose Hilferding. And third, another typoscript of 16 pages (A4 format), titled "Anmerkungen" (Notes). There is no handwritten original of these notes, the manuscript version is probably lost. It is highly probable that Rose Hilferding also typed this text, based on the original manuscript. Only the envelope in which she sent the two typewritten texts to Benedikt Kautsky has been preserved in the Hilferding papers in the IISH, Amsterdam. This 16-page text of "notes", an addition and expansion of Hilferding's first text, has been all but forgotten. They have been mentioned by some

---

[1] See Nikolaevsky 1947: 6. For the circumstances of his death in Paris in late February 1941, see Gottschalch 1968, Kurotaki 1984 and Delacor 1999.

[2] See Hilferding 1948.

[3] In the Rudolf Hilferding Nachlass at the IISG in Amsterdam, the envelope in which Rose Hilferding sent these typoscripts to Benedikt Kautsky in early 1950 from her residence in California to Kautsky's in New York is still preserved. The two manuscripts written by Rudolf Hilferding are in the same map: Hilferding 1941a and Hilferding 1941b.

[4] See Hilferding 1954 and 1956. *Die Zukunft* had been launched in 1946, to replace the theoretical journal *Der Kampf* which had been the most important and influential publication medium of Austro-Marxism. Hilferdings text has been republished in Stephan 1982.

Japanese researchers, but remained completely unknown in the English-speaking world.[5]

Although titled "notes", the text comes without a clear numbering of the paragraphs, nor is there any indication of the places where these additional notes or remarks should have been inserted into the first text. At first glance, we are indeed dealing with a list of additional notes because the text begins with a lot of shorter and longer quotes plus from various authors, complete with references. In the first long version of Hilferding's text, there are just 14 notes and only 3 of them consist of quotes and/or references. Only two sources are mentioned, H.St.L.B. Moss, *La naissance du moyen age*, 1937 and H. Pirenne, *Le movement économique et social*; Friedrich Engels is mentioned in one note but without proper quote or reference. In the text of the "notes" there are 16 different authors and 20 different sources—including Moss who is cited several times, and Pirenne.[6] But, already on page 3, the text changes into a series of shorter and larger complementary remarks to the first manuscript—some being just additions and extensions, some, especially the larger ones comprising a page and more, turning into full-scale attempts to reformulate core thoughts of the original manuscript. In these passages, Hilferding even added some notes, either in brackets or at the bottom of the page with a *). As it is highly unusual to make notes to notes, it seems more likely that in these 16 pages Hilferding had started with an effort to add more quotes and notes to his original manuscript, but very soon switched to rewriting some passages and to extending and/or reformulating the arguments that he had tried to develop in the first version of his text.

Many of these rewritings would fit well into the last two sections of Hilferding's first text: The section on "Marx's conception of history" and the final section on the "objective analysis of relations of production and their psychological processing".[7] There are, however, important differences between the first text and the text of the "notes". Just to mention two: in the text of the "notes", Hilferding criticizes Marx's 1850 shorthand

---

[5] For a recent reference to these "notes", see Krätke 2019 [2018], p. 175. Benedikt Kautsky did not mention them in his short introduction to Hilferding's text when it was first published in 1954, see Kautsky 1954.

[6] The further authors referred to and/or quoted (although not always with complete references) are H. Poincaré (with three different publications), F. Delaisi, H. Heine and J. Romains, A. Siegfried (with two different publications), E. Renan, J.St. Mill, W. Lippmann, L. Rougier, L. Rosenstock-Franck, G.D.H. Cole and R. Postgate, L.Muret and F. Davy.

[7] See Hilferding 1982, pp. 304–311, 311–328.

version of his conception of history much more explicitly than in his first text. And he engages with Lenin's (and Kautsky's) theory about the making of proletarian class consciousness, although inconclusively.

Some Notable Remarks in Hilferding's Complementary Texts

In his very first remark, Hilferding strongly emphasized that in the longer run the social structure of the United States was growing more complicated instead of becoming more simplified. In particular, the great classes, farmers, bourgeoisie and working class, are showing more complicated patterns—due to the emergence and growing importance of intellectuals, rentiers and the ever-stronger differentiation of the farmers.[8]

The two following remarks are referring to the actual war situation and the pre-war situation: Hilferding talks about a war without hatred, obviously misjudging the kind of warfare Nazi Germany was about to unleash in the course of 1941. Second, he remarks that the obvious weakness of international law has enticed the Marxists to underrate the importance of standing up for the concept of law—"in contrast to the declaration made by Marx" in the "Inaugural Address".[9]

Hilferding makes three further remarks which are of general interest regarding his intention of rethinking the basic tenets of the materialist conception of history: First, "ideologies are interacting with each other much stronger than with technology or politics". Although the influence of English Puritanism on the "spirit of capitalism" remains questionable, "in spite of Max Weber", its retarding influence on the development of the arts in England, especially on painting, seems quite obvious.[10] Third, a general warning: it is possible to identify and analyse "interests" pertaining to different social groups. But the researcher should not take the "interests" as he sees them as "directly effective" or take them "immediately as causa movens". People do not just "have" interests, they must become aware of them, even interpret them, and that does imply a "transformation process". Ignoring this process leads to "economic and pseudo-Marxist mysticism".[11]

[8] Hilferding 1941b [1940], p. 1.
[9] Ib., p. 2. [All the translations of Hilferding's text by me, MK].
[10] Ib., p. 2.
[11] Ib., p. 3.

Critique of Marx's Wording of the "Materialist Conception of History" in the Preface of 1859

In the following pages, Hilferding takes issue with the way in which Marx had worded the basic tenets of his "materialist conception of history" in 1859. His critique of this seminal text which was regarded as the classical and authoritative statements of historical materialism by friend and foe alike is much sharper and clearer as in the first version of his manuscript.

What is remarkable, although not surprising for anyone familiar with Hilferding's—and, more broadly, the Austro-Marxist's—thought, he starts with another statement of the "principal progress" that Marx had made in economics: that is the revealing of the "fetish character", the "material appearances" concealing the social relations in modern societies. Demonstrating that "capital" was not a thing, but a social relationship between people, entailed a total transformation of political economy into a science of the "socialisation of man", the socialisation of historical, real man, not false abstracta like "Robinson" or the infamous "homo oeconomicus". And that is where and how Marx's economic analysis is tied together with his conception of history.[12]

However, Marx's statement of one of the core ideas of his conception in his preface of 1859 is flawed, Hilferding argues. In particular, the theorem that the development of productive forces will eventually always get into conflict with the relations of production and "<u>must</u> disrupt them" is a claim going too far "in this generality". What does disrupt relations of production are rather conflicts of interests between social groups - and not all such conflicts are always and to the full extent determined by the development of productive forces. Insisting upon "productive forces", Marx is using "too narrow a formulation", and does not take into account other factors like international trade, war and conquest.[13] In order to explain the differences between the English and French Revolution, one has to consider the difference of the condition of the peasants in both countries. A difference that must be explained by the different positions of state power regarding the peasants in these countries—the difference between a restricted royalty in England and an absolutist monarchy in France. As the

---

[12] Ib., pp. 3, 4. That is exactly the new reading of Marx that Hilferding had already introduced in his very first letter to Karl Kautsky, in 1902, emphasizing the analysis of "fetishism" as the most important part of Marx's theory (cf. Hilferding 1902).

[13] Ib., p. 4.

positions of aristocracy and peasantry were different, so were the outcomes of the revolutions for both classes in these countries. In terms of the productive forces, the countries and their peasants were not so different.[14]

Via a longer detour—an apt critique of the marginal theory of value which ignores the specific nature of relations of production and takes refuge in supposedly eternal psychological laws—Hilferding comes to a critique of the concept of economic laws in Marx's and Engels's thought. They were strongly influenced by the liberal thought of their time and tended to believe in economic laws that could not be altered by state intervention. In his 1859 preface, Marx did not talk about classes and class struggles—but the very peculiarity of his conception of history depends on that and gives it its specific political meaning. Leaving it aside, modifies, even impairs Marx's basic thought. The "sociological base" of it should be maintained. Just the formulation about all previous history being a history of class struggles (from the Manifesto of 1848) meant establishing the nexus with politics.[15]

POLITICS, CLASS AND STATE POWER

Criticizing Marx's misleading and narrow formulations in the preface of 1859, Hilferding has come to the issue of politics and class, or state and class again. In this second attempt to reformulate what Marx and Engels had in mind with their conception of history, he stumbles over the "strange contrast" between the "vagueness" of the categories of the materialist conception of history and the "accuracy and sharpness of Marx's economic concepts".[16] As his essay was meant as a contribution to reformulate the basic tenets of historical materialism in a way more apt for historical research and theorizing, he came back to the relationship between conditions of class—production relations as they presented themselves in specific historical contexts—and state power. How the state powers, the civil services or bureaucracies thought and acted in different national settings,

---

[14] Ib., p. 4. Hilferding comes back to this point and sharpens his argument: it is wrong to take the development of productive forces as the "last causa movens" and to regard it as an autonomous development. Because this development depends itself upon the relations of production and the impetus for development can also come from trade, development of the population and political power (ib., p. 10).

[15] Ib., pp. 5, 6.

[16] Ib., p. 10.

political abstinence in England, a highly political active bureaucracy in France, a bureaucracy shielded against external influences in Prussia, how it was recruited from different groups of society, was decisive.

Moreover, the process by which the interest of the state gained a momentum of its own is different, more or less easily developing, depending on the state's constitution. Hilferding insisted upon distinguishing the constitutional restrictions and the real extension and strength of state power, as the latter could be changed without changing the former. State interests and state power could be changed without changing the production relations—and here Hilferding clearly alludes to the situation in post-war Germany and Austria. The fight for parliamentarism was meant to submit the state to the influence of society—that is the political will resulting from the ongoing class struggle. But under the condition of an "equilibrium of class forces", the state could become more independent than ever.[17]

There are several determinants of the political will in Hilferding's view. As for the class struggle, he insists that it is "rather the resultant of class forces than the expression of the will of one ruling class alone", although the will of the ruling class might temporarily prevail. That is why it is out of the question to identify the will of the state at any moment, that is in the thick of concrete politics, with "the interests of the ruling class"—and one should be very cautious in using the term "class dictatorship".[18]

Class Consciousness—The Most Difficult Question

The second half of the "notes" text is devoted to what Hilferding calls the "most difficult question of Marx's conception of history", the question of the "relationship between class interest and class consciousness".[19] Here, we find a lot of parallels to the last two sections of his first text.

In order to engage with the question of politics and state power in Marxist terms, Hilferding has to explain how classes can turn into political actors, sharing some common ideas about politics and engaging in political conflicts with a shared political will and outlook. Here, again, he finds Marx wanting, generalizing too far and too quickly, suffering from

---

[17] Ib., p. 6. Hilferding is obviously building upon the political theory of his old friend Otto Bauer.

[18] Ib.

[19] Hilferding 1941b [1940], p. 7.

remnants of Hegelianism. Instead, he proposes an analysis of the long and complicated process of transformation in which classes develop first a consciousness of common interests and then, via a further development of ideas and ideologies, a general outlook and general interest which can appeal to the whole of society because it transcends the horizon of the given relations of production. The reformulation of his analysis that we find in his "notes" is rather close to the last section of his first text. Both versions show the same serious intention to provide a new framework to analyse the process of formation and emergence of class consciousness. In a few respects, the text of the "notes" goes beyond the scope of the first text. Hilferding admits that the process of transformation by which the ideas living within a class will eventually grow into "regulative ideas" of the state or of society is not a completely necessary one. It does not have to go until the end—form a consciousness of shared interests to a particular and then to a general class consciousness. The process can be halted, and even if full class consciousness is achieved, it can be reversed. Due to this transformation the consciousness of shared interests can become less unequivocal. That is why class consciousness is less reliable as a determinant of collective political will of the members of the class. On the one hand, it is possible that some of the particular interests of the class can be realized, at least for a part, and such partial realization of shared interests—as in the case of association rights and social-political achievements for members of the working class—can "already partially modify the relations of production". Such partial realizations render the realization of further partial interests more feasible. Hence, and as a consequence of partial success, the transformation process stops short of the formation of full class consciousness.[20] A regression is also possible, when the relations of productions are consolidated instead of overcoming by partial political successes and the members of a class learn that they are able to pursue and assert their shared interests, at least parts of them, without being able to settle all their political claims at once.[21]

Hilferding engages with Lenin's (and Kautsky's) theory of the formation of proletarian class consciousness only with the help of an intellectual avant-garde. Lenin's theory is in conflict with Marx and "too narrow", but Marx's ideas about the inevitable emergence of class consciousness are also wanting. Hilferding admits that the necessary general ideas which

[20] Ib., pp. 9, 10.
[21] Ib., p. 13.

should enter the collective consciousness of a class and transform it have been provided by bourgeois intellectuals. He argues against Lenin and Kautsky referring to the historical example of the struggles for the freedom of association and parliamentary reform in England, as well as to the struggle for the factory laws. In these cases, the consciousness of shared interests within the ranks of the working class was expanded into a clearly political consciousness—because the struggle for material group interests bumped into political obstacles. He leaves the matter unsettled, announcing that he will come back to it later.[22] This remark clearly indicates that he was not finished and wanted to have another go on the text of his essay. History and tradition play a large role in the collective consciousness of social groups and classes; it can be stronger than shared interests based upon the same economic class position. That is why the political consciousness of some social groups and classes can be more unstable than that of others.

At the end, Hilferding returns to the question of state power. Regarding the vagueness, the instability and the incompleteness of the transformation process, he asks himself whether a certain degree of statehood and state centralization should not be regarded as a historical precondition for the emergence and persistence of class consciousness—as only the framework of a state would allow the wider expansion of the consciousness of shared interests within a class. State power, once established, could be considered as the resultant of a "parallelogram of forces", the ever-changing class forces providing the sides of it. It is wrong to identify state power with "the interests of one class". But the image of the parallelogram of forces is not completely correct, as state power itself is one of the forces in this parallelogram, not just a resultant.[23] State power is itself a historical variable, and it can determine the "content of class consciousness", depending upon different features of state power (centralization, malleability, its record of violent behaviour). Class consciousness can be at odds with state consciousness because the economic interests of a class are not enclosed in national or state borders. However, interests in the state will prevail because a class needs the state in order to assert and enforce its economic interests. That is why the international element of class con-

[22] Ib., pp. 13, 14.

[23] Ib., p. 15. Hilferding is presupposing interests of the state powers themselves, including an interest in its self-preservation, and he clearly sees state power in relationships with other social powers, hence as a social relationship.

sciousness will decrease once a class gains influence on the state apparatus.[24] This last remark clearly reflects Hilferding's experience with the labour movement in the Weimar republic.

HILFERDING'S ACHIEVEMENT

In two of his last letters to his life-long friend Karl Kautsky, written in September and in November of 1937, Hilferding mentioned his plan to reconsider the Marxian perspective, in terms of a new class analysis. He explicitly worded his doubts whether "what we have imagined as class consciousness—that is the psychologically compelling result of a certain condition, really has to take shape". This reconsideration should be based upon a new analysis of capitalist development, at least since 1914—and that would be a large and difficult task, and it would include a fresh investigation into the "foundations".[25] The Marxian conception of history in its simplified form had its limits. The basics of Marx's "sociological determinism" were still sound, but the matter was "much more complicated than the vulgar could ever imagine".[26] Did he achieve what he intended—to provide a base for a serious rethinking of the Marxian conception of history? The impact of his essay after its posthumous publication in 1954 and 1956 was rather under—than overwhelming. Even his own son, Peter Milford, was not convinced that his father had actually dealt with the "crucial point" in how far the political superstructure was economically determined and found the text "very unsatisfactory".[27] Benedikt Kautsky agreed with him. He argued that whatever kind of force could be easily understood within the framework of Marx's conception of history, Hilferding's attempt to change it was inappropriate.[28]

[24] Ib.

[25] Hilferding 1937a.

[26] Hilferding 1937b. In one of his last letters, to his old friend Oscar Meyer and his wife, Hilferding described the text he was working on as as "a kind of epilogue and critique of Marxism". Hilferding 1940.

[27] Milford 1955.

[28] Kautsky 1955.

References

Delacor, R.M. 1999. "Auslieferung auf Verlangen"? Der deutsch-französische Waffenstillstandsvertrag 1940 und das Schicksal der sozialdemokratischen Exilpolitiker Rudolf Breitscheid und Rudolf Hilferding. *Vierteljahreshefte für Zeitgeschichte* 47 (2): 217–241.

Gottschalch, W. 1968. *Strukturveränderungen der Gesellschaft und politisches Handeln in der Lehre von Rudolf Hilferding.* Berlin: Duncker & Humblot.

Hilferding, R. 1902. Brief an Karl Kautsky, Mai 21. In Karl Kautsky Nachlass, Amsterdam: IISG, Signature KDXII 581.

———. 1937a. Brief an Karl Kautsky, September 2. In Karl Kautsky Nachlass. Amsterdam: IISG, Signature KD XII 668.

———. 1937b. Brief an Karl Kautsky, November 5. In Karl Kautsky Nachlass. Amsterdam: IISG, Signature KD XII 670.

———. 1940. Brief an Oskar Meyer und Frau, November 30. In Alexander Stein Papers. Amsterdam: IISG, Signature 124.

Hilferding R. 1941a [1940]. *Das historische Problem.* Edited by Rudolf Hilferding Nachlass. Amsterdam: IISG.

Hilferding, R. 1941b [1940]. *Anmerkungen.* Edited by Rudolf Hilferding Nachlass. Amsterdam: IISG.

———. 1948. Brief an Benedikt Kautsky, Juni 8. In Benedikt Kautsky Nachlass. Amsterdam: IISG, Mappe 16.

———. 1954. Das historische Problem. *Zeitschrift für Politik* 1 (4): 294–324.

———. 1956. Das historische Problem. *Die Zukunft, Sozialistische Monatsschrift für Politik, Wirtschaft, Kultur* 10 (2): 48–53; (3): 79–86.

———. 1982. Das historische Problem. In *Zwischen den Stühlen oder die Unvereinbarkeit von Theorie und Praxis,* ed. C. Stephan, 297–328. Bonn: J.H.W. Dietz Nachf.

Kautsky, B. 1954. Einführung zu Rudolf Hilferding. *Das historische Problem* 4: 293–294.

———. 1955. Brief an Peter Milford, Oktober 3. In Benedikt Kautsky Nachlass. Amsterdam: IISG (Mappe 57).

———. 1982. Rudolf Hilferding, Das historische Problem, In Stephan, Cora (ed), Zwischen den Stühlen. Über die Unvereinbarkeit von Theorie und Praxis. Schriften Rudolf Hilferdings 1904 bis 1940. Bonn: J.W. H. Dietz Nachf.: 297–328.

Krätke, M. 2019 [2018]. Austromarxismus und politische Ökonomie. *Beiträge zur Marx-Engels-Forschung* 2018/2019: 165–220.

Kurotaki, M. 1984. Zur Todesursache Rudolf Hilferdings. *Miyagi-Gakuin Joshi-Daigaku Kenkyu-Rombunshu* 61: 1–21.

Milford, P. 1955. Brief an Benedikt Kautsky, October 3. In Benedikt Kautsky Nachlass. Amsterdam: IISG, (Mappe 57).

Nikolaevsky, B. 1947. Hilferdings Vermächtnis. In Neue Volkszeitung I (June 21): 7, II (July 5): 6.

Stephan, Cora, ed. 1982. *Zwischen den Stühlen oder über die Unvereinbarkeit von Theorie und Praxis. Schriften Rudolf Hilferdings 1904 bis 1940*. Bonn: J.H.W. Dietz Nachf.

CHAPTER 17

Rudolf Hilferding: A Born Journalist

Michael R. Krätke

THE UNKNOWN HILFERDING

Until this very day, Hilferding has been regarded as the man of one book, his famous "Finance Capital", published in 1910 for the first time, when its author was just 33 years old. However, he had already made a name for himself before the publication of "Finance Capital" because of his articles published in the *Marx-Studien*, the first publication organ of Austro-Marxism, and the *Neue Zeit*, the leading theoretical publication organ of European Socialism and Marxism of his time. From 1906 onwards, living in Berlin, he became a prolific writer of articles for the socialist papers in Germany while he continued to write for socialist reviews in his native Austria. His journalistic work forms a large part of his legacy. Minoru Kurata has listed several hundred journal articles, written, and published between 1902 and 1940. Kurata's bibliography, although the best and most complete so far, still shows some gaps.[1] As Marx and Engels, as Rosa

[1] Kurata 1974.

M. R. Krätke (✉)
Amsterdam, The Netherlands

© The Author(s), under exclusive license to Springer Nature
Switzerland AG 2023
J. Dellheim, F. O. Wolf (eds.), *Rudolf Hilferding*, Luxemburg
International Studies in Political Economy,
https://doi.org/10.1007/978-3-031-08096-8_17

393

Luxemburg, as Otto Bauer and as many other Marxists, Hilferding never stopped writing for journals and other periodicals (mostly of the Left), sometimes working as editor, sometimes as editor-in-chief as well.

Hilferding had a long career as an editor and journalist. First, from 1904 onwards, he was a regular contributor to the *Neue Zeit* where he published many theoretical essays, some interventions into political debates and quite a lot of book reviews. In early 1907, he joined the editors of the central organ of the German social democratic party (SPD), the "Vorwärts" in Berlin, and worked as its foreign editor until 1915. No later than 1910, he became its editor-in-chief. He continued to write for the theoretical organ of the Austrian social democracy, "Der Kampf", which had been founded in 1908. In those years, he often published under the pseudonym "Karl Emil".

In 1918, returning from the Italian front to Berlin, he became editor-in-chief of the central journal of the USPD, the *Freiheit*. During nearly four tumultuous years, until 1922, when the remnants of the Independent Social Democracy reunified with the majority of the SPD, he wrote many leaders for this journal, serving a public of about half a million people in Germany. Eventually, after he had re-joined the SPD in 1922, he became minister of finance in 1923, at the height of the German hyperinflation, and member of the German parliament in 1924. As the most renowned and widely respected economic and financial specialist of the party, he finally joined the executive committee and co-authored the new programme of the reunified party (the Heidelberg programme of 1925) and appeared as principal or key-note speaker on three-party congresses (Berlin 1924, Kiel 1927 and Magdeburg 1929). He used to give lectures and speeches for the party, for the youth organizations, appeared at congresses of the German trade unions and spoke at international conferences.[2]

In 1924, he became the editor-in-chief of the new review "Die Gesellschaft" which was meant to replace Kautsky's "Die Neue Zeit". Once again, he succeeded in assembling a large group of younger and older intellectuals of the Left, among them Karl Kautsky and some of his Austro-Marxist friends like Otto Bauer. Hilferding did not publish many articles in this journal, but those he did publish were widely read, not only by left audiences but also in conservative intellectual circles and regarded as important contributions to an assessment of the pressing problems of

---

[2] Many of his public speeches were published as brochures and widely distributed among members of the social democratic party and the trade unions.

their times. Hilferding managed to keep the journal on top of the important intellectual and political movements of his time, closely following recent developments of capitalism, changes in the international order, shifts in the balances of power in the Western democracies and major events in the Soviet Union.

When forced into exile, he co-founded and edited the only theoretical journal of the German social democracy in exile of any importance, the *Zeitschrift für Sozialismus*, published from 1933 to 1936. Already in June 1933, he began to write regularly for the party's newspaper in exile, now reduced to a weekly and renamed *Neuer Vorwärts*, edited by Friedrich Stampfer. The bulk of his journal articles were published in this newspaper. His articles in the *Neuer Vorwärts* as well as his pieces published in the *Zeitschrift für Sozialismus* regularly appeared under his most favoured pseudonym "Richard Kern".

Unfortunately, his biographers have largely ignored or neglected his journalistic work[3] with the exception of Alexander Stein. Stein, who worked closely together with Hilferding for many years, has devoted to them several sections of the short biographical sketch of Hilferding which he published in 1946. He described some of the highlights of Hilferding's work as a journalist, especially during his years in exile, but also before, when Hilferding edited the best newspaper of the German left, the *Freiheit*, for four long years. Stein described the main thrust of Hilferding's numerous articles published in the *Neuer Vorwärts* at length, calling him a "born journalist".[4] Rereading more than 300 articles Hilferding published in the newspaper between June 1933 and May 1940, Stein emphasized his long fight against the Nazi regime's rise to power which changed first Germany, then Europe and eventually led to World War II. From the onset of the war in September 1939 until the closing down of the newspaper, Hilferding continued to analyse the strength and weaknesses of Nazi Germany's war effort and its economic base.[5] Gottschalch, in his dissertation on Hilferding,

---

[3] He was not the only one. Karl Marx and Friedrich Engels have shared the same fate. Their economic and political journalism has been largely ignored, much to the detriment of Marxist thought (cf. Krätke 2006). Marxists and Anti-Marxist still today share widely believed myths, for instance that there is no political theory in Marx's or Engels' work, or that Marx and Engels were philosophers and had no talent for nor liked empirical research, or that they were not familiar with the vast economic and historical literature of their time—and so on (cf. Krätke 2022).

[4] Stein 1946, 36.

[5] See Stein 1946, 35–42.

all but neglected Hilferding as a journalist. Only once, in a short paragraph of the biographical chapter of his book, he briefly mentioned the 300 articles Hilferding wrote in exile, most of them dealing with the Nazi economy.[6] Wagner did hardly mention any of his hero's journalism.[7] William Smaldone, however, did more justice to Hilferding the journalist in his biography. He did not only mention the more than 250 articles Hilferding wrote in exile but did refer specifically to 6 articles dealing with the prospects of the Nazis just after their coming to power in 1933. He mentioned the numerous articles in which Hilferding had analysed the expansion of the Germany's war economy, as well as his critique of the ways in which Germany's rearmament was financed by the Nazi government. He even cited an article by Hilferding from the year 1937 where he dared to predict that rearmament would either destroy the German economy or result in total war. Smaldone even took notice of the dozens of articles on foreign policy, including articles on the foreign policy of the Soviet Union, the USA and the other democratic powers. In those years, Hilferding was a rather lone voice in the wilderness of European and American politics where appeasement of the Nazi regime held sway.[8]

CRISES AND CYCLES DURING THE YEARS OF THE LONG PROSPERITY

Before World War I, Hilferding contributed a lot of articles on Marxian political economy, its history and prehistory, and some of its major issues, like the theory of value or the theory of money. Most of these were published in the *Neue Zeit*. Some, like his article dealing with the specific way in which Marx had presented the basic problem of political economy, especially in his theory of value, were extensive statements of the highly peculiar "new reading of Marx" that Hilferding shared with the other Austro-Marxist.[9] But apart from such reflections on economic theory,

---

[6] Gottschalch 1962, 28.

[7] Cf. [nicht besser: "cf."?] Wagner 1996, 167.

[8] Smaldone 1998, 183f, 196, 240f. The work of the Japanese Hilferding-scholars remains rather unknown in the English-speaking world. Some attention has been paid to Hilferding's journalism in the outstanding book of Maasaki Kurotaki (cf. Kurotaki 1998).

[9] Cf. Hilferding 1903, 1904. Both articles, the one dealing with the differences between Marx's theory of value and the ideas of his predecessors, and the one dealing with the specific problem and task Marx had envisaged for his critique of political economy were crucial contributions to new reading of Marx by the Austro-Marxists (cf. Krätke 2019).

Hilferding tackled problem of trade and tariff policy as well as hotly debated political issues, like the general strike.[10] What is more, he contributed a lot of book reviews to the journal.[11] Some of his articles in the *Neue Zeit* and in *Der Kampf* were published under the pseudonym "Karl Emil".

One of his first articles dealing with current events in the capitalist world economy was the text titled "The State of the Economy" (Die Konjunktur), published in 1907, in the year of first worldwide financial crisis occurring after the end of the Great Depression.[12] In the following year, he continued with two further articles, the first dealing with the economic situation in the USA, the second one covering the phenomena of the actual depression in the industries of the major capitalist countries. Both articles were published under a heading in bold letters: Economic Review (Wirtschaftliche Rundschau). A clear indication that the editors of the *Neue Zeit* had entrusted Hilferding with creating and running a new section of the journal. With his two articles, Hilferding opened the new section, following Karl Marx, Friedrich Engels and Rosa Luxemburg in their footsteps.[13] However, after these two contributions by Hilferding, Julian Marchlewski and Hermann Woldt took over. Hilferding's articles are remarkable because they show how proficient he had become in all the matters of the capitalist world economy—down to the smallest detail.

In his article on the crisis of 1907, he explained the financial crisis or panic of 1907 several months before it occurred in October 1907. Although the first symptoms of the crash to come became visible already in advance on the stock markets in Europe and America. It was futile to look for the cause of the coming crisis just in the financial sphere, in

---

[10] Cf. Hilferding 1903a, b, c.

[11] Hilferding's book reviews, mostly dealing with new releases of economic literature, were little essays indeed, and are still today worth reading, although the books he reviewed have long been forgotten. For a (nearly) complete list, see Kurata 1974.

[12] Hilferding 1907.

[13] Hilferding 1908a, b. Marx and Engels had published several articles on the events of the crisis of 1848/1849 and its aftermath, simply called "reviews", in the journal that they launched during the first year of their exile in London, planning to continue the famous *Neue Rheinische Zeitung,* now renamed *Neue Rheinische Zeitung. Politisch-ökonomische Revue* (see Marx and Engels [1850] 2010a, b, and c). In 1898, Rosa Luxemburg had started a series of political-economic reviews of her own in 1898, titled "Wirtschaftliche und sozialpolitische Rundschau". She was able to publish four of these reviews in the social democratic newspaper she edited at that time, the *Sächsische Arbeiter-Zeitung* in Dresden (see Luxemburg [1898] 1970a, b, c, and d).

excesses of speculation or of stock issues. The stock market crash had to be understood as no more than a specific phase in the movement of the business cycle, and this cycle was different compared to the preceding cycle of 1895 to 1900 and 1903. The last upturn did not occur at the same time, and with the same intensity in the major capitalist countries, it came much later in the USA than in continental Europe and was much weaker in England than in other countries.[14] This time, the upswing and the crisis were different, much more extensive in terms of territories, and kept the same pace in Europe and in America. The American industry was in the lead, despite the protective tariffs applied by the US government. Moreover, the movement of money-capital across borders had become more important than ever before in uniting all the different capitalist countries into one worldwide economic area. Money-capital, accumulated by the different national capitalist classes, was being exported and invested across borders in all directions, and became an economic unity. As a consequence of capital export on an ever-growing scale, the unification and harmonization of different areas of capitalism into one capitalist world economy, following the pace of one global business cycle, had made great progress since the end of the Great Depression and the beginning of the new era of prosperity in 1895.[15] Hilferding continued explaining the sources and causes of the present financial crisis—in the development of major sectors of production (like agriculture and construction), in the wave of new companies that were founded and incorporated, and in the sphere of money, credit and stock market speculation. The boom had hit three barriers at the same time: rapidly rising prices of raw materials and rising wages jeopardizing the levels of profit rates capitalists had become accustomed to; pressures on the money markets made it more and more difficult and costly to raise the necessary amounts of credit. This was a major factor due to the nearly simultaneous boom in many industries in all capitalist countries, and the credit crunches were the harbingers of the imminent end of the boom in the capitalist world economy.[16] In the two articles he published a year later, he gave a detailed analysis of the unfolding of the crisis which had started as a financial market crisis in New York and soon spread out over the whole of the capitalist world economy, turning into an industrial crisis and depression, shattering the American indus-

---

[14] Hilferding 1907, 140f.
[15] Hilferding 1907, 141.
[16] Hilferding, 1907, 152–153.

try in particular. The depression in the USA dragged the European industries along into a worldwide slump.[17]

In several articles, published in *Der Kampf* and *Die Neue Zeit* between 1910 and 1913, he addressed more specific issues of economic theory, closely related to his *Finance Capital*. His article on banking practices and payment transactions, published in 1910, did address the question of the division of labour within the banking system. Was banking in capitalism bound to become ever more specialized or could "universal" banks of the German type persist, maybe even prevail in the longer run?[18] His articles on the theory of the concentration process and the formation of corporations were again adding some recent material and further reflections on the formation of big capitalist firms in several sectors.[19] And his article on "money and commodity", published in 1912, was a reaction to some of the criticisms directed against the first section of his *Finance Capital*. Here, Hilferding came back to the basic question: what determines the value of money, if money is a commodity, and what determines the value of money substitutes? How could Marx's theory of money made compatible with the complexities of contemporary currency systems? And how could a recent phenomenon like the continuing inflation haunting several of the most important capitalist countries for many years be explained in accordance with Marx's theory?[20] With this article, he kicked off a major debate among Marxist economists, with the participation of Kautsky, Otto Bauer, Eugen Varga and many others.

1918/1920—The Years of the Revolution That Failed

As the leading expert in Marxism and the only real expert on economic and financial policies, Hilferding became a leading figure in German politics and German journalism again, after he returned from his service in the Austrian army to Berlin in 1918. The old SPD that he knew, had split during the war, and he joined the USPD (Independent Social Democratic Party of Germany) where all his old friends (and some of his enemies) already were. The party made him editor-in-chief of their new central

---

[17] Hilferding 1908a, b.
[18] Cf. Hilferding 1910.
[19] Cf. Hilferding 1912a.
[20] Cf. Hilferding 1912b.

newspaper *Freiheit*, edited and published in Berlin. For nearly four years, he ran this newspaper. His articles were widely read, not only by the members of the USPD but also by many outside the party. In a short series of articles in the *Freiheit*, Hilferding outlined the contours of a tax policy for the socialist Left. A tax policy that should not only support the new republic and help to improve the economic situation of the working class but could also contribute to the expropriation of the propertied classes—and might even support the transition to socialism, redistribute the wealth in society and all that without ruining the very bases of the economy. It is remarkable that Hilferding was one of the very first economists of the Left who already saw the possibilities inherent in a well-constructed tax system to boost the effects of economic policy. A tax system well-built could be used to steer the economic development in a certain direction, influencing the behaviour of producers, consumers and market agents, in addition to creating tax income.[21] His reputation as the leading financial expert of the German Left was well deserved, and he became the first Marxist occupying the Finance Minister's chair in Germany.[22]

What is more, he became one of the leading figures in the struggle for the "socialization" of the German industry. Apart from labour and social policy reforms, the "socialization" was a key point for all the parties of the Left as well as for the trade unions. His party, the USPD, in particular, pushed for a rapid start of the socialization action in the most important branches of the German industry. Hilferding became a member of the first "Socialization Committee" appointed on November 18, 1918, by the provisional government, and he served on the second "Socialization Committee" from March 1920 onwards. He co-authored the final report of the committee, published on September 3, 1920, but he never wrote a longer or shorter treatise on the issue of socialization—despite the fact that he was acting in the middle of the largest public debate in Germany on socialism and the roads to it ever. He did, however, present his views on the issues of socialization—what to nationalize or socialize, how, how quickly, with what consequences—in two long speeches. One, given in the summer of 1919 to the delegates of the 10th Trade Union congress in Nürnberg, the other given to the delegates of the first shop steward's

---

[21] Cf. Hilferding 1919a, b, c.

[22] Hilferding served twice as a minister of finance in a coalition government, in 1923 and in 1928/1929. He had only one predecessor, the Ukrainian Marxist Tugan-Baranovsky who served as minister of finance in the short-lived first Ukrainian Republic in 1919.

congress in October 1920. Both speeches were published as brochures shortly after. Both show that he had carefully read the numerous contributions of his two closest friends, Otto Bauer and Karl Kautsky, who were among the most prolific and influential participants in the debate. He agreed with them on many key points, in particular with respect to the crucial idea that socialization should never become just nationalization but had to go far beyond that.[23] Socialization should open the way for a transformation that would supersede the change of ownership and control and eventually lead to economic democracy.

HILFERDING ON THE GREAT DEPRESSION 1929–1933

As the most renowned economist of the Left, at least in the German-speaking countries, Hilferding was a key figure in the years of the great crisis and depression. Although he was not an uncontroversial figure among the higher circles of politicians and functionaries of the SPD, his advice as an expert in economic and financial policies was still valued and respected. However, from the onset of the crisis, he felt stuck in a dilemma. In a letter to Kautsky, he described his dilemma which he also saw as the dilemma of the social democracy and of the Left. He knew exactly what the sound and correct "capitalist solutions" of the crisis, at least of the international credit crisis, could and should look like, but the capitalists or their political spokesmen were unable and unwilling to impose the necessary measures. On the other hand, the Left was powerless, as there was no clear "socialist solution" to the crisis. The "basic evil of the present situation is that we cannot tell the people in very specific terms how we will get rid of the crisis, which immediate and effective measures we would apply". There is a capitalist way out of the crisis, but "there is no socialist solution", and that makes the situation extremely difficult.[24] Hilferding did not trust the proposals that some of the younger economists from the trade unions developed. Still traumatized by the experience of the post-war hyperinflation, he was wary of risky credit operations and could not see any good in policies that might reduce the rates of unemployment but would, in the end, trigger another hyperinflation. However, he was far from being just an observer on the sidelines.

[23] Cf. Hilferding 1919d, 1920.
[24] Hilferding 1931d.

Fully engaged in parliamentary politics, he remained unusually silent during the first year of the crisis. In 1930, he reminded his social democratic audience, that the economic crisis had already caused a "complete overthrow" of the political situation in Germany. "Based on the history of crises in England, we can study how economic crises in previous times have radicalized the masses and had a progressive political effect", with these words he began his analysis of the interaction of economics and politics in the present crisis.[25] In the past, great crises had triggered mass movements, but that has changed because of the increased level of organization among the working class. Nowadays, a great crisis will weaken the trade unions and will push the working class into the defensive. At the height of the crisis, in 1931, when the crisis turned into an international credit crisis, he returned to the fray with several articles and lectures, trying to explain the course of the crisis to his comrades and to convince them of the actions that still could be taken to avoid further aggravations of the crisis. As he reported to Kautsky in a private letter, he gave a lecture on the credit crisis in public and intended to publish it as a brochure.[26] The lecture was published in the same year. Here, Hilferding gave, first, a very concise summary of the structural changes that had occurred in capitalism, especially in European capitalism, since the 1870s. He insisted on the longer view: the present crisis could only be understood within the context of the structural changes that the recent phase of capitalist development had brought about. Second, he presented his view of the specific nature of the world economic crisis which had begun in October 1929 and was devastating the whole capitalist world. This crisis is an extraordinary one, he emphasized. It was shaking an organized capitalism, dominated by finance capital, a capitalist world system that had become more powerful but also more fragile than ever before.[27] Because industry and credit were more closely tied together than ever before, every industrial crisis must immediately harm the credit system as a whole. And because this type of capitalism was much more dependent upon borrowed capital and short-term industrial credit than in every previous phase of capitalist development. In this capitalist order, the different capitalist countries were much more integrated into a world market—and more dependent upon an international credit system than ever before. When an industrial crisis

---

[25] Hilferding 1930a, 289.
[26] Hilferding 1931i.
[27] Hilferding 1931a, 16, 1930b.

of overproduction hit, it immediately affected also the less industrialized capitalist economies that hinged upon the production and export of raw materials for the big industrial countries. Hence, any industrial crisis would rapidly turn into an international credit crisis, because falling prices of raw materials would destroy trust and credit and incite the creditor countries to withdraw their capitals, that is, to cancel short-term loans instead of prolonging them. Looking at the course of the credit crisis in Europe, Hilferding exhorted his audience not to see the crisis in purely economic terms but also to understand it as a political crisis. After the war, industrial credit between capitalist countries was given first and foremost in the form of short-term loans: because of the war, no one trusted the competitors and rivals from across the borders. But in the moment of crisis, "their economic nature rebelled against their juridical form", as creditors and debtors alike realized that these industrial loans had actually been used as long-term loans for long-term investments.[28] When the first banks fell, when it turned out that the German banks and industrial firms were unable to repay the mass of their short-term debt, the financial centre in London ran into trouble, and the French banks began revoking their credits from England. The inevitable consequence of the credit crises and the bank runs they brought about was the downfall of major currencies, starting with the Pound Sterling. Like a wildfire, the crisis had jumped over and started to devastate the whole monetary and credit organization of the capitalist world.[29]

What is more, in the second part of his lecture Hilferding explained the mechanism of the spreading of the credit crisis, driven by the efforts of the banks to secure their own liquidity, to reclaim loans and to build up reserves. Such actions were perfectly rational from the point of view of the private economic interests of every single bank. But all banks acting in this way at the same time undermined the whole credit organization of the capitalist world and brought money and credit transactions to a standstill. In spite of the credit regulations already existing in most capitalist countries, despite the fact that the capitalist countries already had an instrument at hand to stop such actions and to prevent or stop a credit crisis unfolding—their central banks. Hilferding pointed out how and why the central banks of the largest countries, like the French national bank and the US Federal bank, exacerbated the crisis by following a policy of

[28] Hilferding 1931a, 18, 1931b, c.
[29] Hilferding 1931a, 21–22, 1931e.

keeping their gold treasures in their vaults and not using them.[30] He even gave an outline of the policy alternatives at hand that would lead out of the impasse of the international credit crisis—alternatives to the policies of inflation, devaluation, leaving the gold standard and protectionism that were pursued in different parts of the capitalist world and severely aggravated the crisis. He took this "reformist" stance because he did not believe in an inevitable collapse of capitalism. Capitalism "will not fall because of its own inner contradictions" but only because of the collective will and action of the working classes of the world. Which way out of the crisis? That question was to be decided politically.

In his articles in *Vorwärts* and in the *Gesellschaft* published in the same year, he continued to explain his view of the crisis and to criticize the false, dogmatic policies pursued by governments and central bank directories alike. In the middle of an international credit crisis unfolding, it was necessary to be clear about what was at stake exactly in the present phase of the crisis, to identify the trouble spots and to name and blame those very elements that were impeding a sound crisis policy. So, he took a very close look at the international financial centres, at the financial markets of New York, London and Paris, and at the major central banks in the capitalist world. For Germany, there was a solution to the problem of the bank panic: issuing more banknotes in order to keep payment transactions going. The solution to the international crisis depended upon stopping the capital outflow.[31] The biggest problem was to restore the international credit mechanism, crucial for the world economy. Such a restoration was only possible if central banks acted against the actions of the private banks which were driven by their private interests only. In the modern banking systems, the survival of every single bank hinged upon their command of borrowed capital. Hence, the risk of running a bank could no longer be considered a purely private risk. Central banks were the institutions that could regulate and control private banks. Only central banks could accomplish a turn in bank and credit politics. However, in Germany, the very specific institution of an "independent" central bank allowed its directors to stick to a false and completely dogmatic view of central bank politics— in this case, the view that there was a fixed relation between the gold reserves of the bank and the volume of credit in the economy. Such a relation "did not exist", as Hilferding emphasized. Hence, to overcome the

---

[30] Hilferding 1931a, 27–28, 1931b, e.
[31] Cf. Hilferding 1931f, g.

blockade in German credit politics, it was necessary either to drop the "independence" of the central bank and make it accountable to the government and parliament or to create new institutions outside of the central bank that could regulate and supervise the behaviour of the private banks. Again, Hilferding, with the authority of a former minister of finance, took the "reformist" turn, pleading for a reform of the banking system instead of calling for a revolution in the middle of a panic.[32]

In vain, Hilferding tried to use his influence and international contacts trying to convince the German and the French governments that only a solution of the conflicts between France and Germany, a resettlement, even a cancellation of the war reparations, would allow for a solution for all the crises in trade and currency relations. In his private letters to Kautsky, he complained about the stubbornness on all sides which made conflicts about trade and credit worse and worse.[33] Trying to keep ahead of the toils of daily politics, he reminded the readers of his journal that fascism in Germany owed its upsurge to some structural changes in the fabric of capitalism. First to the war which had shattered the traditional ideas about law and order in the capitalist society because the war economy ended the hegemony of liberalism. For the first time, the state took over and ruled the private economy of private firms and markets, demanding that private interests should be subordinated to the general interest, the interests of national warfare. Capitalist thought was even more shattered by the experience of post-war inflation, a gigantic process of expropriation, a period of turmoil which neither individuals nor the state could control. As a consequence of the increasing sense of insecurity and unpredictability of economic and social life led to a widespread rebellion against capitalism, a rebellion of the "declassed" from all groups and classes of society. A rebellion which fed upon old ideas, reactionary, utopian and radical ones, all thrown together. The Brüning government ruled without parliamentary consent, by means of emergency decrees. According to Hilferding, some of these decrees had demolished another pillar of capitalist thought: the holiness of private contracts. As a consequence, the last base of the legal order upon which capitalism hinged was gone. The world economic crisis had eventually shattered all the ideological bases of the capitalist order.[34]

---

[32] Cf. Hilferding 1931h.
[33] Cf. Hilferding 1932a, b.
[34] Cf. Hilferding 1932c, d.

AFTER THE GREAT DEFEAT—HILFERDING IN EXILE, 1933–1940

As a Jew and prominent socialist and leading intellectual of the Left, Hilferding was among the most hated persons in Germany, on top of all the lists of most wanted persons that the Nazis tried to get their hands on. He left the country in 1933, in early March, first crossing the border with Denmark, then travelling from Denmark via Paris to Zürich. He stayed there for five years, travelling to Prague occasionally to meet with the members of the "Sopade", the newly established executive committee of the SPD in exile. He never became an official member of "Sopade", despite his former position in the SPD. He was, however, made the editor-in-chief of the new theoretical journal, the *Zeitschrift für Sozialismus*. Hence, Hilferding's name was closely linked to the five most important Marxist publications of first half of the twentieth century: *Neue Zeit*, Marx-*Studien*, *Der Kampf*, *Die Gesellschaft* and *Zeitschrift für Sozialismus*. Each of these had a different format, from yearbook to journal, and a different task, geared at different historical contexts.[35] His name was closely linked to three of the most important newspapers in the history of the social democracy and the socialist Left in Germany: to the *Vorwärts*, where he served as editor-in-chief, to the *Freiheit*, the leading newspaper of the USPD, where he again served as editor-in-chief, and to the *Neuer Vorwärts*, where he was by far the most prolific contributor, writing on economic and financial policies, on German affairs, on the world economy, on foreign policies and international affairs for seven years. In early 1938, when Austria and the Czechoslovakian Republic were occupied by Nazi forces, he went to Paris, as did nearly all the members of the "Sopade". During his stay in Paris, he continued his work for the *Neuer Vorwärts*, commenting and analysing the events leading to the outbreak of World

---

[35] As Hilferding described them in a private letter to his friend Paul Hertz in 1933, the articles in the exile journal *Zeitschrift für Sozialismus* had "to be clear and addressed to a general audience". *Die Gesellschaft* had assumed a "scientific format", because it "had the task of introducing new problems especially to the elite of our functionaries", but the new journal had "to be kept readily comprehensible to the masses". Hilferding thought of "roughly in the terms of the *Neue Zeit* during the revisionism debate", but "without the personal attacks" (Hilferding 1933a). As for his work as editor-in-chief of *Die Gesellschaft*, we have a testimony by Hilferding himself: In a letter to Max Quarck he emphasized that the review was not anything like an official publication of the SPD. For my part, Hilferding wrote, "I am striving to keep anything official away" from it (Hilferding 1925).

War II. In May 1940, the exile paper of the SPD ceased publication. Until then, Hilferding commented and criticized the events of the first period of the war.[36] During this period, he rarely published under his own name. Nearly all his journal and newspaper articles appeared under his pseudonym "Richard Kern".

During his years in exile, in Zürich and in Paris, Hilferding regularly analysed and commented on major and minor events in world economics and world politics. The developments of Nazi Germany, the economic, social and political changes that the Nazi regime brought about, clearly were the focus of his attention. After all, he was writing for an audience of German socialists and social democrats who needed information and, above all, guidance in order to make head and tails of the events in Nazi Germany and in the wider world outside of the German borders. The newspaper *Neuer Vorwärts* could be distributed freely outside of Germany and circulated widely among fellow socialists all over Europe. For the comrades who had stayed in Germany, the vast majority of the party members, the newspaper was produced in a special abridged version, under the title *Sozialistische Aktion*, and smuggled over the borders into Germany where they circulated as an underground newspaper. While the *Neuer Vorwärts* was edited by Friedrich Stampfer, the underground paper was edited by Hilferding's friend Paul Hertz.

Regarding the sheer number of articles Hilferding wrote and published in the seven years from 1933 until he was virtually cut off from all possibilities to publish in May 1940, it is not easy to determine the main focuses of his journalistic work during this period. Most of his articles were critical comments on daily events, and one of the subjects he regularly and most frequently dealt with was the economic and financial policies of the Nazi regime in Germany. In the beginning, when he was still convinced that the Nazi regime could not last long and would soon succumb to its own failures—a view widely shared among the exiled Left intellectuals—this was even by far his favourite topic.

However, as the Nazi regime lasted and succeeded in triggering an arms race and even armaments boom in several capitalist countries, he paid more and more attention to the broader picture. Occasionally, he returned to the analysis of the capitalist world economy and to the course of the

---

[36] His oldest and closest friends, Otto Bauer and Karl Kautsky, had died in 1938. Hilferding had been able to attend Bauer's funeral in Paris and, only two months later, Kautsky's funeral in Amsterdam.

world economic crisis since early 1933. Hitler had succeeded to overcome or at least to shift the consequences of the great crisis in Germany, and he was actually supported by many of the big multinational companies engaged in the arms business in one way or the other.

The economic and financial policies of Nazi Germany and other fascist regimes were closely linked to international politics. Especially in the case of Nazi Germany, the success of the rearmament programmes depended upon the reactions of other European powers. So Hilferding devoted a lot of attention to the foreign policies of Nazi Germany and its counterparts in Europe—France, England, the USA—and its potential or actual allies—Italy and Japan. He also dealt with the foreign policies of the Soviet Union which had become an important player in European and world politics. As Nazi Germany's policies were heading towards a new great war in Europe and beyond, Hilferding commented at length upon the efforts of the European democracies to deal with this threat and to accommodate or appease the rising new power in the heart of Europe. Although he thought that another war was inevitable in the end, he did not relent his efforts to assess and criticize the diplomatic attempts to stop the Hitler regime, regardless of their futility.

Occasionally, he added an article on a somewhat different tone, not commenting upon daily events, but trying to introduce some theoretical and principal reflection upon a topic in more general terms. So he wrote on "National Socialism and Anti-capitalism" in January 1934, where he tried to assess the peculiar character of the fascist movement as an "anti-capitalist mass movement".[37] Or, he analysed the changing relations between state powers and the economy, or the power of capital, in several articles, returning to a problem that had already occupied his mind for many years, since World War I. The great depression had led to an upsurge of state interventions into the economies of many advanced capitalist countries, not immediately, but after the traditional concepts of austerity politics had proven to make matters worse instead of overcoming the crisis. Although he remained opposed to the risky financial manoeuvres that the German Reichsbank under its director Hjalmar Schacht performed since Schacht's return to power and continued to warn about a new hyper-inflation, the undeniable fact remained that the capitalist world had changed and was still changing. Not into some kind of "state capitalism", a concept that Hilferding utterly rejected but into a new form of organized

---

[37] Cf. Hilferding 1934c.

capitalism which included state interventions on a regular base and on an unprecedented scale. Repeatedly, he tried to sketch a global picture of the capitalist world as it entered a new period after the second Great Depression had begun to peter out—at least in some of the major capitalist countries, From 1936 onwards, he published a longer review of the economic developments during the previous year, mostly in the first or second issue of January, updating the picture of the capitalist world economy after the crisis from year to year.[38] And, occasionally, he published a general consideration on international politics—like his article on the "basics of foreign policy", published in November 1936.[39] He tried to put the facts he reported and commented upon into the broader framework of political economy, adding some theoretical notions and reflections to his journalism. The new kind of state-controlled and state-regulated capitalist economy the Nazi regime had fostered presented a particular challenge—and Hilferding met it. For instance, by following the qualitative change from an armament economy to a fully fledged war economy that the Nazis were achieving in the longer run, and explaining the "laws of war economy" to his audience in a longer article, published in 1936. Or reflecting upon the changes in the world economy that the economic "autarchy" and decoupling from the world market economy would entail that the dictatorial regimes tried to achieve. Or by explaining the limits of a capitalist war economy and the dead end into which the Nazi regime had driven the German economy.[40] Again and again, Hilferding argued that a war economy was not sustainable, a permanent war economy, cut off from the world market impossible to run—without starting a war. A war, that would not only serve a new imperialist project of subjugating the whole of Europe under Nazi rule but would also be driven by the urgent need to cover the ever-rising costs of war and armament and to use the spoils of war in order to gratify the people supporting the regime.

[38] Cf. Hilferding 1936a, 1937a, 1938a, 1939a.

[39] Cf. Hilferding 1936i.

[40] Hilferding 1935d, 1934d, f, 1936c, e, f, h, l, 1937c, 1938b, d During World War I, Otto Neurath had developed a new branch of economic science focusing upon the phenomena of a war economy. Neurath's pioneering work (see Neurath 1913a, b) was well known because he had connected his findings about the war economy with some optimistic conclusions regarding the future form and functioning of a socialist economy. Hilferding had written an article on the specificities of "war capitalism", published in the *Arbeiter-Zeitung* during the war, in 1915 (see Hilferding 1915). In exile after Hitler's coming to power in Germany, he came back to this topic.

There were alternatives to the economic and financial policies pursued in the countries of dictatorial capitalism. Hilferding paid ample attention to the policies of the government of the "People's Front" in France, led by his old friend Leon Blum, as well as to the experiments of the New Deal policies enacted by President Roosevelt in the USA—against the conventional wisdom of mainstream economics. And he watched and commented upon the economic developments in the Soviet Union, in particular the policies of the first five-year plans. Although he acknowledged what the Soviet Union had achieved in building an industrial base of its own in an extremely short period of time, he watched them with growing scepticism as he was well aware of the human cost of this operation. After a while, he paid more attention to the economic and political developments in other European countries, focusing upon the future adversaries of Nazi Germany, like England and France. And he started to tell his readers more about economic and political events in the USA and in the Soviet Union—both future global players in a theatre of war that would reach beyond the confines of Europe.

Setting the tone, in his first series of articles for the *Neuer Vorwärts*, starting in the summer of 1933, he focused upon the measures taken by the Hitler government to deal with the crisis, in particular with the staggering high levels of unemployment in Germany. Hilferding dismissed many of them as ill-planned, ill-conceived and futile. Already during the first months in exile he realized that the Nazi regime was going to stay for a long time. The Nazis were actually doing what their spokesmen and their grand leader has publicly announced. They were pursuing a policy of rearmament and of rebuilding Germany as a Great Power, carrying out an imperialist project. They were able and willing to change Germany into a fully fledged war economy, and they would inevitably go to war in order to create their new European order under German hegemony. However, taking the rather restricted resources of Germany into account, they would be forced to do this rapidly and to finance the planned resurgence and change of the German economy by hazardous means. In the longer run, the economic and financial policies of the Nazi state would cost the German population dearly.

The Bigger Picture—Analysing the Great Depression and Its Aftermath

Already in the first issue of the *Zeitschrift für Sozialismus*, published in October 1933, Hilferding had tried to take stock of the situation and to assess the effects of the great crisis. He was convinced that the effects of the greatest world economic crisis in the history of capitalism which seemed to be never ending were already shaking the foundations of the capitalist society. An anti-capitalist revolt was in the making already before the onset of the crisis—since the autumn of 1929, it had become manifest. More and more people from all classes, working-class people as well as the members of the middle classes were joining the ranks of anti-capitalist movements. However, the character of these rebellions against capitalism had changed, just because of the masses of middle-class people who had started to turn against the established order.[41]

During the second half of the year 1933, Hilferding had worked on a new political document, trying to outline the basics of a new political strategy for social democracy, a strategy that would fit the new situation after the Nazi's successful bid for power in Germany. In June, he had presented the first draft of a document to the Executive Committee of the SPD in exile in Prague; some weeks later he delivered a second part to this draft paper.[42] In this draft he already outlined many of the ideas which would provide a frame of reference for his political thought and his journalistic work at least until 1936. The "Prague Manifesto", published in

---

[41] Hilferding 1933c, 1–3, 1937d, e. In his articles on Blum's and Roosevelt's economic policies, Hilferding mixed praise with criticism. He wanted to convince his audience that alternative policies were possible and could be successful.

[42] While he was working on his proposal for a new strategic orientation of the party and the labour movement, he continued his discussion with Kautsky on the causes of their defeat in Germany. What had gone wrong? According to Hilferding, most mistakes were made during the formative early years of the Weimar republic, from 1918 to the times of the Kapp-Putsch in March 1920, which showed the last unified mass action of the German labour movement (Hilferding 1933d). Hilferding never shared the illusions about a smooth and safe parliamentary road leading eventually towards socialism. He had lost much of his faith in the intelligence and political capacities of the labour movement but continued to serve it as best he could. Kautsky himself tried to come to grips with the history of socialist/social democratic politics which he had strongly influenced before the war and still during the November revolution and the first years of the Weimar republic. In 1935, he wrote a long manuscript on the politics of the "Marxist centre" within the context of the socialist movement in Germany and Europe. He discussed this text, his political—theoretical "testament", with Hilferding and Hertz. It remained unpublished and was forgotten.

February 1934 in the *Neuer Vorwärts* was the outcome of his rethinking of the strategy for the Left, the only official party document written by Hilferding after he went into exile in March 1933. As Hilferding wrote in his draft assessment, the new phase of capitalist development was posing new problems, not only for Germany but also for the whole capitalist world. The German situation, contrary to appearances, was not fundamentally different from the situation in other capitalist countries, because the world economic crisis had created similar conditions in many countries. In all capitalist countries, the position of the bourgeois class had been shattered; the power of the banks and big industrial corporations had been challenged by the urban and rural middle classes, which had gained political and economic weight, thanks to the transition to a democratic order after World War I. The fight against the rule of the banks and high finance, the fight against inflation, credit crunch and unemployment had gained the upper hand in state policy—and in this respect, the Roosevelt administration was not so far away from the Hitler regime as it appeared. Everywhere in the capitalist world, the state had assumed a leading role, exerting more and more influence on the economy. State interventions had become a new normality and were to be encountered everywhere, restricting the property rights of land and house owners, and establishing market monopolies and price controls. Even ideas about capitalist planning had become widespread. The rebellion against the devastating consequences of the crisis had led to an intellectual, political and economic revolution within the framework of capitalism—and the social democracy should be aware of that. In contrast to what many in the communist movement thought at the time, Hilferding did not share the idea that fascism was a necessary stage of capitalism and could not be overcome without overthrowing the whole capitalist world. In his view, fascism could be defeated, but only by revolutionary means. At that time, he still believed in the possibility to topple the Nazi regime from within, without a war. Contrary to a widespread sentiment among his critics, the Prague Manifesto did not imply any conversion to Leninism on Hilferding's part. He made it very clear, that the goal of any anti-fascist or anti-Nazi revolt would and could never be the establishment of a dictatorship in Soviet style, but the reestablishment of a democratic political and economic order—an order which would require different institutions and different courses of action, but nothing like the state terrorism institutionalized in the Soviet Union.[43]

He accompanied the publication of the "Prague Manifesto" with another article in the *Zeitschrift für Sozialismus*, titled "Revolutionary Socialism". According to its author, the "Prague Manifesto" should initiate a radical break with outdated methods of and ways of political thought and political action that too many people on the Left had embraced far too long. Not prefabricated formulas, no fixed ideas, but a consequent return to the long-forgotten art of Marxist analysis was the order of the day. Taking stock of the facts, respecting the facts, looking for the rationale of strategic political actions not in ideals, wishful thinking or mere personal opinions but in the objective conditions of the objective situation, should be the watchword for the Left. It would be difficult, though, to overcome the difficulties of any attempt to grasp the dynamics of future developments in the capitalist world and to resist the temptation to over-simplify, to jump to conclusions and to ignore the complexities of the new situation.[44] Fascism, as Hilferding put it, did not change any of the foundations of capitalism, but it changed the whole pattern of politics, as well as the whole framework of thought—hence, it changed completely the whole "superstructure" of modern capitalism. Marxists had to learn again how to think and investigate according to the Marxian conception of history.[45] Fascism had come to power as a consequence of the great crisis, but not everywhere, only in some countries—and only because of very specific conditions, conditions that did not exist all over the capitalist world. Hence, the future dynamic of capitalism, the future course of the great crisis would depend upon the interactions between different capitalist powers—dictatorial capitalism and democratic capitalism.

In his first article published in 1936, taking stock and assessing the developments of the previous year, he interpreted the economic events of the year 1935 as a "turning point" in the history of modern capitalism. In

---

[43] This draft text in two parts, written between July and December 1933, has never been published (see Hilferding 1934a). That Hilferding was as opposed to Bolshevism, Leninism and the politics of the Soviet Union as Karl Kautsky from the very beginnings has never been a secret. His private correspondence with Karl Kautsky provides ample evidence for his deep scepticism regarding the prospects of the Russian revolution and the Soviet Union. He never ever shared the optimism of his close friend Otto Bauer with respect to the possibilities of a democratic development in the Soviet Union.

[44] Hilferding 1934b, 145–146.

[45] Hilferding 1934b, 146–147,

1935, the great crisis that started in the fall of 1929 had virtually come to an end. Most capitalist countries, including most colonial countries, had managed to overcome the worst consequences of the crisis and depression. Hilferding pointed to several indicators of a recovery which was already on its way in most capitalist countries. In his view, the recovery was due to a much larger scale and scope of state interventions into the capitalist economies than before the onset of the great crisis. But in some countries, the countries which Hilferding started to deem and to call "countries under dictatorship", large rearmament programmes, the enhanced production of arms, an expansion of the arms industry had become the principal driving factor of an illusory recovery, together with investments in the military infrastructure which triggered a boom in the construction industry. Nazi Germany had led the way into an armaments boom, and some European countries had followed its example, although reluctantly. Hilferding saw them all on the road towards a prolonged arms race. Nazi Germany did enjoy a head start, the democratic capitalist countries following and the biggest industrial power, the USA under Roosevelt, lagging behind.[46]

In the same year, he contributed an article on the "World Economic Crisis", in English, published under his usual pseudonym "Richard Kern" and covering the whole front page of the journal *The New Leader*. In four paragraphs, he recapped the major events and developments during the years of crisis, from the beginning—the initial financial market crash in the fall of 1929, via the collapse of international trade and the international monetary order, following the global credit crunch and banking crisis in 1931, until the belated recovery which he analysed in "Crises and Cycles During the Years of the Long Prosperity" section, and, finally, in the last section on the misery of the dictatorial countries, where he sketched the economic outlook for Nazi Germany and other countries under fascist or authoritarian rule.[47] This was one of the most remarkable contributions to the ongoing debate about this crisis which had occupied the most brilliant minds of the economics profession since 1929. A debate that not only concerned mainstream economists and politicians but did also keep the ranks and files of heterodox economists, including the Marxists, on their

---

[46] Cf. Hilferding 1936a.
[47] Hilferding 1936b.

toes.[48] In the first section of his article on the nature of this crisis, the greatest crisis that world capitalism had experienced so far, he announced the end of the crisis: the "most severe crisis in the history of capitalism" had "come to a standstill, marked by clear signs of recovery". Most economists, including the Marxists, had thoroughly misinterpreted the nature of this crisis, regarding it either as another typical, though more and more widespread cyclical crisis of capitalism, or completely misreading it as a permanent crisis, the last crisis of capitalism entering its final phase. Both were wrong, because they both failed to grasp the specific nature of the epoch which begun with the World War. The war had determined the economic character of the post-war period, leading to state interventions into the capitalist economy of an unprecedented scale and scope.

Hence, the great crisis of 1929 to 1935 had to be understood as a "liquidation crisis" of the war. The most striking characteristics of this crisis could not possibly be understood without taking into consideration the war and its long-lasting effects. As far as the financial aspects of the crisis were concerned, for instance, they were thoroughly influenced by the problem of international reparation payments—a problem which had wrecked the German economy in its relations with other major capitalist economies ever since the Treaty of Versailles and still played a major role in the series of credit crunches and banking crises occurring in 1931 and 1932. That is why Hilferding insisted that it was not a "normal" or "typical" cyclical crisis, but a very special one.

The severity of the crisis was due to the fact that several crises came together since the stock market crash in October 1929: a worldwide agrarian crisis, a crisis of the extractive industries and a crisis of industrial overproduction. A general overproduction in all the important agricultural products was the inevitable result of the vast extension and modernization of agriculture in the non-belligerent countries and in Europe after the war. Sustained efforts by national governments to achieve independence of food supply had exacerbated the overproduction in agriculture. A further,

---

[48] In the same year, Otto Bauer published his seminal book *Between two World Wars?* Its first chapter was devoted to the analysis of the world economic crisis, its origins, its courses and its consequences (see Bauer [1936] 1976). This chapter is based upon Bauer's still unpublished major study on the Great Depression of the 1930s (cf. Krätke 2008). There are quite a lot of similarities between Hilferding's and Bauer's views of the crisis, suggesting that at least Bauer had read some of Hilferding's articles on the crisis. The evidence from the correspondence clearly shows that Hilferding had carefully studied Otto Bauer's book on rationalization, published in 1931.

although unintended result was the dislocation of the old division of labour between the agricultural and industrial countries in the capitalist world, leading to ever more overproduction in most sectors. The war had added enormous disproportions between the key sectors of the economy, boosting arms industries that nobody needed any more after the war ended. Moreover, the war had led to a grave disorganization of the currency and credit mechanisms in the world economy, a disorganization which continued after the war. The destructiveness and intensity of the crisis had been increased by the combination of currency crises, collapse of international credit relations, crippling of the international exchange relations and the consequent impediments to international trade. False state interventions and the rise of nationalist governments in many capitalist countries had aggravated the crisis, which lasted much longer than anybody had expected.

Nonetheless, in 1935, a recovery was on its way in the major capitalist countries. Its signs were strongest in Britain, the Empire and the countries of the Sterling bloc. England took the lead, because in 1931, at the height of the crisis, it abandoned the gold standard and made the transition from free trade to protectionism within its vast Empire. Keeping foreign competitors away allowed for a marked revival of the British and American industries—a revival that went together with a vivid increase of industrial employment, rising wages and an even more marked increase in mass consumption. The recovery in Britain and America led to a recovery in the agricultural and raw material producing countries, with only the countries of the gold-bloc, France, Holland and Switzerland, lagging behind.

For Hilferding, the most remarkable fact about this recovery was the continuing misery in the dictatorial countries, Germany, Italy and Russia. The German dictatorship had created a "purely war economy", at the expense of the consumption industries and the standard of living of the masses. Because such a war economy was not sustainable and could only be financed by measures that would foster another wave of inflation, Hilferding saw the German and the Italian economies heading towards another great crisis, while the rest of the capitalist world was beginning to emerge from the great depression. The disparities between the great capitalist powers were increasing, and as the threat of war was still hanging above the capitalist world, even the countries seeing the first signs of recovery and a new prosperity could not afford to abstain from spending more and more of their wealth for arms and preparations for war.[49]

In this article, based upon the economic data from many capitalist countries which he had studied carefully in the previous years, we find all the core elements of Hilferding's specific view on the great depression and other events in the capitalist world: as in other pieces of the time, despite their journalistic character and framework, he stressed the crucial importance of a longer view, taking into account the long-lasting impact of the great war, emphasizing the lasting effect of state interventions on an unprecedented scale which had become a permanent feature of the capitalist economies in the post-war years. Hilferding did pinpoint the weaknesses ensuing from the uneven developments in different sectors of the capitalist economy, both on the national and on the global level. He had a clear view of the fabric and the dynamics of the world market and a capitalist world economy, comprising several centres, some core regions and several regions on the periphery. He saw the international division of labour which linked highly industrialized capitalist economies to poorly industrialized countries and regions, depending upon the production and export of raw materials. Last but not least, he saw the importance of political actions, including mistakes and errors due to ideological obsessions rampant among politicians and the business elites as well. After 1933, he was changing his previous views about "organized capitalism" in several directions: state interventions had come to stay, but they could operate in different ways and with different outcomes. It was possible to influence and even change the course of slumps and depression, to change the kind and direction of accumulation and economic growth in a country by concerted and sustained state actions. It was no longer likely that the ever-increasing grasp of the state upon the capitalist economy would enhance the socialist possibilities in the future. In the dictatorial states, like Nazi Germany, Fascist Italy and the Japanese Empire, the ever-stronger states had been proven able to overrule any of the established rules that had so far been accepted in the capitalist world. Nationalism and imperialism had won broad support, and large majorities of the people in those countries had adapted to life in a war economy. But the capitalist democracies were not doomed to failure; they also could take decisive actions and were able to overcome the great depression by unconventional means, restoring industrial strength and restructuring capitalist economies on a national base.

[49] Cf. Hilferding 1936b.

418 M. R. KRÄTKE

Hence, speaking in Marxist terms, the whole problematic of cycles, of crises, and of crisis policy had to be reconsidered in the light of the experience that the second great depression in the history of capitalism had provided. Hilferding was one of the few Marxists able and willing to learn the lessons.

In his article reviewing the economic events of the year 1936, Hilferding continued his analysis of the recovery in the democratic capitalist countries. In these countries, as in the dictatorial ones, an increase of armament expenditure and armament production had taken place. But, contrary to the dictatorial countries, the military build-up had not been the decisive driving force of the recovery. In Britain, the recovery had started in the housing sector, and was fostered by a rise in exports, due to protective measures taken and due to the formation of a sterling bloc, comprising several European countries in addition to the Empire. In the USA, the recovery was due to the measures taken by the Roosevelt government. For the capitalist world economy, the arms economy was not decisive. Most important, even crucial for the recovery on a global scale had been the overcoming of the agrarian crisis. Only twice in the history of capitalism, an agrarian crisis and an industrial crisis had coincided. This time, the agrarian crisis had been overcome because of measures taken by the agrarian export countries, the USA, Canada and Argentina, but first and foremost because of a series of bad harvests in the European countries which allowed for the rapid absorption of agricultural overproductions. Second, there was a recovery and even a slight boom in the production of industrial raw materials. And third, the international currency problems had been settled, due to devaluations and thanks to an international currency agreement concluded by the major capitalist countries, France, England, the USA and others. A strong recovery of the core industries had led to a resurgence of world trade, which had, in turn, reinvigorated international credit relations. In stark contrast to the dictatorial countries like Germany, the economic recovery in the democratic countries had reached all sectors and branches of the economy, including the consumption industries. Hence, the big divide between the war economy of the dictatorial countries and the economies of the countries of democratic capitalism has been deepened—as had the political tensions between both camps.[50]

The course of economic developments in the year 1937 was one of the strangest phenomena in the economic history of modern capitalism, as

[50] Hilferding 1937a, e.

Hilferding said in his review article, published in January 1938. The boom continued in most of the industrial countries, and other countries, in particular the countries producing raw materials for export, joined in. Slowly, the restoration of a true world economy was gaining momentum. A world economy, in which the dictatorial countries were participating less, and losing ground because of their sustained pursuit of autarchy. Late, but forceful, came the rise of the industrial boom in the USA, the largest industrial producer in the capitalist world. However, in the last months of the year, the USA saw a stock market crash and an industrial crisis, spreading out all over the country. This time, the crisis in the USA did hardly impair the continuing boom in the industrial countries in Europe. The simultaneity of the economic developments in the major capitalist countries had come to an end. And that was due to the differences of the economic policies applied by the governments in the different countries. In England, the governments[51] restricted their interventions to a minimum. In the USA, however, the governments[52] were driven to take more and more severe actions, so that the American business cycle became much more dependent on the state than in England. Big business in the USA became wary of the changing course of Roosevelt's economic policies, and eventually went on a "capital strike". As a result, the US industry was suffering from a state of "underinvestment" instead of overaccumulation. But this time Hilferding was convinced that the crisis in the USA could be rapidly overcome by a variety of measures encouraging the banks and industrial corporations to engage in investments on a large scale again.[53] In the end, Hilferding had become a supporter of Roosevelt's New Deal policy.

In his next review, however, published in January 1939, he signalled the coming of a new crisis that might bring the boom in the capitalist world to an end. This time, he described a proper political crisis, triggered by the actions of the Mussolini regime in Italy which tried to resolve its colonial quarrels with France in Tunisia and started to invade Ethiopia (then called Abyssinia) again, in order to recover or rebuild something of the long lost Roman Empire in the Mediterranean region.[54] As Hilferding

---

[51] That is, the minority Labour government and the following "national government" (cf. Hilferding 1938b, c).

[52] Already the Hoover administration and the following Roosevelt administration had launched vast support programs for several sectors of the US-economy.

[53] Cf. Hilferding 1938a, d, e, f.

[54] Cf. Hilferding 1939a.

reminded his readers, the civil war in Spain had already pitted the forces against each other which were going to fight each other in the coming European conflict. From now on, the course of economic development would be determined by the hazards of the great war which was to come in due time.

HILFERDING'S CRITIQUE OF THE NAZI ECONOMY

In one of his letters written to Kautsky after he had left Germany, he showed some mixed feelings about the prospects of Nazi Germany. He admitted having misjudged the prospects of the new regime, instead of being a matter of months before it would crumble under the weight of its inner contradictions, the "affair could last for a long time". However, the Nazis had not done anything particular in terms of financial policy and they would "act rather cautiously" after all. Alluding to the old Roman recipe of "panem et circenses", he reckoned that their circus games had so far not been excessively costly and that they were not likely either to offer much bread to the German masses.[55] In the following months and years, he changed his views on the prospects of the regime only slightly. The new Nazi state lasted for longer than anyone on the Left had presumed—but the new Nazi economy was headed towards big troubles. Eventually, the economic and financial policies pursued by the regime would lead to misery and disaster for the German people.[56]

From the very beginning of the Nazi rule, it was quite clear that rebuilding the country's military infrastructure, rearmament and enhancing the ranks of its armed forces were the biggest priority. Everything was subordinated to the goal of regaining sovereignty in military terms, shaking off the fetters that the Treaty of Versailles had imposed upon Germany's military. Already in his first articles written for the *Neuer Vorwärts*, Hilferding predicted that the economic and financial policies of the Nazi regime would lead to a complete bankruptcy of the German state on all levels, from the federal state to the municipalities. The Nazis had eliminated the most important right of the German parliament, its budgetary right, and were handling the state's finances without any form of public

[55] Hilferding 1933b.
[56] For a recent account of the economic history of Germany from 1933 until 1945, see Tooze 2006.

control—which could only lead to shattered finances in due course.[57] Hitler's regime supported the rich and the big corporations; it was dramatically losing ground in terms of exports and could not compensate such losses by means of subsidizing certain branches of the German industry, for instance the car industry.[58] What was more, the Nazi government started to privatize the industrial plants and banks that had *de facto* been nationalized in the first phase of the crisis, when the German state had to come to their rescue and paid for their debts. For Hilferding, this policy not only deprived the German state of a potential lever of control over the economy but did also expose the hollowness of middle-class "anti-capitalism".[59]

Germany's public finances were driven into chaos because rearmament, the core project of the regime, would cost gigantic sums that the country simply could not afford. Deeply concerned about the dire straits the German finances that were due to the amateurism of the Nazi government, Hilferding focused his attention on the financial manoeuvres staged by the Reichsbank and his old enemy Hjalmar Schacht who had been reappointed as director of the German Reichsbank in March 1933.[60] Schacht did not hesitate to turn the German Reichsbank into a money machine on behalf of the Nazi government, using all kinds of financial machinations, creating new instruments of short-term debts and increasing the volume of Germany's floating or unfunded debts beyond all limits and never minding any form of debt consolidation.[61] In Hilferding's view, this meant walking straight into financial chaos and inflation.

Accordingly, he continued to discuss the salient question "who will pay for the rearmament" in many of his articles in the *Neuer Vorwärts*. Germany's inner debt kept rising, as well as the volume of its foreign debts. Heaping deficit upon deficit, and turning Germany's financial

---

[57] Cf. Hilferding 1933e, 1933f.

[58] Cf. Hilferding 1933g.

[59] Cf. Hilferding 1933h, 1933m.

[60] Schacht, acting as director of the Reichsbank from 1923 to 1930, was completely ruthless and had used the Reichsbank as an instrument of his personal ambitions and his anti-socialist crusades. In particular, he obstructed the policies of Rudolf Hilferding, the Marxist that had become minister of finance. In the fall of 1929, at the very beginning of the great crisis, he went as far as obstructing and actually ruining a loan that Hilferding had been negotiating with foreign creditors for the German government. This act of sabotage eventually forced Hilferding to resign as minister of finance in December 1929.

[61] Cf. Hilferding 1933k.

policy into a hazardous gamble, the financial policy of the dictatorship had already run into a blind alley. Regarding the state of the capital markets in Germany, financing the towering deficits by long-term loans was hardly possible. Hence, the regime had to stop its ambitious plans and face the truth that even dictators would not be able to avoid paying for the cost of their actions for ever.[62] Starting an all-out economic war with the creditor countries, the Nazi government had suspended all payments for interest and redemption rates on Germany's foreign debts, short-term and long-term alike, including the payments for reparations. It had prepared this by fending off imports and subsidizing exports but was unable to avoid trade balance deficits. Due to this policy of default, the market value of German government bonds dropped dramatically, allowing German banks to buy them for a pittance. Hilferding saw this as a manoeuvre to force the creditor countries to pay for the Nazi rearmament policy.[63] So far, Hitler had forced the German people, the working class as well as the large majority of the middle classes, to pay for his rearmament programmes. Without a continuous inflow of foreign exchange, in particular US dollars, the rearmament programmes would stall because of the lack of raw materials which could only be imported. The Reichsbank had been losing its foreign exchange and gold reserves rapidly, paying for the growing imports of raw materials and other goods that Hitler needed for the building of his war machine. The "economic miracle" the Nazis boasted of was built upon a swamp of improvisations, hazardous manoeuvres and illusions. The monetary and financial disorder grew by the day. In spite of the much-trumpeted four-year-plans, there was no plan, and the financial chaos was undermining the currency and leading towards increasing inflation.[64] Even Schacht's dictatorship over the monetary and financial policy could not open up a way out of the deepening crisis of the Germany economy. Shifting the increasing burden of the rearmament policy to foreigners or to the future would not work for long.[65] Everything was sacrificed for the sake of the new war machine in the making.[66] As the rearmament gained momentum, the basic economic rule by which the German war economy

[62] Cf. Hilferding 1934e.

[63] Cf. Hilferding 1934k.

[64] Cf. Hilferding 1934g, h, i, j, l, m. Cf. Ritschl 2000, 2002, and Tooze 2006.

[65] Cf. Hilferding 1934n. In addition to his job as director of the Reichsbank, Schacht had also taken office as Minister of Economic Affairs, making him the all-powerful man in Germany's economic and financial policies.

[66] Hilferding 1934o.

17 RUDOLF HILFERDING: A BORN JOURNALIST   423

was run became ever clearer: absolute priority for the development of the means of production industries, at the detriment of the consumer industries. Hilferding demonstrated this in detail with regard to the production of textiles, furniture, shoes and other consumer goods. An increasing part of Germany's labour force was being shifted towards the arms industries while the nominal as well as the real wages sank ever lower.[67] Germany's arms expenditure was much larger than that of any other great country, and Germany's economy had been transformed into a war economy, subject to its laws. Which meant in the German case: more and more employment in the heavy industries, relocation of capital towards the heavy industries and the arms industries, increasing disproportionalities between the industries, lowering of the standards of living, shrinking volumes of foreign trade and financing balance of trade and balance of payments deficits by risky manipulations in order to shift a part of the cost of the German rearmament upon foreigners.[68]

War and armament had played an important role in the history of capitalism. A war economy had some peculiar features which made it unsustainable. Because in the production of arms, labour, material, means of production were used—but what the arms industries produced could neither be used for production nor for consumption. It had use value only in war, resulting in utter destruction of wealth, with no other result than ashes, debris, ruins and human corpses. Hence, selling arms could be profitable for some industrial capitals, but never for a capitalist economy as a whole. Unless a country exported the products of its arms industry, it could only lose from the macroeconomic point of view. The Nazis did not want to export arms but to use them in war. Going to war and using the war machine to acquire and accumulate wealth by dispossessing other capitalist countries by force was the only way to make a profit from it.[69]

As the construction of the German war machine made progress, the inner contradictions of its war economy became more visible. In particular, the growth of the arms industries left all the other industries behind, the increasing import of raw materials reduced the import of foodstuff and other consumer goods, the hazardous financing of arms expenditures by means of an ever-growing mass of uncovered bills of exchange, with the word of the Hitler government as its one and only guarantee—that kind

---

[67] Hilferding, 1935d.
[68] Cf. Hilferding 1935f.
[69] Cf. Hilferding 1935e.

424   M. R. KRÄTKE

of economic policy could not be continued for ever.[70] In the middle of the breeding chaos of an economy driving on unfunded debts, fraudulent manoeuvres in foreign trade, currency manipulations and theft, there was only one thing becoming ever clearer: the war economy the Nazis had created was actually heading for war and the aims of Hitler's war were largely determined by the necessities of maintaining and expanding his war machine, which the German economy could not afford.[71] Germany had the "largest military budget of the world", at the cost of internal and foreign debts of unprecedented heights. For the Nazi regime, rearmament, and the resurrection of German militarism, was a question of life and death. Hence, it would further push rearmament forward, whatever the cost. Because it was able to subdue any resistance by brute force and it managed to deceive and bully its foreign creditors again and again.[72]

The Nazi economy was built upon institutional bases already existing in the times of the Weimar republic or even earlier. Like, for instance, the "independence" of the Reichsbank which made it a perfect instrument to pursue ruthless monetary and financial policies, once it fell into the wrong hands. Or, as Hilferding observed, the organizational structures, the many business associations and networks—one of the main characteristics of "organized" capitalism, German style. Those associations had emerged and established themselves long before the war and had continued to thrive in the Weimar republic. In Germany, not only capital but also labour, peasants and landowners, artisans, shopkeepers and the middle classes in general were used to operate via a variety of associations and had created a veritable hierarchical structure within each branch or field of associations. The Nazi government could easily use this extant structure, occupy the top layers and use them for running the German central bank, manipulate the currency and steering the German economy in the direction it wanted. With the same ease, they used the already existing cartel structure of the German industry and expanded it, creating new cartels and driving the cartelization of more and more industries forward by force.[73] Accordingly, the Nazi regime had strengthened the organization

---

[70] Cf. Hilferding 1935h, i, j, k, m.

[71] Cf. Hilferding 1935l.

[72] Hilferding 1935f, 1936d.

[73] The takeover of existent business and branch organizations and the creation of new ones, incorporating the older ones, by the Nazi regime became a core point in Franz Neumann's analysis of the Nazi economy. His book on the new type of state the Nazis created in Germany was first published after Hilferding's death, in 1942 (see Neumann 2009). But it

of the German economy, creating easy inroads for state control and intervention. While, on the other hand, the economic and financial policies enacted by the regime were continually weakening and undermining the very bases of the industrial and agrarian economy, cutting them off from the world markets, destroying its credit and undermining its currency, the *Reichsmark*.

There were alternatives—in the countries of democratic capitalism. With sympathy, Hilferding observed the politics of the New Deal in the USA. Roosevelt had come to power, supported by a wave of popular anti-capitalist movements emerging under the impact of the great crisis in all quarters of the American society, among farmers, among the middle classes and among the working class. Because of this broad support, the new president could launch a great experiment of reorganizing and restructuring US capitalism, of rehabilitating banks, of introducing first elements of social security schemes, of enhancing wages and reforming labour relations. However, Hilferding saw the danger of inflation lurking around the corner. He did not trust the mobilization of credit as financial base for such an experiment.[74] Roosevelt met a lot of resistance from the US banks and parts of the US industry. But his daring programmes were hailed by a clear majority in the US congress. Hilferding grasped the opportunity to remind his readers of the truism that the leading capitalist groups are not at all able to impose their "dictatorship" in a democratic state, and that "anti-capitalist" groups and layers of society were able to rule over the capitalist economy. However, such groups could lose control again, not because of the failure of political institutions but because their economic policies failed. It was possible to take the reins and to impose an alternative credit policy upon the banks. But a policy of state subsidies and government orders geared to big public works depended upon sound financial policies. Raising enormous amounts of money for public spending by means of loans, creating a huge deficit in the federal budget, was risky and could become impossible under the conditions of inflation, when investors would shy away from government bonds. If inflation got out of control, it could well ruin Roosevelt's great experiment.[75]

---

was Hilferding who had first observed how the Nazi regime was using and incorporating the economic organizations that had flourished in Germany long before World War I (cf. Hilferding 1933l).

[74] Cf. Hilferding 1933j.
[75] Cf. Hilferding 1934e, g.

426 M. R. KRÄTKE

A Critique of International Politics

During his stints as minister of finance in 1923 and in 1927/1928, and during his long years as a member of parliament and an advisor to the social democratic party, to its membership as well as to the party leaders, Hilferding had acquired a profound knowledge of the art of foreign and international politics, as he had attended international conferences and participated in negotiations with foreign powers, in particular with the representatives of Germany's major creditor countries France, England and the USA. He had worked with Stresemann, he became close to Heinrich Brüning, the chief of one of the last governments of the Weimar Republic without participants from the extreme right. Never had the world economy been so closely intertwined with world politics than in the years of the Great Depression and the fragile recovery in some parts of the capitalist world just before the eventual outbreak of World War II. During his long years in exile, Hilferding had to deal with the aggressive foreign policies of Nazi Germany and therefore also with the foreign and international policies of its actual and potential opponents or allies. Accordingly, he did publish articles in which he analysed and criticized the foreign policies of France, of England, of the USA, even of Japan and of the Soviet Union. He had been directly involved in the negotiations for the Young plan in 1929 and had participated in the achievement of other international treaties, so he knew the scene of foreign and international politics well.

When fascism came to power in Italy and Germany, the whole fabric and the very basics of international politics were at peril. Diplomacy was still in use but haunted by the growing tensions between those countries embracing a variety of pacificism after the experience of World War I, and the clearly belligerent countries like Italy, Germany and Japan who wanted to tear up the post-war international order. The League of Nations had lost much of its influence because of the defiant stance and the non-cooperation of many countries. Japan and Germany had left it in 1933, the USA remained outside of it. The Soviet Union joined in 1934 but was expelled because of its attack on Finland in 1939. International law was losing ground because of the ruthless actions of some countries that just ignored it. Hence, the fragile fabric of multilateral agreements, which had stabilized the post-war world economy several times, was in great danger.

In the year 1935, European foreign politics had arrived at a turning point: in 1933, after Hitler came to power, it had still been possible to prevent Germany's rearmament without risk. Two years later, this chance was gone—due to the mistakes made by England and France who gave the Nazi regime time and latitude to pursue the reconstruction of the German army. Caught in the illusion that the Nazi regime could be bound by international contracts, they completely missed the radical change of the very game of international politics that the resurrection of Germany's military might had accomplished. As soon as there are states that deem superior military power, and finally war, as a completely legitimate means of politics and are prepared to go to war by virtue of their form of government, international politics has changed. International treaties, negotiations or agreements no longer can preserve peace, but only the balance of military power. Not equality of rights but the inequality of military power is what determines the course of international politics.[76] The only counter-strategy to Germany's rearmament was the building of alliances among the war-adverse states. A turn which entailed the end of any policy of disarmament and arbitration of conflicts, hence a return to the international politics of the great powers that had led to the catastrophe of World War I. The prospects for reintegrating Nazi Germany into the international order, as it had existed before, were rather dim. England had to keep the peace and avoid confrontations at nearly all costs because it wanted to preserve its Empire and had to reckon not only with Germany but also with the power of Japan and of Russia in the Far East as well.[77] As England retreated again and again in the face of military threats and aggressions (like the aggression of Japan against China), the international peace order had already lost its backbone—and the peace-keeping system in Europe had actually collapsed. Hilferding blamed England, and the Labour Party in particular. Paradoxically enough, British and US foreign policies were not imperialist any more or not imperialist enough, despite the clear threats to the interests of their ruling classes.[78]

Only once, in two articles published in the *Neuer Vorwärts* in November 1936, Hilferding expounded to his readers how and why the very bases of international politics had changed in recent decades. Before the war, the foreign policies of different capitalist countries were still simple to understand. They were determined by the imperialist interests of the dominant fraction of their respective ruling classes. But already before the war, things

---

[76] Hilferding 1935a, 562.
[77] Cf. Hilferding 1935b, 596–601.
[78] Cf. Hilferding 1935c, 627–631.

changed because the politics of imperialism required a strong and well-organized state. More and more, international capitalist competition transformed into a contest between power states. The new power states became more and more independent of society, including the ruling class, and, by the same token, became an omnipresent and omnipotent actor in the economies of these leading imperialist countries. In the post-war dictatorial states, the independence of state power is enhanced again. The influence and power of social classes did not vanish, but besides them a tremendous new power has won its independence, a power to be reckoned with, strong enough to go against even the most powerful class interests. In dictatorial states military power reigns supreme, the economic interests of the country or even of the ruling social classes are subordinated to the interest of the state. What a dictatorial, revisionist and imperialist state like Nazi Germany wants is to enhance its military power and to attain superiority of military might over all actual or potential rivals. Hence, a discrepancy between the economic potential and the military needs arises—and it is bridged only by ever-more risky operations, by inflation, by corruption and by direct interventions into the fabric of the capitalist economy on all levels. In the post-war era, the politics of classical imperialism, as Hilferding saw them, had come to their end: because the urge to export capital had diminished drastically; because the imperialist fractions of the old bourgeoisie had lost their supremacy and because imperialism had met increasing resistance and rebellion in the colonized countries. The new dictatorial states only needed highly developed, already industrialized countries or regions to satisfy their ever-growing appetite for raw materials and energy. Hence, the next clash between the great capitalist powers will be a struggle for the redivision of the world on an unprecedented scale.[79] The foreign policy of the dictatorial states was much more similar to the colonial policies of the early capitalist states in the sixteenth and seventeenth century, when a form of "predatory capitalism" prevailed. It should be regarded as "a new form of primitive accumulation" hinged upon the appropriation of wealth by means of brute force. Only, the new predatory states would consider the wealth of the advanced capitalist countries under democratic government as a tasty prey as well and not hesitate to reach for it.[80]

[79] Cf. Hilferding 1936i, j.
[80] Hilferding 1936i.

British foreign politics continued to avoid confrontations, to sit problems out and to appease the dictators like Hitler, Mussolini and Franco. Hilferding analysed the new dynamics in world politics that ensued from the decline of the League of Nations, the formation of new alliances and "ententes" in Europe and beyond, and the reluctance of the US government to engage in world politics using its full weight. He attacked the failure of British and French foreign politics again and again, judging Chamberlain's efforts to appease Hitler and the Nazi regime as completely misguided.[81] Hilferding never allowed himself to be fooled by the official propaganda. Relentlessly, he exposed the course of Soviet foreign policy. The Stalin regime did just profit from the politics of retreat and non-intervention pursued by Britain and France. Its goal was to drive the rival powers in Europe towards war and stay out of it. The Hitler-Stalin pact of 1939 served exactly that purpose and encouraged the Nazi regime to switch to open warfare. In his view, Stalin's regime was as responsible for the coming war as was Hitler's. But the alliance between the two dictatorial states had finally cleared the fronts between the opposing forces.[82]

The War Is Coming

When Otto Bauer published his seminal book *Zwischen zwei Weltkriegen?* (Between two World Wars?) in 1936, he, like many other socialists in Europe, still harboured hopes that somehow the outbreak of another great war in Europe could be prevented. For Hilferding, it was already clear that the next great war in Europe was inevitable. For more than three years, he had observed, investigated and analysed the build-up of a veritable war economy in Nazi Germany. He had watched and criticized the failures of the democratic states in meeting the challenges coming from the dictatorial states.

Although the Nazi regime had systematically lied to the German people and disguised or rather hushed up the real costs of their rearmament policies, the lack of raw materials and the food shortage were obvious. As Germany had no successful export strategy, the only way to support and to feed an ever-growing war machine was to wage war. War in order to conquer lands in Eastern Europe, first and foremost the Ukraine as future breadbasket of the German Empire or to conquer colonies in other parts

[81] Cf. Hilferding 1936j, 1937b, 1938g.
[82] Cf. Hilferding 1936k, l, 1938g, h, 1939d, e.

of the world. Each of its war aims pitted Nazi Germany against the big colonial powers to the West and to the East. Hence, a world war would follow.[83] When Hitler started to re-militarize the Rhineland in 1936, Hilferding saw the consequences clearly: more and accelerated rearmament, more investment in the war economy, more foreign debts that could never be repaid—except by going to war and plunder the creditor countries.[84] The four-year plan launched by the Nazi government in 1936 was a "plan for war", according to Hilferding. The plan did not offer any solution for the big problems the German economy was grappling with, only aggravated them. It showed, however, that the government was actually preparing for war as the only way out of the trap of a permanent and rapidly growing war economy. A war economy without war could not last.[85]

Few were aware of it, but World War II had already started in 1936—with the invasion of Ethiopia by Italy, with the fascist revolt against the republican government in Spain. It continued with the Japanese invasion of China in 1937. In the summer of 1939, Europe was on the brink of war. In one of his first articles after the invasion of Poland began, in September 1939, Hilferding sketched the economic situation of Germany at the beginning of the war. Germany had no reserves, in fact it had vastly overspent in recent years, investing more than 90 billion Reichsmark in its war industry. As the war began, it was losing millions of able men enrolled in the army, thus reducing the overall productivity in the German industry. War meant that the wear and tear of machinery and industrial plants would increase, while maintenance would become worse and more costly. More and more workers and more and more productive capital would be shifted to the war industry—at the expense of consumer industries and the living standards of the people. As the Nazi regime had cut off the German industry from the world markets, the only way to overcome the enormous lack of raw materials and foodstuff would be to wage a war of plunder, and to conquer the Europe in order to lay hands on the resources the German war industry did not yet have at its disposal.[86] This war was different. It had been inevitable because of the weakness of the international order and because of the many mistakes made in foreign policy since 1933. But it

[83] Cf. Hilferding 1935g.
[84] Cf. Hilferding 1936g.
[85] Cf. Hilferding 1936h, 1937c.
[86] Cf. Hilferding 1939e.

could not be explained by a clash of capitalist interests. Neither the French, or the British, nor the German capitalist class had wanted it. This war was the work of a regime, a state power that emancipated itself from any class power and class will and subdued all powers of economy and society to its will. It had created its own ideological universe, using the specific form and content of German nationalism for its ends. It is a war against the "West", against the very core of modern civil society. Since Stalinist Russia has allied itself with Nazi Germany, it was a war of totalitarian dictatorship against every form of democracy and liberty.[87]

Hilferding did witness the first period of the war, the war in Poland, the war in Scandinavia, the war in Finland and the war in France. Without speculating about the outcome of the war, he noted a new phenomenon: the unification of Britain with its Empire and the French colonial empire into one economic bloc, together with an incomplete customs union, a currency union and joint production for the needs of a war fought together. Hilferding, who had inserted the "United States of Europe" as a long-term goal into the Heidelberg programme of the SPD in 1925, saw this economic bloc as a hint towards the future shape of a European economic order that might be established after the war.[88]

The course of the war proved him right. Nazi Germany, in pursuit of scarce resources, was forced to enlarge the theatre of war ever further. Stalinist Russia launched another war in order to subjugate neighbouring lands—and failed. Again, Hilferding had got it right: the cost of the war was rapidly rising, and the spoils of war and conquest were not enough to pay for it. The Nazi war machine was turning its military aggression against more countries and creating more opponents. In his last article for the *Neuer Vorwärts*, published just when the German attack on the Netherlands had begun, he assessed the war efforts so far: Hitler had suffered the first setbacks in Scandinavia, but the Nazi regime had continued to expand the theatre of war ever further, now looking towards the Balkans and Africa. The future imperial overstretching of the German military reach—from Narvik to Alexandria—was already visible.[89]

[87] Hilferding 1939b, f.
[88] Hilferding 1940d.
[89] Hilferding 1940e. See also Hilferding 1939g, 1940a, b, c.

After World War II: The Future Shape of Europe and the World

On January 29, 1940, Hilferding gave a speech to the members of the Sopade in Paris. The paper he wrote was never published, and is probably lost, but a transcript of his speech has been preserved in the Sopade papers.[90] This was probably the last time that Hilferding met with the members of the executive committee. His speech was the last contribution he made to the enormous task of rebuilding and reorientating the German labour movement. Undaunted, he dared to address the most urgent question—the aims of the war—as well as the questions of the future: the future of democracy in Europa and the world, and the shape of Europe after the defeat of fascism in all its guises.

In Hilferding's view, the fundamental aim of the war was clear: to achieve victory for the allied forces of the democratic countries at all costs, especially after the Soviet Union had joined forces with Nazi Germany. If Hitler and Stalin would win, the "entire basis of the cultural development for which we have worked will no longer exist. We will then have to reckon with a setback of centuries".[91] Regarding the future of Europe and the future shape of the international order after the defeat of Nazi Germany and its allies, Hilferding warned of utopias and speculative ideas. Only democratic institutions were able to restore and maintain the "cultural and spiritual unit" of Europe. But the democratic reorganization of Europe could only take place within the framework of existing power relations. Hence, it was unlikely that Europe could easily be transformed into a federal state—the United States of Europe that the Heidelberg programme of the SPD had propagated in 1925. Such a federal state would lack the necessary centralization of political power. The great powers, like France and Britain, were not likely to give up any of their political or military might and smoothly integrate into a European federal state. Russia, of course, would remain outside any such reconstructed form of European democracy. Economic cooperation, however, would be at the centre of a post-war democratic order, based upon free trade. But in order to build such an economic order in Europe, even in the modest form of a customs union, it would be necessary to deal with the consequences of protectionism and to address the issue of raw materials and natural resources, one of

---

[90] Cf. Hilferding 1940f.
[91] Hilferding 1940f, 1.

the weaknesses of the European economy. Hilferding imagined a transformation process towards a new cooperative economic order in Europe that would take many years to accomplish.

Regarding the future world order, Hilferding pleaded for a new League of Nations, one that should free itself of the illusions and utopias that held sway during the years after World War I. A renewed League of Nations would have to incorporate Great Britain and its Empire, and, in particular, the USA. To make the new League of Nations and a Federated democratic Europe effective, the member states would have to surrender or rather transfer at least parts of their sovereignty to a transnational body. Such a new international order would not provide an "absolute guarantee of peace". Hence, total disarmament would not be feasible, and the Left would have to rethink its traditional stance towards "militarism". Peacekeeping by the use of armed force would not disappear from the post-war world, so it would be crucial to reorganize the state's monopoly of the legitimate use of force.[92] In this speech, summarizing many of the ideas he had already presaged in some of his articles for the *Neuer Vorwärts*, Hilferding did anticipate a lot of what became a staple of social democratic thought after the war. They might not have been aware of it, but leading figures like Willy Brandt marched in the footsteps of the Austrian Marxist who had been the intellectual leader of the Weimar SPD.[93]

REFERENCES

Barclay, D. 1998. Rethinking Social Democracy, the State, and Europe. In *Between Reform and Revolution: German Socialism and Communism between 1840 and 1990*, ed. D. Barclay and E. Weitz. New York and Toronto: Berghahn Books.

Bauer, O. 1976 [1936]. Zwischen zwei Weltkriegen? In *Otto Bauer Werkausgabe*, vol. 4. Wien: Europa Verlag.

Gottschalch, W. 1962. *Strukturveränderungen der Gesellschaft und politisches Handeln in der Lehre von Rudolf Hilferding*. Berlin: Duncker & Humblot.

Hilferding, R. 1902. Zur Geschichte der Werttheorie. *Die Neue Zeit* 21 (1): 213–217.

———. 1903a. Der Funktionswandel des Schutzzolls. *Die Neue Zeit* 21 (2): 274–281.

———. 1903b. Das Zuckerkontigent. Ein Beitrag zum Staatskapitalismus. *Deutsche Worte*, 23.

---

[92] Hilferding 1940f, 3, 4.

[93] Voigt 1987 and Barclay 1998 offer brief discussions of this widely neglected document.

———. 1903c. Brief an Karl Kautsky, 7. September 1903. In IISG Amsterdam, Karl Kautsky Nachlass, Signatur KDXII 583.

———. 1904. Zur Problemstellung der theoretischen Ökonomie bei Karl Marx. *Die Neue Zeit* 23 (1): 101–112.

———. 1907. Die Konjunktur. *Die Neue Zeit* 25 (2): 140–153.

———. 1908a. Die Krisen in den Vereinigten Staaten (Wirtschaftliche Rundschau). *Die Neue Zeit* 26 (1).

———. 1908b. Die industrielle Depression (Wirtschaftliche Rundschau). *Die Neue Zeit* 26 (1): 591–594.

———. 1910. Barzahlung und Bankentrennung. *Der Kampf* 3 (7).

———. 1912a. Zur Theorie der Kombination. *Die Neue Zeit* 30 (1): 550–557.

———. 1912b. Geld und Ware. *Die Neue Zeit* 30 (1): 773–782.

———. 1915. Kriegskapitalismus, in. *Arbeiter-Zeitung* 26: 45.

———. 1919a. Sozialistische und bürgerliche Steuerpolitik. *Die Freiheit* 2: 330.

———. 1919b. Steuern und Wirtschaftspolitik. *Die Freiheit* 2: 332.

———. 1919c. Indirekte Steuern. *Die Freiheit* 2: 336.

———. 1919d. Zur Sozialisierungsfrage. Referat auf dem 10. Deutschen Gewerkschaftskongress vom 30. Juni bis 5. Juli in Nürnberg, Berlin.

———. 1920. *Die Sozialisierung und die Machtverhältnisse der Klassen*. Referat auf dem 1. Betriebsrätekongres, gehalten am 5. Oktober 1920, Berlin.

———. 1923a. Die Aufgaben der Reichsbank. *Vorwärts* 9: 8.

———. 1923b. Die Weltpolitik, das Reparationsproblem und die Konferenz von Genua. *Schmollers Jahrbuch für Gesetzgebung, Verwaltung und Volkswirtschaft* 45.

———. 1924a. Handelspolitik und Agrarkrise. *Die Gesellschaft* 1 (2): 113–129.

———. 1924b. Probleme der Zeit. *Die Gesellschaft* 1 (1): 1–17.

———. 1925. Brief an Max Quarck, 5 October 1925. In Nachlass Max Quarck, FES AsD, 50.

———. 1930a. In der Gefahrenzone. *Die Gesellschaft* 7 (2): 289–297.

———. 1930b. Handelspolitik am Scheideweg. *Magazin der Wirtschaft*, 1, 1.

———. 1931a. *Gesellschaftsmacht oder Privatmacht über die Wirtschaft*. Berlin: Freier Volksverlag GmbH.

———. 1931b. Konsequenzen aus der deutschen Kreditkrise. *Vorwärts*, 25 August.

———. 1931c. Der Zusammenbruch (Englische Kreditkrise). *Vorwärts*, 21 September.

———. 1931d. Brief an Karl Kautsky, 2. Oktober 1931. Karl Kautsky Nachlass, IISG Amsterdam, Signatur KDXII 653.

———. 1931e. Ein Irrweg. Die Inflation, das Interesse an der Sozialreaktion. *Vorwärts*, 4 October.

———. 1931f. In Krisennot. *Die Gesellschaft* 8 (2): 1–8.

———. 1931g. Unheimliche Tage. *Die Gesellschaft* 8 (2): 101–107.

———. 1931h. Probleme der Kreditkrise. *Die Gesellschaft* 8 (2): 233–241.

———. 1931i. Brief an Karl Kautsky, 21. Dezember 1931. Karl Kautsky Nachlass, IISG Amsterdam, Signatur KDXII 655.

17 RUDOLF HILFERDING: A BORN JOURNALIST 435

————. 1932a. Brief an Karl Kautsky, 27. February 1932. Karl Kautsky Nachlass, IISG Amsterdam, Signatur KDXII 656.

————. 1932b. Brief an Karl Kautsky, 16. März 1932. Karl Kautsky Nachlass, IISG Amsterdam, Signatur KDXII 657.

————. 1932c. Unter der Drohung des Faschismus. *Die Gesellschaft* 9: 1.

————. 1932d. *Nationalsozialismus und Marxismus.* Berlin.

————. 1933a. Brief an Paul Hertz, dated 1933. Nachlass Paul Hertz, IISG Amsterdam, Mappe XVII, 1/1933.

————. 1933b. Brief an Karl Kautsky, dated 1933. Karl Kautsky Nachlass, IISG Amsterdam, Signature KDXII 660.

————. 1933c. Die Zeit und die Aufgabe. *Zeitschrift für Sozialismus* 1 (1): 1–11.

————. 1933d. Brief an Karl Kautsky, 23. September 1923. Karl Kautsky Nachlass, IISG Amsterdam, Signatur KDXII 661.

————. 1933e. Totaler Staat—totaler Bankrott. *Neuer Vorwärts,* 1, 18 June.

————. 1933f. Finanzielle Reichszerstörung. *Neuer Vorwärts,* 4, 9 July.

————. 1933g. Verschlechterte Finanzen—Verschlechterte Wirtschaft. *Neuer Vorwärts,* 9, 13 August.

————. 1933h. Kapitulation vor dem Bankkapital. *Neuer Vorwärts,* 14, 17 September.

————. 1933i. Finanzen treiben ins Chaos. *Neuer Vorwärts,* 16, 1 October.

————. 1933j. Das amerikanische Experiment. *Neuer Vorwärts,* 19, 22 October.

————. 1933k. Reichsbank als Geldmaschine. *Neuer Vorwärts,* 20, 29 October.

————. 1933l. Korporationen, Stände und Monopol. *Neuer Vorwärts,* 25, 3 December.

————. 1933m. Das Reich wird ausgeplündert. *Neuer Vorwärts,* 26, 10 December.

————. 1934a. Entwurf. AsD, PV-Emigration (Sopade), Mappe 54.

————. 1934b. Revolutionärer Sozialismus. *Zeitschrift für Sozialismus* 1 (5): 145–154.

————. 1934c. Nationalsozialismus und Antikapitalismus. *Neuer Vorwärts,* 30, 7 January.

————. 1934d. Die deutsche Krise. *Zeitschrift für Sozialismus* 1 (9): 337.

————. 1934e. Finanzpolitik der Diktaturen. *Neuer Vorwärts,* 31, 14 January.

————. 1934f. Revolution der Wirtschaft. *Neuer Vorwärts,* 32, 21 January.

————. 1934g. Das Schicksal des Dollars. *Neuer Vorwärts,* 35, 11 February.

————. 1934h. Verworrene Wirtschaftspolitik. *Neuer Vorwärts,* 39, 11 March.

————. 1934i. Die Krise der Reichsbank. *Neuer Vorwärts,* 41, 25 March.

————. 1934j. Das Schicksal der Mark. *Neuer Vorwärts,* 42, 1 April.

————. 1934k. Wer bezahlt die deutsche Aufrüstung? *Neuer Vorwärts,* 48, 13 May.

————. 1934l. Das Krankheitsbild der Wirtschaft. *Neuer Vorwärts,* 49, 20 May.

————. 1934m. Zwangswirtschaft ohne Plan. *Neuer Vorwärts,* 50, 27 May.

————. 1934n. Schachts Wirtschaftsdiktatur. *Neuer Vorwärts,* 61, 12 August.

————. 1934o. Alles für die Kriegswirtschaft. *Neuer Vorwärts,* 74, 11 November.

436 M. R. KRÄTKE

———. 1935a. Das Londoner Abkommen. *Zeitschrift für Sozialismus* 2 (18): 561–568.

———. 1935b. Macht ohne Diplomatie—Diplomatie ohne Macht. *Zeitschrift für Sozialismus* 2 (19): 593–604.

———. 1935c. Das Ende der Völkerbundspolitik. *Zeitschrift für Sozialismus* 2 (20): 625–637.

———. 1935d. Steigende Rüstung—gedrosselter Konsum. *Neuer Vorwärts*, 92, 17 March.

———. 1935e. Die Gesetzmäßigkeiten der Kriegswirtschaft. *Neuer Vorwärts*, 96, 14 April.

———. 1935f. Was kostet die deutsche Aufrüstung? *Neuer Vorwärts*, 94, 31 March.

———. 1935g. Wolken am braunen Wirtschaftshimmel. *Neuer Vorwärts*, 97, 21 April.

———. 1935h. Fortschreitende Wirtschaftszerrüttung. *Neuer Vorwärts*, 107, 30 June.

———. 1935i. Die Inflationsfinanzierung geht weiter. *Neuer Vorwärts*, 119, 22 September.

———. 1935j. Ausbau der Kriegswirtschaft. *Neuer Vorwärts*, 121, 6 October.

———. 1935k. Das braune Wirtschaftschaos. *Neuer Vorwärts*, 126, 10 November.

———. 1935l. Kriegsziele der Hitlerdiktatur. *Neuer Vorwärts*, 127, 17 November.

———. 1935m. Deutschlands Verschuldung. *Neuer Vorwärts*, 128, 24 November.

———. 1936a. Wirtschaftsjahr 1935. *Neuer Vorwärts*, 134, 5 January.

———. 1936b. The World Economic Crisis. *The New Leader*, 12, 5, 1 February.

———. 1936c. Die Kehrseite der Rüstungskonjunktur. *Neuer Vorwärts*, 136, 19 January.

———. 1936d. Die Höhe der Hitlerschulden. *Neuer Vorwärts*, 138, 2 February.

———. 1936e. Bankrottstimmung in Deutschland. *Neuer Vorwärts*, 141, 23 February.

———. 1936f. Vom Welthandel ausgeschlossen. *Neuer Vorwärts*, 142, 1 March.

———. 1936g. Der Weg in den totalen Krieg. *Neuer Vorwärts*, 144, 15 March.

———. 1936h. Ein Kriegsplan, kein Wirtschaftsplan. *Neuer Vorwärts*, 178, 8 November.

———. 1936i. Grundlagen der auswärtigen Politik. *Neuer Vorwärts*, 179, 15 November.

———. 1936j. Der Block der Diktaturen. *Neuer Vorwärts*, 180, 22 November.

———. 1936k. Die Politik der Sowjetunion. *Neuer Vorwärts*, 182, 6 December.

———. 1936l. Die Konstellation im Osten. *Neuer Vorwärts*, 184, 20 December.

———. 1937a. Weltwirtschaft 1936. *Neuer Vorwärts*, 187, 10 January.

———. 1937b. Mars regiert die Stunde. *Neuer Vorwärts*, 190, 31 January.

———. 1937c. Die Vorbereitung des totalen Krieges. *Neuer Vorwärts*, 193, 21 February.

———. 1937d. Die innere Politik Leon Blums. *Neuer Vorwärts*, 196, 14 March.

————. 1937e. Roosevelt gegen die Diktatoren. *Neuer Vorwärts*, 227, 17 October.

————. 1938a. Das Wirtschaftsjahr 1937. *Neuer Vorwärts*, 239, 16 January.

————. 1938b. Der braune Raubzug. *Neuer Vorwärts*, 249, 27 March.

————. 1938c. Die Wirtschaftswende. *Neuer Vorwärts*, 259, 5 May.

————. 1938d. Wer bezahlt die deutsche Rüstung? *Neuer Vorwärts*, 264, 10 July.

————. 1938e. In der Sackgasse der Kriegswirtschaft. *Neuer Vorwärts*, 270, 21 August.

————. 1938f. Abrüstung oder Aufrüstung. *Neuer Vorwärts*, 281, 6 November.

————. 1938g. Die Politik Chamberlains. *Neuer Vorwärts*, 250, 3 April.

————. 1938h. Der Block der Angreifer. *Neuer Vorwärts*, 256, 15 May.

————. 1939a. Die neue Krise. *Neuer Vorwärts*, 290, 8 January.

————. 1939b. Sturmzeichen. *Neuer Vorwärts*, 293, 29 January.

————. 1939c. An der Schwelle des Krieges. *Neuer Vorwärts*, 316, 9 July.

————. 1939d. Stalins Verantwortung. *Neuer Vorwärts*, 317, 16 July.

————. 1939e. Der Kurs der russischen Außenpolitik. *Neuer Vorwärts*, 324, 2 September.

————. 1939f. Die Wirtschaftslage bei Kriegsausbruch. *Neuer Vorwärts*, 328, 1 October.

————. 1939g. Der Sinn des Krieges. *Neuer Vorwärts*, 341, 31 December.

————. 1939h. Ausdehnung des Krieges. *Neuer Vorwärts*, 340, 10 December.

————. 1940a. Finnland und die Folgen. *Neuer Vorwärts*, 343, 14 January.

————. 1940b. Skandinavien und der Balkan. *Neuer Vorwärts*, 347, 11 February.

————. 1940c. Nach dem finnischen Frieden. *Neuer Vorwärts*, 353, 7 April.

————. 1940d. Krieg und Wirtschaftsgestaltung. *Neuer Vorwärts*, 354, 14 April.

————. 1940e. Von Narwik bis Alexandria. *Neuer Vorwärts*, 358, 12 May.

————. 1940f. Bemerkungen des Genossen Dr. Rudolf Hilferding über die Frage der Kriegsziele und über das Problem der Vereinigten Staaten von Europa (Vorstandssitzung vom 29. Januar 1940). AsD, PV-Emigration, Mappe 3.

Krätke, M. 2006. Marx als Wirtschaftsjournalist. *Beiträge zur Marx-Engels-Forschung*, 2005: 29–97.

————. 2008. Über die Krise der Weltwirtschaft, Demokratie und Sozialismus. Eine unveröffentlichte Untersuchung Otto Bauers über die Weltwirtschaftskrise der dreißiger Jahre. In *Otto Bauer und der Austromarxismus*, ed. W. Baier, L.N. Trallori, and D. Weber. Berlin: Karl Dietz Verlag.

————. 2019. Austromarxismus und politische Ökonomie. *Beiträge zur Marx-Engels-Forschung*, NF 2018/2019: 165–220.

————. 2022. Karl Marx' unvollendetes Projekt. Hamburg: VSA Verlag.

Kurata, M. 1974. Rudolf Hilferding. Bibliographie seiner Schriften, Artikel und Briefe. *Internationale Wissenschaftliche Korrespondenz zur Geschichte der Arbeiterbewegung* 10 (3): 327–347.

Kurotaki, M. 1998. *The Theoretical Legacy of Rudolf Hilferding—from "Finance Capital" to the Posthumous Manuscript* (Japanese). Tokio: Aoki Shoten.

438 M. R. KRÄTKE

Luxemburg, R. 1970a [1898]. Wirtschaftliche und sozialpolitische Rundschau. In *Gesammelte Werke*, vol. 1/1, 278–294. Berlin: Karl Dietz Verlag.

———. 1970b [1898/1899]. Wirtschaftliche und sozialpolitische Rundschau. In *Gesammelte Werke*, vol. 1/1, 308–317. Berlin: Karl Dietz Verlag.

———. 1970c [1899]. Wirtschaftliche und sozialpolitische Rundschau. In *Gesammelte Werke*, vol. 1/1, 326–347. Berlin: Karl Dietz Verlag.

———. 1970d [1899]. Wirtschaftliche und sozialpolitische Rundschau. In *Gesammelte Werke*, vol. 1/1, 352–360. Berlin: Karl Dietz Verlag.

Marx, K., and Engels, F. 2010a [1850]. Review–January–February 1850. *MECW* 10: 257–269.

———. 2010b [1850]. Review, March–April 1850. *MECW* 10: 338–341.

———. 2010c [1850]. Review, May to October 1850. *MECW* 10: 490–531.

Neumann, F. 2009 [1942]. *Behemoth: The Structure and Practice of National Socialism, 1933 – 1944.* Chicago: Ivan R. Dee.

Neurath, O. 1913a. Die Kriegswirtschaftslehre als Sonderdisziplin, in. *Weltwirtschaftliches Archiv* 1: 342–348.

———. 1913b. Probleme der Kriegswirtschaftslehre. *Zeitschrift für die gesamte Staatswissenschaft* 69 (3): 438–501.

Ritschl, A. 2000. Deficit Spending in the Nazi Recovery 1933–1938.

———. 2002. *Deutschlands Krise und Konjunktur 1924–1934.* Berlin: Akademie Verlag.

Smaldone, W. 1998. *Rudolf Hilferding. The Tragedy of a German Social Democrat.* Dekalb: Northern Illinois University Press.

Stein, A. 1946. *Rudolf Hilferding und die deutsche Arbeiterbewegung.* Hannover: Gedenkblätter von Alexander Stein, SPD.

Tooze, A. 2006. *The Wages of Destruction. The Making and Breaking of the Nazi Economy.* London: Penguin Books.

Voigt, K. 1987. Europäische Föderation und Neuer Völkerbund: Die Diskussion im deutschen Exil zur Gestaltung der internationalen Beziehungen nach dem Krieg. In *Deutschland nach Hitler: Zukunftspläne im Exil und aus der Besatzungszeit,* ed. Th. Koerber, G. Sautermeister, and S. Schneider. Opladen: Westdeutscher Verlag.

Wagner, P. 1996. *Rudolf Hilferding. Theory and Politics of Democratic Socialism.* Humanities Press International, Atlantic Highlands.

CHAPTER 18

Postface: From Rudolf Hilferding to Eugen Varga—Towards a Further Book Project

Judith Dellheim and Frieder Otto Wolf

In this book, Frieder Otto Wolf and Nikos Stravelakis have already briefly mentioned Eugen Varga, who intensively studied the writings (and even the speeches) of Rudolf Hilferding. This began out of admiration and it was based upon the realisation that he could learn a lot from the so-called Austro-Marxists. Then, it continued within the framework of an intensive cooperation, which finds a special expression in the Social Democratic journal *Die Neue Zeit*, and finally it took place out of a sharp political and scientific distance to Varga's former role model and comrade. The break occurred in the early 1920s, after the defeat of the Hungarian Soviet Republic, for which Varga was wholeheartedly committed, not least as the finance minister of the People's Republic. Varga, who needed many years to understand the theoretician Rosa Luxemburg, at least to a large extent,

J. Dellheim (✉)
Rosa-Luxemburg-Foundation, Berlin, Germany

F. O. Wolf
Institute of Philosophy, Freie Universität Berlin, Berlin, Germany
e-mail: fow@snafu.de

© The Author(s), under exclusive license to Springer Nature Switzerland AG 2023
J. Dellheim, F. O. Wolf (eds.), *Rudolf Hilferding*, Luxemburg International Studies in Political Economy,
https://doi.org/10.1007/978-3-031-08096-8_18

439

saw himself closely connected to Rosa Luxemburg as a politician and held firmly to the orientation towards a revolutionary overcoming of the capital relation.

The fact that Varga came into close proximity to Stalin after his flight to the Soviet Union and through his work for the Communist International should not lead to a short-circuited identification of Varga as a political Stalinist or as a Stalinist economist. Accordingly, we do take a critical view of Mommen's referring to Varga as *Stalin's Economist* (Mommen 2011, book title). That life under Stalinism shaped Varga's thinking, political and scientific work and above all imposed specific barriers on his writing, has, of course, to be reflected in an informed and critical reading of them. Such a critical reading should also help to better understand the debate on Hilferding's *Finance Capital*, namely on new developments in the capitalist mode of production and in bourgeois society, on problems of the so-called state socialist development as well as on modern socialist theory and politics. Those who dismiss Varga as a Stalinist do an injustice to a courageous person and to a seriously critical scientist—and they deprive themselves of important theoretical and socio-political insights. The fact that he was tolerated and respected by Stalin helped him to save people from a murderous system, and it was also due to several of Varga's qualities such as personal restraint and modesty, objectivity, intelligence and diligence, renunciation of participation in factional struggles and personal integrity.

The following few pages deal exclusively with Varga's critique of Hilferding. Their aim is to raise five central questions:

- Varga's relationship to Marx—as a theoretician, a politician and an activist—and, accordingly, to a critical reading of the written legacy of Marx and Engels;
- the connections between political economy, societal analysis, political activity and forms of political organisation;
- Varga's political-economic analysis of the societal developments since the last years of Marx and Engels;
- Varga's relationship to Rosa Luxemburg's understanding of socialist politics and her politico-economic analysis of imperialism;
- Finally, on how to address, analyse and fully comprehend the failed attempts at a socialist transformation, especially concerning the question of the political and scientific consequences which are to be drawn out of these failures.

18 POSTFACE: FROM RUDOLF HILFERDING TO EUGEN VARGA... 441

Of course, here, these questions cannot be fully discussed—as this would be urgently needed. This is, then, a decisive argument for an invitation to participate in the work on another volume in the series 'Luxemburg International Studies in Political Economy', which will be dedicated to a critical re-reading of Eugen Varga's writings. There, these five problems will have to shape the analytical and theoretical work.

VARGA ON HILFERDING UNTIL 1941

The following brief text provides some more arguments for an invitation to re-read Varga's work. It is historical in nature and begins with two quotations which illustrate the questions just formulated and thereby help to clarify especially Varga's relation to Luxemburg. This text is still rather only a listing of Varga's remarks on Hilferding, as a starting point for some considerations, which will be helpful for our work on the planned book.

The 'great importance of ideology and the political courses of action based on it meant that the soviet dictatorship[1] in Hungary had to include politics and ideology as determining factors at every turn, in dealing with economic problems' (Varga [1920] 1979, p. 75, own translation). This sentence is from Varga's work *Economic Problems of the Proletarian Dictatorship*, which he wrote during his internment and isolation, in 1920, without any access to books and material. These words should make clear that the importance of a politico-economical orientation in political and ideological communication should be fully understood, in order to prevent serious mistakes to be committed in revolutionary action, on the one hand. Concerning the scientific work involved, these words, on the other hand, clearly formulate a challenge also to work on the ideological and political material at hand, by analysing economic constellations and their reflection in the arguments and actions of the different actors and agencies involved. The issue of finance is central here—as it concerns the command over the accumulation of capital, the allocation of resources as well as the relations existing among economic actors and agencies. In Varga's *Economic Problems of the Proletarian Dictatorship* we not only find several positive references to Hilferding's *Finance Capital*, but in particular a productive use of the category 'Finance Capital' in analysing contemporary imperialist development. Varga closely connects this category with that of

---

[1] Varga has begun to address the problems inherent in the very notion of a 'dictatorship of the proletariat' (cf. Balibar 1977) by articulating the economic problems involved.

'finance oligarchy', in order to explain societal development as well as the policies of the most powerful in modern societies. From the time of his *Economic Problems of the Proletarian Dictatorship* onwards, however, Varga has distanced himself from Hilferding—humanly, scientifically and politically. In 1934, this culminated in a clear commitment to Luxemburg and her understanding of the importance of Marx and his literary legacy:

> The bourgeois and the revisionist wing of social democracy openly rejected Marx; the centrists Kautsky, Hilferding, Bauer, etc.—aptly called "harmony apostles" by Rosa Luxemburg—distorted and falsified Marx's teaching to such an extent that nothing remained of its revolutionary content. They paid homage to Marx in words, called themselves and still call themselves "Marxists", but rejected Marx's decisive discoveries. The reason for this rejection is that Marx's doctrine of crisis is inseparable from his doctrine of the historically temporary character and inevitable collapse of capitalism by way of revolution, through the struggle of the proletariat. (Varga [1934] 1982, p. 252, own translation)

It is interesting to note that Varga, who 20 years earlier was rather less appreciative of Luxemburg's *The Accumulation of Capital*, now, amidst a general Bolshevik rejection of Luxemburg, re-articulated the very concern Luxemburg had been pursuing with her book. In this way, Luxemburg became more and more important for Varga's scientific and political life.

In the years before World War I, however, Hilferding had been more significant for Varga than Luxemburg. In the discussion on gold and the gold price already mentioned in Varga's book, Hilferding referred to Varga to reinforce his own positions (Hilferding [1912] 1982, pp. 44–46). However, Varga's two articles are ultimately self-contradictory: on the one hand, they refer positively to Hilferding's 'socially necessary circulation value' embodied by paper money; on the other hand, they defend the idea that the value of commodities must be measured by means of a real money commodity. This money commodity was ultimately still gold at that time. Varga explained in his texts the clear difference between a price increase and an inflation as well as the specificities of the value and price formation of gold as a normal commodity on the market and as a money commodity. In so doing, he consistently applied Marx's theory of value (Varga 1912, pp. 212–220 and 1913, pp. 557–563). However, it seems, he has not been aware of his contradicting stance with regard to Hilferding. In his critique of Irving Fisher's quantity theory, published exclusively in

Hungarian in 1916, he not only relied positively on Hilferding's article in *Die Neue Zeit*, criticised by Kautsky (Kautsky 1912), but explicitly placed the conception of the 'socially necessary circulation value', as represented by paper money, on par with Marx's theory of money (Varga 1916, p. 433). Similarly, Varga wrote in 1914 (and published in 1917) his book *Money. Its Rule in Times of Peace and its Collapse during the War* (Varga [1917], 1979, pp. 1–69). Here, however, Varga dealt more intensively with the problem of money commodities and described, among other things, an interesting observation on the circulation of money and gold by those states which acted as politically and militarily neutral states during World War I: since the central bank stopped buying gold and the mint stopped minting gold coins, gold entered the market like any other commodity. The raw gold and the foreign gold coins began to represent less value than the banknotes to which the currency law applied.

> Therefore the merchants and manufacturers of the neutral countries were now reluctant to accept both the paper money and the gold of the belligerent countries. The merchants prefer that the well-funded citizens of the belligerent countries remain their debtors, pay the interest on their debts and postpone the final settlement until after the war. Moreover, the businessmen of the neutral states like to invest the warring countries' cash accumulated with them in real estate of these states, since they cannot buy other goods because of the shortage. (ibid., p. 66, own translation)

It is about money as a concentrated reflection of power relation. Varga, who especially made use of the analytic strengths of *Finance Capital* in this writing for the political-economic analysis of the development leading up to and during World War I, at that time still imagined a society without a capitalist mode of production to be a society without money (ibid., p. 69). However, this could then neither be a democratic one nor be an economically secure process of societal reproduction.

Varga's scientific and political break with Hilferding can be traced back, on the one hand, to a methodological difference in their analysis in the field of political economy: Varga consistently placed the reproduction of the capital relation, that is the production, appropriation and realisation of surplus value, or the accumulation of capital in concrete economic development, at the centre of his investigation. On the other hand, this break is connected to his politics of a radical critique of modern bourgeois society and its domination by the capitalist mode of production. Around

1922–1923 Varga began to publicly criticise Hilferding as an economist. This was again about gold as a monetary commodity at the time. From August to October 1923, Hilferding served as Germany's finance minister. He wanted to ease the catastrophic economic situation in Germany, where inflation was rampant, above all, by stabilising the mark. For this he wanted to use gold. But Varga accepted Keynes' argument that such measures could not really and sustainably help, because the economic pressure of the reparations to the victors of the World War prevented an upswing of production. So Varga oriented on elementary practical questions: first, economically, towards supplying the population with food and elementary everyday goods and, second, politically, towards easing the German reparation payments by negotiations. 'It testifies to the complete decay of any theoretical understanding in Hilferding personally and in German Social Democracy in general that such a plan (the stabilisation of the mark by gold) could be conceived and adopted by the party. It is surely obvious that the devaluation of the mark is not the cause of the bad economic conditions in Germany, but the reverse' (Varga [1923] 1977, p. 132, own translation). Because of the economic situation of the population and its further deterioration due to concrete monetary and financial policy measures, Varga attacked Hilferding's 'unfortunate plan' (Varga [1924] 1977, p. 24) a short time later. Further, Hilferding wanted to split the Reichsbank into two departments: a goldmark department and a paper-mark department. The goldmark department was to grant capitalists exclusively goldmark loans in the form of banknotes denominated in gold, which would be backed by gold and foreign currency. The paper-mark department, on the other hand, was to continue to meet the needs of the state through paper-mark issuance until the state budget was balanced. 'It was a plan according to the interests of total capital' (ibid.). In his proposals, Hilferding, as a Social Democratic economic and financial politician, increasingly equated economic recovery with general interest, whereby the interests of the bourgeoisie became more important to himself than the interests of the majority of the population. For this turn, Hilferding was sharply criticised by Varga.

We have to see how Hilferding's clear overestimation of the sphere of circulation in relation to the production, distribution and consumption, as expressed in *Finance Capital*, continues and develops its influence on his thinking as well as on his own administrative and political activities.

Sometime later, Varga was outraged that Hilferding 'called the trust-forming capitalists in the Reichstag Committee "Marxists of action"'

(Varga [1927] 1977, p. 287, own translation). This was, however, a consistent intellectual consequence of Hilferding, who separated the formation and development of cartels, trusts and corporations or monopolies from the analysis of the unfolding of capital relations, and thereby decoupled the centralisation of economic activities from the centralisation of capital. An economic monopoly, however, is the result of a high concentration and centralisation of capital, in connection with the development of a financial or capitalist oligarchy. Of course, such processes do go hand in hand with a specific progress of productive forces, that is, by advancing socialisation in a capitalist shell. Hilferding unfortunately linked these processes with automatically making this shell ever thinner and thinner, and ultimately bursting it. He justified this in particular by referring to the following two facts: first, that in large-scale monopolist enterprises internal planning increased in possibilities and weight, which produced a certain counter-tendency to capitalist competition and the resulting anarchy, and, accordingly, the necessity of crises. On the one hand, this also increased the scope for a broader participation of employees and other sections of the population in economic decision-making and in profit sharing. On the other hand, this generated the need for ever more economic policy of the state. Second and by consequence, these large monopolist companies are linked with their partners in 'the state' and in 'politics' much closer than the smaller ones. Their role in the economic life of modern societies, especially in specific branches, promotes a certain kind of administrative and political cooperation which could also be used in the interest of the people working in these companies or living in the locations, where these companies were based. On the other hand, the dominant tendencies of capitalist competition, that is anarchy and crises, could not be restricted by these developments, because the capital relation itself was maintained as such and even 'driven forward'. The dominant tendencies, therefore, unavoidably asserted themselves, from time to time, in crises of increasing dimension. Varga continued to (cf. e.g. already Varga 1926) analyse what was constitutive for the modern capitalist mode of production—that is the striving for profit maximisation, the ever-changing competition, the resulting anarchy and crises, the promotion of trans- and international conquest, conflict and war as well as, of course, the counter-tendencies to such tendencies. Since, on the one hand, with the generalisation of the joint-stock company (or the share capital company), the objective need for capitalists as organisers of social production had ceased to exist, there certainly was a theoretical justification for enquiring about a general crisis of the capitalist mode of production. On the other hand, since the concrete soviet development was historically taking place, it was also allowed to ask questions about a general crisis of modern bourgeois society or, very simplified, 'of capitalism'. Due to the declared progressive 'Bolshevisation' (or, effectively, Stalinisation) of the Communist International, for which Varga worked, it cannot be clearly established what has been the concrete share of the factors of sound economic analysis, scientific error, positive desire, optimism of purpose, ideology, tactics, command and coercion in Varga's work in general and, specifically, in his work on the 'general crisis of capitalism'. In any case, with the financial and economic crisis continuing after the banking crash in early 1931, Varga has complained: 'Hilferding denies the general crisis of capitalism' (Varga [1931] 1977, p. 305, own translation).

The issue of the effective role of the factors enumerated so far, and of their influence on the political positions expressed by Varga, must be linked *a fortiori* in relation to the fateful 'social fascism' thesis, as it was then dominant in Stalinist discourse. But since Hilferding's *Finance Capital* seemed to have been effectively 'falsified' by the banking crisis that openly broke out in 1929, as well as by a sharply rising economic role of the Nazis in Germany, the contradictions between Hilferding and Varga reached a tragic climax: for years, Reich President Paul von Hindenburg and his political partners had sought to eliminate parliament from important political decisions. Constitutional Article 48 permitted this. Heinrich Brüning was the chairman of the centrist faction in the Reichstag, financial expert and proven representative of a national-conservative state. He mentality seemed suitable for their political goals. In the spring of 1930, Hindenburg appointed him Reich Chancellor. Brüning's austerity policy created further social hardship and was exploited politically by the National Socialists. They made dramatic gains in the September 1930 elections. Just a few months later, Brüning used Article 48 for the first time, had the Reichstag dissolved and called new elections because the parliament refused to approve his rigid austerity plans. Hilferding and Co. tolerated Brüning's emergency cabinet, which took about 100 important quasi-legislative decisions. In the 1932 elections, the Nazis had lost 2 million votes (Schleifstein 1977, pp. 136–145). At the turn of 1932–1933, Hilferding wrote: 'The fascist movement has been kept out of state power ... in Germany, thanks to the Social Democracy, which, by its policy of toleration, has avoided the fusion of the bourgeoisie into a reactionary mass under fascist leadership and has prevented the entry of the fascists into government during the rising' (Hilferding 1933, p. 8, own translation). In the same article, Hilferding continued: 'The National Socialists ... are banished to legality, which leaves them only the choice of hastening the incipient descent as a serving member of a bourgeois bloc, or all the more not escaping it in an opposition that disappoints their supporters impatiently waiting for salvation' (ibid., own translation).

Varga did not understand such an assessment of the political situation, a very short time before the German fascists effectively took power in the beginning of 1933. After they had taken it and immediately begun to brutally and bloodily persecute their political opponents and to terrorise the German Jews and other minorities, Varga still spoke of the 'complete theoretical incorrectness of the social-fascist theory that had been promulgated from Bernstein onwards through Kautsky, Hilferding, Braunthal and Leichter—as if the monopolies could alleviate the crisis. The indissoluble connection between the formation of monopolies as the basis of imperialism completely excludes this for the period of the general crisis of capitalism in particular' (Varga [1933] 1977, p. 1709, own translation). In this context, Varga also referred to Hilferding's evidently false claim that the development of monopolies limited the importance of the stock market game: '[F]or never stock prices soared as they had before the crisis' (ibid., p. 1708). However, in actual fact, these 'social fascists' were courageous anti-fascists and Bernstein, Kautsky, Hilferding and Braunthal, like Varga, were themselves Jews. Varga continued his aggressive language in his attacks against the aforementioned categories even after 1933, which was, indeed, highly problematic, politically as well as morally reprehensible—in view of tragic fates, and, especially, with a view towards the need for an anti-fascist unity with the Social Democrats. This judgement cannot and should not be relativised by our remarks on Hilferding's in some way analogous behaviour, in the beginning of this book. However, this statement says a great deal about the poisoned political climate in which Varga always had to fear for his life and at the same time endeavoured to pursue socialist theory and politics. And maybe his attacks against personalities he could not help might confirm his 'political correctness' as a condition for rescuing people from Stalin's madness and from the murderous activities of his henchmen.

In 1937, Varga indirectly returned to the dispute over Rosa Luxemburg's *The Accumulation of Capital*, as he accused Kautsky, Hilferding and their followers of claiming that a crisis-free development of the capitalist mode of production was possible, due to their treatment of Marx's reproduction

448   J. DELLHEIM AND F. O. WOLF

schemes in the second volume of *Capital* and to his later remarks on organised capitalism (Varga [1937] 1982, pp. 7, 31–32).

However, unlike Day (Day 1979/1981, pp. 38–39), the authors explain Varga's reliance on Luxemburg not primarily in terms of her crisis theory, but as a comrade political economist and as a woman who, like Varga, had to suffer in the own party.

A Concluding Remark

Chapter 1 'Introduction: Critically Returning to Rudolf Hilferding' dealt with the complicated personality and the tragedy of the political economist Hilferding, who was a Social Democratic politician and a German statesman. The remarks on Eugen Varga we have made here indicate that we shall also have to deal with a deep historical and human tragedy in the case of this accomplished expert on Marxist political economy who has been a thorough critic of Hilferding's writings, speeches and economic policy actions. But they also should make clear that the criticism of Eugen Varga's literary legacy could help modern readers in better understanding Hilferding's theoretical achievements, as well as his limitations, in order to become capable of critically continuing his analyses, because

- Eugen Varga starts with the phenomena of the capitalist mode of production analysed by Rudolf Hilferding and he starts with Hilferding's analyses. In this context, the questions of money and finance have a special significance, because they essentially mediate the circulation of capital and with its societal reproduction.
- Varga tests Hilferding's analyses on the basis of rich empirical material, and, at the same time, he provides significant empirical material for the continuation of research in economic history and political economy, on societal and especially economic developments in specific countries, world regions and global contexts.
- At the same time, Varga examines Hilferding's analyses on the basis of his own theoretical studies and his own insights into societal and especially economic contexts, corrects these analyses and continues to carry them out.

On this basis, a critical re-reading of Varga's critique of Hilferding and of Varga's other works can help us to better understand *firstly* the course of history and the present historical situation, while, *secondly,* further developing a theoretical approach to analysing societal development, by working on economic categories and essential economic constellations, and by dealing with scenarios and caesuras in historical and in future social developments. And *finally* a careful critical reading of Varga can gain from his rich work, in order to be able to understand and to shape the present more effectively—in such a way that the possibilities of an emancipatory and solidarity-oriented development are identified, preserved and can be progressively made use of. This would be the only possible way of handling Varga's theoretical legacy, starting from a re-reading of the relevant texts by Marx and by Luxemburg, while further focussing especially on the questions of finance in the process of societal reproduction.

References

Balibar, É. 1977. *The Dictatorship of the Proletariat. With an Afterword by Louis Althusser, translated by Grahame Lock*. London: New Left Books.

Day, R. 1981. *The "Crisis" and the "Crash". Soviet Studies of the West (1917-1939)*. Verso.

Hilferding, R. [1912] 1982. Geld und Ware. In: *Zwischen den Stühlen oder über die Unvereinbarkeit von Theorie und Praxis. Schriften Rudolf Hilferdings 1904 bis 1940*, ed. Stephan, C. 44-54. Berlin/Bonn: Verlag J.H.W. Dietz Nachf.

———. 1933. Zwischen den Entscheidungen. In *Die Gesellschaft*, X. Jg. 1933/ Heft 1, 8-9.

Kautsky, K. 1912. Gold, Paper Currency and Commodity. *Die Neue Zeit*, Vol. 30:1, No. 24 & 25, pp. 837-47 and 886-93, translated by Daniel Gaido, https://www.marxists.org/archive/kautsky/1912/xx/gpcc.htm

Mommen, A. 2011. *Stalin's Economist. The economic contributions of Jenő Varga*. Oxon, New York: Routledge.

Schleifstein, J. 1977. Zum historischen Hintergrund der Sozialfaschismus-These. In *E. Varga. Wirtschaft und Wirtschaftspolitik, Vierteljahresberichte 1922–1939, Band 1*, ed. J. Goldberg, 121–148. Westberlin: deb. Verlag das Europäische Buch.

Varga, E. 1912. Goldproduktion und Teuerung. In *Die Neue Zeit: Wochenzeitschrift der Deutschen Sozialdemokratie*. 1911-1912. Band 1 (1912), Heft 7, 212-220, Stuttgart: JHW Dietz-Verlag.

———. 1913. Goldproduktion und Teuerung. In *Die Neue Zeit: Wochenzeitschrift der Deutschen Sozialdemokratie*. 1912–1913. Band 1 (1913), Heft 16, 557-563, Stuttgart: JHW Dietz-Verlag.

Varga, J. 1916. A Pénz Vásárló Erejének Problémája. *Huszadik Század* 1916: 431–438. https://adt.arcanum.com/hu/view/HuszadikSzazad_1916/? pg=859.

Varga, E. [1917] 1979. Das Geld. Seine Herrschaft in Friedenszeiten und sein Zusammenbruch während des Krieges. In *E.S. Varga, Ausgewählte Schriften 1918–1964. Band 1. Der Beginn der allgemeinen Krise des Kapitalismus.* Herausgegeben vom Institut für Internationale Politik und Wirtschaft der DDR, 1-69. Berlin: Akademie-Verlag.

———. [1920] 1979. Wirtschaftspolitische Probleme der proletarischen Diktatur. In *E.S. Varga, Ausgewählte Schriften 1918–1964. Band 1. Der Beginn der allgemeinen Krise des Kapitalismus.* Herausgegeben vom Institut für Internationale Politik und Wirtschaft der DDR, 72-176. Berlin: Akademie-Verlag.

———. [1923] 1977. Internationale Pressekorrespondenz im vierten Vierteljahr 1922. Abgeschlossen am 17. January 1923. In *E. Varga. Wirtschaft und Wirtschaftspolitik, Vierteljahresberichte 1922–1939, Band 2,* ed. Goldberg, J., Nr. 18, 125-142. Westberlin: deb. Verlag das Europäische Buch.

———. [1924] 1977. Wirtschaft und Wirtschaftspolitik im dritten Vierteljahr 1923, Beilage 1924, Wien. In *E. Varga. Wirtschaft und Wirtschaftspolitik, Vierteljahresberichte 1922–1939, Band 2,* ed. Goldberg, J., 1-39. Westberlin: deb. Verlag das Europäische Buch.

———. [1926] 1977. Die Wirtschaft und Wirtschaftspolitik im IV. Vierteljahr 1925. Abgeschlossen am 14.1.1926. In *E. Varga. Wirtschaft und Wirtschaftspolitik, Vierteljahresberichte 1922–1939, Band 3,* ed. Goldberg, J., Nr. 22, 297-329. Westberlin: deb. Verlag das Europäische Buch.

———. [1927] 1977. Die Wirtschaft und Wirtschaftspolitik im IV. Vierteljahr 1926. Abgeschlossen am 20.1.1927. In *E. Varga. Wirtschaft und Wirtschaftspolitik, Vierteljahresberichte 1922–1939, Band 3,* ed. Goldberg, J., Nr. 14, 257-294. Westberlin: deb. Verlag das Europäische Buch.

———. [1931] 1977. Wirtschaft und Wirtschaftspolitik im 4. Vierteljahr 1930. Abgeschlossen am 16.1.1931. In *E. Varga. Wirtschaft und Wirtschaftspolitik, Vierteljahresberichte 1922–1939, Band 4,* ed. Goldberg, J., Nr. 11, 289-320. Westberlin: deb. Verlag das Europäische Buch.

———. [1933] 1977. Wirtschaft und Wirtschaftspolitik im 2. Vierteljahr 1933. Abgeschlossen am 30.7.1933. In *E. Varga. Wirtschaft und Wirtschaftspolitik, Vierteljahresberichte 1922–1939, Band 5,* ed. Goldberg, J., Nr. 30, 1110-1132. Westberlin: deb. Verlag das Europäische Buch.

———. [1934] 1982. Die Große Krise und ihre politischen Folgen. Wirtschaft und Politik 1928–1934. In *E.S. Varga, Ausgewählte Schriften 1918–1964. Band 2. Die Wirtschaftskrisen.* Herausgegeben vom Institut für Internationale Politik und Wirtschaft der DDR, 250-306. Berlin: Akademie-Verlag.

———. [1937] 1982. Die Weltwirtschaftskrisen. In: *E.S. Varga, Ausgewählte Schriften 1918–1964. Band 2. Die Wirtschaftskrisen.* Herausgegeben vom Institut für Internationale Politik und Wirtschaft der DDR, 3-51. Berlin: Akademie-Verlag.

Index[1]

A
Accumulation of Capital, vii, 63, 86, 187, 221, 332, 349, 351, 357, 441, 443
Adler, Max, 12, 279, 290, 294, 295, 325
Aristocracy of labour, 268
Arms race, 64, 407, 414
Austro-Marxism, Austro-Marxists, viii, 12, 14n7, 17, 37, 38, 47, 277–279, 284, 294–296, 299, 385, 393, 394, 396, 439

B
Bank, banking
  banking crisis, 106–108, 414, 446
  central banks, 21, 27–29, 27n19, 35n26, 38, 40, 41, 44, 86, 93, 100, 107, 111, 112, 120, 130, 132, 170, 179, 207, 293, 355, 403–405, 443
Baran, Paul, 53, 54, 73–77, 75n10, 75n11, 246, 264
Bauer, Otto, 12, 15n8, 17, 18, 18n11, 26n18, 35–37, 60–63, 65, 86, 205, 278, 279, 283, 284, 290, 387n17, 394, 399, 401, 407n36, 413n43, 415n48, 429, 442
Bernstein, Eduard, 12, 17–19, 18n12, 86, 253, 254, 294, 296, 336, 337, 350n5, 447
Blum, Leon, 277, 410
Böhm-Bawerk, Eugen, 12, 14, 14n7, 177, 283–291, 285n2, 290n6
Bolshevisation, 2, 446
Braunthal, Julius, 447
Brentano, Lujo, 266, 267, 272
Brunhoff (de), Suzanne, 19n13, 28n20, 109, 206

[1] Note: Page numbers followed by 'n' refer to notes.

© The Author(s), under exclusive license to Springer Nature Switzerland AG 2023
J. Dellheim, F. O. Wolf (eds.), *Rudolf Hilferding*, Luxemburg International Studies in Political Economy,
https://doi.org/10.1007/978-3-031-08096-8

451

Brüning, Heinrich, 317, 356,
426, 446
Bukharin, Nikolai, vii, 62, 64, 65, 70,
86, 177, 206, 216, 222, 223n7
Bureaucracy, 151, 348, 386, 387
Business cycle, 256, 259, 298, 299,
398, 419

C

Capital, vi, x, 11–14, 13n5, 16–20,
24, 25, 29, 29n22, 31, 35–37,
58n4, 62, 78, 115, 121, 125,
144–146, 171, 175, 178, 192,
202, 205, 217, 223, 255, 265,
266, 273, 278, 284, 286, 290,
331, 448
agricultural, 40, 46, 47
commercial, 21, 86, 92, 93, 171,
173, 180
commodity, 33, 46
fictive, fictitious, 25, 32, 39–41,
44–46, 128, 172, 179, 187,
201, 205, 292, 314, 315, 320,
343–345, 348, 361
finance, vii, viii, x, xii, 20, 34–38,
41, 44–47, 56, 57n3, 59,
85–113, 115–137, 141–165,
169–197, 199–227, 245,
246, 263–268, 270–273,
285, 290–294, 307–325,
339, 351, 352,
359, 402
industrial, 14, 18, 24, 25, 30, 31,
33–35, 40, 46, 47, 65, 86, 90,
93, 95, 100, 106, 126, 136,
143, 146, 160, 170–173,
179–183, 186, 187, 189–191,
200, 201, 203–206, 217, 218,
263, 271, 289, 291, 293, 316,
319, 320, 330, 343, 344, 348,
351, 423

interest bearing, 24, 33, 46n29, 58,
58n4, 95, 121, 122, 185, 187,
200, 201, 215, 316, 319, 320,
333, 341, 343, 356
market, market operation, xii, 32,
40, 152, 153, 263, 265, 267,
273, 322, 351, 422
merchant, x, 28, 29, 33, 38, 40, 41,
46, 46n29, 47, 93, 171, 187,
207, 208
money, 85–113, 121, 149, 201,
204, 207, 209, 215, 217, 292,
293, 340
productive, 90, 92, 93, 95, 98, 100,
110, 131, 175, 181, 187, 188,
200, 202, 209, 214, 226, 316,
320, 339, 341, 344, 348, 430
share, 55, 292, 320, 329–362, 445
Capitalism
capitalist socialism, 267
competition, 13, 35, 42, 55, 58, 63,
71, 74, 78, 148, 149, 160,
222, 223, 291, 353, 354,
357, 445
crisis free development, 447
monopoly, xi, 74, 116, 170, 179,
259, 288, 354, 357
organised, 37, 136, 313, 347, 359,
361, 448
state monopoly, 27, 272,
374, 374n25
Carnegie, Andrew, 270
Cartel, cartelisation, xi, 15, 21, 31, 34,
35, 56, 57, 59, 60, 65, 74, 75,
78, 86, 87, 91, 98–100, 106,
147, 163, 180, 184, 185, 193,
200, 205, 215, 215n3, 216, 235,
236, 245, 253–259, 264, 266,
267, 292, 293, 297, 300, 314,
316, 330, 357, 424, 445
Cash, 28, 28n21, 55, 57, 89–92, 105,
119, 178, 345, 443

INDEX 453

Centralisation
of capital, 16, 21, 25, 35, 45, 55,
135, 182, 207–209, 314, 316,
336, 337, 357, 361, 445
of production, 267, 333, 337
Class
capitalist class, 23, 26, 38, 62, 111,
121, 150, 155, 162, 218, 297,
398, 431
class consciousness, 296, 376,
384, 387–390
class dictatorship, 387
class interest, 297, 376, 387, 428
politics and class, 386
working class, 296–299
Colony, colonialism, 18, 60, 186, 190,
195, 289, 330, 429
Commodity, 16, 24–26, 32, 33, 38,
42, 43, 45, 46, 55, 56, 68, 70,
71, 78–79, 88, 89, 98, 99, 101,
102, 104, 106, 111, 119,
122–124, 146, 163, 175–180,
188, 202, 203, 211, 212, 221,
245, 284, 287, 291, 297, 309,
312, 333, 340–342, 341n2, 345,
348, 352, 353, 358, 361,
399, 442–444
Communist International, 2, 440, 446
Competition, ix, 13, 16, 23, 25,
33–35, 42, 43, 55–59, 63, 71,
72, 74, 75n11, 76, 78, 97, 99,
111, 145–149, 152, 156, 160,
161, 164, 174, 182–185, 209,
215, 215n3, 217, 218, 222, 223,
255, 258, 266, 272, 286–288,
289n5, 290, 290n6, 291, 293,
294n8, 299, 300, 313, 316,
319, 324, 332, 333, 340,
347, 348, 352–358, 361,
428, 445
Concentration
of capital, 183, 290, 292, 332

of production, xi, 184, 293
of resources, 361
Corporation, corporations, xi, 16, 25,
26, 31, 34, 35, 37, 38, 41, 42,
44–47, 56–58, 74, 75, 94, 96–98,
110, 133, 141–160, 164, 206,
208, 210, 214, 234–240, 236n6,
243–248, 255, 265, 270, 292,
316, 319, 323, 324, 342,
345–349, 352–357, 359, 361,
399, 412, 419, 421, 445
modern, 239, 240, 243, 245, 246,
255, 263, 292
Credit, viii, 16, 21, 22, 24, 25, 27–31,
29n22, 34, 36–42, 44, 46, 47,
87–98, 100, 101, 103–111,
119–121, 124–126, 128,
133–135, 137, 147, 153, 163,
171, 173–176, 178–180, 184,
187, 188, 190, 191, 193, 195,
196, 201, 205–208, 211, 212,
215–217, 225, 226, 254, 292,
293n7, 299, 312, 316, 332, 334,
339, 341, 342, 345, 346, 348,
349, 353–356, 359, 361, 398,
401–405, 412, 414–416,
418, 425
industrial credit, 29, 120, 134, 179,
180, 182, 191, 402, 403
Crisis
credit, 22, 401–404
economic, ix, 22, 26n18, 54,
59, 61, 62, 68, 116, 225,
253, 256, 284, 285, 292, 300,
355, 402, 405, 408, 411,
412, 446
financial, vi, 14, 36, 37, 81, 87,
116, 118, 150, 156, 213, 214,
216, 247, 352, 397, 398
general, 65, 70, 446, 447
money, 85–113
permanent, 73, 74, 415

454 INDEX

Currency, 16, 19, 22, 27, 38, 45, 70, 88, 91, 104, 112, 172, 176, 177, 216, 399, 403, 405, 416, 418, 422, 424, 425, 431, 443, 444

D

Debt, x, 25, 29, 32, 39, 41, 91, 93, 101, 106, 107, 109, 110, 119, 128, 211, 217, 219, 220, 236n6, 319, 332, 403, 421, 422, 424, 430, 443
Derivative, 129
  commodity derivative, 25, 32, 41, 42, 44, 46, 129
Der Kampf, 17, 394, 397, 399, 406
Die Gesellschaft, 20, 394, 406, 406n35
Dividends, 43, 44, 55, 57, 58n4, 76, 95, 155, 211, 319–323, 345, 349, 360, 361

E

Eloi/Morlocks, 269
Employment, unemployment, 3n1, 39, 60, 73, 148, 246, 251, 255, 401, 410, 412, 416, 423
Engels, Friedrich, vi, viii, 4, 12–14, 13n5, 14n6, 16, 23, 24, 26, 31, 32, 37, 42, 43, 86, 173, 193, 205, 224, 226, 264, 265, 368, 368n7, 370n17, 383, 386, 393, 395n3, 397, 397n13, 440

F

Factory laws, 389
Fascism, 2, 23, 287n3, 299, 367n2, 405, 412, 413, 426, 432
  'social fascism,' 3, 446
Federal Reserve System, 271

Fetishisation, 294, 356
Feudal past, 266
Finance, 5n3, 115, 200, 233, 254n2, 277
  finance market, xii, 127, 128, 201, 203, 204, 206, 208, 211, 244, 245
  finance oligarchy, 442
Finance capital, vii–x, xii, xiii, 2, 4, 11–47, 53 78, 57n3, 85–113, 115–137, 141–165, 169–197, 171n1, 199–227, 233, 245, 246, 252, 254, 259, 263–265, 267, 270–273, 278, 278n1, 285, 289–291, 289n5, 293, 307–325, 330, 331, 336–357, 350n5, 359, 382, 393, 399, 402, 440, 441, 443, 444, 446
  bank based finance capital, 110, 263, 265
Financialisation, x, 47, 54, 77, 87, 115–137, 143, 144, 150–155, 169–197, 211
Fisher, Irving, 442
Foxwell, Herbert, 266

G

Gold
  goldmark, 444
  gold price, 442
  gold standard, 19, 26, 178, 195, 298, 299, 404, 416
  gold treasure, 404
Great Depression, xiii, 14, 22, 37, 53, 59, 70, 111, 281, 296, 299, 397, 398, 401–405, 408, 409, 411–420, 426
Grossman, Henryk, vii, 55, 63, 85–87, 100, 113, 225

INDEX 455

H

Hegelianism, 388
Hertz, Paul, 3n2, 406n35,
   407, 411n42
Hilferding, Rose, 317,
   382, 382n3
Hindenburg, Paul, 446
Hitler, Adolf, 4, 408, 409n40, 410,
   412, 421–424, 426, 429–432
Holland, Henryk, 266, 272
Hungarian soviet republic, 439

I

Imperialism, vii, x, 4, 18, 19, 60–62,
   64, 88, 100, 111, 125, 135, 180,
   185, 195, 199, 200, 206, 208,
   214–216, 218, 222–224, 223n7,
   226, 234, 254, 264, 268, 278n1,
   282, 289, 293, 293n7, 417, 428,
   440, 447
Industrial feudalism, xii, 264–267,
   269, 272, 273
Industrial fluctuation, 255
Insurance, 38, 39, 42, 45, 46, 74, 77,
   98, 208, 342
Intellectuals, vi, x, 53–78, 204, 240,
   252, 272, 273, 277–281,
   283–284, 296, 307, 361, 377,
   384, 388, 389, 394, 395, 406,
   407, 412, 433, 445

J

Joint-stock bank, 190
Joint stock company, xi, 43, 94–97,
   107, 108, 181, 189, 193, 235,
   319, 329–362, 445

K

Kalecki, Michał, viii, xi, 75, 75n10,
   251–259, 253n1, 264, 265

Kautsky, Benedikt, 382, 382n3,
   384, 390
Kautsky, Karl, 12–15, 15n8, 17, 18,
   20, 21, 24, 34n25, 37, 55, 59,
   63, 64, 86, 206, 215, 223n7,
   254, 272, 278, 284, 290, 294,
   296, 318, 341, 385n12,
   388–390, 394, 399, 401, 402,
   405, 407n36, 411n42, 413n43,
   420, 442, 443, 447
Keynes, John Maynard, Keynesianism,
   22, 75, 75n10, 176, 178, 213,
   252, 273, 298, 299, 444
Knapp, Georg, 27
Kowalik, Tadeusz, viii, 223n7,
   252–255, 253n1, 258, 264–266,
   270, 272
Krzywicki, Ludwik, xii, 253, 263–273
Kurata, Minoru, xvii, xviin3, 5, 12n2,
   17, 330, 359, 393, 397n11

L

Lange, Oskar, 263, 271
Large-scale enterprise, xi,
   147, 233–249
Lederer, Emil, xi, 12, 256, 259
Leichter, Käthe, 447
Lenin, Vladimir Iljitsch, vii, 2, 4, 19,
   60, 64, 65, 86, 206–208, 215,
   223n7, 234, 264, 268, 278,
   278n1, 293n7, 299, 369n9, 375,
   384, 388, 389
Liberalism, 243, 281, 282, 289,
   294n8, 300, 372, 405
Lippmann, Walter, 279, 281–283,
   288, 289, 294, 296, 299
Littlefield, Charles, 269, 270
Luxemburg, Rosa, v–vii, xii, xiv, 2, 5,
   6, 15n9, 19, 35, 53–78, 116,
   199, 200, 205, 211, 214,
   216–218, 217n4, 221–227,
   223n8, 234, 251–253, 259,

456 INDEX

318, 330, 356, 357, 359–361,
393, 397, 397n13,
439–442, 447–449

M

Managed capitalism, 256–259
Manager, management, 29, 30, 42,
43, 94, 143, 144, 147, 151–153,
155–160, 158n7, 164, 183, 192,
193, 201, 208, 234, 237, 238,
244, 246, 248, 249, 267, 279,
282, 316, 323, 333, 340, 346,
348, 352, 355
Mandel, Ernest, 67, 117, 137, 225
Marchlewski, Julian, 215n3, 397
Marx, Karl, v–xii, xiv, 4, 5, 6n5, 7,
11–19, 13n5, 14n7, 15n8, 15n9,
19n13, 23–26, 25n16, 28n20,
29–38, 29n22, 29n23, 37n27,
40, 43, 44, 47, 54–56, 56n1,
58n4, 59–62, 61n5, 71, 72, 74,
76, 78, 86, 99, 102, 115,
119–122, 125, 136, 142–146,
145n4, 148, 171–178, 183, 187,
192–194, 196, 200–210, 210n1,
212–214, 212n2, 217, 223,
223n6, 226, 227, 234, 235, 237,
245, 251, 252, 255, 256, 258,
259, 265, 266, 271, 273, 278,
284, 286, 287, 290, 290n6, 292,
294–295, 307, 308, 313, 314,
318, 320, 321, 329–332,
334–336, 335n1, 338, 339, 357,
359–361, 368–371, 370n16,
373–376, 375n26, 376n30,
383–388, 390, 393, 395n3, 396,
397, 397n13, 399, 440, 442,
443, 447, 449

Materialist conception of history, xii,
23, 368–370, 384–386
Milford, Peter, 390
Militarism, militarisation, x, xi,
199–227, 338, 424, 433
Mises, Ludwig von, 12, 256,
282–288, 294, 294n8, 300
Mommen, André, 440
Money, vi, vii, 15, 16, 17n10, 18, 19,
19n13, 21, 22, 24–28, 29n22,
30, 32–34, 37–41, 44, 46,
85–113, 118–123, 135, 146,
153, 171, 172, 174–182, 187,
195, 196, 200–209, 212, 212n2,
215, 217, 238, 245, 258, 284,
287, 288, 290–294, 299, 300,
312, 315, 316, 318–320,
322–324, 333, 339–345, 341n2,
347–349, 351, 353, 355–357,
360, 361, 396, 398, 399, 403,
421, 425, 442, 443, 448
real money commodity, 442
Monopoly
business, 255
capital, xi, 77, 110, 236, 265,
268–271, 322
finance capital, xii,
263–266, 270–273
price, 59, 69, 75, 78, 79, 210, 211,
322, 357
profit, xi, 60, 325, 358
Moody, John, 269
Morgan, J.P., 268–271
Mortgage, 39, 41, 128
Moss, H. St. L. B., 383
Moszkowska, Natali, ix, 54, 58,
70–75
Multinational company/corporation,
151, 408

N

National Socialists, National Socialism, Nazis, Nazi regime, 5n3, 5n4, 23, 256, 277, 278, 296, 299, 350, 356, 395, 396, 406, 407, 409, 410, 412, 420, 422–424, 424–425n73, 427, 429–431, 446, 447
Neoliberalism, 54, 117, 132, 277–300
Neue Zeit, 14, 19, 20, 393, 394, 396, 397, 406, 406n35
New Deal, 150, 237, 410, 419, 425

O

Oligarchy, 26, 171, 208, 265, 315, 348, 352, 354, 356, 445
Over the counter (OTC), 43

P

Paper money, 27, 88, 92, 105, 176–179, 341, 442, 443
Parliamentarism, 338, 387
Participation, 94, 196, 338, 342, 345, 355, 359, 399, 440, 445
Philippovich, Eugen von, 12, 283
Pirenne, Henri, 383
Planning, 69, 70, 144, 148, 149, 152, 160–165, 233, 242, 254, 268, 272, 282, 347, 355, 397n13, 412, 445
Polanyi, Karl, 176, 215, 216, 218, 220, 221
Politics, political actors, 3, 5, 6, 6n5, 20–23, 27, 28, 45, 119, 223, 223n7, 283, 289, 294–298, 300, 331, 338, 339, 347, 352, 369, 369n10, 372, 374–376, 384, 386–387, 396, 399, 402, 404, 405, 407–409, 411n42, 413,

413n43, 425–429, 440, 441, 443, 445, 447
Posner, Stanislaw, 268
Preobrazhensky, Evgeni, 69
Profit
corporate, 57
profit rate, 55–56, 72, 95, 108, 121, 148, 177, 182, 183, 240, 286, 291, 398
promoter profit, xi, 30, 55, 56n1, 57, 96, 97, 120, 180–182, 205, 317–325, 343–345, 348, 349, 361
'Proletarian Dictatorship,' 171, 315, 338, 441n1
Property, x, 31, 34, 59, 107, 113, 121, 143, 145, 146, 187, 189, 192, 193, 201, 202, 204, 210–213, 210n1, 217, 221, 226, 227, 234, 238, 245, 248, 264, 267, 308, 312, 324, 332, 335, 374, 412
Prussia, 224, 339, 387

R

Rearmament, 396, 408, 410, 414, 420–424, 427, 429, 430
Renner, Karl, 12, 29n22, 46, 46n29, 294
Reproduction of the capital relation, 443
Revolution, English revolution, French revolution, xiii, 21, 28, 60, 64, 65, 67, 111, 144, 162, 163, 179, 180, 182, 219, 254, 259, 268, 270, 271, 278, 284, 293–296, 298, 315, 373, 385, 386, 399–401, 405, 411n42, 412, 413n43, 442
Rockefeller, John D., 269, 270
Rodbertus, Karl, 267, 272

458 INDEX

Roosevelt, Franklin Delano, Roosevelt administration, 237, 410, 411n41, 412, 414, 418, 419, 419n52, 425

S
Schacht, Hjalmar, 408, 421, 421n60, 422, 422n65
Schumpeter, Josef, viii, 12, 20, 175, 176, 254–256, 254n2, 283
Schwab, Charles M., 270
Securities, xi, 25, 41, 42, 44, 46, 97–99, 105, 106, 129, 205, 216, 225, 248, 272, 292, 323, 324, 425
Shareholder, xi, 43, 44, 56, 95, 97, 98, 120, 147, 151, 156, 157n6, 158, 159, 189, 211, 234, 236, 236n6, 238, 239, 244, 247, 292, 293, 318, 319, 322, 338, 342, 343, 345, 346, 348, 352, 356, 357, 359–361
Shareholder value, 155, 157, 244, 246
Smaldone, William, 1, 11n1, 277, 278, 278n1, 283–285, 290, 292, 293, 295–298, 359, 396, 396n8
Social democracy, 20, 267, 278, 297, 300, 336, 368, 394, 395, 401, 406, 411, 412, 442, 446
'Social fascism,', 3, 446
Socialism, socialist, socialist transformation, vii, viii, xi, 2, 4–6, 14, 19, 20, 22, 29, 29n22, 59, 60, 64, 69, 86, 100, 111, 144, 148, 160–165, 174, 175, 191–194, 197, 240, 254, 256, 265–268, 272, 277–300, 308–313, 315, 316, 331, 337, 338, 393, 400, 401, 406, 407, 409n40, 411n42, 417, 429, 440, 447

Society, xi, xiv, 4, 7, 7n6, 14, 112, 118, 119, 123, 125, 126, 141–143, 145, 148, 149, 151, 160, 162, 163, 177, 178, 193, 194, 212, 212n2, 222, 236, 239, 243, 245, 248, 249, 264, 265, 267, 286–289, 290n6, 291, 292, 294n8, 297, 307–313, 315, 316, 332, 334–336, 341, 348, 352, 356, 357, 360, 369, 370, 372–375, 376n30, 377, 385, 387, 388, 400, 405, 411, 425, 428, 431, 440, 442, 443, 445, 446
Sociological determinism, 390
'Sopade,', 406, 432
'Soviet Union', soviet development, 4, 68, 69, 76, 395, 396, 408, 410, 413, 413n43, 426, 432, 440
Speculation, speculative, 40, 42, 47, 54, 96–98, 100, 104, 106–109, 111, 129, 133, 174, 189, 193, 194, 291, 321, 332, 356, 398, 432
Stages/phases of capitalist development, 3n2, 64, 86, 102, 105, 106, 125–127, 133, 134, 136, 137, 146, 150, 160, 171, 180, 188, 189, 191, 194, 206, 207, 215, 223n8, 237, 280, 315, 412
Stalin, Josef, 3, 4, 70, 278, 429, 432, 440, 447
Stalinism, Stalinisation, vi, 150, 367n2, 440, 446
Stampfer, Friedrich, 395, 407
State, vi, ix, x, xiii, 14, 21–23, 27, 27n19, 28, 34n24, 37–39, 42, 44, 58, 60, 64, 65, 79, 88–90, 92, 93, 105, 107–109, 111, 124, 128, 129, 132, 142–146, 148, 150, 151, 154, 156, 157,

161–165, 177–180, 185, 187, 191, 193, 194, 201, 213, 216–220, 222–225, 233, 235, 236, 238–240, 247, 256, 258, 267, 268, 272, 278, 282, 288, 289, 291, 293, 294, 296–300, 308, 309, 330, 332, 333, 337, 338, 347, 352, 354, 355, 359, 372–375, 374n25, 377, 386–390, 405, 408–410, 412–417, 419–422, 424n73, 425, 427–429, 432, 433, 443–446

State power, 20, 21, 45, 111–113, 150, 159, 160, 354, 372–375, 385–387, 389, 389n23, 408, 428, 431, 446

State socialism, 161, 308

Steindl, Josef, 75n10, 258

Sternberg, Fritz, vii

Stock market, stock exchange, 14, 15, 25, 31–33, 37, 40, 43, 45, 55, 58, 80–81, 87, 94–98, 104–106, 109, 111, 112, 172, 180, 195, 200, 201, 203, 205, 206, 238, 244, 266, 314, 315, 319, 321, 325, 343, 344, 397, 398, 415, 419

Sugar Trust, 267

Supervisory board, 346, 348, 355

Surplus values, 33, 39, 59, 61, 62, 71, 78, 90, 97, 101–103, 185, 202–204, 210, 210n1, 217, 222, 225, 332–334, 342–344, 349, 351, 358, 360, 361, 443

Sweezy, Paul, ix, 19n12, 53–78, 86, 87, 110, 133, 175, 206, 246, 255, 264, 285n2, 286, 294

Syndicate, 163, 184, 269

T

Transnational company/corporation (TNC), 47, 209, 211, 214

Trotsky, Leon, 2, 17, 65, 67, 69, 70, 130, 173, 206, 278

Trust, trust form, 3n1, 21, 34, 45, 56, 57, 59, 60, 65, 87, 91, 98–100, 124, 125, 150, 180, 184, 215n3, 263, 266–270, 324, 325, 330, 357, 401, 403, 425, 445

Tugan-Baranowsky, Mikhail, 60, 252, 284–287, 289, 291

U

Underconsumption, 7, 70–74, 101, 109, 256, 284

USPD, 2, 394, 399, 400, 406

V

Value

circulation value, 442, 443

commodity value, 345

exchange value, 98, 122, 152, 291, 308

money value, 152

Varga, Eugen, xiii, 65, 70, 71, 374, 374n25, 399, 439–449

Vogelsang, Karl, 266, 267

Vorwärts, 15, 18, 404, 406

W

War economy, xiii, 22n14, 23, 396, 405, 409, 409n40, 410, 416–418, 422–424, 429, 430

Weber, Max, 369–371, 370n16, 384

Weimar, Weimar Republic, xiii, 20, 256, 317, 390, 411n42, 424, 426, 433

Woldt, Hermann, 397

Printed in the United States
by Baker & Taylor Publisher Services